The Evolution of Human Adaptations

Readings in Anthropology

John J. Poggie, Jr.
University of Rhode Island

Gretel H. Pelto
University of Connecticut

Pertti J. Pelto
University of Connecticut

Macmillan Publishing Co., Inc.
New York

Macmillan Publishing Co., Inc.
866 Third Avenue, New York, New York 10022

Collier Macmillan Canada, Ltd.

Library of Congress Cataloging in Publication Data

Poggie, John J.   comp.
  The evolution of human adaptations.

  1.   Anthropology—Addresses, essays, lectures.
I. Pelto, Gretel H., joint comp.   II. Pelto, Pertti
J., joint comp.   III. Title.
GN29.P63   301.2   75–2311
ISBN 0–02–396000–0

Printing: 1 2 3 4 5 6 7 8   Year: 6 7 8 9 0 1 2

Preface

Over a century ago anthropology as a separate area of study developed because of the interest of Europeans and North Americans in the many different exotic cultures of the world, as well as the mysteries posed by the great numbers of archaeological ruins in the Mesopotamian classical lands and the Central American regions of bygone Mayan and Aztec civilizations. The fascination of these topics is powerful and to some extent anthropology became for a time the collection of the quaint, foreign, and exotic. But decades ago anthropologists went beyond simple description of past and present cultures to develop theoretical systems for explaining and understanding biological, cultural, and social processes. At first this theoretical endeavor was carried out in armchair theorizing rather than through careful empirical investigations, but the scientific intent was clear. For the teaching of anthropology there remains to this day an interest in a combination of the presentation of non-Western life-styles and other interesting human phenomena along with the main aspects of a panhuman biocultural science.

Because it is so wide-ranging and comprehensive in dealing with all aspects of the human condition, anthropology has traditionally had wide appeal as a special kind of humanities. Some people view it basically as comprehensive culture history; others would prefer to define our discipline as worldwide comparative social science. It is the only academic discipline that combines features of biology, social science, and the humanities under a single rubric.

Because it is such a wide-ranging discipline, so eclectic, and characterized by diverse schools of thought, it is practically impossible to present the full scope of anthropology within a single collection of readings. The upper limit of papers within a single cover can result only in a poor and frustrating sample of many different aspects of human lifeways and the many different styles of research among anthropologists. In this collection we have taken a particular anthropological frame of reference, built especially around the concepts of biocultural evolution and ecological adaptation. This is a view of human cultural and social behavior in a time perspective that is becoming increasingly central to anthropological thinking, and we find this perspective to be applicable to a very wide range of practical and theoretical questions.

It is also a perspective that articulates effectively with the theoretical ideas of biologists, economists, environmentalists, and other disciplines. Each of our selected papers, therefore, is put here for a distinct theoretical purpose, and not simply as an instance of cultural exotica or as an interesting bit from our fossil past. In our introductory statement we make clear the main features of our theoretical frame of reference, and the introductions to each of the sections are intended to further define the evolutionist-ecological perspective we are assuming. We do not, of course, intend to suggest that this is the only possible view of the human experience. We must recognize that there are competing alternative theoretical perspectives, most of which are well represented in other collections of readings as well as various introductory texts in anthropology. A truly eclectic instructor might consider using this collection of readings, together with a text of different persuasion, as a means of maximizing the view of theoretical diversity. On the other hand, the theoretical views in this reader were constructed to fit closely with the organization of the book *The Human Adventure* by Pelto and Pelto (1976).

Collections of readings such as this one are by their nature very flexible as teaching devices for introductory courses. Instructors should find it easy to rearrange the sections of the book to conform with their own preferences of organization and topical interest. Some instructors may find that in the short time slot of a quarter or trimester they might prefer to omit some of the biological or archaeological materials in favor of a contemporary human-cultures approach. Others may feel it more useful to proceed in the other direction, concentrating on the biological and archaeological materials, and eliminating some of the aspects of culture in favor of selected case studies as supplemental readings. An ideal introductory course frequently is enhanced by the addition of at least a couple of extensive case studies to amplify the topics and cultural forms dealt with somewhat piecemeal in a collection. Case studies that overlap with these readings may be particularly useful; for example, some people might wish to assign Elizabeth Thomas Marshall's *The Harmless People* to tie in with the selection "Veld Food," which we have included in Section 3. In the same vein, the case study of *The Itinerant Townsmen* by Ralph Jacobson might be assigned to fit in with a general modernization focus, tying into the selection on social classes we have included in Section 5. In some cases the easier way to accomplish the same result might be to have several copies of these case studies on reserve for students rather than requiring the purchase of the additional texts.

The papers we have selected to achieve these purposes are for the most part selections that we have found useful in one way or another in our own teaching of introductory courses. Some of these are fairly well known "regulars" in the mainline of anthropological use (for example, the paper by Malinowski), but at the same time we have tried to select papers from the most recent contemporary research. Whenever there was a choice to be made we selected more recent materials.

We have selected the items in our various sections on the basis of theoretical relevance first, but they are also chosen because of their readibility and interest for undergraduates. We have not sacrificed quality, but wherever possible the selections are those that have a flow of style and vocabulary that is in keeping with the levels of experience of beginning college students. Naturally the papers vary in their language and style so that some individual students may dislike certain items and be quite turned on by others—a natural and expected state of human affairs. Certain papers, however, have been selected as "honors work," representing a higher degree of complexity and challenge that can be assigned by instructors to students wishing a deeper penetration into selected theoretical-methodological questions. The average college student can read these honors selections to get the main general points, glossing over details of statistical analysis or other technical material. Naturally instructors will find a wide variety of approaches to these selections. In those many instances where instructors are faced with handling the entire course in a brief ten or twelve weeks the honors papers might be left out of required reading and be used by the instructor as topics for special lectures or selected extra-credit readings.

We owe a large vote of thanks to the original authors of these selections and to their publishers, who have granted us permission to reproduce them here. We had planned to include a number of other papers for which we had been kindly granted permission by their authors and publishers, but space limitations precluded their use here. Kenneth Scott and Joseph Falzone of Macmillan assisted us in many ways. Beth Underwood typed portions of the manuscript and Erika Poggie helped us with many of the editorial tasks. To all of these people we express our sincere thanks in helping us project these materials into a book.

J. J. P.
G. H. P.
P. J. P.

Contents

Introduction

You see, I am alive.
You see, I stand in good relation to the earth.
You see, I stand in good relation to the gods.
You see, I stand in good relation to all that is beautiful.
You see, I stand in good relation to you.
You see, I am alive, I am alive.
   Kiowa Indian Song *

Do you see me! . . .
Do you all help me!
My words are tied in one
With the great mountains,
With the great rocks,
With the great trees,
In one with my body
And my heart.
Do you all help me
With supernatural power,
And you, day,
And you, night!
All of you see me
One with this world!
   Yokut Indian Song *

Much of the time our views of human activity and of ourselves are shaped by daily needs and worries; we philosophize about social things in terms of our own particular cultural and ideological blinders. However, if we want to understand the different ways in which human groups organize their living, then we must learn how to step back from our daily concerns and develop a broader perspective. From the great welter of differences in human lifeways we need to be able to identify panhuman similarities of behavior, cross-cultural similarities in ways of managing fundamental human problems. The social sciences generally are concerned with the bigger patterns—the basic processes whereby human lifeways are transformed by circumstance and environmental challenges. The wide differences in individual ideologies, physical characteristics, technologies, and other components of human adaptation are regarded as variations on the general themes of human behavior.

American anthropology has developed a point of view in which human behavior is studied from a very long time perspective, with a frame of reference in which all cultural systems are considered valid in their own terms. This perspective is unique in that no other

* In the World of the American Indian, ed. Jules B. Billard, National Geographic Society, 1974.

field of study looks at humans from their earliest beginnings, across the full range of different cultures and from a point of view that asks questions about the significance of cultural differences and similarities. While historians study human activity over time, in anthropological theory *historical* time is but a small segment of the total story of *Homo sapiens*. The unfolding of human biological and cultural capabilities required several millions of years, and the full human story can only be understood with this time reference. Industrial societies have occupied only a tiny part of the time span in which humans evolved and lived. Hunting and gathering peoples, herders, and agriculturalists have all been important actors in cultural evolution. To understand humans is to see them in their entirety, over the several millions of years of evolutionary change and in terms of the diverse adaptations they have made to various parts of this planet. It is for this reason that anthropologists pursue the study of what some people think of as "exotic" societies. In their study of contemporary societies anthropologists do not assume any sort of superiority of the western European-North American way of doing things. Monogamy, monotheism, and capitalism are seen as simply a part of the range of variation in marriage, religion, and economic systems.

It is the cross-cultural and long-term perspective that makes the anthropological study of humans different from psychology, economics, political science, and other social sciences. Also, the anthropological perspective is generally more "holistic," and treats human lifeways as complex interdependent systems of family organization, politics, economic arrangements, psychological characteristics, and biological features. Anthropology is, more than most other disciplines, simultaneously cultural-social *and* biological.

On the biological side anthropology takes a Darwinian, evolutionist perspective. The human animal is seen as developing over the past three to five million years through gradual processes of natural selection—developing upright posture, a large complex brain, finely tuned eye-hand coordination, and other human features. The biological adaptation of *Homo sapiens* has been especially notable in the areas of behavioral complexity, the capacity for learning, and the special communications systems by which we transmit our learning from one person to another and from one generation to the next.

On the cultural side we see the evolution, in humans, of cultural tradition—in both social and technological features. Cultural evolution includes increased complexity in social organization in conjunction with improved food getting through cooperative hunting and gathering, sharing of food within small groups, followed by the invention of food production in the form of domestication of plants and animals.

Although our contemporary life-styles are so thoroughly shaped by cultural things, the "big picture" of human evolution is best understood as a process of *biocultural* adaptation. There has been a sequence of intertwined biological and cultural changes beginning some three to five million years ago and continuing to the present day. The evidence for these changes is found in the fossil remains of our ancestors and in archaeological sites—the tools and other works of early humans—as well as in the indirect clues we have in still existing hunting and gathering societies. Study of our nearest primate relatives, the apes and monkeys, also provides valuable information.

Adaptation: Biological and Cultural

Since we have suggested that the development of human lifeways has been a complex process involving both biological and cultural features, it is important to note that the concept "adaptation," basic to an evolutionary perspective, is used in two different ways. *Biological* adaptation is generally defined as genetically transmitted changes in plants and animals that result in an adjustment or "improvement" in the survival changes of the plant or animal population. Thus we speak of the hoof of the horse as having developed as an "adaptation" to an open environment in which speed enhanced the survival chances of individuals. Failure to adapt biologically to environmental changes, new predators, or other actors has generally led to the extinction of the affected populations. The demise of the dinosaurs is probably the best-known example of a failure in biological adaptation.

Nongenetic adaptations, on the other hand, are suggested by common expressions such as "John adapted well to his new job." Or, "The hunters in the Far North have adapted to the Arctic cold through their tailored fur clothing and other cultural items." In these instances, no changes in the genetic codes of individuals are needed to make the adjustments of behavior and equipment. While humans today have very extensive capabilities for nongenetic adaptations, this fact is dependent on the long-term genetic modifications by which humans have come to have far greater cognitive-mental capabilities than any of the other animals.

Although it is true that human cultural adaptation has resulted in greater and greater numbers of our species, and that for some people this represents adaptative success, we do not assume that cultural adaptation, development of new cultural forms, is always positive. We should not label all of our culture history as "progress." For example, many people now believe that the vast numbers of humans in the world today (compared to the hunters and gatherers of fifteen thousand years ago) may be a maladaptive development. We may have damaged the equilibrium of environment irrevocably, and thus built into our future a natural disaster. We certainly cannot make the assumption that "bigger is better," in population or anything else. In the anthropological view simple, complex, and "intermediate" societies are all to be understood in their own terms without invidious comparisons.

The same point, of course, applies as well to discussions of biological evolution in other animals. At certain periods of time animals are supposedly "well adapted" to their environments, yet later they outrun their habitats and available food supplies, to be replaced by other animals better adapted to the changed situations. Thus the now extinct Irish elk and the great dinosaurs were "successful" for a time, but not "successful" in the long run.

The Process of Cultural Evolution

In the past three to five million years of human evolution certain major turning points stand out. The first of these occurred several million years ago, sometime before the Ice Age (Pleistocene) geological period. The "event" has been referred to as the "human revolution" by anthropologists Charles Hockett and Robert Ascher, and was the transition from nonhuman to prehuman animal. In response to the changing environment in Africa our tree-dwelling, vegetable-eating ancestor probably began to adapt its ways to open grasslands. Finding itself at a disadvantage among the large and fierce predators, and swift-footed herd animals, this ancient ape began developing extrasomatic means of adaptation—the first tools of our ancestors. Initially these tools were nothing more than ordinary rocks which, as digging implements and weapons, increased survival chances. The human revolution represents the transition from an essentially arboreal life to a new way of life in which there was great selective advantage for large and complicated brains and a bipedal, upright mode of locomotion.

While that first big turning point in human evolution involved both biological developments and learned cultural processes, the later major changes in human lifeways have been progressively more cultural and less dependent on genetic changes. Sometime during the past million years or so, as the human brain became relatively much larger than that of the apes, our ancestors developed the capabilities of complex symbolic speech using a transformed vocal apparatus. The linguist Philip Lieberman has found that the crucial changes in our vocal system may have developed only during the past two or three hundred thousand years, and such recent fossil hominids as the Neanderthals lacked fully modern speech capabilites. At any rate, some of the most recent dimensions of human evolution are very closely linked to special language capability that is universal among contemporary *Homo sapiens.*

Throughout the "Stone Age" there was a gradual, slow accumulation of tool inventories, but until only fifteen thousand years ago human groups depended entirely on wild game, fish, and vegetable products for food. There were no domesticated plants and animals. Then, a few thousand years ago, human groups developed domestic food plants and meat-producing animals, paving the way for the development of more complicated technologies and social systems. Like the development of human tool-using capabilities millions of years earlier, the transition to domestic plants and animals was a process stretching over many centuries, even though this process has been referred to as the "neolithic revolution."

Unlike that "human revolution" millions of years earlier, the revolution in food production methods did not depend on any genetic changes in the human animal. We already had the capacity for an omnivorous diet of plants and animals, and the technological features needed for exploitation of food resources were transmitted through the generations as cultural ideas. The transformations in the plants and animals themselves, on the other hand, involved genetic changes which included the development of more docile animals as well as the evolution of heartier plants with larger and more complex grains and other edible parts.

The genetic changes in the plants and animals appear to have come about through human "tampering" with the wild species. This neolithic revolution occurred during the centuries between 12,000 and 8000 B.C. in the Near East, perhaps about the same time in Southeast Asia, and several thousands of years later in Central and South America. In some other parts of the world the shift to domesticated plants and animals as major food sources occurred in relatively recent times, through the spread of cultural ideas carried from person to person and from group to group into new environments.

The expansion of food supplies and the more sedentary way of life made possible by the domestication of plants and animals led in time to the growth of population centers and the emergence of the first cities, beginning nearly six thousand years ago in the Near East. This period has been referred to as the "urban revolution." Like the "neolithic revolution," the urban revolution occurred at different times in different parts of the world. Following developments in the Near East, the settled agriculturalists of Egypt soon were building cities and complex social systems of their own, and similar developments in Northwest India extended the spread of ideas and cultural capabilities from the heartland of Mesopotamia. The rise of cities in Europe, around the northern shores of the Mediterranean, took place many centuries later, for the relatively more difficult environments of Greece and the Italian peninsula could not be exploited by the same food-production techniques that worked so well in Sumeria and neighboring regions. New combinations of crops and food animals were required before the rise of Greek civilization was possible.

In the Far East, the beginnings of urbanization and complex political systems in China appear shortly before 1500 B.C. reflecting the spread of cultural ideas and techniques from both the Near East and Southeast Asia. In the Americas the ancestors of modern Indian people had adopted domestication of plants and animals several thousand years before they began building cities. The great city of Teotihuacán rose to prominence in the period from about A.D. 100 to A.D. 600, and, in its time, was apparently larger than Rome. But like Rome, Teotihuacán was burned and sacked (in the seventh century), to be replaced by other cities and population centers. Throughout the centuries, in both the Old World and the New, populations in urban centers increased as more and more peasant farmers migrated to the cities in search of work and other opportunities. In some areas cities grew up mainly as trading centers; in others major military-governmental concentrations provided the basis for metropolitanism.

The growth of more complex sociocultural systems reflects increased energy resources. The food-producing revolution included the use of large animals as sources of power; later, people harnessed water power and the winds for sailing ships, turning wheels, and for other activities. Until just two or three centuries ago, however, the amount of energy harnessed by human groups was sharply limited because of the variations and uncertainties in the unconcentrated energy sources of wind and water. The development of steam power and internal combustion engines in the eighteenth and nineteenth centuries brought about a major transformation. In a relatively short period of time, groups developed the capability of using concentrated fuels (petroleum, coal, etc.) for production purposes. The number of factories multiplied, and already existing cities expanded rapidly with new employment opportunities and new social attractions.

At the same time the manufacturing centers reached out farther and farther into nonurban hinterlands, to sell their goods and to extract raw materials and labor resources. Thus the "industrial revolution" brought about a major "delocalizing" of human activities, and the vastly increased interdependence of populations across time and space.

The growth of factory cities and widespread commercial and resource-exploiting activities have brought the effects of modernization to all parts of the world. European explorers, then armies, and colonial administrators spread to all corners of the globe during the eighteenth and nineteenth centuries, and brought about sharp confrontations between European cultural systems and those of the non-Western peoples. This most recent phase of human cultural evolution is marked by the development of the economic, political, and social systems that have worldwide manifestations. There were, of course, well-developed civilizations in earlier times that had powerful and widespread impacts. In India and China, especially, complex food production systems had made possible accumulation of large populations in vast empires with wealth, complex political and social structures, and dreams of worldwide power. In those preindustrial societies millions of peasants toiled to produce food for the city folks, including the governmental and bureaucratic elites with wealth and governmental power. In most recent times these complex civilizations have themselves become more and more industrialized as the techniques and resources of industrialization are shifted back and forth across continents and nations with greater and greater rapidity.

Collecting Anthropological Information

The earlier phases of human cultural evolution, as we have briefly reviewed earlier here, have been studied mainly from archaeological data, fossil matrials, and other indirect evidence. From the period of the first cities and the beginnings of urbanization, however, more and more of the story of humankind has been available to us through written records. But even the human history of the last two thousand years is, to a considerable extent, a story that unfolded in areas unreached by written histories. Much of the information for Africa, the Americas, and large parts of Asia depends on indirect inferences from archaeological, linguistic, ethnological, and other materials.

During the past hundred years anthropologists have been studying peoples whose past histories have not been written down for posterity. Large amounts of comparative data have been accumulated about different human groups ranging from simplest hunting and gathering peoples to complex states such as the numerous large kingdoms of Africa. In some areas anthropologists have studied the social patterns of pastoral nomads with their herds of animals—camels, reindeer, sheep and goats, cattle, horses—and other forms of food on the hoof.

Practically all peoples engage in some trading with neighbors, but many of the nonindustrialized peoples have relied mainly on local energy resources until very recent times. These groups with localized energy resources are especially important "cases" for anthropologists to understand in detail in order to develop theoretical understanding of human ecological adjustments in preindustrial forms. The range of variation of human societies, from hunting and gathering to large-scale preindustrial societies and on to modern industrialized nations, represents a vast body of information to be used for the interpretation of our prehistoric past as well as the principles of ecological adaptation and evolution which continue to shape our present and future human adaptations.

While cultural anthropologists were devoting their energies to collecting information about the variety of cultural adaptations found among nonindustrial peoples, biological anthropologists have been examining the ways in which these same populations vary in their biological adaptations. Such characteristics as body proportions, hair type, skin pigmentation, nose length, tooth length, and blood type were being studied in relation to particular physical end epidimeological environments of the world. Biological anthropologists also study the behavior and biology of living nonhuman primates—studies that have produced a great deal of information, including data about the nearness of the blood chemistry of modern primates to that of humans. Estimates from this source show the chimpanzees to be our closest living relatives and indicate that our evolutionary separation from them occurred perhaps about four or five million years ago.

In a similar way, anthropological linguists studying the similarities and differences among the world's languages have been able to make estimates and extrapolations about past history. For example, among the Indo-European languages, which have been extensively studied, it is possible to fill in some of the prehistory of populations speaking these languages before the dawn of written history in Europe.

While much specialization in data-gathering techniques and theory building has occurred in each of the subareas of anthropology, the development of a comprehensive understanding of evolutionary processes and adaptive patterns in different environments requires putting together information from many different sources. The study of prehistoric developments in Mesoamerica, for example, requires comparative linguistic information, huge amounts of archaeological work, data from various aspects of physical anthropology, all interwoven with the data about the cultural patterns and social systems of different contemporary or recent Mesoamerican peoples. Moreover, as data from prehistoric populations are linked to the more recent developments, the work of historians, sociologists, and other scholars becomes directly relevant to the generalizing work of the anthropologists.

Often the separate branches of anthropology pursue their various research projects independent of one another, later integrating the information into a larger and more comprehensive synthesis. In recent times, though, large research projects have often been built up of intensive collaboration among these subfields. For example, the ongoing research in the Aleutian Islands, carried out by William S. Laughlin and his associates, has involved a long-term collaboration among biological anthropologists, archaeologists, ethnologists, and linguists, as well as medical people and other professions outside the field of anthropology. Such complex integrations of research activities illustrate the variety of different subspecialities and topical interests found in the complex field of general anthropology.

The Ecological Perspective

A holistic picture of human biocultural evolution provides a framework for understanding our present human condition. This evolutionary point of view focuses our attention on humans as complex culture-bearing animals, adapting to many different environments, extracting energy from available resources, and maintaining complex social forms and institutions. Interaction with the environment is central in this point of view, but in our social and cultural behavior we have created new dimensions. Our human-made environments— our cities, highways, shopping malls, and accompanying *social* systems—have become the forms of our adaptational energies. Whereas hunting and gathering peoples are mainly concerned with the features of their physical environment—climate, terrain, animals and plants, and various features of physical geography—we need only to look around us and examine our day-to-day adaptational decisions to realize how fully our own lifeways are tuned to the social environment—of governmental bureaucracies, unions, multination corporations, chain stores, mass media, and a bewildering variety of other socially mediated resources. Most of our food supplies come from other people's environments; most of our energy resources are transmitted to us long distances from other centers; and our daily affairs are frequently interrupted, or modified, by events in distant places. Our problems with Arab-dominated petroleum resources are but one example of this feature of social environment.

The model of human ecology shown in Figure 1 is a useful scheme for examining human-environment relations. This model is a conceptual map intended to guide the observer along the various pathways of interconnectedness that have to be followed in order to understand human activities in their ecological and social settings. As we look at different societies we find that the "shape" and details of the model differ considerably depending on *which* of the components have the greatest influence in a particular situation in a

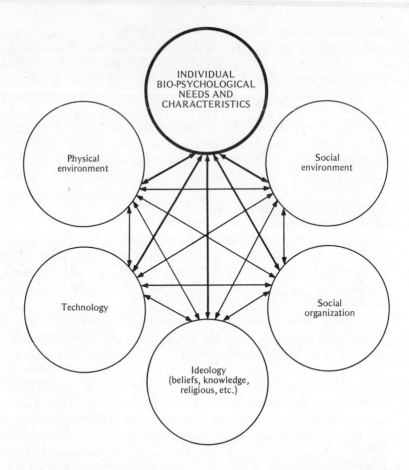

community, region, or nation. For example, among the Innuit peoples of the Canadian Arctic, there is clear primacy of physical environment and technology, with much less impact of ideology.

Some theorists have argued that the human condition is always shaped by technological-economic forces. However, there are many examples of societies in which ideological-religious influences play a primary role in affecting all aspects of life-style. The Hutterite peoples of North America are a society in which the ideological-religious component is a dominating influence in the overall culture patterns. The Hutterites believe very strongly in a set of religious values that influence their work, their material surroundings and possessions, their relationship to the outside world, their family life, their reproductive rate, their political system and leadership, and even the patterning of health and illness.

Looking at other people in the same environment (the Great Northern Plains), we can find other variations in adaptive strategies. The various Plains Indians, before the coming of the Whites, are examples of societies in which *social* environment seems to take on a very important role in affecting the rest of the model of human ecology. For example, the eighteenth- and nineteenth-century Cheyenne Indians have been described as a people who seemed to be responding in many ways to a hostile social environment, in which a number of competing tribes were occupying overlapping territories, using horses to aid the exploitation of bison. It was an area of chronic warfare, in which exaggerated manliness and aggressive warriorship were highly esteemed. There were well-organized and well-defined warrior societies. The Cheyenne people had sacred ceremonials to keep up social solidarity among bands, which were dispersed during the winter months. Certainly the physical environment, the seasonal variation in weather conditions, and the shifts in vegetation and animal life upon which people depended had very important influences on the ecological systems of the Plains Indians. But it is also clear that the *social* environment—of competing tribal groups jostling each other in competition for scarce resources—was a significant factor in the adaptations that evolved in this part of North America.

We should keep in mind that at any one time the various elements in an ecological system are only imperfectly interrelated. The state of "adjustment" among the various components is constantly disturbed by changes in one or another of them, and these changes are not automatically or immediately followed by compensating changes in other components. Strains and contradictions develop whose adjustment is the focus of the wide range of processes in societies. It is often possible to observe the effects of these strains and contradictions.

The effect of horses on Plains Indian life is a good example. Horses were introduced by the Spaniards into North America in the sixteenth century and became naturalized—that is, adjusted to the climate and terrain of North America and reproduced and flourished in this environment. Some of these naturalized horses were captured by various Indian tribes. This introduced a large technological change. It represented a harnessing of nonhuman energy that could be used for human transportation, as well as for hauling various kinds of loads. The effects of this large-scale technological innovation in the Great Plains were enormous. The warrior societies, new definitions of male roles, large-scale tribal solidarity, new ideologies, heightened ethnocentrism, and new religious and ritual systems can all be traced to the effects of the advent of the horse. Thus the model of human ecology is not only useful for understanding a static situation, but it is also useful for understanding patterns of change and adjustment over time within particular cultures or regions.

Perhaps one of the most salient changes in the lives of Americans living in the 1970s has been the ideological growth, quite strikingly, of the "whole earth" ecological movement. People with this point of view see the Earth as a finite system, an "island," and regard *Homo sapiens* as simply part of the system—an animal that must give up its arrogant ways and learn to live in harmony with the rest of the system. All this new ideology is replacing the earlier "frontier mentality" or "unlimited resources" view of our environment. This ideological shift in recent times has, of course, quickly run into opposition with the social organization of "business as usual" and at the same time is having significant effects on technology as industrial engineers are asked to develop exhaust emission controls, smokeless smokestacks, and other devices.

We do not wish to claim that societies "naturally" tend to maintain an equilibrium within their ecological systems. The notion of equilibrium is useful only to a degree. But it is important to understand the interdependence among the parts in the human ecology network. A change in one part necessitates changes in other parts, even if these adjustments are often delayed. All human sociocultural systems are perpetually in a process of change. Also, over the long prehistory of our species there have been numerous cultures that were unable to make the necessary adjustments within their ecological systems and became "extinct."

Modernization and the Contemporary Plight

The new complexities of human adaptation in our contemporary world, including heightened rates of interaction among all parts of the globe, can be understood in the same general terms as the adaptations of peoples in small-scale tribal societies such as the Cheyenne or the peoples of New Guinea. We have reached a stage in the evolution of general culture where the lifeways of all human groups are interrelated. The magnitude of the interrelatedness of human populations around the world is staggering when one considers this in terms of our model of the ecological system.

Taken at the world level, we see the degree of interrelatedness of all the different sectors and groups of nations—the industrialized countries, the developing nations, and the marginal, not-yet-nationalized peoples. There is a constant system of transactions that goes on among the various industrial nations, and a pursuit of various goals and interests. The diplomatic maneuvers of Henry Kissinger point up the complexities of political links and economic interrelationships that shape our world affairs. These, of course, are the most visible ties—those that are reported in the news each day in industrial nations—but there are many less obvious links that range from the migration of peoples from continent to continent, the importation of raw materials on a massive scale, and the shuffling of capital investments around the world.

Given the magnitude of global interaction, adjustments are more and more difficult to carry out within the framework of enormous interdependence among nations with varied interests. Decisions on adaptations that are made in the contemporary world affect more and more people at once, and the effects are transmitted more rapidly. In part this is because of the very large populations that exist in the world today. Whereas in the past the effects of political and economic decisions usually affected only parts of the world (because of the relatively more localized nature of human sociocultural systems), the emergence of a worldwide interrelatedness in this modern period of human evolution means that individual trial-and-error solutions to problems are more costly and dangerous. A great proportion of the world's population is affected by the actions of a few major industrial-political centers, and this means that the consequences of human error are enormously magnified. This is not only true in the domain of political relationships among nations but also holds for the economic, social, and cultural domains as well. This, coupled with the fact that human culture has reached the stage where there is an enormous concentration of energy utilization, brings us closer to potential ecological catastrophe. The recent findings linking vinyl chloride to liver cancer point up the kind of long-term effects built into systems of high energy and vast technology. Some people have interpreted the current scene of human cultural evolution as one in which the great human cultural computer prints out the results of human adaptive decisions at an ever-expanding rate, but there are fewer and fewer people in a position to read the "error messages," and those who can read the errors have less and less time or opportunity to say what should be done about the mistakes.

The complexities of our present stage of cultural evolution, so threatening and so rapidly changing, lead some people to "drop out" of the culture in which they have been living, in a search for ways to "relocalize" their lives. We see individuals turning to small-scale farming; to the utilization of local "archaic" sources of energy such as wood instead of oil in heating homes; we see the emergence of communes and countercultures; we see the emergence of cults and movements such as natural foods devotees and people who fantasize about a different life while reading the *Whole Earth Catalogue*. Other people, equally disenchanted and fearful of the current situation, seek changes both large and small in the social order. We see the emergence of new social movements—some quite localized, others bent on worldwide revolution.

There are those who advocate technological solutions to our current problems. They are the people who feel that bigger and more technology, including nuclear-powered generating plants, larger and more technologically complex refineries, and other complicated energy distribution systems, will bring solutions for our global problems. They call for complicated means of cleaning up technology, through the use of stack scrubbers and complicated systems of water purification. They are also the people who advocate more complicated means of transportation through automated systems of mass transit. They are the "big technology" thinkers in our midst. They propose solutions for the Third World and its hungry people in the form of more and more technology so that the peoples in the Third World can increase their food-producing capacity. Often these "technocrats" have little understanding of the social structure and organization that must support bigger and more complicated technology both in the industrial nations and in the developing nations.

In contrast, there are others who say we must return to a less complicated state of existence in which *low energy* technology is emphasized. They propose that we return to the use of wood stoves rather than placing greater and greater dependence on fossil fuels and electricity for our heating sources. They say that instead of automated mass transit systems, we should make more use of bicycles in getting to and from work and the other places we need to go. Although these may appear to be diametrically opposed positions, it is interesting to note that both of these positions emphasize technology as the way to cope with the situation: either through "big technology" or "little technology."

We do not wish to present an entirely bleak picture of the prospects for our species. We know that *Homo sapiens* has faced a great many problems in the long period of evolutionary change on this earth, in a great variety of environments. So far, our species has been able to adapt to the natural and cultural changes we have faced. Although our present situation is complicated and changing rapidly, there is cause for a certain amount of optimism *if* we can rapidly generate enough understanding and knowledge about the processes of human evolution, and the way things work in the highly elaborated networks of energy, communication, and social linkages around the world. It is important that we generate this knowledge within the framework of a model of human behavior that includes all the components of the ecological system.

It is here that anthropology tries to make its major impact, for anthropology is the discipline in search of understanding of how things work in human adaptation, how an ever-changing combination of ecological, social-cultural, and individual elements fit together in the human experience among different peoples of the world. Anthropology does not seek to be entirely unique among sciences, but it does rely heavily on a holistic perspective that allows us to see the human condition over the past millions of years, and across the varieties of human societies—from small bands, to tribes, peasant communities, fishing communities, to small nation states, to industrial societies. We are biased, but we feel that the most useful information and the greatest understanding of the human condition can come only from a truly pan-world perspective.

1   Anthropology and Science

Anthropology is a unique combination of biological science, social science, history, and humanities. Some anthropologists are deeply involved in the history of graphic arts, while other persons with the same label "anthropologist" are immersed in complicated laboratory research on human blood composition. Still others study contemporary human behavior in a manner similar to the work of sociologists. Overall, however, anthropology is more firmly rooted in the sciences than in the humanities.

In order to place anthropology in perspective, it is useful to review some basic ideas of the scientific approach. The methods of science, involving the testing of hypotheses, the accumulation of careful empirical information, and development of broad theoretical perspectives, are the foundation of our discipline. Anthropological science includes a broad mixture of quantified, statistical research and description of past events, lifeways of peoples, and other quite nonstatistical modes of presenting information. If the whole discipline of anthropology has any one central "problem," it is in maintaining communication among the different parts of our complex and eclectic scription of past events, lifeways of peoples, and other quite nonanthropology, and the presentation of materials in general texts on the subject.

In this first section we will begin with some comment about the principal segments of anthropology in relation to the general domain of modern science. A handy beginning is to describe the four major components of anthropology: physical anthropology, archaeology, linguistics, and social-cultural anthropology. Although we will not give completely "separate but equal" treatment to each of these components in our selection of readings, it is important to note that anthropology is in some respects a "confederacy" of four distinct disciplines with somewhat different histories of scholarship.

The separate bodies of information and frames of reference of physical anthropology, social-cultural anthropology, linguistics, and archaeology can be fitted together only if we adopt a very broad, general theoretical perspective. In recent decades a conceptual scheme has been developed that aids us in putting together such a unified view of human evolution and behavior. General systems theory provides a way of linking together complex empirical materials in a multivariable synthesis. To provide a glimpse of this kind of thinking we are including a paper by Kenneth Boulding titled "General Systems Theory: The Skeleton of Science." This selection may whet the appetites of some students and lead them to further explorations of a very important idea. Others may feel that it is a bit too abstract at this time, preferring to leave the paper for the honors students.

Pertti J. Pelto

The Nature of Anthropology

The broadest and boldest definition of anthropology states simply that "anthropology is the study of man and his works." In the years since that definition was invented many of us have become sensitized to the male-centered cast of this language, and prefer to use the term "human" in this context. And in fact only that very broad definition can include all the varied field studies, theoretical interests, and teaching areas of people who call themselves anthropologists. Under the title "anthropology" in course catalogues of major universities, we notice first that this field of study is usually divided into two main branches—physical anthropology and cultural (or social) anthropology. Most anthropology departments offer two separate introductory courses corresponding to these two aspects of the study of the human animal.

Physical Anthropology

Ever since the great Swedish naturalist Linnaeus published his monumental classification of plants and animals in the eighteenth century, humans have been listed among the animals, and the study of ourselves has been regarded as a branch of natural science. An important aspect of biological anthropology is the examination of the many-sided evidence for human evolution from "lower" forms of animal life. Therefore, introductory courses in physical anthropology often begin with materials on the comparative anatomy of *Homo sapiens* and our nearest "cousins," the apes and monkeys, all fellow members of the order of mammals called *Primates*. Then they may study the fossil evidence of human evolution in the form of fossilized bones of Neanderthal Man, Java Man, and a great number of other fragments from humans and apes that lived hundreds of thousands of years ago. Interest in our biological relationships with the other primates also leads to a comparative study of the social behavior of subhuman primates, such as the gorillas, chimpanzees, and baboons.

The variations among different physical populations of *Homo sapiens*—commonly divided into Mongoloid, Negroid, Caucasoid, and several smaller racial stocks—are another major concern of the physical anthropologists.

Recent developments in the science of genetics have changed the study of racial classifications from a dull cataloguing of obvious traits (color of skin, eye color, head shape, height, etc.) into an exciting search for patterns in the genetic inheritance of blood types, resistance to particular diseases, and examination of biological adaptation to different world climates.

In addition to these two relatively well-known lines of interest, physical anthropology has become increasingly concerned with the study of human growth and constitution, relationships of nutrition to body build, and a number of other physiological problems that bring anthropology into close contact with the special fields of anatomy, radiobiology, serology, physiology, and general medicine.

Cultural (Social) Anthropology

The distinctive feature that makes humans so different from other animals is that the human pattern of life is based on "culture,"—socially learned patterns of behavior, based on symbolic processes. Other animals may have some rudiments of culture, but for us *all* behavior is pervasively cultural. The several different facets of human culture (culture history, language, social structures, personality, etc.) give rise to a series of subfields that may be grouped in a variety of ways in the teaching of anthropology.

Archaeology

Archaeology is sometimes grouped with physical anthropology for teaching purposes. It is clearly cultural rather than biological, however, for the archaeologist studies the information about human dwellings, monuments, objects of art, tools, weapons, and other human works covered over by the soils of time.

Typical course offerings in archaeology can include: "New World Archaeology" (concerned with the prehistoric remains of American Indian cultures); "Old World Prehistory" (study of the stone tools, cave art, and other evidence about human life during the million or more years of the great Ice Ages); "Beginnings of Near Eastern Civilizations," and various specializations within these broad studies.

Since archaeologists are concerned with "digging up our past," they have important connections with history and historians. As a matter of fact, the "classical archaeologists," who dig in the ruins of ancient civilizations of the Mediterranean and Middle East (Troy, Crete, the tombs of Egypt, etc.), are usually found in departments of history or the classics, rather than in anthropology. Concern with the evidence of the past found in the earth's crust also links archaeologists with geologists, palaeontologists, palaeobotanists, and the geophysics.

Linguistics

"Linguistics" is the study of language—our highly elaborated system of communication. This study is not concerned with learning to speak foreign languages fluently but rather is aimed at accurate scientific description and comparison of languages. Probably the earliest strong interest in linguistics was developed around the study of the relationships among languages, particularly when it was discovered that most of the languages of Europe, though mutually unintelligible, are descended from a single common ancestor language—ancient Indo-European.

Recent developments in linguistics have brought the linguists into increasing contact with psychologists, philosophers, and mathematicians, as they pursue such topics as psycholinguistics, metalinguistics, semantics, and communications theory.

Ethnology

"Peoples and Cultures of Africa," "Ethnology of Oceania," "North American Indians," and a number of similar course titles illustrate the cultural anthropologists's concern with the infinite varieties of human behavior that have been found on the face of our globe. From this worldwide range of cultures and peoples, anthropologists search for similarities and differences that provide clues to understanding "human nature" and human culture history.

The courses in which cultural anthropologists present their systematic comparisons and theoretical researches are variously entitled "Comparative Economics," "Comparative Religion," "Culture Change," "Primitive Law and Government," "Social Structure," and so on. When psychological theory is systematically interwoven with these comparative ethnological data, we find courses entitled "Culture and Personality" and "Psychological Anthropology."

Whenever anthropologists are engaged in straightforward description of the cultural patterns of a given society they are concerned with "ethnography." When their materials are organized in terms of social systems, we can label the research (or the course) "Social Anthropology," indicating (among other things) the influence on Americans of some very interesting developments in British anthropology of the past forty years. Other diverse interests of anthropologists are made clear by the names of their course listings: for example, "Ethnomusicology," "Comparative Folklore," and "Primitive Art." Courses in which anthropological knowledge and theory are centered on the practical problems of our complex age are usually titled "Applied Anthropology."

Anthropology Is Fundamentally Cross-Cultural

Very often the first sign of an anthropologist-to-be is a young boy's or girl's fascination with Indians, lost continents, explorations in Africa, and exotic island peoples of the South Seas. The same kind of fascination with the "unusual" and "different" among peoples and cultures has spurred many anthropologists to their first extensive field work. When a thirst for systematic observation and comparative research are grafted onto the earlier romantic impulses, the motivations for a mature anthropology begin to emerge.

Curiosity and fascination with the exotic are not the main justifications for the anthropologist's interests in primitive peoples,[1] however. The more fundamental explanation is that non-Western societies provide a great range of behavioral diversity. Economic institutions, family organization, religious beliefs and practices, magic, artistic achievements, and personality types of every description provide the evidence for establishing the constants and the variants of human culture. The anthropologist feels that the fundamental principles of cultural and social systems can be discovered only through study of the whole range of human behavior patterns. Still another reason for the anthropologist's study of non-Western societies is that these provide him with a sort of "laboratory" setting, where something approaching the total scope of a cultural system can be observed in a relatively compact, localized community that is not just a fragment of a huge, modern society.

Some anthropologists have maintained that their field of study is concerned exclusively with primitive peoples, but most see their discipline as a general bio-cultural study and recent anthropological research of the postwar period has been in the subcommunities and specialized segments of large, literate societies. These include work on rural communities of modern Europe, Latin America, Japan, and India, in addition to anthropological study of topics like "the culture of a psychiatric hospital," "city taverns," "themes in French culture," and "the American kinship system."

The Integration of Anthropology

It is evident that anthropology—however specific it may often be in dealing with data—aims at being ultimately a co-ordinating science, somewhat as a legitimate holding corporation co-ordinates constituent companies. We anthropologists will never know China as intensively as a Sinologist does, or prices, credit, and banking as well as an economist, or heredity with the fullness of the genetic biologist. But we face what these more intensive scholars only glance at intermittently and tangentially, if at all: to try to understand in some measure how Chinese civilization and economics and human heredity, and some dozens of other highly

---

[1] The word "primitive" in casual conversation seems to refer most usually to peoples and practices that "civilized" Europeans and Americans regard as strange, quaint, and (generally) inferior. The anthropologist, when he uses the expression at all, defines "primitive peoples" as people who have no written language—hence, "pre-literate" people. Anthropological researchers generally avoid making value judgments about supposedly "inferior" or "irrational" or "backward" behavior.

developed special bodies of knowledge, do indeed interrelate in being all parts of "man"—flowing out of man, centered in him, products of him.[2]

With these words the late Alfred L. Kroeber, one of the foremost anthropologists of this century, expressed the idea that the stuff of anthropology is drawn from many different areas of knowledge. The research interests and types of courses taught by anthropologists reflect this great diversity, but in many situations today there are tendencies toward the fragmentation of the discipline. Physical anthropology, for example, is becoming increasingly specialized and complex in its researches on the physiology, anatomy, and genetic attributes of humans. Most cultural anthropologists find themselves farther and farther out of touch with the newest research and information in this field. At the same time, scholars in physical anthropology experience great pressures to concentrate their energies on the rapidly developing areas of radiobiology, the chemistry and physics of human genetics, and related fields. Thus they may become comparative strangers to the interests and research of the linguists, cultural anthropologists, and archaeologists who are their fellow staff members in departments of anthropology.

Also, the study of linguistics has become highly specialized, with an intricate vocabulary of description, semimathematical modes of analysis of language structure, and extremely complex philosophical and psychological arguments over fundamental assumptions in the field.

As we view the natural history of different branches of science and philosophy, we see that diversification and separation of fields of study is a natural result of increased knowledge about the world in which we live. It is easy, therefore, to argue that gradual splitting up of the different branches of anthropology into separate disciplines would be just as natural as the differentiation of chemistry, physics, and biology from the earlier unity of general science. But most anthropologists, especially in the United States, cling stubbornly to the "holistic principle" as stated by Dr. Kroeber. For, despite all tendencies toward specialization, the strong interrelatedness of human physical characteristics and behavioral systems cannot be ignored. From whatever angle the nature of the human animal is approached, there is no denying that our economic behavior, religious institutions, and other aspects of culture are deeply influenced by psychobiological characteristics. Similarly, the body as a physical system is affected by one's religion, occupation, family, and other social and cultural facts.

One area of study that graphically illustrates the integration of the study of humanity is concerned with the problems of mental illness. In postwar years important advances have been made in the development of a holistic theory of psychiatric disorder. The development of drugs and other organic treatments demonstrates the relationship of our biological attributes to

[2] A. L. Kroeber (ed.), *Anthropology Today* (Chicago: University of Chicago Press, 1953), p. xiv. Copyright 1953. All rights reserved.

psychologcial functioning. Theoretical developments in the area of psycho-somatic medicine offer additional evidence of these linkages. At the same time, studies of mental disorders among the Eskimos, peoples in Africa, Asia, and other areas, and evidence of different rates and kinds of mental illness in subsections of our own society show the importance of social and cultural factors in problems of mental health.

The integration of biological and cultural data in research on mental illness is particularly well illustrated in Anthony F. C. Wallace's analysis of a mental disorder called *pibloktoq*, found among the Greenland Eskimos. *Pibloktoq* is characterized by compulsive mimicking behavior, "speaking in tongues," shouting, weeping, tearing off clothing, and running away naked in the arctic cold. Rejecting a wholly psychoanalytic interpretation for this disorder, Wallace suggests that it is related to periodic calcium deficiencies in the Eskimo diet. Particular social circumstances trigger the breakdown, however, and the specific contents of the aberrant behavior must be understood in terms of Eskimo psychological and cultural patterns. Clearly, research on problems of this sort requires close collaboration among biological, psycho-logical, and cultural sciences.

Methods of Research: The Qualitative-Quantitative Mix

Anthropologists have been slower than the other bio-social scientists in adopting statistical, quantified methods in research. The reluctance to use statistical analysis and hypothesis-testing appears to be a reflection of a continuing humanities component in anthropology, and the predilection for "holistic depiction" in which we try to describe the full texture of human behavior, rather than reducing peoples' activities, attitudes, and achievements to abstracted tabulations and graphs.

On the other hand, in the past two decades we have become increasingly sensitized to the fallibility, the inevitable biases, in non-quantified descriptive data—especially when the typical situation is still that of one or two individuals (often a husband-wife team) living for some months as partici-pant-observers in the midst of the cultural-social system they are studying. The researcher observer's view of any community is bound to be only a narrow slice from the complex and endlessly varied day-to-day behavior of people. The problem is compounded as anthropologists have shifted their research interests to larger and more complex scenes. How can the *urban* anthropologist, for example, cope with the variety of life-styles, economic activities, and other behavior in the study of city-dwellers?

Emerging research trends in the anthropology of the 1970s still include a considerable component of non-qualified "holistic depiction"; at the same time the use of statistical analysis and scientific hypothesis-testing has seen a rapid growth in anthropology. The shift to more quantification came first in physical anthropology, of course, since this aspect of the study of *Homo sapiens* has always been the most closely allied with biological science.

Archaeologists, too, have for a long time employed numerical analysis in sorting and classifying the often large numbers of material items dug up in their excavations, but only with the advent of the "new archaeology" in the 1960s and 1970s have they turned to large-scale computerized hypothesis-testing and theory-building.

Many cultural anthropologists now employ statistical procedures as part of their inventory of research methods, but their tables, graphs, and frequency distributions are usually combined with rich descriptive materials that give flesh-and-blood context to their hypothesis-testing and theoretical abstractions. The numbers and measurements may take the form of structured interviews, counts of food-production or energy expenditures, prices of goods exchanged, and many other countable features of human action. Also, census reports and other written sources provide anthropologists with complex numerical materials for study of everything from population and economic trends to discrimination in school grades and hiring practices.

The quantitative-qualitative mix of research methods in anthropology reflects continuity of the science-and-humanities combination in the holistic study of mankind.

Relationships with Other Social Sciences

In practice there is a good deal of both theoretical and practical overlap between anthropology and sociology. And the areas of common interest seem to have increased considerably in the past fifteen or twenty years. Nonetheless, some general differences separate the interests of *most* anthropologists from those of *most* sociologists. These differences in tendency include:

1. Most anthropologists prefer to study non-Western peoples (though there are many exceptions); most sociologists prefer to study aspects of Western society and culture. (But growing numbers of sociologists are now immersed in studies of African, Indian, Chinese, and other societies, and more anthropologists are looking at their own cultures.)
2. Most anthropologists prefer to do research on small communities, by means of observations and interviews of people in face-to-face contact. Most sociologists prefer to study larger segments of social systems, using information gathered on questionnaires or extracted from statistics on population, crime rates, employment figures, voting records, and so on. In general, sociologists feel much more at home using statistical analysis than do anthropologists.
3. Anthropologists include physical anthropology as an important part of

their science; sociologists concentrate their studies nearly exclusively on social aspects of the human condition.

4. Most anthropologists consider human culture history to be a central concern of the discipline; the majority of sociologists leave historical studies to others, preferring modern social institutions for research topics.

The differences between anthropology and psychology are much more clearly observable, though again there are growing areas of overlap. Psychologists usually study the behavior of individuals in carefully defined laboratory or experimental situations; thus, psychology is much more an experimental science than is anthropology. Psychologists are, in the main, even less interested than sociologists in study of non-Western peoples. However, the rapidly developing field of social psychology includes cross-cultural studies and other features that are very close to the interests of psychologically oriented anthropologists. Anthropologists and psychologists also have common interests and much potential for joint research on the physiology of the human brain and nervous system. A somewhat unexpected area of co-operation has developed between psychology and anthropology in laboratory and field studies of monkeys and apes.

Anthropology also shares notable similarities of interest with geography. Studies of the spread of domestication of plants and animals; adaptation of peoples to particular kinds of physical environments; social and cultural characteristics of pastoral (animal herding) societies, and a great many other areas of research are studied simultaneously by geographers and anthropologists. In topics such as Islamic culture history, Chinese culture and society, and Latin American culture history we often find anthropologists and historians working on very similar research interests, though methods of study may be different. The full range of anthropological interests and research links the work of anthropologists with that of scholars in many other fields. This is natural and expected, for all scholars accept the principle of the interconnection of the universe, the unity of all life on earth, and the oneness of human history and society. Special areas of study labeled with the names of various "ologies," are, after all, artificial segments of information chopped out of the unified web of events and things. If scholars paid careful heed to the artificial boundaries between areas of study, we might still be in the Dark Ages of human knowledge.

Summary

Since anthropology is "the study of humankind," including social, cultural, psychological, and physical characteristics, anthropological study is partly biological science, partly social science, and in part included among the humanities. In the main lines of their studies, anthropologists may be distinguishable from sociologists, psychologists, physiologists, zoologists, geographers, historians, and others; but the wide-ranging interests of individual scholars make any clear boundaries among these several disciplines impossible to draw. Some of the most exciting areas of modern research are those that play havoc with the boundaries among the various disciplines. Studies of mental health and mental disorder, for example, involve the work of physiologists, psychiatrists, psychologists, sociologists, anthropologists, geneticists, biochemists, and social workers. The general areas of human evolution and cultural history similarly combine work from dozens of different branches of science and humanities.

In the welter of interlaced scientific and historical studies anthropologists have attempted to maintain a broad, holistic approach to their work. Narrow specializations have generally been avoided, and the splitting of anthropology into isolated subcompartments has also been avoided, although the strains involved in this diversity of anthropology sometimes show on the faces of weary and harassed students who must spread their studies over such wide ranges of knowledge.

James Deetz

What Is Archaeology?

Archaeology is the special concern of a certain type of anthropologist.[1] We cannot define archaeology except in reference to anthropology, the discipline of which it is a part. Anthropology is the study of man in the broadest sense, including his physical, cultural, and psychological aspects, and their interrelationships. Archaeology concerns itself with man in the past; it has been called the anthropology of extinct peoples.

Archaeologists are anthropologists who usually excavate the material re-

[1] This [paper] is concerned with archaeology as a part of anthropology. There is a somewhat different type of archaeology, sometimes called classical archaeology, which is primarily concerned with the archaeology of the civilizations of the ancient Mediterranean world. This type of archaeology is usually taught as art history in university art departments. Its beginnings lie in the Renaissance, when man became interested anew in ancient art and dug it from the ground to serve as an example and inspiration. Anthropological archaeology, on the other hand, is only as old as anthropology itself, and is concerned with all the remains of past man, wherever we find them in the world.

mains of past cultures, and through the study of such evidence, attempt to re-create the history of man from his earliest past and to determine the nature of cultural systems at different times and places around the world. Archaeology is similar to history in part of its purpose, that of delineating sequences of events in the past and their importance to mankind today. This kind of reconstruction is called prehistory, a term which stresses a basic difference between archaeology and history. Prehistory treats the time before man learned to write and therefore record his own career on earth. It begins with man's first appearance on this planet, almost two million years ago, and usually ends with the beginnings of written history in all parts of the world. This later date can be as early as *circa* 3500 B.C. in the Near East, or as late as A.D. 1850 in parts of the state of California. While such time limits can be imposed on archaeological studies, they are somewhat flexible and blurred at the later end of the scale. In recent years, archaeologists and historians have become aware of the value of working together in certain situations. The archaeological and historical records combined often yield a richer picture than either would separately. We know from history that Plymouth Colony was founded in 1620, that the ship bringing the first colonists was the *Mayflower*, that separate land grants were given the settlers in the cattle division of 1627, and that the first houses were probably made from sawn clapboards. Yet no known historical documentation tells us exactly what animals were used for food by the Plymouth colonists, what types of dishes were used in the homes, when the first bricks were produced locally, or what types of nails, window cames or door hardware were used in constructing the houses. Archaeological investigation of seventeenth-century house sites in Plymouth has given the answers to all these questions, fleshing out much of the bare bones of the historical accounts.

In the missions of southern California, we know from the historical record that quarters were constructed for the Indian neophytes, and that they were occupied by family groups. Such a structure was built at La Purisima Mission in 1814, but the resident Padre was satisfied with simply noting in his diary that the building had been erected. Archaeological excavation showed it to be 540 feet long, of adobe brick with heavy tile roof. Study of the contents of the apartment units within this barracks structure provided valuable insights regarding Indian life in the missions not forthcoming from the historical record.

If historical documentation is of value at the later end of the archaeologist's time scale, the earliest end leans heavily on the natural sciences. The older the material, the less perfectly preserved it usually is, and the greater the need for supporting interpretations with data drawn from other disciplines. The excavation of a 40,000-year-old site in France requires the assistance of paleontologists, botanists, soil specialists, and geologists, to name but a few of the nonanthropological scholars who work with the archaeologist in the analysis of the materials recovered. Through the application of results from these supplementary fields, the archaeologist is given a good idea of the environment in which man lived at the time, and the types of problems which life presented.

The "where" of archaeological work is as important as the "when." Modern archaeologists are pursuing their investigations in all those places where man lives or has lived at any time in the past. Sites are excavated in the frigid Arctic, in the jungles of tropical America, Africa and Asia, on the open plains of the United States, beneath the streets of London, and even under the waters along the coastlines of many parts of the world.

With the entire world from which to draw his materials, and a two million year span of time represented by them, it is the task of the archaeologist today to integrate this immense yet imperfect corpus of data into a meaningful picture, and in so doing provide an understanding of cultural process in time and space.

Culture

Archaeology seeks to learn about culture from the fragmentary remains of the products of human activity. What, then, is culture? Culture can mean many things: a growth of bacteria in a petri dish, the correct way to behave in various situations, or what we get when we read "good" books, listen to "good" music, or learn to appreciate "good" works of art. To the anthropologist, culture means none of these things. On the other hand, to say just what it does mean to an anthropologist is by no means simple. In fact one entire book has been devoted to the definitions of culture used in anthropology.[2] Assuming that you could find them, ten anthropologists selected at random on the street would probably give ten somewhat different definitions.

Since we are concerned with culture in our discussion of archaeology, we must attempt a definition in the face of so many others; there is some comfort in numbers, however, and our treatment of culture in this case will not be too different from the consensus. Culture can be defined by making several statements about it.

CULTURE IS LEARNED BEHAVIOR. We inherit many things from our ancestors through genes; the color of our hair, our blood type, the shape of our face. Other things are given to us by our ancestors, but not biologically. There is no gene for speaking English, wearing a necktie, calling our mother's sister's children "cousin" or using Arabic numerals. Yet, generation after generation does these things, having learned them by a process separate from the genetic and biological, a process termed *extrasomatic*, apart from the body. We might even say that culture is everything a person would not do were he to grow up completely isolated on a desert island.

[2] A. L. Kroeber, and C. Kluckhohn, *Culture: A Critical Review of Concepts and Definitions* (Papers of the Peabody Museum of American Archeology and Ethnology, Vol. 47, No. 1); Cambridge, 1952.

CULTURE IS UNIQUELY HUMAN. This statement might cause some disagreement. Many species of animals learn certain patterns of behavior in a way not too different from that by which man learns cultural patterns. But man is the only animal who uses culture as his primary means of coping with his environment. Culture is man's adaptive system. While bears and rabbits in the Arctic have developed heavy pelts through biological evolution that protect them against the cold, the Eskimo makes a snug fur suit and lives in an igloo. Over the ages, man has elaborated culture into an ever more complex buffer between him and his world. Remove this cultural screen from the picture, and we would find man so ill adapted to his environment that he would probably become extinct. Even a brief loss of electrical power places urban man in an unfamiliar and uncomfortable relationship to the environment, and an apartment dweller who cannot use his electric can opener is in much the same predicament as an Australian aborigine who has lost all his spears while hunting far from home.

CULTURE IS PATTERNED. The array of habits and customs which make up culture for any group of people is integrated: each part relates to every other part in a systematic manner. Anthropologists categorize culture in certain conventional ways. Language, religion, economics, technology, social organization, art and political structure are typical categories. In any culture, the form of the political structure is in some way contingent on the social structure; art reflects religion, social organization shapes a part of technology, and so on. In studying the nature of cultural patterning, anthropologists have come to understand how culture is structured in hundreds of cases.

SOCIETY IS THE VEHICLE FOR CULTURE. The distinction between culture and society is clear. Societies are groups of interacting organisms, and man is but one species of social animal along with other primates, many insects, and even certain lower forms of life. In the human case, society is the repository of culture; it carries it; its members participate in it; and culture is the dominant determinant of social behavior.

Culture can thus be defined as a uniquely human system of habits and customs acquired by man through an extrasomatic process, carried by his society, and used as his primary means of adapting to his environment.[3]

To this definition we might add one qualification as archaeologists. Culture is highly perishable, and therefore cannot be excavated. No one has ever dug up a political system, a language, a set of religious beliefs, or a people's attitude toward their ancestors. Yet such things as political and religious behavior, language, and social interaction affect what the archaeologist does recover.

[3] Anthropologists also distinguish between culture on the one hand, and individual cultures on the other. This latter, somewhat different use of the term signifies individual groups of people the members of which share in a particular culture system. Thus we can speak of American culture, Chinese culture, Navaho culture, etc. Another definition of culture in these terms would be the shared habits and customs of a single society.

The patterning which the archaeologist perceives in his material is a reflection of the patterning of the culture which produced it. Pots, arrowheads, house floors and axes are the products of culture, not culture in themselves, but they are linked to culture in a systematic manner. It is the archaeologist's task to discover how cultural behavior is shown in its products.

Archaeological Method

An Indian village on the Missouri River in 1750 must have been a lively place. Barking dogs running between large earth-covered houses; children playing on the roofs; women making pots and chatting by the doorways; a party of men returning from a hunting expedition laden with bison meat—all contribute to a picture of confusion, sound, and motion. The same village in 1965 is a silent cluster of dim green rings of grass on the brown prairie, the only sound that of the wind, the only motion and life that of a tumbleweed rolling across the low mounds and depressions, and of a hawk circling high in the sky. The people are gone, and the only things which attest to their former presence are fragments of the objects which they made and used, buried in the collapsed remains of their dwellings.

If you had gone into this village after all the people had left, but before any deterioration had begun, understanding what had taken place there would be difficult enough. The material culture of a people is but a small part of their whole cultural pattern. The behavior which took the form of chatting, playing, and hunting could not be directly observed in their absence. Add to the problem the factor of disintegration over a period of two centuries, and the magnitude of the archaeologist's task becomes painfully clear. He must attempt to say as much as he can about the entire way of life of a people based on the very fragmentary remains of only a fraction of their material products. It is this incompleteness of the archaeological record which demands many of the techniques and methods of archaeology.

Like physicists, chemists, biologists, and other scientists, archaeologists observe, describe, and attempt to explain. Observation, description, and explanation comprise the three levels of archaeological study, and the archaeologist proceeds through these levels in a certain way so that he might finally be able to say many things about past cultures based on their scanty and imperfect remains.[4] The particular operations of archaeology which correspond to these somewhat general levels are the *collection* of data through excavation (observation), the *integration* of the data recovered by placing it in time and space and ordering it according to some type of classification which will permit comparison with similar data (description), and the draw-

[4] For a discussion of analytical levels in archaeology and anthropology, see G. R. Willey, and P. Phillips, *Method and Theory in American Archeology* (Chicago: University of Chicago Press, Phoenix Books, 1962), p. 4.

ing of *inferences* from the patterns seen in the integrated data which serve as explanations of these patterns in cultural terms (explanation).

At the first level, that of excavation, archaeologists have developed a set of field techniques which enable them to gain a maximum amount of useful information from the material buried beneath the earth. Having recovered this material in a carefully controlled way, it is necessary to bring order to it before any logical inferences can be made. At this second level of analysis, the primary goal is to describe the materials according to three variable dimensions, those of space, time, and form.[5] The spatial dimension of archaeological data is usually simply a function of the location of the excavations in terms of geographic space. To place the materials in time, a set of methods exists which enables the archaeologist to say how old his materials are. The formal dimension of archaeological materials consists of their physical appearance. Until the broken pots, remains of houses, flint arrowheads, and other fragments have been described in such a way that they can be compared with others, it is difficult to produce sophisticated inferences. The descriptive level of archaeology then consists of saying where the material was found, how old it is, and what it looks like—a seemingly simple set of operations which is in fact quite complex, and which has posed problems which have required almost philosophical solutions at times.

When he has recovered his evidence, and integrated it according to its spatial, temporal, and formal aspects, the archaeologist turns to the third level, that of asking what his materials mean in terms of the culture which produced them in the distant past. At this level, four important aspects of the data become important for the first time; we can classify these aspects as the contextual, the functional, the structural, and the behavioral.

Let us see how these aspects are used in archaeological inference by considering how they relate to a specific case, a clay bowl for example. The contextual aspect of this bowl refers to the context in which it was found, and all the circumstances of its occurrence, including the animal and plant remains found with it. Inferences concerning the cultural meaning of this bowl would certainly differ if it had been discovered in a burial rather than in a house or on the altar of a ruined temple. In one case, it may have served a very special mortuary function; in the others, it may have been either a domestic object or a ritual one.

The contextual aspect of an object frequently tells us something about its functional aspect. However, it may not if the context of discovery was not identical to its functional context in the culture which used it. Bowls used for ritual, domestic, or mortuary purposes could all find their way into a common trash heap; we would certainly not suggest that this context indicated the use of this type of bowl as trash. The functional aspect of an object

[5] A. C. Spaulding, "The Dimensions of Archaeology," *Essays in the Science of Culture in Honor of Leslie A. White,* ed. G. E. Dole and R. L. Carneiro (New York: Thomas Crowell and Co., 1960).

is at times clarified by the contextual aspect but may involve other considerations, since inferences regarding the function of the object in the culture which produced it involve the consideration of its contextual aspect as well as its functional aspect.

All man-made objects are reflections of the thoughts of the people who made them. The structural aspect of the bowl tells us something of the cultural norms which led to its production. In comparison with other bowls, this one might be seen as "typical" in that it and similar ones resulted from the expression in clay of a set of ideas which were joined by certain "rules" of combination. For example, since all bowls of this type have round bottoms and straight sides, there may have been a "rule" which dictated the repeated combination of round bottoms and straight sides, and bowls with square bottoms and flaring sides would violate such a "rule" and either would not have been made or would have been thought "wrong" by their makers.

The "rules" which govern the structural aspect of the bowl were a part of the cultural system of its makers, and as such were passed along from generation to generation. The repeated application of these "rules" shows a patterning of behavior which is reflected by the behavioral aspect of the bowl. That is, we are now concerned with the relation between the behavioral significance of patterning shown by the material and the behavior which was typical of the producing culture. For example, it has been shown that highly patterned and similar behavior led to the manufacture of similar pottery in an Indian village where women resided in the same dwelling with their daughters. The sharing of behavior patterns by these women, brought about by their common residence, was reflected in the sharing of "rules" as shown by the pottery.

These four aspects of archaeological data which form the basis of inference thus involve the circumstances of discovery of material objects as these might aid in understanding their function, the function served by the objects in the culture which produced them, the rules which dictated their creation, and the behavioral aspects of the sharing and passing on of these rules. At the inferential level, the archaeologist is at last providing the flesh for the bare bones of his data, and, if done with care and imagination, such a procedure makes possible the delineation and ultimate understanding of past cultures.

Excavation

In many ways, the archaeologist's fundamental unit of study is the *site*. In simplest terms, and perhaps in a rather profound sense, a site can be defined as that place where an archaeologist digs. A more specific definition would be a spatial concentration of material evidence of human activity. While sites are frequently the remains of communities, they need not be, and frequently represent activities other than those involved primarily with residence and domestic activity. Examples include cemeteries, frequently adjacent to communities, but at times separate; hunting sites, often called kill sites, where animals were slaughtered by driving a herd over a cliff; ceremonial precincts which were the focus of some type of ritual activity, Stonehenge being a good example; or quarries where stone was removed prior to its fabrication into finished tools.

Archaeologists speak of sites as having *components*, a component being the distinguishable evidence of a discrete occupation or use of that site by a group of people. A single component site would be one which was occupied only once, while a multicomponent site would be one which was occupied repeatedly by the same or different people. That the same people could produce two or more components can be understood through considering the effect of a temporary abandonment of the site of sufficient duration to permit the archaeologist to discern discrete evidence of each occupation. Both time and space can contribute to differences between cultures. It is possible that two neighboring communities differ less at one point in time than does one group of people from its direct ancestors a century removed.

When archaeological investigations are begun in an area where little work has been done in the past, the first step is to conduct a survey. This involves going over the area on foot, by auto, or horseback, inspecting aerial photographs if available, and recording all sites discovered through this process. Frequently, test excavations are made in conjunction with the survey to determine site depth or number of components. Such excavations are usually one or two small pits.

The sites are given numbers, and a form is made out which provides essential information regarding location, size, possible age, state of preservation, and other key facts. Many site-numbering systems are used; one of the most popular is that employed by the Smithsonian Institution, the University of California, and a number of other agencies. Typical site numbers assigned according to this system are 39 BF 2 and 4 SBa 520. An archaeologist familiar with the system knows immediately that the first is in South Dakota and the second in California, since the first number designates the state according to its position in an alphabetized list of states, with California being the fourth and South Dakota the thirty-ninth.[6] The letters designate counties, Buffalo and Santa Barbara respectively. The final number refers to the site within the county according to survey lists. Thus, the first number designates the second site surveyed and recorded in Buffalo Country, South Dakota, and the second the five hundred and twentieth site recorded in Santa Barbara County, California.

When the survey has been completed, certain sites are singled out for excavation. The reasons for such selection are many and varied, and range from the site's apparent importance based on size, depth, or other factors recorded on the survey form to the impending destruction of the site by road construction, dam building, or housing project development.

[6] Hawaii and Alaska, admitted to the Union since this numbering system was devised, are given numbers 49 and 50, thus preserving the other forty-eight number designations.

Having selected a site for excavation, the archaeologist establishes a camp in the site's vicinity, or, if he is lucky, houses his crew in a nearby town. In the United States, the majority of archaeological field work is done during the summer months, and crews are often made up of college students, although local help is frequently used to good advantage. The size of the crew is dictated by the size of the site, the magnitude of the work planned, and the operating budget.

The first step prior to excavation involves the drawing of a scale map of the site, or, in the case of very large sites, the particular area to be excavated and its immediate environs. A point is then located somewhere on or adjacent to the site, and designated the *datum* point. The datum point is marked permanently, either with a cement post, steel pipe, or by locating it on a natural feature such as a small rock outcropping which is not likely to be moved or lost over the years. The datum point is very important, since it is the reference point according to which all excavations are located. In this way, if future work should be done in the same area at some later time it will be possible to determine where previous excavations were carried out. A site not tied in with a datum point is floating in space, and once the dirt has been replaced it is impossible to tell where the excavations had been placed.

The first excavation is usually not on the site at all, but at a point well away from the area thought to contain cultural remains. This pit, often called a *control* pit, is dug in order to learn the nature of the soils and deposits in an undisturbed state. Such a pit is usually excavated to a depth of several feet. Its function is to show the archaeologist what the deposits on his site were like prior to man's disturbance of them. Disturbances observed on the site can then be interpreted in part with reference to the known, undisturbed cross section in the same area.

Having prepared the map, established the datum point, and ascertained the normal condition of the deposits on the site, the archaeologist is ready to begin excavation of the cultural materials. This procedure is a very complex one, and we can only consider excavation in its most general terms. Excellent manuals of field techniques providing specific and detailed information on excavation are available.[7]

In general, one of two approaches is employed, depending on the nature of the site. Both are aimed at maintaining a rigorous control on the location of all material recovered. In one case, there may be no visible evidence of structural remains such as walls, depressions marking the floors of houses, or mounds suggesting some type of building. In this case, one usually begins by laying out a grid on the site, and using the squares of the grid as a guide to the location of excavated materials. For example, if we were to begin excavation in a shell heap on the coast of California, there would be no visible evidence of structures, and past experience would suggest strongly that none

[7] R. Heizer, A Manual of Archaeological Field Methods (rev. ed.; Palo Alto: National Press, 1950).
K. Kenyon, Beginning in Archaeology (rev. ed.; New York: Praeger, 1961).

would be encountered. Lacking such remains, a grid of five-foot squares would be laid out on the site, covering the area which was to be excavated. In this way we are imposing an arbitrary order on an unstructured (to our eyes, at least) area of material. Our imposed, arbitrary order, in the form of grid squares, then serves as a guide to the segregation of specimens according to horizontal location. The squares are usually given co-ordinate numbers of one type or another. The usual procedure is to select an arbitrary point, which may also be the datum point, at the intersection of two lines, and give each square a number-letter code based on the cardinal points of the compass and distance from the point of departure. Thus a square just northeast of the point of departure would be designated N 1 E 1, since it is one square north and one square east of that point (Fig. 1).

Each of these pits is excavated as a unit, and the material from the pit is segregated vertically according to depth below surface. If there is no visible layering of the soil (stratification), arbitrary levels, usually either three or six inches thick, are kept separate. If visible stratification exists, an attempt is made to separate the material from a given pit according to the layer in which it is found. Such stratification usually corresponds with the discrete deposition of materials which could be quite different from level to level. If arbitrary levels are used there is a danger of mixing material from more than one level (Fig. 2). The pits are excavated in this manner until the bottom of the cultural deposits is reached. It is customary to dig some distance below this bottom level, at least in some of the pits, since there may be more cultural material separated from that above by a band of sterile, seemingly undisturbed fill.

The material recovered during excavation is placed in strong paper or cloth bags. Each bag is labeled according to the pit and level which produced the materials. A typical bag might carry the label:

4 SBa 7

N3 W5

0.5 ft – 1.0 ft B.S.

7/16/62

J.W.

The objects in the bag are known to have come from the second level below surface (vertical location within a half foot) in the third square to the north and the fifth square to the west of the key point of the grid (horizontal location within five feet) in the seventh site recorded in Santa Barbara County, California. Such a label provides a precise location of the contents of the bag. The date of excavation is given in the fourth line, and the initials in the fifth line are those of the digger so that, should any question arise concerning the material, the archaeologist will know who to consult (or in some cases, who to blame!).

A slight difference in labeling occurs if there are visible layers. In this case,

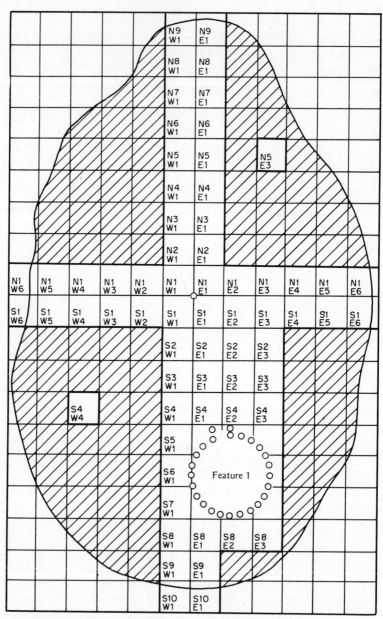

FIGURE 1. A small site (shaded area) showing layout of grid control. House circle (Feature 1) is excavated as a unit. Numbered squares have been excavated.

these layers are numbered, and the vertical location is given according to layer number. Each digger working on a pit also completes a daily report describing the work he did, unusual circumstances noted, and any other in-

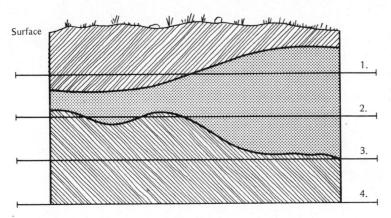

FIGURE 2. The effect of excavating sloping natural strata by arbitrary levels. Level 2 would contain the mixed materials from all three strata.

formation of importance. These notes are filed together and consulted frequently by the archaeologist as work progresses, and in the preparation of the final report of the excavation of the site.

When the presence of architectural features in a site is known, these frequently replace the grid as the main guide to horizontal location. In this case, there is an order inherent in the material, which the archaeologist can see. It is more logical to let this order dictate the location of materials whenever possible. For example, the site might be a multi-room pueblo in the Southwest. The rooms then become the basic units of horizontal location, since a completely random application of a grid could lead to mixing, much as the application of arbitrary vertical levels could produce mixing in the presence of visible stratification. If a square happened to cover parts of two rooms, and if these rooms served quite different functions, or were built and used at different times, unwanted mixing would be certain to result. Grids can be used with success within structural units, however, and often are useful when the structures are large.

Vertical segregation in structures is usually according to visible levels; at least an attempt is made to segregate material from the floor of the structure from the fill, that portion which was introduced at some later time, or through the collapse of a roof (Fig. 3). The difference between material from the floor and fill of a structure is illustrated by a common case encountered in excavating the foundations of earth-covered houses in the Great Plains. In this case, the dirt used by the builders in covering the roof to a thickness of two feet was often removed from areas of the village which contained debris from earlier times. In many instances, this material was hundreds of years older than the house being built. When the village was abandoned, and the house either burned or collapsed, older material was deposited atop the later material on the floor of the house. Failure to segregate specimens

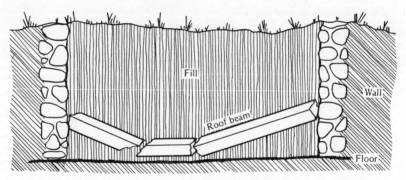

FIGURE 3. Typical controls used in a collapsed room unit.

according to whether they came from the floor or fill overlying the floor results in mixing materials which were made centuries apart.

A bag label from a site with structures might look something like this:

4 SBa 520
structure 22
room 6
floor

Those areas of sites with architectural features which lack such structures are excavated according to a grid system.

In the course of digging, the archaeologist encounters a variety of materials, which can be classified into three broad, general classes: artifacts, features, and non-artifactual materials. When associated, these constitute what is usually termed an archaeological assemblage. Artifacts are man-made objects such as pots, axes, pipes, arrowheads, or beads. Features are culturally produced objects which, unlike artifacts, cannot be taken from the field. They include fire pits, houses, storage pits, and burials, to name but a very few. The artifacts from features can be collected, but the features themselves must be recorded in the field. This is done by making accurate plans, cross-sectional drawings, and photographs of the feature. This information is filed with the other data from the site. Non-artifactual materials include a great variety of things, such as animal bone, seeds, charcoal, shells, pigments, asphaltum, and ash. While not man-made, such material tells the archaeologist much about the former occupants of the site.

When the excavations have been completed, and all records, artifacts, and related materials have been taken into the laboratory, the archaeologist is ready to begin the difficult but often fascinating task of resurrecting a life way of a people from the scraps and pieces which he has spent long hours removing from the earth. Before this can begin, the material must be cleaned and catalogued. Cataloguing is a simple process and involves placing a number on each object taken from the site. These numbers are entered in a catalogue, and the entry tells the location and circumstances of discovery of each object. Once a collection has been catalogued, it can be mixed, sorted, or segregated in any way, and it is still possible to place the objects back in their original relationships with an accuracy which is as great as the accuracy and precision of field location by pit, level, or feature.

Bernard Campbell

Method and Plan in the Study of Human Evolution

Science does not claim to discover the final truth but only to put forward hypotheses based on the evidence that is available at the time of their presentation. Well-corroborated hypotheses are often treated as facts, and such a fact is that of organic evolution. If a hypothesis is fairly general in its presentation, it is difficult to test, but a detailed hypothesis like that of organic evolution is readily susceptible to disproof. The evidence for evolution is overwhelming, and there is no known fact that either weakens the hypothesis or disproves it.

As part of organic evolution, the phenomenon of human evolution also amounts to a fact, but as yet its detailed path is not known with great certainty. We shall not aim merely at showing that human evolution has occurred, for this has already been well demonstrated. My intention here is to examine what evidence we have available for the detailed path of human evolution, in an attempt to discover the origin of man. Such a detailed hypothesis as I have here presented is likely to prove a fallible achievement, but its fallibility will not altogether detract from its value. Not only does the presentation of such a hypothesis have a high heuristic value, but it is by the erection and testing of hypotheses that science progresses. They may indeed be tested and found wanting; science demands only that they should be consistent with the available evidence and as far as possible self-consistent.

With the heuristic as well as the scientific value of the exercise in mind, I have attempted to synthesize into a coherent account the evidence now available of the course of human evolution. This evidence is derived from two sources, from fossils and from living animals. When we examine the

Reprinted from Bernard Campbell, Human Evolution, Second Edition (Chicago: Aldine Publishing Company, 1966); copyright © 1966, 74 by Bernard Grant Campbell. Reprinted by permission of the author and Aldine Publishing Company.

evidence carefully, however, we realize that neither source supplies directly pertinent facts, but inferences from both sources must be made as to what happened in time past. The evidence is always indirect; inference after inference must be made as to the course of the evolution of man. The whole truth will perhaps never be known, but that does not negate the value of making a hypothetical interpretation of what evidence we can lay our hands on.

Our interpretation of the evidence of human evolution rests on three kinds of inference:

1. A first inference, which lies nearest to the facts, may be obtained from a study of fossil bones and teeth. The evidence that these ancient fragments furnish is not *directly* relevant because we cannot tell whether or not any fossil actually belonged to a human ancestor. Indeed, such a coincidence would be unlikely for any particular fossil individual, but whether it be the case or not can never be known for sure. However, even if such fragments do not lie on the main stem of human evolution but are side branches, they can tell us something of the main stem from which they themselves evolved. Their relevance can of course only be understood in the light of the other evidence that we have at our disposal.

Studies of fossil bones and teeth tell us directly of the skeleton and dentition of the animals of which they were a part. We can, however, make a second inference from their structure, which will tell us more about the animal. We can make deductions about the size and form of the nerves and muscles with which they formed a single functional unit. Muscles leave marks where they are attached to bones, and from such marks we can assess the size of the muscles. At the same time, such parts of the skeleton as the cranium give us considerable evidence of the size and form of the brain and spinal cord.

2. Having built up a picture of at least some part of our fossilized creature, we can now make a further inference as to its whole biology and its way of life. In the first place, knowledge of its body will tell us something of its mode of locomotion (swimming, running, jumping, climbing, burrowing, etc.), from which it is not a long step to infer its environment (marine or fresh water, terrestrial or arboreal). At the same time, supporting evidence derived from a study of the geological context of the fossil may confirm the presence in the prehistoric times when it lived off seas, lakes, plains, or forests. Another line of inference also begins with the teeth. These may suggest the diet on which the animal fed (herbage, roots, flesh, etc.), and here again we find some indication of how the animal lived. In this way, by rather extensive deductions, we can build up a picture of the whole biology of the extinct animals.

3. But these interpretations are based on one further and essential line of evidence, that of living animals. This third kind of inferred evidence, though rather remote, will prove of inestimable value. If we assume from the fact of evolution that all animals are related, it is reasonable to deduce that those most similar are most recently descended from a common stock. We must

therefore compare the anatomy and physiology of living animals—and especially the monkeys and apes—with that of living man. This method can also be used to assess the closeness of relationship of different fossils. We can then assume that fossil bones most similar to any living animal are the remains of an ancestor of that animal, or a near relative of that ancestor. In turn, geological data that indicate the age of the fossil deposit will give us some idea of the succession in which the fossils lived. And we can make a further inference from the study of the comparative anatomy of living animals, for it is possible to predict within certain limits what a common ancestor was like, even in the total absence of fossils. Indeed, we can in that way infer the existence of ancient forms and from them infer their way of life.

In view of the methods of studying human evolution outlined above, it is not surprising that our concern [is] mainly with bones and teeth, for they are the only parts preserved as fossils. But that is not as limiting as might be supposed, since the skeleton is the most useful single structure in the body as an indicator of general body form and function. The teeth, in turn, are very valuable in assessing the relationships of animals because their basic form is not affected by the environment during growth. It is, however, a feature of [my approach] to infer from the bones and teeth—by consideration of their function—the maximum possible amount about the body as a whole and the way of life of the animal. In that way we attempt to trace the evolution of the whole human being as a social animal. . . .

In synthesizing evidence to discover the course of human evolution, we therefore draw on three kinds of data; we study living animals, fossil animals, and their geological age. We [also compare] the living primates—man's nearest relatives—with man himself, to gain insight into their differences. We [also] compare their structure with that of fossil remains of their ancestral relatives. The structure of this approach is shown in the accompanying diagram.

The underlying argument should be clear at any stage. The living primates form a series, from the most primitive to the most advanced, which suggests a general trend of evolutionary development. We investigate that trend to

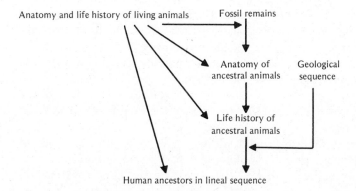

see what light it can throw on the origin of man, who is the most advanced of all primates. On the basis of our varied evidence, we finally postulate how man may have evolved from his primate ancestor. Such a final inference of the origin and evolution of *Homo sapiens* will, as we have said, be valid yet hypothetical: it will always be subject to revision as new evidence becomes available.

The only way to infer the whole life history of an animal from a few fragments of bone is to investigate the function of those fragments. For example, the form of fossil shoulder and arm bones will be informative in that respect only if we try to find how the muscles were attached to the bones and compare them with those of living animals. We may thus be able to determine the difference in function of our fossil bones from that of the bones of living animals. Was this fossil shoulder joint the type associated with animals that walk quadrupedally upon the ground or with animals that hang by their forelimbs from trees? An answer to that question gives us immense insight into the whole life history of the animal, and such insight is gained from our knowledge of living animals.

Organic Evolution

When, in 1858, Charles Darwin and Alfred Russel Wallace published their theory of evolution by natural selection, they provided a rational and convincing explanation of the causes as well as the fact of evolution in plants and animals.

These two naturalists both traveled widely and had observed minutely the variation that clearly existed within each species. Members of species, they observed, are not identical but show variation in size, strength, health, fertility, longevity, behavior, and countless other characters. Darwin, in particular, realized that natural variation was used by man in the selective breeding of plants and animals, for, by selection, man would breed only from the particular individuals possessing the qualities desired by the breeder.

In due course, the key to how a similar kind of selection operated in nature to transform wild species of organisms came to both men, and it arose from the same source. The first edition of a book entitled *An Essay on the Principle of Population*, by an English clergyman, T. R. Malthus, appeared as early as 1798, and in that book the author showed how the reproductive potential of mankind was far in excess of the natural resources available to nourish an expanding population. Malthus showed that in practice the size of populations was limited by such lethal factors as disease, famine, and war, and that such factors alone appeared to check what would otherwise be an expanding population.

Both Darwin and Wallace read Malthus' essay independently, and, remarkably enough, both men record in their diaries how they realized (in 1838 and 1858, respectively) that in that book lay the key to understanding the cause of the evolutionary process. It was clear to both that what Malthus had discovered for human populations was true for populations of plants and animals: their reproductive potential was vastly in excess of that necessary to maintain a constant population size. They realized that the individuals that in fact survived must for that reason be in some way better equipped to live in their environment than those which did not survive. Thus it followed that in a natural interbreeding population any variation would most likely be preserved that increased the organism's ability to leave fertile offspring, while the variations that decreased that ability would most likely be eliminated.

The theory that Darwin and Wallace formulated on that basis (at first, independently of each other) may be stated as four propositions and three deductions. Both propositions (P) and deductions (D) have since been well corroborated by careful observation.

P.1. Organisms produce a far greater number of reproductive cells, and, indeed, young individuals, than ever give rise to mature individuals.

P.2. The number of individuals in populations and species remains more or less constant over long periods of time.

D.1. *Therefore there must be a high rate of mortality both among reproductive cells and among immature individuals.*

P.3. The individuals in a population are not all identical but show variation in all characters, and the individuals that survive by reason of their particular sets of characters will become the parents of the next generation.

D.2. *Therefore the characters of those surviving organisms will in some way have made them better adapted to survive in the conditions of their environment.*

P.4. Offspring resemble parents closely but not exactly.

D.3. *Therefore subsequent generations will maintain and improve on the degree of adaptation realized, by gradual changes in every generation.*

As a result of the weight of evidence presented by Darwin in his famous book of 1859, *On the Origin of Species by Means of Natural Selection, or the Preservation of Favoured Races in the Struggle for Life,* biologists became convinced of the value and truth of the theory of evolution that he and Wallace proposed. Since that date, scientists have closely investigated the processes involved in the different propositions and deductions, and geneticists have come to understand the mechanism that accounts for the origin of variation and the transmission of characters. Of direct interest to students of human evolution are the concepts involved in deductions 2 and 3, for, while the genetic processes of man are no different from those of the rest of the animal kingdom, the selective factors that caused human evolution were unique.

The directing force in evolution is natural selection, and we must satisfy ourselves as to exactly how selective action came to effect the evolution of mankind.

Natural Selection and Fitness

It is clear that only a proportion of individuals in a population survive long enough to reach maturity and in their turn bear offspring. The environment itself determines the fate of each and, in destroying a proportion, selects the remainder. Through its effect upon each individual the environment controls to a decisive extent the direction and rate of evolution, and for that reason it may be considered to be one creative factor in the process of evolutionary change.

Although natural selection acts on individuals, it is the population that evolves, since the genetic plan of an individual is unalterable and remains constant throughout its life. A novel genetic plan arises only in the production of germ cells (*gametes*) and in the fusion of male and female germ cells in sexual reproduction. Not only are successive generations therefore necessary for the introduction of new gene combinations, but they are in fact the source of variation on which natural selection acts. This is not to deny the existence of evolution among animals and plants that reproduce asexually, but the sources of variation are more limited in them. . . .

A series of successive generations reproducing sexually relates individuals not only through the dimension of time but also in the dimension of space. Animals must find a mate among their contemporaries, and if they mate more than once in a lifetime (as most of them do), sexual relationships will be spread widely. Thus, the unit of evolution, the breeding population (or Mendelian population), includes all the individuals able to mate with each other. The size of the population may vary, but it is the breeding unit, with its network of sexual relations, that evolves in the course of time.

The *fitness* of such a population requires not only ability to cope with the existing environment and to reproduce but also the potentiality to evolve in the future in response to environmental change. This potentiality requires not only genetic stability, which reflects the broad stability of the environment, but also genetic variability (consequent upon sexual reproduction), which reflects the instability of the environment. That is to say, a population cannot afford to vary greatly in a stable, competitive, and hostile environment, for random variation may be lethal; the population must remain well adapted. At the same time, the population must be able to change, evolve, in adaptation to environmental change. This necessary genetic stability, accompanied by flexibility in the form of adaptability, is the basis of Darwinian fitness, and the balance struck between these two factors determines how fit a population is.

The dynamic stability of all the genetic components of a population (called the *gene pool*) makes possible adaptation to the environment without losing the possibility of modifying such adaptation in the presence of environmental change in the future. The absence of such modification can result in extinction; a proper balance must be found between stability and flexibility, and it is an alteration in the form of this balance that, among other things, characterizes the evolution of man.

It is clear that every gene, every character of the individual, its anatomy, physiology, and psychology, contributes to the biological fitness of the population, and it is in this sense and this sense only that a particular character is of evolutionary significance. There is no reason to suppose that any character can be neutral in this respect. Whatever characters evolve in a population, it is the contribution that they make to the population's fitness that results in their selection, in their survival. It is the population that evolves, not the individual.

At the same time, since all parts of an organism require energy for their maintenance, any part that ceases to have a function will be rapidly lost in the process of evolution. Not only any part but any process will also be lost. As an example, color vision is believed to have been evolved by the reptiles and then lost in the very early period of mammalian evolution; it was evolved a second time in the evolution of the primates, but other mammals cannot see color because it has not been selected during their evolution. Thus we do not often find characters without functions, a fact that may well apply to so-called vestigial characters; it seems probable that they have at least a reduced function.

The function of a character can therefore be understood fully only as an activity that is necessary and contributes to the overall reproductive advantage of the population in which it has evolved. The function of any character that cannot be interpreted in that light cannot be said to be properly understood. It follows that in order to understand the evolution of man it is desirable to consider the function of each new character that was evolved and to discover how it bestowed upon the population in which it became established a greater probability of survival in a changing environment.

How populations have survived by changing their nature is the story of evolution. The concept of fitness involves both adaptedness and adaptability, but, like evolution itself, though it may be elucidated in the past, it can only be surmised in the present.

Kenneth E. Boulding

General Systems Theory—The Skeleton of Science

General Systems Theory is a name which has come into use to describe a level of theoretical model-building which lies somewhere between the highly generalized constructions of pure mathematics and the specific theories of the specialized disciplines. Mathematics attempts to organize highly general relationships into a coherent system, a system however which does not have any necessary connections with the "real" world around us. It studies all thinkable relationships abstracted from any concrete situation or body of empirical knowledge. It is not even confined to "quantitative" relationships narrowly defined—indeed, the developments of a mathematics of quality and structure is already on the way, even though it is not as far advanced as the "classical" mathematics of quantity and number. Nevertheless because in a sense mathematics contains all theories it contains none; it is the language of theory, but it does not give us the content. At the other extreme we have the separate disciplines and sciences, with their separate bodies of theory. Each discipline corresponds to a certain segment of the empirical world, and each develops theories which have particular applicability to its own empirical segment. Physics, Chemistry, Biology, Psychology, Sociology, Economics and so on all carve out for themselves certain elements of the experience of man and develop theories and patterns of activity (research) which yield satisfaction in understanding, and which are appropriate to their special segments.

In recent years increasing need has been felt for a body of systematic theoretical constructs which will discuss the general relationships of the empirical world. This is the quest of General Systems Theory. It does not seek, of course, to establish a single, self-contained "general theory of practically everything" which will replace all the special theories of particular disciplines. Such a theory would be almost without content, for we always pay for generality by sacrificing content, and all we can say about practically everything is almost nothing. Somewhere however between the specific that has no meaning and the general that has no content there must be, for each purpose and at each level of abstraction, an optimum degree of generality. It is the contention of the General Systems Theorists that this optimum degree of generality in theory is not always reached by the particular sciences. The objectives of General Systems Theory then can be set out with varying degrees of ambition and confidence. At a low level of ambition but with a high degree of confidence it aims to point out similarities in the theoretical constructions of

From Kenneth Boulding, "General Systems Theory—the Skeleton of Science," Management Science, 2 (1956), 197–208. Reprinted with the permission of Management Science and the author.

different disciplines, where these exist, and to develop theoretical models having applicability to at least two different fields of study. At a higher level of ambition, but with perhaps a lower degree of confidence it hopes to develop something like a "spectrum" of theories—a system of systems which may perform the function of a "gestalt" in theoretical construction. Such "gestalts" in special fields have been of great value in directing research towards the gaps which they reveal. Thus the periodic table of elements in chemistry directed research for many decades towards the discovery of unknown elements to fill gaps in the table until the table was completely filled. Similarly a "system of systems" might be of value in directing the attention of theorists towards gaps in theoretical models, and might even be of value in pointing towards methods of filling them.

The need for general systems theory is accentuated by the present sociological situation in science. Knowledge is not something which exists and grows in the abstract. It is a function of human organisms and of social organization. Knowledge, that is to say, is always what somebody knows: the most perfect transcript of knowledge in writing is not knowledge if nobody knows it. Knowledge however grows by the receipt of meaningful information —that is, by the intake of messages by a knower which are capable of reorganizing his knowledge. We will quietly duck the question as to what reorganizations constitute "growth" of knowledge by defining "semantic growth" of knowledge as those reorganizations which can profitably be talked about, in writing or speech, by the Right People. Science, that is to say, is what can be talked about profitably by scientists in their role as scientists. The crisis of science today arises because of the increasing difficulty of such profitable talk among scientists as a whole. Specialization has outrun Trade, communication between the disciples becomes increasingly difficult, and the Republic of Learning is breaking up into isolated subcultures with only tenuous lines of communication between them—a situation which threatens intellectual civil war. The reason for this breakup in the body of knowledge is that in the course of specialization the receptors of information themselves become specialized. Hence physicists only talk to physicists, economists to economists—worse still, nuclear physicists only talk to nuclear physicists and econometricians to econometricians. One wonders sometimes if science will not grind to a stop in an assemblage of walled-in hermits, each mumbling to himself words in a private language that only he can understand. In these days the arts may have beaten the sciences to this desert of mutual unintelligibility, but that may be merely because the swift intuitions of art reach the future faster than the plodding leg work of the scientists. The more science breaks into sub-groups, and the less communication is possible among the disciplines, however, the greater chance there is that the total growth of knowledge is being slowed down by the loss of relevant communications. The spread of specialized deafness means that someone who ought to know something that someone else knows isn't able to find it out for lack of generalized ears.

It is one of the main objectives of General Systems Theory to develop these generalized ears, and by developing a framework of general theory to enable one specialist to catch relevant communications from others. Thus the economist who realizes the strong formal similarity between utility theory in economics and field theory in physics is probably in a better position to learn from the physicists than one who does not. Similarly a specialist who works with the growth concept—whether the crystallographer, the virologist, the cytologist, the physiologist, the psychologist, the sociologist or the economist —will be more sensitive to the contributions of other fields if he is aware of the many similarities of the growth process in widely different empirical fields.

There is not much doubt about the demand for general systems theory under one brand name or another. It is a little more embarrassing to inquire into the supply. Does any of it exist, and if so where? What is the chance of getting more of it, and if so, how? The situation might be described as promising and in ferment, though it is not wholly clear what is being promised or brewed. Something which might be called an "interdisciplinary movement" has been abroad for some time. The first signs of this are usually the development of hybrid disciplines. Thus physical chemistry emerged in the third quarter of the nineteenth century, social psychology in the second quarter of the twentieth. In the physical and biological sciences the list of hybrid disciplines is now quite long—biophysics, biochemistry, astrophysics are all well established. In the social sciences social anthropology is fairly well established, economic psychology and economic sociology are just beginning. There are signs, even, that Political Economy, which died in infancy some hundred years ago, may have a re-birth.

In recent years there has been an additional development of great interest in the form of "multisexual" interdisciplines. The hybrid disciplines, as their hyphenated names indicate, come from two respectable and honest academic parents. The newer interdisciplines have a much more varied and occasionally even obscure ancestry, and result from the reorganization of material from many different fields of study. Cybernetics, for instance, comes out of electrical engineering, neurophysiology, physics, biology, with even a dash of economics. Information theory, which originated in communications engineering, has important applications in many fields stretching from biology to the social sciences. Organization theory comes out of economics, sociology, engineering, physiology, and Management Science itself is an equally multidisciplinary product.

On the more empirical and practical side the interdisciplinary movement is reflected in the development of interdepartmental institutes of many kinds. Some of these find their basis of unity in the empirical field which they study, such as institutes of industrial relations, of public administration, of international affairs, and so on. Others are organized around the application of a common methodology to many different fields and problems, such as the Survey Research Center and the Group Dynamics Center at the University of Michigan. Even more important than these visible developments, perhaps, though harder to perceive and identify, is a growing dissatisfaction in many departments, especially at the level of graduate study, with the existing traditional theoretical backgrounds for the empirical studies which form the major part of the output of Ph.D. theses. To take but a single example from the field with which I am most familiar. It is traditional for studies of labor relations, money and banking, and foreign investment to come out of departments of economics. Many of the needed theoretical models and frameworks in these fields, however, do not come out of "economic theory" as this is usually taught, but from sociology, social psychology, and cultural anthropology. Students in the department of economics however rarely get a chance to become acquainted with these theoretical models, which may be relevant to their studies, and they become impatient with economic theory, much of which may not be relevant.

It is clear that there is a good deal of interdisciplinary excitement abroad. If this excitement is to be productive, however, it must operate within a certain framework of coherence. It is all too easy for the interdisciplinary to degenerate into the undisciplined. If the interdisciplinary movement, therefore, is not to lose that sense of form and structure which is the "discipline" involved in the various separate disciplines, it should develop a structure of its own. This I conceive to be the great task of general systems theory. For the rest of this paper, therefore, I propose to look at some possible ways in which general systems theory might be structured.

Two possible approaches to the organization of general systems theory suggest themselves, which are to be thought of as complementary rather than competitive, or at least as two roads each of which is worth exploring. The first approach is to look over the empirical universe and to pick out certain general *phenomena* which are found in many different disciplines, and to seek to build up general theoretical models relevant to these phenomena. The second approach is to arrange the empirical fields in a hierarchy of complexity of organization of their basic "individual" or unit of behavior, and to try to develop a level of abstraction appropriate to each.

Some examples of the first approach will serve to clarify it, without pretending to be exhaustive. In almost all disciplines, for instance, we find examples of populations—aggregates of individuals conforming to a common definition, to which individuals are added (born) and subtracted (die) and in which the age of the individual is a relevant and identifiable variable. These populations exhibit dynamic movements of their own, which can frequently be described by fairly simple systems of difference equations. The populations of different species also exhibit dynamic interactions among themselves, as in the theory of Volterra. Models of population change and interaction cut across a great many different fields—ecological systems in biology, capital theory in economics which deals with populations of "goods," social ecology, and even certain problems of statistical mechanics. In all these fields population change, both in absolute numbers and in structure, can be discussed in terms of birth and survival functions relating numbers of births and of deaths in specific age groups to various aspects of the system. In all these fields the interaction of population can be discussed in terms of competitive, complementary, or parasitic relationships among populations of different species, whether the species consist of animals, commodities, social classes or molecules.

Another phenomenon of almost universal significance for all disciplines is that of the interaction of an "individual" of some kind with its environment. Every discipline studies some kind of "individual"—electron, atom, molecule, crystal, virus, cell, plant, animal, man, family, tribe, state, church, firm, corporation, university, and so on. Each of these individuals exhibits "behavior," action, or change, and this behavior is considered to be related in some way to the environment of the individual—that is, with other individuals with which it comes into contact or into some relationship. Each individual is thought of as consisting of a structure or complex of individuals of the order immediately below it—atoms are an arrangement of protons and electrons, molecules of atoms, cells of molecules, plants, animals and men of cells, social organizations of men. The "behavior" of each individual is "explained" by the structure and arrangement of the lower individuals of which it is composed, or by certain principles of equilibrium or homeostasis according to which certain "states" of the individual are "preferred." Behavior is described in terms of the restoration of these preferred states when they are disturbed by changes in the environment.

Another phenomenon of universal significance is growth. Growth theory is in a sense a subdivision of the theory of individual "behavior," growth being one important aspect of behavior. Nevertheless there are important differences between equilibrium theory and growth theory, which perhaps warrant giving growth theory a special category. There is hardly a science in which the growth phenomenon does not have some importance, and though there is a great difference in complexity between the growth of crystals, embryos, and societies, many of the principles and concepts which are important at the lower levels are also illuminating at higher levels. Some growth phenomena can be dealt with in terms of relatively simple population models, the solution of which yields growth curves of single variables. At the more complex levels structural problems become dominant and the complex interrelationships between growth and form are the focus of interest. All growth phenomena are sufficiently alike however to suggest that a general theory of growth is by no means an impossibility.

Another aspect of the theory of the individual and also of interrelationships among individuals which might be singled out for special treatment is the theory of information and communication. The information concept as developed by Shannon has had interesting applications outside its original field of electrical engineering. It is not adequate, of course, to deal with problems involving the semantic level of communication. At the biological level however the information concept may serve to develop general notions of structuredness and abstract measures of organization which give us, as it were, a third basic dimension beyond mass and energy. Communication and information processes are found in a wide variety of empirical situations, and are unquestionably essential in the development of organization, both in the biological and the social world.

These various approaches to general systems through various aspects of the empirical world may lead ultimately to something like a general field theory of the dynamics of action and interaction. This, however, is a long way ahead.

A second possible approach to general systems theory is through the arrangement of theoretical systems and constructs in a hierarchy of complexity, roughly corresponding to the complexity of the "individuals" of the various empirical fields. This approach is more systematic than the first, leading towards a "system of systems." It may not replace the first entirely, however, as there may always be important theoretical concepts and constructs lying outside the systematic framework. I suggest below a possible arrangement of "levels" of theoretical discourse.

(i) The first level is that of the static structure. It might be called the level of *frameworks*. This is the geography and anatomy of the universe—the patterns of electrons around a nucleus, the pattern of atoms in a molecular formula, the arrangement of atoms in a crystal, the anatomy of the gene, the cell, the plant, the animal, the mapping of the earth, the solar system, the astronomical universe. The accurate description of these frameworks is the beginning of organized theoretical knowledge in almost any field, for without accuracy in this description of static relationships no accurate functional or dynamic theory is possible. Thus the Copernican revolution was really the discovery of a new static framework for the solar system which permitted a simpler description of its dynamics.

(ii) The next level of systematic analysis is that of the simple dynamic system with predetermined, necessary motions. This might be called the level of *clockworks*. The solar system itself is of course the great clock of the universe from man's point of view, and the deliciously exact predictions of the astronomers are a testimony to the excellence of the clock which they study. Simple machines such as the lever and the pulley, even quite complicated machines like steam engines and dynamos fall mostly under this category. The greater part of the theoretical structure of physics, chemistry, and even of economics falls into this category. Two special cases might be noted. Simple equilibrium systems really fall into the dynamic category, as every equilibrium system must be considered as a limiting case of a dynamic system, and its stability cannot be determined except from the properties of its parent dynamic system. Stochastic dynamic systems leading to equilibria, for all their complexity, also fall into this group of systems; such is the modern view of the atom and even of the molecule, each position or part of the system being given with a certain degree of probability, the whole nevertheless exhibiting a determinate structure. Two types of analytical method are important here, which we may call, with the usage of the economists, comparative statics and true dynamics. In comparative statics we compare two equilibrium positions of the system under different values for the basic parameters. These equilibrium positions are usually expressed as the solution of a set of simultaneous equations. The method of comparative statics is to compare the solutions when the parameters of the equations are changed. Most simple mechanical problems are solved in this way. In true dynamics on the other hand we exhibit the system as a set of difference or differential equations, which are then solved in the form of an explicit function of each variable with time. Such a system may reach a position of stationary equilibrium, or it may not—there are plenty of examples of explosive dynamic systems, a very simple one being the growth of a sum at compound interest! Most physical and chemical reactions and most social systems do in fact exhibit a tendency to equilibrium —otherwise the world would have exploded or imploded long ago.

(iii) The next level is that of the control mechanism or cybernetic system, which might be nicknamed the level of the *thermostat*. This differs from the simple stable equilibrium system mainly in the fact that the transmission and interpretation of information is an essential part of the system. As a result of this the equilibrium position is not merely determined by the equations of the system, but the system will move to the maintenance of any *given* equilibrium, within limits. Thus the thermostat will maintain *any* temperature at which it can be set; the equilibrium temperature of the system is not determined solely by its equations. The trick here of course is that the essential variable of the dynamic system is the *difference* between an "observed" or "recorded" value of the maintained variable and its "ideal" value. If this difference is not zero the system moves so as to diminish it; thus the furnace sends up heat when the temperature as recorded is "too cold" and is turned off when the recorded temperature is "too hot." The homeostasis model, which is of such importance in physiology, is an example of a cybernetic mechanism, and such mechanisms exist through the whole empirical world of the biologist and the social scientist.

(iv) The fourth level is that of the "open system," or self-maintaining structure. This is the level at which life begins to differentiate itself from not-life. It might be called the level of the *cell*. Something like an open system exists, of course, even in physico-chemical equilibrium systems; atomic structures maintain themselves in the midst of a throughput of atoms. Flames and rivers likewise are essentially open systems of a very simple kind. As we pass up the scale of complexity of organization towards living systems, however, the property of self-maintenance of structure in the midst of a throughput of material becomes of dominant importance. An atom or a molecule can presumably exist without throughput: the existence of even the simplest living organism is inconceivable without ingestion, excretion and metabolic exchange. Closely connected with the property of self-maintenance is the property of self-reproduction. It may be, indeed, that self-reproduction is a more primitive or "lower level" system than the open system, and that the gene and the virus, for instance, may be able to reproduce themselves without being open systems. It is not perhaps an important question at what point in the scale of increasing complexity "life" begins. What is clear, however, is that by the time we have got to systems which both reproduce themselves and maintain themselves in the midst of a throughput of material and energy, we have something to which it would be hard to deny the title of "life."

(v) The fifth level might be called the genetic-societal level; it is typified by the *plant*, and it dominates the empirical world of the botanist. The outstanding characteristics of these systems are first, a division of labor among cells to form a cell-society with differentiated and mutually dependent parts (roots, leaves, seeds, etc.), and second, a sharp differentiation between the genotype and the phenotype, associated with the phenomenon of equifinal or "blueprinted" growth. At this level there are no highly specialized sense organs and information receptors are diffuse and incapable of much throughput of information—it is doubtful whether a tree can distinguish much more than light from dark, long days from short days, cold from hot.

(vi) As we move upward from the plant world towards the animal kingdom we gradually pass over into a new level, the "animal" level, characterized by increased mobility, teleological behavior, and self-awareness. Here we have the development of specialized information-receptors (eyes, ears, etc.) leading to an enormous increase in the intake of information; we have also a great development of nervous systems, leading ultimately to the brain, as an organizer of the information intake into a knowledge structure or "image." Increasingly as we ascend the scale of animal life, behavior is response not to a specific stimulus but to an "image" or knowledge structure or view of the environment as a whole. This image is of course determined ultimately by information received into the organism; the relation between the receipt of information and the building up of an image however is exceedingly complex. It is not a simple piling up or accumulation of information received, although this frequently happens, but a structuring of information into something essentially different from the information itself. After the image structure is well established most information received produces very little change in the image—it goes through the loose structure, as it were, without hitting it, much as a sub-atomic particle might go through an atom without hitting anything. Sometimes however the information is "captured" by the image and added to it, and sometimes the information hits some kind of a "nucleus" of the image and a reorganization takes place, with far reaching and radical changes in behavior in apparent response to what seems like a very small stimulus. The difficulties in the prediction of the behavior of these systems arises largely because of this intervention of the image between the stimulus and the response.

(vii) The next level is the "human" level, that is of the individual human being considered as a system. In addition to all, or nearly all, of the characteristics of animal systems man possesses self consciousness, which is something different from mere awareness. His image, besides being much more complex than that even of the higher animals, has a self-reflexive quality—he not only knows, but knows that he knows. This property is probably bound up with the phenomenon of language and symbolism. It is the capacity for speech—the ability to produce, absorb, and interpret *symbols,* as opposed to mere signs like the warning cry of an animal—which most clearly marks man off from his humbler brethren. Man is distinguished from the animals also by a much more elaborate image of time and relationship; man is probably the only organization that knows that it dies, that contemplates in its behavior a whole life span, and more than a life span. Man exists not only in time and space but in history, and his behavior is profoundly affected by his view of the time process in which he stands.

(viii) Because of the vital importance for the individual man of symbolic images and behavior based on them it is not easy to separate clearly the level of the individual human organism from the next level, that of social organizations. In spite of the occasional stories of feral children raised by animals, man isolated from his fellows is practically unknown. So essential is the symbolic image in human behavior that one suspects that a truly isolated man would not be "human" in the usually accepted sense, though he would be potentially human. Nevertheless it is convenient for some purposes to distinguish the individual human as a system from the social systems which surround him, and in this sense social organizations may be said to constitute another level of organization. The unit of such systems is not perhaps the person—the individual human as such—but the "role"—that part of the person which is concerned with the organization or situation in question, and it is tempting to define social organizations, or almost any social system, as a set of roles tied together with channels of communication. The interrelations of the role and the person however can never be completely neglected—a square person in a round role may become a little rounder, but he also makes the role squarer, and the perception of a role is affected by the personalities of those who have occupied it in the past. At this level we must concern ourselves with the content and meaning of messages, the nature and dimensions of value systems, the transcription of images into a historical record, the subtle symbolizations of art, music, and poetry, and the complex gamut of human emotion. The empirical universe here is human life and society in all its complexity and richness.

(ix) To complete the structure of systems we should add a final turret for transcendental systems, even if we may be accused at this point of having built Babel to the clouds. There are however the ultimates and absolutes and the inescapable unknowables, and they also exhibit systematic structure and relationship. It will be a sad day for man when nobody is allowed to ask questions that do not have any answers.

One advantage of exhibiting a hierarchy of systems in this way is that it gives us some idea of the present gaps in both theoretical and empirical knowledge. Adequate theoretical models extend up to about the fourth level, and not much beyond. Empirical knowledge is deficient at practically all levels. Thus at the level of the static structure, fairly adequate descriptive models are available for geography, chemistry, geology, anatomy, and descriptive social science. Even at this simplest level, however, the problem of the adequate description of complex structures is still far from solved. The theory of indexing and cataloguing, for instance, is only in its infancy. Librarians are fairly good at cataloguing books, chemists have begun to catalogue structural formulae, and anthropologists have begun to catalogue culture traits. The cataloguing of events, ideas, theories, statistics, and empirical data has hardly begun. The very multiplication of records however as time goes on will force us into much more adequate cataloguing and reference systems than we now have. This is perhaps the major unsolved theoretical problem at the level of the static structure. In the empirical field there are still great areas where static structures are very imperfectly known, although knowledge is advancing rapidly, thanks to new probing devices such as the electron microscope. The anatomy of that part of the empirical world which lies between the large molecule and the cell however, is still obscure at many points. It is precisely this area however—which includes, for instance, the gene and the virus—that holds the secret of life, and until its anatomy is made clear the nature of the functional systems which are involved will inevitably be obscure.

The level of the "clockwork" is the level of "classical" natural science, especially physics and astronomy, and is probably the most completely developed level in the present state of knowledge, especially if we extend the concept to include the field theory and stochastic models of modern physics. Even here however there are important gaps, especially at the higher empirical levels. There is much yet to be known about the sheer mechanics of cells and nervous systems, of brains and of societies.

Beyond the second level adequate theoretical models get scarcer. The last few years have seen great developments at the third and fourth levels. The theory of control mechanisms ("thermostats") has established itself as the new discipline or cybernetics, and the theory of self-maintaining systems or "open systems" likewise has made rapid strides. We could hardly maintain however that much more than a beginning had been made in these fields. We know very little about the cybernetics of genes and genetic systems, for instance, and still less about the control mechanisms involved in the mental and social world. Similarly the processes of self-maintenance remain essentially mysterious at many points, and although the theoretical possibility of constructing a self-maintaining machine which would be a true open system has been suggested, we seem to be a long way from the actual construction of such a mechanical similitude of life.

Beyond the fourth level it may be doubted whether we have as yet even the rudiments of theoretical systems. The intricate machinery of growth by which the genetic complex organizes the matter around it is almost a complete mystery. Up to now, whatever the future may hold, only God can make a tree. In the fact of living systems we are almost helpless; we can occasionally cooperate with systems which we do not understand: we cannot even begin to reproduce them. The ambiguous status of medicine, hovering as it does uneasily between magic and science, is a testimony to the state of systematic knowledge in this area. As we move up the scale the absence of the appropriate theoretical systems becomes ever more noticeable. We can hardly conceive ourselves constructing a system which would be in any recognizable sense "aware," much less self conscious. Nevertheless as we move towards the human and societal level a curious thing happens: the fact that we have, as it were, an inside track, and that we ourselves *are* the systems which we are studying, enables us to utilize systems which we do not really understand. It is almost inconceivable that we should make a machine that would make a poem: nevertheless, poems *are* made by fools like us by processes which are largely hidden from us. The kind of knowledge and skill that we have at the symbolic level is very different from that which we have at lower levels—it is like, shall we say, the "knowhow" of the gene as compared with the knowhow of the biologist. Nevertheless it is a real kind of knowledge and it is the source of the creative achievements of man as artist, writer, architect, and composer.

Perhaps one of the most valuable uses of the above scheme is to prevent us from accepting as final a level of theoretical analysis which is below the level of the empirical world which we are investigating. Because, in a sense, each level incorporates all those below it, much valuable information and insights can be obtained by applying low-level systems to high-level subject matter. Thus most of the theoretical schemes of the social sciences are still at level (ii), just rising now to (iii), although the subject matter clearly involves level (viii), Economics, for instance, is still largely a "mechanics of utility and self interest," in Jevons' masterly phrase. Its theoretical and mathematical base is drawn largely from the level of simple equilibrium theory and dynamic mechanisms. It has hardly begun to use concepts such as information which are appropriate at level (iii), and makes no use of higher level systems. Furthermore, with this crude apparatus it has achieved a modicum of success, in the sense that anybody trying to manipulate an economic system is almost certain to be better off if he knows some economics than if he doesn't. Nevertheless at some point progress in economics is going to depend on its ability to break out of these low-level systems, useful as they are as first approximations, and utilize systems which are more directly appropriate to its universe—when, of course, these systems are discovered. Many other examples could be given—the wholly inappropriate use in psychoanalytic theory, for instance, of the concept of energy, and the long inability of psychology to break loose from a sterile stimulus-response model.

Finally, the above scheme might serve as a mild word of warning even to Management Science. This new discipline represents an important breakaway from overly simple mechanical models in the theory of organization and control. Its emphasis on communication systems and organizational structure, on principles of homeostasis and growth, on decision processes under uncertainty, is carrying us far beyond the simple models of maximizing behavior of even ten years ago. This advance in the level of theoretical analysis is bound to lead to more powerful and fruitful systems. Nevertheless we must never quite forget that even these advances do not carry us much beyond the third and fourth levels, and that in dealing with human personalities and organizations we are dealing with systems in the empirical world far beyond our ability to formulate. We should not be wholly surprised, therefore, if our simpler systems, for all their importance and validity, occasionally let us down.

I chose the subtitle of my paper with some eye to its possible overtones of meaning. General Systems Theory is the skeleton of science in the sense that it aims to provide a framework or structure of systems on which to hang the flesh and blood of particular disciplines and particular subject matters in an orderly and coherent corpus of knowledge. It is also, however, something of a skeleton in a cupboard—the cupboard in this case being the unwillingness of science to admit the very low level of its successes in systematization, and its tendency to shut the door on problems and subject matters which do not fit easily into simple mechanical schemes. Science, for all its successes, still has a very long way to go. General Systems Theory may at times be an embarrassment in pointing out how very far we still have to go, and in deflating excessive philosophical claims for overly simple systems. It also may be helpful however in pointing out to some extent *where* we have to go. The skeleton must come out of the cupboard before its dry bones can live.

2

Biocultural Evolution: From Ape to Human

Homo sapiens is a special kind of animal. We are primate animals, but within the pattern of primate evolution we have developed some very unusual characteristics. If we are to understand these special features that underlie our humanity and at the same time see ourselves in relation to those other animals, then we should start with some comparisons between humans and the other living primates. The paper by Hans Kummer gives us some of the flavor of this comparison, from the point of view of an ethologist. One of the frustrations of students in introductory anthropology is that each of these topics could be a whole semester's work. This discussion about primate comparisons deals with only some very general main points that some individuals may want to pursue much further.

The second major task in understanding the human animal is to explore something of the fossil evidence concerning our prehuman past. That whole trek into the Ice Ages and beyond, to remains from 3, 4, and 5 million years ago requires attention to geology, as well as understanding of the general principles of biological evolution as set forth in the paper by Campbell in our first section. While there are literally hundreds of different individual fossil finds that make up the as yet incomplete jigsaw puzzle of our evolutionary history, certain of our ancestors stand out as major evolutionary landmarks, and at the same time major points of controversy. Neanderthal, the fossil that first aroused great controversy and new theoretical possibilities over a hundred years ago, is still today much debated. Some anthropologists see Neanderthal as our direct ancestor; others relegate that group of fossils to a side branch or dead end in the evolutionary process.

During the last twenty years the most important set of new evidence of human evolution has been the fossils discovered by Louis B. Leakey and associates in East Africa. That whole story of the fossil materials from Olduvai Gorge in Tanzania is itself a complex and many-sided story. Phillip Tobias has set out some of the main features of this saga in some detail and provides a summary of the range of evidence for what appears to have been an exciting transitional time in our human or prehuman past. We have selected this paper as special "honors material," but the main features of this paper should be read by all students as a summary of very important fossil materials.

Somewhere during the transition from apelike ancestors to the modern upright walking *Homo sapiens,* some of our ancestors developed the capacity for complicated symbolic language. Many people have regarded this symbolic capability, and language use, as the major unique characteristic of our species—up until the 1960s, that is. During the last ten years some of our beliefs about the uniqueness of human symbolic capabilities have been shaken. Several different teams of researchers, including the Gardners at the University of Nevada, have demonstrated that our primate cousins the chimpanzees have impressive and apparently unused capacities for understanding and communicating symbolically. Although their vocal anatomies do not permit them to develop a rich spoken language, the chimps can manipulate objects or use sign language (or even computer keyboards) to put together abstract constructions and complex messages under experimental conditions. These recent discoveries give a whole new dimension to the matter of origins of human symbolic processes. Some of these specially trained chimps have even joked and engaged in word play with their trainers!

Hans Kummer

Man and Primates Compared

Distribution

There are many signs that indicate the success of a species; one of them is simply the size of its geographical range. Even a superficial look at what primates and man have achieved in inhabiting the earth shows that the range of Homo sapiens includes the ranges of all other primate species taken together. It actually extends far beyond their total range, especially toward the poles but also away from the continents to the oceanic islands.

Distributions further suggest that man in some way stands apart from the rest in his ecological needs. In the African rain forests many primate species are sympatric. They can survive in the same habitat because it offers a variety of ecological niches, and so it is not surprising that there is also a niche for man. The picture changes as we leave the rain forests and move into the savannas; the number of primate species that share a common habitat now declines to two or three. Man is still with them. Finally, in the semi-deserts and the colder areas, we find only one monkey species in each area. The semi-deserts of the Red Sea coasts are inhabited only by hamadryas baboons, the cold and barren Ethiopian mountains only by geladas; only anubis baboons are found in the desert mountains of Tibesti, and only the Barbary macaque in the Atlas range. Since no physical barrier prevents other species from colonizing the hamadryas and the gelada areas, we must conclude that their habitats offer primates only one ecological niche. But even here, we find man. Apparently his ecological niche is so different from that of his pioneering fellow primates that both may exist in the same harsh environment.

Traveling farther north, far beyond the ranges of the last nonhuman primate, we continue meeting that same species man that we first saw among scores of other primate species in the equatorial rain forest. Ever changing his survival technique, he seems to fit into every niche on dry land. Nearly naked in the rain forest, man becomes hairy with the hair of animals in the north, and in the arctics, wooden extensions on his feet carry him over the snow and make him, ecologically, a new animal. The tools with which he transforms himself and his niches are his cultures. The geographical mosaic of the nonhuman primates, confined in their narrow species ranges, restricted to their single way of life, contrasts with the pervasive distribution of ecologically polymorphic man.

Diversity of Social Structure

Since ecological polymorphism requires polymorphism of behavior, wide adaptive success should also reveal itself in a variety of social structures. Because the human species survives in more habitats than all other primate species together, one would expect that its social behavior, as far as it is related to ecological conditions, would vary accordingly. Man would then equal the behavioral range not of one but of many primate species. This seems correct in at least one respect: One primate species generally adheres to a single type of social structure. For example, all gibbon populations studied to date are organized into monogamous pairs of one male and one female plus young. So far, all known hamadryas baboons and geladas live in breeding units of one male and several females, and savanna baboons are always organized in larger, promiscuous units. In contrast, the social structures of our own species range from monogamous to polygynous systems and even include polyandry, which is unknown among primates.

Nonhuman primate species may, however, not be quite so homogeneous in structure as would now seem, since only a few populations of each species have been studied. A larger sample might reveal the odd aberration which, like polyandry in man, would not be discovered in a brief survey. We know already that Indian langurs (Presbytis entellus), which form multi-male groups in many areas, can also organize into one-male groups in certain other regions.

If the present impression that most primate species have only one social organization is confirmed, it might be taken as proof of a narrow modification range. But such a conclusion would be premature. Man's technological success has exposed his social behavior to a far greater variety of environments than any other primate deals with. Such variety must have, at one or another time or place, activated nearly every behavioral modification of which humans are capable. If other primate species were exposed to a similar variety of modifying influences they might also reveal a broad potential for diverse social organization. On the other hand, the evidence of hamadryas baboons suggests that the genetic potential of some nonhuman species may indeed be restricted to one type of society which environmental change would hardly alter.

Technology

Man is the animal that not only occupies but also shapes its ecological niches by means of technology. When inspecting the known primate achievements in this respect, one can only be unimpressed. Their lack of elaborate technical skills compares unfavorably with those of many so-called lower vertebrates and many invertebrates. Hundreds of bird species build nests a hundred times more elaborate than the chimp nest, which is the highest achievement of primate building activity. Certain weaver birds build roofs above their nest colonies; primates at best use one when it is already there.

The comparison is somewhat unfair, because the evolutionary trend from birds to mammals tends to replace parental behavior by parental physiology. Primates, being mammals, raise their young first within the mother's body and then feed them with her milk, which makes complex nesting and feeding behavior unnecessary. But rodents are mammals too. Many of them dig burrows and pat them with plant parts carried into the nest from outdoors. Many collect and hoard food. There is not one among the two hundred or so primate species that constructs an ever-so-simple burrow or does much with food but eat it on the spot. Specialized swimmers and divers have evolved among both rodents and carnivores, but not among primates.

Primates are, superficially, as unspecialized and primitive as their insectivorous, bush-dwelling ancestors. They occasionally catch prey to eat, but their hunting techniques cannot match those of the specialized carnivores. They are primarily vegetarians; but they can neither survive a severe winter at high altitudes or latitudes, nor can they go long without water in dry areas, as some ungulates do. Although primates have prehensile hands, their use of tools is modest. Chimpanzees poke at hidden insects with long, thin stalks, but so does a species of Galapagos finch. Some macaques are reported to smash shells with stones. Egyptian vultures open ostrich eggs the same way, and diving California sea otters carry a stone with every mussel to the surface of the sea and there crack the shell. Nobody would have predicted that a primate would develop a technology of human dimension.

Given that no nonhuman primates hunt, build, or store food as elegantly as, say, wasps, how do we interpret the fact that it was a primate that ultimately developed all these behaviors to their greatest extent? If monkeys and apes are at all more human than other mammals with regard to their behavioral substrates, then why have primate field studies depicted their subjects as such poor performers in these domains? And what pressures would have favored the evolution of mental capacities that apparently are not used?

One answer is that some of the most developed primate abilities are manifested only in critical situations so rare that they have never been witnessed by field scientists. Some of the fantastic hunters' tales of baboon burials and other unusual behaviors may contain a grain of truth. Field observation is indeed a poor method for studying rare but important behavior. It takes experiments creating unusual situations to delineate a behavioral repertoire that comes close to the animal's full capacities. No field observation, it seems, could ever have predicted that chimpanzees would collect metal coins of certain colors if they could later exchange them for fruits in a slot machine, but laboratory experiments have shown that they have this ability. A vast body of experimental data has demonstrated an unusual disposition in chimpanzees for tool-using, technical problem solving, and cooperation, essential capacities in human technology.

In contrast to the highly specialized but rigid skills of lower vertebrates, then, primates have a potential for learning broad sets of tasks which neither they nor their ancestors encountered in this particular form. *This flexibility, and not a specialized but genetically fixed skill, prepared the way for culture.* Thus, monkeys and apes are not so far removed from man in their capacities as the study of their everyday life in the wild suggests. Even so, the primates' success in laboratories does not explain why they ever evolved abilities that seem so unimportant or even inapplicable in their habitats.

Among the tentative answers to this problem, I shall report the one I find most convincing. The British ethologist Michael Chance has repeatedly discussed the hypothesis that the large primate cortex and the corresponding ability to use new tools may first have evolved in the context of social behavior and not in the context of technical exploitation of the habitat. Most primates are sexually stimulated and motivated for many months of the year, but the overt behavior of most group members is constantly restricted by the presence of dominant group members. An action is or is not permissible depending on who is watching and who might lend support. Success requires that a monkey know and integrate the status of all group members present, and their alliances and antagonisms toward him and among each other. Thus, a primate, in his relationship with a partner, is able to use a third animal. A female can provoke an attack from a male against an opponent who ranks above her by the trick of presenting to the male while threatening the opponent. Subordinate male macaques approaching dominant males often take along a young infant to inhibit the aggression of the other. Whereas wild monkeys use no technical tools to exploit their habitat, they manifest analogous schemes in their social behavior.

According to Chance, "tool-using" in the social context may have predisposed the ancestors of man to develop technical tools. This speculation has an interesting secondary implication. If the primate ability of predicting combined effects was indeed transferred from the social to the technical context, then this ability was at the same time freed of the ancient compulsions inherent in social behavior, such as aggression and sex. The handling of sticks or wheels is not loaded with the emotions that go with the handling of social partners, and progress in technology could thus be much faster than progress in social behavior. This disparity is a major problem of modern man.

This leads us back to the social skills of nonhuman primates. Skillful behavior in the social field requires that the actor be capable of adapting his own emotional behavior to the situation—which now and then means suppressing it. Without this ability, predicting and combining would be useless. It seems that some primates can indeed suppress certain behaviors even against strong motivations to act. The female anubis baboons that were transferred to a hamadryas troop offer an example. They easily learned that the aggression of the herding hamadryas male could be avoided by staying close to him, but this meant they had to suppress their strong motivation to flee. Most anubis females succeeded in doing so for many hours on end, although sudden compulsive escapes occurred even long after the new social role had been learned.

The ability to predict combined effects and to control one's own behavior may thus be among the primate predispositions for human adaptations. These abilities would have to be generalized and transferable in order to serve as a basis for culture. So far, field studies have been crude in their approach to these abstract aspects of behavior. We do not know how much combination and self-control are worked into the social behavior of primates, and we have not studied their group foraging with special attention to these abilities. This, perhaps, is why we are often left with the impression that behavior and social organization are no more refined among primates than among many other mammals. We may have looked too much at the units of behavior and not enough at its organization. Experimental results from laboratories should receive much more attention from field workers than in the past.

Sexual Differentiation and Group Life

If we now shift to the more ancient levels of social roles and the style of group life, comparisons become more easy and traits more common in primates and man.

The primate male, in general, is more aggressive and more dominant than the female. He is more likely to leave the group and to migrate. This can probably be said of most human societies too. Within the family group, the human male seeks his activities farther from the home base than the female. Whether these are more than superficial similarities is open to question. In general, human cultures seem to push the sexual division of roles much further than nonhuman primate societies.

This differentiation of roles is already significant with primate infants. The play groups of macaques and baboons, for example, generally include more juvenile males than females; in hamadryas play groups the ratio is about eight to one. While the males are out playing, the females often remain with the female adults of their family group. Sociographic analyses further show that male juveniles interact in larger groups than females, who mostly associate with one partner only. Preliminary data based on the same methods reveal a similar pattern in human children.

One promising way of comparing human and primate behavior is to ask: What is the total array of social tendencies evolved in the primate order? And which of these tendencies have passed into the human heritage? The characteristics most interesting to compare are not the simple motor acts and communicative signals cherished by ethologists, but the higher level of behavioral sets such as submission or social exclusion. These sets make use of the communicative acts, but they are highly independent of their particular form and have their own taxonomic distribution. The style of primate group life may exemplify this level of comparison.

The style of primate groups apparently varies along a main gradient, with the macaque-baboon style and the chimpanzee style as the extremes. Baboon and macaque societies are typically characterized by intense dominance. Individuals tend to assert exclusive access to a particular partner. On the group level, this tendency is paralleled by a strong differentiation between group members and outsiders, with avoidance or antagonism between neighboring groups. Thus, the groups are typically closed and live separately, with the hamadryas and the geladas as the only major exceptions. It is still unclear whether dominance and exclusiveness are causally connected parts of the same syndrome. Territoriality, it seems, is not closely associated with either of them.

The group style of chimpanzees and (largely) of gorillas is marked by a low intensity of dominance. Exclusive claims for partners are absent among adults, so that an inferior male can copulate with a female in full view of the dominant male. These great apes do not noticeably discriminate against outsiders. Their society is open, and its members, instead of living as a closed pack of "ins" among slightly inimical neighbors, are socially and spatially mobile. Fights between entire groups have been seen among macaques, baboons, and langurs, but not among the large apes.

One would expect that man, a close relative of the apes, would approach their social style rather than that of baboons. But the overall impression suggests the opposite. Man's latent or overt inclinations for dominance hierarchies, closed groups, and discrimination against outsiders suggest that he approached the baboon type of society, at least at one stage of his evolution. In many respects the hamadryas baboon's society of closed but coordinated family units is a better model of human social structure than that of the chimps. While man seems on the way toward open societies, his rigid social attitudes are often transferred to larger groups, to the level of professions, religions, nations, and races, and they continue to flare up on the level of small groups. The British primatologist Vernon Reynolds, drawing attention to this phylogenetic incongruence, suggests ecological explanations. He points out that such immobile investments of labor as crop fields, stores, cattle, and houses must have worked in favor of territorial behavior, closed food-sharing units, and hierarchies based on exclusive possessions. Regardless of whether man ever passed through a chimp-like stage, it is obvious that behavior sets of this type have a peculiar taxonomic distribution. They are not confined to a closely related group of species but they emerge here and there without apparent systematic continuity. Territorial behavior, dominance, and responses of social exclusion appear to be general vertebrate potentials. They seem to emerge in very similar forms, by evolution or modification, wherever a species is faced with appropriate ecological conditions.

Conclusion

The speculative and deductive character of this text may at times have disappointed the reader as much as it frustrated the author. While thinking and writing, I came to see several reasons why primate field studies have so far failed to present conclusive insights into the ecological functions of societies.

First, social behavior is of two kinds. One kind consists of the behaviors that establish and constantly reestablish the society. These are mating, nursing, fighting, playing, social grooming, and other associative interactions. These behaviors occur mostly at resting places; they are conspicuous and have therefore been well studied. The second category shows the society in function, in its concerted interaction with the habitat. Spatial arrangements in social foraging and traveling, decisions on travel routes, and communication about food sites belong to this class. Its manifestations are subtle and inconspicuous, consisting of a short glance or of a male's sitting down instead of walking on. Studying them is difficult and has therefore been neglected, although it is this class of behavior that passes or fails in the ecological test, not the noisy fights. With respect to the present theme, field students have generally looked at the wrong side of the picture in studying a society's internal physiology instead of its ecological functions. Let us be fair—not all investigators who went to the field intended to study adaptive functions.

Second, it seems that future field studies pertinent to our subject must shift from the easily observable motor patterns of the individual to the higher level of behavioral sets and strategies. These are more relevant to survival than the particular form of a threat or a digging movement. We have seen that the strong point of primate adaptation does not lie in the motor skills of the individual, but in the way things are done in groups.

Third, there is a need for increased experimental research, both in the field and in laboratories, on the range of modification in response to varied environments. It is not enough to describe one variant of a species' social organization that occurs under "natural" conditions. We should investigate the modification potential of a species to its very limits, that is, to the point where the changes induced by the environment are no longer adaptive and homeostatic but lead to breakdown. I can hardly imagine a more urgent research task than to gather such knowledge about man. Insights into the tolerance limits of primates could help us in defining our own.

C. Loring Brace

Ridiculed, Rejected, but Still Our Ancestor Neanderthal

Neanderthal: The word is now so familiar, and its implications of the archaic so clear, that it describes things quite unrelated to its original meaning. Modern writers refer to ultraconservative and moss-backed attitudes in social affairs as "Neanderthal," and occasionally call the holders of such views "Neanderthals"; likewise, so-called Neanderthals in politics are regarded as human fossils, with the further implication that they properly should have become extinct long ago.

As we shall see, this implication of extinction has been developed to a surprising degree by the majority of scientists who have studied the genuine human fossils called Neanderthals. But is this majority right? Did extinction of the Neanderthals come, as we are usually led to believe, because they were too different to qualify as our ancestors? If a Neanderthal existed today, if he appeared in a crowd of the rest of us, what would people say?

Would the robust bony structure, massive chest, and developed musculature be especially noticeable under a modern suit of clothes? Of course, clothes would not hide the broad, thick hands or the massive face beneath the heavy bony brow—particularly if this Neanderthal should smile and display the big front teeth that, more than anything else, hold the key to the difference between a Neanderthal and an average modern man. In his time, in a world where tools were crude, many manipulatory tasks had to be handled by that original built-in, the human dentition. Natural selection favored heavy-duty teeth that could withstand wear and tear; to support such teeth required a face somewhat larger than modern size.

The term Neanderthal itself refers to a valley in the heart of western Germany, through which flows a stream, the Düssel, which joins the Rhine at Düsseldorf. In the seventeenth century, this quiet valley was a favored place for picnics, and was particularly admired by the Düsseldorf organist and composer Joachim Neumann, who signed some of his works "Neander," the Greek translation of his name. After his death, local people began calling the secluded valley, then spelled thal in German, Neanderthal.

By the mid-nineteenth century, industrialism was transforming the Neanderthal with quarrying operations in the limestone cliffs that loomed above the stream bed. In 1856, quarrymen discovered a human skeleton buried in a small cave, the Feldhofer Grotto, but they did not recognize the bones as human; in fact, they unceremoniously shoveled them out of the cave while

Reprinted from C. Loring Brace, "Neanderthal," Natural History (May 1968), 38–45, with permission of Natural History Magazine. Copyright © The American Museum of Natural History, 1968.

preparing it for blasting. However, the quarry owner preserved the bones, and their importance was recognized later by Johann Karl Fuhlrott, a science teacher at the local high school, who was an enthusiastic student of the region's natural history. Unfortunately, the bones were discovered so casually and unprofessionally that only the larger pieces of what must have been a complete human skeleton were preserved. None of the smaller bones, the fragile parts, or the teeth were saved.

Fuhlrott not only realized that the bones were human but also that they were of most unusual and possible "primitive" form. Unlike certain more recent discoverers of important hominid fossils, he also realized that to study and interpret them required training he did not possess. So he enlisted the aid of Herman Schaaffhausen, professor of anatomy at Bonn. Both men then presented their evidence for discussion at a number of scientific society meetings, suggesting that the bones might have belonged to an individual of some antiquity. Actually, the antiquity they had in mind went back only to the pre-Celtic and pre-Germanic inhabitants of northern Europe hinted at in the writings of classical authors—a far cry from the forty thousand years and beyond that we now know must have been the case.

Unfortunately, respected and "competent" opinion on the significance of the Neanderthal skeleton was delivered before a basis existed for appreciating either the extent of human antiquity or the possibility of evolutionary changes and relationships in a biological sense. The relationship between ancient human remains and the course of man's development has always brought a heightened, emotion-laden concern, and even supposedly competent opinion has frequently been less than scientifically objective. This is true even for recent exciting finds in Africa, but perhaps the most bizarre spectrum of opinion concerning a human fossil was that offered in supposed explanation of the original Neanderthal skeleton.

Suggestions that this ancient person had suffered from idiocy, lunacy, rickets, premature ossification of cranial sutures, and various other pathological manifestations came from a series of "experts." Others, reflecting the sense of superiority felt by denizens of such places as London, Paris, Berlin, reflected their prejudices when they compared the supposedly "inferior" traits of the Neanderthaler to features they assumed to be characteristic of people inhabiting various benighted places in the modern world—such as Holland or Ireland. One distinguished German anatomist dismissed the skeleton as that of an "old Dutchman"; an eminent French scholar referred to it as a robust Celt resembling "a modern Irishman with low mental organization."

Possibly the most amusing interpretation was based on the following data about the Neanderthaler: (1) evidently the left elbow had been broken early in life and had healed in such a way that movement was subsequently restricted; (2) the individual was presumed to have suffered from rickets, so it was suggested that pain from the elbow and the rickets had caused the person to knit his brows in a perpetual frown. This became ossified, producing what has become an outstanding characteristic in descriptions of Neanderthal form

—the heavy ridge along the brow. Adding to this pathological "evidence," Schaaffhausen's anatomical colleague from Bonn, Professor Mayer, suggested that the bowed femurs might testify to a lifetime spent on horseback. Assembling all this, Mayer suggested the Neanderthal was a deserter from the Russian forces that chased Napoleon back across the Rhine in 1814 and, more specifically, a rickety Mongolian Cossack who had crawled into the cave for refuge.

The most significant opinion came from Rudolf Virchow, a German who was a recognized leader in cellular pathology and also highly respected as an anthropologist and liberal politician. This critical and uncompromising champion of the strict scientific principles of deduction and inference said that there was virtually no way of determining the antiquity of the find because with it were no associated tools or animal bones. After a detailed, careful review of the notable features of the skeleton, he pronounced it pathological. Naturally, few even thought to question the judgment of one of the world's leading pathologists.

To counter those who claimed great antiquity for the skeleton, Virchow pointed out that it was that of an individual who was past fifty years of age. This argued that the Neanderthaler had belonged to a civilization that cared for, and assured the survival of, the middle-aged and elderly, which would have been most unlikely in the remote prehistoric period that some had suggested. With this logic Virchow increased the probability, so his readers believed, that unusual morphological features of the skeleton could be accounted for only by invoking some sort of pathological involvement. It was a cautious, critical, and skeptical approach; unfortunately, Virchow was using the right reasons to reach the wrong conclusion.

In 1858—two years after the Neanderthal discovery—a visit by British scholars to the site of Boucher de Perthes' archeological researchers in northwest France led to the conviction that man must have been in existence for a substantial period of time prior to the dawn of written history. This conviction was confirmed by groups from both Britain and France in the succeeding year. And in November of the same year, 1859, appeared Darwin's book *Origin of Species*. It changed forever the entire frame of reference for appraising the significance of sequences of prehistoric animals—including the human animal. After a decade of debate, evolution by means of natural selection became a dominant aspect of natural science in both England and Germany.

In France, however, Darwin's reception was quite different. Twenty years after Darwin and A. R. Wallace (who had independently hit on the same ideas) published their preliminary essays, the term "evolution" was cautiously introduced to French biology. But in France, instead of meaning descent with modification by means of natural selection, the concept of evolution was so similar to the theory known as "catastrophism"— featuring extinctions, invasions, and successive creations, supported by Cuvier during the first third of the nineteenth century—that it largely amounted to a relabeling of the earlier view.

At any rate, Darwinian evolutionists were not yet able to do much about the initial Neanderthal interpretations. Still lacking was an adequate basis for appraising either the skeleton's antiquity or its evolutionary significance. And an aura of peculiarity has clung to the Neanderthals ever since. To this day, most professional anthropologists and paleontologists, with myself as one of the unpopular exceptions, repeatedly refer to the Neanderthals as "extreme," "specialized," or "aberrant," and deny that they were ancestors of modern man.

Another decade passed. Then, exactly thirty years after the first Neanderthal discovery, vindication of the Schaaffhausen—Fuhlrott views came from the discovery of two more fossil skeletons, this time in the commune of Spy, in Belgium. Both resembled the original Neanderthal so closely that to claim that their characteristics, too, were explainable by idiocy or pathology was straining coincidence too much for most people, although Virchow continued to cling to his pathological judgment.

The excavation techniques this time had been more careful; the jaws, teeth, and many of the smaller bones were preserved. Not only did the Spy skeletons reinforce the view that the Neanderthal form characterized an entire prehistoric population; the Neanderthal population to which they evidently belonged could now be dated, relatively speaking, for the first time. This was because archeological research during the thirty years had provided a broad framework for the arrangement of prehistoric materials: the most recent of the Stone Age categories was the Neolithic, a period of crude crop tending and polished stone tools; most ancient was the Lower Paleolithic, characterized by heavy hand axes of chipped stone (bifaces) and a hunting mode of existence.

The Spy Neanderthals were fitted into a category one degree less ancient than the Lower Paleolithic, because they were found with tools of a type first recognized in excavations at the southern French village of Le Moustier. With today's radioisotope dating techniques we know that the cultural traditions of the Mousterian Neanderthals extended from about 35,000 B.C. back at least 50,000 years to somewhere between 80,000 and 100,000 years ago. In the 1880's, however, there was no way to make even rough estimates of antiquity other than to note that such-and-such cultural assemblage was older or younger than another one. Hence the Mousterian culture was considered a degree younger than the Lower Paleolithic hand axe cultures, but still much older than that of the earliest cultivators and herdsmen.

Since the Spy discovery, except for narrowing the dates and refining our knowledge of how the Neanderthals provided themselves with clothing and shelter, we retain pretty much the same picture of their life and times that was available by the end of the nineteenth century.

The Spy discovery, followed by others, provided a frame of reference for a few previously uncovered isolated fossils. One of these was a skull found on the north side of the Rock of Gibraltar in 1848. Although that was eight years before the "original" Neanderthal, its importance was not recognized until years later. The excitement over Darwin's book and the English translation of Schaaffhausen's memoir on Neanderthal focused a little belated attention on this Gibraltar skull, which, in the meantime, had been brought to England. After its brief appearance at a couple of scientific society meetings, it was consigned to the Museum of the Royal College of Surgeons in England, where it remained unappreciated until after the end of the nineteenth century. Not until a German anatomist made a detailed comparison with other Neanderthal skeletal material did the English become interested enough to initiate studies themselves.

The other fossils that could be placed in context because of the Spy discoveries were mandibles. The original Neanderthal lacked face, jaw, and teeth, and, although it was suspected that individual robust mandibles found in France, Belgium, and Czechoslovakia came from Neanderthal-like individuals, it remained only a suspicion until the Spy remains raised it to a substantial probability.

Meanwhile, the years between 1856 and 1886 saw the recovery of artifacts and skeletal remains from the period immediately following that of the Mousterian and Neanderthal. The artifacts were more finely made than those of the Mousterian, many more kinds of tools were represented, and tools of worked bone were found for the first time. Some of them were decorated with graceful, realistic engravings showing many of the extinct animals whose bones occurred in the same deposits.

And for good measure, the human skeletal remains from those Upper Paleolithic levels, including the famous Cro-Magnon discovery, displayed aggregates of traits that allowed their describers to claim the creature had differed in no way from modern man. This depended on viewpoint. The skeletons indicated distinctly heavier musculature and larger faces, jaws, and teeth than the *average* modern man has. However, a small but sufficient number of living humans do attain this level of ruggedness. At any rate, the archeological record revealed the ancients were skillful hunters as well as talented artists. And, with their skeletal form suggesting they should be considered ancestors of contemporary Europeans, the modern interpreters studied and discussed the Upper Paleolithic men with an almost familial pride.

Next came an important discovery in the other direction of the time scale. The decade following 1886 brought the discovery and discussion of a very different and far older form—the famous *Pithecanthropus erectus* from Java. When the young Dutch physician, Eugene Dubois, found it in the Far East in 1891–92, opinions varied almost as much as those that greeted the first Neanderthal. By the turn of the century, however, a fair percentage of those qualified to judge had accepted the specimen as representing a true, if primitive, human being. Both *Pithecanthropus* and Neanderthal stood as erect as we do.

Then, at the very end of the nineteenth and for the first five years of the present century, came the discovery and description of the remains of between 14 and 15 Neanderthals from a Yugoslavian site at Krapina in Croatia. But there was not a complete long bone or reconstructible skull; the Krapina population is now known chiefly for adding to our knowledge about the human dentition. A total of 263 individual teeth was found.

It is evident that by the beginning of the twentieth century the modest collection of evidence concerning the course of human evolution was ripe for a thorough appraisal. This was done—in simple, logical, Darwinian fashion—by the Strasbourg anatomist and anthropologist Gustav Schwalbe in his book *Studien zur Vorgeschichte des Menschen* ("Studies on the Prehistory of Man").

He regarded Dubois' *Pithecanthropus* as representing the earliest known human population ancestral to all later men. Today, most scholars accept this part of his conclusions, although few now separate *Pithecanthropus* in a formal taxonomic sense from genus *Homo*. Consequently, *Pithecanthropus* becomes *Homo erectus*, but non-technically we can go on referring to members of this species as pithecanthropines.

Descended from the pithecanthropines are the Neanderthals, whom Schwalbe placed directly in the line of human evolution, first as the separate species *Homo neanderthalensis* and later, for reasons not altogether clear, as *Homo primigenius*. Actually, the general scientific belief today is that the Neanderthals were so like modern men that, if some were alive today, they could interbreed with *Homo sapiens* to produce viable fertile offspring. In other words, most anthropologists now favor classifying the Neanderthals as *Homo sapiens*, the same as modern man; at most, they would only add the subspecific designation *neanderthalensis*. But this does not alter the basic situation. The same people retain the old belief that Neanderthal was too different to qualify as our ancestor.

Schwalbe had been more alert than that. Having classed Neanderthals as a separate species, he then claimed they became extinct, not because they left no descendants, but extinct in the sense that the world today no longer has a distinct population of Neanderthals. For his time, Schwalbe's was the most balanced and logical approach.

Contrast it with the general idea held by zoologists and anthropologists in 1968. Almost no vestige of Schwalbe's appraisal has survived. Instead one reads varying versions of a view that contrasts the Neanderthals with us. They are written off as victims of "specializations"—although just why it is disadvantageous to be extraordinarily robust and to possess heavy brow ridges, faces, and teeth is rarely spelled out. Ultimately these inhabitants of western Europe are said to have succumbed to the invasion of populations of fully modern form who had evolved somewhat mysteriously "in the east."

Why such a change in viewpoint? For an indicator, we turn to reminiscences by the late Sir Arthur Keith, the dominant physical anthropologist in the English-speaking world throughout the first half of the twentieth century: "I had supposed that man's ascent had been made by a series of succeeding stages [but] . . . discoveries were being made in France which indicated to my mind that Neanderthal man could no longer be regarded as an ancestor. The stratum containing his fossil bones was followed at once by one containing the fossil bones of our type—the modern type. Apparently we moderns had invaded Europe and exterminated Neanderthal man."

He was referring to the Neanderthal skeletons found in 1908, one being the famous "old man" of La Chapelle-aux-Saints from Corrèze—the most complete, best-preserved Neanderthaler discovered up to then and for a long time thereafter. This find led to an overwhelming monograph published by paleontologist Marcellin Boule of the National Museum of Natural History in Paris. In sharp contrast to Schwalbe, he concluded that Neanderthal form was too divergent to represent a stage in the evolution of modern man. Every one of Boule's crucial points eventually turned out to be questionable, but in the meantime even Schwalbe inexplicably conceded that the Neanderthals had become extinct without issue. When Schwalbe died two years later, in 1916, his evolutionary views, with a few exceptions, died with him.

Then, fifteen years later, came the discovery of bones at the cave of Mugharet-es Skhul—on the slopes of Mount Carmel in what is now Israel. These bones showed a mixture of Neanderthal and modern traits in proportions so equal that the term Neanderthaloid was coined to acknowledge that here was no full-scale Neanderthal. It had been Boule's verdict that there could be no intermediaries, yet here was an intermediary.

Various hypotheses were offered in explanation. One of them was based on the idea that the Mount Carmel deposits were earlier in date than western Europe's "classic" Neanderthals, so perhaps here in the Middle East were the remains of the population that evolved into modern form—while the classic, or conservative, Neanderthals of the west remained isolated and unchanged.

Since such hypotheses were suggested, circumstances have changed. First, modern dating techniques place the Skhul remains at less than 40,000 years—in other words, right between the classic Neanderthals and the earliest moderns, in time as well as in form. Second, several good classic Neanderthals in the full flower of brows, jaws, and teeth have been found at Shanidar cave in Iraq, the heart of the area "to the east." Also indicating that classic Neanderthals were not isolated in western Europe is the discovery of Neanderthals in Morocco, Greece, Israel, Uzbekistan, and even China—plus candidates for Neanderthal status that have existed for years in Java and Africa as well.

Certainly there is no longer any reason to regard the Neanderthals as an isolated European phenomenon. Nor is there any reason to reject their candidacy for status as the direct ancestors of more recent men. So, in an interpretive sense, we are right back where Gustav Schwalbe left us in 1906. Because the evidence with which Boule contradicted Schwalbe's relatively simple approach was faulty at that time, and has not been supported since then, it is reasonable to ask what impelled him to view the world as he did.

To begin with, we should realize that Marcellin Boule was trained in late nineteenth-century France, where the concept of "evolution" was far more akin to the castastrophism of Cuvier than to the Darwinian views in which Schwalbe and Keith were trained. Boule explained change in the human fossil record by extinctions and invasions with little concern for adaptive response and the mechanics of biological change. His view could be called "hominid catastrophism."

That it should have come to dominate thinking about the course of human evolution in general, and the Neanderthal's role in particular, is due in large part to the accidents of history. Prior to 1914, the most effective attempt to deal with human origins from an evolutionary point of view had been produced in a German academic context and had considerable influence elsewhere. But the invasion of Belgium and the burning of Louvain in 1914—in short, the initiation of World War I—seriously tarnished the civilized and scholarly image that German academia had previously enjoyed. From the point of view of the study of human evolution, it was particularly unfortunate that the tradition associated with Schwalbe should have been located at Strasbourg. Political control of Alsace-Lorraine, which had been in German hands since the Franco-Prussian war of 1870–71, returned to the French after World War I. They promptly fired the German faculty of the university at Strasbourg ending the tradition that had flourished there under Schwalbe.

Also after the war, major works summarizing our knowledge of Boule and Keith, among others; and two subsequent generations of professional students of human evolution have grown up schooled to believe that the prehistoric Neanderthals were a peculiar group, not because of anything pathological as Virchow once thought, but rather because of their assumed failure to adapt.

Our knowledge of the events that occurred in the remote past will always be incomplete, and proof for one or another interpretive hypotheses can never be final. Where the subject of our concern is as rare and fragmentary as Neanderthal skeletal remains, we have seen how the political and intellectual history of the past hundred years has, in some instances, played a more significant role in determining which points of view find favor than do the objective pieces of evidence themselves. From what we actually know, it is probable that if a properly clothed and shaved Neanderthal were to appear in a crowd of modern urban shoppers or commuters, he would strike the viewer as somewhat unusual in appearance—short, stocky, large of face—but nothing more than that. Certainly few would suspect he was their "caveman" ancestor.

Phillip V. Tobias

Early Man in East Africa

Olduvai Gorge in Northern Tanganyika (Republic of Tanzania) has in recent years thrown a flood of light on an early chapter in the evolution of man. Between 1955 and 1963, L. S. B. Leakey, M. D. Leakey, and their sons and helpers uncovered fossil bones representing no fewer than 14 individuals from various levels in the Olduvai strata (1). Although detailed descriptions are yet to be published (2), it is clear that earlier and lower mid-Pleistocene deposits of East Africa contain the remains of at least two different kinds of fossil hominids (that is, members of the Hominidae, the family of man). The first group of fossils fits comfortably into a well-defined category, the australopithecines, which have long been recognized as a partially hominized group, that is, a group possessing some characteristics like those of Homo. The second assemblage has proved most difficult to place in any existing category. After exploring every other possibility, we have been forced to attribute this second group of fossils to a new and lowly species of Homo, namely Homo habilis: this species represents a more markedly hominized lineage than the australopithecines and comprises a hitherto-unrecognized and even unsuspected transitional or intermediate form of early man (3).

In this article I consider the history and some of the characteristics of the new fossils, as well as their cultural and evolutionary position, and propose modifications to some existing schemes of hominid phylogeny in the light of these new discoveries.

The Olduvai Sequence

Before I review the new discoveries in detail, it may be useful to describe briefly the Olduvai stratigraphic succession (Fig. 1).

Olduvai Gorge has been cut by river action through a deep succession of old sediments, tuffs, and lavas. From the exposed strata, a remarkable series of fossils and implements has been recovered, ranging in age from Lower to Upper Pleistocene.

The strata exposed in the walls of Olduvai Gorge were divided by Hans Reck into five beds, numbered I to V, from the lowest upwards. This classification was adopted and the limits of the beds were more precisely defined by Leakey and, more recently, by Hay (4). It should be stressed, however, that

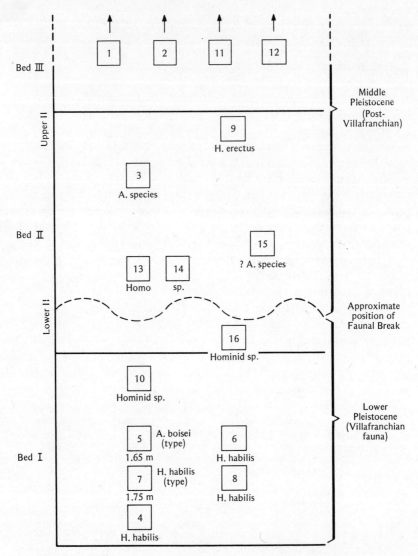

FIGURE 1. Schematic representation of the lower half of the Olduvai sequence, showing the approximate vertical positions of hominid fossils (numerals enclosed in squares). The potassium-argon dates are indicated near the left margin (m = million years).

these beds are not absolute stratigraphic units corresponding to sharp divisions in the Pleistocene sequence of events. Rather they are conveniently mappable units. . . .

In this presentation, the subdivision into five beds will be used to provide a background against which to consider the hominid remains.

Potassium-argon dates are available for several levels within Bed I. The span of time represented by these Beds is suggested by ages 1.75 and 1.65 million years for two levels in the lower half of Bed I. In a word, the chapters of human evolution which are dealt with here cover the period from about 2 million to about half a million years ago.

The Australopithecine Chapter

Exactly 40 years have elapsed since R. A. Dart published a description of a new kind of higher primate which had been recovered from a limestone fissure at Taung in South Africa (6). This discovery was one of the most remarkable, perhaps the most important, in the history of paleoanthropology. Earlier discoveries of fossilized human ancestors had shown unequivocally human affinities: this is true of the Neanderthal group and even of the earlier and morphologically more primitive Java ape-man, *Homo erectus* (or *Pithecanthropus*, as he has been called until fairly recently). But the Taung specimen differed from the others in being so much smaller-brained, bigger-toothed, and in other respects morphologically more archaic, that its precise affinities remained a cause of dispute for decades. Initially, Dart claimed no more than that it was an ape with a number of features suggesting hominization, that is, an advance in a general human direction. He therefore called it *Australopithecus africanus*—simply the "southern ape of Africa."

With the wisdom of hindsight, we are today able to recognize in Dart's fossil the first real proof of the animal origins of man, the first concrete fossil evidence that Darwin's theory of the origin of species by small modifying steps and gradations from other pre-existing species is applicable to man. For here was an apelike creature which showed in its anatomical make-up a greater number of resemblances to hominids than are shown by any of the existing manlike apes of Africa or Asia.

It took time, as well as the discovery of many new specimens of *Australopithecus* (Table 1), the patient study of their anatomical features, and a closer

---

Table 1: Dates of Discovery of Australopithecine Fossils

1924	Tang (S. Afr.)
1936–1949	Sterkfontein Type Site (S. Afr.)
1938–1954	Kromdraai (S. Afr.)
1939	Garusi (E. Afr.)
1947–1961	Makapansgat (S. Afr.)
1948–1952	Swartkrans (S. Afr.)
1955–1959	Olduvai (E. Afr.)
1957–1958	Sterkfontein Extension Site (S. Afr.)
1964	Peninj, Lake Natron (E. Afr.)

---

look at the living great apes, to reach the now widely accepted conclusion that the australopithecines were an early branch of the Hominidae, the family of man, rather than of the Pongidae, the family of the apes. No fewer than eight sites in Africa have yielded australopithecine fossils (Fig. 2).

Most of the African australopithecines belong to deposits which have been classified, on comparative faunal evidence, as Lower Pleistocene. At least three sites have provided evidence that the australopithecines survived in Africa into the Middle Pleistocene—namely Swartkrans and Kromdraai in the Transvaal and Peninj (Natron) in Tanganyika.

Of all early hominid groups, the Australopithecinae are the best represented in our fossil storehouses. From the South African sites alone, no fewer than 315 australopithecine entries have been prepared for the forthcoming new edition of the *International Catalogue of Fossil Man:* some comprise a single isolated tooth, some an almost complete cranium. . . .

Whatever the proper classification, there is an abundance of evidence bearing on the anatomical structure and variation, the behavioral (or cultural) characteristics, and the ecological, geographical, and temporal background of the australopithecines. These lines of evidence concur in demonstrating that

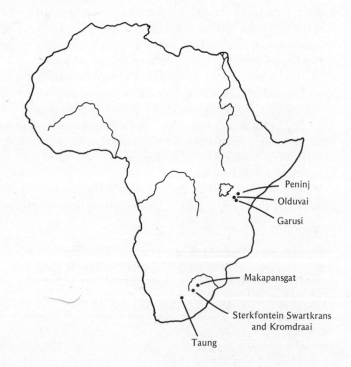

Table 2: Number of Australopithecine Teeth from Various Sites Available for Study

Taung	24
Sterkfontein	162
Kromdraai	39
Swartkrans (35)	311
Makapansgat	55
Garusi	2
Peninj (Natron)	16
Olduvai (7)	16
Total	621

at least some of the known australopithecines, or of slightly earlier creatures of very similar aspect, fulfill the morphological requirements for a hypothetical human ancestor.

East African Australopithecines

Australopithecines have been found at three East African sites, Garusi (1939), Olduvai (1955, 1959, and ?1963), and Peninj (1964), all situated in northern Tanganyika.

The first specimen was found by Kohl-Larsen at Garusi in 1939. It comprises a fragment of upper jawbone containing both premolars. . . .

The most important East African australopithecine is the specimen originally called by Leakey *Zinjanthropus boisei* (11) and now reclassified by Leakey, Tobias, and Napier as a species of the genus *Australopithecus,* namely *A. boisei* (3). For the time being the name *Zinjanthropus* is being retained to designate a subgenus within the genus *Australopithecus.* The specimen comprises a very complete cranium, including all 16 upper teeth; the wisdom teeth or third molars were still in process of erupting, suggesting that the individual was in his late teens at the time of death. A brief preliminary description has been given by Leakey *(1, 11).* Tobias *(12)* has placed on record the cranial capacity as 530 cubic centimeters; that is, the specimen's brain was no larger than that of the small-toothed *A. africanus* child from Taung. . . .

The third site in East Africa to yield an australopithecine is Peninj, on the west side of Lake Natron, about 80 kilometers northeast of Olduvai Gorge. Here, in January 1964, one of Leakey's assistants, Kamoya Kimeu, a member of the expedition led by Richard Leakey and Glynn Isaac, discovered a nearly complete and superbly preserved mandible of a large-toothed australopithecine *(1).* According to Leakey's provisional identification of the fauna from this new site, it is of early mid-Pleistocene age and thus much later than the original *A. boisei* from Olduvai. It would seem to be equivalent in age to the upper part of Bed II, or even to the overlying Beds III and IV, in the Olduvai sequence. . . .

The Gap Between Australopithecus and Homo

Although *Australopithecus* fulfills the morphological requirements for an ancestor of man, there remains a substantial gap between the australopithecines and the most lowly representative of the hominines hitherto recognized (that is, *Homo erectus*, formerly called *Pithecanthropus, Sinanthropus, Atlanthropus*, and so on). The size of this morphological gap may best be illustrated

Table 3: Chronological and Geographical Distribution of Australopithecines. The relative chronological positions of the East and South African sites are uncertain, as indicated by the question marks. Whereas potassium-argon dates are available for Olduvai, none is available for South African sites. Comparisons of fauna are valuable among the sites within each major geographical zone, as exemplified by forthcoming new analyses of fauna from South African sites by H. B. S. Cooke and from East African sites by L. S. B. Leakey. Since comparisons between fauna from the East and South African sites are somewhat vitiated by the large distance and ecological differences between the areas, this scheme must be regarded as highly provisional.

	SOUTH AFRICA	EAST AFRICA
	Kromdraai	?Olduvai II (Upper)
		?Peninj (Natron)
Middle Pleistocene	Swartkrans	?Olduvai II (Middle)
	?Sterkfontein Extension Site	?Olduvai II (Lower)
		?Garusi
Lower Pleistocene	Makapansgat	
	Sterkfontein Type Site Taung	
		Olduvai I

by reference to three parameters which have shown most marked change during the process of hominization in the Pleistocene: brain size, tooth size, and tooth shape. Unfortunately, we cannot use the evidence of hand and foot bones, since we have insufficient evidence bearing on these features in *Australopithecus* and in *Homo erectus*. On the other hand, good samples of teeth and fair samples of braincases and endocranial casts exist for both of these groups.

From seven australopithecine crania it has been possible to make fair estimates of cranial capacity. One of these crania is the Olduvai type specimen of *A. boisei* and six are of small-toothed South African specimens. They include the child from Taung, whose estimated capacity is 500 to 520 cm³: when allowance was made for probable changes with growth, his adult capacity was estimated by various workers *(12)* as 570, 600, and 624 cm³, bigger, in fact, than any australopithecine capacity actually measured. Selecting the median value (600 cm³), we obtain an australopithecine range of 435 to 600 cm³ and a mean of 508 cm³. The range for nine *Homo erectus* crania, including 1000 cm³ for Olduvai hominid 9 *(20)*, is 775 to 1225 cm³ with a mean of 978 cm³. . . .

Figure 3 represents the ranges and the gap between the presently accepted estimates of cranial capacity for *Australopithecus* and *H. erectus*. There is an interval of 175 cm³ between the capacities of the largest-brained australopithecine and the smallest-brained *H. erectus*. However, this difference is rather meaningless unless we consider the estimated body size of the two forms. Jerison has analyzed brain size (to which cranial capacity is an approximation) into two independent components, one of which is determined by body size and the other of which is associated with improved adaptive capacities *(24)*. Given certain assumptions, it has further been possible to estimate the number of cortical nerve cells in the brain as a whole, as well as in each of the two components. The number of "excess" nerve cells—that is, of cells over and above those which can be accounted for by body size—may then be taken as a measure of the real advancement in brain volume, irrespective of body size.

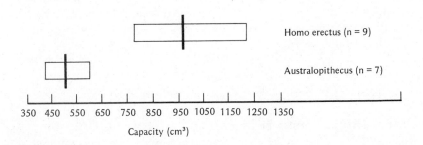

FIGURE 3. The ranges and means of cranial capacity in two early hominids. *Australopithecus* (including both small- and large-toothed forms) and *Homo erectus* (formerly known as *Pithecanthropus*). The largest estimated australopithecine capacity is 600 cm³ and the smallest of *Homo erectus* 775 cm.

The following are estimates of the numbers of excess nerve cells based partly on Jerison's estimates and partly on my own (25):

African great apes	3.4 to 3.6 billion
Australopithecines	4.0 to 5.0 billion
Homo erectus	5.8 to 8.4 billion
Homo sapiens	8.4 to 8.9 billion

If our estimates are correct, there is a bigger gap between *Australopithecus* and *H. erectus* than between the apes and the australopithecines or between *H. erectus* and *H. sapiens*. If, instead of comparing ranges, we compare the mid-values for the groups, we obtain values of 3.5, 4.5, 7.1, and 8.65 billion for the four groups, respectively. Clearly, there is a greater distance between *Australopithecus* and *H. erectus* than between any other two consecutive groups.

To compare dental features of the two groups, it is necessary to point out that on the basis of tooth size, the australopithecines fall into two more or less well-defined subgroups. The first—represented by the fossils from Taung, Sterkfontein, Makapansgat, and Garusi—has somewhat smaller cheek teeth (premolars and molars), but somewhat larger anterior teeth (incisors and canines); this group is called *Australopithecus africanus*. The second—represented by the australopithecine fossils from Swartkrans, Kromdraai, Olduvai, and Peninj (Natron)—has larger cheek teeth and smaller front teeth; this group comprises *A. robustus* and *A. boisei* in the most recent classifications.

On the basis of these three parameters, there is a clear and sizable gap between known australopithecines and *Homo erectus*. Until recently, it has apparently been tacitly assumed that *Australopithecus* graded more or less insensibly into *Homo erectus* in the manner postulated in general terms by Charles Darwin. It is therefore of no small interest to note that so large a gap exists, not only with respect to one parameter, brain size, but, in the same creatures, with respect to dental traits.

It is this gap that has been filled by *Homo habilis*, the newly discovered hominid which, with respect to the three parameters used to characterize the gap, as well as with respect to other morphological markers, lies in a largely intermediate position.

Homo habilis: The Early Pleistocene Hominine

The family Hominidae may be divided into two subfamilies, the Australopithecinae and the Homininae. The term "hominine" is the common or coloquial name connoting a member of the subfamily Homininae.

From at least four levels in Bed I and the lower (Villafranchian) and middle parts of Bed II in the Olduvai succession have come skeletal remains of another type of hominid (Fig. 1). This hominid differs widely from A. *boisei*, the large-toothed australopithecine found in the same beds. For instance, the teeth are appreciably smaller than those of A. *boisei*. While the sizes of the teeth of A. *boisei* in general fall *above* the top of the range for the South African australopithecines, the teeth of this second hominid, especially the premolars, fall at or below the lower end of the australopithecine range (23). Such wide divergence between the two hominids from the same site is far in excess of what can be attributed to sexual dimorphism: in any event, it is accompanied by divergences in shape, proportions, and detailed morphology of the teeth, in cranial shape and curvature, and in cranial capacity. Clearly the second batch of fossils represents another type of hominid. In almost all the departures of the second hominid from the australopithecine morphological pattern, it approaches more closely to the hominine pattern. In other words, the total pattern is more markedly hominized than that of *Australopithecus*. To the Bed I form characterized by these more hominized features we have given the name *Homo habilis*.

The formal naming of the species was announced by Leakey, Tobias, and Napier on 4 April 1964 (3). The generic name implies that this primitive hominid belonged to the genus *Homo*, while the specific name *habilis*, which was suggested by R. A. Dart, means "able, handy, mentally skillful, vigorous," from the inferred ability of the man to make stone tools.

The features which distinguish *H. habilis* remains from those of australopithecines and relate them rather to the more advanced Homininae include the capacity of the braincase, both absolutely and in relation to estimated body size, the size, proportions, and shape of the teeth, the shape and size of the jaws, and the curvature of the cranial bones. In addition, the post-cranial bones help us to obtain a picture of the very hominine morphological pattern of *Homo habilis*, but they do not assist in the taxonomic problem of deciding whether, for instance, the hand of *H. habilis* was closer to that of *Australopithecus* or to that of the Homininae. This is because we do not know enough about the structure of the hand in either the australopithecines or *H. erectus*.

In all those parts for which we do possess adequate comparative material for both australopithecines and early hominines, most of the bones of *H. habilis* fall at the extreme or beyond the range of variation for the australopithecines.

One important example of the greater degree of hominization shown by *H. habilis* is provided by his cranial capacity. Although the cranial vault of the type specimen is incomplete, it has been possible to estimate the capacity of the intact vault (26). The estimates range from 643 to 724 cm^3, with central values 674 and 681 cm^3. This is some 80 cm^3 more than the largest known capacity of *Australopithecus* and 95 cm^3 smaller than the smallest known capacity of *H. erectus*.

When Jerison's formulae (24) are applied to the estimate of 680 cm^3, the body size being estimated from the size of the foot bones, a value of 5.3 to

5.4 billion "excess nerve cells" is obtained. That is, the "intelligence" component of the brain of H. *habilis* has about 0.8 to 1.0 billion more neurons than that of the australopithecines, but about 1.7 to 1.8 billion fewer than that of H. *erectus* (25). Jerison's formulae thus provide striking confirmation of the evidence provided by absolute cranial capacity that H. *habilis* is a more advanced hominid than *Australopithecus* but not so advanced as H. *erectus*.

The parameter of tooth size has the same story to tell. Most of the teeth of H. *habilis* are smaller than those of most australopithecines. Thus, in 30 out of 38 comparisons, the absolute sizes of the H. *habilis* teeth lie at the extreme of the range for *Australopithecus* or outside the range.

Not only the size, but the shape of the teeth is distinctly different from that of *Australopithecus*. Instead of possessing the great breadth characteristic of the teeth of the latter, the teeth of H. *habilis* are narrow and relatively elongated, this departure being found in 20 out of 30 comparisons with the australopithecine teeth. In this respect, the teeth of H. *habilis* resemble those of H. *erectus*.

In sum, H. *habilis* was a pygmy-sized hominid with a relatively large cranial capacity, reduced and narrow teeth, and a number of markedly hominine features in his limb bones. His total structural pattern was that of a creature appreciably more hominized than any of the large group of australopithecines of South and East Africa. The advanced features, moreover, were not those of an individual extreme variant, but characterized all the individuals represented over some considerable time. Clearly, this strain represents a distinct taxon intermediate between the most advanced *Australopithecus* and the most primitive *Homo*.

Cultural Status of Homo habilis

It is accepted that cultural or ethological evidence may be added to morphological evidence in assessing the taxonomic status of a group. We may ask the question: Did H. *habilis* behave like an *Australopithecus* or like a *Homo*?

At each of the levels in Bed I where remains of *Homo habilis* have been found, primitive stone implements have been recovered. These artifacts are commonly made from pebbles or irregular fragments, and the cultural phase represented by the succession of stone industries constitutes the Oldowan Culture, formerly known as the Oldowan phase of the pre-Chelles-Acheul Culture. For long, the identity of the makers of the Oldowan Culture tools has been uncertain: some have maintained that the australopithecines were responsible, others have attributed the tools to early members of *Homo erectus*—but always on the basis of very indirect arguments. When in 1959 the cranium of the Olduvai australopithecine (A. *boisei*) was found on a living floor alongside Oldowan tools, at a time when no other adequate hominid remains were known to be associated with these tools, Leakey claimed that this australopithecine must have been the Oldowan toolmaker (1). This left a difficult problem: Why was the East African australopithecine associated with stone tools, whereas the Makapansgat australopithecine was associated with the bone, tooth, and horn tools described by Dart? Subsequently, however, remains of H. habilis were found on the same living floor as A. boisei and the tools. Furthermore, remains of H. habilis were found on the lower (earlier) living floors in Bed I, in each instance associated with Oldowan artifacts. While it is possible that both A. boisei and H. habilis made tools, it is probable that H. habilis was at least the more advanced toolmaker.

Furthermore, if we make a survey of all the evidence from South and East Africa, we see that Australopithecus alone has not yet been found with stone objects which are undoubtedly tools, except where advanced hominid remains were present as well (20, 25). Six out of 12 deposits have yielded australopithecine remains with no stone tools (27); four sites which have australopithecines and stone tools contain, in addition, indications of a more advanced hominid. The remaining two deposits contain only the more advanced hominid and stone tools. At no site where australopithecine remains are the only hominid remains present are there any stone implements; conversely, at every site which has yielded stone implements and associated hominid remains, these hominid remains include those of a more advanced hominid, whether or not australopithecine remains are present in addition. Furthermore, at every site which has yielded the more advanced hominid, stone tools are present.

It has tentatively been concluded from these associations that no unequivocal evidence exists that Australopithecus made Oldowan stone tools to a set and regular pattern and according to a developing cultural trend. On the other hand, it seems very probable that H. habilis was the maker of the Oldowan stone tools, while H. erectus made the later (Chelles-Acheul) implements.

Dart (28) has demonstrated that the australopithecines were capable of a wide range of cultural activities. It may, however, be argued that all of these activities fall into the categories which Napier (29) has classified as ad hoc tool-using, purposeful tool-using, tool-modifying for an immediate or even for a future purpose, and possibly even ad hoc tool-making. But it may be questioned whether these australopithecine activities constitute cultural tool-making—that is, whether they exhibit a set and regular complex of patterns which, moreover, show developmental trends with the passage of time.

If this interpretation is correct, ethological or cultural evidence could be added to the anatomical evidence which tends to ally H. habilis with the hominines rather than with the australopithecines.

One further probable manifestation of the culture of the early Olduvai hominids is a rough circle of loosely piled stones discovered on a living floor at DK I in the lower part of Bed I (3). It suggests a crude shelter or windbreak and is on the same level as that on which the earliest remains of H. habilis were found (MK I). H. habilis may have been responsible for this rude structure.

Significance of Homo habilis

Both its structure and its place in time impart a unique significance to *Homo habilis*, while, culturally, it seems to provide us for the first time with a knowledge of the makers of the Oldowan Culture.

Structurally, *H. habilis* may be regarded as a most effective link between the Australopithecinae and the Homininae, between which, as has been mentioned, there is a larger gap than has hitherto been recognized. Its very intermediacy is underlined by the fact that some workers would regard the newly discovered form as the most advanced australopithecine and others as the most primitive hominine. Thus, even in the short time since the new fossils

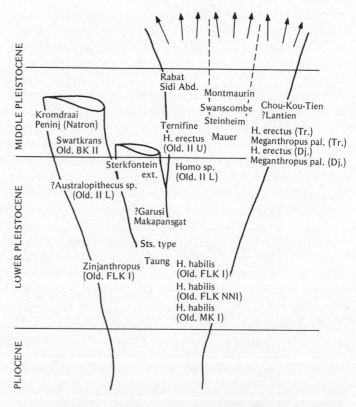

FIGURE 4. Schema of Lower and Middle Pleistocene hominids, showing the position in time and space of the most important specimens discovered to date. The left trunk of the tree represents the large-toothed australopithecine line; the middle trunk the small-toothed australopithecine line; and the right trunk the hominine line leading to modern man. *Sts.,* Sterkfontein; *Sidi Abd.,* Sidi Abderrahman; *Old. II,* Olduvai Bed II; *U,* upper; *L,* lower; *Tr.,* Trinil beds; *Dj.,* Djetis beds.

were discovered, various workers have believed that the habilines were simply another australopithecine (30), a new genus between *Australopithecus* and *Homo* (31), a new lowliest species of *Homo*, namely *H. habilis* (3), and even a new subspecies of *H. erectus*, namely *H. erectus habilis* (32). The position adopted by my colleagues and myself would seem to be a compromise between the extreme views on either side. Although argument on the exact taxonomic position may continue for some time, it seems that there is already fairly general agreement on this virtually uniquely linking position of *H. habilis*.

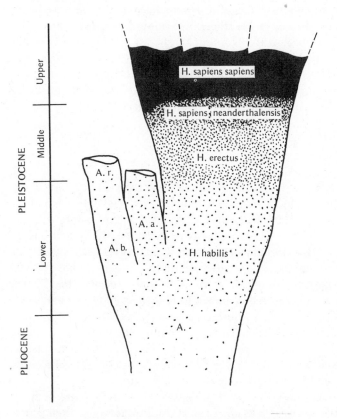

FIGURE 5. A provisional schema of hominid phylogeny from Upper Pliocene times to the Upper Pleistocene. Increasing intensity of shading represents increasing degrees of approach toward the structure and behavior of modern man. A, the hypothetical ancestral australopithecine; A.b., *Australopithecus (Zinjanthropus) boisei*; A.r., *Australopithecus robustus*; A.a., *Australopithecus africanus*. The schema indicates the synchronic coexistence of several different hominids in the Lower and Middle Pleistocene, the australopithecines surviving into the Middle Pleistocene alongside more advanced hominids of the genus *Homo*. This figure should be considered in conjunction with Fig. 4.

Perhaps only *Meganthropus palaeojavanicus* of Sangiran, Java, lies in a similarly intermediate position between the Australopithecinae and the Homininae, albeit a little nearer to the australopithecines than is *H. habilis (17)*.

Chronologically, the recognition of *H. habilis* means that a more hominized line of creatures was evolving alongside the somewhat less hominized australopithecines even in the Lower Pleistocene. Previously, the *H. erectus* remains of the Djetis Beds, agreed by most as belonging to the beginning of the Mid-Pleistocene, represented the earliest recognized hominine. It was still possible then to claim that, if indeed the Homininae stemmed off from an australopithecine ancestral group, this lineage of *Homo* need not have arisen any earlier than the end of the Lower Pleistocene. It now seems clear that, if the habilines are in fact members of the Homininae, then hominines were already present in Africa, and perhaps in Asia, during at least the second half of the Lower Pleistocene. The departure of the hominine line from its presumed australopithecine ancestor must then have occurred as early as at least the Upper Pliocene or the first part of the Lower Pleistocene.

Bearings on Hominid Evolution

As a total morphological complex, *H. habilis* represents a more advanced grade of hominid organization than *Australopithecus*. Have the habilines arisen from the australopithecines? Since they are contemporary with *H. habilis*, the australopithecine populations represented by the actual fossils recovered to date are clearly too late—and possibly slightly too specialized—to have been on the actual human line, unless we are to postulate a polyphyletic origin of the Homininae at varying times from australopithecine stock. Morphologically, the gracile *A. africanus* is closest to *H. habilis* and seemingly least specialized. It would not be rash therefore to suggest that of the various australopithecines *A. africanus* has departed least from the common ancestor of *A. africanus* and *H. habilis*. On the other hand, the large-toothed, specialized *A. robustus and A. boisei* would seem to be far off the common *africanus-habilis* line. Two possible interpretations spring to mind:

1) The Pliocene ancestral australopithecine was large-toothed and perhaps adapted to a vegetarian diet *(33)*; *A. boisei* and *A. robustus* would then represent a conservative line which maintained these qualities right through into the Middle Pleistocene, while *A. africanus* developed different ecological requirements which, perhaps through a more carnivorous or, at least, omnivorous diet, led to a relaxation of selective pressures maintaining large teeth. The gracile *H. habilis* stemmed off from this smaller-toothed line of australopithecines and became selected for increasingly hominine features.

2) The ancestral australopithecine was unspecialized, small-toothed, omnivorous. At some time in the Upper Pliocene, it diversified into macrodontic and megadontic lines (*A. robustus* and *A. boisei*), with specialized dentition, perhaps accompanying a specialized, essentially herbivorous diet. Another line

remained little changed and unspecialized, eventually to dichotomize into a progressively more hominized line represented by H. habilis in Africa and perhaps Meganthropus in Asia and a more conservative residual line (A. africanus) which, because of ecological similarities to H. habilis, did not long outlast the emergence of this hominine.

Which of the two interpretations is correct, or whether other alternatives should be considered, only the direct evidence of Pliocene fossils will determine. Pending their discovery, I incline to favor the second view, on indirect lines of evidence to be presented elsewhere. That is, I tend to regard the large teeth and supporting structures of A. robustus and A. boisei as secondary specializations, rather than as primitive or ancestral features which J. T. Robinson seems to believe (33).

Irrespective of which interpretation we adopt, it seems reasonable to infer that late in the Pliocene, or thereabouts, some populations of ancestral Australopithecus-like hominids moved forward to a further grade of hominization, thus generating the Homininae. We may tentatively conclude that H. habilis is on this direct hominine line. Such is the message of his morphology and his culture, while his position in space and time is compatible with this conclusion (34). As a Lower Pleistocene hominine, he bids fair to provide us with a population, one or more sections of which were ancestral to the mid-Pleistocene hominines (Fig. 5). Nothing in the structure or dating of the relevant fossils rules out the possibility that some populations of H. habilis underwent further hominizing changes by phyletic evolution late in the Lower Pleistocene, to attain the H. erectus grade of hominization.

Such a reconstruction permits us to recognize a series of grades of hominization, within which we may classify the available fossils. Despite wide variation within each grade—only a fraction of which is as yet known for most grades—we may recognize: (i) an australopithecine grade, represented convincingly only in South and East Africa; (ii) a habiline grade from Africa, perhaps corresponding to a meganthropine grade in Asia; (iii) an earlier H. erectus grade, represented in Africa possibly by remains from middle Bed II, Olduvai, and by "Telanthropus" from Swartkrans, and in Asia by the Djetis Beds hominines from Sangiran, Java; (iv) a later H. erectus grade, represented in Africa by "Chellean Man" from upper Bed II, Olduvai and by "Atlanthropus" of Northwest Africa; in Asia by the Trinil Beds and Chou-Kou-Tien hominines; and in Europe possibly by the remains of Mauer; (v) an earlier H. sapiens grade (Neanderthal) widely distributed in the Old World; and (vi) a later H. sapiens grade, ultimately worldwide in distribution. This sequence shows remarkable parallels between Africa and Asia from grade 2 onwards (17).

We see in conclusion that H. habilis has bridged the last remaining major gap in the Pleistocene part of the story of human evolution.

Summary. Recent discoveries of early Pleistocene hominids in East Africa have revealed a new stage in human evolution. The remains of Homo habilis, discovered by L. S. B. Leakey and his family, bridge the hiatus between the most advanced australopithecines and the most primitive hominines. The new species was bigger-brained and smaller-toothed than *Australopithecus*, the fossil apeman from South and East Africa. It is very probable that *Homo habilis* was, as his name implies, a "handyman," maker of the earliest stone culture, the Oldowan.

These primitive hominines were already in existence in the Lower Pleistocene, living alongside a variety of more conservative hominids, the australopithecines. The closeness of morphology between *H. habilis* and *Australopithecus africanus* points strongly to a common ancestry in the Upper Pliocene or the very beginning of the Pleistocene. The large-toothed *A. robustus* and *A. boisei* were already diverging by specialization from the postulated unspecialized ancestral australopithecine. The first hominines must thus have come into being by the beginning of the Pleistocene. Later, some populations of *H. habilis* seemingly underwent further hominizing changes to generate a new species, *Homo erectus*, bigger men with larger and more effective brains, smaller and more modern human teeth, probably more complete adjustment to upright stance and bipedal gait, a more precise manual grip, and an appreciably advanced material culture.

Homo habilis thus fills in the last remaining major gap in the Pleistocene story of human evolution.

References and Notes

1. L. S. B. Leakey, *Nature* **184**, 491 (1959); **189**, 649 (1961); ———— and M. D. Leakey, *ibid.* **202**, 5 (1964).
2. The skulls and teeth have been entrusted to me by Dr. Leakey for detailed study, while Drs. J. Napier, P. Davis, and M. Day of London are studying the other (postcranial) parts of the skeleton. Our detailed reports will appear in a new series of volumes on the Olduvai Gorge to be published by Cambridge University Press.
3. L. S. B. Leakey, P. V. Tobias, J. R. Napier, *Nature* **202**, 7 (1964).
4. R. Hay, *Science* **139**, 829 (1963).
5. L. S. B. Leakey, *Olduvai Gorge 1951–1961*, vol. 1, A *Preliminary Report on the Geology and Fauna* (Cambridge Univ. Press, Cambridge, 1965).
6. R. A. Dart, *Nature* **115**, 195 (1925).
7. There are some 54 additional teeth from Olduvai. Some of them belong to *H. habilis*; some may be australopithecine; while others are as yet of unknown affinities.
8. L. Kohl-Larsen, *Auf den Spuren des Vormenschen* (Strecker and Schröder, Stuttgart, 1943).
9. H. Weinert, *Z. Morphol. Anthropol.* **42**, 113 (1950); **43**, 73 (1951).
10. J. T. Robinson, *Am. J. Phys. Anthropol.* **11**, 1 (1953); **13**, 429 (1955).
11. L. S. B. Leakey, *Nature* **186**, 456 (1960).
12. P. V. Tobias, *ibid.* **197**, 743 (1963).
13. L. S. B. Leakey, *ibid.* **181**, 1099 (1958); J. T. Robinson, *ibid.* **185**, 407 (1960); G. H. R. von Koenigswald, *Koninkl Ned. Akad. Wetenschap. Proc. Ser. B* **63**, 20 (1960); A. A. Dahlberg, *Nature* **188**, 962 (1960).
14. Y. Coppens, *Compt. Rend.* **252**, 3851 (1961); *Bull. Soc. Préhistorique Franc.*

58, 756 (1961); in *Problèmes Actuels de Paléontologie (Evolution des Vertébrés)* (Centre National de Recherche Scientifique, Paris, 1962), p. 455.

15. M. Stekelis, L. Picard, N. Schulman, G. Haas, *Bull. Res. Council Israel* **9G**, 175 (1960).
16. F. Weidenreich, *Amer. Mus. Nat. Hist. Anthropol. Papers* **40**, 1 (1945).
17. P. V. Tobias and G. H. R. von Koenigswald, *Nature* **204**, 515 (1964).
18. G. H. R. von Koenigswald, *Koninkl. Ned. Akad. Wetenschappen Proc. Ser. B.* **60**, 153 (1957).
19. E. L. Simons, *Science* **141**, 879 (1963).
20. P. V. Tobias, *Current Anthropol.*, in press.
21. F. Weidenreich, *Palaeontol. Sinica* n.s. **D10**, 1 (1943).
22. M. Boule and H. V. Vallois, *Fossil Men* (Thames and Hudson, London, 1957).
23. P. V. Tobias, "Festschrift on the 65th birthday of Juan Comas," in press.
24. H. J. Jerison, *Human Biol.* **35**, 263 (1963).
25. P. V. Tobias, in *Proc. 8th Intern. Congr. Anthropol. Ethnol. Sci.*, Moscow, August 1964, in press.
26. P. V. Tobias, *Nature* **202**, 3 (1964).
27. Although cultural material and an australopithecine mandible are known from Peninj (Lake Natron), the implements are not associated with the mandible. I am indebted to Glynn Isaac for the information that excavation of the jaw site itself has yielded no cultural material. Scattered stone artifacts and two early Acheulian sites occur some distance from the mandible site. G. Isaac, *Quaternaria*, in press.
28. R. A. Dart, "The Osteodontokeratic Culture of *Australopithecus prometheus,*" *Transvaal Museum Mem.* 10 (1957).
29. J. R. Napier, in *Classification and Human Evolution*, S. L. Washburn, Ed. (Viking Fund, Chicago, 1963), p. 178.
30. W. E. le Gros Clark, *Discovery* **25**, 49 (1964).
31. G. H. R. von Koenigswald, personal communication.
32. D. R. Hughes, *The Times*, London, 10 June 1964.
33. J. T. Robinson, in *Evolution und Hominisation*, G. Kurth, Ed. (G. Fischer, Stuttgart, 1962), p. 210; J. T. Robinson, *S. African Archaeol. Bull.* **19**, 3 (1964).
34. P. V. Tobias, in *Britannica Book of the Year, 1964* (Encyclopaedia Britannica, Chicago, in press).
35. As a second type of hominid (*Homo erectus* or *Telanthropus*) is known to be present in the Swartkrans deposit, the possibility cannot be excluded that some of the large numbers of isolated teeth from this deposit may *not* belong to the australopithecine.
36. I thank Dr. L. S. B. Leakey for entrusting the fossils to me for study; Prof. G. H. R. von Koenigswald and Dr. D. Hooijer for helpful cooperation; L. P. Morley, A. R. Hughes, Miss J. Soussi, and Mrs. R. W. Levine for technical assistance; the South African Council for Scientific and Industrial Research, the Boise Fund, the Wenner-Gren Foundation for Anthropological Research, Cambridge University, the University of the Witwatersrand, and the National Geographic Society for financial assistance.

F. Clark Howell

The Hominization Process

Modern paleoanthropological studies seek to understand, in both biological and cultural perspective, those factors which effected the evolution of man. The biologically-oriented anthropologist is especially concerned with the nature and adaptive significance of major anatomical and physiological transformations in the evolution of the body from an apelike higher primate to the single variable species, *Homo sapiens*. He must equally concern himself with the origin and evolution of distinctively human patterns of behavior, especially capabilities for culture and the manifestations of such capacities, and not only with their biological bases.

The fossil record of man and his higher primate relatives is still far from adequate. However, in the last several decades significant discoveries have been made which considerably expand our knowledge of ancient human and near-human populations. There is not now a single major range of Pleistocene time from which some one or more parts of the world has not at last yielded some hominid skeletal remains. Hence, there is now some pertinent evidence to suggest the general sequence and relative order of those bodily transformations during this process of hominization. In this process major changes were effected at quite unequal rates, in: the locomotor skeleton, the teeth and their supporting facial structures, the size and proportions of the brain, and the enveloping skull bones. And there were equally significant and accompanying changes in behavior. In the course of the last decade the earlier phases of this process have received considerable investigation. Some significant aspects of that work are to be considered here.

Man is a primate and within the order Primates is most closely related to the living African anthropoid apes. How immediate the relationship, or to put it another way, how far removed in time the point of common ancestry prior to divergence, is still unsettled. Except under special circumstances skeletal remains are not readily preserved in the acid soils of forested habitats; hence fossil remains of anthropoid apes from the requisite late Tertiary time range, some twenty- to a few million years ago, are uncommon, and when found are often very inadequately preserved. Nevertheless, apelike higher primates are known to have had a widespread Eurasiatic distribution (up until five to ten million years ago, by which time such creatures had disappeared from increasingly temperate Europe); they were presumably also common in parts of Africa, although there, fossiliferous beds of that age are singularly rare. Fragmentary jaws and teeth of such creatures indicate their higher primate—indeed, specifically ape—affinities. They also suggest substantial diversity in anatomical structure as well as in over-all size. The rare and fortunate occurrence of other skeletal parts (such as limb bones) indicate that some distinguishing characteristics of modern apes were later evolutionary "specializations" rather than the "primitive" ancestral condition. Several specimens of jaws and teeth, from regions as widely separate as northern India and eastern Africa, and some ten- to fourteen million years in age, show some hominid resemblances. Until more adequately preserved skeletal remains are recovered, these few provocative fragments will remain enigmatic. The antecedents of the hominids, the so-called proto-hominids, are still really unknown, and one can only speculate about the very early formative phases in the process of hominid emergence.

The anatomical-physiological basis of the radiation of the hominids is generally acknowledged to have been a major transformation in structure and function of the locomotor system. The lower limb skeleton and associated musculature were modified under selection pressures eventually to permit a fully erect posture and efficient, habitual bipedal gait. The changes effected in the lower limb were extensive and revolutionary. The characteristic curvature of the loins, the short, broad and backwardly shifted hip bones and their displaced and strengthened articulation with the sacrum, their sinuous distortion to form a basin-like structure about the lower abdomen, as well as the shortened ischial region, were all part of a complex of largely interrelated modifications adaptive for terrestrial bipedalism. There were related changes in the musculature of the hip and thigh, in relative proportions and in structure and function of specific muscle groups, all to afford power to run and to step off in walking, to maintain the equilibrium of the upright trunk during the stride, and to extend fully and to stabilize the elongated lower limb at hip and knee—an impossible stance for any ape. And the foot was fully inverted, with the lateral toes shortened and the hallux enlarged and immobilized, the rigidity of the tarsus enhanced through the angularity of joints and strengthened ligaments, with the development of prominent longitudinal and transverse arches, and the heel broadened to become fully weight-bearing.

The singularity of the erect posture was long ago recognized from comparative anatomical studies of man and the nonhuman primates. Its priority in the hominization process has been fully confirmed by the discovery in Africa of the still earliest known hominids, the australopithecines (genus *Australopithecus*), creatures with small brains, but with lower limbs adapted to the erect posture and bipedal gait, or at least for upright running. Some evidence suggests that the full-fledged adaptation to bipedalism, that which permitted leisurely and prolonged walking, was not yet wholly perfected. The hominid type of dental structure, with small incisor teeth, reduced and spatulate-shaped canines, and noninterlocking canines and anterior premolar teeth all set in a parabolic-shaped dental arch, was also fully differentiated. Brain size, as estimated from skull capacities, was only about a third to two-fifths that of the size range of anatomically modern man. There are several distinct forms of the genus *Australopithecus*, surely distinct species (and probably valid subgenera), with consistent differences in skeletal anatomy as well as in body size. One larger form attained a body weight of some one hundred twenty to one hundred fifty pounds, whereas another was much smaller with a body weight of only some sixty to seventy-five pounds.

Although thus far restricted to Africa, these earliest known hominids were nonetheless fairly widely distributed over substantial portions of that continent. Their ecological adjustments are now known in some measure and can even be paralleled among certain present-day African environments within the same regions. One small South African species is recorded under rainfall conditions some 50 per cent less than that of the present-day (now twenty-eight to thirty inches) in the same region—a rolling, high veld country of low relief and little surface water. Other occurrences testify to more favorable climatic and environmental situations. Generally speaking, the environments were relatively open savanna. In southern Africa remains of these creatures, along with other animals, occur in caves in a limestone plateau landscape where caverns, fissures, and sink holes probably afforded fairly permanent sources of water which was otherwise scarce. But there, and also in eastern Africa, sites were in proximity to more wooded habitats fringing shallow water courses, or mantling the slopes of adjacent volcanic highlands. It is just such transitional zones, the "ecotones" of the ecologist, which afford the greatest abundance and diversity of animal and plant life.

The absolute age of some of these creatures can now be ascertained as a consequence of refinements in the measurement of radioactivity (potassium/ argon or K/A) in some constituent minerals of volcanic rocks. Their temporal range extends back nearly two million years with some representatives apparently having persisted until less than a million years ago. Their discovery has therefore tripled the time range previously known for the evolution of the hominids.

Culturally-patterned behavior appears concurrently with these creatures. In several instances there is direct association with some of their skeletal remains. The field investigation of undisturbed occupation places, maximizing the possibility for the recovery of evidence in archeological context, has culminated in these significant discoveries. Traditional prehistoric archeological studies, on the other hand, were largely preoccupied with the sequential relationships of relics of past human endeavors, often in secondary contexts. The careful exposure of undisturbed occupation places has permitted wholly new inferences into the nature of past hominid adaptations and patterns of behavior. This work has broader implications for it forces complete rejection of the traditional viewpoint of some anthropologists which envisioned the sudden appearance of human behavior and culture at a "critical point" in man's phylogeny.

This most primitive cultural behavior is manifest in several ways. There was a limited capability to fashion simple tools and weapons from stone (and presumably in other media, although perishable materials are not preserved). These objects, the raw material of which was not infrequently brought from sources some distance away, include deliberately collected, sometimes fractured or battered, natural stones or more substantially modified core (nodular) and flake pieces fashioned to produce chopping, cutting, or piercing edges. Several undisturbed occupation places with associated animal bones attest also to the acquisition of a meat-eating diet. It was limited, however, to the exploitation of only a narrow range of the broad spectrum of a rich savanna and woodland fauna. It comprised predominantly various freshwater fish, numerous sorts of small amphibians, reptiles (mostly tortoises and lizards), and birds, many small mammals (rodents and insectivores), and some infants (or the very young) of a few moderate-sized herbivorous ungulates. Vegetal products doubtless constituted a very substantial part of the diet of these predaceous-foragers, but the conditions of preservation prohibit other than inferences as to what these may have been. At any rate carnivorous behavior of these earliest hominids contrasts markedly with the essentially vegetarian proclivities of recent apes (and monkeys).

Such food remains and associated stone artifacts are concentrated over occupation surfaces of restricted extent—in part at least seasonally exposed mud flats around ephemeral lakes adjacent to periodically active volcanoes. These occupational concentrations have a nonuniform distribution over the occupation surfaces; there are dense central clusters of tools and much broken-up and crushed bones (presumably to extract the marrow), and peripherally more sparse occurrences of natural or only battered stones and different, largely unbroken skeletal parts of their prey. In one case a large ovoid-shaped pattern of concentrated and heaped-up stony rubble, with adjacent irregular piles of stone, suggests a structural feature on the occupation surface. These uniquely preserved sites in eastern Africa, sealed in quickly by primary falls of volcanic ash, afford some tantalizing glimpses into the activities of these primitive creatures. Such occupation places may well represent an ancient manifestation of the adjustment to a "home base" within the range, a unique development within the hominid adaptation.

We can now delineate some of the basic features of the early radiation of the hominids to include: (1) differentiation and reduction of the anterior dentition; (2) skeletal and muscular modifications to permit postural uprightness and erect cursorial bipedalism; (3) effective adjustment to, and exploitation of a terrestrial habitat; (4) probably a relatively expanded brain; (5) extensive manipulation of natural objects and development of motor habits to facilitate toolmaking; and (6) carnivorous predation adding meat protein to a largely vegetal diet.

The adaptation was essentially that of erectly bipedal higher primates adjusting to a predaceous-foraging existence. These adaptations permitted or perhaps were conditioned by the dispersal into a terrestrial environment and the exploitation of grassland or parkland habitats. The African apes (and also the Asiatic gibbon), especially the juvenile individuals, show occasional though unsustained efforts at bipedalism; it is highly probable that this pre-adaptive tendency, which developed as a consequence of the overhand arboreal climbing adaptation of semi-erect apes, was pronounced in the still unknown proto-hominids of the Pliocene. Wild chimpanzees are now recognized some-times to eat meat from kills they have made, and also to manipulate inanimate objects, and even to use and occasionally to shape them for aid in the food quest. This would surely suggest that such tendencies were at least equally well developed among the closely related proto-hominids.

Terrestrial environments were, of course, successfully colonized long pre-viously by other primates. These are certain cercopithecoid monkeys, the secondarily ground-dwelling quadrupedal patas monkeys and baboons of Africa and the macaques of Asia (and formerly Europe). Hence their adapta-tions, social behavior, and troop organization provide a useful analogy for inferences into the radiation of the proto-hominids. Comparative investiga-tions of the nonhuman primates, including the increasingly numerous and thorough behavioral and ecological studies of monkeys and apes in natural habitats mentioned by DeVore, have substantially broadened our under-standing of the primate background to human evolution. These studies serve to emphasize those particular uniquenesses of the human adaptation.

A half million or probably nearly a million years ago, hominids were in the process of dispersal outside the primary ecological zone exploited by the australopithecines. In part, this dispersal can be understood only in respect to the opportunities for faunal exchange between the African and Eurasiatic continents, and the prevailing paleogeographic and paleoecological conditions of the earlier Pleistocene. The diverse Saharan zone failed to constitute a bar-rier to this dispersal, or to that of Pliocene and early Pleistocene mammal faunas for that matter. Moreover the extensive seas of the Pliocene and earliest Pleistocene were sufficiently lowered, either due to continental uplift, or, less likely, as a consequence of the incorporation of oceanic waters in extensive arctic-subarctic ice caps, so as to afford substantial intercontinental connec-tions.

Probably within a hundred thousand years, or less, representatives of the genus *Homo* were dispersed throughout most of the Eurasian subtropics and had even penetrated northward well into temperate latitudes in both Europe and eastern Asia. This dispersal involved adjustment to a diverse new variety of habitats. Cultural and perhaps physiological adaptations permitted, for the first time, man's existence outside the tropics under new and rigorous climatic conditions, characterized by long and inclement winters. It was unquestion-ably facilitated by anatomical-physiological modifications to produce the genus *Homo* including prolongation of growth and delayed maturation, and behavioral changes favoring educability, communication, and over-all capabili-ties for culture.

The fully human pattern of locomotion was probably perfected by this time. These final transformations in the hip, thigh, and foot permitted a fully relaxed standing posture, with the body at rest, as well as sustained walking over long distances. The skeletal evidence is unfortunately still incomplete, but some four to six hundred thousand years ago the lower limb skeleton appears not to have differed in any important respect from that of anatomically modern man. Brain size, and especially the relative proportions of the temporal-parietal and frontal association areas, were notably increased to some one-half to two-thirds that of *Homo sapiens* (and to well within that range which permits normal behavior in the latter species). And some further reduction and simplification also occurred in the molar (and premolar) teeth and the supporting bony structures of the face and lower jaw.

Hunting was important as a basis for subsistence. Meat-eating doubtless formed a much increased and stable portion of the normal diet. Much of the mammalian faunal spectrum was exploited, and the prey included some or all of the largest of herbivorous species, including gregarious "herd" forms as well as more solitary species, and a variety of small mammals. Several occupation places of these early and primitive hunters, some of which are quite undisturbed, are preserved and have been excavated in eastern Africa and now also in Europe. These localities preserve prodigious quantities of skeletal remains of slaughtered and butchered mammals. The famous and enormous cave locality (Locality I) of Choukoutien (near Peking) in eastern Asia is a unique occurrence of occupation of a site of this type at such an early time. At Choukoutien, although other ungulate and carnivorous mammals are also present, about 70 per cent of the animal remains are represented by only two species of deer. In Africa the impressive quarry included a number of gigantic herbivorous species, as well as other extinct forms. In two such occupation sites in eastern Africa, over five hundred thousand years old, the very abundant fauna included species of three simians, two carnivores, two rhinos, eight pigs, two to three elephants, sheep and buffalo, two hippos, three giraffids, a chalicothere, six horses, as well as numerous antelopes and gazelles, and other remains of small mammals (rodents), birds, and some reptiles (tortoises). Preferential hunting of certain herd species is recognized at several somewhat younger occupation sites in Europe. At one of two sites in central Spain recently worked by the writer only five large mammalian species are represented, and of these a woodland elephant and wild horse are most numerous, with infrequent wild oxen (aurochs) and stag (red deer), and very rare rhinoceros. The remains of some thirty individual elephants, many of which were immature, are represented in an area of approximately *three hundred* square meters! At another such open-air site, on the edge of the Tyrrhenian sea north of Rome, remains of horse predominated over all other species. Some indication of the level of cultural capability and adaptation, as well as requisite plasticity for local ecological adjustment is afforded by the diversity of game species which were exploited and the corresponding distinctions in occurrence, habitat preference, size of aggregation, and their species-specific patterns of behavior.

Toolmaking capabilities are notably improved along with the establishment of persistent habits of manufacture. These reflect in part at least, more d terous and effective control of manual skills. Corresponding evolutionary changes in the structure and function of the hand, especially development of the fully and powerfully opposable thumb, with expansion and complication of the corresponding sector of the cerebral motor cortex and interrelated association areas, were all effected under the action of natural selection.

Not only was the over-all quantity and quality of the stone tools increased. New techniques were developed for the initial preparation as well as for the subsequent fashioning of diverse and selected sorts of stone into tools (and weapons). New types of stone tools make their appearance, including in particular sharply pointed and cutting-edged tools of several sorts, seemingly most appropriate for butchery of tough-skinned game. Certain stones already of favorable form were deliberately trimmed into a spheroidal shape, it is thought, as offensive missiles. These and other forms of tools subsequently become remarkably standardized. This fact, and the very broad pattern of geographical distribution throughout Africa, southern and western Europe, and through western into southern Asia and the Indian subcontinent, suggest also a sophisticated level of communication and conceivably even the capability of symbolization.

More perishable stuffs, such as wood and fiber, are unfortunately very rarely preserved. However, several such early sites in Europe attest the utilization and working of wood, fashioned into elongate, pointed, and spatulate shapes. The discovery had doubtless been made of the thrusting spear, a major offensive weapon in the pursuit of large, thick-skinned mammals. Again, although traces of the utilization of fire are nearly equally as rarely preserved, there is incontrovertible evidence of its discovery and utilization (whether for heat or cookery is uncertain), both in Europe and in eastern Asia.

The development of a hunting way of life, even at a very unsophisticated level of adaptation, it has been argued, set very different requirements on early human populations. It led to markedly altered selection pressures and was, in fact, responsible for profound changes in human biology and culture. Many workers regard this adaptation as a critical factor in the emergence of fundamentally human institutions. Some of those changes which represent the human (*Homo*) way of life would include: (1) greatly increased size of the home range with defense of territorial boundaries to prevent infringement upon the food sources; (2) band organization of interdependent and affiliated human groups of variable but relatively small size; (3) (extended) family groupings with prolonged male-female relationships, incest prohibition, rules of exogamy for mates, and subgroups based on kinship; (4) sexual division of labor; (5) altruistic behavior with food-sharing, mutual aid, and cooperation; and (6) linguistic communities based on speech.

possible ever to obtain direct evidence of this sort from ogical record. Yet an approach which combines the field of the behavior of living nonhuman primates with terns of adaptation and behavior of human hunter- can enhance enormously the sorts of inferences usually

97

ess

olution: *From Ape to Human*

drawn from the imperfect evidence of paleoanthropological investigations. The favorable consequences of active coöperation between students concerned with the origin and evolution of human behavior, however diverse in background and orientation, is already evident and has considerably advanced understanding of the process of hominization. In the coming years it may be comparable with those advances in paleoanthropological studies effected through the fullest cooperation with colleagues in the natural sciences.

R. Allen Gardner and Beatrice T. Gardner

Teaching Sign Language to a Chimpanzee

The extent to which another species might be able to use human language is a classical problem in comparative psychology. One approach to this problem is to consider the nature of language, the processes of learning, the neural mechanisms of learning and of language, and the genetic basis of these mechanisms, and then, while recognizing certain gaps in what is known about these factors, to attempt to arrive at an answer by dint of careful scholarship (1). An alternative approach is to try to teach a form of human language to an animal. We chose the latter alternative and, in June 1966, began training an infant female chimpanzee, named Washoe, to use the gestural language of the deaf. Within the first 22 months of training it became evident that we had been correct in at least one major aspect of method, the use of a gestural language. Additional aspects of method have evolved in the course of the project. These and some implications of our early results can now be described in a way that may be useful in other studies of communicative behavior. Accordingly, in this article we discuss the considerations which led us to use the chimpanzee as a subject and American Sign Language (the language used by the deaf in North America) as a medium of communication; describe the general methods of training as they were initially conceived and as they developed in the course of the project; and summarize those results that could be reported with some degree of confidence by the end of the first phase of the project.

Reprinted from R. Allen Gardner and Beatrice T. Gardner, "Teaching Sign Language to a Chimpanzee," Science, 165 (August 15, 1969), 664–772, copyright 1969 by the American Association for the Advancement of Science, with permission of Science and the author.

Preliminary Considerations

THE CHIMPANZEE AS A SUBJECT. Some discussion of the chimpanzee as an experimental subject is in order because this species is relatively uncommon in the psychological laboratory. Whether or not the chimpanzee is the most intelligent animal after man can be disputed; the gorilla, the orangutan, and even the dolphin have their loyal partisans in this debate. Nevertheless, it is generally conceded that chimpanzees are highly intelligent, and that members of this species might be intelligent enough for our purposes. Of equal or greater importance is their sociability and their capacity for forming strong attachments to human beings. We want to emphasize this trait of sociability; it seems highly likely that it is essential for the development of language in human beings, and it was a primary consideration in our choice of a chimpanzee as a subject.

Affectionate as chimpanzees are, they are still wild animals, and this is a serious disadvantage. Most psychologists are accustomed to working with animals that have been chosen, and sometimes bred, for docility and adaptability to laboratory procedures. The difficulties presented by the wild nature of an experimental animal must not be underestimated. Chimpanzees are also very strong animals; a full-grown specimen is likely to weigh more than 120 pounds (55 kilograms) and is estimated to be from three to five times as strong as a man, pound-for-pound. Coupled with the wildness, this great strength presents serious difficulties for a procedure that requires interaction at close quarters with a free-living animal. We have always had to reckon with the likelihood that at some point Washoe's physical maturity will make this procedure prohibitively dangerous.

A more serious disadvantage is that human speech sounds are unsuitable as a medium of communication for the champanzee. The vocal apparatus of the chimpanzee is very different from that of man (2). More important, the vocal behavior of the chimpanzee is very different from that of man. Chimpanzees do make many different sounds, but generally vocalization occurs in situations of high excitement and tends to be specific to the exciting situations. Undisturbed, chimpanzees are usually silent. Thus, it is unlikely that a chimpanzee could be trained to make refined use of its vocalizations. Moreover, the intensive work of Hayes and Hayes (3) with the chimpanzee Viki indicates that a vocal language is not appropriate for this species. The Hayeses used modern, sophisticated, psychological methods and seem to have spared no effort to teach Viki to make speech sounds. Yet in 6 years Viki learned only four sounds that approximated English words (4).

Use of the hands, however, is a prominent feature of chimpanzee behavior; manipulatory mechanical problems are their forte. More to the point, even caged, laboratory chimpanzees develop begging and similar gestures spontaneously (5), while individuals that have had extensive contact with human beings have displayed an even wider variety of communicative gestures (6). In our choice of sign language we were influenced more by the behavioral evidence that this medium of communication was appropriate to the species than by anatomical evidence of structural similarity between the hands of chimpanzees and of men. The Hayeses point out that human tools and mechanical devices are constructed to fit the human hand, yet chimpanzees have little difficulty in using these devices with great skill. Nevertheless, they seem unable to adapt their vocalizations to approximate human speech.

Psychologists who work extensively with the instrumental conditioning of animals become sensitive to the need to use responses that are suited to the species they wish to study. Lever-pressing in rats is not an arbitrary response invented by Skinner to confound the mentalists; it is a type of response commonly made by rats when they are first placed in a Skinner box. The exquisite control of instrumental behavior by schedules of reward is achieved only if the original responses are well chosen. We chose a language based on gestures because we reasoned that gestures for the chimpanzee should be analogous to bar-pressing for rates, key-pecking for pigeons, and babbling for humans.

AMERICAN SIGN LANGUAGE. Two systems of manual communication are used by the deaf. One system is the manual alphabet, or finger spelling, in which configurations of the hand correspond to letters of the alphabet. In this system the words of a spoken language, such as English, can be spelled out manually. The other system, sign language, consists of a set of manual configurations and gestures that correspond to particular words or concepts. Unlike finger spelling, which is the direct encoding of a spoken language, sign languages have their own rules of usage. Word-for-sign translation between a spoken language and a sign language yields results that are similar to those of word-for-word translation between two spoken languages: the translation is often passable, though awkward, but it can also be ambiguous or quite nonsensical. Also, there are national and regional variations in sign languages that are comparable to those of spoken languages.

We chose for this project the American Sign Language (ASL), which, with certain regional variations, is used by the deaf in North America. This particular sign language has recently been the subject of formal analysis (7). The ASL can be compared to pictograph writing in which some symbols are quite arbitrary and some are quite representational or iconic, but all are arbitrary to some degree. For example, in ASL the sign for "always" is made by holding the hand in a fist, index finger extended (the pointing hand), while rotating the arm at the elbow. This is clearly an arbitrary representation of the concept "always." The sign for "flower," however, is highly iconic; it is made by holding the fingers of one hand extended, all five fingertips touching (the tapered hand), and touching the fingertips first to one nostril then to the other, as if sniffing a flower. While this is an iconic sign for "flower," it is only one of a number of conventions by which the concept "flower" could be iconically represented; it is thus arbitrary to some degree. Undoubtedly, many of the signs of ASL that seem quite arbitrary today once had an iconic origin that was lost through years of stylized usage. Thus, the signs of ASL are neither uniformly arbitrary nor uniformly iconic; rather the degree of abstraction varies from sign to sign over a wide range. This would seem to be a useful property of ASL for our research.

The literate deaf typically use a combination of ASL and finger spelling; for purposes of this project we have avoided the use of finger spelling as much as possible. A great range of expression is possible within the limits of ASL. We soon found that a good way to practice signing among ourselves was to render familiar songs and poetry into signs; as far as we can judge, there is no message that cannot be rendered faithfully (apart from the usual problems of translation from one language to another). Technical terms and proper names are a problem when first introduced, but within any community of signers it is easy to agree on a convention for any commonly used term. For example, among ourselves we do not finger-spell the words *psychologist* and *psychology*, but render them as "think doctor" and "think science." Or, among users of ASL, "California" can be finger-spelled but is commonly rendered as "golden playland." (Incidentally, the sign for "gold" is made by plucking at the ear-lobe with thumb and forefinger, indicating an earring—another example of an iconic sign that is at the same time arbitrary and stylized.)

The fact that ASL is in current use by human beings is an additional advantage. The early linguistic environment of the deaf children of deaf parents is in some respects similar to the linguistic environment that we could provide for an experimental subject. This should permit some comparative evaluation of Washoe's eventual level of competence. For example, in discussing Washoe's early performance with deaf parents we have been told that many of her variants of standard signs are similar to the baby-talk variants commonly observed when human children sign.

WASHOE. Having decided on a species and a medium of communication, our next concern was to obtain an experimental subject. It is altogether possible that there is some critical early age for the acquisition of this type of behavior. On the other hand, newborn chimpanzees tend to be quite helpless and vegetative. They are also considerably less hardy than older infants. Nevertheless, we reasoned that the dangers of starting too late were much greater than the dangers of starting too early, and we sought the youngest infant we could get. Newborn laboratory chimpanzees are very scarce, and we found that the youngest laboratory infant we could get would be about 2 years old at the time we planned to start the project. It seemed preferable to obtain a wild-caught infant. Wild-caught infants are usually at least 8 to 10 months old before they are available for research. This is because infants rarely reach the United States before they are 5 months old, and to this age must be added 1 or 2 months before final purchase and 2 or 3 months for quarantine and other medical services.

We named our chimpanzee Washoe for Washoe County, the home of the University of Nevada. Her exact age will never be known, but from her weight and dentition we estimated her age to be between 8 and 14 months at the end of June 1966, when she first arrived at our laboratory. (Her dentition has continued to agree with this initial estimate, but her weight has increased rather more than would be expected.) This is very young for a chimpanzee. The best available information indicates that infants are completely dependent until the age of 2 years and semidependent until the age of 4; the first signs of sexual maturity (for example, menstruation, sexual swelling) begin to appear at about 8 years, and full adult growth is reached between the ages of 12 and 16 (8). As for the complete life-span, captive specimens have survived for well over 40 years. Washoe was indeed very young when she arrived; she did not have her first canines or molars, her hand-eye coordination was rudimentary, she had only begun to crawl about, and she slept a great deal. Apart from making friends with her and adapting her to daily routine, we could accomplish little during the first few months.

LABORATORY CONDITIONS. At the outset we were quite sure that Washoe could learn to make various signs in order to obtain food, drink, and other things. For the project to be a success, we felt that something more must be developed. We wanted Washoe not only to ask for objects but to answer questions about them and also to ask us questions. We wanted to develop behavior that could be described as conversation. With this in mind, we attempted to provide Washoe with an environment that might be conducive to this sort of behavior. Confinement was to be minimal, about the same as that of human infants. Her human companions were to be friends and playmates as well as providers and protectors, and they were to introduce a great many games and activities that would be likely to result in maximum interaction with Washoe.

In practice, such an environment is readily achieved with a chimpanzee; bonds of warm affection have always been established between Washoe and her several human companions. We have enjoyed the interaction almost as much as Washoe has, within the limits of human endurance. A number of human companions have been enlisted to participate in the project and relieve each other at intervals, so that at least one person would be with Washoe during all her waking hours. At first we feared that such frequent changes would be disturbing, but Washoe seemed to adapt very well to this procedure. Apparently it is possible to provide an infant chimpanzee with affection on a shift basis.

All of Washoe's human companions have been required to master ASL and to use it extensively in her presence, in association with interesting activities and events and also in a general way, as one chatters at a human infant in the course of the day. The ASL has been used almost exclusively, although occasional finger spelling has been permitted. From time to time, of course, there are lapses into spoken English, as when medical personnel must examine Washoe. At one time, we considered an alternative procedure in which we would sign and speak English to Washoe simultaneously, thus giving her an additional source of informative cues. We rejected this procedure, reasoning that, if she should come to understand speech sooner or more easily than

ASL, then she might not pay sufficient attention to our gestures. Another alternative, that of speaking English among ourselves and signing to Washoe, was also rejected. We reasoned that this would make it seem that big chimps talk and only little chimps sign, which might give signing an undesirable social status.

The environment we are describing is not a silent one. The human beings can vocalize in many ways, laughing and making sounds of pleasure and displeasure. Whistles and drums are sounded in a variety of imitation games, and hands are clapped for attention. The rule is that all meaningful sounds, whether vocalized or not, must be sounds that a chimpanzee can imitate.

Training Methods

IMITATION. The imitativeness of apes is proverbial, and rightly so. Those who have worked closely with chimpanzees have frequently remarked on their readiness to engage in visually guided imitation. Consider the following typical comment of Yerkes (9): "Chim and Panzee would imitate many of my acts, but never have I heard them imitate a sound and rarely make a sound peculiarly their own in response to mine. As previously stated, their imitative tendency is as remarkable for its specialization and limitations as for its strength. It seems to be controlled chiefly by visual stimuli. Things which are seen tend to be imitated or reproduced. What is heard is not reproduced. Obviously an animal which lacks the tendency to reinstate auditory stimuli—in other words to imitate sounds—cannot reasonably be expected to talk. The human infant exhibits this tendency to a remarkable degree. So also does the parrot. If the imitative tendency of the parrot could be coupled with the quality of intelligence of the chimpanzee, the latter undoubtedly could speak."

In the course of their work with Viki, the Hayeses devised a game in which Viki would imitate various actions on hearing the command "Do this" (10). Once established, this was an effective means of training Viki to perform actions that could be visually guided. The same method should be admirably suited to training a chimpanzee to use sign language; accordingly we have directed much effort toward establishing a version of the "Do this" game with Washoe. Getting Washoe to imitate us was not difficult, for she did so quite spontaneously, but getting her to imitate on command has been another matter altogether. It was not until the 16th month of the project that we achieved any degree of control over Washoe's imitation of gestures. Eventually we got to a point where she would imitate a simple gesture, such as pulling at her ears, or a series of such gestures—first we make a gesture, then she imitates, then we make a second gesture, she imitates the second gesture, and so on—for the reward of being tickled. Up to this writing, however, imitation of this sort has not been an important method for introducing new signs into Washoe's vocabulary.

As a method of prompting, we have been able to use imitation extensively to increase the frequency and refine the form of signs. Washoe sometimes fails to use a new sign in an appropriate situation, or uses another, incorrect sign. As such times we can make the correct sign to Washoe, repeating the performance until she makes the sign herself. (With more stable signs, more indirect forms of prompting can be used—for example, pointing at, or touching, Washoe's hand or a part of her body that should be involved in the sign; making the sign for "sign," which is equivalent to saying "Speak up"; or asking a question in signs, such as "What do you want?" or "What is it?") Again, with new signs, and often with old signs as well, Washoe can lapse into what we refer to as poor "diction." Of course, a great deal of slurring and a wide range of variants are permitted in ASL as in any spoken language. In any event, Washoe's diction has frequently been improved by the simple device of repeating, in exaggeratedly correct form, the sign she has just made, until she repeats it herself in more correct form. On the whole, she has responded quite well to prompting, but there are strict limits to its use with a wild animal—one that is probably quite spoiled, besides. Pressed too hard, Washoe can become completely diverted from her original object; she may ask for something entirely different, run away, go into a tantrum, or even bite her tutor.

Chimpanzees also imitate, after some delay, and this delayed imitation can be quite elaborate (10). The following is a typical example of Washoe's delayed imitation. From the beginning of the project she was bathed regularly and according to a standard routine. Also, from her 2nd month with us, she always had dolls to play with. One day, during the 10th month of the project, she bathed one of her dolls in the way we usually bathed her. She filled her little bathtub with water, dunked the doll in the tub, then took it out and dried it with a towel. She has repeated the entire performance, or parts of it, many times since, sometimes also soaping the doll.

This is a type of imitation that may be very important in the acquisition of language by human children, and many of our procedures with Washoe were devised to capitalize on it. Routine activities—feeding, dressing, bathing, and so on—have been highly ritualized, with appropriate signs figuring prominently in the rituals. Many games have been invented which can be accompanied by appropriate signs. Objects and activities have been named as often as possible, especially when Washoe seemed to be paying particular attention to them. New objects and new examples of familiar objects, including pictures, have been continually brought to her attention, together with the appropriate signs. She likes to ride in automobiles, and a ride in an automobile, including the preparations for a ride, provides a wealth of sights that can be accompanied by signs. A good destination for a ride is a home or the university nursery school, both well stocked with props for language lessons.

The general principle should be clear: Washoe has been exposed to a wide variety of activities and objects, together with their appropriate signs, in the hope that she would come to associate the signs with their referents and later make the signs herself. We have reason to believe that she has come to understand a large vocabulary of signs. This was expected, since a number of chimpanzees have acquired extensive understanding vocabularies of spoken words, and there is evidence that even dogs can acquire a sizable understanding vocabulary of spoken words (*11*). The understanding vocabulary that Washoe has acquired, however, consists of signs that a chimpanzee can imitate.

Some of Washoe's signs seem to have been originally acquired by delayed imitation. A good example is the sign for "toothbrush." A part of the daily routine has been to brush her teeth after every meal. When this routine was first introduced Washoe generally resisted it. She gradually came to submit with less and less fuss, and after many months she would even help or sometimes brush her teeth herself. Usually, having finished her meal, Washoe would try to leave her high chair; we would restrain her, signing "First, toothbrushing, then you can go." One day, in the 10th month of the project, Washoe was visiting the Gardner home and found her way into the bathroom. She climbed up on the counter, looked at our mug full of toothbrushes, and signed "toothbrush." At the time, we believed that Washoe understood this sign but we had not seen her use it. She had no reason to ask for the toothbrushes, because they were well within her reach, and it is most unlikely that she was asking to have her teeth brushed. This was our first observation, and one of the clearest examples, of behavior in which Washoe seemed to name an object or an event for no obvious motive other than communication.

Following this observation, the toothbrushing routine at mealtime was altered. First, imitative prompting was introduced. Then as the sign became more reliable, her rinsing-mug and toothbrush were displayed prominently until she made the sign. By the 14th month she was making the "toothbrush" sign at the end of meals with little or no prompting; in fact she has called for her toothbrush in a peremptory fashion when its appearance at the end of a meal was delayed. The "toothbrush" sign is not merely a response cued by the end of a meal; Washoe retained her ability to name toothbrushes when they were shown to her at other times.

The sign for "flower" may also have been acquired by delayed imitation. From her first summer with us, Washoe showed a great interest in flowers, and we took advantage of this by providing many flowers and pictures of flowers accompanied by the appropriate sign. Then one day in the 15th month she made the sign, spontaneously, while she and a companion were walking toward a flower garden. As in the case of "toothbrush," we believed that she understood the sign at this time, but we had made no attempt to elicit it from her except by making it ourselves in appropriate situations. Again, after the first observation, we proceeded to elicit this sign as often as possible by a variety of methods, most frequently by showing her a flower and giving it to her if she made the sign for it. Eventually the sign became very reliable and could be elicited by a variety of flowers and pictures of flowers.

It is difficult to decide which signs were acquired by the method of delayed imitation. The first appearance of these signs is likely to be sudden and unexpected; it is possible that some inadvertent movement of Washoe's has been interpreted as meaningful by one of her devoted companions. If the first observer were kept from reporting the observation and from making any direct attempts to elicit the sign again, then it might be possible to obtain independent verification. Quite understandably, we have been more interested in raising the frequency of new signs than in evaluating any particular method of training.

BABBLING. Because the Hayeses were attempting to teach Viki to speak English, they were interested in babbling, and during the first year of their project they were encouraged by the number and variety of spontaneous vocalizations that Viki made. But, in time, Viki's spontaneous vocalizations decreased further and further to the point where the Hayeses felt that there was almost no vocal babbling from which to shape spoken language. In planning this project we expected a great deal of manual "babbling," but during the early months we observed very little behavior of this kind. In the course of the project, however, there has been a great increase in manual babbling. We have been particularly encouraged by the increase in movements that involve touching parts of the head and body, since these are important components of many signs. Also, more and more frequently, when Washoe has been unable to get something that she wants, she has burst into a flurry of random flourishes and arm-waving.

We have encouraged Washoe's babbling by our responsiveness; clapping, smiling, and repeating the gesture much as you might repeat "goo goo" to a human infant. If the babbled gesture has resembled a sign in ASL, we have made the correct form of the sign and have attempted to engage in some appropriate activity. The sign for "funny" was probably acquired in this way. It first appeared as a spontaneous babble that lent itself readily to a simple imitation game—first Washoe signed "funny," then we did, then she did, and so on. We would laugh and smile during the interchanges that she initiated, and initiate the game ourselves when something funny happened. Eventually Washoe came to use the "funny" sign spontaneously in roughly appropriate situations.

Closely related to babbling are some gestures that seem to have appeared independently of any deliberate training on our part, and that resemble signs so closely that we could incorporate them into Washoe's repertoire with little or no modification. Almost from the first she had a begging gesture—an extension of her open hand, palm up, toward one of us. She made this gesture in situations in which she wanted aid and in situations in which we were holding some object that she wanted. The ASL signs for "give me" and "come" are very similar to this, except that they involve a prominent beckoning movement. Gradually Washoe came to incorporate a beckoning wrist movement into her use of this sign. In Table 1 we refer to this sign as "come-gimme." As Washoe has come to use it, the sign is not simply a modification of the

Table 1: Signs used reliably by chimpanzee Washoe within 22 months of the beginning of training. The signs are listed in the order of their original appearance in her repertoire (see text for the criterion of reliability and for the method of assigning the date of original appearance).

SIGNS	DESCRIPTION	CONTEXT
Come-gimme	Beckoning motion, with wrist or knuckles as pivot.	Sign made to persons or animals, also for objects out of reach. Often combined: "come tickle," "gimme sweet," etc.
More	Fingertips are brought together, usually overhead. (Correct ASL form: tips of the tapered hand touch repeatedly.)	When asking for continuation or repetition of activities such as swinging or tickling, for second helpings of food, etc. Also used to ask for repetition of some performance, such as a somersault.
Up	Arm extends upward, and index finger may also point up.	Wants a lift to reach objects such as grapes on vine, or leaves; or wants to be placed on someone's shoulders; or wants to leave potty-chair.
Sweet	Index or index and second fingers touch tip of wagging tongue. (Correct ASL form: index and second fingers extended side by side.)	For dessert; used spontaneously at end of meal. Also, when asking for candy.
Open	Flat hands are placed side by side, palms down, then drawn apart while rotated to palms up.	At door of house, room, car, refrigerator, or cupboard; on containers such as jars; and on faucets.
Tickle	The index finger of one hand is drawn across the back of the other hand. (Related to ASL "touch.")	For tickling or for chasing games.
Go	Opposite of "come-gimme."	While walking hand-in-hand or riding on someone's shoulders. Washoe usually indicates the direction desired.
Out	Curved hand grasps tapered hand; then tapered hand is withdrawn upward.	When passing through doorways; until recently, used for both "in" and "out." Also, when asking to be taken outdoors.

Hurry	Open hand is shaken at the wrist. (Correct ASL form: index and second fingers extended side by side.)	Often follows signs such as "come-gimme," "out," "open," and "go," particularly if there is a delay before Washoe is obeyed. Also, used while watching her meal being prepared.
Hear-listen	Index finger touches ear.	For loud or strange sounds: bells, car horns, sonic booms, etc. Also, for asking someone to hold a watch to her ear.
Toothbrush	Index finger is used as brush, to rub front teeth.	When Washoe has finished her meal, or at other times when shown a toothbrush.
Drink	Thumb is extended from fisted hand and touches mouth.	For water, formula, soda pop, etc. For soda pop, often combined with "sweet."
Hurt	Extended index fingers are jabbed toward each other. Can be used to indicate location of pain.	To indicate cuts and bruises on herself or on others. Can be elicited by red stains on a person's skin or by tears in clothing.
Sorry	Fisted hand clasps and unclasps at shoulder. (Correct ASL form: fisted hand is rubbed over heart with circular motion.)	After biting someone, or when someone has been hurt in another way (not necessarily by Washoe). When told to apologize for mischief.
Funny	Tip of index finger presses nose, and Washoe snorts. (Correct ASL form: index and second fingers used; no snort.)	When soliciting interaction play, and during games. Occasionally, when being pursued after mischief.
Please	Open hand is drawn across chest. (Correct ASL form: fingertips used, and circular motion.)	When asking for objects and activities. Frequently combined: "Please go," "Out, please," "Please drink."
Food-eat	Several fingers of one hand are placed in mouth. (Correct ASL form: fingertips of tapered hand touch mouth repeatedly.)	During meals and preparation of meals.
Flower	Tip of index finger touches one or both nostrils. (Correct ASL form: tips of tapered hand touch first one nostril, then the other.)	For flowers.
Cover-blanket	Draws one hand toward self over the back of the other.	At bedtime or naptime, and, on cold days, when Washoe wants to be taken out.
Dog	Repeated slapping on thigh.	For dogs and for barking.

cont.

Table 1 *cont.* Signs used reliably by chimpanzee Washoe within 22 months of the beginning of training. The signs are listed in the order of their original appearance in her repertoire (see text for the criterion of reliability and for the method of assigning the date of original appearance).

SIGNS	DESCRIPTION	CONTEXT
You	Index finger points at a person's chest.	Indicates successive turns in games. Also used in response to questions such as "Who tickle?" "Who brush?"
Napkin-bib	Fingertips wipe the mouth region.	For bib, for washcloth, and for Kleenex.
In	Opposite of "out."	Wants to go indoors, or wants someone to join her indoors.
Brush	The fisted hand rubs the back of the open hand several times. (Adapted from ASL "polish.")	For hairbrush, and when asking for brushing.
Hat	Palm pats top of head.	For hats and caps.
I-me	Index finger points at, or touches, chest.	Indicates Washoe's turn, when she and a companion share food, drink, etc. Also used in phrases, such as "I drink," and in reply to questions such as "Who tickle?" (Washoe: "you"); "Who I tickle?" (Washoe: "Me.")
Shoes	The fisted hands are held side by side and strike down on shoes or floor. (Correct ASL form: the sides of the fisted hands strike against each other.)	For shoes and boots.
Smell	Palm is held before nose and moved slightly upward several times.	For scented objects: tobacco, perfume, sage, etc.
Pants	Palms of the flat hands are drawn up against the body toward waist.	For diapers, rubber pants, trousers.
Clothes	Fingertips brush down the chest.	For Washoe's jacket, nightgown, and shirts; also for our clothing.

Cat	Thumb and index finger grasp cheek hair near side of mouth and are drawn outward (representing cat's whiskers).	For cats.
Key	Palm of one hand is repeatedly touched with the index finger of the other. (Correct ASL form: crooked index finger is rotated against palm.)	Used for keys and locks and to ask us to unlock a door.
Baby	One forearm is placed in the crook of the other, as if cradling a baby.	For dolls, including animal dolls such as a toy horse and duck.
Clean	The open palm of one hand is passed over the open palm of the other.	Used when Washoe is washing, or being washed, or when a companion is washing hands or some other object. Also used for "soap."

original begging gesture. For example, very commonly she reaches forward with one hand (palm up) while she gestures with the other hand (palm down) held near her head. (The result resembles a classic fencing posture.)

Another sign of this type is the sign for "hurry," which, so far, Washoe has always made by shaking her open hand vigorously at the wrist. This first appeared as an impatient flourish following some request that she had made in signs; for example, after making the "open" sign before a door. The correct ASL for "hurry" is very close, and we began to use it often, ourselves, in appropriate contexts. We believe that Washoe has come to use this sign in a meaningful way, because she has frequently used it when she, herself, is in a hurry— for example, when rushing to her nursery chair.

INSTRUMENTAL CONDITIONING. It seems intuitively unreasonable that the acquisition of language by human beings could be strictly a matter of reiterated instrumental conditioning—that a child acquires language after the fashion of a rat that is conditioned, first, to press a lever for food in the presence of one stimulus, then to turn a wheel in the presence of another stimulus, and so on until a large repertoire of discriminated responses is acquired. Nevertheless, the so-called "trick vocabulary" of early childhood is probably acquired in this way, and this may be a critical stage in the acquisition of language by children. In any case, a minimal objective of this project was to teach Washoe as many signs as possible by whatever procedures we could enlist. Thus, we have not hesitated to use conventional procedures of instrumental conditioning.

Anyone who becomes familiar with young chimpanzees soon learns about their passion for being tickled. There is no doubt that tickling is the most effective reward that we have used with Washoe. In the early months, when we would pause in our tickling, Washoe would indicate that she wanted more tickling by taking our hands and placing them against her ribs or around her neck. The meaning of these gestures was unmistakable, but since we were not studying our human ability to interpret her chimpanzee gestures, we decided to shape an arbitrary response that she could use to ask for more tickling. We noted that, when being tickled, she tended to bring her arms together to cover the place being tickled. The result was a very crude approximation of the ASL sign for "more" (see Table 1). Thus, we would stop tickling and then pull Washoe's arms away from her body. When we released her arms and threatened to resume tickling, she tended to bring her hands together again. If she brought them back together, we would tickle her again. From time to time we would stop tickling and wait for her to put her hands together by herself. At first, any approximation to the "more" sign, however crude, was rewarded. Later, we required closer approximations and introduced imitative prompting. Soon, a very good version of the "more" sign could be obtained, but it was quite specific to the tickling situation.

In the 6th month of the project we were able to get "more" signs for a new game that consisted of pushing Washoe across the floor in a laundry basket.

In this case we did not use the shaping procedure but, from the start, used imitative prompting to elicite the "more" sign. Soon after the "more" sign became spontaneous and reliable in the laundry-basket game, it began to appear as a request for more swinging (by the arms)—again, after first being elicited with imitative prompting. From this point on, Washoe transferred the "more" sign to all activities, including feeding. The transfer was usually spontaneous, occurring when there was some pause in a desired activity or when some object was removed. Often we ourselves were not sure that Washoe wanted "more" until she signed to us.

The sign for "open" had a similar history. When Washoe wanted to get through a door, she tended to hold up both hands and pound on the door with her palms or her knuckles. This is the beginning position for the "open" sign (see Table 1). By waiting for her to place her hands on the door and then lift them, and also by imitative prompting, we were able to shape a good approximation of the "open" sign, and would reward this by opening the door. Originally she was trained to make this sign for three particular doors that she used every day. Washoe transferred this sign to all doors; then to containers such as the refrigerator, cupboards, drawers, briefcases, boxes, and jars; and eventually—an invention of Washoe's—she used it to ask us to turn on water faucets.

In the case of "more" and "open" we followed the conventional laboratory procedure of waiting for Washoe to make some response that could be shaped into the sign we wished her to acquire. We soon found that this was not necessary; Washoe could acquire signs that were first elicited by our holding her hands, forming them into the desired configuration, and then putting them through the desired movement. Since this procedure of guidance is usually much more practical than waiting for a spontaneous approximation to occur at a favorable moment, we have used it much more frequently.

Results

VOCABULARY. In the early stages of the project we were able to keep fairly complete records of Washoe's daily signing behavior. But, as the amount of signing behavior and the number of signs to be monitored increased, our initial attempts to obtain exhaustive records became prohibitively cumbersome. During the 16th month we settled on the following procedure. When a new sign was introduced we waited until it had been reported by three different observers as having occurred in an appropriate context and spontaneously (that is, with no prompting other than a question such as "What is it?" or "What do you want?"). The sign was then added to a checklist in which its occurrence, form, context, and the kind of prompting required were recorded. Two such checklists were filled out each day, one for the first half of the day and one for the second half. For a criterion of acquisition we chose a reported frequency of at least one appropriate and spontaneous occurrence each day over a period of 15 consecutive days.

In Table 1 we have listed 30 signs that met this criterion by the end of the 22nd month of the project. In addition, we have listed four signs ("dog," "smell," "me," and "clean") that we judged to be stable, despite the fact that they had not met the stringent criterion before the end of the 22nd month. These additional signs had, nevertheless, been reported to occur appropriately and spontaneously on more than half of the days in a period of 30 consecutive days. An indication of the variety of signs that Washoe used in the course of a day is given by the following data: during the 22nd month of the study, 28 of the 34 signs listed were reported on at least 20 days, and the smallest number of different signs reported for a single day was 23, with a median of 29 (12).

The order in which these signs first appeared in Washoe's repertoire is also given in Table 1. We considered the first appearance to be the date on which three different observers reported appropriate and spontaneous occurrences. By this criterion, 4 new signs first appeared during the first 7 months, 9 new signs during the next 7 months, and 21 new signs during the next 7 months. We chose the 21st month rather than the 22nd month as the cutoff for this tabulation so that no signs would be included that do not appear in Table 1. Clearly, if Washoe's rate of acquisition continues to accelerate, we will have to assess her vocabulary on the basis of sampling procedures. We are now in the process of developing procedures that could be used to make periodic tests of Washoe's performance on samples of her repertoire. However, now that there is evidence that a chimpanzee can acquire a vocabulary of more than 30 signs, the exact number of signs in her current vocabulary is less significant than the order of magnitude—50, 100, 200 signs, or more—that might eventually be achieved.

DIFFERENTIATION. In Table 1, column 1, we list English equivalents for each of Washoe's signs. It must be understood that this equivalence is only approximate, because equivalence between English and ASL, as between any two human languages, is only approximate, and because Washoe's usage does differ from that of standard ASL. To some extent her usage is indicated in the column labeled "Context" in Table 1, but the definition of any given sign must always depend upon her total vocabulary, and this has been continually changing. When she had very few signs for specific things, Washoe used the "more" sign for a wide class of requests. Our only restriction was that we discouraged the use of "more" for first requests. As she acquired signs for specific requests, her use of "more" declined until, at the time of this writing, she was using this sign mainly to ask for repetition of some action that she could not name, such as a somersault. Perhaps the best English equivalent would be "do it again." Still, it seemed preferable to list the English equivalent for the ASL sign rather than its current referent for Washoe, since further refinements in her usage may be achieved at a later date.

The differentiation of the signs for "flower" and "smell" provides a further illustration of usage depending upon size of vocabulary. As the "flower" sign became more frequent, we noted that it occurred in several inappropriate contexts that all seemed to include odors; for example, Washoe would make the "flower" sign when opening a tobacco pouch or when entering a kitchen filled with cooking odors. Taking our cue from this, we introduced the "smell" sign by passive shaping and imitative prompting. Gradually Washoe came to make the appropriate distinction between "flower" contexts and "smell" contexts in her signing, although "flower" (in the single-nostril form) (see Table 1) has continued to occur as a common error in "smell" contexts.

TRANSFER. In general, when introducing new signs we have used a very specific referent for the initial training—a particular door for "open," a particular hat for "hat." Early in the project we were concerned about the possibility that signs might become inseparable from their first referents. So far, however, there has been no problem of this kind: Washoe has always been able to transfer her signs spontaneously to new members of each class of referents. We have already described the transfer of "more" and "open." The sign for "flower" is a particularly good example of transfer, because flowers occur in so many varieties, indoors, outdoors, and in pictures, yet Washoe uses the same sign for all. It is fortunate that she has responded well to pictures of objects. In the case of "dog" and "cat" this has proved to be important because live dogs and cats can be too exciting, and we have had to use pictures to elicit most of the "dog" and "cat" signs. It is noteworthy that Washoe has transferred the "dog" sign to the sound of barking by an unseen dog.

The acquisition and transfer of the sign for "key" illustrates a further point. A great many cupboards and doors in Washoe's quarters have been kept secure by small padlocks that can all be opened by the same simple key. Because she was immature and awkward, Washoe had great difficulty in learning to use these keys and locks. Because we wanted her to improve her manual dexterity, we let her practice with these keys until she could open the locks quite easily (then we had to hide the keys). Washoe soon transferred this skill to all manner of locks and keys, including ignition keys. At about the same time, we taught her the sign for "key," using the original padlock keys as a referent. Washoe came to use this sign both to name keys that were presented to her and to ask for the keys to various locks when no key was in sight. She readily transferred the sign to all varieties of keys and locks.

Now, if an animal can transfer a skill learned with a certain key and lock to new types of key and lock, it should not be surprising that the same animal can learn to use an arbitrary response to name and ask for a certain key and then transfer that sign to new types of keys. Certainly, the relationship between the use of a key and the opening of locks is as arbitrary as the relationship between the sign for "key" and its many referents. Viewed in this way, the general phenomenon of transfer of training and the specifically linguistic phenomenon of labeling become very similar, and the problems that these phenomena pose for modern learning theory should require similar solutions. We do not mean to imply that the problem of labeling is less complex than has generally been supposed; rather, we are suggesting that the problem of transfer of training requires an equally sophisticated treatment.

COMBINATIONS. During the phase of the project covered by this article we made no deliberate attempts to elicit combinations or phrases, although we may have responded more readily to strings of two or more signs than to single signs. As far as we can judge, Washoe's early use of signs in strings was spontaneous. Almost as soon as she had eight or ten signs in her repertoire, she began to use them two and three at a time. As her repertoire increased, her tendency to produce strings of two or more signs also increased, to the point where this has become a common mode of signing for her. We, of course, usually signed to her in combinations, but if Washoe's use of combinations has been imitative, then it must be a generalized sort of imitation, since she has invented a number of combinations, such as "gimme tickle" (before we had ever asked her to tickle us), and "open food drink" (for the refrigerator—we have always called it the "cold box").

Four signs—"please," "come-gimme," "hurry," and "more"—used with one or more other signs, account for the largest share of Washoe's early combinations. In general, these four signs have functioned as emphasizers, as in "please open hurry" and "gimme drink please."

Until recently, five additional signs—"go," "out," "in," "open," and "hear-listen"—accounted for most of the remaining combinations. Typical examples of combinations using these four are, "go in" or "go out" (when at some distance from a door), "go sweet" (for being carried to a raspberry bush), "open flower" (to be let through the gate to a flower garden), "open key" (for a locked door), "listen eat" (at the sound of an alarm clock signaling mealtime), and "listen dog" (at the sound of barking by an unseen dog). All but the first and last of these six examples were inventions of Washoe's. Combinations of this type tend to amplify the meaning of the single signs used. Sometimes, however, the function of these five signs has been about the same as that of the emphasizers, as in "open out" (when standing in front of a door).

Toward the end of the period covered in this article we were able to introduce the pronouns "I-me" and "you," so that combinations that resemble short sentences have begun to appear.

Concluding Observations

From time to time we have been asked questions such as, "Do you think that Washoe has language?" or "At what point will you be able to say that Washoe has language?" We find it very difficult to respond to these questions because they are altogether foreign to the spirit of our research. They imply a distinction between one class of communicative behavior that can be called language and another class that cannot. This in turn implies a well-established theory that could provide the distinction. If our objectives had required such a theory, we would certainly not have been able to begin this project as early as we did.

In the first phase of the project we were able to verify the hypothesis that sign language is an appropriate medium of two-way communication for the chimpanzee. Washoe's intellectual immaturity, the continuing acceleration of her progress, the fact that her signs do not remain specific to their original referents but are transferred spontaneously to new referents, and the emergence of rudimentary combinations all suggest that significantly more can be accomplished by Washoe during the subsequent phases of this project. As we proceed, the problems of these subsequent phases will be chiefly concerned with the technical business of measurement. We are now developing a procedure for testing Washoe's ability to name objects. In this procedure, an object or a picture of an object is placed in a box with a window. An observer, who does not know what is in the box, asks Washoe what she sees through the window. At present, this method is limited to items that fit in the box; a more ingenious method will have to be devised for other items. In particular, the ability to combine and recombine signs must be tested. Here, a great deal depends upon reaching a stage at which Washoe produces an extended series of signs in answer to questions. Our hope is that Washoe can be brought to the point where she describes events and situations to an observer who has no other source of information.

At an earlier time we would have been more cautious about suggesting that a chimpanzee might be able to produce extended utterances to communicate information. We believe now that it is the writers—who would predict just what it is that no chimpanzee will ever do—who must proceed with caution. Washoe's accomplishments will probably be exceeded by another chimpanzee, because it is unlikely that the conditions of training have been optimal in this first attempt. Theories of language that depend upon the identification of aspects of language that are exclusively human must remain tentative until a considerably larger body of intensive research with other species becomes available.

Summary

We set ourselves the task of teaching an animal to use a form of human language. Highly intelligent and highly social, the chimpanzee is an obvious choice for such a study, yet it has not been possible to teach a member of this species more than a few spoken words. We reasoned that a spoken language, such as English, might be an inappropriate medium of communication for a chimpanzee. This led us to choose American Sign Language, the gestural system of communication used by the deaf in North America, for the project.

The youngest infant that we could obtain was a wild-born female, whom we named Washoe, and who was estimated to be between 8 and 14 months old when we began our program of training. The laboratory conditions, while not patterned after those of a human family (as in the studies of Kellogg and Kellogg and of Hayes and Hayes), involved a minimum of confinement and a maximum of social interaction with human companions. For all practical purposes, the only verbal communication was in ASL, and the chimpanzee was maximally exposed to the use of this language by human beings.

It was necessary to develop a rough-and-ready mixture of training methods. There was evidence that some of Washoe's early signs were acquired by delayed imitation of the signing behavior of her human companions, but very few if any, of her early signs were introduced by immediate imitation. Manual babbling was directly fostered and did increase in the course of the project. A number of signs were introduced by shaping and instrumental conditioning. A particularly effective and convenient method of shaping consisted of holding Washoe's hands, forming them into a configuration, and putting them through the movements of a sign.

We have listed more than 30 signs that Washoe acquired and could use spontaneously and appropriately by the end of the 22nd month of the project. The signs acquired earliest were simple demands. Most of the later signs have been names for objects, which Washoe has used both as demands and as answers to questions. Washoe readily used noun signs to name pictures of objects as well as actual objects and has frequently called the attention of her companions to pictures and objects by naming them. Once acquired, the signs have not remained specific to the original referents but have been transferred spontaneously to a wide class of appropriate referents. At this writing, Washoe's rate of acquisition of new signs is still accelerating.

From the time she had eight or ten signs in her repertoire, Washoe began to use them in strings of two or more. During the period covered by this article we made no deliberate effort to elicit combinations other than by our own habitual use of strings of signs. Some of the combined forms that Washoe has used may have been imitative, but many have been inventions of her own. Only a small proportion of the possible combinations have, in fact, been observed. This is because most of Washoe's combinations include one of a limited group of signs that act as combiners. Among the signs that Washoe has recently acquired are the pronouns "I-me" and "you." When these occur in combinations the result resembles a short sentence. In terms of the eventual level of communication that a chimpanzee might be able to attain, the most promising results have been spontaneous naming, spontaneous transfer to new referents, and spontaneous combinations and recombinations of signs.

References and Notes

1. See, for example, E. H. Lenneberg, *Biological Foundations of Language* (Wiley, New York, 1967).

2. A. L. Bryan, *Curr. Anthropol.* **4**, 297 (1963).
3. K. J. Hayes and C. Hayes, *Proc. Amer. Phil. Soc.* **95**, 105 (1951).
4. K. J. Hayes, personal communication. Dr. Hayes also informed us that Viki used a few additional sounds which, while not resembling English words, were used for specific requests.
5. R. M. Yerkes, *Chimpanzees* (Yale Univ. Press, New Haven, 1943).
6. K. J. Hayes and C. Hayes, in *The Non-Human Primates and Human Evolution*, J. A. Gavan, Ed. (Wayne Univ. Press, Detroit, 1955), p. 110; W. N. Kellogg and L. A. Kellogg, *The Ape and the Child* (Hafner, New York, 1967; originally published by McGraw-Hill, New York, 1933); W. N. Kellogg, *Science* **162**, 423 (1968).
7. W. C. Stokoe, D. Casterline, C. G. Croneberg, *A Dictionary of American Sign Language* (Gallaudet College Press, Washington, D.C., 1965); E. A. McCall, thesis, University of Iowa (1965).
8. J. Goodall, in *Primate Behavior*, I. DeVore, Ed. (Holt, Rinehart & Winston, New York, 1965), p. 425; A. J. Riopelle and C. M. Rogers, in *Behavior of Nonhuman Primates*, A. M. Schrier, H. F. Harlow, F. Stollnitz, Eds. (Academic Press, New York, 1965), p. 449.
9. R. M. Yerkes and B. W. Learned, *Chimpanzee Intelligence and Its Vocal Expression* (William & Wilkins, Baltimore, 1925), p. 53.
10. K. J. Hayes and C. Hayes, *J. Comp. Physiol. Psychol.* **45**, 450 (1952).
11. C. J. Warden and L. H. Warner, *Quart. Rev. Biol.* **3**, 1 (1928).
12. The development of Washoe's vocabulary of signs is being recorded on motion-picture film. At the time of this writing, 30 of the 34 signs listed in Table 1 are on film.
13. The research described in this article has been supported by National Institute of Mental Health grants MH-12154 and MH-34953 (Research Scientist Development Award to B. T. Gardner) and by National Science Foundation grant GB-7432. We acknowledge a great debt to the personnel of the Aeromedical Research Laboratory, Holloman Air Force Base, whose support and expert assistance effectively absorbed all of the many difficulties attendant upon the acquisition of a wild-caught chimpanzee. We are also grateful to Dr. Frances L. Fitz-Gerald of the Yerkes Regional Primate Research Center for detailed advice on the care of an infant chimpanzee. Drs. Emanual Berger of Reno, Nevada, and D. B. Olsen of the University of Nevada have served as medical consultants, and we are grateful to them for giving so generously of their time and medical skills. The faculty of the Sarah Hamilton Fleischmann School of Home Economics, University of Nevada, has generously allowed us to use the facilities of their experimental nursery school on weekends and holidays.

3   Hunting Societies

Shifting our attention from the physical-physiological changes that produced our modern human species, our understanding of the human past in cultural terms begins with the realization that at least 99 percent of our cultural history occurred *before* the invention of food-growing techniques, complex technologies, and the other elaborations of material things now so prominent in human life. The fact is that during most of the past three to four million years *all* our ancestors were hunters and gatherers who were able to make a living without domesticated plants or animals.

What kind of life was it in those long millennia before people had gardens and fields to cultivate, and domesticated animals to herd and to exploit when they needed food? Until very recent times most people have believed that the hunting-gathering way of life of long ago was "nasty, brutish, and short." The mental images we call up of the hunting way of life are frequently of semistarvation and the long hours of search for elusive prey, the constant specter of hunger hanging over the small bands of people. That image is vivid in the selection from John Tanner's narrative which is the portrayal of life among the Ojibwa Indians in the decades after the Revolutionary War. This narrative gives something of the flavor of what it is like to be dependent on hunting in the dead of winter in the northern forests of North America. We note, though, that John Tanner was a white man, influenced by the white peoples' perceptions of the hunting way of life. Recently Marshall Sahlins and others have argued that hunting peoples frequently do rather well for themselves, and may enjoy a bountiful way of life without being constantly on the verge of starvation—especially in certain kinds of environmental situations. The evidence, of course, is scant concerning the "affluence" or "poverty" of different hunting and gathering peoples in our own evolutionary past. Much of the evidence is entirely gone and we can only speculate about the ways of life of people who lived many thousands of years ago. However, our aim in anthropology is to eliminate as much as possible our distorted modern value concepts from our speculations, and to search always for further circumstantial information to strengthen our theories about our cultural past.

The only physical evidence we have of our prehistoric past comes from the slim collections of archaeological materials painstakingly dug up and analyzed in relation to the climatic conditions and available plants and animals of times gone by. Fortunately there are still some peoples in the world who make stone tools and weapons and use them in their daily activities. Richard Gould, who is an archaeologist and ethnologist, has studied some of the features of stone tools among Australian aboriginal peoples, searching for data from the present to apply to past cultural evolution.

The common view is that hunting peoples have diets consisting largely of products of the hunt, that is, a lot of saturated fats and proteins. Our selection about veld food gives a somewhat more balanced view, for a number of recent studies have demonstrated that most hunting and gathering peoples have diets consisting of 60 to 80 percent vegetable materials, and only perhaps 20 or 30 percent meat from the hunt. Our understanding of the hunting way of life requires this important corrective.

John Tanner

John Tanner's Narrative

With the deep snow and thick ice, came poverty and hunger. We were no longer able to take beaver in traps, or by the ordinary methods, or kill moose, though there were some in the country. It was not until our sufferings from hunger began to be extreme, that the old woman had recourse to the expedient of spending a night in prayer and singing. In the morning she said to her son and Waw-be-be-nais-sa, "Go and hunt, for the Great Spirit has given me some meat." But Wa-me-gon-a-biew objected, as he said the weather was too cold and calm, and no moose could be approached so near as to shoot him. "I can make a wind," answered Net-no-kwa, "and though it is now still and cold, the warm wind shall come before night. Go, my sons, you cannot fail to kill something, for in my dream I saw Wa-me-gon-a-biew coming into the lodge with a beaver and a large load of meat on his back." At length they started, having suspended at their heads and on their shot pouches the little sacks of medicine which the old woman had provided for them with the assurance that, having them, they could not possibly fail of success. They had not been a long time absent, when the wind rose from the south, and soon blew high, the weather, at the same time, becoming warmer. At night, they returned, loaded with the flesh of a fat moose, and Wa-me-gon-a-biew with a beaver on his back, as the old woman had seen him in her dream. As the moose was very large and fat, we moved our lodge to it, and made preparations for drying the meat. This supply of our wants was, however, only temporary, though we found a few beaver, and succeeded in killing some. After about ten days we were again in want of food. As I was one day hunting for beavers at some distance from our lodge, I found the tracks of four moose. I broke off the top of a bush, on which they had been browsing, and carried it home. On entering the lodge, I threw it down before Waw-be-be-nais-sa, who was lying by the fire, in his usual indolent manner, saying, "Look at this, good hunter, and go and kill us some moose." He took up the branch, and looking at it a moment, he said, "How many are there?" I answered, "four." He replied, "I must kill them." Early in the morning he started on my road, and killed three of the moose. He was a good hunter when he could rouse himself to exertion; but most of the time he was so lazy that he chose to starve rather than go far to find game, or to run after it when it was found. We had now a short season of plenty, but soon became hungry again. It often happened, that for two or three days we had nothing to eat; then a rabbit

Reprinted from John Tanner, John Tanner's Narrative, pp. 54–68 (Minneapolis: Ross and Haines, 1956); copyright © 1956 by Ross and Haines. Reprinted by permission of the publisher.

or two, or a bird, would afford us a prospect of protracting the suffering of hunger for a few days longer. We said much to Waw-be-be-nais-sa to try to rouse him to greater exertion, as we knew he could kill game where any thing was to be found; but he commonly replied that he was too poor and sick. Wa-me-gon-a-biew and myself, thinking that something might be found in more distant excursions than we had been used to make, started very early one morning, and travelled hard all day; and when it was near night we killed a young beaver, and Wa-me-gon-a-biew said to me, "My brother, you must now make a camp, and cook a little of the beaver, while I go farther on and try to kill something." I did so, and about sunset he returned, bringing plenty of meat, having killed two caribou. Next day we started very early to drag the two caribous through all the long distance between us and our camp. I could not reach home with my load, but Wa-me-gon-a-biew having arrived, sent out the young woman to help me, so that I arrived before midnight. We now saw it would not be safe for us to remain longer by ourselves, and this small supply enabling us to move, we determined to go in quest of some people. The nearest trading-house was that at Clear Water Lake, distant about four or five days' journey. We left our lodge, and taking only our blankets, a kettle or two, and such articles as were necessary for our journey, started for the trading-house. The country we had to pass was full of lakes and islands, swamps and marshes; but they were all frozen, so that we endeavoured to take a direct route.

Early one morning on this journey, Waw-be-be-nais-sa, roused perhaps by excessive hunger, or by the exercise he was compelled to take to keep along with us, began to sing and pray for something to eat. At length he said, "to-day we shall see some caribou." The old woman, whose temper was somewhat sharpened by our long continued privations, and who did not consider Waw-be-be-nais-sa a very enterprising hunter, said, "And if you should see caribou you will not be able to kill them. Some men would not have said, 'we shall see game to-day,' but 'we shall eat it.'" After this conversation, we had gone but a little distance when we saw six caribous, coming directly towards us. We concealed ourselves in the bushes, on the point of a little island, and they came within shot. Wa-me-gon-a-biew flashed his piece, when he intended to fire, and the herd turned at the sound of the lock, to run off. Waw-be-be-nais-sa fired as they ran, and broke the shoulder of one of them; but though they pursued all day, they returned to camp at night without any meat. Our prospect was now so discouraging that we concluded to lighten ourselves by leaving some baggage, in order to make the greater expedition. We also killed our last dog, who was getting too weak to keep up with us; but the flesh of this animal, for some reason, the old woman would not eat. After several days we were bewildered, not knowing what route to pursue and too weak to travel. In this emergency, the old woman, who, in the last extremity, seemed always more capable of making great exertions than any of us, fixed our camp as usual, brought us a large pile of wood to keep a fire in her absence, then tying her blanket about her, took her tomahawk, and went off, as we very well knew, to seek for some method by which to relieve us from our present distress. She came to us again on the following day, and resorting to her often-tried expedient to rouse us to great exertion, she said, "My children, I slept last night in a distant and solitary place, after having continued long in prayer. Then I dreamed, and I saw the road in which I had come, and the end of it where I had stopped at night, and at no great distance from this I saw the beginning of another road, that led directly to the trader's house. In my dream I saw white men; let us, therefore, lose no time, for the Great Spirit is now willing to lead us to a good fire." Being somewhat animated by the confidence and hope the old woman was in this way able to inspire, we departed immediately; but having at length come to the end of her path, and passed a considerable distance beyond it without discovering any traces of other human beings, we began to be incredulous, some reproaching and some ridiculing the old woman; but afterwards, to our great joy, we found a recent hunting path, which we knew must lead to the trader's house; then redoubling our efforts, we arrived on the next night but one, after that in which the old woman had slept by herself. Here we found the same trader from whom we had a credit of one hundred and twenty beaver skins at Rainy Lake, and as he was willing to send out and bring the packs, we paid him his credit and had twenty beaver skins left. With these I bought four traps, for which I paid five skins each. They also gave the old woman three small kegs of rum. After remaining a few days, we started to return in the direction we came from. For some distance we followed the large hunting path of the people belonging to the trading-house. When we reached the point where we must leave this road, the old woman gave the three little kegs of rum to Waw-be-be-nais-sa, and told him to follow on the hunter's path until he should find them; then sell the rum for meat, and come back to us. One of the little kegs he immediately opened, and drank about half of it before he went to sleep. Next morning, however, he was sober, and started to go as the old woman had directed, being in the first place informed where to find us again. Wa-me-gon-a-biew accompanied him. After they had started, I went on with the women to Skut-tah-waw-wo-ne-gun, (the dry carrying place,) where we had appointed to wait for him. We had been here one day when Wa-me-gon-a-biew arrived with a load of meat; but Waw-be-be-nais-sa did not come, though his little children had that day been compelled to eat their moccasins. We fed the woman and her children, and then sent her to join her husband. The hunters with whom Waw-be-be-nais-sa had remained, sent us an invitation by Wa-me-gon-a-biew to come and live with them, but it was necessary, in the first place, to go and get our lodge, and the property we had left there. As we were on our return we were stopped at the dry carrying place with extreme hunger. Having subsisted for some time almost entirely on the inner bark of trees, and particularly of a climbing vine found there, our strength was much reduced. Wa-me-gon-a-biew could not walk at all, and every one of the family had failed more than the old woman. She would fast five or six days, and seem to be little affected by it. It was only because she feared the other members of the family would perish in her absence that she now consented to let me go and try to get some assistance from the trading-house, which we believed to be nearer than the camp of the hunters. The former we knew was about two ordinary days' journey; but, in my weak condition it was doubtful when I could reach it. I started very early in the morning. The weather was cold, and the wind high. I had a large lake to cross, and here, as the wind blew more violently, I suffered most. I gained the other side of it a little before sunset, and sat down to rest. As soon as I began to feel a little cold, I tried to get up, but found it so difficult that I judged it would not be prudent for me to rest again before I should reach the trading-house. The night was not dark, and as there was less wind than in the day time, I found the travelling more pleasant. I continued on all night, and arrived early next morning at the trader's house. As soon as I opened the door they knew by my face that I was starving, and immediately inquired after my people. As soon as I had given the necessary information, they despatched a swift Frenchman with a load of provisions to the family. I had been in the trader's house but a few hours, when I heard the voice of Net-no-kwa outside, asking, "is my son here?" And when I opened the door she expressed the utmost satisfaction at sight of me. She had not met the Frenchman, who had gone by a different route. The wind had become violent soon after I left our camp, and the old woman, thinking I could not cross the lake, started after me, and the drifting snow having obscured my track, she could not follow it, and came quite to the trading-house with the apprehension that I judged it would not be prudent for me to rest again before I should reach remainder of the family came in, having been relieved by the Frenchman. It appeared, also, that the Indians had sent Waw-be-be-nais-sa with a load of meat to look for us at the dry carrying place, as they knew we could not reach their encampment without a supply, which it was not probable we could procure. He had been very near the camp of our family after I left, but either through wilfulness, or from stupidity, failed to find them. He had camped almost within call of them, and eaten a hearty meal as they discovered by the traces he left. After remaining a few days at the trading house, we all went together to join the Indians. This party consisted of three lodges, the principal man being Wah-ge-kaut, (crooked legs.) Three of the best hunters were Ka-kaik, (the small hawk,) Meh-ke-nauk, (the turtle,) and Pa-ke-kun-ne-gah-bo, (he that stands in the smoke.) This last was, at the time I speak of, a very distinguished hunter. Some time afterwards he was accidentally wounded, receiving a whole charge of shot in his elbow, by which the joint and the bones of his arm were much shattered. As the wound did not show any tendency to heal, but, on the contrary, became worse and worse, he applied to many Indians, and to all white men he saw, to cut it off for him. As all refused to do so, or to assist him in amputating it himself, he chose a time when he happened to be left alone in his lodge, and taking two knives, the edge of one of which he had hacked into a sort of saw, he with his right hand and arm cut off his left, and threw it from him as far as he could. Soon after, as he related the story himself, he fell asleep, in which situation he was found by his friends, having lost a very great quantity of blood; but he soon afterwards recovered, and notwithstanding the loss of one arm, he became again a great hunter. After this accident, he was commonly called Kosh-kin-ne-kait, (the cut off arm.) With this band we lived some time, having always plenty to eat, though Waw-be-be-nais-sa killed nothing.

When the weather began to be a little warm, we left the Indians and went to hunt beaver near the trading house. Having lately suffered so much from hunger, we were afraid to go any distant place, relying on large game for support. Here we found early one morning, a moose track, not far from the trading house. There was now living with us, a man called Pa-bah-mew-in, (he that carries about,) who, together with Wa-me-gon-a-biew, started in pursuit. The dogs followed for an hour or two, and then returned; at this Pa-bah-mew-in was discouraged, and turned back; but Wa-me-gon-a-biew still kept on. This young man could run very swift, and for a long time he passed all the dogs, one or two of which continued on the track. It was after noon when he arrived at a lake which the moose had attempted to cross; but as in some parts the ice was quite smooth, which prevented him from running so fast as on land, Wa-me-gon-a-biew overtook him. When he came very near, the foremost dog, who had kept at no great distance from Wa-me-gon-a-biew, passed him, and got before the moose, which was now easily killed. We remained all this spring about one day from the trading house, taking considerable game. I killed by myself twenty otters, besides a good many beavers and other animals. As I was one day going to look at my traps, I found some ducks in a pond, and taking the ball out of my gun, I put in some shot, and began to creep up to them. As I was crawling cautiously through the bushes, a bear started up near me, and ran into a white pine tree almost over my head. I hastily threw a ball into my gun and fired; but the gun burst about midway of the barrel, and all the upper half of it was carried away. The bear was apparently untouched, but he ran up higher into the tree. I loaded what was left of my gun, and taking aim the second time, brought him to the ground.

While we lived here we made a number of packs and as it was inconvenient to keep these in our small lodge, we left them, from time to time, with the traders, for safe keeping. When the time came for them to come down to the Grand Portage, they took our packs without our consent, but the old woman followed after them to Rainy Lake, and retook every thing that belonged to us. But she was prevailed to sell them. From Rainy Lake we went to the Lake of the Woods, where Pa-bah-mew-in left us. Here, also, Waw-be-be-nais-sa rejoined us, wishing to return with us to Rainy Lake; but Net-no-kwa had heard of a murder committed there by some of his relations that would have been revenged on him, for which reason she would not suffer him to return there. At the invitation of a man called Sah-muk, an Ottaw-waw chief, and a relative of Net-no-kwa, we returned to Rainy Lake to live with him. Wa-me-gon-a-biew, with the two women, and the children, went on to Red River. Sah-muk treated us with much kindness. He built and gave us a large bark canoe, intended for the use of the fur traders, and which we sold to them for the value of one hundred dollars, which was at that time the common price of such canoes in that part of the country. He also built us a small canoe for our own use.

The river which falls into Rainy Lake, is called Kocheche-se-bee, (Source River,) and in it is a considerable fall, not far distant from the lake. Here I used to take, with a hook and line, great numbers of the fish called by the French, dory. One day, as I was fishing here, a very large sturgeon come down the fall, and happening to get into shallow water, was unable to make his escape. I killed him with a stone, and as it was the first that had been killed here, Sah-muk made a feast on the occasion.

After some time we started from this place with a considerable band of Ojibbeways, to cross Rainy Lake. At the point where we were to separate from them, and they were to disperse in various directions, all stopped to drink. In the course of this drunken frolic, they stole from us all our corn and grease, leaving us quite destitute of provisions. This was the first instance in which I had ever joined the Indians in drinking, and when I recovered from it, the old woman reproved me very sharply and sensibly, though she herself had drank much more than I had.

As soon as I recovered my wits, and perceived into what a condition we had brought ourselves, I put the old woman in the canoe and went immediately to a place where I knew there was good fishing. The Ojibbeways had not left us a mouthful of food, but I soon caught three dories so that we did not suffer from hunger. Next morning I stopped for breakfast at a carrying place where these fish were very abundant, and while the old woman was making a fire and cooking one that I had just caught, I took nearly a hundred. Before we were ready to re-embark, some traders' canoes came along, and the old woman, not having entirely recovered from her drunken frolic, sold my fish for rum. The traders continued to pass during the day, but I hid away from the old woman so many fish as enabled me to purchased a large sack of corn and grease. When Net-no-kwa became sober, she was much pleased that I had taken this course with her.

In the middle of the Lake of the Woods is a small, but high rocky island, almost without any trees or bushes. This was now covered with young gulls and cormorants, of which I killed great numbers, knocking them down with a stick. We selected one hundred and twenty of the fattest, and dried them in the smoke, packed them in sacks, and carried them along with us. Thence we went by way of the Muskeeg carrying place to Red River. As we were passing down this river, I shot a large bear on shore, near the brink of the river. He screamed out in a very unusual manner, then ran down into the water, and sank.

At this place, (since called Pembinah,) where the Nebeninnah-ne-sebee enters Red River, had formerly been a trading house. We found no people, whites or Indians; and as we had not plenty of provisions, we went on all night, hoping soon to meet with some people. After sunrise next morning, we landed, and the old woman, while collecting wood to make a fire, discovered some buffaloes in the woods. Giving me notice of this, I ran up and killed a bull, but perceiving that he was very poor, I crept a little farther and shot a large fat cow. She ran some distance, and fell in an open prairie. A bull that followed her, no sooner saw me enter the open prairie, at the distance of three or four hundred yards from her, than he ran at me with so much fury that I thought it prudent to retire into the woods. We remained all day at this place, and I made several attempts to get at the cow, but she was so vigilantly watched by the same bull that I was at last compelled to leave her. In the rutting season, it is not unusual to see the bulls behave in this way.

Next day we met the traders coming up to Nebeninnah-ne-sebee,[1] and gave them a part of the meat we had taken from the bull. Without any other delay, we went on to the Prairie Portage of the Assinneboin River, where we found Wa-me-gon-a-biew and Waw-be-be-nais-sa, with the other members of our family from whom we had so long separated.

Waw-be-be-nais-sa, since they left us, had turned away his former wife, and married the daughter of Net-no-kwa's sister, who had been brought up in our family, and whom the old woman had always treated as her own child. Net-no-kwa no sooner understood what had taken place, than she took up what few articles she could see in the lodge, belonging to Waw-be-be-nais-sa, and throwing them out, said to him, "I have been starved by you already, and I wish to have nothing more to do with you. Go, and provide for your own wants; it is more than so miserable a hunter as you are, is able to do, you shall not have my daughter." So being turned out, he went off by himself for a few days, but as Net-no-kwa soon learned that his former wife was married to another man, and that he was destitute, she admitted him again into the lodge. It was probably from fear of the old woman that he now became a better hunter than he had been before.

That winter I hunted for a trader, called by the Indians Aneeb, which means an elm tree. As the winter advanced, and the weather became more and more cold, I found it difficult to procure as much game as I had been in the habit of supplying, and as was wanted by the trader. Early one morning, about midwinter, I started an elk. I pursued until night, and had almost overtaken him, but hope and strength failed me at the same time. What clothing I had on me, notwithstanding the extreme coldness of the weather, was drenched with sweat. It was not long after I turned towards home that I felt it stiffening about me. My leggins were of cloth, and were torn in pieces in running through the brush. I was conscious I was somewhat frozen, before I arrived at the place where I had left our lodge standing in the morning,

[1] Nebeninnah-ne-sebee—High Craneberry River; since called Pembinah. The Indian name is derived from that of the viburnum, with large red edible berries, somewhat resembling the craneberry; thence called v.oxycoccus. "Red River" is from the Indian Miskwawgumme-wesebee.

and it was now midnight. I knew it had been the old woman's intention to move, and I knew where she would go, but I had not been informed she would go on that day. As I followed on their path, I soon ceased to suffer from cold, and felt that sleepy sensation which I knew preceded the last stage of weakness in such as die of cold. I redoubled my efforts, but with an entire consciousness of the danger of my situation, it was with no small difficulty that I could prevent myself from lying down. At length I lost all consciousness for some time, how long I cannot tell, and awaking as from a dream, I found I had been walking round and round in a small circle, not more than twenty or twenty-five yards over. After the return of my senses, I looked about to try to discover my path, as I had missed it, but while I was looking, I discovered a light at a distance by which I directed my course. Once more, before I reached the lodge, I lost my senses, but I did not fall down. If I had, I should never have got up again, but I ran around and round in a circle as before. When I at last came into the lodge, I immediately fell down, but I did not lose myself as before. I can remember seeing the thick and sparkling coat of frost on the inside of the pukkwi lodge, and hearing my mother say that she had kept a large fire in expectation of my arrival, and that she had not thought I should have been so long gone in the morning, but that I should have known long before night of her having moved. It was a month before I was able to go out again, my face, hands, and legs, having been much frozen.

The weather was beginning to be a little warm, so that the snow sometimes melted, when I began to hunt again. Going one day with Waw-be-be-nais-sa a good distance up the Assinneboin, we found a large herd of probably 200 elk, in a little prairie which was almost surrounded by the river. In the gorge, which was no more than two hundred yards across, Waw-be-be-nais-sa and I stationed ourselves, and the frightened herd being unwilling to venture on the smooth ice in the river, began to run round and round the little prairie. It sometimes happened that one was pushed within the reach of our shot and in this way we killed two. In our eagerness to get nearer, we advanced so far towards the center of the prairie that the herd was divided, a part being driven on the ice, and a part escaping to the high grounds. Waw-be-be-nais-sa followed the latter, and I ran on to the ice. The elks on the river, slipping on the smooth ice, and being much frightened, crowded so close together that their great weight broke the ice, and as they waded towards the opposite shore, and endeavoured in a body to rise upon the ice, it continued to break before them. I ran hastily and thoughtlessly along the brink of the open place, and as the water was not so deep as to swim the elks, I thought I might get those I killed, and therefore continued shooting them as fast as I could. When my balls were all expended, I drew my knife and killed one or two with it, but all I killed in the water were in a few minutes swept under the ice, and I got not one of them. One only, which I struck after he rose upon the ice on the shore, I saved. This, in addition to the others we had killed on the shore made four, being all we were able to take out of a gang of not less than two hundred. Waw-be-be-nais-sa went immediately, under the pretence of notifying the traders, and sold the four elks as his own, though he killed but two of them.

At this time, Wa-me-gon-a-biew was unable to hunt, having, in a drunken frolic been so severely burned, that he was not able to stand. In a few days, I went again with Waw-be-be-nais-sa to hunt elks. We discovered some in the prairie, but crawling up behind a little inequality of surface which enabled us to conceal ourselves, we came within a short distance. There was a very large and fat buck which I wished to shoot, but Waw-be-be-nais-sa said, "not so, my brother, lest you should fail to kill him. As he is the best in the herd I will shoot him, and you may try to kill one of the smaller ones." So I told him that I would shoot at one that was lying down. We fired both together, but he missed and I killed. The herd then ran off, and I pursued without waiting to butcher, or even to examine the one I had killed. I continued the chase all day, and before night had killed two more, as the elks were so much fatigued that I came up to them pretty easily. As it was now night, I made the best of my way home, and when I arrived, found that Waw-be-be-nais-sa had brought home meat, and had been amusing the family by describing the manner in which he said he had killed the elk. I said to them, "I am very glad he has killed an elk, for I have killed three, and to-morrow we shall have plenty of meat." But as I had some suspicion of him, I took him outside, and asked him about the one he had killed, and easily made him acknowledge, that it was no other than the one I had shot, from which he brought in some of the meat. He was sent to the traders to call men to bring in the meat, and again sold all three as his own, when he had not helped to kill even one of them. The old woman, when she became acquainted with this conduct, persecuted him so much that he was induced to leave us. Wa-me-gon-a-biew, also, who had married an Ojibbeway woman in the fall, now went to live with his father-in-law, and there remained in our family only the old woman and myself, the Bowwetig girl, Ke-zhik-o-weninne, the son of Taw-ga-we-ninne, now something of a boy, and the two small children. I was now, for the first time, left to pass the winter by myself, with a family to provide for, and no one to assist me. Waw-be-be-nais-sa encamped about one day from us. I had, in the course of the fall, killed a good many beavers and other animals, and we had for some time enough to supply all our wants. We had also plenty of blankets and clothing. One very cold morning in the winter, as I was going out to hunt, I stripped off all my silver ornaments and hung them up in the lodge. The old woman asked me why I did so. I told her that they were not comfortable in such extreme cold weather, moreover, that in pursuing game I was liable to lose them. She remonstrated for some time, but I persisted, and went to hunt without them. At the same time I started to hunt, the old woman started for Waw-be-be-nais-sa's lodge, intending to be absent two days. The lodge was left in the care of Skawah-shish, as the Bowwetig girl was called, and Ke-zhik-o-weninne. When I returned late at night, after a long and unsuccessful hunt, I found these two children standing, shivering and crying by the side of the ashes of our lodge, which, owing to their carelessness, had been burned down, and every thing we had consumed in it. My silver ornaments, one of my guns, several blankets, and much clothing, were lost. We had been rather wealthy among the Indians of that country; now we had nothing left but a medicine bag and a keg of rum. When I saw the keg of rum, I felt angry that only what was useless and hurtful to us was left, while every thing valuable had been destroyed, and taking it up, threw it to a distance. I then stripped the blanket from the Bowwetig girl, and sent her away to stay by herself in the snow, telling her that as her carelessness had stripped us of every thing, it was but right she should feel the cold more than I did. I then took the little boy, Ke-zhik-o-weninne, and we lay down together upon the warm ashes.

Very early the next morning I started out to hunt, and as I knew very well how the old woman would behave when she came to a knowledge of her misfortune, I did not wish to reach home until late at night. When approaching the place where our lodge had been, I heard the old woman scolding and beating the little girl. At length, when I went to the fire, she asked me why I had not killed her when I first came home and found the lodge burned down. "Since you did not," said she, "I must now kill her." "Oh my mother do not kill me, and I will pay you for all you have lost." "What have you to give? how can you pay me?" said the old woman. "I will give you the Manito," said the little girl, "the great Manito shall come down to reward you, if you do not kill me." We were now destitute of provisions, and almost naked, but we determined to go to Aneeb's trading-house, at Ke-new-kau-neshe way-boant, where we obtained credit for the amount of one pack of beaver skins, and with the blankets and cloth which we purchased in this way, we returned to Wa-me-gon-a-biew's lodge, whence he and his wife accompanied us to our own place.

We commenced to repair our loss by building a small grass lodge in which to shelter ourselves while we should prepare the pukkwi for a new wigwam.[2] The women were very industrious in making these, and none more active than Skwah-shish, the Bowwetig girl. At night, also, when it was too dark to hunt, Wa-me-gon-a-biew and myself assisted at this labour. In a few days our lodge was completed, and Wa-me-gon-a-biew, having killed three elks, left us for his own home.

After a little time, plenty and good humour were restored. One evening the old woman called to her the little Bowwetig girl, and asked her if she remembered what promise she had made to her when she was whipped for burning the lodge. Skwah-shish could make no answer, but the old woman took the opportunity to admonish her of the impropriety of using the name of the Deity in a light and irreverent manner.

[2] Pronounced by the Indians, We-ge-wham.

Marshall Sahlins

The Original Affluent Society

If economics is the dismal science, the study of hunting-gathering eco-nomics must be its most advanced branch. Almost totally committed to the argument that life was hard in the Paleolithic, our textbooks compete to convey a sense of impeding doom, leaving the student to wonder not only how hunters managed to make a living, but whether, after all, this was living? The specter of starvation stalks the stalker in these pages. His technical in-competence is said to enjoin continuous work just to survive, leaving him without respite from the food quest and without the leisure to "build culture." Even so, for his efforts he pulls the lowest grades in thermo-dynamics—less energy harnessed per capita per year than any other mode of production. And in treatises on economic development, he is condemned to play the role of bad example, the so-called "subsistence economy."

It will be extremely difficult to correct this traditional wisdom. Perhaps then we should phrase the necessary revisions in the most shocking terms pos-sible: that this was, when you come to think of it, the original affluent society. By common understanding an affluent society is one in which all the people's wants are easily satisfied; and though we are pleased to consider this happy condition the unique achievement of industrial civilization, a better case can be made for hunters and gatherers, even many of the marginal ones spared to ethnography. For wants are "easily satisfied," either by producing much or desiring little, and there are, accordingly, two possible roads to affluence. The Galbraithean course makes assumptions peculiarly appropriate to market economies, that man's wants are great, not to say infinite, whereas his means are limited, although improvable. Thus the gap between means and ends can eventually be narrowed by industrial productivity, at least to the extent that "urgent" goods became abundant. But there is also a Zen solution to scarcity and affluence, beginning from premises opposite from our own, that human material ends are few and finite and technical means unchanging but on the whole adequate. Adopting the Zen strategy, a people can enjoy an unparalleled material plenty, though perhaps only a low standard of living. That I think describes the hunters.[1]

The traditional dismal view of the hunter's fix is pre-anthropological. It

Reprinted from Richard B. Lee and Irven DeVore, editors, Man the Hunter (Chicago: Aldine Publishing Company, 1968); copyright © 1968 by the Wenner-Gren Foundation for Anthropological Research, Inc. Reprinted by permission of the author and Aldine Pub-lishing Company.

[1] I realize that the Netsilik Eskimo as described by Balikci constitute an exception in point. I shall not speak to this case here.

goes back to the time Adam Smith was writing, and maybe to a time before anyone was writing. But anthropology, especially evolutionary anthropology, found it congenial, even necessary theoretically, to adopt the same tone of reproach. Archeologists and ethnologists had become Neolithic revolutionaries, and in their enthusiasm for the revolution found serious shortcomings in the Old (Stone Age) Regime. Scholars extolled a Neolithic Great Leap Forward. Some spoke of a changeover from human effort to domesticated energy sources, as if people had been liberated by a new labor-saving device, although in fact the basic power resources remained exactly the same, plants and animals, the development occurring rather in techniques of appropriation (i.e., domestication). Moreover, archeological research was beginning to suggest that the decisive gains came in stability of settlement and gross economic product, rather than productivity of labor.

But evolutionary theory is not entirely to blame. The larger economic context in which it operates, "as if by an invisible hand," promotes the same dim conclusions about the hunting life. Scarcity is the peculiar obsession of a business economy, the calculable condition of all who participate in it. The market makes freely available a dazzling array of products all these "good things" within a man's reach—but never his grasp, for one never has enough to buy everything. To exist in a market economy is to live out a double tragedy, beginning in inadequacy and ending in deprivation. All economic activity starts from a position of shortage: whether as producer, consumer, or seller of labor, one's resources are insufficient to the possible uses and satisfactions. So one comes to a conclusion—"you pays your money and you takes your choice." But then, every acquisition is simultaneously a deprivation, for every purchase of something is a denial of something else that could have been had instead. (The point is that if you buy one kind of automobile, say a Plymouth fastback, you cannot also have a Ford Mustang —and I judge from the TV commercials that the deprivation involved is more than material.) Inadequacy is the judgment decreed by our economy, and thus the axiom of our economics: the application of scarce means against alternate ends. We stand sentenced to life at hard labor. It is from this anxious vantage that we look back on the hunter. But if modern man, with all his technical advantages, still hasn't got the wherewithal, what chance has this naked savage with his puny bow and arrow? Having equipped the hunter with bourgeois impulses and Paleolithic tools, we judge his situation hopeless in advance.

Scarcity is not an intrinsic property of technical means. It is a relation between means and ends. We might entertain the empirical possibility that hunters are in business for their health, a finite objective, and bow and arrow are adequate to that end. A fair case can be made that hunters often work much less than we do, and rather than a grind the food quest is intermittent, leisure is abundant, and there is more sleep in the daytime per capita than in any other conditions of society. (Perhaps certain traditional formulae are better inverted: the amount of work per capita increases with the evolution of culture and the amount of leisure per capita decreases.) Moreover, hunters seem neither harassed nor anxious. A certain confidence, at least in many cases, attends their economic attitudes and decisions. The way they dispose of food on hand, for example—as if they had it made.

This is the case even among many present marginal hunters—who hardly constitute a fair test of Paleolithic economy but something of a supreme test. Considering the poverty in which hunter and gatherers live in theory, it comes as a surprise that Bushmen who live in the Kalahari enjoy "a kind of material plenty" (Marshall, 1961, p. 243). Marshall is speaking of non-subsistence production; in this context her explication seems applicable beyond the Bushmen. She draws attention to the technical simplicity of the non-subsistence sector: the simple and readily available raw materials, skills, and tools. But most important, wants are restricted: a few people are happy to consider few things their good fortune. The restraint is imposed by nomadism. Of the hunter, it is truly said that this wealth is a burden (at least for his wife). Goods and mobility are therefore soon brought into contradiction, and to take liberties with a line of Lattimore's, the pure nomad remains a poor nomad. It is only consistent with their mobility, as many accounts directly say, that among hunters needs are limited, avarice inhibited, and—Warner (1937 [1958], p. 137) makes this very clear for the Murngin—portability is a main value in the economic scheme of things.

A similar case of affluence without abundance can be made for the subsistence sector. McCarthy and McArthur's time-motion study in Arnhem Land (1960) indicates the food quest is episodic and discontinuous, and per capita commitment to it averages less than four hours a day. The amount of daytime sleep and rest is unconscionable: clearly, the aborigines fail to "build culture" not from lack of time but from idle hands. McCarthy and McArthur also suggest that the people working under capacity—they might have easily procured more food; that they are able to support unproductive adults—who may, however, do some craft work; and that getting food was not strenuous or exhausting. The Arnhem Land study, made under artificial conditions and based only on short-run observations, is plainly inconclusive in itself. Nevertheless, the Arnhem Land data are echoed in reports of other Australians and other hunters. Two famous explorers of the earlier nineteenth century made estimates of the same magnitude for the aborigines' subsistence activities: two to four hours a day (Eyre, 1845, 2, pp. 252, 255; Grey, 1841, 2, pp. 261–63). Slash-and-burn agriculture, incidentally, may be more labor-intensive: Conklin, for example, figures that 1,200 man hours per adult per year are given among the Hanunóo simply to agriculture (Conklin, 1957, p. 151: this figure excludes other food-connected activities, whereas the Austrialian data include time spent in the preparation of food as well as its acquisition). The Arnhem Landers' punctuation of steady work with sustained idleness is also widely attested in Australia and beyond. Lee reported that productive members of !Kung Bushman camps spend two to three days per week in subsistence. We have heard similar comments in other papers at the symposium. Hadza women were said to work two hours per day on the average in gathering food, and one concludes from James Woodburn's excellent film that Hadza men are much more preoccupied with games of chance than with chances of game.

In addition, evidence on hunter-gatherers' economic attitudes and decisions should be brought to bear. Harassment is not implied in the descriptions of their nonchalant movements from camp to camp, nor indeed is the familiar condemnations of their laziness. A certain issue is posed by exasperated comments on the prodigality of hunters, their inclination to make a feast of everything on hand; as if, one Jesuit said of the Montagnais, "the game they were to hunt was shut up in a stable" (Le Jeune's *Relation* of 1634, in Kenton, 1927, 1, p. 182). "Not the slightest thought of, or care for, what the morrow may bring forth," wrote Spencer and Gillen (1899, p. 53). Two interpretations of this supposed lack of foresight are possible: either they are fools, or they are not worried—that is, as far as they are concerned, the morrow will bring more of the same. Rather than anxiety, it would seem the hunters have a confidence born of affluence, of a condition in which all the people's wants (such as they are) are generally easily satisfied. This confidence does not desert them during hardship. It can carry them laughing through periods that would try even a Jesuit's soul, and worry him so that—as the Indians warn—he could become sick:

I saw them [the Montagnais] in their hardships and their labors, suffer with cheerfulness. . . . I found myself, with them, threatened with great suffering; they said to me, "We shall be sometimes two days, sometimes three, without eating, for lack of food; take courage, *Chihine*, let thy soul be strong to endure suffering and hardship; keep thyself from being sad, otherwise thou will be sick; see how we do not cease to laugh, although we have little to eat" (Le Jeune's *Relation* of 1634, in Kenton, 1927, 1, p. 129).

Again on another occasion Le Jeune's host said to him: "Do not let thyself be cast down, take courage; when the snow comes, we shall eat" (Le Jeune's *Relation* of 1634, in Kenton, 1927, 1, p. 171). Which is something like the philosophy of the Penan of Borneo: "If there is no food today there will be tomorrow"—expressing, according to Needham, "a confidence in the capacity of the environment to support them, and in their own ability to extract their livelihood from it" (1954, p. 230).

References Cited

CONKLIN, HAROLD C., (1957) *Hanunóo Agriculture: a report on an integral system of shifting cultivation in the Philippines*, Vol. 2, Rome: Food and Agriculture Organization of the United Nations.

EYRE, EDWARD JOHN (1845) *Journals of expeditions of discovery into Central Australia and overland from Adelaide to King George's Sound, in the years 1840–41*, London: T. and W. Boone.

GREY, GEORGE (1841) *Journals of two expeditions of discovery in northwestern and western Australia, during the years 1837, '38 and '39*, London: T. and W. Boone.

KENTON, EDNA (ed.) (1927) *The Indians of North America*. In the Jesuit relations and allied documents; travels and explorations of the Jesuit missionaries in New France 1610–1791. New York: Harcourt Brace. (First published Burrows, 1896).

MARSHALL, LORNA K. (1961) Sharing, talking and giving: relief of social tension among !Kung bushmen, *Africa*, 31, 231–49.

McCARTHY, FREDERICK D. AND MARGARET McARTHUR (1960) The food quest and the time factor in aboriginal economic life. In Charles P. Mountford (ed.), *Records of the American-Australian Scientific Expendition to Arnhem Land*, Vol. 2, *Anthropology and Nutrition*, Melbourne: Melbourne University Press.

NEEDHAM, RODNEY (1954) Siriono and Penan: a test of some hypotheses, Southwestern Journal of Anthropology, 10(3):228–32

SPENCER, BALDWIN AND F. J. GILLEN (1899) The Native Tribes of Central Australia, London: Macmillan.

WARNER, WILLIAM LLOYD (1937) A Black Civilization: a study of an Australian tribe, New York: Harper & Row.

Elizabeth Marshall Thomas

Veld Food

With the warm air came a series of long, fat clouds sailing from the north like slow dirigibles, some of them showering down a few drops of rain. We were amazed to see rain in winter, the dry season, something we had not seen before, and we asked Ukwane about it. He said that it was not unusual for rain to come in the wintertime but very hard on the people of the desert, as it fools the wild vegetables from which the Bushmen get their water.

There are many kinds of wild roots which can be eaten in winter, and each is marked among the grass blades by an almost invisible dry thread of a vine. The roots are swollen with liquid by which the plants preserve their life during the drought. When the plants feel the onset of spring, warm air and raindrops, the dry vines suck moisture out of the watery roots, turn green, and put out tiny leaves, and in this way, if the false spring lasts, the roots are soon sucked dry entirely. Bushmen cannot get enough water from eating the vines and leaves. The plants do not bear fruit until summer; the spring-season vegetables, such as little onions, pods like pea pods, and leafy green vegetables that taste like rhubarb, have not grown in yet; and so the Bushmen must go thirsty. People have died of thirst in these false seasons.

Gathering veld food is the work of the Bushman women, and I used to go with them quite often on their trips. We sometimes stayed in the veld all day eating roots instead of drinking water. One day my brother came along to film the gathering of veld food, and as we were getting ready to leave, Gai also joined us. It is customary for Bushmen never to let a group of their women go anywhere with a Bantu or a European man unless a Bushman man goes with them to protect them. Gai sauntered along behind us in his role of guardian, quite unhampered, as he had nothing with him but his loincloth. Dasina, Twikwe, and Tsetchwe walked in front, each with a digging-stick thrust in her belt like an enormous knife, each wearing a heavy cape, and Tsetchwe carrying her baby, who rode, carefree and swinging his feet, on her shoulder. John and I walked in the middle of the procession, and at the end came the three young boys, who did not stay in single file but ran all over the veld, ran circles around us, and shouted to each other happily.

We walked across the pan of Ai a ha'o through the fine, soft grass, which left tiny, barbed seeds sticking to our legs. We walked through the brush on the opposite side and then over a wide plain, where we saw a herd of wilde-beest. No one was armed, and when the wildebeest saw us, put down their heads, and ran, we could only watch helplessly as all that meat galloped away.

We walked until we came to a patch of tsama melons, perhaps twenty of them lying together, shiny, smooth, and green in the grass. The vine that once had nourished them had dried away and already some of the melons were turning yellow, overripe, ready to open and release their seeds.

The women stopped and began to gather up the green melons, Twikwe picking them with a mechanical, stereotyped gesture. She first slipped her hand under a melon; then, twisting her elbow, she lifted the melon and held it pinched between the heel of her hand and her forearm, and with a scoop slipped it into the pocket of her kaross on the side. In a moment the side of her kaross was full, and she stood erect for an instant, looked at the sky, shifted her weight, and suddenly the melons rolled to the back of her kaross, leaving the side free for more. She was very efficient. In a moment she had a load. I was a little surprised at her, however, for now she would have to carry the melons with her all day whereas she might have gathered them on the way home. But Bushman women do not seem to mind this.

The women left behind the yellow melons which would have been bitter and rotten, touching them disappointedly with their toes instead. The false spring was hastening the time when all the melons would be gone, forcing the Bushmen to eat roots as a staple diet, not as desirable because of the uses that tsama melons have. Melons are eaten as both food and water, their pulp is added to meat which needs liquid for boiling, their seeds are roasted and eaten or ground into powder and used as flour, their rinds serve as mixing-bowls, as containers for small, loose objects, as cooking-pots with or without the pulp inside, as urine-containers for curing hides, as targets for the children's shooting practice, as children's drums, as resonators for musical instruments, and all this amounts to a serious loss for Bushmen when the melons rot or dry.

We went on until we were about two miles from camp. We were going to an almost imperceptible small hill, a place, said Twikwe, where a great deal of veld food grew. On the way a moving shadow caught our attention, and we looked up to see a white-breasted, black-winged vulture sailing not far above our heads, not stirring himself but riding the drafts and currents of the air. He was looking at us with hard eyes, his red face turned to look down, and suddenly he closed his great wings under his body, sweeping them down so far that the long wing feathers brushed together four feet under his belly. Then his wings swept up again and bore him on. I had never seen a vulture do that before. He did it only once, then made a circle all around us, looking down at us, his eyes cool in their red wrinkles; he rose higher and higher and soon he was gone. All over Africa the sky is full of vultures, but so high that you can seldom see them; any time you look up with binoculars, however, you will probably be able to see one sailing, waiting up there for a disaster.

We were going particularly to look for *bi*, a fibrous, watery root that is the mainstay of the Bushmen's diet during the hot season when the melons are gone. From the end of August, when the spring begins, the heat increases in intensity until December and January, when the rains come, relieving the drought. During this hot, dry season the sand reflects the sun until the air all over the veld shudders and dances, until human beings and animals alike gasp for air and water. This is the hardest season of all for the Bushmen, yet most of them remain alive by going into the veld early in the morning in the cooler light of dawn to gather bi. The bi they find is brought back to the werf before the sun is hot; it is scraped, and the scrapings are squeezed dry. The people drink the juice they squeeze. Then they dig shallow pits like graves for themselves in the shade. They urinate on the bi scrapings and line the pits with the now moist pulp, then lie in the pits and spend the day letting the moisture evaporating from the urine preserve the moisture in their bodies. They lie still all day and at dusk go into the veld again to gather food, perhaps a few roots or cucumbers, returning to their werf before it is utterly dark, for in the hot season the big snakes, too, move only at night, the mambas and the cobras out of their holes.

By the end of the season the Gikwe are emaciated from hunger and thirst, and it is because of this season that the Gikwe hear the jackals on the plains cry "Water, water."

When we reached the little hill Twikwe had mentioned we found no bi root, but we found other kinds of veld food: a bush with red berries, several kinds of roots, and spiny cucumber not three inches long, round and bristling with its spines like a sea urchin, handsome in its light-brown, yellow-striped skin. The young boys found five of these cucumbers lying in a crooked row on the sand, all put there by a vine which had mostly dried and shriveled away. We picked them and ate them. They have a watery green flesh which looks just like the flesh of a cucumber as we know it but which is sweet.

Witabe, noting the direction of the vine by the way it had deposited its cucumbers, traced it to its source and found a bit of it left above the ground, below the branches of a whitethorn bush. He said there would be an edible root there, and when he dug, there was.

Meanwhile, Gai had found a solid, stiff vine like a stalk among the roots of a gray bush which was the home of a small flock of birds. Just for fun, Gai chased the birds out; they would have gone anyway, but, frightened by him, they flew like little pellets in every direction, leaving behind a pale, soft grass nest blowing in the wind. Gai sat down facing the bush with the branch shadows all over him and dug with a digging-stick in the sand between his legs. The branches around his head got in his way, tickling his ears, causing him to slash impatiently at them with his digging-stick, and when this did no good he endured the nuisance for a moment, then flung himself down on his back, put up his long legs like a fighting cock, and kicked the branches down.

He dug out a great deal of earth, throwing it behind him, and finally uncovered a *ga* root, big and dark with a warty surface all covered with lumps like a toad or a stone; a fascinating thing, for although it was large and nondescript, brownish gray in brown-gray sand, marked only by an old dry vine, it was life itself to Bushmen, bitter but quite moist even in the hottest season. Tsetchwe put the root in her kaross and we went off, Gai generously carrying the baby, taking him from Tsetchwe by the forearm and swinging him up to his shoulder. The baby rode astride Gai's neck with the soft kaross he wore draped over Gai's head. From the rear they were an apparition, as this made the baby's head, not much higher than Gai's, look like a tiny head on a man's tall, slender body.

We wanted very much to find a *bi* root, and while Gai, the baby, and my brother went off to look for one I waited behind with the women. We rested in a small circle in the dim shade of the grass, which, when we were sitting, came high above our heads so that all we could see was a circle of sky and, in the circle, the ragged, waxing moon. It had risen luxuriously in the daytime and was a pale, large crescent, pearl-colored in the sun. The moon is a root with a climbing stalk, a vine. It can be eaten.

Giamakwe began to urinate right in our midst, crouching and pulling his loincloth aside. Although the adults are slightly inhibited about this, the children are not, sometimes simply turning aside to urinate as one might turn aside to cough. Presently the young boys got up and ran away, and when they did Tsetchwe herself got to her feet, stepped aside, and urinated also, standing up but leaning forward. Bushman women sometimes do this, but Bushman men crouch to urinate. "It is our law," they say.

While the women rested they had refreshed themselves with one of Twikwe's melons which Twikwe chopped for them by holding the melon between the soles of both feet and mashing its pulp with her digging-stick, which she held in both hands. Then they got up from their grass nest, sharpened their digging-sticks with Twikwe's knife, and set out to begin the search for food. They each chose a different direction and soon they were out of sight. I followed Twikwe to see what she would find, hurrying to keep up as she trampled ahead of me on those spindly, awkward legs of hers, which she kicked out with each step in a walk like the walk of a clown. She kept her back straight, for it was still early and the load in her kaross was light.

As I could not speak many words of Gikwe, she didn't even try to talk, but paused from time to time instead to show me things. Once she crouched among the branches of a thorn bush and beckoned to me to show me a tiny vine winding around the bush's trunk. I nodded. It marked an edible root. She pinched the base of the vine where there was a faint touch of green, then, grasping her digging-stick, began to dig. The ground was quite hard, but she dug rapidly, her slender back curved as she squatted over the hole and the muscles of her thin arms swelling. After a long time she threw down her digging-stick and tugged at something in the bottom of the hole. She sat back, and in her hands was a huge stone, which she heaved aside.

"Look," she said, and I crawled beside her into the bush. She had made a hole three feet deep, a foot across, and at the bottom, dim in shadow, lay an immense gray root wedged securely between two stones. "Ga," she said. She ripped the severed vine from the bush it clung to and tossed it into the sunlight. "Look," she said again, assuming that I would now recognize a ga vine when I saw one; but although I examined it closely, it still looked like any other vine to me.

Again she bent over the hole, leaning over so far that her head came between her knees, and grasped the huge root with both hands. She tugged so hard that I heard her joints crack, but the root was wedged and she couldn't move it. She took up her digging-stick again, panting now, and struck the rocks, and the point of her digging-stick splintered.

"Ai," she said, exasperated, sitting back on her heels to carve a new point with her knife. She bent again, pried at the rocks, pried at the root, but it was useless, she couldn't move it. Then she relaxed, resting for a moment as she rubbed her sore shoulders before she got to her feet and walked away, beckoning with her head for me to follow. We would leave it.

We wandered about haphazardly for a time, looking for a vine, and presently I saw one twisted around some grass blades, binding them together in a tuft. I pointed it out to her, but she smiled and shook her head, turning her hands palm upward in the gesture for nothing. She meant that it was a useless species of vine, marking nothing below. Later, as we walked along, she laughed. Twikwe was charmed by the mistakes the members of our expedition made, for they were always elementary and, to her, very diverting.

Keeping her eyes on the ground, Twikwe noticed a tiny crack in the sand. She scooped at it with the point of her digging-stick, tipped out a truffle, and picked it up almost without stopping. As we walked on she broke it in half, put half in her kaross, and offered half to me. I ate it. It was light brown and had a delicious, salty flavor. Truffles grow an inch or so below hard-surfaced ground and have no leaf nor stalk nor vine to show where they are, only the tiny crack made by the truffle swelling, which the Bushmen notice.

We had crossed a barren stretch of plain where only grass was growing and were in another patch of low bushes where veld food also grew. The great plains of the Kalahari may seem undiversified, but really they are divided into countless little patches, some barren, some fertile, depending probably on the soil. In this veld-food patch Twikwe found another vine tangled in the lower branches of a thorn bush and she crawled in after it and began to dig. The thorns around her head, all smooth and shining white like jewels, were tickling her, but, unlike Gai, she delicately put up just one hand and picked off the very thorns that pricked her.

She resumed her digging and after perhaps twenty minutes as she followed down the vine she uncovered another ga root also wedged among stones. This ga was not as large as the other one, nor was it wedged as tightly, and when she grasped it, arched her back, and tugged, clenching her teeth and straining her thin arms, the rocks suddenly gave way and the ga flew loose, sending Twikwe crashing back among the thorns. She wiped the perspiration from her forehead with her thumb before she crawled out of the bush, dragging her root and her digging-stick. I noticed that the root was very wrinkled, as if it had shrunk. Twikwe struck at it with the point of her digging-stick, chipping out a fragment, which she put in her mouth. Then she spat, stood up, and walked away from it. When I, too, tasted it to see what was the matter I found that it was flaccid, dry, and very bitter, quite inedible. I looked inside the bush and saw that its vine had begun to turn a little green.

We went on, and passed a few dry melons on our way, yellow and empty, perhaps bitten by an antelope some time ago. I kicked at one of them and a gray lizard ran out, straight and fast as an arrow. Then it turned around and ran back in again, having no place else to go.

Soon Twikwe found a third root and, after digging it out and tasting it, found it quite acceptable; putting it in her kaross, she went on to find a fourth. We found old, dry holes where Bushman women had dug out roots seasons ago, a few dry vines with bitter, useless roots below, and three more roots that proved to be edible, as well as two more melons, a few spiny cucumbers, a handful of berries from a tiny bush, and one more truffle. This would feed Twikwe and her two sons for one or two days, or perhaps would be shared with Ukwane and Kutera because Kutera, that day, had not felt well enough to gather food of her own. Bushmen help each other, each Bushman woman contributing to the support of her own family and perhaps to the well-being of some very old people as well.

When Twikwe considered that she had enough, we turned back to find the others, and presently we came to the plain where we had left them. Twikwe called, and was answered by three or four voices very near by. Then, right in front of us as if from nowhere, the three boys, Tsetchwe, and Dasina appeared standing, having been crouching in the long grass. Twikwe and I joined them, and the Bushmen passed Twikwe's pipe, the short, wide antelope bone stuffed with tobacco. When it was passed to me I puffed it, too, but it was so strong and rank that it made me dizzy.

Soon we heard a wail, a sad crying out in the veld, and it was Gai and John returning with Nhwakwe, who had begun to miss his mother or want to go home. Gai looked cross and walked rapidly with his little burden riding on his shoulder, and even John seemed somewhat annoyed because of the noise and because they had not found a bi root. When they came up to us Gai swung Nhwakwe down, dangling him by the arm as he handed him to Tsetchwe, who took him at once and let him nurse. Bushman babies do not like to go for veld food because the sun is hot, there is nothing to eat except the raw roots, and there is nobody to play with, yet they do not like to be left at home alone either. This is a constant and insoluble problem for Bushman mothers.

After asking Gai more questions and, at his suggestion, roaming from one point to another over the veld in search of a bi, it came to John and me that he did not want to show us where one was growing. We understood this, for the bi roots of the veld are naturally limited and if we took one when the Bushmen did not need it, it would not be there when they did. We assured Gai that we did not want to eat it, only to see its vine, and at last he remembered, he said, where one was, far out in the veld and on the way to Okwa. But we were not discouraged and set off in that direction, and after a while we found it far away but not as far as Gai had said. It took us an hour to reach it, but we had traveled slowly because the women had stopped to gather melons along the way.

When we came to the center of an enormous plain with no tree or bush to mark the place, Gai stopped and, glancing around for a moment, pointed suddenly with his toe. After trying hard to see, we noticed a tiny shred of a vine wound around a grass blade; no part of the vine still touched the ground, as the vine had dried and parts of it had blown away. Gai had known where the bi was, he told us, because he had walked by it months ago in the last rainy season when the vine was still green, and he had remembered. He had assumed that it was still there because only his own people used the territory around it and if one of them had taken it he would have heard. Bushmen talk all the time about such things. He had had it in his mind to come back and get it when the tsama melons were gone, but now, perhaps when he saw its vine there and thought about it under the ground, he changed his mind. Squatting near the vine and digging with his hands, he soon had exposed it, two feet down and dark in shadow. He seized it and tore it from the earth.

It was shaped like a monstrous beet, with its vine coming from the top like a little stalk and its root bristling from the bottom like a tassel. It had a hard, bark-like crust and it was gray and hairy. Gai held it daintily by its vine, and, as dirt was still dropping off it he slapped and brushed it to clean it; then he held it high above the big cavity it had filled, looked at it with a rather satisfied smile, and said what nice water it would be.

We went home then, walking again in single file in a straight course over the veld, veering only once toward a fallen tree, where the women stopped to gather firewood. The women, walking first, were heavily loaded now with melons, roots, and firewood. Tsetchwe loaded most heavily of all because the baby rode on her shoulder. The women used their digging-sticks as canes because their knees were bending, and walked quickly, trying to get home as soon as possible. After the women came the young boys carrying nothing, and last of all came Gai, holding his bi by its tassel of root. Before long he hurried and caught up to Tsetchwe, and once again he took a turn with Nhwakwe, swinging him from Tsetchwe's shoulders to his own, where Nhwakwe rode happily, his tiny hands pressed over his father's eyes.

Richard A. Gould

Chipping Stones in the Outback

Click! Click! The thin sound of stones being struck together reached me through the hot summer air as I walked along the bottom of the dry creek bed toward camp in the Clutterbuck Hills of the desert area of Western Australia. Rounding the last bend I found an aboriginal man, sitting cross-legged, striking flakes from a water-worn pebble. I realized as I watched him that I was witnessing a scene that has taken place repeatedly throughout the whole of human history, from the time of earliest man to the present. Stone chippings like these, mundane artifacts to be sure, have been one of the most important sources of evidence for archeologists studying the cultures of ancient man. Indeed in some places they are the only evidence. Because of their importance, archeologists constantly have sought ways to interpret how these ancient tools were made, their functions, and their role in prehistoric cultures. Furthermore, the archeologist has often used these same tools to distinguish one group of prehistoric people from another.

Most archeologists begin their interpretations along strictly archeological lines. By this I mean they examine the artifact itself in an attempt to determine its method of manufacture and its use.

Reprinted from Richard A. Gould, "Chipping Stones in the Outback," Natural History (February 1968), 42–48, with permission of Natural History Magazine. Copyright © The American Museum of Natural History, 1968.

A stone arrowhead, for example, is usually easy to identify by inspection. Other kinds of stone tools may be harder to interpret, requiring close and at times microscopic analysis of such things as breakage and wear patterns, weight, size, raw material, and different kinds of chipping.

Archeologists also check their excavation notes to see if the artifact might be associated with something else that will provide clues. If, for instance, a certain style of projectile point is characteristically found associated with the remains of a certain species of game, the archeologist may infer not only the basic function of the artifact but also its role in a special pattern of hunting.

Inevitably, archeologists must turn to historical or ethnographic sources for ideas on which to base any but the most superficial of interpretations. How much harder it is to understand the ancient arrowheads you have uncovered if you do not know about the bow and arrow!

The reports left by early explorers and chroniclers as well as by trained ethnographers do not always supply the needed background information. These explorers and chroniclers may have been more interested in finding gold, looking for good pasture and farming land, or other practical matters than in collecting facts about the industries of the aboriginals they encountered. Ethnologists, while they are interested in the native peoples of an area, tend to be more concerned about ceremonies, kinship systems, language, and other matters than with the parts of the culture that are likely to leave behind tangible remains—such as stone tools, pottery, and other material "hardware"—for archeologists to excavate and study.

Today there is a growing interest in the lives and behavior of ancient people who lived by hunting and gathering wild foods. Most of human prehistory is the story of hunter-gatherers, and it is therefore no surprise to find that many archeologists have directed their efforts entirely toward recovering the cultures of ancient hunter-gatherers. But these archeologists, like myself, have discovered gaps in our knowledge of living, present-day hunter-gatherers. The Congo Pygmies, the Bushmen of the Kalahari Desert, and the aborigines of the Australian desert are about the only people left in the world today who still live entirely this way, and in all three cases rapid changes in their cultures are coming about through contact with Europeans. The time is fast drawing to a close when people like these can still be found living in their normal habitat, depending on their traditional foraging economy.

Although archeologists spend much of their time classifying the stone tools they uncover, hardly anyone has ever attempted to learn how the native peoples themselves classify their stone tools. It has been argued that archeologists should try to make their systems of classification conform to those of the people who originally made and used the artifacts. Thus the acheological ordering of the materials would be more realistic, for it would reflect what went on in the mind of the native user rather than simply what went on in the mind of the archeologist, and would thereby increase the prospect for meaningful interpretation. This is a good argument, but it presupposes that there is a body of evidence on how native people do, in fact, classify their artifacts. Such evidence is generally lacking, especially for hunter-gatherers.

Of the three societies available for study, only the aborigines of the Gibson Desert of Western Australia were known to make and use stone tools as a regular part of their behavior. My wife and I went there in 1966 and lived with aboriginal families both in the desert and on Aboriginal Reserves for about fifteen months.

Owing to their isolation in this arid country, direct contact with Europeans came only in the last two or three years for some of these aborigines, with at least one family being contacted by government patrols as late as July, 1967. These are mainly Ngatatjara and Pintupi people, all of whom speak various dialects of Pitjantjatjara, a language in use over wide areas of the western desert of Australia. In the desert, these people live entirely by hunting and collecting wild foods, moving on foot over long distances from one water source to another. The nomadic nature of their existence puts a premium on portability in their material culture.

The desert aborigines classify their flaked stone tools into two categories, basing this distinction on the cross-sectional shape of the working edge (*yiri*) of the stone flake from which the tool is fashioned. A fairly thick flake with a steep working edge suitable for adzing or scraping in making wooden objects is called *purpunpa*. A knifelike flake with a thin, sharp edge suited for slicing or cutting is termed *tjimari*. In nearly every case, adze flakes (the term "adze" used here is not to be confused with the much larger adze more commonly thought of as used by shipwrights or by native woodworkers in some parts of New Guinea) are retouched along an edge to provide a sharp scraping surface. They are almost always hafted to the base of a wooden club or spear-thrower. In appearance, they resemble prehistoric stone tools (called scrapers by archeologists) from other parts of the world. Perhaps some of these were also hafted for use as woodworking tools.

Knives are retouched only if the cutting edge needs it, and this retouching is always done on one side of the edge only. In most cases, however, the extremely sharp edge of the freshly struck flake is regarded as sufficient. Flakes used as knives are sometimes given a "handle" by attaching a lump of gum, made either from spinifex (*Triodia* sp.) or blackboy (*Xanthorrhoea thorntonii*) resin, to the blunt edge of the flake.

Sometimes, if the worker is in a hurry, a sharp flake is selected, used for the immediate task, and discarded afterward. This often occurs during the butchering of kangaroos and emus, when the man doing the butchering grasps the flake between his thumb and forefinger while slitting the animal's belly, cutting leg tendons, and removing the feet and tail.

Adze flakes are the most distinctive and widespread class of stone artifacts made by the desert aborigines. Among the Pintupi and Ngatatjara people those tools are made in three different ways. First, there is the technique of direct percussion by means of a small hammerstone. The flake is held horizontally, bulbar face upward, in one hand (before being hafted) while sharp blows are directed downward along the edge with a small stone, usually a smooth, rounded pebble. While doing this the worker generally steadies himself by propping the elbow of the arm holding the adze flake against his knee while seated in a cross-legged position. In a matter of from ten to twenty seconds, a row of tiny flakes is removed from the underside of the edge, and the flake is then ready to be hafted to a club or spear-thrower.

Often, however, the flake is first hafted and then trimmed by means of

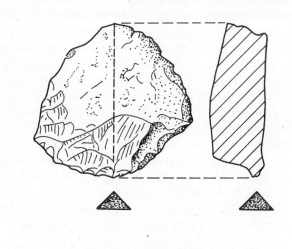

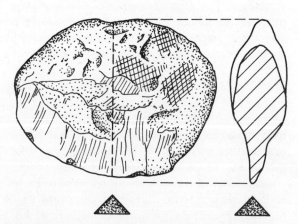

FIGURE 1. The two basic categories of flaked stone tools are the broad-edged adzing tool (*purpunpa*), top, and the narrow-edged knife (*tjimari*), bottom, shown both in full view and cross section. The knife is set in a gum "handle." Arrows indicate the cutting edges.

gentle blows struck with a wooden stick. In this case the hafted flake is cradled, bulbar face upward, in the hollow of one hand with the working edge cushioned against the fleshy part of the thumb. The other hand taps a stick along the edge of the flake, detaching a row of small flakes in about twenty seconds.

Finally, there is the most remarkable technique of all—that of biting the flake in order to trim the edge. This practice, which apparently does not damage the teeth, has been observed before among the desert aborigines by Professor Donald Thomson, but it has not been studied in detail. The only other mention of this technique I know of comes from Coronado's chronicler, Casteñada, who observed this method of stone flaking on the Great Plains of North America in 1541. To accomplish this technique successfully the worker must have "flat teeth," that is, teeth with the crowns worn down to a flat, rather than a serrated, surface. This is a common physiological feature among people who normally eat foods containing large amounts of grit.

Another prerequisite for this technique is exceptionally strong jaw muscles. In this respect, too, the desert aborigines are well endowed, for their diet contains many tough foods, particularly meat that would be regarded as grossly undercooked by European standards.

As a woodworking tool the hafted stone adze is surprisingly efficient. It takes a desert aborigine only about twice as long to complete a woodworking task with a stone adze as with metal chisels and axes. Using metal tools he can produce an undecorated wooden spear-thrower in about four to five hours of continuous work; with a hafted stone adze the same task can take about eight and a half to nine hours.

Perhaps the supreme test of the stone adze comes in making a transverse cut across the grain of a mulga (*Acacia aneura*) stave to form the tip of a digging stick. It is fairly easy to shave away the wood surface if one is working with the grain of the wood, but working across the grain of this hard wood is difficult and requires a special technique. The tip of the digging stick is placed in a small fire and allowed to char. The char is scraped away with the stone adze until the surface is clean, then it is charred and scraped again, and the process is repeated until the point on the tip of the digging stick is completed.

Some archeologists have speculated on the possible advantages of "fire hardening" of spear tips and digging sticks recovered from ancient sites in Europe and elsewhere, but the behavior of the desert aborigines indicates that, far from hardening the wooden tip, this technique of charring serves to soften the outer surface of the wood and makes it easier to scrape away with a stone adze or abrading stone.

During use there is a tendency for the center of an adze flake to wear faster than the outer edges, resulting in a slightly concave edge. Retouching is aimed at straightening and sharpening and may occur as many as twenty times during the course of making one undecorated spear-thrower. Usually the flake is reversed in the haft during the job, and the flake is finally worn down to an absolutely characteristic slug. Under magnification these worn slugs have minute "ridges" running across the steep face of the flake. They are among the most common artifacts in aboriginal campsites.

There is one type of adzing tool used by these aborigines that has never been reported before from the Australian desert. This is a small engraving tool that is included within the range of artifacts called *purpunpa*, but which is also given a special term, *pitjuru-pitjuru*. It consists of a small flake with a fairly thick but narrow tip. In about half the cases I observed, this flake was given some secondary trimming after being hafted, but otherwise it was not retouched until it grew dull from use. It is set into a gum haft at the end of a short handle, 10 to 16 inches long. Unlike ordinary adzes, this tool is regarded as a sacred object and is never shown to women, children, or uncircumcised men. It is the most specialized stone tool made by the desert aborigines and is used exclusively for making the incised decorations on sacred boards and decorated spear-throwers.

All flake knives are called *tjimari*, regardless of their size (which ranges from ¾ to 4 inches in length and ½ to 2½ inches in width) or the degree to which they are treated as sacred. The larger flake knives (generally without a handle) may serve more mundane functions, such as cutting up small game, sinews, and a variety of other domestic purposes. Unlike smaller knives that are used mainly for circumcising male novices, these large knives have no sacred connotations and can appear openly in camp with no restrictions on who can see or use them.

In most cases these knives are discarded after only a few uses, and no effort is made to resharpen them. Thus they rarely show much in the way of secondary trimming and could be extremely difficult for an archeologist to recognize once the gum handle has decomposed. At times the hafted adze may be used as a cutting tool in butchering game, but this is unusual and happens only when no flake knives are readily available.

A *yalkara*, or hand ax, generally consists of nothing more than a hand-held rock with a sharp edge, picked up off the ground when needed and thrown away after use. On every occasion when I have been present, these have been used only for woodworking tasks, such as cutting spear shafts or detaching wooden slabs for shaping into spear-throwers or sacred boards. This latter task is accomplished with wooden wedges and either a large rock or a piece of wood used as a hammer. My informants say that sometimes they trimmed the working edge of the hand ax with rough percussion flaking, but this has been less frequent since steel axes have become available.

One of the usual explanations for the use of Paleolithic hand axes in Africa and Europe has been the suggestion by many archeologists that they were used in butchering large game. In most cases, there is no reason to doubt this interpretation, but it is interesting to point out that the desert aborigines butcher all their large game (kangaroos, euros, emus) by means of wooden wedges, using untrimmed rocks or logs for pounding and small stone flakes or flake knives for cutting the skin and tendons. Among these people stone hand axes are used almost entirely for woodworking. Perhaps wooden-wedge butchering was a more widespread or even typical technique in the past.

Although the aborigines do not attempt to enhance the appearance of stone tools by careful trimming, they do tend to place an esthetic value on cherty materials of different color and texture. All agree that rough, grainy white quartzite is poor material, and they will use it only when absolutely nothing else is available. Natives from the Warburton Range area prefer the white chert found in quarries near there. The Pintupi and northern Ngatatjara men prefer the yellowish quartzites and creamy yellow cherts found in their region. These preferences have little to do with the actual working qualities of the different materials, for all are satisfactory materials for stone chipping. Rather, they reflect the close totemic ties each man has to the particular region from which he comes. The localities of these quarries often figure as places where "dreamtime" heroes, or *wati tjukurpa*, performed creative acts, and are venerated by men who believe themselves to be patrilineally descended from these ancestral beings. Thus a man may have a sense of kinship with some of these chert quarries, and he will value the stone material from them as a part of his own being.

In March, 1967, I met an extended family of twelve Pintupi people near Tjalpu-tjalpu waterhole. One of the men in the party carried a small bag containing yellow quartzite flakes from Partjar, some fifty miles to the northwest. Another man in the party had left a pile of sixteen small, round pebbles in front of his shelter at Tika-tika, the previous campsite. He had transported these from Partjar and intended to use them as hammerstones.

Here again, the aborigines have provided the archeologist with an interesting explanation for a problem he has most often explained by trade. Perhaps much of the occurrence of materials from distant areas was a matter of personal preference on the part of the individual who collected the material.

Formal instruction in the art of stone chipping and related techniques is at a minimum. Little conversation occurs at these times, but the children watch closely and sometimes try later on to imitate their parents' actions, using scraps of stone or wood lying about the campsite.

Since the making of stone tools does not apparently depend on conversation, those archeologists who have from time to time inferred the beginnings of speech from the complexity of the artifacts found at early sites might well profit from this observation. It might be added, however, that conversation does play an important part in the selection of raw material for tools. At such times the conversation is highly animated, as the virtues of this and that chert are hotly debated.

When contrasted with sacred activities, the chipping of stone tools is regarded by these aborigines as an art of little importance, the way Americans might, for instance, treat the matter of tying one's shoelaces. This casual attitude can raise certain problems for the archeologist. For one thing, there is a tendency for these people to pick up ancient stone tools from the surface of sites where they are camped and reuse these implements. Small, finely made, crescent-shaped tools of chert, along with other small, rather elegantly made stone tools (loosely classed as "microliths"), occur on the surface of many old campsites, and recent stratigraphic work near Warburton has shown that these tools predate the present culture of this region.

On one occasion I saw a Pintupi man at Partjar pick up an unusually thick lunate and haft it to his spearthrower. He called this *yiraputja,* and I learned that any obviously worked but unidentified stone item like this, as well as any substance foreign to the area such as pearl shell, is classed by this term. It includes any substance these people think was left behind by the totemic beings in their dreamtime travels. This category is distinctly different from *kanti,* a word used to define any unworked, chertlike material suitable for making stone tools.

Reutilization of already ancient materials may have been fairly common behavior among prehistoric peoples in many parts of the world. It can result in the discovery of early tools in much later levels in an ancient site and is another possibility the archeologist must consider if he is to interpret his finds correctly.

Once my wife went out to collect honey ants with some Ngatatjara women from the Laverton Reserve. While they were out, one of the women's dogs chased and killed a kangaroo. One woman picked up a natural flake of rough quartzite from the ground and used it to slit the animal's belly and cut the intestines. Then the stone was thrown away (and later collected by my wife). On another occasion, I was traveling near Mount Buttfield, about two hundred miles northeast of Warburton, in the company of two Ngatatjara men from that region. These men had caught several goannas early in the day. In camp late that afternoon they roasted these lizards and ate the fleshy parts. Then they placed the backbone, head, shoulders, and tail on top of a small rock, which they used as a kind of anvil. With handheld stones, they pounded the cartilaginous bone and scraps of meat together into a pulpy mass, which they then ate.

At times I have seen men pick up an untrimmed flake of chert and use it as a kind of spokeshave by gripping it between thumb and forefinger and scraping wood from the shaft or point of a spear. This usually happens when a man, for one reason or another, does not have a hafted adze with him. Generally the flake is tossed away when the task is finished.

In all of these cases, completely untrimmed rocks were used as tools. Also, with the possible exception of the spokeshave, they were not used long enough to cause any appreciable wear. Unless such items were found in clear association with other cultural materials, it might be impossible for an archeologist to recognize them as tools. In their simplicity these instant tools are on a par with the controversial eoliths debated by archeologists for many years, and they are a persistent feature of the stone technology of the desert aborigines.

At every turn, the desert aborigines present us with the unexpected. Archeologists do not ordinarily classify stone tools on the basis of the working edge (shape and size are usually thought to be more important), but the aborigines do. Archeologists do not ordinarily consider wooden wedges as possible butchering tools, but the aborigines do. Although there is nothing else in the world today quite like the aborigines' hafted stone adze, this kind of woodworking tool may have been more widespread in the ancient past. It has become an established archeological convention to speak of fire hardening of ancient wooden spear tips and digging sticks, yet the aborigines fire soften theirs! Evidence of transport of lithic materials is common in ancient sites throughout the world. Trade is often invoked to account for it, along with simple carrying of the stone from one place to another. But why do people do this? The aborigines unique reason is that they are motivated by sentiments of kinship toward particular totemic beings close to the source of the stone. The desert aborigines chip stone with their teeth. Perhaps this technique, too, was more widespread in ancient times, as suggested by Casteñada's account.

In short, the desert aborigines present archeologists with a set of new possibilities to use in interpreting the lithic remains of prehistoric hunting-and-gathering people. The opening up of these new possibilities is the chief value of continued ethnographic studies by archeologists. In four or five years the opportunity for studies of this kind will probably vanish as the aborigines adjust to life on reserves and in nearby towns.

4 Neolithic Revolution: Horticulture, Pastoralism, and Fishing Peoples

Somewhere around 8000 B.C., hunting and gathering populations began to tamper with the life cycles of wild plants and animals, and thus began the process of the domestication of plants and animals. The cumulative effect of this involvement with plants and animals is called the Neolithic Revolution. It represents the transition from hunting and gathering to a state of cultural evolution wherein humans produced their food instead of depending on gathering what nature provided. The consequences of the Neolithic Revolution are profound. Development of domesticated food supplies provided for enormous increases in population of our species, as well as much greater specialization and complexity in social organization. To study the processes of the Neolithic Revolution we can turn first to the Near East, for it is in that part of the world that we have the greatest amount of archaeological information. Frank Hole provides us with an interpretation of the emergence of civilization in Mesopotamia, starting with the earlier stages of the Neolithic Revolution, extending over a period of some five thousand years. Although the details of this period are still not fully known, it seems from the evidence at hand that the process involved considerable experimentation with different kinds of social and cultural organization in response to the environmental diversities of that part of the world.

Although there is evidence that the Neolithic Revolution occurred first in the Near East, and is best known from this area of the world, there is also considerable evidence that this transition took place independently in several other parts of the world. We can say with certainty that food production evolved independently in southeast Asia, and in the Americas (centered in Mexico and Peru). In each of these areas different cultigens and animals were utilized. However, the general consequences of food production on human population size and societal complexity appeared to be broadly similar in the several areas of the world. It also seems likely that food production was invented independently in West Africa and possibly in other areas as well.

When we refer to food production we generally think primarily of plow agriculture, but there are several other important types of food domestication. These include pastoralism—the utilization of animals as a way of converting vegetable material into high-grade animal protein, as well as the "slash-and-burn" horticultural system in which there is utilization of forested areas by means of burning, cropping, and then abandonment for periods of time.

The slash-and-burn technique as described by Russell was practiced widely both in prehistoric times, when it provided support for many people in prehistoric Europe, and continues in contemporary times as a very important means of cultivation for millions of peoples in tropical and subtropical regions. This technique is characterized by Russell as a very effective adaptation to forest areas, and may be much less damaging to the environment than the type of cropping of large continuous areas utilized by European agriculturalists in the mid-latitudes.

A mode of food production which is rapidly disappearing from the modern world is that of pastoralism. Pastoralists require large areas of open range for their animals, and in a world where nations are pushing farther and farther into their unexploited hinterlands, this mode of extensive ecological exploitation cannot persist. Thus it is only in a few areas of the world where the nomadic way of life can be found today. The Turkmen nomads described by Irons are such a group who still preserve something of the independence and individualism characteristic of pastoralists.

Fishing is technically similar to hunting and gathering, for it does not depend on domestication of the food sources. Some peoples did develop fishing equipment and techniques during the latter part of the Ice Ages, but specialized fishing economic systems were probably developed after the Ice Ages were over. Most fisher populations in recent times have been partially dependent on farming for some of their food. The coastal Lapps described by Robert Paine are an example of such a dual fishing-farming system.

Frank Hole

Investigating the Origins of Mesopotamian Civilization

In southwest Asia, between 8000 and 3000 B.C., human society developed from self-sufficient bands of nomadic hunters to economically and politically integrated city dwellers who specialized in a variety of occupations. A central archeological problem is to try to discover the factors that triggered these fundamental changes in man's way of life. For want of evidence and for want of a satisfactory model of the conditions existing during the period in question, searching for origins and attempting to discover the course of events that led to civilization is difficult. Prehistorians deal with nameless cultures, trusting to reconstructions from physical remains for their picture of life in ancient times. They must work directly with geographic, technological, and demographic factors and only indirectly infer ideologies and philosophical concepts. Archeologists are thus limited in what they can hope to learn by the nature of their data and the tools they have for interpreting them. Within these limits, however, it is possible to construct some plausible theories about the origins of civilization and to test them through controlled programs of excavation and analysis. In this article I define the problem under consideration in ecological terms, review the current evidence, and suggest topics for further study.

Mesopotamian (Sumerian) civilization began a few centuries before 3000 B.C. and was characterized by temples, urban centers, writing, trade, militarism, craft specialization, markets, and art. Inferred characteristics are a class-stratified society and well-defined mechanisms for regulation of production and distribution of resources. To be sure, Sumerian civilization must have had many other important but intangible characteristics, but most of these cannot be inferred from archeological data (1).

The early Mesopotamian civilizations were restricted to southern Mesopotamia, the alluvial plain that stretches south from Baghdad to the Persian Gulf. Remains of immediately antecedent cultures have been excavated in the same area, and still older cultures have been excavated in the surrounding Zagros mountain valleys of Iraq and Iran and on the steppes at the verge of plain and mountain in Khuzistan, southwest Iran (2).

Intensive agriculture is a precondition for civilization. The Sumerian societies for which we have some historical records were sustained by cultivation of irrigated barley and wheat, supplemented by crops of dates, and the production of sheep, goats, cattle, pigs, and fish. In 8000 B.C. people were just beginning to plant cereals, raise animals, and live in permanent villages; their societies were small, self-sufficient, egalitarian groups with little differentiation of occupation or status. These people had fewer of the artifacts and qualities of civilization than the Sumerian city dwellers had 5000 years later. In this article I use 8000 B.C. as a convenient base line and attempt to assess some 5000 years of culture history (see Table 1).

Theories of Development

Recognizing the obvious changes in society that occurred during the 5000 years, archeologists and others have proposed causal factors such as characteristics of geography to account for them. The most detailed examination of the relationship between geographic features and social forms has been made by Huntington (3), but other scholars working with data from Southwest Asia have had more influence on archeologists. For example, in attempting to explain the origins of agriculture, Childe proposed climatic change, specifically desiccation, as the initiating event and set off a chain of thought that is still favored by some authors (4). Childe argued that "incipient desiccation . . . would provide a stimulus towards the adoption of a food-producing economy. . . ." Animals and men would gather in oases that were becoming isolated in the midst of deserts. Such circumstances might promote the sort of symbiosis between man and beast implied in the word *domestication*. Although Childe's theory is attractive, there is no conclusive evidence that the climate in Southwest Asia changed enough during the period in

Table 1: Generalized Chart Showing the Chronology of Phases and Sites Mentioned in the Text (39).

DATE (B.C.)	SETTLEMENT SUBSISTENCE TYPE	CULTURAL PHASE	ETHNIC GROUP
2500		Early Dynastic III	Sumerians
		Early Dynastic II	Sumerians
		Early Dynastic I	Sumerians
2900	Walled cities	Jamdet Nasr	Sumerians
3500	Cities	Uruk	?
4000	Towns	Ubaid	?
5300	Temples	Eridu	?
5500	Irrigation	Sabz	
5800		Mohammad Jaffar	
6500	Food production	Ali Kosh	
8000	Food production and small, settled villages	Bus Mordeh	
Pre-8000	Nomadic hunters	Zarzian	

question to have affected the beginnings of agriculture and animal husbandry (5).

It was once fashionable to think of culture as inevitably rising or progressing, and this trend was thought to be analogous to biological evolution. Except in a most general way, however, modern prehistorians do not think of universal stages of cultural development (6). Rather than focusing on evolutionary stages, many scholars have examined the role of particular social and economic activities in triggering the emergence of complex forms of society. For instance, Marxists have explained the form of society (government, broadly speaking) on the basis of modes of production. Marxist evolutionists even today explain the development of social classes and political states in similar terms. They argue that, as people gained control over the production of food, the concept of private property crept in, and later the mass of people were exploited by the propertied few. "The creation of a state was necessary simply to prevent society from dissolving into anarchy due to the antagonisms that had arisen" (7). Information on the emergence of Sumerian civilization that might support this idea, however, is lacking.

Another attempt to correlate technological systems and social advances was made by Karl Wittfogel in *Oriental Despotism*. He contended that, where people had to depend on irrigation, they inevitably led themselves into an escalating dependence on an organizational hierarchy which coordinated and directed the irrigation activities. "The effective management of these works involves an organizational web which covers either the whole, or at least the dynamic core, of the country's population. In consequence, those who control this network are uniquely prepared to wield supreme political power" (8). Although Wittfogel's analysis seems valid in many instances, archeological investigation in both Mesopotamia and the Western Hemisphere leads to the conclusion that there was no large-scale irrigation at the time of the emergence of the first urban civilization (9).

An Ecological Approach

Single factors such as technology are unquestionably important, but they can be understood only within the cultural, social, and geographic context. A more comprehensive view that takes into account the interrelation of many factors is called human ecology. In a consideration of cultural development, the relevant concept in human ecology is adaptation, hence the approach is to try to discover how particular factors influence the overall adaptation of a society. By means of the general approach, human ecology attempts to understand what happened in the histories of particular cultures. It does not address itself to making general statements about cultural progress or evolution.

In an ecological approach, a human society is treated as one element in a complex system of geography, climate, and living organisms peculiar to an area. To ensure survival, various aspects of a human society must be complementary and the society itself must be successfully integrated with the remainder of the cultural and physical ecosystem of which it is a part (10). From the ecological view, such factors as technology, religion, or climate cannot be considered apart from the total system. Nevertheless, some parts of the system may be considered more fundamental in the sense that they strongly influence the form of the other parts (11). Anthropologists, through their study of modern societies, and archeologists, through inference, find that such factors as geographical features, the distribution of natural resources, climate, the kinds of crops and animals raised, and the relations with neighboring peoples strongly influence the forms that a society may take. These factors comprise the major elements of the ecosystem, and societies must adapt themselves to them.

Archeological Evidence

For the period 8000 to 3000 B.C., archeological data are scattered and skimpy. This naturally limits the generality of any interpretations that can be made and restricts the degree to which we can test various theories. Ideally we would wish to work with hundreds of instances representing the range of environmental and cultural variation; instead, for the whole of Southwest Asia we can count fewer than 100 excavated and reported sites for the entire range of time with which we are dealing. Of course the number of unexcavated or unreported sites about which we know something is far greater, but we cannot but be aware of how little we know and how much there is to find out.

In all of Southwest Asia only about 15 villages that date to 8000 B.C. have been excavated, and only two of these, Zawi Chemi and the Bus Mordeh levels at Ali Kosh, give good evidence of the use of domesticated plants or animals (12). In short, data for the time of our base line are woefully inadequate. We have much fuller information about the villages of 5000 B.C., but, unfortunately, for periods subsequent to 5000 B.C. the *kind* of data we have changes drastically. Thus, although there is historical continuity in the series of known sites, there is discontinuity in some of the data themselves because few archeologists have worked sites spanning the whole period from 8000 to 3000 B.C. Most of the sites dating to about 3000 B.C. were excavated by "historic" archeologists who struck levels that old only incidentally as they plumbed the depths of the cities they were digging. These scholars depended far less on artifacts than on history for their interpretations. The earliest sites were dug by prehistorians who based their inferences on results generated by an array of scientific experts. In order to understand the origins of civilizations, we thus need to bridge two quite different "archeological cultures." Archeologists and their various colleagues working in the early villages painstakingly teased out grains of charred seeds, measured metapodials and teeth of early races of sheep or cattle, and analyzed the chemical and mineral constituents of obsidian and copper; their counterparts working in the historic sites busied themselves with the floor plans of temples, the funerary pottery in the graves, the esthetics of an art style, and the translation of cuneiform impressions in clay (13).

Bearing in mind the reservations I have already expressed, we can begin to try to pick a coherent path through 5000 years of history. In dealing with Mesopotamia, it is usual to regard the presence of towns, temples, and cities as indicative of civilization. If we do so, we can divide our history into two parts, beginning with small food-producing villages and following with more complex societies that include towns and cities. In the ensuing discussion I assess the available evidence and, for both forms of community, outline the characteristics and indicate how the community developed.

Food-Producing Villages

Small food-producing villages have had a long history, but here we are chiefly interested in those that existed between 8000 and 5000 B.C. None of these communities is known thoroughly, and the following descriptions are based on data from several excavated sites and from surface surveys. The fullest data come from the phases represented in Ali Kosh and Tepe Sabz, in southwest Iran, and from Jarmo, Sarab, and Guran in the Zagros mountains. Additional data derive from extensive surveys in Khuzistan and the valleys of the Zagros (14, 15).

During this period villages are small and scattered, typically less than 1 hectare in size and housing perhaps 100 to 300 people. They are situated on the best agricultural land in regions where farming is possible without irrigation. From a handful of sites known to be about 10,000 years old, the number of settlements had increased by 5000 B.C., when many villages were within sight of one another and almost every village was within an easy day's walk of the next. There is no evidence of great migrations or any serious pressure of population during this time. By 4000 B.C. some villages occupy areas as large as 2 hectares (14, 16).

The increase in population appears to have been a direct consequence of improved agricultural techniques. In 8000 B.C., only primitive, low-yield races of emmer wheat and two-row barley were grown; sheep and goats were both in the early stages of domestication. By 5000 B.C. a modern complex of hybrid cereals and domesticated sheep, goats, cattle, and pigs were being exploited, and irrigation was practiced in marginal agricultural areas such as Deh Luran (17). The effects of developed agriculture are soon apparent, for, by 4000 B.C., settlement of new areas by prehistoric pioneers can be shown clearly in such places as the Diyala region to the east of Baghdad (18, 19). The age of the earliest settlements in southern Mesopotamia proper is unknown, but it would be surprising if groups of hunters and fishers had not lived along the rivers or swamps prior to the introduction of agriculture. The oldest settlement, Eridu, has been dated to about 5300 B.C., but there are no contemporary sites. In fact, there are few villages known in southern Mesopotamia that antedate 4000 B.C.

Towns and Cities

The millennium between 4000 and 3000 B.C. saw the rapid growth of towns and cities. Villages were also abundant, but some evidence suggests that they were less numerous than in earlier periods. "In part at least, the newly emerging pattern must have consisted of the drawing together of the population into larger, more defensible political units" (14). The trends I describe here pertain almost exclusively to southern Mesopotamia; in the north and in the valleys of the Zagros, the pattern remained one of small villages and—emerging later than their counterparts in the south—townships (20).

From southern Mesopotamia, archeological data for the period before 3000 B.C. are skimpy. Deep soundings at the bases of such sites as Eridu, Ur, Uqair, Tello, Uruk, and Susa and test excavations at Ubaid, Ras al-Amiya, and Hajji Mohammad are about all we have (2). Only at Ras al-Amiya is there direct evidence of agriculture, although at Eridu a layer of fish bones on the altar of temple VII suggests the importance of the sea and of fishing. Archeological evidence from several of the remaining sites consists either of temple architecture or pottery, the latter serving more to indicate the age of a site than the social or cultural patterns of its inhabitants. Some temple plans are known, but published data on domestic architecture are few, and the sizes of the communities can be inferred only roughly.

There are extensive enough excavations at sites like Uruk, Khafajah, Kish, Ur, and Nippur to indicate the scale of urbanism and many of its more spectacular architectural and artistic features for the period after 3000 B.C. The largest Early Dynastic site was evidently Uruk, where 445 hectares are enclosed by the city wall; contemporary Khafajah and Ur comprise 40 and 60 hectares, respectively. By contrast, the Ubaid portion of Uqair had about 7 hectares (2).

Historical Reconstructions

Pictographic writing began by about 3400 B.C., but it is difficult to interpret, and in any case early writing tells little about society; it is confined to bookkeeping (21). Nevertheless, by depending on myths, epics, and tales written some 1000 years later, scholars have attempted historical reconstructions of the emerging urban societies (22–24).

The oldest texts that characterize the Sumerian community are no earlier than 2500 B.C. and were written at a time when the "Temple-city" had already become the characteristic feature of the Mesopotamian landscape (25). In the view of many authors (26), the city was an estate belonging to gods of nature and maintained on their behalf by completely dependent and relatively impotent mortals. Controversy centers around the degree to which the temple controlled the economy. The extreme view is that it controlled everything while the more popular moderate view is that it controlled only part of the economy. In the Early Dynastic period, it seems clear, some, if not all, people were responsible to a temple which in turn directed most of the production and redistribution of goods and services. For practical purposes there was no distinction between the economic and the religious roles of the temples, but their administrators may not have had much political influence. Some temples listed large staffs of attendants, craftsmen, laborers, and food producers, but the precise relationship of these people to the temple is by no means clear. Moreover, such staffs would have been associated with the largest temples and not with the host of lesser temples and shrines that seem to have been present in the larger cities. Political control was vested variously in the *en* (lord), *lugal* (great man, or king), or *ensi* (governor-priest), depending on the historical period, the city referred to, and the translator of the text. In early times religious and secular titles seem not to have been held by the same person. Jacobsen describes, for pre-Early Dynastic times, a "primitive democracy" with the leader appointed by and responsible to an assembly of citizens (27). The arguments about the nature of Sumerian cities are summarized by Gadd (28): "The issues barely stated here have been discussed with much elaboration and ingenuity, but only a notable increase of contemporary evidence could raise the conclusions to a possibility of much affecting our conception of Sumerian government."

Environment and Subsistence

By combining the geographic, economic, and historical data, we can construct some plausible theories about the course of development and the situations that triggered it (29). The remarkable thing, from an ecological view, is the change in relations between men and products, and then between men and their fellows during the 5000 years. If we return for a moment to the pre-agricultural ways of life, we find small bands of hunters exploiting the seasonally available resources of a large territory by wandering from one place to another. Each community was self-sufficient, and each man had approximately the same access to the resources as his fellows. The earliest villagers seem to have maintained this pattern, although, as agriculture and stock breeding became more developed and important economically, the villagers tended more and more to stay put. People settled down where they could raise large amounts of grain, store it for the future, and exchange it for products they did not produce. In return for dependability of food supply, people gave up some of their dietary variety and most of their mobility. From a pattern of exploiting a broad spectrum of the environment, there developed a pattern of exploiting a relatively narrow spectrum (30).

As long as people stayed where they could find sufficiently varied resources through hunting and gathering, they could be self-sufficient. When people settled in villages away from the mountains, out of the zone of rainfall agriculture, they were no longer independent in the sense that they personally had access to the varied resources they desired or needed. Psychologically and sociologically this marked a turning point in man's relations with his environment and his fellows. Southern Mesopotamia is a land with few resources, yet in many ways this was an advantage for the development of society. In a land without timber, stone, or meals, trade was necessary, but the role of trade in the emergence of civilization should not be overemphasized. Date palms and bundles of reeds served adequately instead of timber for most construction, and baked clay tools took the place of their stone or metal counterparts in other areas. On the other hand, travel by boat is ancient, and extensive land and sea trade is attested in early documents. It was easy to move goods in Mesopotamia (31).

In order to live as well as the farmers in Deh Luran did, the Sumerians had to cooperate through trade, barter, or other means with their fellow settlers. We should remember that the barren vista of modern Mesopotamia on a dusty day does not reveal the full range of geographic variation or agricultural potential of the area. Swamps and rivers provided fish and fowl and, together with canals, water for irrigation and navigation. With sufficient water, dates and other fruits and vegetables could be grown. The unequal distribution of subsistence resources encouraged the beginnings of occupational specialization among the various kinds of food producers, and this trend was further emphasized after craftsmen started to follow their trades on a full-time basis (32).

Economics and Management

Because of the geographic distribution of resources and the sedentary and occupationally specialized population, a social organization that could control production and redistribution was needed. Clearly, any reconstruction of the mechanics of redistribution in emerging Mesopotamian civilization is subject to the severe limitations of the evidence. If we recognize this, however, we may then seek in contemporary societies analogs that may help us imagine appropriate redistributional structures. In modern economies, money markets act as the agency of redistribution, but in virtually all "primitive" societies where surpluses or tradeable goods are produced, a center of redistribution of another kind grows. The "center" can be a person (for example, the chief); an institution, like a temple and the religious context it symbolizes; or a place, like a city with some form of free markets (33). Jacobsen suggests that in Sumeria temples served as warehouses, where food was stored until times of famine.

Sahlin's (34) studies in modern Polynesia are also relevant to this point. He found that there is a close relation between surplus production and the degree of social stratification in Polynesia—that in a redistributional economy, the greater the surplus is, the greater is the degree of stratification. Of course we can only speculate about Mesopotamia, but, granting this and following Sahlins's findings, we may say that the chief of the Mesopotamian town would have acted as the center of redistribution. In Mesopotamia, most of the surplus labor or food went directly or indirectly into building and maintaining temples. One would also have expected the chief to use a good bit of the surplus to support himself and his family, to pay the wages of craftsmen, and to buy the raw materials that were turned into artifacts, such as jewelry and clothing, that served to distinguish his rank. Others in the lord's biological or official family would also have profited from his control of the resources and ultimately have become recognized as a social class entitled to special prerogatives. This social stratification would have been associated with a similarly burgeoning system of occupational differentiation.

In an emerging system where both technology and governmental forms are relatively simple but susceptible of improvement, there is a maximum opportunity for feedback. That is, if a certain level of production will support a certain degree of social stratification, efficient management by the social elite may result in more productivity (34, p. 110). It is interesting to speculate on how much the construction of enormous irrigation systems during later Mesopotamian history may have depended on the rising aspirations of the ruling elite.

Although the need for management of production might in itself have been sufficient cause for a developing social stratification, other factors were probably contributory. Turning now to law and politics, I should point out that, with the establishment of irrigation and the concentration of population in urban centers, man's basic attitudes toward the land must have changed. The construction of irrigation systems, even if primitive, makes the land more valuable to the builders, and this, if it did nothing else, would lead to some notions of property rights and inheritance that had not been necessary when abundant land was available for the taking. An irrigation system also implies that some men may have more direct control over the supply of water than others. This could have led to an increase in the power of individuals who controlled the supply of water, and it certainly must have led to disputes over the allocation of water. It seems inevitable that a working system of adjudicating claims over land would then have been necessary, and the task may have fallen to the chiefs (lords) (35).

The presence of "neighbors" also has ecological implications; it is worth recalling that property invites thievery. Adams argues that the "growth of the Mesopotamian city was closely related to the rising tempo of warfare," and Service points out that the integration of societies under war leaders is common, and clearly an adaptation to social-environmental conditions. Several Early Dynastic II cities had defensive walls, attesting to conflict between cities and perhaps between settled farmers and nomadic herders, but the historical evidence for warfare begins only about 2500 B.C. (36).

If we consider both the agricultural system and the wealth, we see conditions that enhanced opportunities for leadership and, ultimately, for direction and control. With these situations, the emerging systems of rank and status are understandable without our resorting to notions of "genius," "challenge and response," or immigration by more advanced peoples.

Religion

The role of religion in integrating emerging Mesopotamian society is frequently mentioned. By 3000 B.C. texts and temples themselves attest to the central place of religion in Sumerian life; theoretically, at least, cities were simply estates of the gods, worked on their behalf by mortals (26). How closely theory corresponds to fact is a question that cannot be answered. Although we cannot date their beginnings precisely, we know that temple centers were well established by 5000 B.C., and that towns and temples frequently go together. Whether towns developed where people congregated because of religious activities or whether temples grew in the market centers where the people were cannot be decided without more data. Both interpretations may be correct. Historic evidence suggests that economic activities were controlled by the temples, but this evidence says nothing about the original relationships between the two. Furthermore, the interpretation of the historical documents is open to question. As Gadd (28, p. 39) points out, the picture of Sumerian economy that the various authors use is based on the "detailed records of one temple (Lagash) over a rather short period."

In regard to this limited view of the role of religion, it is well to recall that major settlements had several temples. At Khafajah, for example, perhaps as early as 4000 B.C. there were three temples, and a fourth was added later. Our image of the Sumerian temple is nevertheless likely to be that of the large temple oval at Khafajah or Ubaid rather than that of the smaller temples that were contemporary and perhaps just as characteristic. The temple oval appears to have housed a society within a city, but many temples had no auxiliary buildings. More impressive even than the temple ovals were the great ziggurats erected on artificial mounds—at Uruk 13 meters high and visible for many kilometers. Again this was only one of several temples at the same site. In Ubaid, Eridu, and Uqair, for example, where temples were originally associated with residential settlements, the towns were later abandoned and only the temples with cemeteries were maintained (37).

Summary

It seems unlikely that Mesopotamian society took a single path as it approached the rigidly organized, hierarchal civilization of Early Dynastic times. Rather, we imagine that there was considerable experimentation and variety in the organization of society as people adapted to their physical environment and to the presence of other expanding communities.

Some towns and cities probably arose as the demographic solution to the problem of procuring and distributing resources. It would have made sense to have central "clearing houses." Similarly, it would have made sense to have the craftsmen who turned the raw materials into finished products live close to their supply (probably the temple stores). Temple centers are natural focal points of settlements. Cities and towns, however, are not the only demographic solutions to the problem of farming and maintaining irrigation canals. Both of these tasks could have been carried out by people living in more dispersed settlements. City life in Mesopotamia probably also presented other benefits. For example, as warfare came to be a recurrent threat, the psychological and physical security of a city must have been a comfort for many. Finally, to judge from some historical evidence, Mesopotamian cities were places of diversity and opportunity, no doubt desiderata for many people as long as they could also gain a suitable livelihood (38).

In considering the development of civilization, an ecological approach forces us to consider multiple factors. Seeking isolated causes among the many factors possibly involved ignores the central concept of adaptation, with its ramifications of interaction and feedback. Still, we are a long way from fully understanding the emergence of Mesopotamian civilization. In particular, we need a great deal more archeological data that relate to the 2000 years preceding 3000 B.C. in southern Mesopotamia. Specifically, there are three projects which ought to have high priority in the planning of future archeological work in this area. First, we need thorough surveys in order to determine the early history of settlement in Mesopotamia. By means of these surveys in and around the early cities, we would try to determine the duration of occupation, and the variety and location of additional sites. Second, we need extensive excavation of selected smaller sites and portions of larger ones in order to determine the characteristics of different settlements. We would like to know in what way the cities, towns, temple centers, and villages were integrated to form a socioeconomic network. A third question, which gets at the crux of the matter, is, What structural form did the emerging Sumerian society take? Answers to this question must depend in large part on the results of future surveys and excavations of the kind suggested above. Then, selective excavations focusing on successive periods should yield data on the relative roles of economic and religious activities and on social differentiation and stratification. These data, after they are eventually pieced together, will comprise the story of the emergence of the world's first civilization.

References and Notes

1. Archeological criteria: V. G. Childe, *Town Planning Rev.* **21,** 3 (1950). Sociocultural criteria: R. M. Adams, in *City Invincible,* C. H. Kraeling and R. M. Adams, Eds. (Univ. of Chicago Press, Chicago, 1960), pp. 30–31; E. R. Wolf, *Peasants* (Prentice-Hall, Englewood Cliffs, N.J., 1966) ["It is the crystallization of executive power which serves to distinguish the primitive from the civilized . . . when the cultivator becomes subject to the demands and sanctions of power-holders outside his social stratum" (p. 11)]. The "form" of civilization: H. Frankfort, *The Birth of Civilization in the Near East* (Doubleday, Garden City, N.Y., 1956), chap. 2.
2. Relevant sites are Ubaid, Eridu, Ras al-Amiya, Ali Kosh, Guran, Sarab, and Jarmo. For a bibliography of publications on Mesopotamia and Iran, see articles by E. Porada and R. H. Dyson in *Chronologies in Old World Archaeology,* R. W. Erich, Ed. (Univ. of Chicago Press, Chicago, 1965), pp. 133–200, 215–256.
3. E. Huntington, *Mainsprings of Civilization* (Wiley, New York, 1945).
4. V. G. Childe, *New Light on the Most Ancient East* (Praeger, New York, 1952), p. 25; J. Mellaart, *Earliest Civilizations of the Near East* (Thames and Hudson, London, 1965), pp. 19–20.
5. Studies based on archeology, paleontology, geography, palynology, and geology fail to disclose post-Pleistocene climatic changes that would have been of major cultural significance. See R. J. Braidwood and C. A. Reed, *Cold Spring Harbor Symp. Quant. Biol.* **22,** 19 (1957); K. W. Butzer, in *Cambridge Ancient History* (Cambridge Univ. Press, Cambridge, 1965), vol. 1, chap. 2; K. V. Flannery, *Science* **147,** 1247 (1965); H. E. Wright, Jr., *Eiszeitalter Gegenwart* **12,** 160 (1960); W. van Zeist and H. E. Wright, Jr., *Science* **140,** 65 (1963). Moreover, as I discuss more fully later, the development of urban civilizations doubtless depended more on sociocultural factors such as trade, surplus production, and economic interdependence than on geography *per se* [see R. M. Adams, in *City Invincible,* C. H. Kraeling and R. M. Adams, Eds. (Univ. of Chicago Press, Chicago, 1960), p. 291].
6. For a general discussion of these ideas, see R. J. Braidwood in *Evolution and Anthropology: a Centennial Appraisal* (Anthropological Society of Washington, Washington, D.C., 1959), pp. 76–89; S. Piggott, in *Evolution After Darwin,* S. Tax, Ed. (Univ. of Chicago Press, Chicago, 1960), vol. 2, pp. 85–97.
7. M. W. Thompson, *Antiquity* **39,** 108 (1965).
8. K. A. Wittfogel, *Oriental Despotism* (Yale Univ. Press, New Haven, Conn., 1957), p. 27.
9. R. M. Adams, in *City Invincible,* C. H. Kraeling and R. M. Adams, Eds. (Univ. of Chicago Press, Chicago, 1960).
10. It is misleading to think that at any moment all parts of a system are necessarily functioning harmoniously, let alone perfectly. One finds situations that can only be understood as a result of historical accident. For example, immigrants may carry with them customs and practices that are inappropriate to new circumstances.
11. For examples of the effect of environmental conditions on socio-political integration, see J. H. Steward, *Bull. Bur. Amer. Ethnol.* **120,** (1938); M. D. Coe, *Comp. Studies Soc. Hist.* **4,** 65 (1961).
12. R. L. Solecki, *Intern. Congr. Quaternary, 6th* (1964), vol. 4, pp. 405–412; F. Hole, K. V. Flannery, J. A. Neely, *Current Anthropol.* **6,** 105 (1965). Since this article is restricted to Mesopotamia, I have ignored such spectacular and

large early sites as Catal Hüyük in Anatolia and Jericho in Jordan. These developments were essentially independent of Mesopotamia and must be explained in their own contexts.

13. Kramer expressed the view of many Sumerologists when he spoke of "Mesopotamian archeology in all its aspects: architecture, art, history, religion, and epigraphy" [S. N. Kramer, *The Sumerians* (Univ. of Chicago Press, Chicago, 1964), p. 28]. Historical archeologists often base their interpretations of culture on less tangible factors than those discussed in this article—on catastrophe, invasion and destruction, migration, religious inspiration, inventive genius, moral decadence, and the like.

14. R. M. Adams, *Science* 136, 109 (1962).

15. R. J. Braidwood, *Illustrated London News* 237, 695 (1960); F. Hole, *Science* 137, 524 (1962).

16. For an example of the spacing of settlements and their relation to subsistence patterns, see F. Barth, "The land use pattern of migratory tribes of South Persia," *Norsk Geograf. Tidsskr.* 17 (1959).

17. K. V. Flannery, *Science* 147, 1247 (1965).

18. R. M. Adams, *Land Behind Baghdad* (Univ. of Chicago Press, Chicago, 1965).

19. As agricultural techniques improved and the social organization for exploiting them developed, the population increased and settlement expanded slowly into the less favorable areas, a process that continues even today with the introduction of moldboard plows, tractors, and motor-driven water pumps.

20. A. J. Jawad, *The Advent of the Era of Townships in Northern Mesopotamia* (Brill, Leiden, 1965).

21. A. Falkenstein, *Archaische Texte aus Uruk* (Harrassowitz, Berlin, 1936).

22. A. Deimel, *Sumerische Templewirtschaft zur Zeit Urukaginas und seiner Vorgänger* (Päpstliches Bibelinstitut, Rome, 1931).

23. A. Falkenstein, *Cahiers Hist. Mondiale* 1, 784 (1954).

24. H. Frankfort, *The Birth of Civilization in the Near East* (Doubleday, Garden City, N.Y., 1956), chap. 3; S. N. Kramer, *The Sumerians* (Univ. of Chicago Press, Chicago, 1964); T. Jacobsen, *Z. Assyriol.* 52, 91 (1957). For a criticism of the Templewirtschaft, see N. M. Diakonoff, *Sumer: Society and State in Ancient Mesopotamia* (Academy of Sciences, Moscow, 1959) (in Russian, with English summary). A summary of the views of Russian scholars is given in F. I. Andersen, *Abr-Nahrain* 1, 56 (1959–60).

25. For a general review of Sumerian history, see C. J. Gadd, in *Cambridge Ancient History* (Cambridge Univ. Press, Cambridge, 1962), vol. 1, chap. 13. General accounts of Sumerian life are given in S. N. Kramer, *The Sumerians* (Univ. of Chicago Press, Chicago, 1964) and ——, *History Begins at Sumer* (Thames and Hudson, London, rev. ed., 1961). The cuneiform texts take Sumerian history back to the ruler Mesilim, about 2500 B.C. A summary of the kind of texts available is given in T. Jacobsen, *Z. Assyriol.* 52, 91 (1957).

26. See especially A. Deimel (22) and A. Falkenstein (23).

27. T. Jacobsen, *J. Near Eastern Studies* 2, 159 (1943); *Z. Assyriol.* 52, 91 (1957).

28. C. J. Gadd, in *Cambridge Ancient History* (Cambridge Univ. Press, Cambridge, 1962).

29. Many of the ideas in this section are derived from the work of R. M. Adams; see 9, 14, 18.

30. For an analogous situation, see M. D. Coe and K. V. Flannery, *Science* 143, 650 (1964).

31. The desirability of trade is an effective stimulus to demographic consolidation

and political integration; see M. D. Coe, *Comp. Studies Soc. Hist.* **4**, 65 (1961). A clay model at Eridu gives the earliest evidence for boats; see S. Lloyd, *Illustrated London News* **213**, 303 (1948). For a summary of early trade, see C. J. Gadd (28, p. 41).

32. R. M. Adams (9, p. 276) discusses the Sumerian subsistence base. Sumerian texts make poignant reference to famine and the insecurity of life in Mesopotamia [see T. Jacobsen, *Proc. Amer. Phil. Soc.* **107**, 476 (1963)].

33. K. Polanyi, in *Trade and Market in the Early Empires*, K. Polanyi, C. M. Arensberg, H. W. Pearson, Eds. (Free Press, Glencoe, Ill., 1957), pp. 250–256; for a discussion of chiefdoms, see E. R. Service, *Primitive Social Organization* (Random House, New York, 1962), pp. 144–152. The practical consequence of redistribution in the Mesopotamian case was the development of a tributory peasant society as a distinct social stratum [see E. R. Wolf, *Peasants* (Prentice-Hall, Englewood Cliffs, N.J., 1966), pp. 10–11; T. Jacobsen, *Proc. Amer. Phil. Soc.* **107**, 476 (1963)].

34. M. D. Sahlins, *Social Stratification in Polynesia* (Univ. of Washington Press, Seattle, 1958).

35. On the role of lords, see C. J. Gadd (28, p. 13); T. Jacobsen, *Z. Assyriol.* **52**, 91 (1957). On the development of political authority, see R. M. Adams (9, p. 278); K. A. Wittfogel (8); M. Fried, in *Culture in History*, S. Diamond, Ed. (Columbia Univ. Press, New York, 1960), pp. 713–731.

36. Part of Jacobsen's reconstruction of kingship emerging from a base of primitive democracy is based on the need for a rapidly mobilized defense and the holding of power by war leaders; see T. Jacobsen, *Z. Assyriol.* **52**, 91 (1957); R. M. Adams, *Sci. Amer.* **203**, 153 (1960); E. R. Service, *Primitive Social Organization* (Random House, New York, 1962), p. 114.

37. Abandonment of any city with irrigated fields would be unlikely unless the water failed or the fields became too salty for use. Both of these circumstances have been important in Mesopotamia since settlement began, and we may not be able to infer much about the role of religion in society from the lack of settlements around temples that were probably maintained for a time out of a sense of tradition by people living elsewhere.

38. S. N. Kramer, *The Sumerians* (Univ. of Chicago Press, Chicago, 1964), p. 89.

39. Table 1 is based in part on E. Porada, in *Chronologies in Old World Archaeology*, R. W. Erich, Ed. (Univ. of Chicago Press, Chicago, 1965). Since there is archeological continuity from Eridu times into the Sumerian period, there is probably biological continuity in the population, too. Strictly speaking, however, *Sumerian* is a term that refers to the language and not to the people.

40. The research in Iran was supported by NSF grants GS-67 and 724 and by the University of Chicago and Rice University. The Archeological Service, Musée Bastan, Tehran, granted permission to excavate and provide assistance in the field. I thank Edward Norbeck and Barbara Stark for advice in preparing the manuscript and Steve Wood for the drawings.

W. M. S. Russell

The Slash-and-Burn Technique

From the layers of plant pollen found buried in Danish and Irish bogs we know the kinds of vegetation that grew there during successive periods of time. An examination of the deposits also tells the story of a simple farming method that reached Europe about 5000 B.C., and that still persists in various parts of the world.

Before the Europeans could begin raising crops, something had to be done about the great forests. They did it by slashing and burning the trees. Evidence of the burning shows in the pollen record as a layer of oak charcoal. On the cleared plot the ancient agriculturists then grew wheat and barley for anywhere from ten to twenty-five years, until the declining yield showed that the soil was exhausted. Whereupon they moved on to open up a new area in similar fashion, leaving the old clearing to become overgrown by brush, and then trees. Years later, others might again clear the same plot by the slash-and-burn method, thus beginning a new cycle.

This kind of shifting cultivation was a natural one for simple farmers in their first encounter with tree-covered land. A similarly mobile type of agriculture appeared nearly 7,000 years later when the first European corn-growing pioneers plunged into the temperate-zone forests of North America. Eventually, of course, the growth of settlements and increase of population made it necessary to clear the forest permanently for the continuous use of the same patches of land. In Europe the requirements of this settled type of agriculture were gradually met by an increasingly elaborate balance of mixed farming, with crop rotations and animal manure serving to keep the soil fertile. In North America's forest belt, such permanent settlement developed much faster, and not without disastrous impoverishment of some of the land. At any rate, on both continents today a choice is made: The old temperate-zone woodlands are either conserved, for their timber-growing potential or for recreation, or else they are permanently cleared, for a settled agriculture equipped with all the resources of modern technology.

Only in the cold far north of Europe did temporary clearing linger on to any marked extent. One reason was that the oak forests there gave way to damp spruce and pine woods growing on poor, sandy soils. The trees were cut, the litter was burned to make a thick layer of mineral-rich ash, the ground was hoed (in later periods, plowed) between the tree stumps, and oats or rye (which tolerate the cold) were grown for a while; then the farmers moved elsewhere, leaving the deserted plot to birch and alder, and at last to the returning pines. This was the same method that had been used in the oak forests. It lasted into the late nineteenth century in northern Russia, until 1918 in northern Sweden, and persists today in parts of Finland.

For the Finns, the farm in the clearing must long have been a familiar sight; in their ancient national epic, *Kalevala*, the voice of the old hero Väinämöinen is said to stumble like the hoe among the pine roots. But certainly by A.D. 1781, and probably much earlier, some Finns had transformed the old, casually shifting cultivation into a regular rotation of forest farming. In the first year, they felled the trees. In the second, they burned them. For the next four to six years they grew crops among the stumps. For twenty to thirty years after that they allowed the clearing to revert to forest, then they returned to the same plot and same cycle. Such systematic rotation appeared in Sweden, too, probably brought by Finnish immigrants.

But this way of farming eventually declined, along with the older, casual procedure, as the demand for northern timber increased among peoples farther south and as modern methods made settled agriculture more productive even in the north.

Although forest farming is dying in temperate lands, it remains much alive in the rain forests and savanna woodlands that exist on either side of the Equator, covering vast areas in Central and South America, Africa, Asia, and the islands of the Pacific. Such farming is not a curiosity for anthropologists, a quaint survival among a few backward tribes; it is the way of life for a substantial fraction of the human race. Figures for 1957 estimate that farming on temporary clearings was practiced by over 200 million people (nearly 1 in 12 of the world population), on 14 million square miles (about 30 per cent of the world's cultivable land).

A few isolated tribes with rather simple cultures, for instance in the Amazon Basin and on the uplands of Burma and Thailand, practice the haphazard shifting cultivation of the pioneers. But most forest farmers long ago adopted systematic land use. The area under crops shifts its position, but any given plot is regularly rotated between cropping and fallow. In the fallow period the forest returns, hence this system is sometimes called forest fallow rotation.

Systematic slash-and-burn agriculture has evolved independently in all tropic regions. The farming system and the cleared plot are usually known by the same name, but this varies with locality, so the same practice is called by many names. From Central and South America we have milpa, coamile, ichali, conuco, roça; from Africa, masole, chitemene, tavy; and from the Far East, chena, djum, bewar, dippa, erka, jara, kumari, podu, prenda, dahi, parka, taungya, tamrai, rây, hwajon, djuma, humah, tagal, ladang, kaingin. English-speaking scientists have coined several additional terms, including slash-and-burn, fire agriculture, and forest fallow rotation; they now generally call the typical plots in all these places swiddens (from an old English country word for burned clearings), and the system is swidden farming.

The basic practice is similar all over the tropics. A swidden site is carefully selected. Trees are either felled, usually leaving the stumps, or completely stripped of their branches; creepers and underbrush are slashed away; and the resulting litter, or slash, is spread over the swidden. This is done in the dry season, so the debris soon dries out. It is then set on fire (sometimes with precautions to prevent the fire spreading). This leaves the swidden covered with a layer of ash, ready for planting crops in time to take advantage of the coming rains.

In Europe, and even more so in North America, a farm field conveys the idea of rows and rows of crop plants all of the same kind. By contrast, a swidden is generally like a North American vegetable garden run wild, covered with all sorts of crop plants that will be harvested at different times. In a typical Central American swidden, for instance, squash vines spread over the ground surface, cornstalks rise into the air, beans climb up the cornstalks. The most sophisticated swidden farmers known are the Hanunóo on Mindoro Island in the Philippines, who are impressive botanists. About 1,200 plant species are known in their region, but the Hanunóo themselves distinguish 1,600 different kinds—evidently their classification goes down to plant varieties. Of this number, they actually breed more than 400 kinds in their swiddens. Various other species reproduce themselves. To protect these when the swidden is burned, the farmers wrap them in green plant material.

Generally, among such peoples the swidden is cultivated intensively for a year or so, then gradually less intensively, and finally abandoned. For instance, in Ondo Province, Nigeria, one practice is to clear the swidden in February and burn soon after. Yams and corn are planted with the first rains, together with pumpkins, melons, and calabashes. When the farmers harvest the first corn, in June, they plant beans, manioc, okra, and cocoyams. In September–October they harvest the yams; in October–November they harvest a second crop of corn, which was planted in August. A third corn crop may be planted in the next rainy season, and the farmers may return for a year or two thereafter to dig the manioc and cocoyams, but they generally do not immediately plant this plot again. Fruit trees are often included among swidden crops, and their fruit may be harvested for several years after the swidden is abandoned. Meanwhile, through regeneration from stumps (which are left three feet high in Nigeria for this purpose) and by growth of seeds from the surrounding bush, the swidden gradually reverts to forest. It will not be cleared again for some time. In the interval, other swidden sites are cleared and go through the same cycle.

The periods under intensive cropping and under fallow vary in different places, but when the system is working effectively the cropping period is always relatively short, and the fallow period relatively long, as seen in the chart below.

REGION	YEARS UNDER INTENSIVE CROPPING	YEARS UNDER FALLOW
Philippines (Hanunóo)	2–4	8–10
New Guinea	1	15–20
Ceylon	1–3	8–20
Sierra Leone	2	12–15
Ghana	1–3	10–15
Nigeria (rain forest)	1–2	8–14
Nigeria (savanna woodland)	4	Up to 30

The method of selecting new swidden sites has been studied in detail among the Hanunóo. These people choose sites where the composition of the fallow vegetation has reached the stage ready for slash-and-burn. This may be from eight to ten years after the previous cropping period. The expert Hanunóo do not work with map and calendar. They are guided by botanical criteria that are flexible and highly relevant for their purpose. This method allows for local differences (between soils for instance) and ensures that the fallow period has lasted long enough.

In some parts of the tropics, specially modified forms of swidden farming are practiced, such as the system characteristic of Zambia but found in many other woodland areas of East Africa. In this chitemene system, the farmers slash and burn not only the trees and underbrush of the swidden; they add branches brought in from the surrounding woods. In Sudan, several tribes omit burning the swidden, and instead take advantage of the fact that termites quickly reduce the woody litter to powder. Also in this region are the Dinka, who practice a kind of termite-chitemene system—they collect wood from some distance and pile it in the swidden for the termites.

Not all swidden farmers are people with extremely simple cultures. The Hanunóo, for instance, can write, so they post notices warning neighbors to avoid walking into a clearing that has been slashed but not yet burned. However, the actual farming method is basic to the way of life of all these peoples. It is also encumbered with considerable ritual. To early European observers, the whole procedure seemed senseless, primitive, and a gross waste of land.

Yet there is often method, even in the rituals. The Hanunóo drive a hollow bamboo stick into the ground at a possible swidden site. If the soil does not rise high enough inside the stick, they discard the site and clear elsewhere. Although they regard this as a purely magical test, it can be a crude agronomic way of appraising the soil's structural readiness for tillage. And on many points, these and other swidden farmers can often give excellent scientific reasons for their practices.

Many Europeans must have had the experience that Bishop Mackenzie described to fellow missionary and explorer Dr. David Livingstone in the mid-nineteenth century. "When telling the people in England what were my objects in going out to Africa," said the Bishop, "I stated that, among other things, I meant to teach these people agriculture; but I now see that they know far more about it than I do."

Furthermore, the swidden system is extraordinarily suitable for the tropical environment. Considerable experimental work in Africa, for example, indicates how the system conserves soil fertility. To begin with, the heavy rains keep many tropical forest and woodland soils poor in nitrogen, phosphorus, and other mineral elements that plants need. Nitrogen is normally present in soils either in an insoluble form unusable to plants, in organic matter, or in soluble forms (chiefly nitrates) that plants can take up. Every year, in the tropical rainy season, much of the nitrogen in organic matter is converted by soil bacteria into nitrate. Some of this is used by the plants, but much, being soluble in the rain water, is washed out of the topsoil. This means the stock of available nitrogen is steadily diminished. Phosphorus and other mineral nutrients are also leached down beyond reach of the plant roots.

This leaching problem often also affects the damp, sandy pinewoods of northern Europe, and the benefits of forest fallow have been experimentally demonstrated in Finland as well as in Africa. When leached soils are continuously cropped without manuring, the available nutrient elements are soon used up; crop yields fall and eventually fail. This had begun to happen by 1933, for instance, in parts of Zambia where continuous cash crops of corn had replaced the chitemene system.

Forest fallow restores fertility in at least two ways. First, it constantly returns plant material to the soil as litter (leaves, dead branches, and so forth); then soil bacteria, stimulated by the tropical warmth, quickly convert the litter to organic matter, where the nitrogen content is safe from leaching. Thus the reserves of soil nitrogen gradually increase. Secondly, deep tree roots bring back phosphorus and other mineral nutrients that were leached down to lower depths, and concentrate them at the soil surface or in plant growth— "living fallow." If the fallow is allowed to remain long enough, the topsoil is much enriched in organic matter and mineral nutrients by the next time the plot is cleared.

Early European visitors supposed that burning the slash must be harmful. But agronomists have shown the reverse to be true. The phosphorus and other minerals stored in growing trees are all deposited in the ash, which makes an excellent fertilizer (especially when the forest outside the swidden is also exploited, as in the chitemene system). Although nitrogen in the growing trees is lost to the atmosphere when they are burned, very little of the new store of organic matter in the soil is destroyed by the fire. Experiments in Malawi, Sierra Leone, and Zambia have shown that the burning is in itself beneficial, for burning slash on the swidden gives a higher crop yield than burning it elsewhere and bringing the ash to the swidden. Experiments in Brazil suggest that burning affects soil bacteria (by killing some and stimulating others) in just the right way to improve the soil nitrogen cycle. It is because of this that the crops on a swidden grow and yield well for a few years—until the rebuilt stores of nutrients are exhausted.

Swidden farming can offer other benefits in the tropics. A frequent problem, for example, is actual destruction of the soil by erosion resulting from heavy tropical rains. Where soil is unprotected by fallow, the raindrops may break up part of the surface, and batter the rest to form a waterproof cap. Then the rain water, instead of soaking into the soil, runs down slopes. This runoff may finally tear away the soil in sheets or gouge it into deep gullies.

On steep slopes, one elaborate answer to this problem is building terraces to check the force of the runoff and allow time for water and silt to accumulate on the terrace steps where the crops are grown. Terrace building is laborious, however, and not usually done on a plot used for only a few years at a time.

The swidden system is easier and has many built-in safeguards against soil erosion. When choosing a site for clearing, the Hanunóo carefully avoid uneven ground and unstable soils vulnerable to erosion; for this they use their elaborate classification of soils, which agrees well with results of scientific soil analysis. Then, during the critical period when the newly cleared swidden is exposed to the danger of wind erosion, the drying slash is spread over every square foot of soil as a dead cover, or mulch. (Hanunóo teen-agers who find this chore a nuisance are lectured by their elders about soil erosion.) Creeping, erect, and climbing plants protect the soil during cropping. Afterward the new covering of forest fallow takes over: the foliage and litter break the rain's force, so that it sinks gradually into the soil.

But there is another tropical hazard—the rank growth of weeds, including grasses. Within a year or two after it is cleared, the swidden may become choked by these light-loving plants. Indeed, this often is why the swidden is abandoned so soon. If the forest fallow is able to regenerate, the shade of the trees will eventually suppress the weeds. A way to aid this process is to leave tree stumps and protect some trees during the fire, so they can provide shade for the tree seeds coming from outside the clearing. The stumps serve another purpose: new growth often sprouts directly from them.

By this method the swidden farmers give the forest a chance to return and compete successfully with the weeds. But if cropping goes on too long, the soil may become too poor for trees to get started, and grass weeds may get too much of a grip. The balance now tips in favor of grass against trees, and the plot becomes grassland.

In parts of Africa, swidden farming has become adapted for grassland fallow. But in tropical rotations the grasses are less satisfactory than trees. Their roots are too shallow to reach mineral nutrients leached into the lower soil. Furthermore, the grass supplies little litter for making organic matter.

Grass fallow rotation generally supports only low-yielding, small-grained cereals like the millets, and only on the least-leached soils. Finally, tough, tall grasses like *Imperata cylindrica*, called cogon in the Far East, are liable to take over, turning the plot into a cogonal—an intractable sod that cannot be farmed (at least by ancient methods).

Proper swidden techniques, on the other hand, are admirably adapted to the tropical environment. But they accomplish their purpose only when the ratio of fallow period to cropping period remains high. This requires a great deal of land for each family. For example, if the cropping period is two years and the fallow period is eighteen years, then only 10 per cent of the land is under crops at one time. Hence the system will only support a very low population density—generally about 130 people per square mile, according to an estimate made in Java and widely accepted for the tropics as a whole. The system worked, therefore, during the thousands of years when tropical populations were kept low by parasites and infectious diseases.

But in the twentieth century, modern medicine caused a dramatic increase in populations all over the tropics. Inevitably, a greater proportion of the land was used to meet the need for more food. Also inevitably, the cropping period grew longer and the fallow period shorter. By 1964, for instance, the forest fallow period in parts of Sierra Leone had shortened drastically. It had lasted from twelve to fifteen years; it became three or four years. By 1955, it had shortened in Iboland (Nigeria, rain forest zone) from between eight and fourteen years to three or four years. On parts of the Jos Plateau (Nigeria, savanna woodland zone), a sequence of four years under crops and up to thirty years of woodland fallow became four to six years under crops and one to two years under grass fallow—the woodlands had disappeared.

With this changing ratio of cropping to woodland fallow, the fallow often ceased to fulfill its functions, and eventually was unable to regenerate at all. Crop yields steadily declined as the fallow period shortened. In Benue Province (Nigeria), this deterioration was already noticeable by 1927. Today, over large areas of land, forest has been replaced by cogon grass and has become useless for food production; such cogonals cover 18 per cent of all land in the Philippines. Over other large areas, especially in Africa, India, and Burma, soil has been altogether lost by erosion.

Thus, throughout the tropics, the swidden system is tending to break down under the weight of rising populations. This, of course, is only one aspect of the growing population crisis throughout the world. Between 1958 and 1964, world agricultural production was spectacularly increased by prodigies of technological effort; but production per head remained constant because of the swelling population. Even assuming that the population problem will be solved, however, the swidden method faces reappraisal.

One answer may be to replace it with new farming methods. Although many swidden families have settled homes (however much they shift their plots in the surrounding forest), their way of life is difficult to integrate with that of modern civilization. And it will certainly be desirable to make vast areas of land more productive, capable of contributing more to mushrooming urban societies. To this end, intensive efforts are being made to find better forms of tropical farming. But even with all the resources of modern technology, the task is difficult and the problem far from solved (a tribute to the limited but real achievements of swidden farming, which were made without any of these resources).

In the drier parts of tropical regions, continuous cropping may well prove possible on a large scale. Experiments in savanna areas of Africa have shown that continuous cropping with compost, animal manure, or chemical fertilizers is far more productive than rotation with the grass fallows to which many such areas have been reduced. In surviving savanna woodlands, too, such methods may be better than swidden farming, although it is likely that the chemical fertilizers would have to include more nutrients than the conventional nitrogen, phosphorus, and potassium, which generally suffice for soils of temperate zone lands. The development of mixed farming (providing abundant animal manure) is perhaps the most hopeful solution. This would require introducing improved breeds of animals and (in Africa) eliminating the tsetse flies, harbingers of human and animal disease.

But in the heart of the rain forest there can be another answer. Much research is now directed toward developing a modernized swidden system. It would rely on a fallow made by deliberate planting of selected trees (or sometimes creeping plants), which will either restore soil fertility better and faster than natural fallows, or make possible a new combination of farming with forestry. So far, the attempts have shown little improvement over natural fallow, but research continues. It may well be that, in some such modernized form, man's oldest way of forest farming will continue to prove its worth.

William Irons

The Turkmen Nomads

Until a century ago, Turkmen nomads migrated seasonally over the Central Asian steppe in search of pasture, their mobility preserved by their independence from neighboring sedentary governments. Today they have lost their independence, but in remote areas many still cling to their nomadic way of life.

The Turkmen inhabit a region divided between three countries—Afghanistan, Iran, and the Soviet Union—and their population is a million and a half. Although they have all been brought under the control of these countries, conquest and settlement were accomplished piecemeal, affecting some areas sooner and more drastically than others. Among those who have remained nomadic, tradition is largely intact, and when I began my study of the Turkmen in the winter of 1965, I decided to concentrate on this group.

The devotion of these people to a migratory way of life can be understood only in historic perspective. The Turkmen are by tradition a pastoral people, and for them nomadism is a way of using sparse and seasonably variable pasture for livestock production. But it was, in the past, something more: a means of resisting firm government control. Such resistance was a consciously maintained tradition among the Turkmen, and nomadism was the chief means to this end.

Their eagerness to resist the power of sedentary states grew out of an understanding of what government control meant to settled people. In the harsh social environment of the traditional Middle East and Central Asia, settled people were frequently exploited through the imposition of heavy taxes and rents.

The Turkmen not only avoided such exploitation, but by raiding and collecting tribute from their sedentary neighbors, they went a step further and put themselves in the position of the exploiter. A century ago they were notorious as brigands and especially as slave raiders. Slaving activities were conducted primarily in northeastern Persia (now Iran): Turkmen raiding parties ambushed caravans or attacked villages, retreating quickly with their captives to their own territory.

The portion of the Central Asian steppe inhabited by the Turkmen stretches east from the Caspian Sea to the Amu Darya, a large river that empties into the Aral Sea. The central part of this area is the Kara Kum, or "black sand," a vast, largely uninhabited and uninhabitable desert. The majority of the Turkmen are concentrated in two somewhat more fertile regions bordering the

Kara Kum. One area consists of the banks of the Amu Darya; the other is a long strip of plains and low mountains, lying south of the Kara Kum and separating it from the Iranian Plateau. My study was carried out in a section of the latter area—in the Gorgan Plain of northern Iran.

All nomadic Turkmen are divided into residential groups known as *obas*, and my research was focused on a single *oba* consisting of sixty-one households. This group migrates within the Gokcha Hills, a patch of low hills that protrudes into the Gorgan Plain. An *oba* is associated with a definite territory, and all of its members share common rights over that territory, including the right to use the pastures and any natural source of water there. All have the right to dig wells, but once such wells have been dug they become the private property of the persons who expended their labor in digging them. Similarly, all may plow up virgin land for cultivation, but once someone plows a section it becomes his private property.

Throughout the year these nomads live in yurts, a Central Asian tent, which consists of a hemispherical wooden frame covered with felt. They make their living primarily by raising sheep and goats, and their pattern of migration is largely determined by the needs of their animals and by variations in pasture and water supply. The climate of the Gorgan Plain is characterized by definite wet and dry seasons. The wet season begins in the winter, and during this season the Gokcha Hills and surrounding steppe are covered with a short, but relatively thick, crop of grass giving the appearance of a vast, freshly mowed lawn. Winter temperatures are mild, rarely dipping below the freezing point. The rain-water, as well as occasional melted snow, collects in scattered depres-

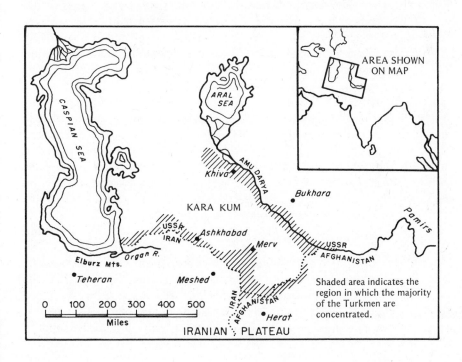

Shaded area indicates the region in which the majority of the Turkmen are concentrated.

sions to form pools from which water is taken for household needs. During this season, the nomads camp where water and suitable pasture can be found. Ample pasture is usually available close to their dry-season location, so that most of their migrations are quite short. In this respect, they differ considerably from many of the pastoral peoples in and around the Iranian Plateau who make long seasonal moves ranging over vastly differing ecological zones.

Among the Turkmen, the seasonal migrations of camps differ from the movements of livestock. The nomad camps of the Gokcha Hills alternately collect at wells and disperse over the surrounding territory, while the livestock move between the Gokcha Hills and the Gorgan River, thirty miles to the south, thus covering a larger area. This means that the Turkmen camp near their herds only during a portion of the year.

The reason for this lies in the needs of their livestock. During the latter part of the winter, the lambing season begins and the Turkmen must be near their herds to assist in cases of difficult birth and to care for the lambs, which are kept inside the yurts at night to protect them from the cold. Because the lambs are too weak to travel far, they must be pastured near the camp. Even after the young animals are weaned, the adult females must be milked daily, and for this reason, the nomads still keep the livestock near their camp.

With the onset of summer, the dry season begins, and the green pastures of spring are gradually transformed to a barren brown. The rainwater pools disappear, and now the nomads must camp near their wells. When the pastures become sparse and desiccated, the animals stop giving milk, and it is no longer necessary to keep them nearby. They are then sent south to the banks of the Gorgan River, where they graze the stubble of harvested fields. The younger men of each household accompany their family's livestock and live separately from the rest of the household, with only a small lean-to-like tent for shelter.

This division of labor is possible because herding, as well as other forms of economic production, is organized by extended families, consisting of an older man and his wife, his married sons with their wives and children, and his unmarried sons and daughters. Each family produces only a part of what it consumes: milk and milk products, meat, felts and carpets for their yurts, and a small amount of grain. In hope of a late spring harvest, wheat and barley are planted during the winter in valley bottoms or other depressions where water tends to collect. This is a gamble, however, since often the crop does not develop, but when a crop can be harvested, the yield is generally sufficient to make up for the losses of grain put down as seed in bad years.

The rest of their needs must be purchased. Cash income comes from the sale of wool, felts, carpets, and animals for meat. The basic item in their diet is bread, and they purchase the bulk of the wheat from which the bread is made. Rice, tea, and sugar must all be bought. Clothing, cloth, metal tools, and nowadays, a hand-powered sewing machine and a transistor radio, are other items that a typical nomadic Turkmen family buys. About once a month, two or three men from each *oba* travel to the nearest city to purchase supplies and to sell their products: animals, wool, and carpets. Thus, the pastoral economy of the Turkmen is market-oriented, even though production is organized along family lines.

The organization of the extended family reflects a strong emphasis on descent in the male line, which runs through all Turkmen social institutions. When a man's daughters marry they go to live with their husbands' families, whereas his sons bring their wives into his household, where they assume the dual role of wife and daughter-in-law. A man's grandchildren in the male line grow up in his household, and he commonly refers to them as his "sons" and "daughters." When, with the passing of generations, his grandsons become old men and the heads of extended families of their own, they will camp together and co-operation between them will be extensive. If any one of them is offended by an outsider, the group will band together to seek redress. Small patrilineages of this sort provide the model in terms of which the larger political units of Turkmen society are organized.

The older men, who make the important decisions, know their genealogies well. Each of them can, on the basis of his genealogy, identify a group of people who share with him a common ancestor in the male line four generations back, and a slightly larger group of people descended from a common ancestor five generations back, and so on, until he has identified himself with descent groups including thousands of families. Ultimately all Turkmen believe they are united by their genealogies as the descendants of a single man, Oghuz Khan. Although the remoter generations of these genealogies are vague and legendary in character, this is of no practical importance since the Turkmen take them seriously as a basis for arranging their social obligations.

Traditionally, the primary function of these descent groups was defense of the individual's rights through violence, or the threat of violence. Defending one's patrilineal kinsmen when their rights were violated was a basic duty in Turkmen social life. This was extremely important, because the absence of state control and of tribal offices with sufficient authority to enforce law and order meant that the strength of a Turkmen's patrilineage was the only guarantee of his rights.

When someone violated a Turkmen's rights by robbing him, injuring him, or killing him, his patrilineal kinsmen were obligated to seek redress by whatever means was necessary, even including violence. In cases of murder, for example, either the murderer or one of his lineage-mates was killed in revenge. Who sought redress for the victim and who defended the culprit were matters determined by genealogy and by the gravity of the affair. Small problems could be handled by the immediate families of the victim and the culprit. As matters increased in seriousness, a wider and wider circle of people who shared common patrilineal descent was called upon for assistance.

Those who were, on the basis of their genealogy, close to neither party also had a prescribed role. It was their obligation to attempt to bring about a peaceful settlement and, if possible, to prevent bloodshed. If the offense was slight, they merely advocated peaceful discussion and suggested compromise. In cases of murder, the neutral party aided the culprit by hiding him from the victim's kinsmen and by helping to arrange his escape to some distant place of refuge. Protecting those who came seeking refuge was part of the obligation of neutral parties to prevent bloodshed. The Iranian government has been attempting to eliminate this traditional system of self-help and to enforce law and order itself; in remoter areas, however, it has not always been successful.

The composition of Turkmen *obas*, like many other aspects of Turkmen social structure, reflects the importance of patrilineal descent. Most of the men of any *oba* are closely related in the male line; in addition, there are usually a number of unrelated families who have come to the *oba* fleeing feuds in their home territory. While these refugees reside there, the *oba* will protect their rights of person and property against outsiders.

The men of an *oba* traditionally selected a headman, who took charge of all dealings with the outside world. Today, in theory, he is appointed by the government, but in practice the local officials usually allow the men of the *oba* to indicate the man they want as their headman. The headman has no authority, but merely acts as a spokesman for the *oba* as a whole. Any important decision must be based on consensus; it must be preceded by discussion by all the men of the *oba*. Usually a headman is selected for his intelligence and integrity and for his ability to speak Persian, the language of the government officials with whom he must deal.

Ordinarily a group of fifteen to thirty *obas*, which belong to the same descent group and occupy contiguous tracts of land, form what the Turkmen call an *il*, a word best translated as tribe. In the days of intertribal warfare, the *obas* of such a tribe were usually on peaceful terms with one another. Tribes that adjoined were usually hostile, and there was much raiding between them.

One of the functions of the Turkmen tribe that has not survived government control is the practice of protecting neighboring sedentary villages. These villages were especially vulnerable to the raids of the Turkmen, and to gain a measure of security and protection each village paid tribute to the Turkmen tribe nearest it. In return, the tribe agreed not to raid the village, and to prevent raids by other Turkmen tribes. They also agreed to compensate the village for losses if they were unsuccessful in preventing raids by other tribes. In effect, the exchange of protection for tribute was a peaceful substitute for raiding.

The Turkmen were able to resist government control, to raid, and to collect tribute because their nomadic way of life made them an effective military force. They were good horsemen and were well supplied with horses. Raids, both of sedentary villages and of other nomads, were frequent events and provided the Turkmen with excellent military conditioning. When clashes with the Persian military forces occurred, normally hostile tribes would unite to turn out a large body of cavalry. This seasoned cavalry could usually hold its ground against the Persian forces, but even when met by superior strength, the Turkmen did not surrender. Instead, they would retreat into the desert north of the Gorgan River, taking their families and livestock with them.

Thus, mobility preserved the power and independence of the Turkmen; this was why they consistently avoided anything that would compromise it. Much of the territory they inhabited was naturally fertile and was crossed by numerous streams. The construction of irrigation works and the practice of intensive agriculture could have made this land more productive. Permanent houses at their dry-season locations could have increased their comfort. The Turkmen, however, would not accept such trends away from nomadic life. They concentrated instead on livestock production, on raiding, and on the collection of tribute.

During the last century, the political independence of the Turkmen has gradually been whittled away. Advances in military technology have shifted the balance of power between the nomadic tribes and settled society and have led to the conquest of the nomads by sedentary powers. Most of the Turkmen were conquered by the Russians during the latter half of the nineteenth century. Those on Iranian soil were subdued and brought under firm control in 1925.

The objective of conquering governments has been to encourage a transition to a more sedentary and peaceful way of life. Such a transition, however, could rarely be accomplished at once. The nomads viewed settlement as a consolidation of governmental authority over them, and were not eager to take up sedentary life. For this reason, in the thirties the Iranian government began a policy of forced settlement not only of the Turkmen but of all of the Iranian tribes. The nomads I studied had been forced to build permanent houses at their dry-season locations in 1936. For five years, under the watchful eyes of government authorities, they lived in these houses during the dry season and migrated with their yurts only during the wet season. This form of semisedentary life developed naturally out of their pattern of pasturing sheep away from their dry-season camps. That it caused no economic difficulties is revealing. The nomads had maintained a completely mobile existence for political rather than for economic reasons, and a transition to a semisedentary existence could be made without economic difficulty.

In 1941, Russia occupied northern Iran because it was fearful of Iranian co-operation with the Germans, and the process of settlement was reversed. The Iranians had been interested in modernization, but the Russians were interested only in sufficient order to keep their supply lines to their Western allies open. Many of the Turkmen who had resented forced settlement reverted to nomadism. The people with whom I recently lived destroyed the houses they had been forced to build and returned to living year-round in yurts. Security deteriorated, and banditry became rife in the remoter and more arid regions, such as the Gokcha Hills.

After the Second World War, the authority of the Iranian government was restored in the Gorgan Plain and efforts to modernize the Turkmen were renewed. The government had come to understand the limited value of the type of force measures used in the thirties. Its objective was not to reduce the Turkmen to the traditional position of exploited peasantry, but rather to integrate them into a society that was on the way to becoming a modern nation. This meant the terms would have to be satisfactory to the Turkmen themselves. In line with this policy, persuasion was used rather than force. Great progress was made in the fertile and populous region south of the Gorgan River.

In the Gokcha Hills, things changed more slowly. By 1960, the government had eliminated banditry, clearing the way for further progress. The Turkmen of this region, however, have remained nomadic to the present. Nevertheless, there are indications that they too will eventually be caught up in the trend of modernization.

The Gokcha Hills Turkmen are beginning to realize that their nomadic way of life has no place in the future. In 1967, when I left the *oba* that I had studied, their headman had begun to discuss the need of a school for their children. He is an intelligent man, aware that his own children will have new opportunities if they become literate. He is convinced, however, that they cannot persuade a government school teacher to live in a community that consists only of yurts. He has been telling the men of his *oba* that they need a school, and that in order to have one they will have to build houses as they did in 1936.

The headman will find that winning the men of his *oba* to this view is a difficult task. Eventually, however, they will build houses and a school, and ultimately they will be drawn into the mainstream of Iranian national life.

Robert Paine

Coast Lapp Fishing

1. Winter Cod Fishing

The winter cod fishing is the most important of the various fishing seasons of the year; indeed, for Revsbotn, it alone is of greater importance than all the other fishing of the year.

If there are already fish in the bay, the season may begin in November. At all events, a holiday period, involving a complete break in the fishing, is

Reprinted from Robert Paine, Coast Lapp Society, Tromsø Museum Skrifter, vol. IV (1957), 98–109, with permission of Tromsø Museum and the author.

taken over the Christmas-New Year week. Early in the New Year the fishing begins again in earnest (some families may not have fished before the New Year), and it may be continued up to Easter. Easter is an important festival and always marks the end of the cod season.

Obviously however, any schedule depends on the arrival of the fish, and it may happen that there is no fishing before January and sometimes (in 1953, for instance) not before February. The length of the season can also be further curtailed through the date of Easter falling early.

The cod are normally fished with nets. These days the nets are usually bought, but each year extensive repair work, taking up much time, is carried out on them. The nets are initially tied together in a «piece» of 12 nets, each member of the boatscrew has some nets (usually either 6 or 4) in each piece. Then several pieces are commonly made into one «length». This length, that may be composed of 24 or 36 or 48 individual nets, is set and dragged as one. A team of three men may have, say, 120 nets between them, composed of 10 pieces which are fished in 3 or 4 lengths. I could not observe any particular rule concerning where the separate lengths should be set and whether they should all be set in the same area. Commonly a team tried two different grounds at a time and set their lengths in two different places, but it was never convenient for these places to be far separated from each other.

A rough-and-ready buoy made out of a piece of wood, which is bound to a glass ball and may have a small flag attached to it, is secured to each length of net. There is no deliberate system of marking, although most buoys do have their own distinctive cut and few mistakes are made. Each fisherman can recognize his own buoy from a distance, but is not necessarily able to recognize all the other buoys.

The average number of nets per fisherman is 40; it can be more, and when fishing from a motor-boat there are usually not less than 60 per fisherman. A normal fishing team (boatscrew) consists of either 2 or 3, more rarely 4, men. On the whole, two is the most popular number, it exacts more labour from each member of the team than in the case of a team of three, but is obviously more favourable financially.

The labour involved in cod fishing can be considerable, besides the discomfort. The discomforts of fishing from an open boat in the weather and latitude of Finmark need no elaboration. Suffice it to say that these discomforts, accentuated through absence of any cover and means of cooking a warm drink, are beginning to be remarked upon by the younger fishermen, and, where there is an alternative present, sometimes lead to their forsaking this type of fishing.

The labour is mainly in the dragging of the nets. The nets become heavier the emptier they are—the fish in a net can «float» a net in the water. Weather permitting, the cod nets should be dragged and set every day. Thus it is natural that the fisherman normally favours the nearer and the shallower grounds. But here again, he must often defer to the elements. Bad weather can keep him on land for over a week, paucity of fish can force him farther from home than he would wish. In 1953 many Revsbotn boats were fishing around Jåvik; [1] this is a long pull out and back, especially if the wind is un-favourable for the use of sail and if the boat is loaded with a cargo of fish. When out at Jåvik—and having to return to Revsbotn for food and sleep and with but poor chances of reasonable catches—the nets were visited no more than two or three times a week.

On coming ashore, a team sets about the gutting and hanging of their fish.

Some of the fishermen of a village, in the latter half of a bad season, may decide to continue fishing with lines and forsake the net fishing (as happened in 1953). The closing of the period of the net fishing is more usually deter-mined not by the retreat of the fish, but by the return of daylight to the heavens. A net can only be used properly while there is insufficient light for the fish to be able to see its mesh. By the beginning of April, the nets may begin to be virtually empty when they are dragged; there are still fish about but there is already too much light. If Easter should come late, and there are still fish in the fjord, then the nets may, nevertheless, be left out, but dragged only every third day or so. Alternatively, the fishing during the final week of the season is sometimes with lines alone.

It is as well that it be emphasized that the heaviest and the most crucial work of the year is done during the period that is the coldest and in which the hours of daylight are least. The conditions of winter fishing entail personal hazard and, inevitably, heavy wear and tear of equipment. The gale that keeps the fisherman land-bound for several days may loosen his nets from their moorings and drag them along the bottom. This fishing, we have pointed out, has not been the practice for so long. The changes to nets from lines, and to the winter season from the summer, were in response to various external changes and to economic need.

2. The Fisherman's Knowledge

Precisely how many fishing grounds there are inside Revsbotn fjord would be difficult to estimate, but the Revsbotn fisherman probably possesses more detailed topographical knowledge about the bottom of his fjord than he does about the land about him. Perhaps, indeed, his mental map of the sea bottom, and of the «bearings» of each of the many fishing grounds in the fjord, is as detailed and complex as the similar mental map that the Mountain Lapp has of the hundreds of topographical features of a particular pasture area.

Young and old people possess this knowledge equally. This is not to say that some of the older inhabitants of the fjord believe the knowledge of the tricks of the trade possessed by some of the younger fishermen, or by one married into the community only six or seven years ago, to be equal to their own. Particularly concerning the reading of the weather signs, the axiom «experience pays» seems to be acknowledged in Revsbotn fjord.

[1] See Fig. 1, p. 186.

Ordinarily, the area used by the fishermen of Revsbotn bay for their winter cod season is that inside Fugløy (Bird island) and the Lillefjord light. Within this area no fisherman would know less than, say, 50 different fishing grounds. In the course of a few minutes, and quite *ex tempore,* a young man of twenty-seven was able to name, and locate on a map, up to thirty fishing grounds inside the fjord.

The Coast Lapps' faculty of being able to impart exact knowledge to a fellow fisherman (a faculty which they share in common with most fishing societies and which they have developed in much the same way as have the Norwegians of this coast) depends upon an intricate system of «bearings».

To each of the known and used fishing grounds are fixed a set of bearings. These have been taken from the fishing ground itself onto prominent and obvious topographical features of the surrounding landscape, e.g. onto a mountain top several kilometres away and a distinctive cleft in the side of the fjord. In this way a man who has set his nets out in the fjord—at, say, *dâvve bod'ne:* «north ground»—and on returning to land falls ill, is able to tell a friend simply that his nets lie on *dâvve bod'ne.* This information will be sufficient to enable his friend to row straight out to the approximate area and, through reference to the already known bearings, quickly find the nets, which he will then drag for the sick man.

More commonly, an observer is able to see how this exact system is used daily—in the village shop or in the home—in the important exchange of fishing news: of which grounds are being used, of which ground is fishing well and so forth.

Such news is exchanged freely, any exceptions to this practice of *bonhomie* being regarded with disdain by the remainder of the fishermen. Indeed, I knew only one such exception among the 42 households around Revsbotn bay. So far as I could judge, there existed little or no competition between the fishermen of the same village who were using the same fishing grounds. When one side of the fjord was fishing better than the other, all would quickly come to know of this, and all the nets of the village might well come to be set almost on top of one another on the same few grounds. It has happened that a 1000 nets, of more than 15 boatscrews, be set on two, or even one, of the well-favoured grounds in Russelv bay.

The villagers of Revsbotn believe that this amicable exchange of information and common use of knowledge and of the grounds themselves, injures no one and benefits all. If there is little fish in the fjord, then the fishing for all will be bad (and each will stand in need of the common pool of knowledge); if there is a lot of fish in the fjord, then all will get their good share.

We may notice that this point of view is consonant with the local circumstances of the fishing. One may usually depend safely upon the regular appearance of winter cod at the base of the fjord in sufficient numbers for all. When there is a bad year, it does not just mean that there is no cod in the fjord, but that throughout the whole of the two to three month period of the winter season there is *little* cod. The season is long enough, and the fishing grounds sufficiently localized, for all to make the best of a bad season and for all to make the very best of a good season. Partly because of this, and partly because of the general practice of goodwill, the results of a winter's fishing among the people of Revsbotn do not differ considerably from one boat to another. These differences are least after a bad season (e.g. 1953–54) and slightly greater after a favourable season (e.g. 1952–53)—when it is said that so and so had «better luck». This is because a season with an excess of fish in the fjord affords greater chances to the keener and more energetic among the boatscrews. This last fact dispels any idea that might have arisen as to an actual egalitarian practice among local fishermen.

A second aspect must be included here. As is shown on the accompanying Sea chart (Fig. 1), the fishing area of Revsbotn bay has been divided into two areas: A and B. Area A is one in which seine-fishermen are afforded preference over fishermen working with nets *(garn)*. The latter may set their nets in area A, but at their own risk. Area B is reserved for the net fishermen only; seiners may not fish in area B. Outside areas A and B no restrictions apply.

This is a piece of state legislation, of the law of 6/5 1938 and, to the best of my knowledge, it is in force in most fjordal areas along the Norwegian coast; in Revsbotn it has been enforced since 1/1 1952.

I am satisfied that the fishermen of Revsbotn themselves had no part in the making of this division, although their fishing committee has on occasions written to the Harbour Master of Hammerfest concerning its details. While it is of practical importance to them, I never managed to elicit much original

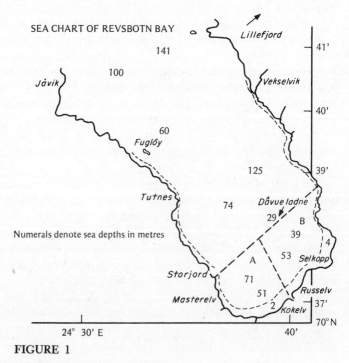

SEA CHART OF REVSBOTN BAY

Numerals denote sea depths in metres

24° 30' E

FIGURE 1

comment from the villagers on the subject of this division of the bay. They agree with the principle and approve of its exercise. It endeavours to protect the local in-shore fishing from the activities of motor-cutters that might come from as far afield as Nordland province.

For a fisherman from Masterelv, it means that he is really bound to row over the bay to Russelv to set his nets. But then the best cod grounds are on this side of the fjord, which is why it was selected as area B. The man from Masterelv is not *compelled* by any legislation to set his nets in area B, the legislation advises him to do so in his own interest, which he has quickly appreciated.

3. Summer Fishing

In the period between the two World wars, the summer season in the Coast Lapp fjords of Finnmark was one of less serious endeavour. The present situation differs in several respects.

The increasing importance of salmon fishing in Finnmark is fairly reflected in Revsbotn fjord. In effect, salmon fishing can mean a new type of professional fishing within the fjord. Yet most owners of salmon nets still take part in the cod fishing in the winter. The salmon net remains, at the moment, a source of extra income in the summer and of extra labour too, at a time when much work must be put into the land.

As the conditions for salmon fishing are generally more favourable at the head of a fjord than around its base, one finds appreciably more salmon nets out at Slotten than in Revsbotn bay. By the time the salmon reach the bottom of the fjord «they have become too wary and move too quickly in their progress up to the freshwater.» There are three families who fish salmon in Revsbotn, two with one net each and the third with two nets. Two of the nets are set inside the bay while one is set out at Fugløy and the fourth as far out as Jåvik. This last net has the best position and is visited by motor-boat.

In many places in Finnmark one is unable to find a suitable site for a salmon net near the home village. In these cases, the fisherman is often prepared to resort to a limited type of summer transhumance. He will build a fishing hut on the selected fishing site, and will spend much of his summer based on this hut, returning possibly only for week-ends and for the harvesting of his grass.[2]

Each owner of a net must have an authorization to use it, he must pay 10 Norwegian kroner a year for the use of a site. No net may be placed within 200 metres of another. By law, salmon nets should not be fished over the week-

[2] An example of this is the case of a man and his son-in-law in Brensvik. Between them they fish three salmon nets out at Kvalvikneset, between Repparfjord and Revsnes. Salmon fishing is their main summer employment, and they spend most of the summer out at Kvalvikneset, where they have a summer hut. They make regular trips to either Revsnes or Kvalsund to sell the salmon.

ends (this is not a Sabbath Day injunction, but one made as a protective measure to salmon fishing).

Brief notice must be given here to some of the other fishing that occurs inside the fjord.

A few individuals from each village attempt some flatfish fishing during the summer. The net used is similar to a cod net, but has a finer mesh and is weighted with small stones, or small bags of sand. While the distribution of the flatfish tends to be rather local, it fetches a very fair price when sold fresh to one or other of the shopmen in the fjord. (Some of those who own motor-boats fish flatfish in the fjord during the winter. One Revsbotn family often concentrates on this fishing to their neglect of the cod fishing.)

Halibut is another species that is fished locally during the summer by a few families. Both in Selkopp and Storjord, for example, a halibut line is set with some regularity most summers. It should be visited every 24 hours.

Although in recent years coalfish fishing has come to be carried on almost exclusively from the larger motor-boats with seine-nets, a few in Revsbotn still set nets (*garn*) in the bay. But the poor results obtained only illustrate the imperative need for mobility in this type of fishing.

It is in this mobile and perambulating (*inter-fjordal*) coalfish fishing that more Coast Lapps are each year becoming engaged—another fairly new endeavour of the summer months.

No fewer than three family groups in Kokelv own seine-nets. This is rather more than what one might expect in a village at the base of a fjord. No one of these three family groups owns a motor-cutter; the expense in itself may be prohibitive at the moment, and anyway, there is no harbour in the bay. Each one of them takes part in the normal way in the local, winter cod fishing. Their seine-nets are only in use during the summer and autumn months, when they rent a motor-cutter and, for the most part, crew it with men from the village. Up to 1952 they had never sold their catches in the village (to the shopman), although, since the Co-operative quay has been built (1953–54), to do so has become a more practical proposition. But it is still not very convenient, for the quay lies too far inside the fjord and too far away from the likelier fishing grounds.

Despite the possibilities of an extra thousand or two *kroner* from this summer fishing, the young men of Revsbotn bay are not on the whole particularly interested in the proposition. They have fished through the winter and wish to be at home for the summer—in the village and about their farms. However, while summer fishing in Revsbotn is inclined to be the fishing of a minority only, it does happen. It takes Revsbotn men out of the fjord in the larger, mechanized types of craft; it approaches the <Lillefjord type> in character (see section 2). Losing much of the isolated and simple character of the Revsbotn winter fishing, it is not so strongly corporate in character. By this I mean that it is not the activity of the village, for the life of the village is not arranged around it, as is the case with the winter fishing when nearly every household in Revsbotn is engaged in it.

The point requiring emphasis, then, is as follows: In the winter, Revsbotn bay is visited by a calculable number of cod for a calculable period of time, but in the summer, fish (other than salmon) only appear *inside the fjord* (or in Revsbotn bay) fortuitously. These may be fished spasmodically for personal needs or for casual cash-returns, but the serious fishermen have to go farther afield in that season of the year.

4. Who Fishes?

In conclusion to this chapter I would consider the proportions of Table 1, concerning the winter fishing in Revsbotn and Lillefjord.

Out of a combined total of 88 active males, there are only 9 who do not fish at all and 7 who are sometimes (some winters) not engaged in fishing. These figures take account of the few non-Lapps in the fjord, and their number provides 3 of the 9 non-fishing population. These three are: the schoolmaster at Kokelv and the Lillefjord shopman and his assistant.

The remaining 6 of these 9 persons are all Coast Lapps. All of them are from Kokelv, they are: the shopman and his junior partner, a professional salmon fisherman for over 20 years, a previous owner of a café in Havøysund who has now come to retire in the village of his wife's parents, an officer in the local mail-boat service and an active young married man who refuses to fish on account of seasickness. The young married man takes various winter jobs on land, the salmon fisherman either works as a cobbler during the winter or on a local fish-quay.

Among the 7 who sometimes do not take part in the winter fishing, there are a few youths of between sixteen and eighteen years who have not yet fully entered the adult labour cycle, and a few men besides, who are able to earn steady money most winters at some trade work, usually carpentry or, in the case of one of them, on a fish-quay.

This nearer look at the non-participants but serves to underline the traditional importance of the winter fishing season in a Coast Lapp village. It also indicates the absence of much occupational professionalism outside fishing and reflects the economic interest that these villagers have in the sea. Even in the instances of those who do not actually fish, their work is related, in a fashion never very indirect, to the sea.

Of recent years there has been a real change in emphasis in the mode of fishing. Still with reference to Table 1, it is illuminating to compare Revsbotn and Lillefjord in this respect.

The combined, actual fishing population is 75,[3] of these nearly two-thirds

[3] The number 75 represents the actual figure for a particular year but, as it happens, it is also the statistical mean over a number of years of A (72 + 7) of Table 1.

Table 1: An Analysis of the Winter Fishing in Revsbotn and Lillefjord—Its Type and Distribution.

A.	REVSBOTN	LILLEFJORD	TOTAL
Total number of active male adults (born between 1882 and 1936)	68	20	88
Total number active in fishing	56	16	72
Total number not fishing	7 + (5)	2 + (2)	9 + (7)

B.

I. Fishing from Rowing-Boats, IN the Fjord

	REVSBOTN	LILLEFJORD	TOTAL
Total	42	6	48
Owners or part-owners of boats	33	4	37
No. of boats	18	3	21
With own nets	38	4	42
Without own nets	4	2*	6

II. Fishing from Motor-Boats, IN the Fjord

	REVSBOTN	LILLEFJORD	TOTAL
Total	9	11	20
Owners or part-owners of boats	5	8	13
No. of motor-boats	3	4	7
With own nets	9	11	20
Without own nets	—	—	—

III. Fishing OUT of the Fjord

	REVSBOTN	LILLEFJORD	TOTAL
Total	4	3	7
In Finmark	1	3	4
with own nets	—	—	—
In Lofoten	3	—	3
with own nets	1	—	3

Notes.

Section A of this Table is compiled as an average from the data for various winter periods of 1951, 1952 and 1953.

Section B represents a specimen year, the figures are those of the year for which the fullest data were available.

In section A account had to be taken of the slight variance from year to year. The figures that follow in brackets represent this variance. See text for nature of these exceptions.

* These two have no nets.

(48) are engaged in rowing-boats, while just over one-third (27) fish from one or another type of motor-boat. But when the figures for Revsbotn and Lillefjord are considered separately, two very divergent results appear. The respective figures for Revsbotn are 42 and 13, while for Lillefjord they are 6 and 14. In other words, while three-quarters of the Revsbotn fishermen use rowing-boats, over two-thirds of the Lillefjord men work from motor-boats.

Lillefjord has a well-sheltered harbour while Revsbotn bay lies open and exposed to all wind and storm. The sheltered harbour early attracted capital and a fish-quay. Revsbotn has only just now (in 1953) obtained a fish-quay and is still, of course, without a safe harbour. We notice their conversion of what originally were simple differences in physical geography into those of activity, and hence of economy and human attitudes too.

The consideration has left no room for doubt as to the basis of the present Coast Lapp economy. Although the balance in their economy is always shifting, these people remain fishermen primarily. During the time of the Russian Trade, the emphasis was almost exclusively on fishing. Then, in the most recent years of all, with the introduction of serious farming as a secondary occupation in place of hunting, the dual basis of their economy has been properly restored.

5 Dimensions of Social Behavior

In the long course of human evolution more and more complex forms of social organization have emerged, particularly as modes of food production made possible larger and larger settlements, and denser populations. Small hunting and gathering bands, with perhaps no more than thirty or forty people in the local group, and population densities of less than one person per 10–20 square miles, have generally been able to organize their work and play without complex bureaucracies or other specialized organizational features. But with the growth of sedentary populations and division of labor, human cultural evolution has seen the growth of elaborate systems of kinship relations, complexes of lineages, clans, and other groups, as well as a great variety of nonkin associations, societies, clubs, and other organizations. Often we discuss human social groups as if they have an existence of their own, apart from the individuals that comprise them. Sometimes when we discuss the conflicts between Republicans and Democrats, or relationships among nations, discussions become so abstract that the individual actor seems remote indeed. To understand human behavior in complex organizational frameworks, however, we should start with the realization that organizations accomplish their objectives, and perpetuate themselves through time because of the activities and efforts of real persons. At the same time, if we are to understand the adaptative strategies and styles of individuals in different cultural scenes we need to think of persons as relating to other people in a variety of different ways, sometimes through individual ties, sometimes through membership in organizations.

In Nancy Modiano's description of "A Chamula Life," the day-to-day activities and long-term life-cycle transitions of an individual illustrate the many ways in which personalized histories are embedded in complex social systems.

No matter how complex the social system, most societies have basic social units built around some form of family. In many respects the core part of any human family (and among other animals as well) is the mother-plus-child unit. In practically all human societies, however, the family organization has a variety of other significant persons in the picture, as "husbands," "father," "brothers and sisters," and a variety of other types of kin are included in the family group. The basic family unit in many societies is the "nuclear family," consisting of a woman and her husband plus unmarried offspring. On the other hand, a great many peoples around the world permit, or perhaps prefer, multiple spouses, often individual males having more than one wife. Whatever the particular details of family arrangements, the basic core family unit is most significant as the group in which reproduction of offspring takes place, sexual arrangements among adults are regulated, children are nurtured and socialized, and in many cases the basic economic cooperating unit is the family group. Often the basic political unit, too, is the family group.

Some anthropologists would disagree with Kathleen Gough when she says that "the family is a human institution, not found in its totality in any prehuman species." In fact, descriptions of baboon groups by Hans Kummer (see our Section 1) suggest that something like "family clusters" are present among those other primates. And some people would argue that the pride of lions in the East African grasslands is a sort of "family." It is, after all, a matter of definition. In any case, it is important to keep in mind the basic panhuman dimensions of family life, no matter how complex the social organizations that are added on in our more densely populated and complex societies.

In addition to relationships of kinship as basic structures of all human groups, most food-producing societies, whether industrialized or not, have differences of economic means, social status and prestige, and other features that separate out people into social levels or "social classes." Frequently such "classes" are relatively fluid and there may be a lot of mobility from one group to another. In other societies, on the other hand, membership in particular classes is much more fixed and unchanging, and may be so rigid and hereditary that we refer to them as "caste systems." The coming of industrialization and "modernization" in non-Westernized parts of the world has often resulted in changes of class structure and stratification. In our selection by David Jacobson on social classes in an East African town we note the development of new dimensions of social class with the coming of modern administrative bureaucracies, formal systems of education, and a money economy. Class differences, like many other social cleavages, are usually marked by differences in language use. While the characteristic of language use is panhuman, people almost always use subtle language differences as marks of status and prestige. Dialect differences among people speaking the same language may represent geographical separation, but they can also represent the social separation of different social groupings within our modern cities.

In recent times there has been much study of diverse ways of speaking English among North Americans. The study of Black English has demonstrated that a language that is often looked down on by teachers in our city schools is a complex and rich means of communication, developed by a socially deprived minority adapting to conditions of life outside the American mainstream. Often our school systems have stigmatized various "nonstandard" dialects of English as if there were only one "correct" standard that everyone should speak, greatly complicating and hindering the process of communication and education for a significant part of our population.

In industrialized societies one often has the impression that ties of kinship have become totally unimportant and secondary in peoples' lives. In fact, the study of the social dimensions of contemporary life frequently jumps from the nuclear family to complex associations and political structures, leaving out any discussion of the ties of kinship beyond the family. However, ties to kin outside one's nuclear family are still of great importance for people in their job getting, education, and other activities. Kin persons beyond the family are a significant network of social support, expressive interaction, and economic help. The dimensions of kin relations beyond the family have not been much studied in our contemporary social scene, but there is increasing evidence of a general shift toward a "matrilateral asymmetry" in kin relations of urbanized peoples. There are some exceptions to this general pattern, and some urban peoples maintain fairly complex patrilineal, patrilateral relations, but even very strongly male-dominated family systems appear to shift toward an emphasis on matrilateral kinship ties as individual mobility and economic independence increase under industrialization.

Nancy Modiano

A Chamula Life

Shalik * came into the world in the dead of night, bawling, protesting. His mother, Loshah, groaned; his father, Molshun, hugged and pressed the bulging belly; Loshah's mother pushed; and the baby dropped onto the little mound of clothes. For the next two years he probably spent most of his time on Loshah's back, observing the world òr sleeping. When he whimpered from hunger the woolen sling was shifted, and from under her arm he would grab at her breast; this was his only "real" food. At night they slept side by side on a hard, wooden platform. He seldom crawled on the dirt floor of their hut, but as he grew he would sit on a blanket, always within her grasp. First steps were encouraged and a stick was held out to guide and support him, but he was not considered able to walk until he could manage the slippery mud trails near home. At first he was dressed in soft, woolen rags, but within a few months, when it appeared that he would live, Molshun bought him a flannel shirt. When he was about a year and a half old and could walk, and Loshah saw that he would not dirty himself too much, she began to weave the first of the rough woolen tunics that would be his principal garment throughout life. At times she talked and played gently with him. At about seven months, for he was a bright baby, he said his first words. .

Tortillas and cooked corn gruel were gradually introduced into his diet, and one day he was not allowed on Loshah's back nor was he allowed to nurse. "The breast is dirty; it is full of excrement," she said. He whimpered a bit, then was silent and did not protest. And then another baby, a little girl to help Loshah, was born. When she died a few months later Shalik must have been blamed, at least in part, for the people feel that a displaced child may have such strong ties to his mother that he or the baby may die. The next child, born when he was about four, was again a girl, and she survived. In all, nine of Loshah's ten children lived: seven boys—of whom Shalik was third— and two girls, covering a span of twenty-four years.

As a baby he was very tractable, and therefore good, but as he grew he became very active and more difficult. He was careless of his clothes, fought with his brothers, and was always playing; a naughty little boy in a world that expected conformity. That he learned to observe the world keenly, to mimic

Reprinted from Nancy Modiano, "A Chamula Life," Natural History (January 1968), 58–63, with permission of Natural History Magazine. Copyright © The American Museum of Natural History, 1968.

* The names of all persons mentioned herein, with the exception of Shalik, have been changed out of respect for their custom of not readily divulging their true names; Shalik asked that his name appear as it does.

all about him with great exactness, and to speak and joke with skill were traits not particularly commended by his parents. They called him "little parrot"; told him to be quiet, to stop pestering.

Soon he began to help with work about the house. At about four he was taught to take grains off an ear of corn and feed the chickens. When Molshun went for firewood, a small bundle would be fitted up with a rope and slung about his head. Much of the time he followed in his mother's tracks or played near the house.

When it was warm out he liked to play with the frogs near the well, and so he helped by carrying a little jug of water. But if ordered to accompany Loshah in cold weather or before sunup, he refused and cried and was scolded and perhaps spanked. He accompanied her to mind the sheep, and he watched Molshun farm or carve wood near the house. As Loshah sat in the field, pasturing, she spun, and showing Shalik how to do it, left him a piece of thread. Soon Shalik began to learn. By the age of six he was turning out the coarser threads and carding the uncombed wool.

More and more he was sent to mind the sheep, sometimes with his next-older brother, increasingly alone, and always he was given a job of carding or spinning. In addition, he was told to make the grass ropes with which to tie the sheep. But the ropes, and the sheep, were often forgotten as he became more and more involved in his games.

At times he tracked animals and birds, and eventually he developed quite a skill with the slingshot. He trapped many a rat with ropes and stones. Many times he joined in play with other little shepherds. "We would make a swing with a grass rope. If we found a board, we would make a slide. We liked to turn and turn and spin around until we were dizzy and fell down. We liked to jump over ravines and see how brave we were and how wide and deep a ravine we could leap. Sometimes we would pile up a lot of leaves under a tree and burn them; we would climb the tree and stay up there until we couldn't stand the smoke any more and then jump down. If a boy had his back to another, the second might jump up on the first with his hands clasped like a tumpline, to see if he could carry him; or one might grab the arm of another and spin him around and around until they both got dizzy and fell down. We had a game like marbles, but we used little fruits; we would shoot for a small hole, and every time a boy got his marble in all the others would have to give him a fruit. Sometimes we would make a game of planting some dried straw to see if it would grow; if another child pulled it out the next day there would be a big argument.

"We also had a game where one child would close his eyes; the others would hide and then call out that they were ready. The first one would try to find the others, but when he got close they would try to scare him and then run out. Then the one who had scared him first would close his eyes, and all the others would hide.

"Another game was that of burying people. One of the children would take off his tunic, and that would serve as the stretcher. We would gather together some of the tortillas that we had been given, and we would eat them. There are some special herbs that we would gather and use in place of the dead one, and we would bury them. And about a week later we would open the grave and see how the herbs were.

"Sometimes we made a heat bath. We would get together a lot of wood, especially little branches, and light them. And we would sit as close to the fire as we could until we were burning with the heat. All the time we should have been looking after the sheep.

"Most of all I liked to organize the others to build houses. First we would dig a hole in the ground, then find branches and build the roof frame. We would gather grass and tie on the thatching, and perhaps even build one or two walls of branches. The houses were about four feet high and sheltered us from the rain. If the weather was very cold and dry, we would burn the house to warm ourselves. A house stood for a few days, then it was time to burn it and build another. If they discovered us, we were scolded because the hole we dug tore up pasturage or was in somebody's forest plot. I always organized and worked with fear in my heart. But I always built houses.

"As a child, I played a great deal; I had no respect for anybody. I did not understand."

Fire always fascinated him. One day he went to play in the woods, carrying some matches he had bought at the market. He lit some dry grass. It caught, and the fire began to spread. Soon the flames reached the lower branches of the berry trees, and neared the houses. The neighbors were threatened, and men ran out to extinguish the fire. The struggle soon grew desperate, or so Shalik recalls it. He was severely scolded by his father and mother and the neighbors, and his aunts, his uncles, his grandparents, all poured out their fear and wrath.

Once the fire had died he slunk off and squatted near the hearth of his hut. For days he sat, barely moving, not eating, not responding to others. At last his parents took fright and relented, and the *curanderos* ("healers") were called. Herbs were gathered, the correct number of candles and requisite bottle of liquor bought, and three eggs selected. The actual ceremony took place where he had been scolded and overcome with fright, but since he could not move, his shirt was sent in his stead. Candles were lit, prayers said, one egg was broken and buried there, and the liquor was consumed. The other two eggs were returned to the house and cooked; one was fed to Shalik, and the other was shared by the rest. The herbs were also cooked, and after he was anointed with them, more prayers were chanted, and so he was cured and able to run about with the other shepherds.

It was shortly after this that a wedding took place at a neighbor's house. He and his oldest brother went to watch. It was very cold, and the two boys shivered in the icy fog. Nearby, at the edge of the forest, was a little stone cave, and they made a fire to warm themselves. Before going home they very carefully put out the flames, or so they thought. The next morning when Loshah went out she found their grandfather cursing in front of his house while trying to put out a forest fire. Although he worked as hard as he could, he could not stop the flames. He called the neighbors. The people came from the wedding party. Shalik's parents tried to help. All were furious, they blamed him and cursed him. The grandfather said that if this fire could not be extinguished quickly, he would burn the little boy. Shalik protested and cried he had not done it, but they would not listen; they said they had seen him there. Meanwhile all worked to put out the flames; Shalik ran back and forth, carrying the heavy water jugs. At last they succeeded, the flames were dead, the ground barely smoking, and again Shalik retreated to the hearth, staring ahead, not speaking, not eating. Again the *curanderos* were called, again the candles lit and prayers raised to the gods, and again he was cured.

The monetary demands of the ever growing family pressed hard on Molshun, and more and more he and the two older boys went to the hot country to work for wages on the plantations. One day Shalik was taken to a house in San Cristobal, told to obey the mistress, and left there.

"When I was very very little I began to work for wages in San Cristobal. I was just about six [he was probably about nine], and I cried all day long. I couldn't understand the people at all because they spoke Spanish. By noon I begged to be allowed to leave. 'The day is over,' I said, but they told me to go back to work. By one o'clock I had picked up my tortilla bag and headed toward the door, but they would not let me go. They showed me a clock and said some words, but I did not understand. I had to stay until four."

That afternoon he went streaking up the mountain, but the next day he was returned to the same house. For days tears poured down his face. "I asked for food. They answered, but I did not understand. They gave me fifty cents a day [$.04 U. S. currency], and I swept up their shop.

"Then I began to understand a bit of what they wanted and the strange sounds they said, and I was less afraid. They began to send me on errands, and I found the work easier. They doubled my pay and gradually kept raising it. I spent many days in that house without leaving. Some days my mother would bring me tortillas, some days they gave me food; I had to spend all my time there.

"When I got home on Saturday evening, my parents would ask me for my money. I would tell them what I had spent. If it was for little things that didn't cost much it was all right. If I wanted bigger things I told them, and sometimes they would buy them for me. So I finally got a leather belt, a hat, a cotton shirt and trousers, but no huaraches [all standard items of Chamula dress]. I have never stopped working since."

Soon Molshun began to take Shalik off to work on the coffee plantations. "We traveled by bus and I was sick for the entire journey. At the plantation I was afraid, for I did not understand the work. In the seven weeks I was there I barely earned any money. But gradually I began to understand what they wanted of me. I returned often, sometimes with my father, sometimes with an older brother. When we went by train I was afraid that I would fall between the cars and be killed. You make good money on the coffee plantations, especially during the harvest.

"There is a weed that grows there. We used to play games by throwing it at each other to see on whose clothes it would stick. When we lined up at 4:00 A.M. for roll call we would push and poke at one another and make a game of it, to see if we could make someone fall and break his food bowl. I was always a little afraid when they called my name. After roll call they would give us breakfast—beans, tortillas, corn gruel, and coffee. At five-thirty we would go out into the fields. At two o'clock we came back for lunch, handed in our work slips, and were given tortillas and beans. In the afternoon we were free to sleep or to wash clothes or go looking for birds or to the store or just rest or do whatever we liked. They also gave us supper: coffee and tortillas, rice once a week, and on one plantation meat once a week. We could buy bread and vegetables on Saturdays. On Sundays people came to sell us food and clothing.

"I was very eager to learn to read and write. My father would not let me go to school; he needed the money I could earn. Nor did my parents dress me well. It was only after I was bringing in my own money that I got a complete outfit. But they have always given to my brothers and sisters."

As he grew Shalik took increasing pride in his ability as a strong and steady worker, one who could always be relied upon to fill in the family's perennial financial crises. Later this same ability would create many difficulties as he became more and more attracted to the material things of the outside world, exceptionally skilled at manipulating in it, yet unwilling to tear himself away from the increasingly illusory emotional warmth of his family.

He would often speak with relish of life on the plantations, but did not want to go back ever. Between stints in the hot country, and steadily thereafter, he worked in San Cristobal—as houseboy, general laborer, gardener, or at whatever he could get. He liked to garden and, even more, to be sent to market. He learned many skills and began to understand the mysterious Spanish better and better. He could command up to all of five pesos a day ($.40 U. S. currency), but liked best the jobs where a meal was included in his salary. In this way he began to know other foods in addition to the beans, tortillas, corn gruel, and boiled vegetables of his house. He even came to eat the taboo lamb.

"On one job I worked as a gardener for the family of a school teacher. I was given a book and a little explanation of the sounds of the letters. But I did not like the job; the people were very unpleasant and dirty. My oldest brother once tried to explain the sounds of the vowels, but I did not understand. Then on another job, I came across a friend, a mestizo, who showed me again that letters can stand for sounds, and I began to understand." In keeping with tradition he brought gifts of sweet potatoes and beer in lieu of payment. Then he became ill and so the lessons ended. The little that he had learned, he repeated over and over. Later he found another teacher, a carpenter, who charged him two pesos for each four-hour class. Shalik was frightened by the cost and had trouble explaining such a high expense at home, so he left the classes. By then he had begun to read, laboriously but incessantly. On another job where he was able to continue his studies, he saw how to use a typewriter, continued to read, and began to write. His use of Spanish improved, especially as he became interested in a mestizo maid in that house. He began to hear words in English and German, and always the facile imitator, he soon mimicked these words. But Shalik had a strong temper and after a year and a half, furious at being scolded, he left. Next he worked for an American anthropologist from whom he learned more English. He began to understand that numbers written with symbols could be added.

As Shalik's earnings increased he began to contribute a part of them to his family, in addition to the corn he regularly bought; from about the age of fifteen he began to save money. He would soon probably be getting married, his father said.

At about eighteen he began to search for a wife. He knew of two girls who might be available. With relatives, friends, and a special spokesman, with gifts of liquor and money, he stated his request at the first house. The group was quickly and severely rebuffed. To the second house they went many times, with much ceremony. Although it looked as though the people there would eventually give in, he was impatient and fearful of the protracted negotiations. He searched in his heart for a solution. He asked *curanderos*, who assured him that some day he would be married.

One day, thinking of another resource, he invited a friend for a few drinks. After they had both mellowed he asked the crucial question: Was there an eligible girl? And so Shalik heard of Catalina. With more drinks he wrangled an invitation to the friend's house, for the friend and Catalina's father were neighbors. On a second visit he spied the girl and discovered that her father was a friend, that they had farmed near each other previously. After more visits the girl appeared to notice him, and her father asked, "What's that fellow doing around here so much?"

He spied her in the streets of San Cristobal. Another time he saw her at a fiesta in Chamula and pointed her out to his parents. "She looks all right but she's awfully short," they remarked. And she seemed to notice him and not disapprove. At last he decided to make his move, for he was very impatient. For an extra gift he might get her right away. So he bought the usual liquor, the bread, the meat, and gathered all his money (less than $30 U. S. currency). At two o'clock one morning the same group—the community elder, Molshun, Loshah, some relatives, and his friends, all with their wives—started out across the hills. They reached Catalina's house by the first rays of daylight.

The elder spoke. "Good morning, Uncle."

No answer.

"Good morning."

"Oh hell, who is it?"

"Me."

"What do you want?"

"To speak to you."

"What do you want?"

The headman gave a muttered answer and began the formal, chanted request.

"You think I have a daughter? She's not here. Who sent you? How did you find this house?" All were very angry questions.

But the elder stood in the doorway, and the family could not get out. Catalina's father continued scolding, but at last he tired. "You want to see my daughter," and he let the group in to see the girl. The liquor was passed around and they toasted one another. Shalik gave ten quarts of liquor.

Then the father asked, "When are you going to take her away?"

"Why not now?" Negotiations were begun as to how much money and what other things would be given, and all the while they got drunker and drunker. At last a deal was struck, and the local elders were called. Their decision was that according to custom Shalik would have to stay there for at least three days, the first day at the party, the second and third working for her father. But he could not stay, for he was working in San Cristobal. Then one said that he could take Catalina right away, which was what he wanted. At last permission to leave was given, with the stipulation that they would return for a formal visit within three weeks, and that Catalina would not take all of her clothing with her. That same morning, well before noon, Shalik led his bride to Molshun's house, where again drinks were passed around.

The wedding ceremony was over. Shalik had made no special preparations for his bride. Many years before he had made a bed for himself, for he did not like to sleep with his little brothers, saying that they were dirty and had lice. Nor did the family make any particular preparations. Shalik remained in San Cristobal six nights a week on his job. On returning home he was met by complaints from his parents and the other children that the new wife, aged all of fourteen or sixteen, was lazy, flirtatious, and worthless. Nor did the two have many moments alone, for when he was at home he was not to sit idle and talk; there was wood to be cut and carried, farming, and many other tasks about the house. Molshun had already tired of work; shortly thereafter he would announce his retirement from the world. Even when Shalik sat within the house he was separated from his wife, for he sat with the men on their side of the fire and she crouched near their bed, far from the flames. She cried a great deal, Loshah scolded, and Shalik was torn between the two.

It was at this point that he changed jobs and began working for me as a guide on numerous trips into the mountains. He had to be away for even longer periods, and he did not enjoy his work. In the beginning he had to hike and carry, which annoyed him. Later, with a horse for his own use and other horses for the baggage, he continued to dislike the traveling. The physical rigors were not unpleasant; it was fear of the unknown, of witchcraft.

During the first and the longest of the trips he became ill, with what, at the time, I thought of as increasing depression. He tired easily and slept longer and more profoundly every day, but cried out in his sleep. He had many bad dreams dealing with sickness and death, involving his animal-soul, his true being. After three weeks he went home for a visit, to find his father and a younger brother ill, and to hear tales of Catalina's possible infidelity. He returned to work with tears in his eyes. After that there were more nightmares, but in one dream a man assured him that he could be cured. Shalik knew that dreams forecast happenings and tell one what to do. He decided to look for a *curandero*. Then he discovered a family enemy at a nearby market, far from home. He believed that the man must have come to set witchcraft against his family. Shalik remained outwardly very polite, dressed himself neatly, and tried to smile. But his eyes became very sad and small, usually bloodshot or yellowed. He looked for a *curandero* wherever we went. Finally he found one and impatiently awaited the time of the ceremony. He bought a quart of liquor, thirteen dozen tiny white candles, a box of cigarettes, a bit of salted meat, and, in addition to these purchases, borrowed some money to pay the *curandero*. The whole bill came to approximately $2.50 in U.S. currency. That evening, as it became dark, he set out to spend the night in the *curandero*'s house. The next morning, reassured that he was not going to die, he returned and dreamed a good dream. He said he would become handsome again, and that for the first time on the trip he felt like himself.

As we traveled through the mountains he thought continually of his wife, of her unhappiness, and of how his father was exploiting him. His temper, never very stable, mounted. Within a few months it exploded in a drunken rage against Loshah. He struck her, an unthinkable act in Chamula. The family was shocked, but he was drunk and not to be held responsible for his behavior. A sister-in-law ran up to hold him back, but he struck her down, too. At last the other men, his older brothers and his father, grabbed hold of him and threw him out of the house, where he lay sobbing in the mud. Catalina crouched near him weeping.

"Let him sleep it off there, and he is never to come back into this house," ruled his parents. They gathered up some of his belongings and threw them out into the mud after him. That afternoon, when he woke up and was told what had happened, he fled with his wife to her father's house, where they were allowed to spend the night. To beg forgiveness of his parents he bought the requisite liquor and carried it to their house, expecting that they would accept his apologies and the liquor, that all would drink together and the argument would be over. But Loshah would not touch the gift. She was furious, as was Molshun. So Shalik and Catalina gathered together the things that had been thrown out into the rain and came down to San Cristobal to spend the night. They were very upset; this was the first time they were alone together.

Shalik now laid claim to some land he had bought years before, almost by accident, in obedience to Molshun's orders. There he would build his home. Meanwhile a neighbor allowed him to occupy an abandoned hut. On Christmas Day, carrying all their possessions on two tumplines, the young couple set off for their land. Within one month the roof was up and it was time to make the first of the ceremonies to the gods. Musicians were hired; liquor, bread, and meat were bought; and all who had helped with the house were invited, with their wives. The elder was among those who had helped. He led the chanting, the dancing, and the drinking. All night they celebrated, until they fell asleep in drunken stupors. The next day the work on the walls began. Within another two weeks they too were up, and the second ceremony was held. This time Shalik invited his parents, and they came, but they squabbled with his in-laws. Nevertheless the gods were propitiated, the house would be a happy one, the devils would avoid it. That night all slept in the new house, but the hard feelings remained, between parents and son, between brothers.

Today, having found another job as gardener, Shalik stands a handsome young man, well aware of his charm, using many wiles to gain his ends against the mestizos of San Cristobal. Anger, a search for dignity, playing on his handsomeness and charm, an occasional retreat from the pressures of life into the blameless infantilism of drunkenness, and most of all, an overriding fear of gossip, which can turn to panic, are major themes in his life.

Life in Chamula and in the neighboring hamlets is closeknit. The gods must be honored, mostly by good behavior. That which excites the gods, especially envy, may bring accusations of witchcraft; once thought of as a witch your time is marked. If you do not leave the settlement, the warmth and mothering of Chamula, sooner or later you will be murdered. Most flee to the big and unfriendly world of San Cristobal, but Shalik does not want to make this move, or to shake off his family, his friends, his whole supportive world. So he tries to behave in outwardly correct forms and to hide his many departures from the accepted, for the mestizo world, with its many purchasable objects, fascinates him.

He is prone to extremes of mood: elation alternating with depression, fury with joy, humility with the heights of vanity. One should always smile, one should always have happiness in his heart, and Shalik tries to feel that way. Yet there is much sadness in life, and much fear—of gossip, of anger with his parents, of irritations with his wife and employers—and so many a time his eyes become small and bloodshot or yellowed, his words harsh and hostile, and the joking almost desperate in tone. He battles to contain his fury and sometimes almost weeps in desperation. He may seek release in drunkenness. Yet, especially compared with our own older adolescents, he has a realistic picture of his world and has not yet learned to successfully repress all the "improper" emotions; many of his feelings burst out into the open.

Chamula's culture is patriarchal. Authority structures are clearly built and clearly defined. Totik is the principal god, the President of Chamula is the principal priest and secular authority, the father is the ruler of his home (although the mother, being present at all times and responsible for the care of house and children, in actuality is often the dominant person). Authority figures are to be respected and obeyed without question. When a person does not wish to obey, he must be out of the ken of the authority; flight is the most common form of avoidance. When a man has been selected for the Chamula government and chooses not to serve, he flees to the coffee plantations. When a child does not wish to obey his parents, he hides in the forest until he thinks they have forgotten, relented, or gone to sleep. In the presence of authority figures one should be humble and childlike. The most polite tone of voice is that of a child; a person in a formal situation playing the subservient role raises his voice, looks down, and bends over a bit, so that he may appear to be as a child in the eyes of his father.

Shalik handles these authority situations with ease, with a great show of submission and overwhelming modesty, unless his ire has been aroused. Then he becomes rebellious, says hostile things, but stands up for his rights. When facing hostile mestizos in San Cristobal he demands respectful treatment; this is unusual among Indians. Indeed he is one of the few who has learned to deal successfully in both the Indian and mestizo worlds.

What matters to him most today? To work, to earn money, to be able to buy the attractive things of the mestizo world; most of all, to live in peace with the gods and his neighbors.

"The most important thing that has happened to me? When I learned how to work and I was able to work by myself in San Cristobal, and when I went to the hot country with my oldest brother. Yes, to work is the most important thing."

The Chamulas know themselves to be Totik's only true children, and yet since the time of the Spanish Conquest they have introduced into their folk-lore stories of how Indians were born to be humble, to be servants, how it is the mestizo and the Spaniard who use their brains to work, but they are the only ones, while the Indian was made to be a bearer of burdens or a worker with his arms and back. Shalik is an unusually intelligent man, yet when he is drunk he says, "I am stupid. I am ugly. I am dark. I am an Indian."

"You are horrible, you are truly a devil," someone once teased him. "That is your real name, devil."

"No," he laughed, "I am a god." And so he might be, for Shalik becomes Salvador in Spanish—the Savior, the Son, Jesus Christ, and the father of us all, Totik; and so he tries to walk in peace with his gods.

Kathleen Gough

The Origin of the Family

The trouble with the origin of the family is that no one really knows. Since Engels wrote *The Origin of the Family, Private Property and the State* in 1884, a great deal of new evidence has come in. Yet the gaps are still enormous. It is not known *when* the family originated, although it was probably between two million and 100,000 years ago. It is not known whether it developed once or in separate times and places. It is not known whether some kind of embryonic family came before, with, or after the origin of language. Since language is the accepted criterion of humanness, this means that we do not even know whether our ancestors acquired the basics of family life before or after they were human. The chances are that language and the family developed together over a long period, but the evidence is sketchy.

Although the origin of the family is speculative, it is better to speculate with than without evidence. The evidence comes from three sources. One is the social and physical lives of non-human primates—especially the New and Old World monkeys and, still more, the great apes, humanity's closest relatives. The second source is the tools and home sites of prehistoric humans and proto-humans. The third is the family lives of hunters and gatherers of wild provender who have been studied in modern times.

Each of these sources is imperfect: monkeys and apes, because they are *not* pre-human ancestors, although they are our cousins; fossil hominids, because they left so little vestige of their social life; hunters and gatherers, because none of them has, in historic times, possessed a technology and society as primitive as those of early humans. All show the results of long endeavor in specialized, marginal environments. But together, these sources give valuable clues.

Defining the Family

To discuss the origin of something we must first decide what it is. I shall define the family as "a married couple or other group of adult kinsfolk who cooperate economically and in the upbringing of children, and all or most of whom share a common dwelling."

This includes all forms of kin-based household. Some are extended families containing three generations of married brothers or sisters. Some are "grand-

Reprinted from "The Origin of the Family," Journal of Marriage and the Family, Vol. 33, No. 4 (November 1971): 760–71. Reprinted by permission of National Council on Family Relations and author.

families" descended from a single pair of grandparents. Some are matrilineage households, in which brothers and sisters share a house with the sisters' children, and men merely visit their wives in other homes. Some are compound families, in which one man has several wives, or one woman, several husbands. Others are nuclear families composed of a father, mother and children.

Some kind of family exists in all known human societies, although it is not found in every segment or class of all stratified, state societies. Greek and American slaves, for example, were prevented from forming legal families, and their social families were often disrupted by sale, forced labor, or sexual exploitation. Even so, the family was an ideal which all classes and most people attained when they could.

The family implies several other universals. (1) Rules forbid sexual relations and marriage between close relatives. Which relatives are forbidden varies, but all societies forbid mother-son mating, and most, father-daughter and brother-sister. Some societies allow sex relations, but forbid marriage, between certain degrees of kin. (2) The men and women of a family cooperate through a division of labor based on gender. Again, the sexual division of labor varies in rigidity and in the tasks performed. But in no human society to date is it wholly absent. Child-care, household tasks and crafts closely connected with the household, tend to be done by women; war, hunting, and government, by men. (3) Marriage exists as a socially recognized, durable, although not necessarily lifelong relationship between individual men and women. From it springs social fatherhood, some kind of special bond between a man and the child of his wife, whether or not they are his own children physiologically. Even in polyandrous societies, where women have several husbands, or in matrilineal societies, where group membership and property pass through women, each child has one or more designated "fathers" with whom he has a special social, and often religious, relationship. This bond of *social* fatherhood is recognized among people who do not know about the male role in procreation, or where, for various reasons, it is not clear who the physiological father of a particular infant is. Social fatherhood seems to come from the division and interdependence of male and female tasks, especially in relation to children, rather than directly from physiological fatherhood, although in most societies, the social father of a child is usually presumed to be its physiological father as well. Contrary to the beliefs of some feminists, however, I think that in no human society do men, as a whole category, have *only* the role of insemination, and *no* other social or economic role, in relation to women and children. (4) Men in general have higher status and authority over the women of their families, although older women may have influence, even some authority, over junior men. The omnipresence of male authority, too, goes contrary to the belief of some feminists that in "matriarchal" societies, women were either completely equal to, or had paramount authority over, men, either in the home or in society at large.

It is true that in some matrilineal societies, such as the Hopi of Arizona or the Ashanti of Ghana, men exert little authority over their wives. In some, such as the Nayars of South India or the Minangkabau of Sumatra, men may even live separately from their wives and children, that is, in different families. In such societies, however, the fact is that women and children fall under greater or lesser authority from the women's kinsmen—their eldest brothers, mothers' brothers, or even their grown up sons.

In matrilineal societies, where property, rank, office and group membership are inherited through the female line, it is true that women tend to have greater independence than in patrilineal societies. This is especially so in matrilineal tribal societies where the state has not yet developed, and especially in those tribal societies where residence is matrilocal—that is, men come to live in the homes or villages of their wives. Even so, in all matrilineal societies for which adequate descriptions are available, the ultimate headship of households, lineages and local groups is usually with men.[1]

There is in fact no true "matriarchal," as distinct from "matrilineal," society in existence or known from literature, and the chances are that there never has been.[2] This does not mean that women and men have never had relations that were dignified and creative for both sexes, appropriate to the knowledge, skills and technology of their times. Nor does it mean that the sexes cannot be equal in the future, or that the sexual division of labor cannot be abolished. I believe that it can and must be. But it is not necessary to believe myths of a feminist Golden Age in order to plan for parity in the future.

Primate Societies

Within the primate order, humans are most closely related to the anthropoid apes (the African chimpanzee and gorilla and the Southeast Asian orangutan and gibbon), and of these, to the chimpanzee and the gorilla. More distantly related are the Old, and then the New World, monkeys, and finally, the lemurs, tarsiers and tree-shrews.

All primates share characteristics without which the family could not have developed. The young are born relatively helpless. They suckle for several months or years and need prolonged care afterwards. Childhood is longer, the closer the species is to humans. Most monkeys reach puberty at about four to five and mature socially between about five and ten. Chimpanzees, by contrast, suckle for up to three years. Females reach puberty at seven to ten; males enter

[1] See David M. Schneider and Kathleen Gough, eds., *Matrilineal Kinship*, Berkeley, 1961, for common and variant features of matrilineal systems.

[2] The Iroquois are often quoted as a "matriarchal" society, but in fact Morgan himself refers to "the absence of equality between the sexes" and notes that women were subordinate to men, ate after men, and that women (not men) were publicly whipped as punishment for adultery. Warleaders, tribal chiefs, and *sachems* (heads of matrilineal lineages) were men. Women did, however, have a large say in the government of the longhouse or home of the matrilocal extended family, and women figured as tribal counsellors and religious officials, as well as arranging marriages. (Lewis H. Morgan: The League of the *Ho-de-ne Saunee or Iroquois*, Human Relations Area Files, 1954.)

mature social and sexual relations as late as thirteen. The long childhood and maternal care produce close relations between children of the same mother, who play together and help tend their juniors until they grow up.

Monkeys and apes, like humans, mate in all months of the year instead of in a rutting season. Unlike humans, however, female apes experience unusually strong sexual desire for a few days shortly before and during ovulation (the oestrus period), and have intensive sexual relations at that time. The males are attracted to the females by their scent or by brightly colored swellings in the sexual region. Oestrus-mating appears to be especially pronounced in primate species more remote from humans. The apes and some monkeys carry on less intensive, month-round sexuality in addition to oestrus-mating, approaching human patterns more closely. In humans, sexual desires and relations are regulated less by hormonal changes and more by mental images, emotions, cultural rules and individual preferences.

Year-round (if not always month-round) sexuality means that males and females socialize more continuously among primates than among most other mammals. All primates form bands or troops composed of both sexes plus children. The numbers and proportions of the sexes vary, and in some species an individual, a mother with her young, or a subsidiary troop of male juveniles may travel temporarily alone. But in general, males and females socialize continually through mutual grooming [3] and playing as well as through frequent sex relations. Keeping close to the females, primate males play with their children and tend to protect both females and young from predators. A "division of labor" based on gender is thus already found in primate society between a female role of prolonged child care and a male role of defense. Males may also carry or take care of children briefly, and non-nursing females may fight. But a kind of generalized "fatherliness" appears in the protective role of adult males towards young, even in species where the sexes do not form long-term individual attachments.

Sexual Bonds Among Primates

Some non-human primates do have enduring sexual bonds and restrictions, superficially similar to those in some human societies. Among gibbons a single male and female live together with their young. The male drives off other males and the female, other females. When a juvenile reaches puberty it is thought to leave or be expelled by the parent of the same sex, and he eventually finds a mate elsewhere. Similar de facto, rudimentary "incest prohibitions" may have been passed on to humans from their prehuman ancestors and later codified and elaborated through language, moral custom and law. Whether this is so may become clearer when we know more about the mating patterns of the other great apes, especially of our closest relatives, the chim-

[3] Combing the hair and removing parasites with hands or teeth.

panzees. Present evidence suggests that male chimpanzees do not mate with their mothers.

Orang-utans live in small, tree-dwelling groups like gibbons, but their forms are less regular. One or two mothers may wander alone with their young; mating at intervals with a male; or a male-female pair, or several juvenile males, may travel together.

Among mountain gorillas of Uganda, South Indian langurs, and hamadryas baboons of Ethiopia, a single, fully mature male mates with several females, especially in their oestrus periods. If younger adult males are present, the females may have occasional relations with them if the leader is tired or not looking.

Among East and South African baboons, rhesus macaques, and South American woolly monkeys, the troop is bigger, numbering up to two hundred. It contains a number of adult males and a much larger number of females. The males are strictly ranked in terms of dominance based on both physical strength and intelligence. The more dominant males copulate intensively with the females during the latters' oestrus periods. Toward the end of oestrus a female may briefly attach herself to a single dominant male. At other times she may have relations with any male of higher or lower rank provided that those of higher rank permit it.

Among some baboons and macaques the young males travel on the outskirts of the group and have little access to females. Some macaques expel from the troop a proportion of the young males, who then form "bachelor troops." Bachelors may later form new troops with young females.

Other primates are more thoroughly promiscuous, or rather indiscriminate, in mating. Chimpanzees, and also South American howler monkeys, live in loosely structured groups, again (as in most monkey and ape societies) with a preponderance of females. The mother-child unit is the only stable group. The sexes copulate almost at random, and most intensively and indiscriminately during oestrus.

A number of well known anthropologists have argued that various attitudes and customs often found in human societies are instinctual rather than culturally learned, and come from our primate heritage. They include hierarchies of ranking among men, male political power over women, and the greater tendency of men to form friendships with one another, as opposed to women's tendencies to cling to a man.[4]

I cannot accept these conclusions and think that they stem from the male chauvinism of our own society. A "scientific" argument which states that all such features of female inferiority are instinctive is obviously a powerful weapon in maintaining the traditional family with male dominance. But in fact, these features are *not* universal among non-human primates, including some of those most closely related to humans. Chimpanzees have a low degree

[4] See, for example, Desmond Morris, The Naked Ape, Jonathan Cape, 1967; Robin Fox, Kinship and Marriage, Pelican Books, 1967.

of male dominance and male hierarchy and are sexually virtually indiscriminate. Gibbons have a kind of fidelity for both sexes and almost no male dominance or hierarchy. Howler monkeys are sexually indiscriminate and lack male hierarchies or dominance.

The fact is that among non-human primates male dominance and male hierarchies seem to be adaptations to particular environments, some of which did become genetically established through natural selection. Among humans, however, these features are present in variable degrees and are almost certainly learned, not inherited at all. Among non-human primates there are fairly general differences between those that live mainly in trees and those that live largely on the ground. The tree dwellers (for example, gibbons, orang-utans, South American howler and woolly monkeys) tend to have to defend themselves less against predators than do the ground-dwellers (such as baboons, macaques or gorillas). Where defense is important, males are much larger and stronger than females, exert dominance over females, and are strictly hierarchized and organized in relation to one another. Where defense is less important there is much less sexual dimorphism (difference in size between male and female), less or no male dominance, a less pronounced male hierarchy, and greater sexual indiscriminacy.

Comparatively speaking, humans have a rather small degree of sexual dimorphism, similar to chimpanzees. Chimpanzees live much in trees but also partly on the ground, in forest or semi-forest habitats. They build individual nests to sleep in, sometimes on the ground but usually in trees. They flee into trees from danger. Chimpanzees go mainly on all fours, but sometimes on two feet, and can use and make simple tools. Males are dominant, but not very dominant, over females. The rank hierarchy among males is unstable, and males often move between groups, which vary in size from two to fifty individuals. Food is vegetarian, supplemented with worms, grubs or occasional small animals. A mother and her young form the only stable unit. Sexual relations are largely indiscriminate, but nearby males defend young animals from danger. The chances are that our pre-human ancestors had a similar social life. Morgan and Engels were probably right in concluding that we came from a state of "original promiscuity" before we were fully human.

Judging from the fossil record, apes ancestral to humans, gorillas and chimpanzees roamed widely in Asia, Europe and Africa some twelve to twenty-eight million years ago. Toward the end of that period (the Miocene) one appears in North India and East Africa, Ramapithecus, who may be ancestral both to later hominids and to modern humans. His species were small like gibbons, walked upright on two feet, had human rather than ape corner-teeth, and therefore probably used hands rather than teeth to tear their food. From that time evolution toward humanness must have proceeded through various phases until the emergence of modern *Homo sapiens*, about 70,000 years ago.

In the Miocene period before Ramapithecus appeared, there were several time-spans in which, over large areas, the climate became dryer and sub-tropical forests dwindled or disappeared. A standard reconstruction of events, which I accept, is that groups of apes, probably in Africa, had to come down from the trees and adapt to terrestrial life. Through natural selection, probably over millions of years, they developed specialized feet for walking. Thus freed, the hands came to be used not only (as among apes) for grasping and tearing, but for regular carrying of objects such as weapons (which had hitherto been sporadic) or of infants (which had hitherto clung to their mothers' body hair).

The spread of indigestible grasses on the open savannahs may have encouraged, if it did not compel, the early ground dwellers to become active hunters rather than simply to forage for small, sick or dead animals that came their way. Collective hunting and tool use involved group cooperation and helped foster the growth of language out of the call-systems of apes. Language meant the use of symbols to refer to events not present. It allowed greatly increased foresight, memory, planning and division of tasks—in short, the capacity for human thought.

With the change to hunting, group territories became much larger. Apes range only a few thousand feet daily; hunters, several miles. But because their infants were helpless, nursing women could hunt only small game close to home. This then produced the sexual division of labor on which the human family has since been founded. Women elaborated upon ape methods of child care, and greatly expanded foraging, which in most areas remained the primary and most stable source of food. Men improved upon ape methods of fighting off other animals, and of group protection in general. They adapted these methods to hunting, using weapons which for millennia remained the same for the chase as for human warfare.

Out of the sexual division of labor came, for the first time, home life as well as group cooperation. Female apes nest with and provide foraged food for their infants. But adult apes do not cooperate in food getting or nest building. They build new nests each night wherever they may happen to be. With the development of a hunting-gathering complex, it became necessary to have a G.H.Q., or home. Men could bring meat to this place for several days' supply. Women and children could meet men there after the day's hunting, and could bring their vegetable produce for general consumption. Men, women and children could build joint shelters, butcher meat, and treat skins for clothing.

Later, fire came into use for protection against wild animals, for lighting, and eventually for cooking. The hearth then provided the focus and symbol of home. With the development of cookery, some humans—chiefly women, and perhaps some children and old men—came to spend more time preparing nutrition so that all people need speed less time in chewing and tearing their food. Meals—already less frequent because of the change to a carnivorous diet—now became brief, periodic events instead of the long feeding sessions of apes.

The change to humanness brought two bodily changes that affected birth and child care. These were head-size and width of the pelvis. Walking upright produced a narrower pelvis to hold the guts in position. Yet as language developed, brains and hence heads grew much bigger relative to body size. To compensate, humans are born at an earlier stage of growth than apes. They are helpless longer and require longer and more total care. This in turn caused early women to concentrate more on child care and less on defense than do female apes.

Language made possible not only a division and cooperation in labor but also all forms of tradition, rules, morality and cultural learning. Rules banning sex relations among close kinfolk must have come very early. Precisely how or why they developed is unknown, but they had at least two useful functions. They helped to preserve order in the family as a cooperative unit, by outlawing competition for mates. They also created bonds *between* families, or even between separate bands, and so provided a basis for wider cooperation in the struggle for livelihood and the expansion of knowledge.

It is not clear when all these changes took place. Climatic change with increased drought began regionally up to 28 million years ago. The divergence between pre-human and gorilla-chimpanzee stems had occurred in both Africa and India at least 12 million years ago. The pre-human stem led to the Australopithecines of East and South Africa, about 3,000,000 years ago. These were pygmy-like, two footed, upright hominids with larger than ape brains, who made tools and probably hunted in savannah regions. It is unlikely that they knew the use of fire.

The first known use of fire is that of cave-dwelling hominids (Sinanthropus, a branch of the Pithecanthropines) at Choukoutien near Peking, some half a million years ago during the second ice age. Fire was used regularly in hearths, suggesting cookery, by the time of the Acheulean and Mousterian cultures of Neanderthal man in Europe, Africa and Asia before, during and after the third ice age, some 150,000 to 100,000 years ago. These people, too, were often cave dwellers, and buried their dead ceremonially in caves. Cave dwelling by night as well as by day was probably, in fact, not safe for humans until fire came into use to drive away predators.

Most anthropologists conclude that home life, the family and language had developed by the time of Neanderthal man, who was closely similar and may have been ancestral to modern *Homo sapiens*. At least two anthropologists, however, believe that the Australopithecenes already had language nearly two million years ago, while another thinks that language and incest prohibitions did not evolve until the time of *Homo sapiens* some 70,000 to 50,000 years ago.[5] I am myself inclined to think that family life built around tool use, the use of language, cookery, and a sexual division of labor, must have been established sometime between about 500,000 and 200,000 years ago.

[5] For the former view, see Charles F. Hockett and Robert Ascher, "The Human Revolution," in *Man in Adaptation: The Biosocial Background*, edited by Yehudi A. Cohen, Aldine, 1968; for the latter, Frank B. Livingstone, "Genetics, Ecology and the Origin of Incest and Exogamy," *Current Anthropology*, February 1969.

Hunters and Gatherers

Most of the hunting and gathering societies studied in the eighteenth to twentieth centuries had technologies similar to those that were wide-spread in the Mesolithic period, which occured about 15,000 to 10,000 years ago, after the ice ages ended but before cultivation was invented and animals domesticated.

Modern hunters live in marginal forest, mountain, arctic or desert environments where cultivation is impracticable. Although by no means "primeval," the hunters of recent times do offer clues to the types of family found during that 99 percent of human history before the agricultural revolution. They include the Eskimo, many Canadian and South American Indian groups, the forest BaMbuti (pygmies) and the desert Bushmen of Southern Africa, the Kadar of South India, the Veddah of Ceylon, and the Andaman Islanders of the Indian Ocean. About 175 hunting and gathering cultures in Oceania, Asia, Africa and America have been described in fair detail.

In spite of their varied environments, hunters share certain features of social life. They live in bands of about 20 to 200 people, the majority of bands having fewer than 50. Bands are divided into families, which may forage alone in some seasons. Hunters have simple but ingenious technologies. Bows and arrows, spears, needles, skin clothing, and temporary leaf or wood shelters are common. Most hunters do some fishing. The band forages and hunts in a large territory and usually moves camp often.

Social life is egalitarian. There is of course no state, no organized government. Apart from religious shamans or magicians, the division of labor is based only on sex and age. Resources are owned communally; tools and personal possessions are freely exchanged. Everyone works who can. Band leadership goes to whichever man has the intelligence, courage and foresight to command the respect of his fellows. Intelligent older women are also looked up to.

The household is the main unit of economic cooperation, with the men, women and children dividing the labor and pooling their produce. In 97 percent of the 175 societies classified by G. P. Murdock, hunting is confined to men; in the other three percent it is chiefly a male pursuit. Gathering of wild plants, fruits and nuts is women's work. In 60 percent of societies, only women gather, while in another 32 percent gathering is mainly feminine. Fishing is solely or mainly men's work in 93 percent of the hunting societies where it occurs.

For the rest, men monopolize fighting, although interband warfare is rare. Women tend children and shelters and usually do most of the cooking, processing, and storage of food. Women tend, also, to be foremost in the early household crafts such as basketry, leather work, the making of skin or bark clothing, and in the more advanced hunting societies, pottery. (Considering that women probably *invented* all of these crafts, in addition to cookery, food storage and preservation, agriculture, spinning, weaving, and perhaps even house construction, it is clear that women played quite as important roles as men in early cultural development.) Building dwellings and making tools and ornaments are variously divided between the sexes, while boat-building is largely done by men. Girls help the women, and boys play at hunting or hunt small game until they reach puberty, when both take on the roles of adults. Where the environment makes it desirable, the men of a whole band or of some smaller cluster of households cooperate in hunting or fishing and divide their spoils. Women of nearby families often go gathering together.

Family composition varies among hunters as it does in other kinds of societies. About half or more of known hunting societies have nuclear families (father, mother and children), with polygynous households (a man, two or more wives, and children) as occasional variants. Clearly, nuclear families are the most common among hunters, although hunters have a slightly higher proportion of polygynous families than do non-hunting societies.

About a third of hunting societies contain some "stem-family" households —that is, older parents live together with one married child and grandchildren, while the other married children live in independent dwellings. A still smaller proportion live in large extended families containing several married brothers (or several married sisters), their spouses, and children.[6] Hunters have fewer extended and stem families than do non-hunting societies. These larger households become common with the rise of agriculture. They are especially found in large, pre-industrial agrarian states such as ancient Greece, Rome, India, the Islamic empires, China, etc.

Hunting societies also have few households composed of a widow or divorcee and her children. This is understandable, for neither men nor women can survive long without the work and produce of the other sex, and marriage is the way to obtain them. That is why so often young men must show proof of hunting prowess, and girls of cooking, before they are allowed to marry.

The family, together with territorial grouping, provides the framework of society among hunters. Indeed, as Morgan and Engels clearly saw, kinship and territory are the foundations of all societies before the rise of the state. Not only hunting and gathering bands, but the larger and more complex tribes and chiefdoms of primitive cultivators and herders organize people through descent from common ancestors or through marriage ties between groups. Among hunters, things are simple. There is only the family, and beyond it the band. With the domestication of plants and animals, the economy becomes more productive. More people can live together. Tribes form, containing several thousand people loosely organized into large kin-

[6] For exact figures, see G. P. Murdock, World Ethnographic Sample, *American Anthropologist*, 1957; Allan D. Coult, *Cross Tabulations of Murdock's World Ethnographic Sample*, University of Missouri, 1965; and G. P. Murdock, *Ethnographic Atlas*, University of Pittsburgh, 1967. In the last-named survey, out of 175 hunting societies, 47 percent had nuclear family households, 38 percent had stem-families, and 14 percent had extended families.

groups such as clans and lineages, each composed of a number of related families. With still further development of the productive forces the society throws up a central political leadership, together with craft specialization and trade, and so the chiefdom emerges. But this, too, is structured through ranked allegiances and marriage ties between kin groups.

Only with the rise of the state does class, independently of kinship, provide the basis for relations of production, distribution and power. Even then, kin groups remain large in the agrarian state and kinship persists as the prime organizing principle within each class until the rise of capitalism. The reduction in significance of the family that we see today is the outgrowth of a decline in the importance of "familism" relative to other institutions, that began with the rise of the state, but became speeded up with the development of capitalism and machine industry. In most modern socialist societies, the family is even less significant as an organizing principle. It is reasonable to suppose that in the future it will become minimal or may disappear at least as a legally constituted unit for exclusive forms of sexual and economic cooperation and of child-care.

Morgan and Engels (1942) thought that from a state of original promiscuity, early humans at first banned sex relations between the generations of parents and children, but continued to allow them indiscriminately between brothers, sisters and all kinds of cousins within the band. They called this the "consanguineal family." They thought that later, all mating within the family or some larger kin group became forbidden, but that there was a stage (the "punaluan") in which a group of sisters or other close kinswomen from one band were married jointly to a group of brothers or other close kinsmen from another. They thought that only later still, and especially with the domestication of plants and animals, did the "pairing family" develop in which each man was married to one or two women individually.

These writers drew their conclusions not from evidence of actual group-marriage among primitive peoples but from the kinship terms found today in certain tribal and chiefly societies. Some of these equate all kin of the same sex in the parents' generation, suggesting brother-sister marriage. Others equate the father's brother with the father, and the mother's sisters with the mother, suggesting the marriage of a group of brothers with a group of sisters.

Modern evidence does not bear out these conclusions about early society. All known hunters and gatherers live in families, not in communal sexual arrangements. Most hunters even live in nuclear families rather than in large extended kin groups. Mating is individualized, although one man may occasionally have two wives, or (very rarely) a woman may have two husbands. Economic life is built primarily around the division of labor and partnership between individual men and women. The hearths, caves and other remains of Upper Paleolithic hunters suggest that this was probably an early arrangement. We cannot say that Engels' sequences are completely ruled out for very early hominids—the evidence is simply not available. But it is hard to see what economic arrangements among hunters would give rise to group, rather than individual or "pairing" marriage arrangements, and this Engels does not explain.

Soviet anthropologists continued to believe in Morgan and Engels' early "stages" longer than did anthropologists in the West. Today, most Russian anthropologists admit the lack of evidence for "consanguineal" and "puna-luan" arrangements, but some still believe that a different kind of group marriage intervened between indiscriminate mating and the pairing family. Semyonov, for example, argues that in the stage of group marriage, mating was forbidden within the hunting band, but that the men of two neighboring bands had multiple, visiting sex relations with women of the opposite band.[7]

While such an arrangement cannot be ruled out, it seems unlikely because many of the customs which Semyonov regards as "survivals" of such group marriage (for example, visiting husbands, matrilineage dwelling groups, widespread clans, multiple spouses for both sexes, men's and women's communal houses, and prohibitions of sexual intercourse inside the huts of the village) are actually found not so much among hunters as among horticultural tribes, and even, quite complex agricultural states. Whether or not such a stage of group-marriage occurred in the earliest societies, there seems little doubt that pairing marriage (involving family households) came about with the development of elaborate methods of hunting, cooking, and the preparation of clothing and shelters—that is, with a fully-fledged division of labor.

Even so, there *are* some senses in which mating among hunters has more of a group character than in archaic agrarian states or in capitalist society. Murdock's sample shows that sex relations before marriage are strictly prohibited in only 26 percent of hunting societies. In the rest, marriage is either arranged so early that pre-marital sex is unlikely, or (more usually) sex relations are permitted more or less freely before marriage.

With marriage, monogamy is the normal *practice* at any given time for most hunters, but it is not the normal *rule*. Only 19 percent in Murdock's survey prohibit plural unions. Where polygyny is found (79 percent) the most common type is for a man to marry two sisters or other closely related women of the same kin group—for example, the daughters of two sisters or of two brothers. When a woman dies it is common for a sister to replace her in the marriage, and when a man dies, for a brother to replace him.

Similarly, many hunting societies hold that the wives of brothers or other close kinsmen are in some senses wives of the group. They can be called on in emergencies or if one of them is ill. Again, many hunting societies have special times for sexual license between men and women of a local group who are not married to each other, such as the "lights out" games of Eskimo sharing a communal snowhouse. In other situations, an Eskimo wife will spend the night with a chance guest of her husband's. All parties expect this as normal hospitality. Finally, adultery, although often punished, tends to be common

---

[7] Y. I. Semyonov, "Group Marriage, its Nature and Role in the Evolution of Marriage and Family Relations," *Seventh International Congress of Anthropological and Ethnological Sciences*, Volume IV, Moscow 1967.

in hunting societies, and few if any of them forbid divorce or the remarriage of divorcees and widows.

The reason for all this seems to be that marriage and sexual restrictions are practical arrangements among hunters designed mainly to serve economic and survival needs. In these societies, some kind of rather stable pairing best accomplishes the division of labor and cooperation of men and women and the care of children. Beyond the immediate family, either a larger family group or the whole band has other, less intensive but important, kinds of cooperative activities. Therefore, the husbands and wives of individuals within that group can be summoned to stand in for each other if need arises. In the case of Eskimo wife-lending, the extreme climate and the need for lone wandering in search of game dictate high standards of hospitality. This evidently becomes extended to sexual sharing.

In the case of sororal polygyny or marriage to the dead wife's sister, it is natural that when two women fill the same role—either together or in sequence—they should be sisters, for sisters are more alike than other women. They are likely to care more for each other's children. The replacement of a dead spouse by a sister or a brother also preserves existing intergroup relations. For the rest, where the economic and survival bonds of marriage are not at stake, people can afford to be freely companionate and tolerant. Hence premarital sexual freedom, seasonal group-license, and a pragmatic approach to adultery.

Marriages among hunters are usually arranged by elders when a young couple are ready for adult responsibilities. But the couple know each other and usually have some choice. If the first marriage does not work, the second mate will almost certainly be self selected. Both sexual and companionate love between individual men and women are known and are deeply experienced. With comparative freedom of mating, love is less often separated from or opposed to marriage than in archaic states or even than in some modern nations.

The Position of Women

Even in hunting societies it seems that women are always in some sense the "second sex," with greater or less subordination to men. This varies. Eskimo and Australian aboriginal women are far more subordinate than women among the Kadar, the Andamanese or the Congo Pygmies—all forest people.

I suggest that women have greater power and independence among hunters when they are important food-obtainers than when they are mainly processors of meat or other supplies provided by men. The former situation is likelier to exist in societies where hunting is small-scale and intensive than where it is extensive over a large terrain, and in societies where gathering is important by comparison with hunting.

In general in hunting societies, however, women are less subordinated in certain crucial respects than they are in most, if not all, of the archaic states, or even in some capitalist nations. These respects include men's ability to deny women sexuality or to force it upon them; to command or exploit their labor or to control their produce; to control or rob them of their children; to confine them physically and prevent their movement; to use them as objects in male transactions; to cramp their creativeness; or to withhold from them large areas of the society's knowledge and cultural attainments.

Especially lacking in hunting societies is the kind of male possessiveness and exclusiveness regarding women that leads to such institutions as savage punishments or death for female adultery, the jealous guarding of female chastity and virginity, the denial of divorce to women, or the ban on a woman's remarriage after her husband's death.

For these reasons, I do not think we can speak, as some writers do, of a class-division between men and women in hunting societies. True, men are more mobile than women and they lead in public affairs. But class society requires that one class control the means of production, dictate its use by the other classes, and expropriate the surplus. These conditions do not exist among hunters. Land and other resources are held communally, although women may monopolize certain gathering areas, and men, their hunting grounds. There is rank difference, role difference, and some difference respecting degrees of authority, between the sexes, but there is reciprocity rather than domination or exploitation.

As Engels saw, the power of men to exploit women systematically springs from the existence of surplus wealth, and more directly, from the state, social stratification, and the control of property by men. With the rise of the state, because of their monopoly over weapons, and because freedom from child care allows them to enter specialized economic and political roles, some men—especially ruling class men—acquire power over other men and over women. Almost all men acquire it over women of their own or lower classes, especially within their own kinship groups. These kinds of male power are shadowy among hunters.

To the extent that men *have* power over women in hunting societies, this seems to spring from the male monopoly of heavy weapons, from the particular division of labor between the sexes, or from both. Although men seldom use weapons against women, they *possess* them (or possess superior weapons) in addition to their physical strength. This does give men an ultimate control of force. When old people or babies must be killed to ensure band or family survival, it is usually men who kill them. Infanticide—rather common among hunters, who must limit the mouths to feed—is more often female infanticide than male.

The hunting of men seems more often to require them to organize in groups than does the work of women. Perhaps because of this, about 60 percent of hunting societies have predominantly virilocal residence. That is, men choose which band to live in (often, their fathers'), and women move with their husbands. This gives a man advantages over his wife in terms of familiarity and loyalties, for the wife is often a stranger. Sixteen to 17 percent of hunting societies are, however, uxorilocal, with men moving to households of their wives, while 15 to 17 percent are bilocal—that is, either sex may move in with the other on marriage.

Probably because of male cooperation in defense and hunting, men are more prominent in band councils and leadership, in medicine and magic, and in public rituals designed to increase game, to ward off sickness, or to initiate boys into manhood. Women do, however, often take part in band councils; they are not excluded from law and government as in many agrarian states. Some women are respected as wise leaders, story tellers, doctors, or magicians, or are feared as witches. Women have their own ceremonies of fertility, birth and healing, from which men are often excluded.

In some societies, although men control the most sacred objects, women are believed to have discovered them. Among the Congo Pygmies, religion centers about a beneficient spirit, the Animal of the Forest. It is represented by wooden trumpets that are owned and played by men. Their possession and use are hidden from the women and they are played at night when hunting is bad, someone falls ill, or death occurs. During the playing men dance in the public campfire, which is sacred and is associated with the forest. Yet the men believe that women originally owned the trumpet and that it was a women who stole fire from the chimpanzees or from the forest spirit. When a woman has failed to bear children for several years, a special ceremony is held. Women lead in the songs that usually accompany the trumpets, and an old woman kicks apart the campfire. Temporary female dominance seems to be thought necessary to restore fertility.

In some hunting societies women are exchanged between local groups, which are thus knit together through marriages. Sometimes, men of different bands directly exchange their sisters. More often there is a generalized exchange of women between two or more groups, or a one-way movement of women within a circle of groups. Sometimes the husband's family pays weapons, tools or ornaments to the wife's in return for the wife's services and later, her children.

In such societies, although they may be well treated and their consent sought, women are clearly the moveable partners in an arrangement controlled by men. Male anthropologists have seized on this as evidence of original male dominance and patrilocal residence. Fox and others, for example, have argued that until recently, *all* hunting societies formed out-marrying patrilocal bands, linked together politically by the exchange of women. The fact that fewer than two-thirds of hunting societies are patrilocal today, and only 41 percent have band-exogamy, is explained in terms of modern conquest, economic change and depopulation.

I cannot accept this formula. It is true that modern hunting societies have been severely changed, de-culturated, and often depopulated, by capitalist imperalism. I can see little evidence, however, that the ones that are patrilocal today have undergone less change than those that are not. It is hard to believe that in spite of enormous environmental diversity and the passage of thousands, perhaps millions, of years, hunting societies all had band exogamy with patrilocal residence until they were disturbed by western imperialism. It is more likely that early band societies, like later agricultural tribes, developed variety in family life and the status of women as they spread over the earth.

There is also some likelihood that the earliest hunters had matrilocal rather than patrilocal families. Among apes and monkeys, it is almost always males who leave the troop or are driven out. Females stay closer to their mothers and their original site; males move about, attaching themselves to females where availability and competition permit. Removal of the wife to the husband's home or band may have been a relatively late development in societies where male cooperation in hunting assumed overwhelming importance.[8] Conversely, after the development of horticulture (which was probably invented and is mainly carried out by women), those tribes in which horticulture predominated over stock raising were most likely to be or to remain matrilocal and to develop matrilineal descent groups with a relatively high status of women. But where extensive hunting of large animals, or later, the herding of large domesticates, predominated, patrilocal residence flourished and women were used to form alliances between male-centered groups. With the invention of metallurgy and of agriculture as distinct from horticulture after 4000 B.C., men came to control agriculture and many crafts, and most of the great agrarian states had patrilocal residence with patriarchal, male-dominant families.

Conclusions

The family is a human institution, not found in its totality in any pre-human species. It required language, planning, cooperation, self-control, foresight and cultural learning, and probably developed along with these.

The family was made desirable by the early human combination of prolonged child care with the need for hunting with weapons over large terrains. The sexual division of labor on which it was based grew out of a rudimentary pre-human division between male defense and female child care. But among humans this sexual division of functions for the first time became crucial for food production and so laid the basis for future economic specialization and cooperation.

Morgan and Engels were probably right in thinking that the human family was preceded by sexual indiscriminacy. They were also right in seeing an

---

[8] Upper Paleolithic hunters produced female figurines that were obvious emblems of fertility. The cult continued through the Mesolithic and into the Neolithic period. Goddesses and spirits of fertility are found in some patrilineal as well as matrilineal societies, but they tend to be more prominent in the latter. It is thus possible that in many areas even late Stone Age hunters had matrilocal residence and perhaps matrilineal descent, and that in some regions this pattern continued through the age of horticulture and even—as in the case of the Nayars of Kerala and the Minangkabau of Sumatra—into the age of plow agriculture, of writing, and of the small-scale state.

egalitarian group-quality about early economic and marriage arrangements. They were without evidence, however, in believing that the earliest mating and economic patterns were entirely group relations.

Together with tool use and language, the family was no doubt the most significant invention of the human revolution. All three required reflective thought, which above all accounts for the vast superiority in consciousness that separates humans from apes.

The family provided the framework for all pre-state society and the fount of its creativeness. In groping for survival and for knowledge, human beings learned to control their sexual desires and to suppress their individual selfishness, aggression and competition. The other side of this self-control was an increased capacity for love—not only the love of a mother for her child, which is seen among apes, but of male for female in .enduring relationships, and of each sex for ever widening groups of humans. Civilization would have been impossible without this initial self-control, seen in incest prohibitions and in the generosity and moral orderliness of primitive family life.

From the start, women have been subordinate to men in certain key areas of status, mobility and public leadership. But before the agricultural revolution, and even for several thousands of years thereafter, the inequality was based chiefly on the unalterable fact of long child care combined with the exigencies of primitive technology. The extent of inequality varied according to the ecology and the resulting sexual division of tasks. But in any case it was largely a matter of survival rather than of man-made cultural impositions. Hence the impressions we receive of dignity, freedom and mutual respect between men and women in primitive hunting and horticultural societies. This is true whether these societies are patrilocal, bilocal, or matrilocal, although matrilocal societies, with matrilineal inheritance, offer greater freedom to women than do patrilocal and patrilineal societies of the same level of productivity and political development.

A distinct change occurred with the growth of individual and family property in herds, in durable craft objects and trade objects, and in stable, irrigated farm-sites or other forms of heritable wealth. This crystallized in the rise of the state, about 4000 B.C. With the growth of class society and of male dominance in the ruling class of the state, women's subordination in- creased, and eventually reached its depths in the patriarchal families of the great agrarian states.

Knowledge of how the family arose is interesting to women because it tells us how we differ from pre-humans, what our past has been, and what have been the biological and cultural limitations from which we are emerging. It shows us how generations of male scholars have distorted or over-interpreted the evidence to bolster beliefs in the inferiority of women's mental processes— for which there is no foundation in fact. Knowing about early families is also important to correct a reverse bias among some feminist writers, who hold that in "matriarchal" societies women were completely equal with or were even dominant over men. For this, too, there seems to be no basis in evidence.

The past of the family does not limit its future. Although the family probably emerged with humanity, neither the family itself nor particular family forms are genetically determined. The sexual division of labor—until recently, universal—need not, and in my opinion should not, survive in industrial society. Prolonged child care ceases to be a basis for female subordination when artificial birth control, spaced births, small families, patent feeding and communal nurseries allow it to be shared by men. Automation and cybernation remove most of the heavy work for which women are less well equipped than men. The exploitation of women that came with the rise of the state and of class society will presumably disappear in post-state, classless society—for which the technological and scientific basis already exists.

The family was essential to the dawn of civilization, allowing a vast qualitative leap forward in cooperation, purposive knowledge, love, and creativeness. But today, rather than enhancing them, the confinement of women in homes and small families—like their subordination in work—artificially limits these human capacities. It may be that the human gift for personal love will make some form of voluntary, long-term mating and of individual devotion between parents and children continue indefinitely, side by side with public responsibility for domestic tasks and for the care and upbringing of children. There is no need to legislate personal relations out of existence. But neither need we fear a social life in which the family is no more.

References

Coult, Allan D. (1965) Cross Tabulations of Murdock's World Ethnographic Sample. University of Missouri.

Fox, Robin (1967) Kinship and Marriage. London: Pelican Books.

Hockett, Charles F., and Robert Ascher (1968) The Human Revolution. In Man in Adaptation: The Biosocial Background, Yehudi A. Cohen (ed.). Chicago: Aldine.

Livingstone, Frank B. (1969) "Genetics, ecology and the origin of incest and exogamy." Current Anthropology (February).

Morris, Desmond (1967) The Naked Ape. Jonathan Cape.

Murdock, G. P. (1957) World Ethnographic Sample, American Anthropologist.

——— (1967) Ethnographic Atlas. University of Pittsburgh.

Schneider, David M., and Kathleen Gough (1961) Matrilineal Kinship. Berkeley: University of California Press.

Semyonov, Y. I. (1967) "Group marriage, its nature and role in the evolution of marriage and family relations." In Seventh International Congress of Anthropological and Ethnological Sciences. Vol. IV. Moscow.

David Jacobson

Mbale Social Classes

Africans in Mbale confine their friendships to their separate social worlds. The boundaries of these worlds, therefore, provide a context for the analysis of friendship behavior. Of these boundaries, the most important is that of social class, which is evident both in what people say and in what they do. The values, beliefs, and norms about social stratification, as well as the behavior of the upper-class Africans separate them from lower-class Africans and are consistent with the socio-economic differences that divide these two groups.

A Folk Model of Social Classes

Elite Africans talk about two classes of African townsmen. They label these classes in different ways: "higher" or "upper class" and "lower class," the "educated" and the "uneducated," the "big people" and the "porters," and they describe them in interactional terms. The statements of upper-class informants illustrate their beliefs about the separation between the classes:

There are classes in Mbale, but they don't mix. The lower-class man moves with his own people, his fellow tribesmen, and he fights with others. Upper-class men, the educated people, speak English, so they can get together, regardless of their tribes.

People go with people from their own level. The villagers and housing-estate people couldn't move with people in the senior quarters. They couldn't keep up with them when it came to giving parties or going to bars.

These comments conceptualize differences in life-style and leisure-time behavior which elite Africans believe characterize the two classes. Furthermore, they indicate which socio-economic attributes elite Africans think sepa.ate them from other Africans in Mbale.

Of these different attributes, upper-class Africans attach special significance to formal education. It provides an idiom in which they distinguish themselves from "uneducated" non-elite Africans. In their view it also legitimates elite status, which becomes apparent where there is an inconsistency between upper-class status and educational achievement. As one informant suggested:

From David Jacobson, Itinerant Townsmen: Friendship and Social Order in Urban Uganda, "Social Classes," pp. 38–55, copyright © 1973, Cummings Publishing Company, Inc., Menlo Park, California.

Those in the [government's] higher salary scale are upper class. But you have people in that class who are not well educated. There are some police officers who have only a junior secondary school education, and they don't fit.

The importance of education as a basis of legitimacy is further evident in another informant's interpretation of what he describes as a discrepancy between superior education and subordinate position:

The upper class are those with big jobs in the government, all regional and district officers. The junior officers are often better educated than some of the senior officers, but get less money. It doesn't seem right.

Their views reinforce one another. One believes that wealth ought to be accompanied by high educational achievement, the other, that a superior education ought to insure a higher ranking position and greater wealth.

The discrepancies which some men resent follow from the fact that they are essentially a "new" elite. They hold senior positions in the bureaucracies of government, in which recruitment and advancement are based largely on high educational qualification. Most of these jobs first became available to Africans in the late 1950's and early 1960's when the colonial administration, in anticipation of independence, began withdrawing its expatriate officers, thereby creating high-level openings. Prior to that, Africans could get no further than the lower echelons, and that they did on a junior secondary school education and long years of loyal service. Thus, the openings which independence created were first filled by older but less educated men who had seniority. Moreover, until recently, there were few highly educated Africans available to fill those positions. Educational opportunities for Africans were quite limited until the rapid expansion of secondary school instruction which began in the 1950's. In 1948, only 84 African students completed the examinations which come at the end of secondary school training. One year less than a decade later, that number had increased almost six-fold (Goldthorpe 1965:5) and by 1961, it had grown almost eight-fold (Hunter 1963:11). Today, the young university graduate who enters the civil service often begins as an assistant to an older but considerably less educated administrator.

To say that they are a new elite, however, does not mean that they are unrelated to traditional elites, that is, to the influential men in the "tribal" society. The fathers of 25 percent of the new elite men held or hold the rank of "chief" in one of the higher administrative units (county or sub-county) into which Uganda is divided. The fathers of another 19 percent were lower level chiefs. Another 22 percent of the fathers of the new elite men were themselves employed by the protectorate administration in skilled jobs such as medical and clerical assistants or were clergymen and teachers. The fathers of the others (36 percent) were subsistence level cultivators or pastoralists. Similarly, the wives of the present elite men, though generally not as well-educated as their husbands, are the daughters of traditional elites, again mostly higher ranking chiefs.

Furthermore, at least in the beginning of their careers, some of their behavior is influenced by the fact that they are essentially the first generation of the new elite. For example, although most of them were married in church and their spouses were not chosen for them by their families, they still went through traditional ceremonies as well. One elite informant who first met his wife (J) in England where they were both students described his marriage:

We were married in church, and there were two hundred guests at a 'western style' reception afterwards. I had to foot the bill for that myself and I am economizing for it. But before the church wedding, I went to see her father to pay him bride wealth. I also had to pay for that by myself, because my father said to me when I was young that since he was paying my school fees that he wouldn't be able to pay for my bride wealth. [I asked him how he decided on the amount to pay. Here follows his description of the initial stages of the exchange.]

I got a team together to go to J's father's house to talk about the marriage. My father, his brother, my cousin [his father's brother's son], and myself. My cousin was the spokesman. I didn't say anything, and I'm not supposed to do any bargaining, nor is my father, only my spokesman. So we went to be introduced.

J's father also had a team. Besides the father there was his eldest brother, who was too old to say anything, another uncle, and J's brother, who would become my brother-in-law. We went to J's house and entered. We sat on one side and they sat on the other side. J was outside with a whole group of women from the area, and she came in to introduce me, though she didn't speak, a girlfriend of hers did. She said 'this is A.N., the District Educational Officer.' [1] At this point there was a lot of clapping and yelling from the women sitting outside. Then J was asked by her uncle if she knows me, so that she wouldn't be surprised about the marriage talk, and she said yes and for how long—in the U.K. Then J left and sat outside the house. Then J's uncle began by welcoming us and asking what we wanted. My spokesman then answered, as though he wanted to marry J instead of me, 'It's very cold at night and I have been looking for a warm blanket and I have seen a beautiful one in this house and I have come to get it.' The uncle then said, 'That is good and well spoken. The blanket is beautiful. It has many decorations.' That means that J had been to school and the U.K. The uncle continued, 'I will be very sorry to see it go, and I think you should contribute towards its decorations, since you are taking it away and I may never see it again.' My spokesman said, 'Agreed. What is the contribution?' Her uncle said, '2,500/=' [$350]. I was shocked by that figure. I expected about 1,000/= [$140]. J, who was sitting outside, yelled in, 'Father, do not sell me. My husband needs the money to begin life with.' Then my spokesman said to the uncle, 'That is well spoken. We have come here to discuss the contribution and I hope that we can speak at leisure and reach a compromise. 2,500/= is very much, I would like to contribute 800/= [$112].' The uncle said, 'Well, you have come here and we will discuss: 2,000/= [$280].' My spokesman said, 'I am glad to see that you have come down, and we will go up: 1,000/= [$140].' The uncle said, 'Well spoken, and I am glad that you have come up; we will come down: 1,500/= [$210].' My spokesman replied, 'Well spoken.' Well, I was prepared to pay 1,000/=, so I leaned over to my spokesman and said, what's 200 more shillings, go to 1,200/= [$168]. My spokesman turned to the uncle, 'We will go up to 1,200/=.' The uncle said, 'Well spoken, you have come up. 1,200/= is agreed.' Then we all had a feast and drank. [Did you pay then?] No. Even if I had it then, I wouldn't have paid for it. J's family now knew me, but my family had to meet hers. Later they came to my house, had a feast, and were presented with the money.

[1] I have changed the informant's occupation to preserve his anonymity.

Although this man went through a traditional marriage custom, it does not mean that he feels tied to other traditional customs nor bound to return to village life. In another discussion the same informant said, in response to my question of whether he would retire to a village or stay in some town, "I couldn't go back to a village, though I would like to get some land just outside a town, where I would be close enough to get its facilities and services. Right now, I am looking at some land where I wouldn't have to pay ground rents, premia, and other town taxes, but where I could bring in water and electricity." As will be seen, this intention to remain a townsman and not to return to the land characterizes the elite and separates them from non-elite Africans.

Notwithstanding their ties with rural kin, and perhaps because of them, elite urban Africans clearly distinguish themselves from the traditional elite. Further indication of both the importance of education in the class concepts of elite Africans and of their status as a new urban elite is manifest in their discussion of differences between elite status in towns and elsewhere. They say that in Mbale recruitment into upper-class jobs is based on educational achievement, although "big men" in the villages may be uneducated. One informant contrasted elite status in urban and rural areas:

To village people the chief is important, but to town people, the chief is unimportant. In town, the educated man is more important. It's his education which makes him respected.

Upper-class Africans see income as another important attribute of social stratification. They describe it as a means to a life style which connotes elite status. As one informant remarked:

People only meet with others who can afford to do the same things, or who have the same interests. Differences in income are basic in choosing friends.

Another man made the same point in a different way:

Upper-class Africans don't think about income, though it is important. When people drink, if a man is known not to have money, his friends will buy for him. But he has to return the drinks sometime. If he doesn't, or won't be able to in the future, those people will stop buying for him.

These men think wealth is important for elite status because it provides the means for sustaining reciprocity, which is itself a most significant feature in the elite Africans' views of social stratification.

The divergent life styles which their different incomes allow them to pursue are indicated in the household budgets of elite and non-elite Africans. Elite Africans, for example, spend approximately five times as much as non-elite Africans do on both food and leisure-time activities. Moreover, a non-elite African who earns less than $336 per year, and 75 percent of all male adult African workers in Mbale earn less than that amount, spends his money on rent, food, and remittances to kin. Anything he spends on leisure-time activities must be deducted from the amount he has to spend on those items.

He does try to reduce his expenses by going home every week, if he is able to and can afford the fare, to get plantains and other food staples (maize meal, cassava, millet, or yams) from his garden. Even then he is unable to cut his costs on items such as paraffin, charcoal, tea, sugar, milk, and any bits of fish and meat which he adds as relish to his meals. The details of the upper- and lower-class budgets are also interesting in other ways, as will be seen. Here it can be noted that upper- and lower-class Africans give to their kinsmen about the same amount of money in absolute terms, but that elite Africans give a much smaller proportion of their cash incomes. Correspondingly, upper-class Africans spend approximately 5 percent of their incomes on life insurance policies which on their retirement will pay a monthly sum that in part will enable them to remain financially independent of their kin.

Wealth alone, however, does not justify elite status. Upper-class Africans say that educational achievement and financial success should be combined, and they do not include wealthy but uneducated Africans within their ranks. Goldthorpe noted this pattern in his general survey of elite Africans in Uganda (Goldthorpe 1965:21), and in Mbale, one informant said:

There are very few wealthy self-employed Africans in Mbale. M is the only one I can think of, but he is uneducated and doesn't move with the civil servants, who are all educated.

In this view, as in those of other upper-class informants, elite status is confirmed by interaction with social equals, and equality is not judged on the basis of income alone.

Upper-class Africans see occupation as the link between education and income. They characterize themselves and others in terms of their jobs, as often as they do by educational levels. Indeed, in their conversations, the two are interchangeable. For example, non-elite status is exemplified by the label "porters," while elite status is typified by that of "civil servants."

In contrast to education, occupation, and income, upper-class Africans do not claim that ethnicity, or tribal identity, is a basis for elite status. This is evident in their comments about the interactional dimension of social stratification, as indicated above: they say that upper-class Africans are "educated" and "can get together regardless of their tribes." It is also indicated in the way they describe themselves: in all their descriptions of an African upper class, no informant qualified elite status by a tribal adjective. They speak of an African upper class, not of a Ganda elite, an Acholi elite, or a Gisu elite.

Their use of English is related to both the importance they attach to education and to the unimportance they ascribe to tribal identity. Upper-class informants state that their use of a common language, English, is significant to the division between themselves and other Africans:

We can't talk to porters because they want to speak their own language and they don't know English.

It is noteworthy that the porters' "own language" is often the same as an elite African's mother tongue. Saying that lower-class Africans "want" to speak their own languages detracts from the fact that elite Africans choose not to speak with them, even when otherwise possible. Elite Africans speak English both in work contexts, where it is required by their duties, and in leisure-time situations, when they choose to use it as a sign of elite status and as a way of talking with elite Africans from tribal backgrounds different than their own.

Although upper-class Africans include socio-economic attributes in their standard of elite status, they view contrasting life styles as certain indicators of social class differences. Of particular significance to them are the political events people follow. They say, for example, that lower-class Africans are only interested in and talk about parochial issues, such as neighborhood scandals and local events, whereas they follow national and international politics. In fact, the major topics of conversation among elite Africans in 1965–66 were Rhodesia's unilateral declaration of independence and Britain's failure to respond to it militaristically, the overthrow of Nkrumah in Ghana, and the "Obote revolution" in Uganda. Non-elite Africans were concerned about the latter event, but did not talk about international politics.

The elite also interpret differences in aspirations as evidence of the line which separates the two classes. One man summarized these differences: "The big people want education and the poor want land." Another informant said:

The major differences between the big people and the porters is what they want: education for the educated, a piece of land for the peasants.

A third informant expanded on this theme:

To the upper class, education is most important. Villagers want a house and land, because they know they won't be able to afford an education for their children and want the income from the land. Also, without education, their children must have a place to go. The people on the housing estates think they have enough education, and they don't place much importance on it. For them, land is important as a source of income, which they think will make them more like the upper class.

The statements of these informants indicate fairly accurately what many elite Africans in fact say are their priorities: almost 50 percent said that educating their children was most important, but only 10 percent place this emphasis on acquiring land. Their beliefs about what other Africans want fit less well with the facts: 33 percent of the lower-class Africans did place first importance on land, but an equal number attached highest priority to educating their children.

Upper-class Africans frequently use modes of personal conduct as indices of social class position. For example, they say that class differences are expressed in the patterns of interaction within each class:

I think that the lower class people are more interdependent and they can more easily beg from one another. Upper-class people are more independent, and I would never borrow anything. We are more restrained, and people are more sensitive to others' privacy.

His evaluation of the two classes is clear in his characterization of informal exchange: he refers to "begging" among lower-class Africans, but to "borrowing" among elite Africans.

Elite Africans also feel superior to non-elite Africans. Their comments about class differences and drinking customs express this attitude. One man, for example, describes what he referred to as the "subjective" side of social stratification:

Not everyone goes to all bars. I don't go to Friends or Rafiki [bars], because the people there sing along with the jukebox. And besides, I would feel uncomfortable at Friends, and the chaps who drink there would feel uncomfortable at the Elgon Hotel [an elite bar].

His assumption that elite and non-elite Africans would "feel uncomfortable" with one another underlines the social distance which upper-class Africans perceive between themselves and other African townsmen. Other informants express this same attitude in terms of expected discomfort and feelings of superiority and inferiority between the classes:

The classes in Mbale don't mix because they don't feel comfortable with each other. They don't talk about the same things or in the same way.
People group together by status. Feelings between the classes are not the same. They don't visit each other, don't keep company. The lower class feels inferior.

This attitude of superiority on the part of elite Africans was also noted some fifteen years earlier by the Sofers in their study of Jinja township. They record that among the African townsmen they surveyed, an emerging elite felt so superior to lower-class Africans as almost not to be of the same race (Sofer and Sofer 1955:69). It is unlikely that in today's independent Uganda any elite African would declare himself a "black European," but the basic sense of superiority appears to be similar.

The elite Africans' thoughts about the subjective aspects of the social distance between social classes are related to their ideas about the lack of leisure-time interaction between them. Upper-class Africans, as described above, characterize people in terms of the bars and dance halls they go to and in terms of the ways in which they behave in these public places. One informant describes different bars and drinking patterns which he associates with elite and non-elite Africans:

The upper-class people drink at the Elgon and Jimmy's. The others drink at Kikuyus, Friends, Rafiki, and Lumumba. They don't mix because they behave differently. The lower-class types like loud music, yelling, shouting, and fighting over women. We talk quietly and drink slowly.

Another informant makes similar distinctions:

Saldanha's, Jimmy's, and the BCU are not bad to go to. The other places are too noisy, tough, and the people who go there are wild. That's where people throw bottles and have knife fights.

The elite Africans' correlation of class status and bars frequented is consistent with actual practice. Most upper-class Africans patronize four bars in Mbale: Jimmy's, Saldanha's, the "BCU" (housed in the Bugisu Co-operative Union building) and the bar in the Mt. Elgon Hotel, located in the upperclass residential area. Non-elite Africans prefer different bars: Maluku, Rafiki, Friends, Lumumba, Kiteso, Kikuyu, and other smaller places located in the rural areas of town.

The two sets of bars frequented by the two classes also differ physically and legally. The sharpest contrast is between bars in the developed part of Mbale and those elsewhere in the town. For example, in the rural areas a bar will often be a room in someone's mud and wattle hut, and by law it is allowed to serve only "native" beer (made from either corn, bananas, or millet). Within the center of town, the bars all look similar, being glass-fronted stores with either one or two rooms, but they differ in the number of patrons they try to accommodate. For example, two elite bars, Jimmy's and Saldanha's, each have six tables with about four chairs to a table, and twelve bar stools. In two non-elite bars, Friends and Maluku, with about the same area of floor space as the two elite bars, the former has nineteen tables, forty-one chairs, eight bar stools, and the latter has thirteen tables, thirty-eight chairs, and seven bar stools. In fact, as elite Africans contend, the non-elite bars are more crowded and are noisier.

The elite Africans' idea that lower-class people are noisy and that upper-class people are quiet is a central theme in their conceptualization of social class differences. It is manifest in their beliefs that educated people are more reserved than the uneducated and that lower-class men of different tribes only fight with one another, in contrast to the tribally heterogeneous elite who get along well together. These elements are interrelated: the educated speak a common language which they sometimes give as a "reason" for their "quietness." They are reserved in their public behavior, and they are united among themselves, despite their ethnic differences.

Thus, the statements of upper-class Africans express their view of the division, along several dimensions, between the two classes of African townsmen in Mbale. They distinguish each class by differences in education, occupation, income, use of English, and other aspects of life style. Indeed, they commonly speak of the division in interactional terms. Moreover, they think of themselves as distinct and solidary; they are aware of themselves as a social class. However, their ideas, which constitute their folk model of social stratification, are based on a combination of received knowledge, preferences, and normative understandings. In fact, their folk model is relatively accurate and is extremely useful to the observer unfamiliar with actual practices, as a guide to further empirical enquiry. The degree to which the folk model is a valid representation may be seen in the interactional divisions between the two classes.

References Cited

GOLDTHORPE, J. E. (1965) *An African Elite*, Nairobi: Oxford University Press.
HUNTER, GUY (1963) *Education for a Developing Region*, London: George Allen and Unwin Ltd.

Robbins Burling

Black English

Origins of Diversity

An American who first hears of caste dialects and of the stylistic switching that is so common in India is likely to react with dismay if not outright horror. Polydialectism seems a poor basis upon which to build a unified nation, and the variability of language along caste lines seems downright undemocratic. Yet many of these same phenomena can be found in America too, and indeed, once we recognize how easy it is for linguistic cues to come to symbolize sociological or situational differences, it should be surprising if American social class divisions were not reflected in the way we use language. In particular, we ought to look at our sharpest sociological cleavage— the division between blacks and whites—and ask whether it is not marked by linguistic variables.

Most white Americans probably believe that they could distinguish Negro speakers from white even while blindfolded. Some may imagine that whatever linguistic differences they perceive are simply the result of underlying racial differences. They may suppose that Negro mouths are built differently from white mouths or that Negroes are simply incapable of such clear and accurate articulation as whites. Such racial notions can easily be disproved, for when northern whites are asked to judge taped samples of speech they often mistake a southern white for a Negro, but conversely they will identify the voice of the rather rare Negro who grows up in an otherwise white northern community as belonging to a white speaker. It is unquestionably the experience of the speaker, particularly his experience in early childhood, that determines how he will speak, not his race.

It is easy to dispose of this racist explanation for Negro-white differences, but a contrary linguistic myth is also current among many Americans today that is more difficult to deal with. A good many well-meaning Americans would like to maintain a sort of dogmatic faith that Negro and white speech is in all essentials identical. Many white Americans, who feel deeply that discrimination is wicked and who insist that Negroes be offered all the same opportunities as whites, are eager to deny any difference at all between the two groups, for they are afraid any admission of cultural differences would provide a rationalization for discrimination. But the fear of offending egalitarian ideals should not stand in the way of an investigation of dialectical variability, and when such an investigation is made, it is abundantly clear that most Negroes in the United States today do have features in their speech that separate them from their white neighbors. Indeed, when we remember the history of black Americans and understand the conditions of segregation in which they have lived and continue to live in both the north and the south, it would be startling if important differences were not found. Unfortunately, serious studies of dialects used by Negroes have begun only very recently.

The first and most obvious generalization to make about the English of many Negroes is that it shows abundant characteristics of the southern United States. Throughout the South, where most Negroes once lived, their speech has probably approached in considerable degree the varieties of English spoken by their white neighbors. They need not have spoken identically to these whites, and indeed the segregated conditions of their lives would almost force us to guess that important linguistic differences would separate the speech of the two groups.

In recent decades, as southern Negroes have surged into northern cities, they have brought along their varieties of southern speech. Since they have largely been forced to live in segregated ghettos, often shut off even more completely from association with whites than in their southern homes, their dialects have been perpetuated and passed on to their northern-born children. What had been geographically distinctive features have been converted into ethnic features. Most northern urban Negroes, for instance, fail to distinguish /i/ from /e/ before /n/, so that words like *pin* and *pen* become homonyms. This is characteristic of most southern speech, both black and white, but in a northern city like New York it is hardly found except among Negroes. Most whites do distinguish those two sounds, but only the rare Negro who grows up in a predominantly white neighborhood learns to do so. As a result a New Yorker could guess the race of a fellow New Yorker with a good chance of being correct simply by hearing him pronounce these two words. Many other southern features, besides the collapse of the *i/e* contrast, have no doubt become generalized as ethnic features in the north. Certainly the totality of features is so pervasive that more often than not northern urban Americans can distinguish Negroes from whites simply by hearing them talk.

Not all the special characteristics of northern urban Negro speech are simply southern, however. The ghettos create their own social climate and evoke their unique linguistic signals. The ghettos, after all, draw upon many southern areas, so the migrants do not arrive with a single uniform dialect. Features that have originated from one southern area can be generalized and accepted by other speakers, while other southern features are dropped as people adjust to their new surroundings. As a result, the recent migrant from the South is clearly marked off from older residents by his purer southern traits, and as the years pass, a new and unique dialect, a synthesis of southern and northern forms with some added local innovations, becomes characteristic of many urban Negroes. Instead of a geographically based dialect we can only speak of one that is ethnically based.

It even seems that in some northern cities the speech of Negroes and whites has been becoming more distinct in recent decades. Southern Negroes have been moving north in such large numbers that their speech has tended to swamp out the more northern dialects of their northern Negro predecessors. In Washington, D.C., immigration of whites from the north has tended to shift white dialects in the opposite direction. In some northern cities the differences between black and white speech have now become so clearly marked that radio stations which carry programs and advertising directed toward a Negro audience sometimes use announcers who have recognizably Negro characteristics in their speech. Perhaps this should be no more surprising than the use of Spanish for programs directed to Puerto Ricans in New York or of Navaho for some programs in the Southwest, but the use of Negro English dialects does constitute an almost unique exception to the bland uniformity of most broadcast English in the United States.

A common southern background and a common reaction to ghetto life in the north can account for many of the differences between Negro and white dialects. But it is also worth noting that a number of striking linguistic features, which are not found in either southern or northern white dialects, seem to be common among Negroes in all northern urban areas. Not all the features that tend to set off the kind of English used wherever Negroes are concentrated in large numbers are simply southern. It may be that the seemingly unique character of black English can only be understood as deriving from a long separate history from white English. It may even be that the English of some black Americans still shows the influence of the time when slaves were first imported into this country or even a few traces of their African origin.

When slaves were brought to the Americas, men and women of diverse linguistic background were thrown together with relatively little chance to learn the English of their masters, but with no way of communicating with one another except by means of some approximation to English. The situation would seem to have been ideal for the development of a pidgin language based upon English, and then for its subsequent creolization in the generation that grew up in America knowing no other language but learning to speak by imitating the imperfect English of their parents. A pidgin is a contact language, native to no one, and generally used in a limited range of situations. It may be simple in structure and may show varied influences from the diverse languages of those who use it. When children grow up basing their speech upon such a pidgin, they can be expected to elaborate it and adapt it to all the varied situations of life. But having been filtered through the distortions of the contact period, this newly developed creole, while a full and flexible medium of communication in its own right, can be expected to differ quite markedly from the original language upon which its ancestral pidgin had been based.

A few New World Negro populations continue to speak forms of English that are so divergent as to be recognized as creoles. The only true creole to survive in the United States today is the so-called Gullah dialect spoken along the coast of South Carolina, but others are found in the West Indies and in Surinam on the north coast of South America. It is remarkable that all these creoles seem to resemble each other to some degree, and a few of their features are even reflected in the less deviant English spoken by many Negroes in the United States.

Hints about the characteristics of the English spoken by Negroes over the past two and a half centuries can be found in fragments of dialogue that have periodically appeared in print and purport to reflect the speech of Negroes. It is not uncommon in such dialogue for *me* to be used even as the subject or possessive form of the first person pronoun. A copula is often missing from sentences in which standard English would always have a form of the verb *be*, though *be* itself sometimes appears where it would not be used in standard English. Some words also suggest an avoidance of final consonants or of complex final clusters, either by dropping or simplifying the consonants or by adding vowels at the end, thus shifting the former final consonant into a prevocalic position. These various features appear, among other places, in the dialogue attributed to a Virginia Negro in the play "The Fall of British Tyranny" written by John Leacock of Philadelphia in 1776. A conversation between a certain "kidnapper and the Negro Cudjo" goes as follows,

Kidnapper	What part did you come from?
Cudjo	Disse brack man, disse one, disse one, disse one, came from Hamton, disse one, disse one, come from Nawfok, me come from Nawfok too.
Kidnapper	Very well, what was your master's name?
Cudjo	Me massa name Cunney Tomsee.
Kidnapper	Colonel Thompson—eigh?

Cudjo	Eas, massa, Cunney Tomsee.
Kidnapper	Well then I'll make you a major—and what's your name?
Cudjo	Me massa cawra me Cudjo.[1]

Similar features appeared in dialogues attributed to Negroes, supposedly coming from the West Indies and Surinam. But, in English-speaking areas of the New World, Negro dialects were never taken seriously enough to be systematically described. We can only infer their characteristics from scattered literary sources. Surinam, however, was ruled by Holland, and here Dutch immigrants had to do their best to communicate with Negroes who spoke an English-based creole. To assist the Dutchmen, grammars of this creole were printed as early as the late 18th century, and these suggest features of the language found all the way north to the United States.

The English spoken by Negroes in the United States today is certainly not a close replica of an 18th century creole, but at least a few details of present day Negro American English may be attributable to an earlier period of pidginization and creolization, followed by persistent modifying influences from standard English. As I will point out, the attrition of final consonants is an important feature of the speech of many Negroes in the United States, and the copula is often missing where it would occur in standard English. One cannot help asking if all forms of New World Negro English might not have a common origin and if centuries of segregation might not have allowed common features to be perpetuated down to the present time. It has even been argued that Negro dialects can be traced all the way to the slave ports of west Africa, where African and European speakers first had to devise makeshift forms of communication. The pidgin English established in these ports would have been carried everywhere in the New World where Africans used English. In subsequent centuries the language would only slowly be modified in proportion to the contact between blacks and speakers of more standard English.

We should even be willing to wonder whether traces of African languages might not have managed to survive the centuries. Certainly African lexical items live on in the more extreme creoles such as Gullah. More tentatively it is tempting to ask if the attrition of final consonants and simplification of final clusters that is so characteristic of much of Negro English is not a distant reflection of the influence of west African languages, for these often have few final consonants. Conceivably this feature of west African languages has even reached out to affect white speakers as well as their Negro neighbors, for in spite of the great status differences dividing

---

[1] Quoted by William A. Stewart in "Sociolinguistic Factors in the History of American Negro Dialects," *Florida FL Reporter* (Spring 1967), p. 24.

blacks from whites in this country, some influences can have gone in both directions. It may not be mere coincidence that certain final consonant clusters are more often simplified in southern white dialects than in those of the north. The *t* of northern pronunciations of the final clusters *-pt* and *-ft* is omitted by some southern white speakers, for instance, with the result that *slept* becomes *slep*, *stopped* becomes homonymous with *stop* (unless the *t* is reintroduced by analogy with other past tense forms) *left* becomes *lef*, and *loft* becomes *lof*.

Just how important the influence of African languages is in the speech of either Negroes or whites in the United States today must remain an open question until far more has been learned both about the various dialects spoken today and about their antecedents. But it does at least seem clear that many features widely distributed among Negroes today can only be understood as a result of their long and special history.

A Stigmatized Dialect

The diverse patterns of English would be no more than linguistic curiosities if they were accepted as the social and cultural equivalent of standard patterns. Americans tend to be relatively tolerant of most regional dialects, but Negro speech patterns have been closely associated with their inferior social position and, like the dialectical specialties of lower-class whites, their patterns have become stigmatized. Many people look upon them not simply as divergent but as inferior. This is true not only of whites. Those Negroes who have themselves struggled for an education and fought to acquire the linguistic symbols associated with education may have little patience with the language of the lower class. Indeed, it is sometimes educated Negro teachers, themselves managing very well with standard English patterns, who most strongly resist any suggestion that the special characteristics of their black student's dialects deserve respect or attention. It may be difficult for some of them to accept the notion that the speech they have worked so hard to suppress is anything but just plain wrong.

To dismiss his speech as simply incorrect or inferior burdens the Negro child who grows up in a northern ghetto with a nearly insuperable problem. To speak naturally with his parents and to compete with his contemporaries on the street, he simply must learn their variety of English. Indeed, if in some miraculous way, he could learn standard English, he would be nothing but an impertinent prig to use it with his parents, and surely his contemporaries would rapidly tease it out of him. The language the child first learns is a rich and flexible medium in its own terms, and it can be used effectively in most of the situations he encounters in daily life. No wonder teachers have only meager success when they try to persuade him to abandon his own easy language in favor of an unnatural—almost foreign—medium. Inevitably, many students simply reject their education and all it stands for.

Years of classroom drilling, exposure to movies and radio, and the brute necessities of trying to get a job do eventually have their effect. While few Negroes from the ghetto fully achieve the middle-class goal of their teachers, many learn to go part way, and many northern Negroes are accomplished dialect switchers. They move toward middle-class standards where that seems to be called for, but they relax into more natural patterns when speaking with their families or close friends, or whenever pretensions would be out of place. They act a bit like speakers in those situations that have been called diglossia. Like Swiss Germans, Negro children first learn a dialect suitable for their home and their close friends. Only in school, if at all, do they learn the standard dialect, which then becomes appropriate for certain kinds of educated discourse, for writing, or for communicating with people outside their own group. Yet in German-speaking Switzerland the two dialects are more clearly recognized as distinct. Each is admired in its own sphere and each can be clearly referred to by its own name. No Swiss, whatever his education, is unwilling to use Swiss German in his home or with close friends. Every Swiss is proud of his dialect, proud of its very distinctiveness from standard German, and no one in Switzerland simply stigmatizes the Swiss dialects as inferior and debased. Although a Swiss switches back and forth as the occasion demands, he is generally clear about his choice, speaking full Swiss German when that is called for but approximating standard German quite closely at other times. He is not likely to glide indecisively between them.

Northern urban Negro dialects are more recent, in more rapid flux, and more consistently despised by speakers of standard English. This has made it difficult for Negroes to develop the pride in their own dialect that the Swiss have in theirs, and most speakers probably slide along more of a continuum than do the Swiss. At one end of the continuum is a speech style close to the standard language and this is the style toward which formal education aims. Students of Negro speech in Washington, D.C., have called this the "acrolect" and have contrasted it with the "basilect" that lies at the opposite and most humble extreme. Ghetto children first hear and speak the basilect, and many Negroes in Washington seem to take it for granted that this is the natural way for small children to talk, just as Javanese expect their children to learn the lowest level of speech first. As children grow older, they learn new or alternative forms and develop more or less skill in switching toward the acrolect.

Consciously or unconsciously, many Negroes learn to slide back and forth along this continuum of styles, though individual speakers vary greatly in the range through which they can switch. The most recent southern migrant, the most severely segregated, the man with the least formal education, may not be able to get far from the basilect. The long-term northern resident, the educated member of the middle class who has daily contact with white speakers of standard English, may use the acrolect easily but be unable to get all the way to the basilect; but many speakers shift over a considerable range. The fluidity of this shifting makes it extremely difficult to make a serious investigation of Negro speech patterns. The middle-class investigator, particularly if he is white, may have great trouble eliciting realistic examples of the more relaxed Negro styles, since the very formality of the investigation encourages informants (whether consciously or not) to shift as far toward the acrolect as they can manage. Where Negroes have adjusted to prejudice and discrimination by accommodating outwardly to the whims of whites, they may be ready to support white stereotypes by guessing at the information the investigator wants and then providing it. They may deliberately conceal the characteristics of their in-group language. Partly for these reasons, though even more through sheer neglect, we have had tragically little reliable knowledge of the speech of lower-class Negroes. By the late 1960s, however, as part of an increasing concern over the fate of segregated Negro children in our educational system, investigations in several cities had finally begun. It is at last possible to sketch a few of the major differences between standard middle-class English and the speech of many urban Negroes. There can be no doubt that the differences extend to every part of language, phonological, grammatical, lexical, and semantic.

Phonological Contrast

One set of features that distinguishes the speech of many Negroes is the obscuring of certain phonological contrasts found in standard English, spoken in the northern United States. In final position standard /θ/ often merges with /f/, and standard /ð/ merges with /v/. As a result, words like *Ruth* and *death*, which northern white speakers virtually always pronounce with final interdental fricatives, are often pronounced by Negroes with labiodental fricatives so that they become homonymous with *roof* and *deaf*.

The standard vowels /ay/ and /aw/ as in *find* and *found* may lose their dipthongal qualities and merge with /a/ of *fond*, and all three of these words become homonymous. A number of other vowels may fall together when preceding /l/ or /r/, so that pairs like *boil* and *ball*, *beer* and *bear*, *poor* and *pour*, are often homonyms. In all these cases, as in the loss of contrast between, the vowels in *pin* and *pen*, many Negroes simply have a few more sets of homonyms in their speech than do most northern whites. Perhaps it is some compensation that a good many southern Negroes do make a distinction between the vowels in *four* and *for*, or *hoarse* and *horse*, which most northern whites confound, though even this distinction tends to be lost by northern migrants.

The existence of these extra homonyms in the speech of Negro children presents them with a few special reading problems, though these should not be insuperable. All English speakers have many homonyms in their speech, and in learning to read English everyone must learn to associate different orthographic sequences with identically pronounced but semantically distinct words. This is one of the barriers we all must overcome in becoming literate. For the most part, a Negro child simply has a somewhat different and larger set of homonyms to cope with. They will give him serious problems only if his teacher fails to understand that these words *are* homonyms in the child's natural speech.

If a student sees the word *death* and *reads* [def] he is correctly interpreting the written symbols into his natural pronunciation, and he deserves to be congratulated. If his teacher insists on correcting him and telling him to say [deθ], she is pronouncing a sequence of sounds that is quite literally foreign to the child, and he may even have trouble hearing the difference between his own and his teacher's versions. Unwittingly, the teacher is correcting the child's pronunciation instead of his reading skills. The child can only conclude that reading is a mysterious and capricious art. If he has enough experiences of this sort he is all too likely to give up and remain essentially illiterate all his life. It is clearly of the utmost importance for anyone who is teaching such children to understand their system of homonyms and to distinguish cases of nonstandard pronunciations from real reading problems.

In other ways Negro speech often differs more dramatically from that of whites, ways that may pose even more serious barriers to literacy. The most important of these seem to involve the loss of final consonants and the simplification of final clusters. Several related developments are involved in this simplification, and they deserve to be considered individually.

-r In many Negro dialects, (as in some white dialects, of course, both in the north and south) post vocalic and preconsonantal *-r* tends to be lost. As in some white dialects, this can result in the falling together of such words as *guard* and *god*, *sore* and *saw*, *fort* and *fought*. Negro speech, however, may go even further than other *r*-less dialects by also losing the intervocalic *r*'s that are preserved in most white dialects, certainly in those of the North. For instance, most New Yorkers in a relaxed mood pronounce *four* without *r* constriction when it occurs finally or before a consonant, as in *fourteen* or *four boys*. But they generally do have *r* constriction when the same word occurs before a vowel as in *four o'clock*. This gives a white New York child some hint about the orthography he must learn, and it must help to rationalize the spelling of the word for him, even in those positions where he would not actually pronounce the *r*. To many Negroes, however, these *-r*'s are absent under all conditions. They may say [fɔ'ɔklak] with as little *r* constriction as they use in [fɔtiyn]. Even an intervocalic *r* occurring in the middle of the word may be omitted, a pronunciation that has been reflected in dialect spellings such as "inte'ested." The name *Carol* may be pronounced identically to *Cal*, and *Paris* and *terrace* become homonymous with *pass* and *test*. A Negro child who first learns this *r*-less dialect has no clue in his own speech about why these words should be spelled with an *-r*, and so he has one extra hurdle to cross if he is to learn to read and write.

-l Although English *l* is phonetically rather like *r* being similar in its distribution within the syllable and even in its effect upon preceding vowels, it is less often completely lost than *-r*. In most English dialects *l* may be replaced, when preceding a consonant, by a back unrounded glide which amounts to little more than a modification of the preceding vowel, as in the rapid pronunciation of *ball game*. But the complete loss of post vocalic *l* and merger of words spelled with *l* with others that are not are largely Negro phenomena. It is not uncommon for Negroes to fail to make a distinction between such words as *toll* and *toe*; *tool* and *too*; *help* and *hep*; *all* and *awe*; *fault* and *fought*.

SIMPLIFICATION OF FINAL CLUSTERS. Final clusters may be simplified by losing one of the elements in the cluster. The most common simplification is the loss of the final /t/ or /d/ from such clusters as *-st, -ft, -nt, -nd, -ld, -zd, -md*. Individual speakers vary in the degree and regularity with which these are simplified, and most Americans, both white and black, sometimes simplify them in certain positions (particularly before consonants) or in certain styles of speech, but the tendency toward simplification is more pronounced in the speech of some Negroes. For many Negroes *past* and *pass*; *meant, mend* and *men; wind* and *wine; hold* and *hole* have become homonyms. Cluster simplification can even be combined with loss of *-l* so that such words as *told, toll* and *toe* may all become homonyms. Clusters with final *-s* or *-z* such as *-ks, -mz, -lz, -dz, -ts* are somewhat less frequently simplified, and these give rise to more complex situations for sometimes it is the first element of the cluster, sometimes the second, that is lost. It is at least possible, however, that the loss of final *-s* or *-z* will reduce such words as *six* and *sick* to homonyms.

It is often difficult to be sure whether the simplified final cluster that we hear really reflects the underlying form of the word as the speaker knows it, or whether we hear only the surface manifestation of a more complex underlying form. One particular case is instructive however: the word *test* seems to be pronounced without the final *t* by many Negroes. Words ending in /t/ in English regularly take an additional /s/ to show the plural, but words ending in /s/ are pluralized by /-iz/. For some Negro speakers the plural of *test* is [tesiz] and the plural of *ghost* is [gosiz]. This seems to demonstrate conclusively that for these speakers, *test, ghost,* and many other words completely lack any trace of the *t* of our orthography or of the standard pronunciation.

OTHER FINAL CONSONANTS. Final *-r, -l* and clusters ending in *-t, -d, -s* and *-z* are those most frequently reduced, but a few Negroes go even further. Final *-t* may be realized as a glottal stop (as in many white dialects), or it may completely disappear. Final *-d* may be devoiced or disappear. Less often *-k* and *-g* may suffer the same fate. Final *-m* and *-n* may be weakened although they usually leave a residue behind in the form of a nasalized vowel. At its most extreme, this reduction in final consonants can go so far that a few individuals seem predominantly to use open syllables, initial consonants followed by a vowel with hardly any final consonants at all. But even for speakers with less extreme reduction, the final parts of words carry a considerably lighter informational load than for speakers of standard English.

Loss of Suffixes

Even moderate consonant reduction may give speakers rather serious problems in learning the standard language, for it happens that it is the tongue-tip consonants /r,l,t,d,s,z/ that are most often lost. These carry a great semantic burden in standard spoken English, since they are used to form the suffixes. Not only are the plural, possessive, past, and third person singular of the verb shown by one or another of these tongue-tip consonants, but so are most of the colloquial contractions that speakers of the standard use orally, though they write them infrequently. Standard speakers most often indicate the future by a suffixed *-ll*, as in *I'll go, you'll go, where'll he go?*, and so on. The colloquial contractions of the copula generally consist of *-r, -z*, or *-s: you're a boy, he's a boy, we're boys, they're boys, the book's good*. If a regular phonological rule leads to the loss of these final consonants, then the grammatical constructions would also be in danger of disappearing. This would imply a series of important ways in which the English of some Negroes would deviate from that of most whites. At least some grammatical changes like these seem to have occurred, although the details appear to be very complex, and are so far only partially understood.

That grammatical change has not been simply the automatic consequence of phonological change is shown by the varying treatment of the plural and of the third person singular marker, which, of course, are phonologically identical in standard English. If loss of suffixes were nothing but a simple result of regular phonological change, then we would expect the plural *-s* and the third person singular *-s* to have suffered exactly the same fate. In fact, the plural marker is usually as well preserved as any suffix, and it shows little if any tendency to be lost. By contrast, in the speech of many Negroes, the third person singular verb suffix is completely absent. These speakers simply lack this suffix, under all conditions, even in cases in which the usual phonological rule for the loss of *-s* would not apply. The easiest way to view this situation in historical perspective is to imagine that both suffixes were first lost under the same conditions, particularly when occurring after other consonants where to have retained them would have resulted in an unpronounceable cluster. When either suffix was added to a root, ending in a vowel, it should have been more readily pronounceable. Upon the identical results of this regular phonological rule, divergent analogical processes could then have brought divergent consequences. If the third person singular marker (which, after all, carries a rather meager semantic load) could be skipped in some positions, it might be skipped elsewhere and so dropped by analogy even from verbs that posed no phonological problem. The plural marker carries a far more significant semantic load, and here, perhaps, the plural signs that survived phonological reduction could serve as a model by which plurals could be analogically reintroduced even onto nouns where a difficult consonant cluster would result. The actual historical processes, by which the plural survived but the third person singular was lost, were no doubt a good deal more complex than this simple scheme would suggest, but the results seem understandable only in terms of both phonological and analogical change.

Other suffixes have suffered varied and complex fates. Contracted forms of the copula often fail to be realized in Negro speech, so instead of *you're tired* or *they're tired*, some Negroes say *you tired* and *they tired*. This much conforms to the regular phonological loss of final *-r*, but when *he's tired* appears as *he tired*, an analogical extension of the missing copula is likely to be involved since loss of final /-z/ when it is not part of a cluster is unusual. Absence of the copula is frequently cited as a characteristic of Negro speech, and this seems to suggest a rather fundamental altering of the organization of tenses. One form of the copula seems not to be lost, however, for the *'m* of *I'm* seems to survive, perhaps because /-m/ has much less tendency for phonological reduction, even than /-z/.

Some possessive pronouns can become identical to the personal pronouns: *your* and *you* may become homonyms as may *their* and *they*. The school child who reads *your brother* as *you bruvver* is actually doing a skillful job of translating the written form into his dialect. Teachers ought to be equally skilled so as to reward rather than to punish such evidence of learning. The noun possessive written *'s* is frequently omitted, even in words ending in a vowel. The possessive forms of some pronouns do survive: *my, our, his, her*, usually remain distinct, and since nobody says *I book* by analogy with the common *they book* and *you book*, the possessive cannot be said to be completely lost even if it is far less frequent than in standard English.

With cluster simplification, the past forms of the verb often became identical to the present forms. *Walked* becomes homonymous with *walk, pass* with *passed*, *drag* with *dragged*, and similarly for a great many verbs. Nevertheless, the past tense is preserved by irregular verbs, for the loss of the past-present distinction has not been carried by analogy so as to eliminate such distinctions as *tell* from *told*. The irregular verbs, of course, are extremely common in ordinary conversation so the past tense is well preserved in colloquial Negro speech, but the regular verbs are still common enough to reduce the amount of information conveyed by the past tense markers.

The phonological loss of final *-l* is related to a frequent loss of the contracted form of the future. This, of course, does not mean that Negroes are unable to convey notions of future time. Expressions with *going to* are common, for instance, but beyond this, the full and uncontracted from of *will* (perhaps pronounced without a final *-l*) is available and regularly used. A

Negro child may be able to say *I go* with an implication of future time, and to be more emphatic, he can say *I will go* or *I wi' go*, but he may never use *I'll go*. For such a child, a reader that uses what appears to a speaker of standard English as the slightly stilted construction "I will go" may be considerably easier to read than a book which uses "I'll go."

Grammatical Change

It is clear that some dialects spoken by Negroes have come to contrast with the dialects of most whites in many ways: the loss of phonological contrast particularly at the ends of words, the weakening of suffixes, and the analogical extension of the resulting patterns. Similar changes are known to have occurred in many languages. They represent the kinds of processes which have been active in every family of languages whose history is at all well known. It is proper, therefore, to view these dialects as exhibiting entirely normal and understandable historical developments from an earlier form of the language, a form that standard English continues to approximate a bit more closely. Like many historical developments in language, it is possible to look upon some of these modifications of the Negro dialects as though they involved a degree of simplification in the language, but if historical changes could only bring increasing simplicity, then sooner or later languages would simplify themselves out of existence. There must be countervailing mechanisms that reintroduce complexity. Recognizing the apparent simplification of some aspects of the Negro dialects, it is tempting to ask whether there are balancing ways in which those same dialects have become more complex than standard English.

It is impossible to give any confident answer to this question, partly because Negro dialects have been so imperfectly studied but even more because we have such meager means of measuring complexity. Still, one cannot help wondering whether the near disappearance of the possessive 's is not compensated for by other devices, if by nothing else but a more consistent use of the possessive with *of*. When the past and future tenses are partially lost and when the copula construction is weakened, one must wonder if other tenses have not appeared to take their place. One set of contrasting constructions that has been recognized as common among Negroes but which is missing from white dialects, is represented by the contrast between *he busy* which means 'he is busy at the moment' and *he be busy* which means 'he is habitually busy.' The use of *be* allows the easy expression of a contrast between momentary and habitual action that can be introduced only by rather cumbersome circumlocutions in standard English. Here is one place where the speech of many blacks has a useful resource surpassing the speech of whites.

Many other constructions, typical of Negro speech, suggest other tenses not found in the standard dialect: *he done told me; it don't all be her fault;*

I been seen it; I ain't like it; I been washing the car (which is not simply a reduced form of the standard 'I have been washing the car'); *he be sleeping.* Such sentences surely utilize rules exceeding the limits of standard English. Unquestionably the rules governing them are as orderly and rigid as those of the standard, but they are just as surely different in important ways. From the viewpoint of the standard language, it may look as though these dialects lack certain familiar mechanisms. From the complementary viewpoint of the dialects, other mechanisms seem to be lacking in the standard. Certainly standard rules are not rich enough to generate the examples cited here.

Ghetto Education

The language of many Negro children of the northern ghettos is divergent enough from standard English to present educators with a terrible dilemma. Everyone agrees that these children deserve an education that is at least as rich as that of the children in the white suburbs. Negro children ought to be able to take pride in their own background and should not be burdened with shame for cultural differences that are not of their making, and which are inferior only in the sense that people with power happen to have different patterns. If black children are to compete successfully with their white suburban contemporaries in the practical if unjust world of the present day United States, they may have to learn the standard language. But if in learning it, they are forced to reject their own native dialect and to accept the dominant society's view that their native language habits are simply inferior, the experience may do them more psychic harm than social good.

Some would argue that Negroes are no worse off today than the generations of children of European immigrants who entered English-speaking schools knowing nothing but Italian, Greek, or Yiddish. These children too were faced with a strange language, which they had to learn to speak and to read. For some, their education may have been traumatic, but many succeeded, and they or their children have been progressively assimilating into the mainstream of American life. Why, it may be asked, are Negroes any worse off? There are at least two reasons.

First, the economic opportunities for a man with a poor knowledge of standard English have declined. Automation has been progressively eliminating unskilled jobs. More than ever before, a man needs an education. But even more than this, the child of the European immigrant spoke a language that both he and his teacher regarded as a real language. It had a literature, it had its own dictionaries, and it had a writing system all its own. These children were not accused of speaking an inferior variety of English; they spoke something entirely different, and their teachers knew they had to start at the beginning with them. It is easy to be deluded into imagining that Negro children simply speak careless English, to conclude that their language patterns are the result of their own laziness, or stupidity, or cussedness.

Some of their teachers never realize that they face a situation with similarities to instruction in a foreign language. Even the child may hardly grasp the truth that his own dialect has its own patterns and structure, and he may all too easily accept his teachers' judgment that he is incapable of learning the "proper" way of speaking. In a just world it would seem fairer to ask others to accept Negro speech as a respectable dialect, one that is as valuable and flexible as any other, than to demand that Negroes, already burdened with problems enough, should have to struggle to learn a different dialect. But such a laudable ideal is probably too remote a dream to be taken seriously.

The problems of ghetto education might be clarified if its various objectives were clearly distinguished. The first goal of language teaching is surely to teach children to read, but it is a depressing truth that thousands of Negro children sit through years of school without ever becoming effectively literate. One important reason for their failure is surely the divergence of the language they bring to school from the language of their teachers and from the language reflected in their textbooks. But whatever the defects of the English spelling system, it has at least one virtue: it does not idiosyncratically favor a single English dialect. Northerners, southerners, Americans, and Englishmen read the same written forms, but each pronounces what he reads in his own way. Our written conventions are not identical to any single spoken dialect, so everyone must learn to translate between the written word and his own native speech habits. To the extent that spoken dialects differ, children come to the task of gaining literacy from various vantage points, and it might seem that the task of the Negro child is not much different from that of other children who have also first learned a particular spoken dialect. The Negro child, however, is likely to be seriously handicapped in two ways. First, his spoken dialect is likely to be even further from the written form than is that of most white children, and inevitably this causes him more difficulty when learning to read. Even more important, his teacher may fail to appreciate the children's special dialect. The teachers of most white children speak dialects enough like that of their students to make their learning problems immediately understandable. A teacher readily understands and sympathizes with a northern middle-class child who has trouble remembering when to write *four* and when to write *for*. She does not balk at her students' easy conversion of the written *hit you* into the spoken colloquial [hičuw]. She will probably not be upset when her students use *'em* when speaking naturally instead of *them*. The same teacher may be utterly mystified by a Negro student's apparent inability to know when to write *toe, toll,* and *told,* or by the apparent capriciousness with which he interprets the past tense, the third person singular, or the possessive suffix. The task of teaching ghetto children to read should benefit greatly from an understanding of what spoken Negro dialects are really like and from reading programs that are specifically designed for speakers of this dialect. One would hope that such a program could avoid stigmatizing the children's own dialect while opening the literate world to them.

Such a reading program will not teach these children standard pronunciation or to speak with standard grammar. That is really a quite separate task, and perhaps it is one that should wait until children are older and until they themselves feel it to be necessary. To try to teach the standard dialect to segregated slum children who have no chance to practice it in their home or on the street, seems to have little more promise of success than the teaching of foreign languages in monolingual America. An older child who has already learned to read and who, from watching television and visiting the movies, has acquired a passive understanding of the standard dialect, may also have both more motivation and more opportunity to escape the restrictions of the ghetto. The prospects may be better for helping him to add active control of the standard to his linguistic repertory, particularly if the curriculum could take realistic account of the language patterns the students start with. What is needed is an instructional program that borrows a few techniques from methods of foreign language instruction and no more than in a foreign language course, need such instruction carry with it the implication that the students' own native language is inferior.

In recent years many of those who have been concerned with education in the ghettoes have come to feel that their realistic goal should be to encourage bidialecticalism, to capitalize upon the skill in dialect switching that many Negroes already have, and to develop ways by which they can learn to do it systematically and well. It is not only arrogant but no doubt utterly useless to ask them to stop speaking with their friends and families in the natural way that they have learned first. They can learn the appropriate time and place for the intimate language and the appropriate time and place for the standard, but they should not have to reject either. The first step in developing such an attitude in students, however, is probably to persuade the thousands of teachers of Negroes that the native dialects of their students have an irreplaceable value to them. These dialects deserve respect and understanding for what they are, not blind and uncompromising opposition.

John J. Poggie, Jr., and Pertti J. Pelto

Matrilateral Asymmetry in the American Kinship System [1]

I. Introduction

American anthropologists have shown a strong preference for non-Western societies in their examination of kinship systems. This may in part be a result of the supposed greater importance of kinship in the behavior of non-Western peoples, but it also reflects the anthropologist's tendency until recent times to leave the study of Western cultural and social forms to the sociologists. In a recent presidential address before the American Anthropological Association, Leslie A. White urged American anthropologists to devote more attention to the study of American culture (White 1965).

Anthropological studies of the American kinship system have centered on examinations of kinship terminology, both in terms of componential and other formal analyses (e.g., Wallace and Atkins 1960; Goodenough 1965; Romney and D'Andrade 1964) and examination of patterning of alternate terms of address (Schneider and Homans 1955). Studies by anthropologists which have examined American kinship in ways other than analyses of terminology include such works as Cumming and Schneider's (1961) study of sibling solidarity, Codere's genealogical study of kinship in the United States (1955), Aberle and Naegele's study of middle-class fathers' occupational role (1952), and Coult and Habenstein's study of extended kinship ties in urban society (1965). The literature on American kinship includes a long list of works by sociologists, notably T. Parsons, B. Farber, M. Zelditch, Jr., W. Goode, M. Sussman, M. Straus, R. Hill, D. A. Sweetser and K. Davis, to name only a few.

Until fairly recently it has been generally accepted that the American kinship system is "symmetrically multilineal" in type, as, for example, described by Parsons (1943) and others. However, some modifications of this point of view have been suggested by researchers who find that, in practice, American families tend to emphasize relationships with maternal relatives.

Schneider and Homans (1955) examined the patterning of informal terms of address and noted some features which suggest greater emphasis on the matrilateral side of kin relations. Robins and Tomanec (1966) asked ques-

Reprinted from John J. Poggie, Jr., and Pertti J. Pelto, "Matrilateral Assymmetry in the American Kinship System," Anthropological Quarterly, 42:1 (January 1969), 1–15, with permission of the Anthropological Quarterly.

[1] The co-authors wish to thank Frank C. Miller and Murray A. Straus for scholarly counsel related to this paper; Barbara Larson and the social anthropology class for help in preparing and carrying out the questionnaire; and Erika R. Poggie for help in data tabulation and typing of questionnaire and manuscripts.

tions concerning "closeness to blood relatives" of a sample of 140 informants at a Mid-Western private coeducational university. They found that "female relatives tend to be closer to ego than male relatives, and relatives to whom he is related through his father" (1966:140).

The sociologist-anthropologist team of Leichter and Mitchell (1967) carried out an extensive analysis of kin relations among both clients and caseworkers associated with a Jewish family service agency in New York City. They found extensive evidence that females tend to be more kin-oriented than males, and that there tends to be a bias toward interaction with the wife's relatives among the clients' families. The same tendency toward a "matrilateral bias" was noted in the caseworker sample; however, the reseachers unfortunately did not control for the fact that most of the caseworker sample was female. While Leichter and Mitchell's research involves a considerable array of data about the structuring of extended kin relations, it should be kept in mind that their population of New York Jews (85–90% of whose parents were born in Europe) cannot easily be taken as representative of general trends in American society.

Coult and Habenstein (1965) also report finding what they refer to as a "matrilateral orientation in American kinship," which they do not believe has been previously noted among white Protestant urban residents. Their study involved "representative samples of blue collar and white collar classes in Kansas City, Missouri" (Habenstein and Coult 1965:2).

Dorrian Apple Sweetser (1966) has assembled data from a number of studies in support of her hypothesis that matrilateral bias in intergenerational kinship solidarity is characteristic of industrial societies. She feels that ". . . where there is succession in male instrumental roles, solidarity will be greater between the nuclear family and the lineal relatives of men, and where there is no succession, solidarity will be greater with the wife's family" (1966:156). She presents data from Japan, Finland, England and the United States showing that as societies become industrialized, and occupational succession from fathers to sons diminishes, there is a shift toward matrilateral kinsmen in the expression of intergenerational solidarity. Her data on intergenerational solidarity include household sharing, residential proximity, interaction and ties of sentiment, and reciprocal aid.

Sweetser's theoretical formulation appears to us to be a useful point of departure for examination of matrilateral bias in American kinship patterns. However, in this paper we will extend her concept of intergenerational solidarity to a more general consideration of extended kinship relations at all generational levels. Hence, in part, this study provides a replication of portions of Sweetser's materials, although in our theoretical analysis we will present somewhat different emphases.

Our objectives in this paper are: (1) to add to the growing body of empirical data by presenting evidence concerning matrilateral orientation in yet another population, and (2) to suggest a theoretical formulation to interrelate and explain "gynocentricity" and "matrilateral bias" in American kinship behavior. We feel that it is important to conceptually distinguish gynocentricity in kin behavior from any observed tendency toward an asymmetry of kin behavior which favors the matrilateral side of the kindred.

By gynocentricity of kinship behavior we mean the tendency for females to be more emotionally involved and active in kinship interaction than are males. Matrilateral bias, on the other hand, refers to the tendency for interaction with kinsmen to be more frequent and intensive with the "mother's side" than the "father's side" of a nuclear family's extended kinship network.

II. Gynocentricity of Kin Relations

Our first task in this study will be to examine evidence concerning gynocentricity by testing the following hypotheses:

1a. Females "enjoy seeing" a greater number of kinsmen than do males.

1b. Female respondents spontaneously list a larger number of kinsmen than do male respondents.

1c. Females write letters to relatives more frequently than do males.

1d. Females telephone more frequently with kin outside the nuclear family than do males.

In order to suggest a causal link between gynocentricity and matrilateral bias we will examine the possibility that, in addition to being more kin-oriented than males, females give preference to interaction with their matrilateral kin. This tendency would appear to be developed in the nuclear family as daughters learn patterns of kin behavior from their mothers. The specific hypotheses that we will test are:

2a. Female egos enjoy seeing more matrilateral kinsmen than patrilateral kinsmen. Male egos enjoy seeing more patrilateral kinsmen than matrilateral kinsmen.

2b. Females write more frequently to matrilateral than to patrilateral kinsmen of their nuclear families. Males write more frequently to patrilateral than to matrilateral kinsmen of their nuclear families.

2c. Females telephone more frequently with matrilateral than patrilateral kin of their nuclear families. Males telephone more frequently with patrilateral than matrilateral kinsmen of their nuclear families.

If in our data we find support for these first two propositions, we would expect that the effects of these tendencies would be to bring about an asymmetry in patterns of kinship interaction which takes the form of a matrilateral bias, viewed from the perspective of individual nuclear families.

The explanation of asymmetry in the American kinship system that we are proposing is based on differentiation in sex roles. In part a sex role differentiation which favors a preponderance of kinship interaction by females could be a "natural" outgrowth of female emotional interest in relatives, if our first four hypotheses are supported by the evidence. Since we are suggesting that this tendency may be an outgrowth of "emotional interest," the nature of the resulting sex role differentiation can be seen in terms of the contrast between *instrumental* and *expressive* behavior as postulated by Stephens, Zelditch and others.[2]

In a study entitled "Role differentiation in the nuclear family: a comparative study" Morris Zelditch, Jr. (1955) has shown that there are cross-cultural regularities in sex role differentiation and that these tend to be patterned in terms of contrasts between instrumental and expressive roles. Zelditch's data show that men assume *instrumental roles* related mainly to achieving tasks, making big decisions, being the ultimate disciplinarian, and taking responsibility for the family's economic security. Women, on the other hand, are said to assume *expressive roles*, which are mainly concerned with nurturance ("feeding everyone, caring for the children, keeping house, plus the emotional concomitants of these nurturant tasks").[*]

In a cross-cultural survey of sex differences in socialization, Barry, Bacon and Child (1957) have produced evidence that supports Zelditch's findings. They have shown that most human societies stress nurturance, obedience, and responsibility among female children and place greater stress on achievement and self-reliance in training male children. These aspects of socialization would appear to be logical concomitants of the instrumental-expressive contrast.

One might question whether differentiation of role behavior along sex lines exists in middle class American families, for in our society there is supposedly a norm of equal authority in nuclear families. However, Zelditch (1955) notes that in spite of a generalized appearance of role uniformity, there is a clear underlying differentiation:

In the distribution of instrumental tasks, the American family maintains a more flexible pattern than most societies. Father helps mother with the dishes. He sets the table. He makes formula for the baby. Mother can supplement the income of the family by working outside. Nevertheless, the American male, by definition, must "provide" for his family. He is responsible for the support of his wife and children. His primary area of performance is the occupational role, in which his status fundamentally inheres; and his primary function in the family is to supply an income, to be the breadwinner. There is simply something wrong with the American adult male who doesn't have a "job." American women, on the other hand, tend to hold jobs before they are married and to quit when "the day" comes, or to continue in jobs of a lower status than their husbands. And not only is the mother the focus of emotional support for the American middle class child, but much more exclusively so than in most societies (as Margaret Mead has pointed out in her treatment of adolescent problems). The cult of the warm, giving "mom"

[2] In her explanation of matrilateral bias in kinship relations in industrial societies, Sweetser (1966) emphasizes the same contrasts in sex roles and also suggests that mother-daughter dependency is a contributing factor.

[*] These formulations seem to us to involve serious biases. In terms of human biological adaptation, "feeding, caring for children, keeping house . . ." appear to be *instrumental* tasks. [Eds.]

stands in contrast to the "capable," "competent," "go-getting" male. The more expressive type of male, as a matter of fact, is regarded as "effeminate" and has too much fat on the inner side of his thigh (1955:339).

If the instrumental-expressive differentiation in sex roles is operative in the domain of kinship interaction, we would suggest that males would have greater responsibility for maintaining ties with kinsmen in societies where extended kin groups have great importance in such "practical" activities as political decision-making, maintenance of economic activities and properties, and carrying on warfare and defense. On the other hand, in societies where many of these activities are carried out by nonkinship organizations, maintenance of kin networks might take on more of the quality of expressive behavior and would be predominantly a female activity.

In the American kinship system, as compared with the situation in numerous non-Western societies, interaction with kinsmen outside the nuclear family tends not to be vitally involved with economic concerns or political decision-making. Familial corporate control of estates, factories, occupations and other economic interests is exceptional in American society, though it does occur, particularly in some segments of the socioeconomic elite. Similarly, instrumental activities in the political sphere tend not to involve corporate bodies of kinsmen in our social system. On the other hand, great interaction does occur along kinship lines, as is particularly visible at Thanksgiving, Christmas, Easter and other expressive ceremonial occasions.

It can be argued, in fact, that the decrease in instrumental significance of the American kinship system frees the American nuclear family for greater expressive interaction in the kinship network. If this is true, and if there is a pan-human tendency for expressive behavior to be defined as a female domain, then we would expect that the communications in the kinship network would be handled mainly by females. Such a female predominance in kinship interaction would account for the suggested matrilateral bias if, as we are hypothesizing, females in American middle class families tend to prefer interaction with matrilateral relatives.

III. Matrilateral Bias in American Kin Networks

We can now turn our attention to the predicted effects of gynocentricity and female kin preferences, namely, an asymmetry within bilateral kin networks which takes the form of a general matrilateral bias as viewed from the nuclear family as a unit (more interaction with mother's side than father's side).

Since our hypothesis concerning matrilateral bias in the American kinship system should apply most strongly to activities that are in themselves expressive acts, we will examine kinship interaction in a series of behaviors which we feel are predominantly expressive in character. Therefore, we will consider the following hypotheses:

3a. Nuclear families tend to visit more frequently with matrilateral than patrilateral kinsmen on holidays.

3b. Matrilateral kinsmen are found living with nuclear families more frequently than are patrilateral kinsmen.

3c. Nuclear families tend to spend vacations more frequently with matrilateral than with patrilateral kinsmen.

3d. The kinsmen who come to nuclear families to spend their vacations are more frequently matrilateral than patrilateral relatives.

IV. Method of Research

A questionnaire was devised to obtain data on kinship interaction. Since the questionnaire was administered in the form of a required report in a social anthropology class at a large Mid-Western university, it was possible to ask the respondents to supply a relatively complete chart of their bilaterally extended kinship networks. The directions in the questionnaire included the following statement: ". . . draw a complete kinship diagram of all of your kinsmen, *consanguineal* and *affinal* . . . be sure to identify yourself as ego . . . number consecutively all of your kin in the diagram."

A series of questions concerning correspondence, visiting, telephoning, vacations and others pertaining to our hypotheses were answered by each respondent in terms of the behavior of his nuclear family. He was also asked to indicate the distance in miles from his nuclear family to each of the kinsmen on the chart. The students in the class (mainly juniors and seniors, most of whom were not majoring in anthropology) were encouraged to take home the questionnaire in order to get complete and accurate information from their families. The point of reference was usually the family of orientation of ego, although students who had been married for at least five years had the option of responding in terms of their family of procreation.

A total of 38 females and 45 males returned completed reports. The fact that these respondents were students in a state university which draws its enrollment mainly from urban areas suggests a strong bias toward "middle class urban" in the sample. Occupations and income data in the questionnaire support this suggestion, for 17% of male heads of households are professionals, 46% are white collar, 32% are blue collar and laborers, and 5% are farmers. The mean reported income is $8,800. This study deals with a population of higher income and occupational level than the populations of the other studies cited earlier in this paper.

In the following analysis all of the consanguineal kin (and their spouses) of the mother in the nuclear family are considered "matrilateral"; all consanguineal kin (and their spouses) of the father of the nuclear family are considered "patrilateral." Interaction *within* the nuclear family was not considered in this analysis.

V. Results [3]

The results of the tests of hypotheses 1a, 1b, 1c, and 1d (tables I–II) give strong support to our gynocentricity hypothesis, in that females "enjoy seeing" a greater number of kinsmen than do males, they spontaneously report a greater number of kinsmen than do males, and they communicate more with kinsmen than do males.

Our next series of hypotheses are concerned with the postulated tendency for females to prefer interaction with, and carry out most interaction with, matrilateral kin of the nuclear family. This may be conceptualized as *individual* matrilateral bias. The results of the tests of hypotheses 2a, 2b, and 2c indicate that females do indeed prefer interaction with the "mother's side of the family," whereas the male preferences and interaction tendencies are not as strongly skewed toward the patrilateral side of the kin network. It is particularly revealing to note that males show only a slight tendency to prefer patrilateral kinsmen, thus lending support to the suggestion that any matrilateral biases result from asymmetry in kin preferences of females rather than asymmetry in preferences of both males and females. This suggests that studies of this type should control carefully for the factor of sex of respondents. In these hypotheses, it should be noted, letter writing and telephoning refer to the activities of *all of the members* of the nuclear families, while the responses concerning kinsmen they "enjoy seeing" refer only to the 83 respondents who filled out the questionnaires.

Our hypotheses 3a, 3b, 3c, and 3d concern behavior which may be seen as matrilateral bias in kin behavior of the nuclear family taken as a group. Although, as noted above, the sample is slightly biased toward males (45 to 38), the statistical computations have been based on the assumption of equal numbers of male and female respondents. This slight male predominance would tend to work against our matrilateral bias hypothesis, but as the tables below indicate, three out of four of these hypotheses are supported at a statistically significant level in spite of the handicap. The one that is not supported is a special case and will be dealt with below in our discussion.

As seen in the statistical tests of hypotheses 3a, 3c and 3d, matrilateral kinsmen strongly predominate among the families who are visited by our 83 nuclear families on holidays and on vacation trips. Matrilateral kinsmen also strongly predominate among those relatives who came to these families on their vacations.

The results of hypothesis 3b are in striking contrast to the other results. Matrilateral kinsmen do *not* predominate significantly among those relatives who now live or in the past have lived in the households of the 83 nuclear families.

[3] All statistical tests of hypotheses follow Chi-square techniques as described in Siegel (1956). Null hypotheses will be rejected at probability levels of .05 or less.

From the foregoing tests of individual hypotheses there appears to be strong evidence for the predicted matrilateral bias in expressive kinship interaction.

VI. Discussion

Before going on to discuss our general theory of a "matrilateral bias" in kinship relations, an alternative hypothesis about these data should be examined. It has been suggested that there is a "matrilocal bias" in middle class residence patterns, in that married couples tend to settle near the *wife's* kinsmen. Such a residential bias could explain the matrilateral tendencies we have found. The tendency toward matrilocal residence has, for example, been reported from a middle class New England town (Fischer and Fischer 1966:16). Sweetser (1966) notes tendencies to matrilocality in some American populations. Her data were taken from the United States Census.

We have examined the composition of those kinsmen living within 50 miles of our respondents' families. We find that this group of relatives is almost equally divided between matrilateral (51%) and patrilateral (49%) kinsmen, and we therefore reject the hypothesis that a matrilocal bias accounts for the results of the hypotheses tested above. Thus, even though matrilocality *may* occur as part of the syndrome of matrilateral bias, it would appear that it cannot be regarded as a direct causal factor in our research population.

Our hypotheses concerning female predominance in interactional tasks, female preference for matrilateral kin and a general matrilateral bias in kinship interaction, particularly in expressive interaction, are strongly supported.

It is particularly interesting to notice that hypothesis 3b is not supported. Matrilateral kin do *not* predominate among relatives living with the nuclear family to the extent that the general matrilateral bias in other aspects of behavior would predict. This finding deserves comment, for it would appear that it is in support of our general hypothesis. An outside kinsman living with the nuclear family is a special situation, of a different order from telephoning, visiting, and vacationing. Such a special arrangement, which is generally disapproved of in our society, represents not an expressive interaction, but a relatively enduring *instrumental* solution to the problem of dependent (usually aged) kinsmen. Our general theory would predict that, since an instrumental act—of economic support—is involved, the decisions about such an arrangement would involve equal participation by males and females in the family, or even some male predominance.[4] Although the gen-

[4] Leichter and Mitchell do find matrilaterality in patterns of "outside kin" living with nuclear family in their sample of New York Jews (1967:250). On the other hand, it was noted in this study that if the husband was in business with kin, it was with his own kin. Furthermore, Adams (1964) in a study of parental aid to married children notes that young couples just starting out, or in the early stages of child-rearing, got direct financial aid such as loans more often from the husband's family, in both a blue-collar and a white-collar American sample.

eral matrilateral bias might provide a slightly larger list of potential candidates from the matrilateral side, we find that 75% of the kinsmen living within the nuclear families in our sample came from the local area (50 mile radius) in which there is a reported near equal number of matrilateral and patrilateral kinsmen (see table II).

Summarizing our findings, it can be stated that when a person in a middle class Mid-Western nuclear family telephones or writes a kinsman outside his nuclear family, it is most likely to be a female and that she is contacting one of the nuclear family's matrilateral kinsmen (as defined above). When a nuclear family stops to visit relatives during a vacation trip it will most likely be spending time with matrilateral kinsmen, and when relatives come to spend their vacation in the home of our hypothetical nuclear family, they will most likely be the wife's kinsmen. Along these same lines, the preponderance of holiday visits by the nuclear family will be with matrilateral kin.

It should be emphasized again that these data were gathered from a predominantly urban, middle class, Mid-Western sample. Taken together with the data from other segments of the American society discussed above, a pattern begins to emerge suggesting pervasive tendencies toward matrilateral biases in American kinship behavior. However, possibilities of regional differences in these patterns should not be ruled out, and replication of studies of this sort in other parts of North America should be carried out.

Our results suggest that in studies of American kinship behavior misinterpretations of the data can result if males and females are not separated in the analysis of the data. In the Robins and Tomanec study, for example, the observed tendencies toward "individual matrilaterality" could have come about because the sample contained more females than males. Also, when indicators of kinship interaction such as visiting and other communications, mutual financial aid, patterns of inheritance and the like are lumped together it is possible that important patterns are obscured because some of these activities are expressive acts, while others have a much more instrumental character. Our data would suggest that these categories should be considered separately.

In the formulation of instrumental vs. expressive role tasks there has been an unfortunate tendency to emphasize the supposed pragmatic characteristics of the male instrumental role with the resulting implication that the female role is somehow of less practical importance. However, it should be emphasized that both kinds of role enactments clearly have practical consequences.

While we do not intend to present a thorough exploration of possible consequences of matrilateral asymmetry in the American kinship system, it is likely that some of the most important concomitants of this bias may be in the socialization and personality formation of the children in the nuclear family. Bernard Farber (1966) has presented evidence concerning one of the possible consequences of kin network asymmetry. In comparing a sample of families of "disturbed" children with a matched sample of "normal" children, he found that the families of the disturbed children showed a significantly greater asymmetry in "feelings of closeness" to kinsmen outside the nuclear family. Farber suggests that optimum power relationships (and hence optimum psychological health) within the nuclear family depend on a relatively balanced bilateral network of kinsmen that provide the larger emotional context within which the nuclear family functions. He feels that:

. . . in a bilateral system, when marked tendencies toward asymmetry occur, there are no formal mechanisms for adjusting disequilibrium in power relations in the nuclear family. This disequilibrium would be especially disruptive to family relations when equalitarian norms are supposed to govern husband-wife interaction. The disequilibrium creates personal problems for family members. These personal problems may result in emotional disturbance in children (Farber 1966:77–78).

While Farber's suggestions are based on a rather small sample (20 cases), his hypothesis may be of great importance if, as the evidence increasingly indicates, asymmetry of kinship interaction is a prevalent feature of the American social system. Asymmetry, of course, is a matter of degree, and research is needed on the effects (social, psychological and economic) of varying degrees of asymmetry. In any case, the several studies that have confirmed a matrilateral asymmetry in our kinship system point to the importance of empirical research on real kinship behavior as against the "ideal models" developed through data-less theorizing. It would appear, for example, that the "symmetrical multilineal" or "onion ring" model of middle class American kinship is of limited theoretical value when it comes to predicting the actual interactions within American kinship networks.

Table I: Statistical Tests of Hypotheses

HYPOTHESIS	MALE	FEMALE	SIGNIFI-CANCE
1a. Number of kin respondents "enjoy seeing"	141	285	.001
1c. Number of persons who write to kin	106	338	.001
1d. Number of persons who telephone kin	151	303	.001
	MATRI-LATERAL	PATRI-LATERAL	
3a. Laterality of holiday household visits with kinsmen (1964 and 1965)	819	422	.001
3b. Laterality of kinsmen "living in"	35	27	N.S.
3c. Laterality of vacations in kinsmen's homes	216	84	.001
3d. Laterality of vacation visits from kinsmen	240	138	.001

Table II

HYPOTHESIS	MALE HIGH	FEMALE HIGH	MALE LOW	FEMALE LOW	SIGNIFI-CANCE
1b. Sex of respondents/ number * of kinsmen reported	13	21	13	16	.05

	MATRILATERAL		PATRILATERAL		SIGNIFI-CANCE
HYPOTHESIS	MALE	FEMALE	MALE	FEMALE	
2a. Sex of respondents/ laterality of kin they "enjoy seeing"	65	140	76	45	.001
2b. Sex of respondents/ laterality of kin they write to	41	214	65	124	.001
2c. Sex of respondents/ laterality of kin telephoned	45	207	106	96	.001

* Defined in terms of above or below mean for sample.

References Cited

ABERLE, DAVID F., AND KASPER D. NAEGELE (1952) Middle-class fathers' occupational role and attitudes toward children. The American Journal of Orthopsychiatry 22:366–378.

ADAMS, BERT N. (1964) Structural factors affecting parental aid to married children. Journal of Marriage and the Family 26:327–331.

ALDOUS, JOAN, AND REUBEN HILL (1965) Social cohesion, lineage type, and intergenerational transmission. Social Forces 43:471–482.

BARRY, HERBERT A., MARGARET K. BACON, AND IRWIN L. CHILD (1957) A cross-cultural survey of some sex differences in socialization. Journal of Abnormal and Social Psychology 55:327–332.

CODERE, HELEN (1955) A genealogical study of kinship in the United States. Psychiatry 18:65–80.

COULT, ALAN D., AND ROBERT W. HABENSTEIN (1965) The prediction of inter-family ties in the American kinship system. In The function of extended kinship in urban society, Habenstein and Coult, eds. Kansas City, Community Studies, Inc., pp. A–1–15.

CUMMING, ELAINE, AND DAVID M. SCHNEIDER (1961) Sibling solidarity: a property of American kinship. American Anthropologist 63:498–507.

FARBER, BERNARD (1966) Kinship laterality and the emotionally disturbed child. In Kinship and family organization, Bernard Farber, ed. New York, John Wiley & Sons, pp. 69–78.

FISCHER, JOHN L., AND ANN FISCHER (1966) The New Englanders of Orchard Town, U.S.A. New York, John Wiley and Sons, Inc.

GOODENOUGH, WARD H. (1965) Yankee kinship terminology: a problem in componential analysis. American Anthropologist, Special Publication Part 2, 67:259–287.

Habenstein, Robert W., and Alan D. Coult (1965) The function of extended kinship in urban society. Community Studies, Inc., Kansas City.

Leichter, Hope Jensen, and William E. Mitchell (1967) Kinship and casework. Russell Sage Foundation, New York.

Murdock, George Peter (1937) Comparative data on division of labor by sex. Social Forces 15:551–553.

Parsons, Talcott (1943) The kinship system of the contemporary United States. American Anthropologist 45:22–38.

Robins, Lee, and Miroda Tomanec (1966) Closeness to blood relatives outside the immediate family. In Kinship and family organization, Bernard Farber, ed. New York, John Wiley & Sons, Inc., pp. 134–141.

Romney, A. Kimball, and Roy Goodwin D'Andrade (1964) Cognitive aspects of English kin terms. American Anthropologist, Special Publication No. 3, Part 2, 66:146–170.

Schneider, David M., and George C. Homans (1955) Kinship terminology and the American kinship system. American Anthropologist 57:1199–1208.

Siegel, Sidney (1956) Nonparametric statistics for the behavioral sciences. New York, McGraw-Hill.

Stephens, William N. (1963) The family in cross-cultural perspective. New York, Holt, Rinehart and Winston.

Sweetser, Dorrian Apple (1963) Asymmetry in intergenerational family relationships. Social Forces 41:346–352.

——— (1964) Mother-daughter ties between generations in industrial societies. Family Process 3:332–343.

——— (1966) The effect of industrialization on intergenerational solidarity. Rural Sociology 31:156–170.

Wallace, A. F. C., and J. Atkins (1960) The meaning of kinship terms. American Anthropologist 62:58–79.

White, Leslie A. (1965) Anthropology 1964: retrospect and prospect. American Anthropologist 67:629–637.

Zelditch, Morris, Jr. (1955) Role differentiation in the nuclear family: a comparative study. In Family, socialization and interaction process, Talcott Parsons and Robert F. Bales, eds. Glencoe, Illinois, The Free Press, pp. 307–315, 338–42.

Political and Economic Dimensions of Adaptations

6

Every human group must deal with matters of "politics"—control of economic and social relationships within the group, decisions about adaptive strategies, and relationships to their neighbors. In the technologically simplest societies, such as the Australian Aboriginal hunter-gatherers, relationships within the group and to neighbors often involved conflicts over women as potential spouses, and the retaliations for alleged acts of witchcraft. These two primary problems—women and witchcraft—have been priority items in political relations among many small-scale societies. There are not many alternatives open to such small human groups in controlling the actions of their neighbors, but frequently some kind of avenging expedition, organized by groups of kin, is carried out to right the supposed wrongs of "those people over in the next valley." Some writers have described these avenging parties as a form of warfare, but the description of the *atninga* among the tribes of central Australia should make clear that this kind of conflict is very different indeed from the mass killing and annexation of territory characteristic of more complex societies. It is instead a means of executing justice in societies where there are no centralized judicial systems, police, courts, or other legal institutions.

Of course relationships to neighboring groups far more often involve peaceful trading of economic goods, exchanges of marriageable individuals for spouses, and other nonaggressive transactions. In some areas with high diversity of resources and effective means of transportation, complex trading systems have developed. The islands of the Melanasian area represent something of an all-time high in such preindustrial exchange networks. Thomas Harding's discussion of trading relationships among the people of the Vitiaz Strait demonstrates that people do not trade goods simply for economic profit and accumulation. Noncommercialized trading systems are often tightly interwoven with political relations, as well as the accumulation of prestige through generosity and wealth display.

From the point of view of Western peoples, economic and political systems are usually considered two separate domains. That is, we tend to think of economic leaders and political leaders as two different kinds of people. This distinction is not necessarily true in our own society, nor is it accurate for preindustrial societies. Heider's discussion of the ideal Dani leader gives us a glimpse of the complex combination of political, physical, and economic skills which make up the ideal leader in this preindustrial society in New Guinea. Leaders in New Guinea societies such as the Dani are at the same time entrepreneurs, politicians, and field marshals. There is little indication of specialization in social, military, or political domains.

Many discussions of political leadership give the impression that in all human societies males are the politicians, except for a few aberrations like Queen Elizabeth and Katherine the Great (not to forget Ella Grasso, Golda Meir and Indira Ghandi). However, in many societies women have exercised political control and been prominent as heads of state to varying degree. African societies have often been thought of as heavily male-dominated in social tendencies, yet women have been politically important even in some of the most male-dominated African social systems. The discussion by Annie M. D. Lebeuf explains some of the context and role situations within which females have exercised political control in non-Europeanized Africa. It is an interesting possibility that African societies may have had more leeway for accepting women's political leadership *before* the coming of Europeans than after. At any rate, it is significant that she notes in summary that "African women have a tradition of practical participation in public affairs."

Political complexity developed early in the Near East, following the rise of complex agricultural systems many thousands of years ago. Our Euro-American distorted view of history sometimes gives us the impression that complex political systems have been a product mainly of the European scene and perhaps China and Japan. Descriptions of Africa, for example, often give the impression of simple "tribal" social organization, with a heavy emphasis on kinship relations and small communities. Before the coming of Europeans, however, many African groups had developed complex kingdoms and administrative bureaucracies rivaling their counterparts in Europe. A number of these have been described in detail in the anthropological literature. The Bunyoro case (John Beattie) is one of these. It is not possible to describe a complex European nation in a few pages, and to the same degree the brief description by Beattie of the Bunyoro kingdom is a very small piece of a very complex system. Nonetheless, we hope that it is enough to illustrate some of the dimensions of governmental structure that evolved in the African scene almost totally separated from Eurasian feudalism and kingdoms.

It is, of course, a mistake to overemphasize the similarities in all of the lines of development politically and economically from simple societies to complex social organization. Whenever we focus on the main convergences and parallels, we miss the texture and interest of the specialized features that mark the very diverse and different forms of society humans have developed. Perhaps our emphasis here on certain similarities of evolutionary processes will spur students to explore the importance of the diversities.

Baldwin Spencer and F. J. Gillen

The Avenging Party in Central Australia

Very often one group of natives, that is, the members of the tribe inhabiting a particular locality, will quarrel with the members of some other group either belonging to the same or to some other tribe. The quarrel is usually due to one of two causes: either some man has stolen a wife from some other group, or else the death of a native is attributed by the medicine man to the magic of some member of a distant group. When this is so, the aggrieved party will arrange to make an attack upon the men who are regarded as the aggressors. Most often the attackers, armed with spears and spear-throwers, boomerangs, and shields, will march up to the enemies' camp, and the quarrel will be confined to a wordy warfare, lasting perhaps for an hour or two, after which things quiet down, and all is over; but in some cases a regular fight takes place, in which severe wounds may be inflicted. In other cases the attacking party will steal down upon the enemy, and, lying in ambush, will await an opportunity of spearing one or two of the men without any risk to themselves.

The following incident which happened recently will serve to show what often takes place.

The men living in the country round about Alice Springs in the Macdonnell Range were summoned by *Inwurra*, that is, properly accredited messengers carrying Churinga, who had been sent out by the Alatunja of the group to assemble for the purpose of making war upon the Iliaura tribe, which occupies the country between eighty and a hundred miles to the north of the Ranges.

For a long time the northern groups of the Arunta tribe had been in fear of the Iliaura, who had been continually sending in threatening messages, or at least it was constantly reported that they were doing so, for it must be remembered that imagination plays a large part in matters such as these amongst the natives. Several deaths, also, which had taken place amongst the Arunta, had been attributed by the medicine men to the evil magic of certain of the Iliaura men. When the messengers and the men summoned had assembled at Alice Springs a council of the elder men was held, at which it was determined to make a raid on the Iliaura, and accordingly a party was organised for the purpose. Such an avenging party is called an Atninga.

When all was prepared the Atninga started away for the north, and, after travelling for several days, came upon a group of Iliaura men, consisting of about a dozen families, near to whom they camped for two days.

As usual on such occasions, the Iliaura sent some of their women over to the strangers' camp, but the fact that the use of the women was declined by the visitors at once indicated that the mission of the latter was not a friendly one. The women are offered with a view of conciliating the Atninga men, who, if they accept the favour, indicate by so doing that the quarrel will not be pursued any further.

In the Iliaura community were two old men, and with them matters were discussed by the elder men amongst the Arunta at a spot some little distance from the camp of the latter. After a long talk extending over two days, during which the strangers set forth their grievances and gave the Iliaura men very clearly to understand that they were determined to exact vengeance, the two old men said, in effect, "Go no further. Our people do not wish to quarrel with your people; there are three bad men in our camp whom we Iliaura do not like, they must be killed. Two are *Iturka* (that is men who have married within the forbidden degrees of relationship); the other is very quarrelsome and strong in magic and has boasted of killing your people by means of Kurdaitcha and other magic. Kill these men, but do not injure any others in our camp, and we will help you."

These terms were accepted by the Arunta, and it was agreed between the old men of the two parties that an attempt should be made to kill the three men on the next day. At daylight the old men of the Iliaura went some little distance away from their camp, and there made a fire, and called up the other men of their party. This special fire, at which it is intended to surprise and kill the men who have been condemned and handed over to the tender mercies of their enemies, is called *Thara* (the ordinary word for fire being *Ura*). At the Atninga camp another fire, also called *Thara*, was lighted at the same time. Shortly after daylight a number of the Arunta, led by an old man, went over to the *Thara* of the Iliaura, all of them being unarmed, and here they took special care to engage the condemned men in conversation. The remainder of the Atninga party in full war-paint, with whittled sticks in their hair, their bodies painted with red ochre, carrying spears, boomerangs, and shields, and each one wearing the magic *Kirra-urkna* or girdle made of a dead man's hair, crept up unseen and, suddenly springing up, speared two of the condemned men from behind. The third man—one of the two *Iturka* —had grown suspicious during the night and had accordingly decamped, taking his women with him.

A large number of spears were thrown into the bodies of the men who were killed. When they were dead the Atninga party danced round the bodies, and taking the whittled sticks or *Ilkunta* from their heads, broke them up and threw the pieces on to the bodies. These *Ilkunta* are always worn by certain groups of the Northern Arunta when they really mean to fight, and amongst the same natives also under these circumstances little curved flakes are cut by means of flints on their spears about a foot from the pointed end.

The Iliaura men looked on quietly while the killing took place, and when all was over, the spears were taken out of the bodies by the men of the Arunta who had acted as decoys, and were handed back to their respective owners. It is supposed that if the latter themselves removed them some great evil would befall them, as the body and anything in contact with it of a victim killed in this way is strictly tabu to the killer.

When this had been done, the Arunta went to the main camp of the Iliaura and took the *Unawa* of one of the dead men, and she became and is now the property of the old man who seized her, she being a woman of the class into which he could lawfully marry. One girl child was annexed by one of the younger men, who carried her on his back for the greater part of the return journey for about a hundred miles. The two women who belonged to the *Iturka* man were away, but no attempt was made to capture them, as being themselves *Iturka*, they would not be taken as wives by the men of the avenging party. They would when captured meet with severe punishment at the hands of the Iliaura men and in all probability would be put to death. Had they been the proper *Unawa* of the dead man, they would, if present, have been appropriated by men of the Atninga party to whom they were also *Unawa*. The special name of *Immirinja* is given to the men who actually took part in the spearing, those who acted as decoys and who thus merely took a passive part, being called *Alknalarinika* which means "onlookers."

Travelling back to the Arunta country, the Atninga party separated into various contingents, each of which went to its own locality, upon arrival at which certain ceremonies had to be observed. The Alice Springs contingent, which will serve to illustrate what took place in each instance, halted some distance away from the main camp and decorated their bodies, painting them all over with powdered charcoal and placing on their foreheads and through the septum of the nose small twigs of a species of Eremophila. As soon as they came in sight of the main camp they began to perform an excited war-dance, approaching in the form of a square and holding and moving their shields as if to ward off something which was being thrown at them. This action is called *Irulchiukiwuma* and is intended to beat off the *Ulthana* or spirit of the dead man.

Thomas Harding

Trade with the Hinterland

Traditionally, Sio [off the coast of New Guinea] received imported food-stuffs and tobacco from the nearest inland villages—Old Mula, Sambori, and Nimbako. In addition, these bush traders brought pigs, dogs, net bags, bows and arrows, stone adzes, painted bark-cloth robes, and dogs' teeth. For food and tobacco they received Sio pots, fish, and coconuts. For other goods they acquired Tami and Rai Coast bowls, *tambu* shell, boars' tusks, obsidian, and red and black pigments. From the densely settled upper Komba and Selepet, the bush middlemen received sweet potatoes, yams, bows, net bags, stone adzes, and pigs and dogs in return for such coastal and overseas products as pots, boars' tusks, *tambu*, wooden bowls, and lime. In spite of the fact that locally produced food is sufficient, the middlemen accept sweet potatoes and yams for pots and other goods. They explain: "They don't bring taro, which we have plenty of. We don't need more food, but they are our kin and we accept what they bring." The Sios also, of course, frequently accept goods which they do not need at the time. When I asked one Sio man why he had four bows (most men have more than one), he replied: "If a bush friend comes with a bow, you have to help him."

To provide an idea of modern trading between Sio and its hinterland, we may examine a number of recent transactions reported by Sio and Komba informants:

(a) 4 pots, 8 coconuts	= 2 *bilums* Singapore taro, 3 packets of tobacco
(b) 1 large pot, 12 coconuts, 1 *laplap*, 2s.	= 1 *bilum* Singapore taro, 1 bunch of bananas, 4 stalks of sugar cane, 1 bundle of greens
(c) 1 large pot, 1 small pot, 8 coconuts, 1s., 1 piece women's clothing (6s.), 2 *laplaps* (8s.), 1 pair short trousers (3s.)	= 1 *bilum* Singapore taro, 1 bundle of lettuce, 3 packets of tobacco
(d) 1 pair trousers (£1)	= 6 packets of tobacco
(e) 1 s.	= 1 bamboo container of lime
(f) 1 pot, 4 coconuts, 1 *laplap* (12s.)	= 5 packets of tobacco
(g) 1 small pot, 1 large pot, 16 coconuts, 1 *laplap*, 1 pair short trousers	= 5 packets of tobacco, 20 Singapore taro, 5 large taro, some bananas

From Thomas Harding, Voyagers of the Vitiaz Strait, pp. 109–117. Copyright © 1967 University of Washington Press. Reprinted by permission of the publisher.

(h) 5 coconuts	= 1 *bilum* of Singapore taro
(i) 5 coconuts, some fish	= 2 *bilums* of taro
(j) 1 pot	= 1 packet of tobacco
(k) (no return gift)	= 1 *bilum* of taro and Singapore taro, 3 packets of tobacco
(l) 1 pot, 8 coconuts	= 3 large packets of tobacco (200–350 leaves)
(m) (no return)	= 2 packets of tobacco
(n) £1	= 1 female piglet
(o) 3 pots, 2 *laplaps*, £5	= 1 two-year-old pig
(p) 1 large machete	= 2 *bilums* of sweet potato, taro and Singapore taro, 4 packets of tobacco

All of these transactions except (e) occurred between trade-friends at Sio. It is apparent that informants' statements regarding rates of exchange offer only the roughest guidelines, and that no series of transactions of this kind will illuminate any implicit rates of exchange. If a balance, according to some standard, exists over the long run, it could only be shown by examining a number of series of transactions between particular sets of trade-friends extending over a period of years. The manner in which exchanges are made and the social ethic guiding exchange combine to make informants' memories of past transactions of the run-of-the-mill sort rather hazy. Transactions involving pigs, dogs, and ornaments, however, are remembered well.

Many of the transactions outlined above are incomplete, that is, they are but an episode in a continuing series. In the case of (c), the Sio man explained his generosity as follows: "The bushwoman's husband died recently and I felt sorry for her. Besides, I thought of all the food that she will bring next time." In (h) it was conceded that five coconuts were only part-payment for the *bilum* of food received. In (k) the bushman had an expectation but received no specific promise of a future return. Transaction (m) illustrates the common practice whereby a bushman sends tobacco to a Sio trade-friend via another trader along with a message as to what he wants in the future. By resorting to a third party, the man may make a specific request, something he is loath to do when he meets his trade-friend face to face. In (n) the bushman was dissatisfied with the one pound received for the pig—this is the stated rate of exchange—and this combined with other unsatisfactory transactions caused him to break off the relationship. A Komba trader reported transaction (p) as evidence of the generosity of his Sio trade-friends.

Transaction (l), one pot and eight coconuts for three large packets of tobacco, is unbalanced in favor of the Sio side of the exchange. A small pot is worth three to six shillings while one shilling is the widely recognized equivalent for one "rope" of coconuts (four). The Sios regard an ordinary packet of tobacco containing at least several dozen leaves to be worth one shilling, while a large packet is worth three or four shillings (sometimes tobacco is made up in packets three feet long, which are worth five pounds or a pig). In these terms, the goods exchanged were of unequal value—five to eight shillings' worth of pots and coconuts for at least ten to twelve shillings' worth of tobacco—and the Komba partner was highly dissatisfied. Increasingly, younger men feel that prices for tobacco, in particular, should correspond more closely to town market prices, where six leaves may be sold for one shilling. In this case the Komba man did not calculate values on this basis, but regarded the three packets of tobacco together to be worth eighteen shillings, while he put the cash value of the pot and coconuts at five shillings. This comparison was made in the course of illustrating the general point that the Sios are unfair when it comes to paying for tobacco. His dissatisfaction in this particular case, however, stemmed mostly from the fact that he wanted not pots or coconuts but a *laplap*. In general, people travel to Sio with specific needs in mind, but sometimes they receive as gifts things which they do not want at the time. Similarly, Sio people are generally more pleased by a gift of taro than of sweet potato, or of tobacco rather than bows or net bags, of which they may have plenty. Thus, dissatisfaction may arise on both sides even though—unlike transaction (1)—the exchange is objectively balanced.

Division of Labor Related to Trading

Most trade between Sio and the hinterland is conducted between trade-friends, and most exchange between trade-friends takes place at Sio. Therefore, the transport of goods, one of the main burdens of labor in trading, is borne by the inland people, especially the women. A comparison of the activities performed by the different groups, and men as opposed to women, indicate that Sio men do the least, while Komba and Sio women do the most. The various trade-related activities are distributed as follows:

Komba women: The bulk of transport; taro planting and weeding, harvesting for trade; manufacture of net bags.

Komba men: Heavy work in gardening; cultivation of tobacco, curing and wrapping of tobacco leaf; bow making; on trading trips men carry their personal belongings and the lightweight packets of tobacco; sometimes a man carries a single *bilum* of food while his wife carries two.

Sio women: Pottery making, fishing, transport to markets, cooking; collection and grinding of *tambu* shell for ornaments; cleaning of coconut groves, preparation of sun-dried copra (cash from copra sales used in trade).

Sio men: Fishing; cleaning coconut plantations and processing of copra.

The position of Sio men, in particular, seems enviable. When a trade-friend arrives, the Sio becomes a gracious host. His wife cooks the meals, brings down pots from their overhead storage racks, and if any fish are to be provided she probably catches them. Children are dispatched to collect coconuts. Meanwhile, the head of the household fulfills his obligations by sitting in the company of his friends on the veranda.

At the same time, as money, bush knives, and *laplaps* have become more important in local trading, the burden of Sio men increases. The cash returns of hard labor as a wage worker or in copra production must be diverted from other uses to sustain trade relationships.

Comparisons with Gitua

Moving east from Sio along the *kunai* littoral, one finds that the coast is sculptured into a remarkable series of grassy terraces rising in regular tiers to heights of several hundred feet. The terrace land is visible from Siassi, thirty to forty miles away, as a yellowish swath. The heart of the swath is barren, dry, and oppressively hot. It is this protruding part of the mainland coast, from Fortification Point to Cape King William (named by Dampier who in March, 1700, saw the "smokes" of the pig hunters from the other side of the Strait), which helps to produce the "funnel effect" of the Vitiaz Strait that is noted by European seamen during the Southeast season. On land, too, the winds reach high velocities, and gardens near the beach are walled off with wind screens to protect the yams against salt spray. The three large communities of Sio, Gitua, and Sialum all formerly lived on small offshore islands, as if they intended to dissociate themselves somehow from the inhospitable character of the coastal strip itself.

Gitua (population 415) is twelve miles east of Sio, closer to the heart of the terrace land, and in major respects environmental conditions are less favorable than at Sio. Timber and building materials for houses and canoes are in short supply; the fringing reef is small; wild pigs are few; extensive stands of sago palms are lacking; there are much fewer coconuts than at Sio; and bush areas favorable for taro planting are very restricted. Finally, the terms of the inland trade are much less favorable than at Sio.

As at Sio, local trade takes place both at markets and through visits of trade-friends. A much larger proportion of trading at Gitua, however, is performed in markets. According to the market rate, the Gituans say, a clay pot currently brings three to four taro, while in dealing with trade-friends a pot is worth five to ten taro (more comparable to Sio). The difference between Sio and Gituan rates of exchange may be largely a matter of geography. The hinterland villages of Gitua—Kumukio, Kinalakna, Bambi, Gitukia, Sikikia, Wetna, Ezanko, and others—are all a walk of two hours or less from the beach. Meeting places for trade are therefore convenient to both the Gituans and mountain villagers. A trading trip that begins in the morning can be concluded well before midday—and much of the exchange of inland for coastal products takes place at these midway sites. From Sio, on the other hand, the nearest inland village of Balup is three and one-half to four hours away. Sometimes Balup people visit Sio and return in a day, but more often they stay overnight. Traders from Mula, Sambori, Nimbako, or more remote villages must plan on spending at least one night at Sio. The traders therefore require hospitality—food and lodging—and for this reason most trade is conducted on the much more sociable lines of trade-friendship.

Coast-inland exchange at Sialum, twenty-five miles east of Sio, probably closely resembles the situation at Gitua. Stolz, who lived at Sialum between 1907 and 1911, states that fish was the main item moving inland (Sialum did not manufacture pottery at this time) in return for taro, sweet potato, tobacco, betelnut, and bows. He observed that "Strange to say, the trade is carried on only by old women."

The Trade System Viewed from Sio

Before leaving the mainland of New Guinea for the archipelago, we can appropriately scan the trade system from this vantage point. Looking out over the waters of the Strait from the Sio beach in early morning, or late afternoon, the outer islands stand out in bold silhouettes. Arop Island, Tolokiwa, Umboi, and beyond Umboi the two great mountains which stand guard at the western tip of New Britain, appear much closer than they really are. Beyond Sio to the south loom the towering ridges of the Sarawaged Range. Prior to the advent of Europeans, the Sio world was bounded by these ranges, the outer islands, and the lines of clouds visible on the horizon. This world, corresponding approximately to the territory of the trade system, was not necessarily or inherently hostile, for it was interlaced by social connections radiating from Sio. The Sios found their enemies closer to home, the nearby communities of Gitua, Kumukio, Kiari, and the Komba. People from afar were friends.

To the people of the hinterland, Sio is known as *aman topne*, the source of pots. In return mainly for their clay pots, the Sios receive all the specialized products that the Vitiaz Strait has to offer. From the interior comes food when it is most needed—taro, sweet potatoes, and bananas. Also from the interior come bows and arrows, net bags, pigs, dogs, bark cloth, pandanus rain capes, dogs' teeth, and tobacco. From the Rai Coast come wood bowls, black pigment, bark cloth, dogs' teeth, *Canarium* almonds, and, when required, yams, taro, and bananas. Arop Island provides the finest hand drums and betel mortars. In addition to pots, some of these goods—such as tobacco, Rai Coast bowls, bows, net bags, pigs, and dogs' teeth—are passed on by the Sios to the Siassi traders in return for pandanus mats, coconuts, boars' tusks, disc beads, sago, red ochre, obsidian, and wooden bowls.

Trade was often the occasion for gala festivals, or the two events were timed to coincide. When the members of the Hamburg Expedition visited Sio Island in 1909, a festival—an inter-*mbawnza* distribution and *singsing*—was about to get under way. Present as guests were Arop Islanders, Siassis, and small, timid men from the interior, probably Kombas. At such crossroads of trade as Sio, then, people from different parts of the "world" met face to face, and there is nothing to suggest that such mixed gatherings were unusual.

The regular voyages of the Siassi Islanders bring them to the Sio Coast once or twice annually, during the change of seasons. For example, in November they take advantage of the tag end of the Southeast Trade winds to make the crossing, and return by the first winds of the Northwest Monsoon.

Karl G. Heider

The Ideal Dani Leader

Dani statements about leadership are worth noting, even though they do not particularly correspond to observable reality. The invariable Dani answer to the question, "Why is (X) such a big man?", is "He has killed many people in war." Secondary replies mention his many wives and pigs. But in fact, the lists of killings attributed to the various men of the Neighborhood are greatly inflated or at best describe general participation in a killing. (If they were real, one would have expected that their enemies had long since been completely eradicated.) The number of wives a man has is more a result of influence, especially economic influence, than a cause of it. And leaders in fact often have fewer pigs on hand than many less important men.

Skill in oratory, which figures so prominently in the leadership pattern of nearly every other New Guinea society, is quite unimportant to the Dani. There are no speeches at public events. The leaders of a ceremony will mumble incantations at ghosts or shout names to identify givers or receivers of goods, and at battles it is most often the young and unimportant men who shout the most hilarious obscenities. The persuasiveness of a leader is exercised privately, in small groups or tête-à-tête.

The confederation-level leaders are all gentle men of strength and skill. To some extent these Dani leaders correspond to [Kenneth] Read's description of the leaders of the Gahuku-Gama in East New Guinea. But while Read suggests that this gentleness is a mark of autonomy, of standing somewhat

Reprinted from Karl G. Heider, The Dugum Dani (Chicago: Aldine Publishing Company, 1970); copyright © 1960 by Wenner-Gren Foundation for Anthropological Research, Inc. Reprinted by permission of the author and Aldine Publishing Company.

outside a system in which the primary male virtue is aggressiveness, in the Dani case it is this gentleness which seems to be the dominant virtue. Read has said of New Guinea Highlanders in general that

they seem to be continually on the verge of some more or less violent and unexpected outburst, and continual close association with them becomes a strain.

This description certainly does *not* fit the Dugum Dani. Their aggressiveness in warfare is a different matter. It is not so much interpersonal aggression for the purpose of domination, but much more a tactical skill whose result may be the death of an enemy. The Dani simply do not live in the tense, aggressive atmosphere that Read and many others since have reported from the Highlands of New Guinea.

I think that when the Dani describe their leaders as killers with many wives and pigs, they are referring to a general quality of skill or competence: Personal aggressiveness and brutality, even against an enemy, is not valued; but one often hears the cry "*Hat hotiak*" ("you are clever") said approvingly to both children and adults, referring to this skillful competence.

Means of Gaining Influence

There are no formalized requirements or institutionalized paths to leadership and influence. Likewise, there is no status or rank that a man at some point in his career assumes and later relinquishes. All normal men are big men (*ab gogtek*) to some degree. Those I call leaders are those with the greatest influence. The Dani themselves have no comparable term to separate out this category of leaders.

Since the means of increasing one's influence are implicit, we must look to those men who have greater or less influence and attempt to discover the reasons for their position in the continuum.

[Leopold] Pospisil has stated of the Ekagi (Kapauku) that "pig breeding constitutes the only way to become rich and to acquire prestige, achievements which in turn enable a man to become an influential politician," and that "wealth and skill in oratory constitute the prerequisites for assumption of the political leadership of a village." For the Dugum Dani wealth is certainly a factor in achieving leadership, but skill in oratory apparently does not play an important role. There seem to be four major factors in the development of influence for the Dugum Dani.

SKILL IN WARFARE. Skill in warfare is a major factor in the prestige of a man. The number of kills a man has to his credit is probably not so important. Rather, his bravery or his fearlessness is important. This quality may be demonstrated in different ways. A man like Wejaklegek, or the cripple Alheto, demonstrate it on the front line of battle, never retreating and courting enemy arrows. On the other hand, the powerful Um'ue is rarely seen on the front lines—he fights on the side, in the bush, where cleverness is more important than brute courage.

The younger men are judged by their skill and courage in the face of the enemy. For those men who have enough influence to call a battle or raid, much of their prestige rides on their skill in assuring the success of the venture.

ECONOMIC COMPETITION AND HOUSEHOLD SIZE. Economic power is gained not so much by accumulation of wealth as by skillful manipulation of wealth in the complex exchange system—in participating in the exchange which takes place at funerals and other ceremonies. An unimportant man such as Egali happens to have many more pigs but less prestige than an important man like Um'ue.

The number of wives a man has does not directly affect his prestige; rather the number of women—wives, older relatives, and young girls—and boys in his household has a direct effect on his economic power: The pigs are cared for primarily by women and boys, and so if a man has few women and boys, his ability to maintain a large herd is diminished. In practice this is not a limiting factor: Egali, with one wife and one son, maintains a herd of about fifteen pigs; Um'ue, although there are perhaps ten women and boys in his household, is never able to increase his herd much beyond ten because he is involved in so much exchange at funerals. Women are further important because salt, which is traded for feathers, furs, exchange stones, and net materials from the Jale, is prepared exclusively by the women; too, the exchange nets are made exclusively by women.

An indication of the influence of a man is the number of youths—boys and sometimes even girls—who come to live in his compound on the basis of the kinship structure, and in particular the *ami* relationship. The *ami* is the mother's brother, but also includes all men of the mother's sib or even moiety. The *opase*, strictly the father, but extended to all men of the father's sib and even moiety, functions similarly. A youth can claim either *opase* or *ami* relationship with any man of the area, and, if there is a friendly relationship, can live in that man's compound, sharing the work of the compound, and eventually expects the man to assist in the marriage exchange, or in exchange at the cremation of one of the youth's closer relatives, and even in disputes. These youths, between age ten and the time they are married (around the age of twenty) lead highly mobile lives, drifting from one compound to another. An important man like Um'ue may have up to three or four such youths staying in his compound, but there is nothing formalized in these relationships.

HEREDITY AND INHERITANCE. An important factor in prestige not recognized explicitly by the Dani is heredity. Heredity has an indirect effect on prestige: A man is not important simply because his father was a leader; but several factors make it easier for such a man to rise in importance, make it more likely that a leader will be the son of a leader.

Since the more important men tend to have more wives and therefore more sons than the less important men, perhaps probability favors an important man having an important father. But more significant is the fact that the important man will be able to give his sons pigs, and his sons will have a share in his other wealth. When the time comes for them to marry, they will have easier access to wealth for the marriage exchange than the son of a poor man.

CHARISMA. The factor of charisma is easy to exaggerate in a situation such as the Dugum Dani, where the other factors are so vague. However, it is certainly present. Personal charisma must be a factor in almost any culture except where there is a purely hereditary kinship or a leadership based on certain special talents such as shamanism.

In the Dani case, charisma is not demonstrated by the orator, but rather by the man acting within the small group—in his conversation in the men's house or the watchtower shelter.

There is no Dani term for charisma, but it is related to the Dani concept of *edai-egen*, the physiological heart; also the soul of the living man; and, most pertinent in this sense, it may be described as the "goodness" of a person. A man with a short temper, who is easily provoked into hurting people within his group (as opposed to the valued killing of the enemy), is described as *edai-egen dlek*, having no heart. The leader is also the man with a great *edai-egen*, a man kind to children, hospitable to all.

This concept contradicts to some extent the category of *hunuk balin*, in which are found those who are particularly ruthless in war and who are also sometimes said to have no *edai-egen*. For example, Husuk, an important leader of the Gosi-Alua, is *hunuk balin* but is also noted for his kindness.

PRESTIGE AND INFLUENCE. Prestige does not necessarily imply influence as a leader. For example, Asikhanedlek has prestige because of his fighting ability, but he has little influence. Like his father before him, he is relatively poor. He has one wife, and rarely more than one pig. Most important, he is a loner. He lives with his wife and daughter alone in a compound, one of the two one-family compounds in the Neighborhood. He chooses solitude, which is rare among the highly gregarious Dani.

Oaklia also has prestige without influence. Although he also has only one wife, his compound attracts several other older women, a girl, and several youths. He is a member of the powerful Wilil sib. Economically he is well off. But he does not excel in warfare. Although other men often come to his men's house, he rarely visits other men's houses.

Leadership and Spheres of Influence

Leadership among the Dani may be reduced to influence; the extent to which a man is a leader is determined by the kinds of activities in which he can exercise effective influence on the behavior of others. The spheres of influence pertinent to the Dani are cooperative work projects, warfare, and various ceremonies.

COOPERATIVE WORK PROJECTS. Most work is done by men working alone or together with the men of a single household or compound. However, there are some jobs—in particular, thatching a roof and smearing mud on a garden—that are usually done by a larger group of men, a dozen or more. If the man or men who own the house or garden have enough influence to call (*jogo*) the group together it is a sign of influence.

In the case of house building, influence is never a problem. Any man with enough influence to have a house of his own will have enough influence to summon the necessary helpers. This is not always true in the case of a garden. Even boys as young as ten may have their own gardens. Most boys from the age of fifteen or so do have their own gardens. Most men, and even some boys of fifteen, are able to call a crew of men and boys to help them in the mudding. There are a few exceptions: Asikhanedlek does most of his own mudding, although he is occasionally helped by his counsin, Huoge. One man, even more of a loner than Asikhanedlek, had no help at all in mudding his large garden. However, nearly all men have enough influence to call a mudding crew together.

WARFARE. War itself is an alliance affair, but the events of war, the raids and battles, are usually carried out on the confederation level.

The leaders in warfare are those who have the influence to initiate, or call (*jogo*), a raid or battle. The members of a raiding party are usually drawn from among friends living in a single neighborhood; the participants in a battle are drawn from the entire confederation. However, both the raid and the battle are called by leaders of confederation stature—men whose influence extends beyond the neighborhood. There is considerable disagreement as to how many men are able to call raids. But in practice, raids are called only by a few men in the confederation. Of these, only Weteklue or Nilik call battles. However, since in a battle called by a Wilihiman-Walalua leader, the warriors are usually joined by the allied Gosi-Alua, this man may be said to have influence beyond the federation.

CEREMONIES. The only man whose influence is alliancewide is Gutelu of the Dloko-Mabel Confederation. Some men from the Dloko-Mabel often drift over to battles on the southern front, and occasionally Wilihiman-Walalua men participate in battles on the northern fronts. However, only one event is truly alliancewide. This is the *ebe akho*, the great pig feast that takes place every four or five years. In 1963 Gutelu proved to be the only man able to initiate this ceremony.

Another ceremony, intermediate in size between the *ebe akho* and individual cremations is the *je wakanin* (carrying of the exchange stones) which, in October 1961, involved the Wilihiman-Walalua, the Gosi-Alua, the Phaluk-Matian, and several other confederations, but not the Dloko-Mabel. This was initiated by Sula, the leader of the Phaluk-Matian, and Weteklue of the Wilihiman-Walalua.

A further indication of influence is the custody of war trophies. Until 1961 all trophies captured by any members of the alliance were taken into custody by Gutelu. By May 1961, however, the influence of Gutelu in this matter over the southern members of the alliance was weakening, and Weteklue took custody of trophies captured by the Wilihiman-Walalua on the southern front.

Funerals provide a frequent opportunity for the public exercise of leadership on the confederation or even neighborhood level. A cremation is held in the compound in which the person died. To some extent, the number of mourners and the number of gifts brought to the cremation and the later *ilkho* ceremony terminating the mourning period are determined by the influence of the dead person and the circumstance of death. The cremation of a person killed by an enemy will draw considerably more attention than that of a person who has died of natural causes, because of the greater need to placate the ghosts after a war death. For example, although the cremation of the young boy Wajakhe, killed in a raid, was held in the compound of the unimportant Halihule and was run by Asilanedlek and Huoge, both uninfluential young men, a large number of gifts was brought because of the circumstances of the death.

To some extent, however, the number of gifts is determined by the influence of the men in whose compound the cremation is held. At the cremation of Asikhanedlek's father, in his compound, there were pitifully few gifts; at the cremation of Jagik, formerly an influential man and father of two influential sons, Nilik and Elabotok, held in Nilik's compound, there was an exceptionally large number of gifts. During a period of six months, in 1961–1962, there were seven cremations in the neighborhood, five of them in Um'ue's compound. Of these, three were for people who did not live in the compound but who had come there a few days or weeks before they died. It was said that they expected there would be a better cremation if it were run by Um'ue. This reflects both the financial ability of the host, who must sacrifice more of his own pigs than the visitors, and his influence in being able to call gifts to a cremation for which he is responsible.

To the largest cremations, gifts and visitors come from most of the neighborhood, and a few may come from outside the neighborhood.

Influence Groups

Within the groups of Dani social organization described above, it is possible to speak of three separate but interrelated realms of influence and leadership: men, children and boys, and women. The mainstream of social leadership, which is confined to the men, has been described above.

The leadership of children's play groups lies with boys up to an age of about fifteen. Until this age children have no influence in the economic or any other aspect of the culture. They do participate to the extent of herding pigs or helping with minor jobs around the compound such as baby-sitting, but they work in a strictly noninfluential capacity. Groups of boys in a neighborhood frequently play together, in more or less organized play. The core of these groups are boys ten to thirteen years of age, but the groups also include smaller brothers and sisters on the fringes. Play is often war games—mock battles with grass spears, or shooting at rolling hoops with wooden spears; *waik*, where spears are skidded along the ground to achieve the greatest distance; or expeditions to kill birds with sticks or crude bows and arrows. In this play the leaders are primarily the boys with the greatest skill—such as Juwa, the twelve-year-old son of the unimportant Loliluk.

LEADERSHIP AMONG THE WOMEN. Women seldom act as a group. They tend to stay in their compounds or to work individually in gardens. Thus there are no women with broad neighborhood or confederation influence comparable to that of the men. However, women do exert considerable influence on their husbands and even on their grown sons. This influence is related to the important role of women in the economy. They have the primary responsibility for maintaining the gardens, cooking food, and tending the pigs. The degree of independence of Dani women, and therefore their influence, depends to a great extent on their personality. Generally speaking, Dani women are highly independent. In many instances a woman prefers simply to leave her husband or father's household rather than to remain in a stressful situation where influence is necessary. In most cases, however, the women will stay and exert influence even on an influential husband. Um'ue, for example, who in 1963 already had considerable influence in the affairs of the Neighborhood and the local Wilil sib members, was in turn subject to the active influence of his wife Egabue, (It was she who insisted he build a compound in the mountains so she would not have to live with two other of his wives). His strong-willed old mother, Aneakhe, and his young daughter Hagigake both could publicly win their way over him in minor matters of daily life.

Exceptions to the generally limited influence of women in Dani culture are the women with special curing powers, the *he phatphale*. During a curing ceremony a *he phatphale* takes charge of the ceremony, entering the men's house and directing the activities of even the most important men.

Conclusions

Although the patrilineal ideology expressed in moiety and sib membership and in kinship terms is a prominent and explicit feature of Dani social structure, it has little coercive effect on Dani behavior. The one area where ideology is definitive is in marriage, in which moiety exogamy is rigidly observed. Attendance at ceremonies is not defined by descent, although the forms of the prestations are. Residence is a matter of choice, and although most men live in a confederation which has a strong representation of their own sib, the sibs have considerable geographical distribution, so even this limitation leaves room for option.

Like the economic aspect of Dani life, the social and political aspects show little specialization; that is, there are no classes and there is little concentration of power in the hands of the leaders. However, while economic production is so generalized that there are virtually no specialized kinds of goods to be exchanged for other specialized kinds of goods within the society, moiety exogamy creates a social specialization which assures a complex network of social ties. Along these ties flow gifts valuable because of their general scarcity, not because of their specialization. Dani society, if one takes the 5,000-person alliance as a unit, consists of a large interacting group, but it is not a complex group in the sense of containing much division of labor in an absolute sense. The ties that make up the social network are an arbitrary socially defined division of labor. For example, moiety exogamy rules say in effect that one's own moiety produces no marriageable women, and wives must be obtained from the opposite moiety. At a funeral, shell gifts are necessary and they must be obtained from the sib of the dead person's mother. In short, the Dani social network is widespread but egalitarian.

Annie M. D. Lebeuf

The Role of Women in the Political Organization of African Societies

Among the Kotoko of the Chari delta, it is the daughter of the chief official of the kingdom, the *Iba*, chief of the land, on whom the title is bestowed. In distinction to the other royal wives, she must never have any children, and she does not live in the same part of the palace as they do. She lives in the southern part of the building, according to a strict system of correspondence between functions and spatial directions. Along with the *Magira* she rules over the women of the kingdom, and she helps to choose some of the officials, in particular the army leaders whom she appoints personally, having chosen them from among the officials attached to her own house. She plays an important part in the septennial ceremonies for ensuring the perpetuation of the kingdom. She is associated with the morning star, the mother of all the stars, and is regarded by the people as the mythical mother of all the nobles.

In general, her power is such that it provides a constant counterbalance to that of the king, the entire political system being conceived as a delicate balance between masculine and feminine, right and left, north and south, that must be maintained in the power-relations of individuals, in all their activities, and even in their spatial location.

In all the political systems which have either one or two women at the top of the hierarchy, these women belong to a very restricted group drawn from a social class which already confers on them, even before they occupy their special roles, rights and privileges which are in marked contrast to those of the rest of the female population. The woman who fills the chief role always belongs to the generation senior to that of the king, and her position in the royal lineage, whatever it may be, is just as important as the kinship relation between her and the king. In general, she is regarded as his "mother," and acts as guide, protector, or initiator. Almost everywhere, it is she who has to choose the woman who will play the second role in sharing power with the king. This second woman, either a classificatory sister of the king or the daughter of some powerful family in the kingdom, is, with the exception of the sister of the *Mugabe* of Ankole, his official "wife." But as wife she has a completely different status from that of the other wives, which places her on an entirely different level. Emphasis is everywhere laid on the importance of both these roles, closely linked with the king as they are, either through his life, or in the period from the opening of his reign until the enthronement of his successor. When the women who fill them die, they are replaced by another member of their family, except in the case of the *Ngasa*, whose death entails that of the king.

In general, the relations between the two queens and the king, whether he be their son, their brother or their spouse, are of an exceptional nature, quite without parallel in the ordinary course of life. Thus to understand the association of all three, it is necessary not only to determine the position they occupy in relation to each other, but also to see this within the whole pattern of the royal lineage system.

We have seen that queens may take their full share in the responsibilities of power, either by performing the same functions as the king, or by carrying out tasks which are complementary to his; or they may have a restricted field in which they operate, although this in no way impairs their authority.

There is no doubt, however, that it is in the moral and ritual spheres that their importance lies. Or at any rate it is here that we can most easily observe the importance of their role, for these are the spheres that have suffered least from the recent political upheavals, since the spiritual values on which institutions are based long outlast the institutions themselves. But it would be wrong to view the queens' participation in state affairs from this angle alone and make them out to be nothing more than performers of sacred rites. If this function now eclipses all their other functions, this is because of the collapse of the system as a whole; and it may well be the case that this aspect of the queens' role has acquired increased significance because of the restrictions placed upon their judicial and administrative activities.

In political systems such as these, characterized as they are by a pronounced hierarchical structure, most women who either belong to, or have affinal ties with, the royal lineage, enjoy various prerogatives which often have political implications. They are frequently given positions of territorial authority, having one or several villages under their control or full powers over a district, in which latter case succession in the female line may be involved, as with the Bemba. The rights usually assigned to them place them apart from the rest of the female population, and enable their behaviour to approximate more closely to that of the male sex than to that of their own.

They enjoy greater freedom and authority in matrilineal than in patrilineal societies, but here, too, their position is similar, although the rule of patrilineal descent imposes restrictions of varying severity on rights acquired through marriage. In the kingdoms situated in the region of the Great Lakes, the daughters of the king are prohibited by their very rank not only from having an official husband, but also from bearing children; and should a Shilluk princess, bound by the same rules, dare to infringe them, she is liable to be put to death on giving birth to a child. This, however, is an extreme case. Most tribes have been able to arrive at a compromise, and, as in the case of the Bagirmians or the Bamileke, either recognize the children of princesses as belonging to the king, whoever their father may have been, or, as with the Nupe, confer a status upon the members of the aristocracy which is transmissible through women as much as through men, both to their husbands and to their descendants.

Many chiefs are able to strengthen their position by arranging diplomatic marriages for the women of the royal lineage, thus helping to seal alliances with foreign tribes and provide ambassadors with special privileges; and even if a chief's wives have little to do with state affairs, they can nevertheless act as guarantee for alliances that have been formed. Thus marriage among African chiefs can play the same sort of role as it did for the monarchs of our own *ancien régime*.

In Bagirmi, for instance, the *Maiarami*, daughters of the king, were married to the most important nobles of the kingdom and held a position of absolute authority over them. If a noble happened already to have a wife, he was obliged to divorce her, as polygyny was forbidden.

It was by means of similar systems of marriage alliances, in which kinship and political ties are intertwined, that many royal families were able to establish their authority and extend it over tribes which had originally been strangers to them. We have seen how the Lovedu queen used a system of this kind. The Swazi royal family provide another interesting example. All the king's wives were chosen from different clans, whose members thus acquired affinal ties with the reigning family, while the king gave his female relatives in marriage to important chiefs, even foreign ones. Because of their origin, these women held special positions in the households of their husbands, and were the potential mothers of their heirs.

It is a fairly widespread practice for members of a group to present one or two of their daughters to the king of another group as a mark of allegiance. The small kingdom of Ngoio was where the Vili king's chief wife came from, and the four oldest Maba families provided the Sultan of Wadai with his chief wives, while it was the Buffalo clan that supplied the wife of the Kabaka who bore the title of *Nanzigu*. Among the Ngoni, a quarrel between the chief and his wife was enough to create a state crisis.

It sometimes happens in systems of this kind that a power structure similar to that of the central government is found at the district level, with a woman giving full assistance to the local chief in his duties, or with female officials helping him in his decisions.

Among the Ashanti the head of each village has at his side a senior woman (*obaa panin*) chosen by him and his elders to direct the affairs of the community. The Kotoko afford another example, every town having two *Mra Saba*, whose role among the local women is similar to that of the *Magira* and the *Gumsu* among the women of the capital. They are appointed by the members of their own sex, one for the northern districts and one for the southern, to direct their work and leisure activities, to settle quarrels, and to look after their interests. These women also take the lead in certain fishing expeditions in which they are the only women to take part along with the men. In the same way, at Bida, among the Nupe, the *Sonya* organizes the women of low birth as the *Nimwoye* and the *Sagi* do for the women of the aristocracy. She is elected by the married women of the town, who treat her with great respect, and her rank is confirmed by the *Etsu*. She organizes all the work that is done collectively and supervises the market. Formerly she levied a due on all commercial transactions, a portion of which she returned to the queen.

Again, in every village a woman is elected by her companions to fulfil similar tasks, and given the title of *Sagi* originally reserved for one of the two leading female figures in the kingdom. This title seems to have replaced an earlier one, that of *Lelu*, which used to be conferred on the woman who was believed to be the most powerful witch in the village and who, by thus being used officially in the service of the village, could be of benefit to it.

In societies where the political system is based on kinship organization, the opportunities open to women for participation in public affairs are no longer so clear cut, but extend to a larger number of them. In a few isolated cases women are found at the head of a community, but it is mainly indirectly, by the tasks which they perform and by their preponderant role in spiritual matters, that they are able to exert a profound influence on the life of the community.

Those cases in which women do act as village heads or local chiefs, or are at the head of a larger unit corresponding to the lineage or the clan, are found among tribes of great apparent diversity, and scattered over a wide area, always excepting those which have adopted Islam, where women are usually precluded from taking part in activities regulated by the precepts of the official religion.

When women exercise functions of this kind, it is generally because they have inherited them. In the absence of a male heir, many groups permit a woman to inherit the functions of her father or her husband. A more rare occurrence is when chiefs, during their lifetime, designate a sister or a daughter to succeed them rather than a son. She is then invested with the same powers and occupies the same position as if she were a man. She presides over religious ceremonies to which formerly she was not admitted, and may even be leader of the hunt and on occasion war leader. Masculine behaviour of this kind extends even to matrilineal societies such as the Lovale, for instance. In patrilineal societies women who fill such roles are not, as a rule, permitted to have an official husband, the status conferred upon them being incompatible with the normal relations between husband and wife; but they may have children, which will belong to their own family, the father losing all rights over them. In some tribes, such as the Venda, a woman who has inherited the headship of a village or even a chiefdom is allowed to marry if she wishes, in which case her husband maintains his rights over his children, who cannot then claim succession to their mother. But she is also entitled to divorce, whereupon she will make an official marriage with another woman whose bridewealth she herself pays. She chooses one of her kin to be father of this woman's children, who will be regarded as her own children. The father will have no rights over them, and one of them, either male or female, will be chosen as successor. We have already seen that the Lovedu queen proceeds in a similar fashion.

Also among the Venda, as with the Mboshi (Congo), the Luba (Katanga) and the Mende (Sierra Leone) and other tribes, certain groups, in contradistinction to the usual tribal practice, are reported as having a woman as hereditary chief. Apparently the explanation of this institution, as given by the groups concerned, is that the spirit of a female ancestor is believed to reside in the place where the woman is chief. The Bachama (Northern Nigeria) give a similar explanation for the fact that the town of Njimoso is always governed by a woman, her main responsibility being the maintenance of the cult of the local tutelary deity. The Chamba Tsugu town of Debbo apparently follows the same pattern.

Among the Luba there is a district in the neighbourhood of Kamina which is governed by the *Mwadi,* two women who at every new moon are always possessed by the spirit of a former ruler. In the days when the kingdom still existed they had been closely associated with him, their special function having been to supply the paramount chief, the *Mulopwe,* with his supply of kaolin for ritual purposes. This duty shows what an important position they must have held, for the transfer of kaolin always implies that the giver is the superior of the receiver.

Thus we see that on kinship or ritual grounds women may fulfil functions normally performed by men.

The frequency with which cases of this kind occur varies greatly from region to region. It does not seem to have anything to do with the rule of descent obtaining or with the position of women in the community; but possibly occurrences tend to increase in certain circumstances where economic and historical factors play a determining role, as for instance among the Mende. There, the number of women in positions of authority increased in consequence of the troubles arising from the British occupation, having been put forward by the people so as to obviate reprisals. The fact that the conquerors had a woman—Queen Victoria—as sovereign may also have been a contributing factor.

Some tribes have special institutions that enable women to play an important part in the accession of a chief (whether standing in a kinship relation to him or not), and in supervising women's activities and controlling relations between villages.

Such is "the wife of the district" among the Tonga, a Bantu tribe of the South-East. The title arises because the woman who holds it has become a wife of the chief owing to the marriage payment having been made by his subjects in the hope that she will be the mother of his heir. She organizes the women of the community, particularly in their agricultural work, and performs the rites for the women's cults. Between the Kwilu and the Kasai, the Pende, Bunda, Dinga and Lele have an institution called the *hohombe* or *ngalababola,* usually translated: "wife of the village", which, until recently, gave the women concerned a position of paramount importance. The "wife of the village" was not in any sense a prostitute. She was of high rank, enjoyed certain privileges, and both she and her children held a special status. There were various ways in which she might come to hold the position. She might be directly chosen by the villagers, either after having been captured by them from a neighbouring group, or, on the other hand, after she had come to them seeking sanctuary; or she might be the daughter or relative of a chief chosen by him at the time of her birth to occupy the position, when the time came, in a neighbouring village.

For some time after she had taken up her duties she did not do any of the work usually done by women, but took part in all male activities, even hunting. She then took a small number of husbands and went to live beyond the boundaries of the village, and was then at the disposal of all its inhabitants. Her children were regarded as "the children of the village". The villagers as a group supplied her sons with the amount required for the payment of bride-wealth. The bride-price asked for by her daughters was much higher than average, and to become a "son-in-law of the village" meant acquiring a position of influence and bearing insignia similar to those of a chief.

These relations were stabilized by a rule of succession whereby the father of every family has the right to his daughter's daughter, either for himself, or to give in marriage to his brother, nephew, or grandnephew. This system, as applied to "the wife of the village", meant that a daughter borne by her daughter would take the place of her (i.e. the daughter's daughter's) maternal grandmother, and that the "son-in-law" of the village (the daughter's daughter's father) would in turn lay claim to her daughter, either to marry her or give her in marriage to one of his close kin.

Most of the local chiefs made use of this institution to strengthen their position, giving their own daughters to whatever villages they chose, thereby placing the inhabitants in the relation of son-in-law to them, while themselves standing in the relation of son-in-law to these villages in the following generation.

Although it is a well-known fact that in most tribes women are organized into age-classes or associations of a ritual or initiatory character, extraordinarily little is generally known about the actual activities of such groups.

To each age-class belong duties, collective tasks and ritual obligations, but everywhere age brings increasing authority, and an old person of either sex is always treated with respect and asked for advice. Very often women past child-bearing age become elders, and take part in their discussions.

Sometimes there are mixed associations such as the *Butwa* of certain Lunda groups for instance, in which old people of both sexes, the *Mangulu*, are included in the highest grades, and thus enjoy direct participation in all public affairs. But more often the women's organizations are parallel to those of the men and each operates within its own sphere.

Associations such as the *Nimm* of the Ekoi of Southern Nigeria, or the

Akejuju of their neighbours, the Bini, give women powers which are in some respects greater than those of the men, who dread the effects that might result. Among the Ube, Gere and Wobe on the Ivory Coast the village head is obliged to consult the leader of the association of women initiates, mainly concerning the agricultural work.

The *Sande* society has considerable influence among the Mende, representing for the women what the *Poro* is for the men, an initiation group that bears entire responsibility for education and for general behaviour. Its leader, the *Majo*, is in a position to exercise a direct influence over the attitude of the men towards its members. Also among the Mende are found the *Njayei* and *Humoi* societies, formed to look after the mentally sick and to ensure the fertility of the soil by adopting the appropriate procedures, and they are at the service of every community. These women have techniques both for promoting the development of the personality and for encouraging self-confidence. Chiefs often ask them for advice, and they take part in the election of candidates for office. Their leaders bear hereditary titles and sometimes acquire such a high standing locally that the English, when the protectorate treaties were being signed, often mistook them for political chiefs.

While it is a general tendency for women to form groups for the purpose of carrying out their various activities, in wealthy and populous areas like Southern Nigeria, such groups, owing to the importance of women in commerce and agriculture, have become powerful organizations which have been in existence for a long time.

An example of a complex system of groups of this kind is provided by the Yoruba. Its development was partly due to the existence of large towns, and its objectives are mutual aid, defence of common interests, and the organization of markets, for the attainment of which women in every town have formed producers', sellers', and buyers' associations. The Oyo associations are called *Egbe Iyalode* (literally: association of the *Iyalode*), the *Iyalode* being the title of the leader of these associations; and they are consulted by the political authorities. An *Iyalode* is often an important figure. The *Iyalode* of Ibadan, for instance, was a member of the Council of State down to 1914.

Ibo villages all have their women's councils, and in large towns each district nominates its own spokeswoman, these together forming the council. There is no hierarchy between the various councils, but their members maintain permanent relations with each other as between one urban or village area and another. Each council is presided over by a woman elected, not on account of her seniority or wealth, but because of her personality and experience. These councils are responsible for everything concerning agriculture and the interests of women in general. They fix the timetable for all the important agricultural tasks, look after the protection of crops, and regulate all the ceremonies involved. If anyone, man or woman, contravenes any of their decisions, they can take sanctions against them, and they have great authority in judicial matters. When the interests of a woman have to be defended, the council meets to discuss the matter with her family, or, if she is married, with her husband's family.

Although their powers are not so great as they used to be, their strength and cohesion can be measured by the widespread nature of the movement for the assertion of their rights which they organized in 1929, which was known as "the Aba Riots" or "the war of the women". Following upon a rumour that the government was on the point of introducing a tax on women's property, they started making demonstrations which broke out first in Aba and then spread through the two provinces of Owerri and Calabar, mobilizing more than two million people, very few of whom seem to have been men. The rapidity with which the trouble spread and the gravity of the situation which resulted illustrate the tremendous strength of the women's organizations.

African women have a tradition of practical participation in public affairs. Among many peoples the very conceptions on which power is based associate them closely with the exercise of power, and although it is usually men who are called upon to rule, the norms which regulate the position of individuals within a community often permit a woman, under special circumstances, to take the place of a man. In general, the profound philosophical ideas which underlie the assignment of separate tasks to men and women stress the complementary rather than the separate nature of these tasks. Neither the division of labour nor the nature of the tasks accomplished implies any superiority of the one over the other, and there is almost always compensation in some other direction for the actual inequalities which result from such a division.

J. H. M. Beattie

Bunyoro: An African Feudality?

In a recent article . . . Dr. Jack Goody discussed the utility of applying the concepts and vocabulary of Western feudalism to traditional African states. He pointed out that the term 'feudalism' has been used in many senses even by European historians, and he concluded that although the specific institutions into which feudalism (however defined) may be broken down

Reprinted from "Bunyoro: An African Feudality?" *by J. H. M. Beattie,* Journal of African History, *V:1 (1964), 25–36, by permission of Cambridge University Press.*

may often usefully be compared, the kind of overall comparison that is invited by words like 'feudalism' is best avoided at this stage.

In this paper I adduce corroborative evidence for Goody's thesis from my own study of a traditional African kingdom. I give a brief account of some of the main structural features of the interlacustrine Bantu state of Bunyoro, in western Uganda, as they existed in pre-European times. And in doing so I consider the usefulness, in the context of the Nyoro polity, of feudal ideas.

First, for the purposes of this essay, at least some content must be given to the general concept of feudalism. As Goody noted, some authors, though not as a rule professional historians, have written as though any society with a ruler, a rough hierarchy of chiefs, and a subordinated peasantry were *ipso facto* feudal. Some of the earlier anthropologists, and Potekhin in his paper on Ashanti feudalism, took such a view. On it, a vast number of past and present states in Africa and elsewhere throughout the world are feudal; the difficulty is, of course, that so vague and all-inclusive a formulation is analytically useless. Unless the feudal analogy can provide some clear criteria for distinguishing some kinds of 'traditional' states from others, there is little point in adopting it. The view of feudalism which stresses specifically a particular kind of land-holding is somewhat more useful. On this view feudalism is a form of polity based on the relation of vassal and superior arising from the holding of land 'in feud', that is, in consideration of service and homage from vassal to lord. This formulation selects only one element in the complex of medieval European feudal institutions, and that one not always considered essential. But it does point to the reciprocating, contractual element in feudalism, and so to the personal nature of the relationships involved and the stress on personal loyalty between inferior and superior. Thus Maquet stresses the personal bond between two persons unequal in power, involving protection on one hand, fealty and service on the other. These criteria do conveniently, if broadly, distinguish such polities from those in which specialized political authority either is altogether lacking or is distributed on an impersonal, bureaucratic basis. But although such simple characterizations may have some descriptive value, they omit reference to certain important features of European feudalism which are lacking in states like Bunyoro. So unless what is and what is not implicit in the notion of feudalism is carefully specified, they too may lead to misunderstanding.

Probably the clearest summary of what are most usefully regarded as the essential characteristics of feudalism is Marc Bloch's, quoted by Goody in his article. Bloch, it will be remembered, specified five fundamentals. These were: (1) the fief, usually but not essentially land; (2) the personal nature of the bond of political dependence; (3) the dispersal of authority—rulers have to delegate and they have to make loyalty worth while. These criteria fit many African kingdoms, including Bunyoro, well enough. But then he has also: (4) a reference to a specialized military class, something that is not found in Bunyoro or in many of the African polities which have been described as feudal; and (5) the reference to the survival in some form of the idea of the state.

This last point is important: if European feudalism in its beginnings implied the weakening, even the breakdown, of the state, and the distribution of powers formerly held by it among private individuals, in most African states there has been no such breakdown. In fact, as Goody remarks, many if not most of the polities which have been described in feudal terms represent a trend towards rather than away from centralization. Far from expressing the breakdown of a formerly more strongly centralized authority, they represent, in many cases, what appear to be the first beginnings of such authority. Thus among the Alur, described by Southall, hitherto chiefless communities have in historical times come voluntarily under the dominion of chiefly lines, and the evidence suggests that in the case of at least some of the interlacustrine Bantu kingdoms intrusive minorities imposed centralized forms of government on preexisting segmentary societies.

A further important point of difference between European feudalism and some types of 'African feudalism' relates to the question of which categories of persons were linked as subordinate and super-ordinate. In Europe the characteristic feudal bond was between the tenant or fief-holder and a nearby chief or lord, from whom he held his fief and to whom he looked for protection; there was no direct link between the fief-holder and the king. Thus the king's links with his subjects were only indirect, and for the most part they were only of secondary importance. In Bunyoro and kingdoms like it, however, the case was very different. Although subordinate chiefs were sometimes powerful and revolt was by no means unknown, loyalty to and dependence upon the person of the king himself were explicit and universal values at all levels, and these values were constantly expressed and reinforced in service, homage and ritual. Virtually all political rights in the kingdom were held, and were seen as being held, directly of the king, and at his pleasure. Although he was by no means an 'absolute' ruler, he was regarded by all as the sole original source of political authority. In Bunyoro, as in some other African kingdoms, the polity sometimes called 'feudal' was really a means to achieving and sustaining a system of centralized administration; in no sense was it a symptom of the breakdown of such a system.

A brief examination of some of the typical political institutions of traditional Bunyoro, and some consideration of how the system worked, may enable us to decide whether, and how far, the basic categories of feudalism are helpful in understanding it. For these purposes, it is useful to regard the Nyoro state as entailing a balance of opposing forces: those of centralization on the one hand, which have the effect of expressing and reinforcing the king's power; and those of decentralization on the other hand, the effect of which is to strengthen the power of chiefs and subjects as against the central authority. In this equation, the chiefs inevitably played a double role, being at the same time an intrinsic part of and a potential threat to the kingship. Traditional

Bunyoro was a centralized polity of some stability (though it was less centralized and less stable than the neighbouring and territorially more compact kingdom of Buganda), so centripetal forces will demand more attention than centrifugal ones.

The latter can be dealt with fairly briefly. They comprise, first, the degree of independence exercised by the chiefs and, second, the effectiveness of the indigenous regional groupings at the community level; families, lineages, clans and neighbourhoods. I deal first with the chiefs. Like other traditional rulers, the king (*Mukama*) of Bunyoro could only retain his power by giving some of it away. Some writers, such as Murdock, have regarded kingdoms like Bunyoro as 'African despotisms', African despotism being a sort of counterpart of Oriental despotism, even though not hydraulic. Certainly some African rulers have at some times acted despotically; but with a widely dispersed population, poor communications and a simple technology (especially in regard to weapons), it is difficult to maintain for long, if at all, any very high concentration of political power. Always there were some institutionalized checks on the abuse of power by the central authority. In Bunyoro the great territorial chiefs, of whom in historical times there were a dozen or more, enjoyed a good deal of autonomy, governing their areas rather like private estates. Their rights over these territories and their inhabitants, which they held from the king as his subordinates and on condition of tribute payment and homage to him, were subject to restrictions, but within their areas these chiefs were accorded high prestige, and received homage and tribute similar to, but on a much smaller scale than that paid to the king, whose representatives they were. But they did not possess these powers in their own right. They enjoyed them only because they were the king's nominees, 'the Mukama's spears'. Nevertheless they could and did claim a considerable measure of independence, especially if they were remote from the capital. In several recorded instances this extended to actual revolt, and to the setting up of independent units. The neighbouring kingdom of Toro originated early in the nineteenth century in rebellion by the dissident Nyoro prince Kaboyo, and in Baker's time and later one of the king's agnates, Ruyonga, maintained (with some European support) virtual independence in the north of Bunyoro for many years. So although the chiefs were indispensable to the effective functioning of the centralized Nyoro political system, at the same time they were, and were recognized to be, a constant threat to it. I show below how this threat was met.

The chiefs were an essential component of the Nyoro administrative system; the localized groups of clansmen and neighbours who made up the Nyoro community were not; rather they stood in opposition to it. There is no clear evidence that Nyoro society was ever of the acephalous, segmentary kinship-based type described for many other parts of Africa (including some neighbouring areas) but for what it is worth it may be speculated that it may well have been so in the remote period before the present ruling line or its predecessors had appeared on the scene. At any rate, what is certain is that while there can be no centralized state without subordinate political authorities and subjects, it is perfectly possible for a segmentary society to exist without chiefs or specifically political functionaries at all. African peoples like the Nuer and the Tallensi have done so up to very recent times. Where, as in Bunyoro, a centralized government is superimposed on a community which retains many of the 'segmentary' characteristics of a clan and lineage system (for example, a hundred or more exogamous 'totemic' clans with a tradition of former localization, and many of the social usages and values appropriate to such a system), there must be some kind of adaptation between the two elements; the state must somehow come to terms with the community. I consider below some of the means traditionally adapted to this end in Bunyoro. Here I wish to stress that Nyoro themselves are well aware of the difference, even the opposition, between the state and the central government on the one hand, and the local community or neighbourhood on the other. For the first they use the terms *obukama* (kingship) and *obulemi* (rule or government); the second they refer to by such terms as *obunyaruganda* (clanship), *obuzaranwa* (kinship) and *obutahi* (neighbourhood). Often they consciously oppose these two fields of social interaction. From the Nyoro peasant's viewpoint, the first is something external, even oppressive—the root *lema* means 'to bear down upon', 'to be too heavy for', as well as 'to rule'—the second provides the intimate and familiar context of everyday village life. And in fact the demands of the king and his chiefs on the one hand, and of clansfolk, kin and neighbours on the other, may and often do conflict. Nyoro see their social structure as dual, not monolithic, and the problem of reconciling its two components is quite explicit in Nyoro culture.

These, in brief, are the major divisive forces in Nyoro political structure, opposing the king to his chiefs on the one hand, and the kingship or state to the local community on the other. How are these gaps bridged? I consider, rather arbitrarily, those institutions which I call centripetal under two heads: first, those which relate to the king's (and the chiefs', so far as they are, as it were, political extensions of the king) relations with the people as a whole, and second, those concerned more specifically with the king's relations with his territorial chiefs. Again rather arbitrarily, I list five institutions under the first head and five under the second. Other institutions could no doubt be identified, and some of the ones here recorded could probably be further broken down. However, the ten listed are of key functional importance, and also they are particularly characteristic of Bunyoro, and in some degree of other similar states.

I begin with those institutions which relate the kingship with the people as a whole. First, the kingship is hereditary in the male line; only the son of a king can become a king. But not the eldest son; we shall see the point of this below. Thus the institution of kingship is (I am using the historical present here and elsewhere) the enduring focus and centre of Nyoro society; it provides a central political value and a symbol of national identity for all Nyoro. Succession is not predetermined; any son of a king except the eldest may inherit: which one does so depends on the support he can command. Often two, sometimes three or more, eligible princes have competed for the succession after their father's death. So, in Bunyoro as in some other kingdoms, there was a period of lawlessness and anarchy between reigns, an interregnum during which warring factions made life for ordinary people dangerous and uncertain. To them, it was plain that the maintenance of the kingship was a condition of security and of national well-being, for when it was suspended the country was reduced to chaos and confusion.

It has just been noted that the king's first-born son could not succeed him, and this provides the second institutional means of integrating king and people. The eldest son automatically assumed the office of *Okwiri*, the headship of the Bito, that is, of the numerous and powerful clan (or perhaps congeries of clans) of which the king was a member. In strongly stratified Bunyoro, where the gap between the ruling Bito and the ordinary peasants (Iru) was universally recognized and strongly marked, an effect of this institution was, as it were, to detach the king from his identity with his own agnatic group, and so to free him for his role as ruler and leader of all Nyoro, not just of his own group, the Bito. The gap is one which must be bridged wherever a ruling clan or other group achieves dominance over a subordinated majority of supposedly different stock, and Bunyoro's office of *Okwiri* provides one means of rendering the kingship acceptable to the mass of the governed.

Third, the value of the kingship is stressed in tradition, myth, ritual and ceremonial. Tradition links the ruling Bito dynasty, through the two earlier Cwezi and Batembuzi dynasties, with the very beginnings of the world. Although there is strong evidence that the present Bito rulers are Nilotic intruders who have been in Bunyoro for two or three centuries at most, they claim, and Nyoro do not dispute the claim, that they are descended in an unbroken paternal line from the earliest rulers. This 'mythical charter' effectively makes the kingship an acceptable, even unquestioned, institution. The king's importance to the country as a whole is further expressed in the familiar idiom of 'divine kingship': he is mystically identified with his kingdom, and his well-being is as indispensable to it as it is to him. His importance and uniqueness are stressed in numerous usages, of most of which accounts are available elsewhere. He has his special drums, spears and other regalia; distinctive forms of greeting are reserved for him and may not be used to anyone else; his more important doings are described in a court vocabulary applicable only to him; his accession and death are marked by elaborate and special ceremony. Everybody approaches him humbly and submissively; even today his senior chiefs kneel to hand him anything or to receive anything from his hands. All these usages impress on everybody's minds the paramountcy of the kingship and its absolute superiority over every other force or faction in the state. In an almost literal sense, everything is seen as depending on or derived from it. To traditionally minded Nyoro, the kingship is indispensable.

Fourthly, as in other African kingdoms, the king's economic role was an important centripetal or integrating force in the Nyoro state. Mauss has classically demonstrated the ubiquity of prestation or gift exchange as a means to social integration, and the Nyoro king was the centre of such an exchange system. Not only the chiefs but any Nyoro could visit the king, and he would not come empty-handed; women, cattle, beer and grain were continually passing into his hands. Reciprocally, as well as presenting cattle or women to persons to whom he was obliged or who were in need, the king gave feasts at frequent intervals. Some of his special praise-names stress his open-handedness. Thus he is called *Agutamba* (he who relieves distress), and *Mwebingwa* (he to whom people run for help); the first name is part of his official title. The Mukama's role as the greatest giver and receiver in the country played a major part in binding his people to him in mutual interdependence. It should be stressed that the obligation to give to, and the right to receive from, the king extended (in theory at least) to all his subjects; it was not restricted to his chiefs. Although, as the Mukama's representatives, the chiefs were themselves the centres of similar but very much smaller-scale systems of exchange, every man, and especially every man who held any kind of authority above the family level, stood potentially if not actually in a direct personal relationship with the king. Even the lowest grades of chiefs were not appointed by the senior chiefs but by the king himself: this might sometimes amount to little more than the confirmation of a chief's nomination, but this confirmation was indispensable. In the case of important chiefs, a formal ceremony of installation had to be performed by a special agent of the king, and all recipients of political authority were, in theory, required to bind themselves to the Mukama by a ceremony of 'drinking milk' with him. In former times even succession to a clan headship had to be validated by the king. All of these appointments and confirmations required that the recipients of authority should make gifts to the king: since authority itself was a gift no less than material goods, there was a reciprocal element in these transactions. The continuing network of exchanges thus involved must have served as a powerful integrative force in the traditional kingdom.

Finally, the constitution of the royal household itself provides a significant means of bringing people and kingship together. The king maintained, and maintains to the present day, a great number of palace officials, including ritual experts, keepers of the various regalia, musicians, cooks, bath attendants, herdsmen, and many others. These far exceed the numbers needed for practical purposes. Among them are representatives of all of the few specialist occupations in the country, such as pottery, barkcloth making and iron-working. Even more important, these officials also represent many of the hundred or more clans to one or other of which every Nyoro belongs. Many of the palace offices are traditionally tied to particular clans, and each is jealously guarded as the exclusive prerogative of that clan; in this way the kingship absorbed the clan system, to which it stood in opposition, into itself. Even today, the hereditary tenure of such an appointment (which is far from onerous, involving perhaps attendance at the palace for a few days each month) is highly valued. When I was in Bunyoro a young man of good education holding such a post, which required him to live near the palace, turned down an offer of lucrative employment outside the kingdom rather than give up his hereditary position at the palace.

Even the king's selection of his 'wives' may be regarded as serving a similar end. Nyoro kings were traditionally polygynous, often extremely so. It is not recorded how many wives Kabarega, the last independent Nyoro king, had, but the names of 140 children begotten by him are on record. The Mukama could take his women from any of the clans, with one or two exceptions, and a son of any of these women was eligible to succeed him. Thus not only was the whole clan honoured (and many clans have been so honoured) by having given a 'wife' to the Mukama, but a girl so given might conceivably become the mother of the next king. If she did, the whole of her clan would become 'mothers' and 'mother's brothers' to the new king, and would acquire extremely high status in the kingdom, as well as being rewarded by offices and estates.

These are some of the institutions through which the Nyoro people as a whole were bound to the kingship in common recognition of its importance and indispensability. I now go on to consider some of the ways in which the king's chiefs themselves were bound to the king in a relationship, more or less stable, of subordination and personal obligation.

First, Nyoro chiefs are not hereditary. At all levels, as was noted earlier, they are individually appointed, or their appointments are confirmed, by the king. Traditionally, proprietary rights over particular areas and their peasant occupants were allotted as a mark of royal favour, often as a reward for service. In the pre-European era this service might have been military; in more recent times it is more likely to have been economic or domestic. Even a few years ago loyal service in the royal household, for example, as cook or regalia-keeper, was sometimes rewarded with a minor chiefship. In Bunyoro, as in medieval England, 'personal service to the king brought a rich reward'. Obviously such appointments are less appropriate in the conditions of the twentieth century (modern administration calls for learned skills not taught in the Mukama's kitchen or bathroom) than they were in traditional times, and in the 1950s they were giving rise to some resentment among educated Nyoro. But what they stressed was the fact that political authority was traditionally thought of as being in the last resort the personal property of the Mukama. The very word Mukama means the master or owner of anything—or everything. Subordinate authority is accordingly his gift, and like most gifts it is not given unconditionally. Chiefs retained their rights over the territories allotted to them and their inhabitants only on condition of service and homage to the king, and he could and sometimes did dismiss them summarily.

Second, the importance of the allocation of authority, and its origin in the person of the Mukama, are emphasized by ritual. The delegation of authority is not a purely administrative, secular affair; it is also a rite. The king, like other persons and events which have the quality of being both extraordinary and potentially dangerous, is believed to possess a special ritual potency, called *mahano*, and when he delegates his authority he gives away at the same time some of his own *mahano* or essence. This is expressed in the traditional rite, already referred to, of 'drinking milk' with the Mukama, in recent times replaced by the ceremonial handing of a roasted coffee berry by the king to the person who is being vested with subordinate authority. The symbolism involved is plain. The king's sacred herd of cattle and the milk from it were traditionally most intimately linked with both his and the country's well-being, and roasted coffee berries, often handed round in Nyoro homes when specially favoured or distinguished guests are entertained, are associated also with the institution of blood partnership, the closest bond conceivable between men. Coffee berries, the two segments of which are closely united in the same husk, aptly symbolize a particularly close attachment. If ritual is a language, a way of saying something held to be important, then these usages express, and so tend to reinforce, the value attached to the central political power in Bunyoro and to its delegation.

A third way in which senior chiefs and other eminent persons (these categories were traditionally hardly distinguishable) might be bound to the king and the kingship was through a system of what may be called 'ennoblement'. Traditionally the king might award elaborate beaded 'crowns' or headdresses, decorated with coloured beads and cowrie shells and bearded with colobus monkey skins, to senior chiefs or other persons whom he wished particularly to distinguish. This was the highest gift which the king could bestow, and was awarded only to persons who had served with particular distinction, or who had achieved conspicuous military success. It was also traditionally awarded to the king's 'mother's brother', that is, to the head of his mother's clan. As well as his crown (*kondo*), the person thus ennobled received extensive proprietary territorial rights over some part of the country, so that if he was not already a chief, as he most likely was, he was made one by the award.

Even more than the grant of political authority, the grant of a crown implied the bestowal, so to speak, of some part of the potency of the kingship itself. This is clear from the rigorous ritual prohibitions which possession of a crown implied. Thus crown-wearers were subject to ritual food prohibitions (they were debarred from eating low-status foodstuffs like sweet potatoes or cassava) similar to those observed by the king himself. Unlike ordinary political office, crowns were hereditary in the male line, though an heir would have to be confirmed in his succession by the king himself. The institution is now dying out; no crown has been awarded for many years. This is not surprising. The king has not been the ultimate source of political power in Bunyoro since the last century; the territorial rights that formerly accompanied the award no longer exist in their traditional form, and in any case they are no longer at the Mukama's personal disposal.

Fourthly, the major chiefs were required to maintain houses at or near the capital as well as in the territories allotted to them, and they had to attend the king's court constantly. Failure to do so was noticed, and laid the negligent chief open to suspicion of rebellious intentions. When a chief left the capital, he had to leave behind him a deputy (*mukwenda* or *musigire*), who assumed all his titles and represented him at court during his absence. In the same way the chief would be represented in his own area by a *musigire* while he was absent at court. When the chief is absent from the royal court, his deputy in a real sense *is* the chief. So in theory the senior chiefs were always in attendance upon the king, while at the same time they were always engaged in the discharge of their duties as the king's territorial administrators. In this way the *musigire* system enabled the senior chiefs to sustain at the same time two scarcely compatible roles. A chief is essentially a 'king's man', and must, by constant attendance, continually express his personal devotion to and dependence upon the Mukama. At the same time he is also a territorial ruler, personally responsible for the good government of the region allotted to him. The importance of the requirement of constant attendance at the palace as a check to centrifugal tendencies is obvious. It is worth noting, also, that it also provided the king with a more or less permanent group of advisers: in systems of this kind there is no need for a separate royal council or 'secretariat'; the same people can serve both as councillors and administrators.

Fifthly and finally, the king himself did not reside permanently at his capital, which itself was frequently changed in traditional times. Like William I of England, he frequently undertook protracted tours around his kingdom, accompanied by numerous retainers, staying for days and even weeks at the headquarters of one or other of his chiefs. It fell upon the local population to build, on the model of the palace itself, the necessary accommodation for him and his entourage, and to provide ample supplies of food and drink for the royal party. In return, the king provided feasts of meat and beer for the local people. These frequent tours (which were carried out in considerable state even when I was in Bunyoro ten years ago) enabled the Mukama to keep an eye on the local activities of his chiefs of all ranks, and also to keep a finger on the pulse of public opinion.

On the basis of this summary account of some of Bunyoro's most important traditional political institutions, can we say whether Bunyoro is 'feudal' or not? Indeed, is there any point in asking such a question? If, with Maquet, we regard as feudal any political system centred on face-to-face relations between persons of unequal power, one offering protection, the other service and loyalty, then Bunyoro is indeed feudal. But so, it might seem, are most, if not all, small-scale, pre-industrial states. For political relations are by definition between persons of unequal power, of whom one gives orders and the other obeys; they must offer some mutual advantage if they are to persist; and in societies lacking writing, post offices and telephones, political relations, like all other social relations, must be face-to-face ones. If, alternatively, with the *Shorter Oxford English Dictionary* (and perhaps with more etymological propriety) we hold feudalism to consist essentially in the holding of land, and of the authority associated with such tenure, by an inferior from a superior 'in feud', on conditions of service and homage, then, also, Bunyoro is a feudal state. But even here, it is evidently clearer and more helpful to say that in Bunyoro the allocation of land and of territorial authority is of a type similar to that found in the feudal polities of medieval Europe, than it is to say roundly that Bunyoro is a feudal state. For if (say) Norman England was a feudal state, then Bunyoro resembles it—and quite strikingly—in some respects, and differs from it—perhaps a little less obviously—in others.

Like Goody, I consider it to be more useful and illuminating to retain the term 'feudalism' and its associated vocabulary for the complex European polities to which they were first applied (and perhaps to such other systems, like the Japanese one, which can be shown to resemble it in all or most of its essential features), and to describe the political institutions of traditional Bunyoro and of other African kingdoms as far as possible in their own terms. This of course is not to deny the usefulness of drawing attention to analogies with European feudalism where these are found, or the importance for field-work of knowing, from historical sources, how other peoples, at other times and in other conditions, have dealt with the problems of government in small-scale societies. But although traditional Bunyoro had much in common with the feudal states of medieval Europe, it also differed from them in very important respects. If we are to describe it as a feudal state, however we restrict or modify our definition of feudalism, we shall, in underlining the similarities, inevitably tend to ignore or at best to understress the differences.

Summary

In terms of Marc Bloch's celebrated definition, the traditional interlacustrine Bantu kingdom of Bunyoro, in western Uganda, is 'feudal' in some respects but not in others. This is shown by a survey of Bunyoro's traditional political institutions, some of which tended to decentralize, others to centralize, political power and authority. Of the first, the most important were the considerable degree of independence enjoyed by the chiefs, and the largely self-sufficient community relationships of neighbourhood and kinship. Of the centripetal institutions, some linked the people to the kingship, others bound the chiefs to the king. Examples of both types are described. It is concluded that although traditional Bunyoro shared some features with European 'feudal' states, it also differed from them in important respects. Thus it would be misleading to refer to it, without a good deal of qualification, as a 'feudality'.

7 Individuals in Adaptation: Physical and Psychological Characteristics

Any theory of biological or biocultural evolution must focus in part on the characteristics and behaviors of *individuals* in their adaptive processes. The crucial question in adaptation is self-maintainance and survival. Self-maintainance includes getting enough food and shelter, as noted in earlier sections, but there are also problems of health maintainance and psychological well-being. All human societies have medical systems for dealing with the insults and threats to the body posed by the environment. In all societies people get sick; in all societies people injure themselves or get bashed physically and mentally by their enemies. Also, in every society there are disease vectors—the insects and other carriers of illness that penetrate the defenses of the human body from time to time. In most human groups the physical ills that beset people are not a sharply separate category from psychological ills, or the social problems such as marital conflict and certain kinds of social stresses. The common denominator in all of these—whether physical, psychological, or social—is that people feel bad and seek help from someone, usually a specialist in healing.

The oldest profession is certainly that of the healer, if we allow for the fact that the healer in most simpler societies (and in our own prehistoric past) has generally been a practitioner of religious functions as well. Thus, the shaman is a special role found in all human societies, and is almost always a combination of ritual specialist, healer, finder of lost objects, futurologist, and sometimes social arbiter or "judge." Since nonmodern peoples generally could not have discovered anything like the "germ" theory of disease (because they did not have microscopes), their explanations for sickness and cures for sickness have had to be constructed from other sources. Indeed, "we moderns" didn't have much use for any germ theory of disease until a little over a hundred years ago. Most human groups have regarded illness as coming from supernatural forces, and even in modern times many Europeans and North Americans have considered sickness to be one of the consequences of violating the wishes of the supernaturals, or, conversely, evidence of the foul play by the devil or other supernaturally evil people. Most of our hospitals, of course, were established by religious groups and their names refer to Christian-Judaic supernaturals (St. Luke, Mt. Sinai, the Good Shepherd Hospital), illustrating the longtime connection between healing and religion. And when European-American people suffer that ultimate illness—death—the last rites are turned over to the hands of religious practitioners.

The bodily healers in most human societies have generally practiced a very eclectic medical style. While incantations and supernatural ritual may loom important in their therapies, the use of herbs and other naturalistic remedies is almost equally widespread. Also common is the shamanistic bedside manner which includes some manipulation of the patient's social network and social relations to bring comfort and relief from social problems as well as from the sicknesses thought caused by evil spirits, violation of taboos, or other events. To practice these eclectic therapies shamanistic healers usually derive a large portion of their powers from contacts with the supernaturals—the helping spirits, or deities who pass on some of their mystical powers to selected individuals to be redistributed to those in need.

David Werner's description of healing in the Sierra Madre is a rich example of eclectic medicine. As he notes, some of the herbal remedies in this Indian medical system appeared to have "proven curative property," although many of their other medical practices seem much more magical than naturalistic. Among the people of the Sierra Madre, as elsewhere, methods of curing are adopted from a wide variety of sources, and most folk healers are fairly open to adoption of new practices, even giving injections of penicillin along with their more traditional remedies.

The practice of modern university-based "scientific" medicine has spread rapidly to the remote areas of the world during the past two or three decades. Practically all Indian groups in North America, and most of those of Latin America, nowadays have some contact with modern medical services. Often the practitioners of "modern medicine" (doctors, nurses, and public health authorities) have taken the view that they should eradicate those traditional practices seen as detrimental to health and basically unscientific. The recipients of new medical systems, however, have usually taken a much more eclectic view, combining acceptance of modern medicine with maintenance of faith in large portions of their traditional healing practices. In most recent times medical authorities have recognized the value of aspects of traditional medical practices, and have sought to develop working relationships with traditional healers. A notable instance of this new view of medicine is seen in Robert Bergman's description of a school for medicine men, in which traditional Navajo medical practitioners are being trained in part in traditional terms, partly by medical doctors from our public health service. It is the opinion of some of these public health authorities that the traditional medical practices are especially efficacious in connection with illnesses of psychological origin, and for other socially induced problems that have been well handled by the traditional Navajo medicine men.

The special profession or social role of shaman in nonmodern societies has always fascinated scholars and lay people. The psychological characteristics of shamans and healers have often suggested that something very complicated about personality "abnormalities" is involved in the training and the original preselection of individuals to this socially important activity. Certainly in some societies the shaman appears to have been "half crazy" in behavior. That is the argument of Waldemar Bogoras, who lived for a number of years among Siberian peoples at the turn of the century. His observations certainly suggest that Chukchee individuals were quite different from their fellow humans in psychiatric characteristics, but we should quickly note that in many other societies shamanistic curers have not been nearly as aberrant as those Siberian cases must have been. It could be argued, though, that the position of healer is itself a focus of great tension and concern among peoples and that in most societies people have very ambivalent feelings toward the individual on whom they are dependent for their maintenance of well-being.

Practically all societies recognize some relationships between the foods we eat and the illnesses we suffer. Most peoples have various food taboos or food prescriptions in connection with their therapeutic practices. Also, most people regard certain foods as dangerous to the health or as contributing to sickness under particular circumstances. David McKay's article about medical practices in west Malasia illustrates a particularly close relationship between food and health in one society. This paper reminds us of the need in contemporary industrialized and urbanized societies for much greater attention to interactions between nutritional and health problems.

Many of the communities and peoples that anthropologists study are nowadays in somewhat marginalized situations in rural areas, in city slums, or other economically and socially and psychologically difficult environments. In a rural poverty area of the midwest, for example, the facts of low income and awareness of supposed advantages and attractions "out there" in mainline North American society can produce feelings of insecurity and inferiority in some people, and coupled with other problems may have serious consequences for mental health. Again, when people from rural areas or from reservation areas move into cities, they often find that jobs are not available, they are discriminated against, and various other problems may make them wish they had stayed "down on the farm" or "back on the reservation." In fact, many of the city migrants do return to their home areas permanently or at least for extended visits, in coping with or reacting to the problems and stresses of the city.

The general frame of reference we have employed in this section is intended to suggest that psychological features of individuals are part of the system of explanation for why different people engage in different kinds of behaviors or may have diverse adaptive styles within similar environments. The psychological features, of course, interact in complex ways with economic facts, technological equipment, and physical and social environments. At the same time, social events and cultural and economic forces or situations can affect people's psychological well-being and have strong impact on personalities. Thus in some of our materials here we are looking at personality features or psychological characteristics as *outcomes* of other forces; whereas we also consider the ways in which these psychological features may themselves have effects on other aspects of culture and society. These materials are intended to illustrate the point in our adaptational diagram on page 10, that the arrows between individual characteristics and other parts of the ecological system are in *both* directions. Neither the individual bio-psychological nor the other "boxes" in the diagram are thought of as being "first causes" in explaining human behavior.

First Symptoms of a Shamanistic Calling

The shamanistic call begins to manifest itself at an early age, in many cases during the critical period of transition from childhood to youth. It is also the period of rapid and intense growth; and it is well known that many persons of both sexes manifest during this time increased sensitiveness, and that the mind often becomes unbalanced. It is easy to understand that this critical period of human life, which is always full of unexpected changes and developments, is peculiarly adapted to the first implanting of shamanistic inspiration.

Nervous and highly excitable temperaments are most susceptible to the shamanistic call. The shamans among the Chukchee with whom I conversed were as a rule extremely excitable, almost hysterical, and not a few of them were half crazy. Their cunning in the use of deceit in their art closely resembled the cunning of a lunatic.

The Chukchee say that young persons destined to receive shamanistic inspiration may be recognized at a very early age, even in their teens, by the gaze, which, during a conversation, is not turned to the listener, but is fixed on something beyond him. In connection with this, they say that the eyes of a shaman have a look different from that of other people, and they explain it by the assertion that the eyes of the shaman are very bright, which, by the way, gives them the ability to see "spirits" even in the dark. It is certainly a fact that the expression of a shaman is peculiar,—a combination of cunning and shyness; and by this it is often possible to pick him out from among many others.

The Chukchee are well aware of the extreme nervousness of their shamans, and express it by the word niñi'rkɪlqin ("he is bashful"). By this word they mean to convey the idea that the shaman is highly sensitive even to the slightest change of the psychic atmosphere surrounding him during his exercises. For instance, the Chukchee shaman is diffident in acting before strangers, especially shortly after his initiation. A shaman of great power will refuse to show his skill when among strangers, and will yield only after much solicitation: even then, as a rule, he will not show all of his power. He is shy of strange people, of a house to which he is unaccustomed, of "alien" drums and charms which are hidden in their bags, and of "spirits" that hover around. The least doubt or sneer makes him break off the performance and retire.

Reprinted from Waldemar Bogoras, The Chukchee, Memoirs of The American Museum of Natural History, No. 11, 1953, by permission of The American Museum of Natural History.

The shamanistic "spirits" are likewise described as "fleeting," meaning that they want to flee before every unusual face or voice. When too many strange visitors come to the shaman, the "spirits" are shy of appearing, and, even when they do come, they are all the time anxious to slip away. Once when I induced a shaman to practise at my house, his "spirits" (of a ventriloquistic kind) for a long time refused to come. When at last they did come, they were heard walking around the house outside and knocking on its walls, as if still undecided whether to enter. When they entered, they kept near to the corners, carefully avoiding too close proximity to those present.

"Ke′let belong to the wilderness," say the shamans, "just as much as any wild animal. This is the reason that they are so fleeting." Ke′let of the animal kind have this shyness to an extreme degree. When coming at the call of the shaman, they sniff and snort, and finally, after some short exercise on the drum, flee back to the freedom of the wilderness. All this, of course, is brought about by ventriloquism. Even the ke′let of diseases, especially those who cannot harm man much,—as, for instance, rheum or cold,—are described as very "fleeting." Thus, in one tale, the rheum, before mustering sufficient courage to enter a human habitation, makes several attempts, and each time goes back overcome by its shyness. When caught on the spot, it manifests the utmost fear, and in abject terms begs for freedom.

The Chukchee generally are highly susceptible to any physical or psychical impressions of a kind to which they are unused; as, for instance, to unfamiliar odors. This is especially the case in regard to diseases; and the saying, "The Chukchee people are 'soft to die' " (nuthiwi′qin), is frequently heard among them. Thus, though they are able to endure excessive hardships, they succumb quickly to any contagious disease brought from civilized countries. This sensitiveness is shared by other native tribes of northeastern Siberia, and even by the Russian creoles, who are just as susceptible to psychic influences of an unusual character; for instance, to warning received in dreams or from strange people, to threats on the part of shamans or high officials, etc. During the last epidemic of measles, a creole in Gishiga lived but one night after having been told by an official, who meant no harm, that in a dream he had seen him die. There have been several instances of suicide among the cossacks and Russianized natives as the result of reproof on the part of officials. In other cases, native guides of Lamut or Yukaghir origin, travelling with parties of Russian officials on exploring expeditions, have, on losing their way in the uninhabited country, run away from fear and despair, and every trace of them thereafter has been lost. Suicides are also frequent among the Chukchee.

It seems to me that Mr. Jochelson has in mind the same high degree of susceptibility when he calls attention to the fact that the young men of the Yukaghir were said in ancient times to be exceedingly bashful, so much so that they would die when a sudden affront was given them, even by their own relatives. The shamans possess this nervous sensitiveness in a still higher degree than other people. This finds expression in the proverb that shamans are even more "soft to die" than ordinary people.

While speaking of this subject, let me add, that the slightest lack of harmony between the acts of the shamans and the mysterious call of their "spirits" brings their life to an end. This is expressed by the Chukchee when they say that "spirits" are very bad-tempered, and punish with immediate death the slightest disobedience of the shaman, and that this is particularly so when the shaman is slow to carry out those orders which are intended to single him out from other people.

On the other hand, apart from the displeasure of his ke'let, a shaman is said to be "resistant to death" and especially "difficult to kill," even when vanquished by enemies. Thus, in a description of a murder which took place in the Anui country in the nineties of the last century, the native, whose words were written down verbatim, says,—

"With an incantation of theirs they made him sleep. While he was sleeping, they attacked him from both sides. One cut his throat; the other stabbed him in the direction of the heart, the source of life and death. Nevertheless he jumped up. But he had no arms. They were also "knowing people"; and thus they induced him, likewise by incantations, to leave the camp unarmed. If he had had only a small knife, perhaps he would have been able to overpower them. Now, though he (being a shaman) stood up, with what could he fight them, except with his teeth and nails? Thus they stabbed him; but his wounds immediately healed and he was as before. For a very long time they could not kill him. At last they fell upon him from both sides, and, throwing him down, scooped out his eyes, pierced the eyeballs with a knife and flung them far away. Then they cut his body here and there; also the heart they tore away and cut to pieces. All these pieces they buried in the ground in separate places, because they were afraid to bury them together, lest he should revive."

Another account of similar kind says,—

"She [the murderer] came to her neighbor, a woman, who was busy with her fireboard, trying to make a fire. She stabbed her from behind. But the girl continued to work on the fire, because she was a shaman-girl, a woman able to stab herself (in shamanistic performance). Therefore she could not kill her, but only severed the tendons of her arms and legs."

A third account, referring to the small-pox epidemic of 1884 in the country of the western Kolyma, says,—

"Then A'mče began to think about his son-in-law, because his daughter left him ill in the vacant camp. A'mče said, 'Let us go and visit him.' He said, 'He is one able to resist death, he is a shaman.'"

The shamanistic call manifests itself in various ways. Sometimes it is an inner voice, which bids the person enter into intercourse with the "spirits." If the person is dilatory in obeying, the calling "spirit" soon appears in some outward, visible shape, and communicates the call in a more explicit way. For instance, Aiñanwa't says that at one time, after a severe illness, when his soul was ripe for inspiration, he saw several "spirits," but did not give much heed to the fulfilment of their orders. Then a "spirit" came to him. He was gaunt, and black of color, and said that he was the "spirit" of reindeer-scab. Aiñanwa't felt himself very much drawn toward that "spirit," and wanted him to stay and become his constant companion. The "spirit" hesitated at first, and then refused to stay. He said, however, "I may consent, if your desire for my company is strong enough,—if you wish me enough to take the drum, to handle it for three days and three nights, and to become a shaman." Aiñanwa't, in his turn, refused, and the "spirit" immediately vanished.

The shamanistic call is also manifested by various omens, such as meeting a certain animal, finding a stone or a shell of peculiar form, etc. Each of these omens has in itself nothing extraordinary, but derives its significance from its mystical recognizance in the mind of the person to whose notice it is brought. This process resembles the finding of amulets; and, indeed, the stone found, or the animal met, becomes the protector and the assistant "spirit" of the person in question.

Young people, as a rule, are exceedingly reluctant to obey the call, especially if it involves the adoption of some characteristic device in clothing or in the mode of life. They refuse to take the drum and to call the "spirits," leave the amulets in the field, etc.

The parents of young persons "doomed to inspiration" act differently, according to temperament and family conditions. Sometimes they protest against the call coming to their child, and try to induce it to reject the "spirits" and to keep to the ordinary life. This happens mostly in the case of only children, because of the danger pertaining to the shamanistic call, especially in the beginning. The protest of the parents is, however, of no avail, because the rejection of the "spirits" is much more dangerous even than the acceptance of their call. A young man thwarted in his call to inspiration will either sicken and shortly die, or else the "spirits" will induce him to renounce his home and go far away, where he may follow his vocation without hindrance.

On the other hand, it is entirely permissible to abandon shamanistic performances at a more mature age, after several years of practice; and the anger of the "spirits" is not incurred by it. I met several persons who asserted that formerly they had been great shamans, but that now they had given up most of their exercises. As reason for this, they gave illness, age, or simply a decrease of their shamanistic power, which in the course of time manifested itself. One said that because of illness he felt as if his arms and legs were frozen, and that thereafter they did not thaw, so that he was unable to "shake himself" well upon the drum. Another said that he and his "spirits" became tired of each other. Most of the cases, probably, were simply the result of recovery from the nervous condition which had made the persons in question fit subjects for the inspiration. While the shaman is in possession of the inspiration, he must practise, and cannot hide his power. Otherwise it will manifest itself in the form of bloody sweat or in a fit of violent madness similar to epilepsy.

Training of the Shaman

There are parents who wish their child to answer the call. This happens especially in families rich in children, with large herds, and with several tents of their own. Such a family is not inclined to feel anxious about a possible loss of one of its members. On the contrary, they are desirous of having a shaman of their own,—made to order, so to speak,—a special solicitor before the "spirits," and a caretaker in all extraordinary casualties of life.

A shaman by the name of Tei'ñet, in the country near the Wolverene River, told me that, when the call came to him and he did not want to obey, his father gave him the drum and induced him to begin the exercise. After that, he continued to feel "bashful" for several years. On days of ceremonials he even fled from the camp and hid himself, lest his relatives should find him out and bring him back to camp, to show to the assembled people his newly acquired and growing skill.

For men, the preparatory stage of shamanistic inspiration is in most cases very painful, and extends over a long time. The call comes in an abrupt and obscure manner, leaving the young novice in much uncertainty regarding it. He feels "bashful" and frightened; he doubts his own disposition and strength, as has been the case with all seers, from Moses down. Half unconsciously and half against his own will, his whole soul undergoes a strange and painful transformation. This period may last months, and sometimes even years. The young novice, the "newly inspired," loses all interest in the ordinary affairs of life. He ceases to work, eats but little and without relishing the food, ceases to talk to people, and does not even answer their questions. The greater part of his time he spends in sleep.

Some keep to the inner room and go out but rarely. Others wander about in the wilderness, under the pretext of hunting or of keeping watch over the herd, but often without taking along any arms or the lasso of the herdsman. A wanderer like this, however, must be closely watched, otherwise he might lie down on the open tundra and sleep for three or four days, incurring the danger, in winter, of being buried in drifting snow. When coming to himself after such a long sleep, he imagines that he has been out for only a few hours, and generally is not conscious of having slept in the wilderness at all. The accounts of such prolonged sleep are, of course, greatly exaggerated.

The Chukchee, however, sometimes, in case of sickness, fall into a heavy and protracted slumber, which may last many days, with only the necessary interruptions for physical needs, and which may, perhaps, end in death, though this is by no means assured. For instance, two years before my coming to the Anadyr, one Rıke'whi, a Chukchee living at Mariinsky Post, and his wife, both had an attack of grippe, which ravages the country at short intervals. The woman died. The man slept it out for more than two months. During this time he took but little food, mostly dried fish, and very rarely could he have a hot meal prepared for him by sympathetic women among his neighbors. All this was corroborated by the Russian cossacks living at Mariinsky Post, in close proximity to the natives.

The before-mentioned Aiñanwa't also told me that in 1884 he lost his whole family by small-pox, but slept it out himself for two weeks, during which time he conversed with "spirits." It is also believed that the "spirits" communicate with novices during their slumbers, and gradually assert their power over their minds and their whole persons.

The process of gathering inspiration is so painful to young shamans, because of their mental struggle against the call, that they are sometimes said to sweat blood on the forehead and the temples. Afterwards every preparation of a shaman for a performance is considered a sort of repetition of the initiative process: hence it is said that the Chukchee shamans during that time are easily susceptible to hemorrhage and even to bloody sweat. I myself witnessed two cases of bleeding from the nose among Chukchee shamans before their performances. As regards the bloody sweat, I knew of only one case, and even in that I was suspicious that the shaman in question, having an attack of nose-bleed, had happily thought to smear his temples with blood in order to increase our respect for his shamanistic powers. At least, he kept repeating that he was not like the modern shamans, but that he was the equal of the ancient "genuine" shamans, who sweated blood from the strain of their inspiration. He was, however, a typical specimen of a Chukchee shaman,—a very unsteady, excitable nature; and after all, I am not quite sure that he tricked us with his bloody sweat.

The preparatory period is compared by the Chukchee to a long, severe illness; and the acquirement of inspiration, to a recovery. There are cases of young persons who, having suffered for years from lingering illness (usually of a nervous character), at last feel a call to take to shamanistic practice, and by this means overcome the disease. Of course it is difficult to draw the line of demarcation, and all these cases finally come under one and the same class. The preparatory period of inspiration is designated by the Chukchee by a special term, meaning "he gathers shamanistic power" (the verb tewitɪ'ñɪrkɪn and its derivatives). With weaker shamans and with women, the preparatory period is less painful, and the call to inspiration comes mainly in dreams.

To people of more mature age the shamanistic call may come during some great misfortune, dangerous and protracted illness, sudden loss of family or property, etc. Then the person, having no other resource, turns to the "spirits," and claims their assistance. It is generally considered that in such cases a favorable issue is possible only with the aid of the "spirits": therefore a man who has withstood some extraordinary trial of his life is considered as having within himself the possibilities of a shaman, and he often feels bound to enter into closer relations with the "spirits," lest he incur their displeasure at his negligence and lack of gratitude.

The single means used by the Chukchee shamans, novice or experienced, for communication with "spirits," is the beating of the drum and singing. As said before, the usual family drum is employed with a drum-stick of whalebone, while a wooden drum-stick is used chiefly in ceremonials. Some drums have two whalebone drum-sticks, of which the extra one is supposed to be intended for the use of "spirits," when they approach and want to "shake themselves"; that is, to beat the drum.

The beating of the drum, notwithstanding its seeming simplicity, requires some skill, and the novice must spend considerable time before he can acquire the desired degree of perfection. This has reference especially to the power of endurance of the performer. The same may be said of the singing. The manifestations continue for several hours, during all which time the shaman exercises the most violent activity without scarcely a pause. After the performance he must not show any signs of fatigue, because his is supposed to be sustained by the "spirits"; and, moreover, the greater part of the exercise is asserted to be the work of the "spirits" themselves, either while entering his body, or while outside his body. The degree of endurance required for all this, and the ability to pass quickly from the highest excitement to a state of normal quietude, can, of course, be acquired only by long practice. Indeed, all the shamans I conversed with said that they had to spend a year, or even two years, before sufficient strength of hand, and freedom of voice, were given to them by the "spirits." Some asserted that during all this preparatory time they kept closely to the inner room, taking up the drum several times a day, and beating it as long as their strength would allow.

The only other means of training for inspiration, of which I am aware, is abstention from all fat and rich foods, as well as great moderation in eating. The same strictness is observed ever afterwards in the preparation for each individual performance, in which the shaman tries to abstain wholly from food.

Various tricks performed by the Chukchee shamans, including ventriloquism, have to be learned in the preparatory stage. However, I could obtain no detailed information on this point, since the shamans, of course, asserted that the tricks were done by "spirits," and denied having any hand whatever in proceedings of such a character.

In some cases, evidently, the old men have taught the younger generation, who are said to have received their power from them. The transfer is final, and cannot be revoked. The man who gives a part of his power to another man loses correspondingly, and can hardly recover the loss afterwards. To transfer his power, the older shaman must blow on the eyes or into the mouth of the recipient, or he may stab himself with a knife, with the blade of which, still reeking with his "source of life," he will immediately pierce the body of the recipient. These methods are also supposed to be used by shamans in the treatment of their patients.

David Werner

Healing in the Sierra Madre

In a small Mexican village I was shaken awake one night by a young *campesino* whose sister had just been stung by a scorpion. He pleaded with me to come quickly. Armed with an injection of antivenin I hurried to the family's adobe house, but found that the treatment had already begun. The young woman's husband had hunted down the offending scorpion on the dirt floor, chopped off its tail, split the animal open on its ventral side, and bound the still-wriggling creature to his wife's stung finger.

In the barrancas, the steep ravine country of the Sierra Madre of eastern Sinaloa, northeast of Mazatlan, such a treatment is typical. Here, many small farms are a day's journey or more from the closest road, and in the summer rainy season, weeks may pass when communication with the outside world is impossible. Although the Mexican government has taken large steps toward providing rural health centers in isolated sectors, the remote reaches of the Sierra Madre have no such services as yet. The people are forced to rely on their own ingenuity, plus the traditional folk cures handed down from the past.

While the modern medical aid I have been providing for the past five years is usually gratefully accepted, the villagers are understandably reluctant to give up the folk cures in which they have placed their faith and hope for centuries. Many come for help only after their attempts with home remedies have failed, and if modern medicine seems too slow or unpromising to them, they may suddenly switch back to traditional remedies. More often, however, folk medicine is applied simultaneously with whatever treatment I recommend.

On the surface there seems to be more madness than method behind the array of herbal cures and folk treatments found in the barrancas. But I have learned from the *curanderas*, as female herbal healers are called, that many cures are guided by time-honored assumptions. For example, the treatment for scorpion sting described above reflects a local saying that "every poisonous animal also has an antipoison."

Such home brew "antivenins" are common. One broad-spectrum remedy, claimed effective against many different bites and stings, is prepared by heating one scorpion, one centipede, and one black widow spider in alcohol. To give it potency, villagers insist that the brew be exposed overnight to the dew. Other remedies are specific for particular poisonous creatures. For

Reprinted from David Werner, "Healing in the Sierra Madre," Natural History (November 1970), 61–66, with permission of Natural History Magazine. Copyright © The American Museum of Natural History, 1970.

rattlesnake bite, for example, some villagers cut open the live snake, remove the gall bladder, and smear the bile on the bite. Others claim it is more effective for the victim simply to catch the snake and quickly bite a piece out of it, although I have yet to see this done.

"The more poisonous the animal, the more potent its antipoison," is another folk rule of the barrancas. Since the Mexican beaded lizard—a close relative of the venomous Gila monster—is feared as the most deadly of all animals, it is understandably revered as an antidote against every type of animal toxin. Its shed skin is applied against the poisoned bite or sting to effect a cure.

Although the villagers believe, quite rightly, that the beaded lizard is highly poisonous, they also maintain, erroneously, that this lizard can spit large distances and that its saliva is the cause of *pinto*, a piebald skin condition of the aged. Piebald skin is also reputedly caused by eating pork and drinking milk at the same meal or by getting angry after taking a purgative. This sort of explanation for ailments, especially skin conditions, is common in the barrancas. For example, ringworm of the scalp is said to result from a butterfly landing on one's hair. Ringworm of the body, however, is attributed either to moth's urine or to the bite of a mosquito that has previously sucked a toad's blood.

These odd and unfounded explanations for otherwise inexplicable maladies call to mind the American folk myth that "toads cause warts." In the barrancas, toads are, in fact, considered deadly, but they are not accused of causing warts. Nevertheless, one must be careful never to kill a toad, as this may cause the rains to fail in the summer planting season. As for warts, every *campesino* "knows" they are caused by contact with iguana blood.

In the pharmacology of the barrancas, the application of venomous animals extends far beyond their use as antivenins. The rattlesnake, or *víbora de cascabel*, for example, is a crawling medicine chest. Rare is the village hut that does not have a coil of *víbora* hanging by a leather thong over the cooking fire within handy reach in case of medical emergency. Various anatomical parts of the rattlesnake are used for infirmities ranging from boils to bronchitis. While the treatment of tonsillitis requires a species of rattlesnake found only in the high sierra, for most cures any rattlesnake will do. Most of the prescriptions are very explicit. Consider the treatment for miner's cough (silicosis). "Cut off the head and tail of the rattlesnake, powder the remains, mix with water and drink. For best results, tease the snake before killing it, as this potentiates the 'antimicrobial' action." The rattlesnake has even entered the realm of preventive medicine. When I asked a mother why she hung a necklace of rattlesnake bones around her baby's neck, she replied, "To prevent the diarrhea caused by teething, of course."

The use of venomous animals to treat venomous bites is representative of the homeopathic, or "like cures like," principle, which crops up time and again in the folk medicine of the Sierra Madre. Some aspect of the curative agent usually resembles or strongly suggests the infirmity it is supposed to counter. Such resemblances probably inspired the discovery of the treatment in the first place, although perhaps unconsciously, for the *curanderas*—who gain knowledge of a new cure in a trance or dream—seem totally incognizant of the homeopathic relationship. Nevertheless, it is often quite evident. The rattle of the rattlesnake, for example, is pulverized and placed in the ear for treatment of earache. The fang is used for curing toothache, the tip being inserted into the offending cavity.

Many quasi-homeopathic cures can be cited. To prevent a dog bite from becoming infected, the hair from the tip of the dog's tail is boiled and the wound washed with the water. If, however, the victim wishes to revenge himself against the dog, he plasters a poultice of red chili pepper against the bite. Being hot, the chili pepper is supposed to "bite back" and cause the dog's death.

Absurd as it may sound to us, this sort of "remote control" seems probable to the villager whose life is rich with witches, demons, and other supernatural beings. In his world there are many similar examples. The infected fissures that develop on a cow's teats because of poor milking hygiene are attributed to spilling some of the cow's milk over hot coals; therefore the villagers always heat milk with great caution. When a fishbone sticks in someone's throat, he must hurry to the cooking fire and turn a flaming fagot so that the unlit end ignites; this will dislodge the fishbone.

Many of the herbal as well as animal remedies reflect the quasi-homeopathic principle. There are literally hundreds of herbal folk medicines, for another saying goes, "Every plant has a curative function, if one can but discover what it is." Fortunately, many of the plants give away their secret function through some telltale characteristic of their morphology. Thus we find that *yedra*, a crimson red wood fungus once prized as tinder by the Indians, is used in the treatment of nosebleed and hemorrhage. The broad conical spines, or "bumps," on the bark of *pochote* (wild kapok) are ground up and fed to a child with measles in order to make the spots come out, for it is believed that when the spots bud the disease ceases to be dangerous. *Guaco*, a serpentine vine with a strange, dark flower shaped like the head of a reptile, is widely used in the treatment of snakebite and other poisoning.

Consistent with the homeopathic trend of folk medicine, unpleasant maladies often have unpleasant cures. The more revolting the infirmity, the more repulsive the cure tends to be. For goiter, the unsightly protrusions that bulge from the throats of many of the highlanders as a result of iodine deficiency, there exist a variety of such remedies: tear open a freshwater crab (common in the mountain streams) so that its innards exude, then bind it against the goiter; smear the brains of a turkey vulture upon the goiter three times a day; stroke the goiter with the hand of a dead child; or plaster the goiter with *yerba sin raiz*, "herb without roots," a euphemism for human excrement used medicinally.

In the barrancas, scatology has become a medical art. Animal as well as human excrement is used in scores of specific treatments. Recently I was called to the aid of a three-year-old child who had stumbled into a vat of boiling lard and burned 40 percent of his body. By the time I arrived on muleback, the boy was already suffering from severe electrolyte imbalance and had begun to convulse. As I entered the dark adobe room where the boy was sheltered, I smelled and then saw a platter of fresh cow manure beside the cot. The boy's distraught mother explained that it should be spread on the child's hand, but unable to remember whether the dung should be smeared on the right hand or the left, she hadn't dared apply it. I talked the mother out of the dung cure and administered a balanced salt solution. The child responded, and fortunately, the burns developed no infections.

Urine, like excrement, is a common constituent of barrancan pharmaceutics. Its application ranges from the use of human urine in the emergency cleansing of wounds to a tonic for bronchitis prepared from horse urine. Some of the treatments have mythological overtones. For example, washing the face with human urine controls acne effectively only when done for nine consecutive days beginning with a full moon.

I, myself, once had the dubious fortune to be the recipient of a folk cure using child's urine. I had fallen from a rock wall at night and broken several ribs. An old *curandera* was called at once to my aid. She spread out a sackful of corn from which she selected the most rotten and shriveled grains. These she charred over the cooking fire, then ground them into a powder in a big bowl. She then bade her six-year-old granddaughter urinate in the bowl, and when the child had shyly obliged, she mixed the charred powder and urine into a dark, evil-smelling paste. Plastering this over my ribs, she said, "This will prevent the injury from developing *pasmo* or cancer." (Both *pasmo* and *cancer* are terms used to define severe infections. *Cancer*, as a folk term, bears no relation to carcinoma.) The remedy did, indeed, prove successful, insofar as no infection resulted. As for side effects: it itched!

Creatures renowned for their ferocity are also frequently credited with medicinal powers. The meat of the peccary (wild boar) is cooked and eaten as treatment for general debility. Lard of mountain lion is smeared on painful joints to relieve arthritis.

In addition, animals that are in some way odd or atypical may be blamed for otherwise unexplained infirmities, and therefore used in curing them. The praying mantis is accused of causing cattle bloat. The bat is reputed to cause blindness by urinating in the eyes of sleeping persons. Glowworms are thought to be deadly and are blamed when someone who has slept in the fields dies unaccountably.

The list of animal remedies goes on and on, and as I flip through the file I have drawn together, I find, for example, the following annotations under louse: place a human louse in the eye to remove a foreign object. And, throw a pig louse in the ear of a mule to cure it from rearing its head back when the bit is put in its mouth. Under pig, I find: to cure your husband's alcoholism, secretly sneak one thimbleful of pig's milk into his liquor. Under iguana: for depression, eat fried iguana meat, *but not the meat of the green iguana.* Green iguana is thought poisonous and is blamed, along with the devil, for staggers in cattle.

With this kaleidoscope of folk cures, the question arises as to how many, if any, of these remedies have medicinal value. Apart from their psychological benefits, the efficacy of many of the treatments is at best dubious, yet some have definite merit.

As a general rule, I find the greater the number of folk cures enlisted for one malady, the lesser the likelihood that any will be effective. (The same is true, of course, for modern medicine. One need but review recent medical literature on tetanus or snakebite to see how varied and contradictory are the findings and recommendations when dealing with such often fatal, yet enigmatic, maladies.) Few, if any, of the antipoisons have merit in the treatment of venomous reptile and arthropod bites. Therefore, one finds an astonishing array of additional remedies: animal, herbal, fecal, mineral, and even musical. Violin music is prescribed for the bite of poisonous spiders! (The latter treatment was perhaps suggested by the violin-shaped marking on the cephalothorax of the deadly brown recluse spider.)

On the other hand, if one single cure exists for a malady, and especially if that cure is widely practiced, there is a fair chance that it may be effective. In the treatment of cuts and other wounds, the astringent juice of the cactus *Pachycereus pecten-aboriginum* is apparently effective in checking bleeding. I have seen this demonstrated many times, and now I even prescribe mouthwashes of the juice of this cactus, with good results, in cases of severe bleeding following tooth extraction.

Chemical analysis has validated the medicinal properties of certain of the local plants of the barrancas. The herbs with proven curative properties, however, are usually not those with telltale characteristics relating them to the maladies they serve. The same is true of animal cures: the more obvious the homeopathic link between malady and remedy, the less likely it is that the cure has any physiological value.

There are, however, some curious folk cures worthy, at least, of further investigation. The small amount of venom that remains on the rattlesnake's fang may, in fact, have an anesthetic function for toothache. Crayfish, eaten whole and alive to increase lactation in women do, no doubt, provide needed calcium. In some cases, the use of cow's urine mixed half-and-half with milk and taken on an empty stomach apparently is effective in the expulsion of intestinal worms. One cure for arthritis, that of letting a bee sting the affected joint seems improbable; yet, before the introduction of corticoids, some European doctors used honeybee venom to treat joint disease.

The use of oil of *vagre,* "catfish," in the late stages of bad burns deserves special study. Gross scarring in severely burned villagers treated with catfish oil is often dramatically less than that of patients with equivalent burns treated in the best American hospitals. This is of special interest in light of similar results described in studies of Eskimos, who also use fish oils to treat burns.

The villagers may even be on to some unique biological medicines. For infections in postpartum women, they brew a tea from underground fungus gardens of leaf-cutting ants. Like penicillin, this fungus may combat bacterial infection. Conversely, fresh cow dung, plastered on a child's scalp to control fungal infection, sometimes seems to work, perhaps due to the action of fungus-suppressing bacteria so abundant in fecal material.

If some of the folk remedies of the barrancas have probable merit, others are regrettably harmful. With few possible exceptions, the use of feces, for example, is of no benefit, and when applied to open sores or wounds may be the source of tetanus or other disastrous infections. No less detrimental to health is the so-called *dieta*, or regimen, prescribed for a wide variety of ailments. Most illnesses are classified according to their cause as either *caliente*, "hot," or *fresco*, "cold," and foods used in treatment are classified in the same way. This classification is arbitrary, and bears no relation to either the temperature or spiciness of the food. For some illnesses hot foods are to be avoided, for others, cold foods. If a person has a bad cold, for instance, he should under no circumstances eat an orange, as oranges are *muy fresco* and may produce *congestión*. (*Congestión*, for which there exists a formidable gamut of causes and remedies, is a catch-all infirmity covering everything from appendicitis to heart failure and tetanus.)

One of the most far-reaching and devastating *dietas* is that which a postpartum mother must follow. She must not bathe for fifteen days following childbirth. She must not eat eggs for twenty days. For forty days she must not eat any fruits or vegetables, including beans, the villagers' main source of protein. During these forty days, the new mother may eat young roosters, but not hens—and not roosters that have begun to mate. She must avoid going barefoot or handling moist earth. For twenty days she must avoid eating venison because it is "very cold." In short, about all the postpartum mother ends up eating is corn and, if available, white rice. As most of the women in the barrancas are anemic even before pregnancy, the nutritional deficiencies that result from the *dieta* lower even more their resistance to hemorrhage and infection. If the mother succumbs, the distraught villagers search her past for some violation of the *dieta*, and only when an answer has been guessed at and irrevocably confirmed by repeating it many times do they rest easy once again.

One must wonder about the origin of many of these beliefs and folk remedies. How old are they? From where do they stem? The *campesinos* live intrinsically off the land, and the land, with its unique flora and fauna, its torrential rains and droughts, its absolutes and uncertainties, goes far in shaping the lore of its people. The folk medicine of the barrancas is not static, but slowly evolving, like the landscape itself.

Historically, however, there are three conspicuous sources of the local medical lore. Out of the past have come the myths and medicines of the endemic Indian civilization and of the invading Spanish civilization, whose merger produced the present mestizo population. In addition, there are smatterings of modern science. The influences from these three sources have been turned and twisted until they can exist side by side in the minds of the people. It is not uncommon to see a woman with a migraine headache first bind her brow with the leaf of a wild arum lily, as did her Indian predecessors; then consult a *curandera* to have the causative hex lifted, as did her Spanish ancestors in the Dark Ages; and finally go to a modern quack in the next village to have herself injected, because "injections are good."

From the former Indian culture have come not only the basic herbal cures, but also an intriguing moon lore. Older villagers recall that the full-blooded Indians would sleep with their wives only during the waning moon so that their offspring would be strong and live long. Although this custom has gone out of vogue, the villagers today still cut timber for huts and fences only when the moon is waning, insisting that timber cut during the waxing moon rots more quickly. They still believe, also, that the light of an eclipsing moon will cause developing fruit to shrivel before it matures, but that flying a piece of red cloth from the tip of the tree may prevent this "eclipsing" of the fruit. Once, on my return from the upper villages, I found my favorite red shirt flapping from the top of the mango tree outside my dispensary. In like manner, birth deformities are reputedly engendered when the light of the eclipsing moon falls on a pregnant woman. The danger exists when the moonlight strikes one side of a woman only. As a preventive measure, pregnant women (and often nonpregnant ones, just to be sure) go outside during the eclipse and turn around three times.

Though the Spanish side of the ancestry come other ideas and legends. The oldest relic of folklore pathology in the barrancas traces back to the notorious basilisk of the ancient Greeks. This mythological dragon, alleged to have caused instant death to anyone who looked upon it, has shrunken noticeably in the 2,500 years of its evolution. Today in the Sierra Madre, the *basilisco* is said to be a strange little animal, rarely—or more probably, never—encountered, which hatches from the undersized egg of a chicken that has mated with the soil instead of a rooster. It is said that one has only to look at this ugly, lizardlike apparition and he will go as blind as if he had been urinated upon by a bat.

A number of mythological ailments and their treatments stem from traditions of medieval Spain. One, *caida de mollera*, means "fallen fontanel." When infants get severe diarrhea—as they frequently do in villages where the only sanitary facility is the omnivorous pig—tissue dehydration from fluid loss may cause the fontanel, or unclosed portion of the cranium, to sag inwards. The villagers, observing this, have put the cart before the horse by concluding that the child has diarrhea because its brains have slipped downward. Treatment consequently consists of elevating the brains back into place. Each *curandera* has her own procedure. These include holding the baby upside down over a bowl of hot cooking oil and slapping the bottoms of its feet three times to jolt the brains back into position. Or, moistening the baby's crown with hot oil and sucking upward three times on the fontanel to lift the brains into position. Another recommendation is to open the baby's mouth and push upward on the palate with the forefinger to hoist the baby's brains back into position.

It is surprising how many babies not only survive this treatment, but show improvement afterwards. A few, however, die.

Whatever merits and demerits it may have, the medical lore of the bar-rancas is not wanting in ingenuity or imagination. The one concept utterly lacking in folk medicine, however, is that very concept upon which modern medicine is founded: scientific method. True, the *campesinos'* desire for an-swers equals that of the modern researcher. When confronted by an in-firmity, they also search for both cause and cure, and find them. Often their line of reasoning is both logical and complex. But there is no provision for checking a rational answer against physical events, no allowance for testing a hypothesis. Rather, the hypothesis is transmuted into a conclusion by the process of simple repetition. "Might it have been this?" becomes, "It must have been this," and finally, irrovocably, "It was this!" Thus we find, because someone's great-grand-mother, years ago, ate an orange in the evening and that night died of a heart attack, that today no one in the barrancas will touch an orange after sundown.

Similar conclusions from coincidental events have given rise to folk beliefs that "eggs eaten after dark cause *congestión*," that "the bite of the green iguana poisons calves," and to many other causes and cures for maladies. By the same token, it is no surprise that the *dieta* of postpartum mothers is so limited. The incidence of puerpeural mortality is high, largely due to lack of sterile techniques by midwives, and the resultant infections are invariably blamed on some violation of the *dieta*. If no violation can be found, a new source of the problem is sought. "It must have been the mango she ate," is quickly abbreviated to, 'It was the mango," and from that day on the mango is included on the blacklist. And so the list is expanded until the *dieta* itself becomes a contributing factor in maternal mortality.

Yet never is an attempt made to systematically gather evidence that will either support or disprove a proposed cause or remedy. To search for evidence is to admit uncertainty, and in the Sierra Madre, as anywhere, uncertainty is difficult for man to tolerate. It is easier to live in dread of something spe-cific—even if mythological—than to admit that one does not know the direction in which the danger lies.

Fear of the unknown is the greatest fear of all, and in the prescientific world of the barrancas, the unknown looms large indeed. The *campesino* has neither the equipment nor the know-how to decipher even the simpler enigmas of nature. If he did not buffer his reality with a battery of rational, if sometimes ill-founded, explanations, the maze of unforeseen dangers and inexplicable events would soon be overpowering. Thus we find that in the barrancas, the villagers are devoted, not so much to seeking causes and cures that are valid, but to securing clear-cut causes and cures for everything.

Robert L. Bergman

A School for Medicine Men

This paper is an account of how a Navajo community set up its own medical school and how a non-Indian psychiatrist became involved in it. In order to understand what happened one must have some acquaintance with the nature of Navajo medicine. This subject has received an enormous amount of attention from anthropologists and other behavioral scientists. I will make no attempt here to review the extensive anthropologic literature except to recommend the great works of Haile (1), Reichard (2), and Kluckhohn and associates (3–6). The psychiatric literature is less extensive. It includes the early article of Pfister (7), which seems to me to be remarkably insightful and sound in spite of having been based on very little and quite second-hand evidence. The Leightons (8) in 1941 described Navajo ceremonials beautifully and explained many of their beneficial elements. Sandner (9) reported his work with Navajo medicine men to the APA three years ago. Almost everyone agrees that the ceremonies work.

Background

Navajo practitioners generally fall into three categories. The herbalists know a variety of medicinal plants, which are used primarily for symptomatic relief. The diagnosticians are shamans who work by inspiration. By one of several techniques, such as hand trembling, crystal gazing, or star gazing, they divine the nature and cause of an illness and make an appropriate referral to a member of the third and highest status group, the singers. The singers (I will use the terms "ceremonialist," "medicine man," and "singer" synonymously) do the only truly curative work, and it is a school to train them that I will be discussing.

Navajo nosology classes diseases by etiology; identical illnesses often have similar symptoms, but they need not. Note that psychiatric nosology is similar, e.g., depression is often characterized by insomnia, but sometimes the reverse can be true. A seriously oversimplified statement of Navajo etiology is that disease is caused by a disharmony with the universe, including the universe of other men. A singer restores this harmony by performing a ceremony proper to the case. Little or no reliance is placed on herbs or other

Reprinted from Robert L. Bergman, "A School for Medicine Men," American Journal of Psychiatry, *130:6 (1973), 663–666, copyright 1973 the American Psychiatric Association,* with permission of the American Psychiatric Association and the author.

medicines and, as is the case with psychiatry (at least from the psychoanalytic viewpoint), this absence of organic measures confers high status.

No one seems to know precisely how many ceremonies there are, but there are many. Important ones last five or nine nights and are difficult and elaborate to a degree approached among us physicians, I think, only by open heart surgery. The proper performance of a major sing requires the presence of the entire extended family and many other connections of the patient. The immediate family must feed all of these people for days. Many of the people present have important roles in the performance, such as chanting, public speaking, dancing in costume, leading group discussions, and many other prescribed activities of a more or less ritualized nature. For the singer himself the performance requires the letter-perfect performance of 50 to 100 hours of ritual chant (something approaching the recitation of the New Testament from memory), the production of several beautiful and ornate sand paintings, the recitation of the myth connected with the ceremony, and the management of a very large and difficult group process.

Non-Navajo explanations of why all this effort helps anyone tend to be rather offensive to the medicine men themselves, and *their* explanations, if they should feel like giving any, tend to be unsatisfying to us since they are based on the supernatural. The difference may not be as great as it appears, however. Traditional Navajos talk frequently in symbols: "We are glad you came from Washington to talk with us. There are many mountains between here and Washington," which translates as, "Communication with the federal government is difficult. We are glad you are making an effort to improve it." They also reject the notion that they are using figures of speech. They do not attach as much significance to the distinctions among different levels of reality as we do, and like some poets, they reject as stupid and destructive any attempt to translate their words into ordinary language. Though it seems to me that their myths and chants are symbols of human social-psychological forces and events, they would regard such a statement as silly and missing the point. Nevertheless, I will make a slight attempt in that direction.

The Rituals

For the past six years, I have been practicing psychiatry among the Navajo people. I have often referred patients to medicine men (who in turn occasionally refer patients to me). I have also often consulted medicine men, and patients have often told me about the medicine men's traditional cures and their feelings about these cures. It seems to me, although my knowledge of the sings is very limited, that the ceremony performed is almost always symbolically appropriate to the case. Pathologically prolonged grief reactions, for example, are almost always treated with a ceremony that removes the influence of the dead from the living and turns the patient's attention back toward life. "Treatment of a dream by a dream," Pfister called it.

It seems to me that the singers and we psychiatrists are the converse of one another with regard to our attitude toward ritual. To them ritual is the main focus: What is unvaryingly their practice from one case to another is at the center of their thought. Informal interaction with the patient and his family is considered important in an informal sort of way. This kind of interaction is not what is taught explicitly but only what is taught by the by. Our ritual, which I would argue is fairly elaborate, is not taught as the central part of psychiatry; rather, the more varying interaction is taught explicitly to psychiatry residents—ritual being taught by the by. In any event the singers do manage an intricate family interaction that, I think, has several important effects: (1) the patient is assured that his family cares for him by the tremendous effort being made; (2) the prolonged and intense contact makes it inevitable that conflicts are revealed and, if things are handled skillfully, resolved; and (3) a time of moratorium and turning point are established.

At the time I first heard of the medicine-man school in 1967, I was already quite convinced of the value of Navajo medicine. Aside from the cases I had seen, I was greatly influenced by my contact with a singer named Thomas Largewhiskers. Mr. Largewhiskers, who is now 100 years old, agreed to be my consultant and to teach me a little of what he knew. I first looked him up after seeing a formerly psychotic patient who attributed her remarkable and well-documented improvement to him. At the time of our first meeting I tried to explain what I do and said that I wanted to learn from him. He replied, "I don't know what you learned from books, but the most important thing I learned from my grandfathers was that there is a part of the mind that we don't really know about and that it is that part that is most important in whether we become sick or remain well." When he told me some of his life story it impressed me that he had become interested in being a singer when, as a young man, he had had an accident and the singer who took care of him explained that it had been unconsciously determined.

Mr. Largewhiskers and many other extremely old men are still practicing very actively. There is a growing demand for their services—growing because the population is increasing and their belief in traditional medicine is continuing. The trouble is that younger people are not becoming singers. The reasons behind the lack of students are largely economic. To learn to perform even one short ceremony takes at least a year of full-time effort. To learn a major ceremony takes much longer, and many medicine men know several. Since the end of the old herding economy, almost no one can afford to give up earning a living for such a long time. At the time of starting the school for medicine men Yazzie Begay, one of its founders, said, "I have been acquainted with several medicine men who have recently died. They were not able to teach the ceremonies which they knew to their grandchildren or to anyone else. Today their sacred instruments and paraphernalia are sitting unused."

The School

The school is at Rough Rock, Ariz., a community near the center of the Navajo Reservation. It is part of the Rough Rock Demonstration School, the first community-controlled Indian school. The Demonstration School was started in 1965, when the Bureau of Indian Affairs (BIA) gave the buildings and equipment to a nonprofit corporation of Navajo leaders called Dine, Inc. Dine helped the Rough Rock chapter of the tribe set up and elect its own board of education (no one on the original board could speak English and all were ceremonialists) and then contracted with the board to operate an elementary boarding school. BIA contributed funds that would have been equal to the budget of such a school if they had been operating it; funds also came from the Office of Economic Opportunity (OEO) and other sources. Soon after the school began operations in 1966, the people became convinced that their ideas really were taken seriously in its daily workings, and several local people suggested setting up the medicine-man school to the board. It was pointed out at a board meeting that white people have medical schools and give students scholarships to attend them and that what was needed most on the reservation were new medicine men. Therefore they felt Rough Rock should set up a school for singers and provide scholarships.

The idea was taken up enthusiastically by the board, and the details were worked out over the course of the next year. It was decided to alter the traditional method of teaching and learning sings as little as possible. (The old way is by apprenticeship and takes place in the teacher's home.) It was also decided that each medicine man would teach two apprentices of his own selection, that is, application for admission to the school would be made by trios consisting of a medicine man and two trainees. The school board would select among them on the basis of the medicine man's reputation, the trainees' apparent ability, and the importance of and threat of extinction to the ceremony that was proposed to be taught. The medicine men were to be paid a very modest salary and the trainees considerably less for their subsistence.

Obtaining Funds

Ever since the Demonstration School started, I had been going there once a month or more to consult with the guidance counselor and teachers. At one time the school administration, at the direction of the board, was preparing a project proposal in an attempt to obtain funds; I was asked to attend a meeting about the project, and here my support for the proposal was enlisted. This was the first of several project discussions in which I took part, and ultimately the board kindly included me in the proposal. It was decided that I should meet regularly with the trainees to discuss non-Navajo medicine, particularly psychiatry. I strongly suspect that my inclusion was a move to make the project look more reasonable to funding agencies.

I flatter myself that from time to time my colleagues in the school and the trainees have been glad to have me around, but I am sure that I have gained much more from this than they have. Before the project could materialize, however, we had to obtain funds.

The first proposal was made to OEO, which turned it down. The second proposal went to the Training and Special Projects Branch of the National Institute of Mental Health (NIMH). This one was accepted, although not, I suspect, without some trepidation. At the time of the site visit by NIMH it became apparent how many mountains there really were between Rough Rock and Bethesda, Md. First of all, the weather became very bad and the site visitors felt they were stranded in Albuquerque, which is 250 miles away from Rough Rock. Luckily the school board was able to go to Albuquerque, so we had a meeting. Two incidents seemed to me to epitomize the meeting. The first was a question from the visitors: "How can a project that supports the continuance of superstition promote mental heath?" The reaction of the ceremonialist school board members was more restrained than I had expected. They answered at length, and I added my endorsement. The visitors seemed satisfied. Later one of them, in leafing through the documents, said, "The project director is to be full-time, and the salary listed here is $5000. Can that possibly be right?" When that question had been translated, Mr. John Dick, the director in question, who was a medicine man and a former school board member, asked anxiously, "Is it too much?" I am very grateful that the project was funded, and I know that the board is also appreciative.

The Training Program

The work began in September 1969 and is still continuing. There are six medicine men and 12 trainees. Most of the original trainees are still in the program. One of the faculty members died during the first year and was replaced. The ceremonies being taught so far have been one and two nights in length, and almost all of the trainees have completed learning them. Soon they will be performing them for the first time. They will then go on to major ceremonies. Although the lessons (excluding the ones I teach) are conducted at various homes scattered over considerable territory in which there are no paved roads, Mr. Dick as director maintains close supervision. He travels to each home and watches over the teaching and its results. As the trainees have progressed, he and other medicine men have tested them. My only criticism has been that Mr. Dick's supervision seems rather harsh at times. He has demanded continuous effort and has been very hard on some people whom he surprised when he thought they should be working and they weren't. Still, apart from minor professional jealousy, the group's morale seems high. The program has been well accepted, and there clearly will be a demand for the services of the graduates. Other communities are trying to start similar schools. Recently one of the medicine men had one of his students perform a sing over him.

My sessions are a full day every two weeks. Before I started holding them I met with the medicine men to describe what I intended to do and to ask their permission. To my great pleasure they not only agreed to my plans but said they would like to attend along with the trainees. Attendance has varied from time to time, but usually most of the trainees are present as well as three to five of the medicine men. During the first year I talked about somatic medicine, attempting to cover elements of anatomy, physiology, pathology, diagnosis, and treatment. I discovered that the entire group, including the trainees, had considerable knowledge of anatomy and some of physiology. The sessions were lively. The medicine men and the trainees enjoyed trying out stethoscopes, otoscopes, opthalmoscopes, and blood-pressure cuffs. Microscope slides of blood smears and pathology specimens were also very popular. In return I was learning more about ceremonial practice, although not as much as I was to learn the next year when we began discussing psychology.

One of the high points of the first year was a visit that the group made to the Gallup Indian Medical Center. It was characteristic, I thought, that the two things the medicine men most enjoyed seeing at the hospital were an operation and a particularly good view of a sacred mountain peak from the windows of the psychiatric ward. They also had criticisms and suggestions. They were horrified by the pediatric ward because the children were so lonely. They kept asking, "Where are the parents?" They urged that better provisions be made for parents to stay with their children. They also suggested that we build two hogans at the hospital for ceremonial purposes. They remarked that they all had performed brief ceremonies in the hospital but that they could do more in a real hogan. They said that the medical staff could see the patients during the sing and could go back and forth if necessary. Their suggestion still has not been followed, but I hope that it will be soon.

During the second year I began discussing psychiatry, and in this area there has been more of a two-sided interchange. We have spent much time on European and Navajo notions of the unconscious, a subject in which difficulties in translation have been great. Navajo metapsychology still largely eludes me, but it is clear that the medicine men know about the dynamic interpretation of errors and dreams. We spent a great deal of time discussing dreams and were pleased to discover that all of us followed the same custom with regard to them. We all, it turned out, spend our first waking moments in the morning contemplating and interpreting our dreams. One of the medicine men gave an example. He had dreamt about an automobile accident and said that that kind of a dream meant something serious was going on within him and that in order to prevent some disaster from happening to him, it was important to perform a chant about it.

There has been a good deal of case presentation on both sides, particularly, for some reason not clear to me, regarding returned Viet Nam veterans. My feeling of trust and closeness to this group ultimately became such that I presented my own case, describing some things that had led me to enter my analysis and something of the analysis itself. When I finished this rather long account, one of the singers asked me the name of my analyst and where he is now. When I told him, he said, "You were very lucky to find a man who could do so much for you. He must be a very intelligent person."

Another high point for me was demonstrating hypnosis. The group ordinarily looks half asleep—as seems to be the custom with medicine men in meetings. This was unnerving at first, until I found out from their questions and comments that they had been paying very close attention. When hypnosis was demonstrated, however, they were obviously wide awake, although at times I wondered if they were breathing. Working with a carefully prepared subject (I was unwilling to face failure before this audience), I demonstrated a number of depth tests, somnambulism, age regression, positive and negative hallucinations, and some posthypnotic suggestions. When I was done, one of the faculty members said, "I'm 82 years old, and I've seen white people all my life, but this is the first time that one of them has ever surprised me. I'm not surprised to see something like this happen because we do things like this, but I am surprised that a white man should know anything so worthwhile." They also pointed out the resemblance of hypnosis to hand trembling, a diagnostic procedure in which the shaman goes into a trance and his hand moves automatically and indicates the answers to important questions. After we had discussed the similarity, they asked that my subject, a young Navajo woman, diagnose something. I objected, saying that neither she nor I knew how to do this and that it was too serious a matter to play with. They insisted that we try, however, and finally we decided that a weather prediction was not too dangerous to attempt. They were particularly interested in the weather at that time because we were in the midst of an especially severe drought, and someone in the community had predicted that it would continue for another year. When my subject was in a deep trance, I instructed her to visualize the weather for the next six months. She predicted light rain within the week, followed by a dry spell of several months and finally by a good rainy season in late summer. I make no claim other than the truthful reporting of facts: She was precisely correct.

My involvement in this project has, of course, been extremely interesting to me. It is hard, however, to assess the effects of the project on the medicine men and on me. The medicine men say that they know better when and how to refer patients to the white doctors, and I think they feel more kindly toward us. In turn, I feel better able to understand my Navajo patients and know better when to refer them to medicine men. I have adopted some Navajo styles of thought, I think. I use hypnosis more than I used to. And one of my Navajo colleagues in the Indian Health Service Mental Health Program claims that I try to act like a medicine man all the time.

References

1. Haile BOFM: Origin Legend of the Navaho Enemy Way. Publications in Anthropology No. 17. New Haven, Yale University Press, 1938
2. Reichard GA: Navajo Religion. New York, Bollingen Foundation, 1950
3. Kluckhohn C, Leighton D: The Navajo. New York, Doubleday & Co., 1962
4. Kluckhohn C, Wyman LD: An Introduction to Navajo Chant Practice with an Account of the Behaviors Observed in Four Chants. Memoirs of the American Anthropological Association No. 53. Menasha, Wis, American Anthropological Association, 1940
5. Kluckhohn C: The Great Chants of the Navajo. Societies Around the World. Edited by Sanders IT and others. New York, Dryden Press, 1956
6. Kluchhohn C: Navajo Witchcraft. Boston, Beacon Press, 1967
7. Pfister O: Instinctive psychoanalysis among the Navajos. J Nerv Ment Dis 76: 234–254, 1932
8. Leighton AH, Leighton D: Elements of psychotherapy in Navajo religion. Psychiatry 4:515–523, 1941
9. Sandner D: Navajo medicine men. Read at the 123rd annual meeting of the American Psychiatric Association, San Francisco, Calif, May 11–15, 1970

David A. McKay

Food, Illness, and Folk Medicine: Insights from Ulu Trengganu, West Malaysia *

Introduction

The use or restriction of specific foods to preserve health or ameliorate illness has been a part of the medical art throughout its history. Science has judged various precepts as wise or foolish; still others remain as unproved items of medical common sense, embedded in the customs of even the most sophisticated societies. A scant 60 years ago, Osler (1909) hailed as the most "remarkable triumph of modern hygiene" Takagi's elimination of beri-beri from the Japanese Navy by "allowing a larger portion of nitrogenous food and forbidding the use of fresh fish altogether"—a mixture of fact and fancy instructive to our present perspective. More recently, Ingelfinger (1966) has noted the prevalence of unproven dietary precepts in the contemporary treatment of peptic ulcer. Indeed, after reviewing the limited scientific basis for various dietary regimens in gastrointestinal disease, the Council on Foods and Nutrition on the American Medical Association (1961) concluded that most "must be regarded as based on unverified impressions and traditional lore. Such bases, like much folklore, must contain veins of truth, but to find them in a mountain of rubble is a task for tomorrow."

In the tradition-oriented cultures of rural villages throughout much of the world, indigenous systems of folk medicine are only beginning to be affected by urban-centred scientific medicine. The precepts of both types of medicine derive from empiric perceptions interpreted in the light of pre-existing theory or custom. The difference lies in the relative likelihood of theory being modified by new experience or of the conflicting observations being interpreted in such a way as to become harmonious with accepted custom. Folk medicine is not restricted to the villages of developing nations; but in such settings its importance may be more readily apprehended.

Reprinted from David A. McKay, "Food, Illness, and Folk Medicine: Insights from Ulu Trengganu, West Malaysia," Ecology of Food and Nutrition, 1:1 (November 1971), 67–72, with permission of Gordon and Breach Science Publishers, New York.

* Supported by the University of California International Center for Medical Research and Training (UC ICMRT, G. W. Hooper Foundation, San Francisco) with funds from Grant A1 10051, National Institutes of Health, U.S. Public Health Service, and carried out within the Division of Rural Health Research, Institute for Medical Research, Kuala Lumpur, Malaysia.

Ulu Trengganu: Background of the Studies

Ulu Trengganu is a rural, inland district in West Malaysia, located some 250 miles northeast of Kuala Lumpur. An ancient site of Malay-Islamic civilization,[1] the district remained relatively isolated from the effects of British rule, including concomitant immigrations. Most of its present population of about 30,000 are Malay villagers. It was found to have the highest 1–2 year old age-specific mortality rate of West Malaysian districts (McKay & Lim, 1969), and special nutritional and parasitological studies were carried out during 1968 and 1969 in 12 of its more remote and economically underdeveloped villages (McKay, 1970, McKay et al., 1971, and unpublished data). These study villages, located 25–35 miles inland on the fringe of the uninhabited central mountain wilderness, comprised a population of about 2,000 engaged in subsistence-level farming of rice and rubber.

The following synopsis of the interaction of food and illness in the local folk medicine is drawn from observations made during periodic visits to these villages over an 18-month span. Impressions are collated from many conversations with villagers and from more formal interviews, near the end of the study period, with five leading indigenous health practitioners (*orang bomoh*).

The Role of the Bomoh

The skill of a *bomoh* in these villages derives from his knowledge of:

locally-available herbs or roots (*ubat akar kayu*) considered therapeutic for certain illnesses;

local spirits (*hantu-hantu*) which must sometimes be placated to prevent, or end, illness or ill fortune;

traditional magical incantations (*jampi*) used in exorcising evil spirits, giving healing qualities to water (*ayer jampi*) or other substances, or in certain important ceremonies such as planting rice or building a house;

ways in which food and other substances should be used or avoided to preserve or restore health.

These complex forms of knowledge usually pass from grandfather to grandson, and one man, or one lineage, may specialize in one function, or in treating one form of illness. Of these four areas of expertise, only the last concerns us here, and this is least exclusively the preserve of the *bomoh*. The proper uses of foods in relation to illnesses are matters of common knowledge, but differences of opinion sometimes arise; then the villagers turn

---

[1] The earliest evidence of Malay language and Islamic civilization in the Malay Peninsula is an inscribed stone dated in the Islamic year 906 (A.D. 1486) and known as the 'Trengganu stone' (*batu surat*). It was found at Kuala Brang, the district seat of Ulu Trengganu. This, among other things, led Wheatley (1964) to speculate that Kuala Brang was the famed China-trade *entrepôt* center, Fualan, of the Sri Vijaya era.

to the *bomoh* for authoritative judgment. He may thus be viewed not only as a healer but also as a standard source of conventional wisdom in matters related to health.

The Categories of Food

Food, in the context of Malay folk medicine,[2] can usually be considered in several categories:

Rice is in a class by itself. It is for Malays, as for many southeast Asian peoples, more than the dietary staple; it is a super-food (Jelliffe, 1966), often virtually synonymous with the idea of food. Thus to eat rice (*makan nasi*) means to have a real meal, in contrast to a snack. It is the life-giving food for all ages, often given in the second or third months of life as a pounded porridge (*bubor*), or even earlier to a child who seems sickly. A parent will say of an apparently healthy older child, presented to a physician because his appetite for rice seems poor, "He doesn't eat rice; how can he be healthy?"

Foods eaten with rice are termed *lauk*, and are usually served in a spicy curry or other sauce (*kuah*). These include various vegetables, fish, meats, and eggs. Sometimes only a simple *lauk* of hot chili peppers mixed with a salty soy sauce (*ketchap*) or with a fermented fish or shrimp preparation (*budu* or *belachang*) is taken with rice. This is especially likely if the family is poor. The more expensive animal protein foods are valued for both taste and nutritive qualities; but their primary purpose is to improve the taste of rice, and such foods (especially meat or eggs) are usually eaten only in small quantities.

Other foods are eaten mainly as snacks, used to tide oneself or the children over until the next major (rice) meal. This category includes, in addition to homemade cakes (*kueh*) and commercial products such as biscuits, tea, coffee, sugar, condensed milk, and soft drinks, a wide variety of local fruits, boiled chunks of cassava (*ubi kayu*), sections of raw sugar cane (*tebu*), and the water from fresh coconuts. These snack foods, along with the *lauk*, the with-rice foods already noted, possess a variety of qualities specifically beneficial or deleterious in relation to health. In contrast, rice is never other than good.

Finally, some foods are taken purely for medicinal purposes, such as honey for a cough, or chicken liver for night blindness. Also, herbal or commercial medicines, in the present context, have certain attributes of food.

[2] A detailed comparison of the Malay food beliefs outlined here with those reported elsewhere is beyond the scope of this paper. Work by Wilson (1970, 1971), Wolff (1965, a & b), Firth (1966), and McArthur (1962) detail such beliefs as encountered elsewhere in West Malaysia. Colson's (1969) detailed analysis of indigenous preventive medicine in a Pahang village also provides interesting comparisons with the role of the Ulu Trengganu *bomoh* as briefly described herein.

Food Attributes Affecting Health

Quite apart from being tasty (*sedap*) or nutritious (having *zat*), many foods affect health in other ways that influence their use. Best known are heating and cooling properties, derived from a traditionally perceived effect of food on the body, a concept common in the folk medicine of many tropical countries. In Trengganu, individual opinions vary as to the heating or cooling properties of a given food, but some foods, such as the fruit papaya and many green and yellow vegetables, are widely considered cooling (*benda sejok*); others, including cassava (*ubi kayu*) and most kinds of mammalian meat, are considered heating (*benda panas*). Still other foods are grouped together by certain physical properties—such as having a scaly (*bersisek*) or fuzzy (*miang*) surface; or being pointed in shape; or having a sour (*asam*) or sweet (*manis*) taste. Different effects are attributed to these properties. Thus, for example, corn (*jagong*), fern shoots (*puchok paku*), and the fruit *langsat* (*Lansium domesticum*) all are *miang* and provoke coughing. The *langsat* together with other sour-tasting fruits (*asam*) has a bad effect on malaria. Fern shoots, and other non-fuzzy but sharp-pointed shoots produce abdominal pains in pregnancy. Both *langsat* and fern shoots, but not corn, are also bad for worms because they are cooling. Other deleterious effects of foods derive from intrinsic properties that are less easily perceived or grouped.

Food and Illness

Illness relates to food in several ways. Some illnesses are believed to be directly caused by what is ingested. Thus malaria is often considered to result from eating sour fruits or drinking water that has not been heated. Goiter, and the lymphedema or hydrocele of filariasis, are both considered part of the disease *uluran*, a swelling in the body which may result from excessive intake of cooling foods. Other illnesses are the result of taking food at an improper time; for example, a malarial fever may be precipitated by eating cooling food when one is hot from working in the sun. Illnesses in children are often attributed to an injudicious diet of the mother during pregnancy. Thus the offspring of a mother who indulges in sour fruits, generally prohibited in late pregnancy, will suffer from malaria, and skin problems will afflict the child whose mother has broken the taboo against certain fish such as *ikan ayuh*. The condition *mabok* which is usually translated as intoxication is characterized by nausea, vomiting, dizziness, and often (purportedly) prostration and death. It is widely held to result from eating two foods which oppose (*lawan* or *belaga*) each other. The indescribably pungent flavored *durian*, no doubt the most esteemed fruit in Southeast Asia, is most prominent in this category. Throughout Malaya it is said that a dire form of *mabok* results from taking *durian* with any alcoholic beverage. Of more importance for the abstaining Muslims of Trengganu is the combination of *durian* with cassava, or of either of these with the medicine chloroquine. Combining Chinese melon with honey (*ayer madu*), or papaya with *tapai*, a locally popular sour dough snack, is also certain to make one terribly *mabok*.

The most important relationship of food to illness in the folk medicine of Ulu Trengganu is the concept that certain normally acceptable foods become detrimental (*bisa*) in time of specific illness.[3] The food, or group of foods, considered *bisa* not only exacerbates a specific overt illness but may even precipitate an illness that was not known to be present. Therefore foods considered *bisa* for common illnesses of childhood, like malaria or skin infections, are given sparingly, if given at all, even to apparently well children who may (who can tell?) be about to become sick. In an initial (1968) malaria survey of the 1–3 year old children in these villages, 125 of 152 (82%) children examined were infected at the time of survey. Thus the chances that any one child might develop malarial fever on any given day are high. This is appreciated by parents who are consequently reluctant to give a child a cooling food (*benda sejok*) or sour fruits (*asam*) that might precipitate an attack that day. Unfortunately, *benda sejok* and *asam* include many of the carotene-rich foods potentially available to the child.

Similarly, since eggs and many kinds of fish and meat are generally considered *bisa* for skin infections (*kudis*), this common ailment of rural childhood, and the food prohibitions that accompany it, may become significant factors in limiting protein intake. Foods considered *bisa* in common childhood illnesses therefore gain a stigma of not being good foods for children in general. Papaya, an inexpensive plentiful source of carotene often recommended by health educators, is notably viewed this way. Not only is it a potent cooling food, but if taken with *tapai* it will surely make a child *mabok*. Since one can't be sure a child is not about to develop malaria or "eye worm," for which papaya is very bad (*kuat bisa*), or that he will not unknowingly pick up and eat some *tapai*, it is much safer to keep papaya away from children all together.

Interestingly, many government-provided pills are considered heating and may be used, or *not* used, for this property rather than for the purpose intended by the dispenser. In this district with hyperendemic malaria, the most important of these medications is chloroquine, whose dramatic effect on the cold (shaking) fever of malaria (*demam sejok* or *ketar*) may in part explain the heating qualities attributed to other pills. In a village where the children had been receiving weekly chloroquine chemosuppression with excellent cooperation, the parents refused to give the pills (a heating substance) when measles (a hot fever) broke out. Although much desired for its demonstrable efficacy in preventing malaria, the medicine became temporarily *bisa* for a

[3] The word *bisa* in Malay literally means *poisonous*, as in *ular bisa* for a poisonous snake; its meaning in this context is similar, but less strong. It has no relation to the paradoxical common use of the same word in Indonesian (generally the same langauge as Malay) to mean *is able!*

child who had, or risked having, measles. Chloroquine administration also became difficult during the *durian* season because of the fear, already mentioned, of becoming *mabok* if the fruit and drug were taken at the same time. Patients could be convinced that the chloroquine was more important and would refrain from eating the beloved *durian* if they needed chloroquine. But assurances from the doctor that the two could be mixed with impunity, supported by a statement that he himself had tried it without ill effect, usually only made the patient doubt his physician's wisdom.

Table 1 gives a representative list of foods interacting adversely with certain illnesses. Some relationships have already been alluded to, but a more detailed example may better clarify the potential significance of such beliefs. Intestinal roundworms are common in these villages [4] and are generally considered a congenital condition. The worms are blamed for various abdominal pains and distension, and worm-expelling medicines are exceedingly popular. A more serious syndrome in children attributed to worms, usually small, thin worms (*chaching hallus* or *kerawait*), is marked by roughening of the skin, irritation and drying of the eyes, and night blindness. A white scale (*sisek*) develops in the eye as the condition advances and eventually the eye may become cloudy (*kelabu*) and vision may be lost completely. Obviously, this disease corresponds closely to *xerophthalmia*, a form of malnutrition that I noted in about 10% of 1–3 year old children during an initial examination in May, 1968. But to the mother, these signs were simply attributable to *chaching* (worms) and would be made worse, and may even have been precipitated, by giving common green or yellow vegetables or fruits that are either cooling or sour-tasting. The rationale seems to be that these foods irritate the disease-causing worm to greater activity and may provoke it to ascend from the gut, thus affecting the eye. A specific preventive charm, the *tongkit chaching*, is often worn about a child's neck to impede the worm in its ascent. As one *orang bomoh* dramatically explained, if a child, who did not see well one night, ate a food that was strongly *bisa*, such as papaya, the next morning his eyes would be clouded. The curious and unfortunate effect of this belief is to decrease the marginal intake of vitamin A at the very time the child is in most dire need of it. In contrast, several *orang bomoh*, when asked concerning therapy for this eye condition, responded that a whole chicken liver broiled in the sap of the papaya, or an egg baked in a certain kind of tuber (*gandong*), were often efficacious. Alas this striking folk wisdom in therapeutics seemed far less widely accepted than the folk folly that produced carotene restriction, consequently *xerophthalmia* was a major health hazard.

---

[4] Faeces examined from 141 1- to 3-year-olds in May, 1968, contained eggs of *Ascaris* in 88% of the specimens, *Trichuris* in 50%, and *Necator americanus* in 23%.

Table 1: Foods Believed to Exacerbate Specific Illnesses in the Folk Medicine of Ulu Trengganu, West Malaysia

Type of Food:	Xerophthalmia ("worms")	Cough	Skin Infection (kudis)	Malaria	Measles	Diarrhoea	Uluran [a]
				ILLNESS			
Wild fern shoots, pumpkins, many other green or yellow vegetables (generally cooling foods)	+	±	±	+	+	+	++
Ikan ayuh (and several other common salt water fish)	++	++	++	±	++	++	±
Freshwater fish with scales (ikan bersisek)	++	±	+	0	+	++	0
Hens' eggs	±	±	+	0	+	+	0
Miang (substance with fine, hairlike fuzz)	±	++	±	±	+	±	±
Asam (sour fruits, such as mango, citrus fruits)	+	±	±	++	++	++	±
Papaya (fruit)	++	±	±	+	++	++	++

++ = very strongly contraindicated
+ = usually considered contraindicated (bisa)
± = sometimes thought undesirable, opinions vary
0 = usually considered to be of no consequence

[a] A condition characterized by localized swelling of the body (including lymphedema, hydrocoele, or goiter), generally attributed to excessive coldness or air in the body.

Nutrition Education and Cross-Cultural Understanding

The attitude of the villagers towards the eye condition (*chaching*) which is indicative of hypovitaminosis A, provides a lesson for the health worker dealing with an alien culture. Initially, when I encountered a child with this condition, I would, after giving an injection of vitamin A, explain to the mother and other onlookers why this child needed to eat more of the common green and yellow vegetables and fruits found in the village. The listeners would nod appreciatively, grateful for the medicine provided and happy that this foreigner was speaking to them in their language. They would willingly forgive him for not understanding that such cooling foods would undoubtedly make the child's condition worse. Since other noncooling sources of vitamin A were potentially available such as *chekur manis*, a local small-leafed vegetable, these foods would be acceptable as special medicinal foods in the same manner as chicken liver or specially prepared eggs. With prolonged contact, one might well convince some villagers, especially the younger ones, that certain cooling foods could also be used. Progress in health education is more rapid however when one can reinforce or modify concepts which do not contradict firmly held beliefs.

In health, the professional often assumes that his own concepts are universally applicable and that health education is simply a matter of effective communication. However the professional is often an alien, even to compatriots of different ethnic background. As such, he may fail to recognize his incongruity as an educator until he has achieved an understanding of the indigenous concepts of the people with whom he is working.

Jelliffe and Bennett (1961) suggested that, from a public health viewpoint, local customary practices be considered in four categories pertaining to their effects: beneficial, harmful, neutral, and of uncertain significance. Although some practices may seem so clearly detrimental that they should be discouraged as rapidly as possible, the outside assessor should be quicker to commend the beneficial than to condemn the harmful. Probably most practices described in this paper belong in the fourth category, of uncertain significance, since they are derived from a stream of experience not readily perceived and evaluated.

A system of folk medicine should be viewed as an expression of a people's encounter with their environment and, as such, be appreciated for the insights into human ecology that the system provides. The health educator thus enters into dialogue with its proponents, learning as well as teaching, being slow to attack as fallacious those precepts whose significance he can only incompletely grasp. Gradually, he then may blend such of his own precepts as may seem relevant into the knowledge of the people with whom he works.

References

AMERICAN MEDICAL ASSOCIATION COUNCIL ON FOOD AND NUTRITION (1961) Diet as related to gastrointestinal function. *J. Amer. Med. Assoc.* 176:935–941.

COLSON, A. (1969) The prevention of illness in a Malay village: an analysis of concept and behavior. Doctoral dissertation, Stanford University.

FIRTH, R. (1966) *Housekeeping amongst Malay Peasants.* London: Athlone Press, University of London, 242 pp.

INGELFINGER, F. J., A. S. RELMAN, M. FINLAND (Eds.) (1966) *Controversy in Internal Medicine.* Philadelphia and London: W. B. Saunders Co., pp. 171–179.

JELLIFFE, D. B. (1966) *The assessment of the nutritional status of the community,* WHO Monograph Series, No. 53. World Health Organization, Geneva.

JELLIFFE, D. B., AND F. J. BENNETT (1961) Cultural and anthropological factors in infant and maternal nutrition. *Fed. Proc.* 20 (Suppl. No. 7):185–187.

McARTHUR, A. M. (1962) *Assignment Report, Malaya* 12. Wld. Hlth. Org. Regional Office for the Western Pacific WPR/449, 62.

McKAY, D. A. (1970) Anthropometry in action V: age assessment in village anthropometric studies. *J. Trop. Pediat.* 16:24–27.

McKAY, D. A., R. K. H. LIM, K. H. NOTANEY, AND A. E. DUGDALE (1971) Nutritional assessment by comparative growth achievement in Malay children below school age. *Bull. Wld. Hlth. Org.* (in press).

McKAY, D. A. AND R. K. H. LIM, Nutritional epidemiology in West Malaysia Proc. First SEAMEC Regional Nutrition Seminar, Djakarta, October, 1969.

OSLER, W. (1909) *In* A. M. HARVEY, AND V. A. McKUSICK, (Eds.) (1967) *Osler's Textbook Revisited: Reprint of Selected Selections with Commentaries.* New York: Appleton-Century-Crofts, pp. 361.

WHEATLEY, P. (1964) *Impressions of the Malay Peninsula in Ancient Times.* Singapore: Eastern Universities Press, Ltd., 254 pp.

WILSON, C. S. (1970) Food beliefs and practices of Malay fisherman: an ethnographic study of diet on the east coast of Malaya. Doctoral dissertation, University of California, Berkeley.

WILSON, C. S. (1971) Food beliefs affect nutritional status of Malay Fisherfolk. *J. Nutr. Educ.* Winter, 1971, pp. 96–98.

WOLFF, R. J. (1965a) Modern medicine and traditional culture: confrontation on the Malay peninsula. *Human Organization* 24:339–345.

WOLFF, R. J. (1965b) Meanings of food. *Trop. Geogr. Med.* 17:45–51.

Gretel H. Pelto

Adaptation to Economic Marginality: A Psychosocial Model

Under pressure from a number of sources American anthropologists are increasingly turning their attention to the study of our own society. The crises of the cities and of interethnic conflict have, understandably, moved into the foreground of concern, particularly since the demands for a "relevant" social science are most likely to come from city voices. But the rural hinterlands are part of our cultural scene and have their problems too. Marginal rural areas such as northern Minnesota—the focus of this research—are beset with economic decline, out-migration and the resulting cultural and psychological depression in populations that feel they have been left out of the mainstream of action.

A few years ago an extensive research project was initiated by the Upper Mississippi Mental Health Center in northern Minnesota. The research program was practical and applied in its origins, since the clinical staff wanted to find out more about the populations they serve, especially the factors associated with the types of problems they were confronted with in their daily routines. At the same time they recognized that the answers to the questions they were asking involved relatively broad range theoretical research. The research team, therefore, defined the problem as the generation of an empirically derived model of psychosocial adaptation in an economically depressed area.

The Mental Health Center serves a five-county area in the "cut-over" region in the north-central part of Minnesota. The area has experienced a steadily worsening economic situation for several decades. In the mid-1960s it was characterized by low income (the median income in the research population was just over $3000 per year), high unemployment with significant seasonal fluctuations, and a declining population in which most young people leave as soon as they graduate from high school, if not before.

A series of communities was selected for study, chosen to represent the range of variation in the area in terms of economic affluence, degree of tourism, ethnic-religious background, and several other characteristics. Fieldworkers took up residence in the selected research communities in order to gather ethnographic data through participant observation and informal interviewing techniques.

The smallest of the communities, Ashville, is in the most serious condition in terms of its economic position and future prospects. By Northern Min-

An original paper published with the permission of the author.

nesota standards, the town is relatively heterogeneous in ethnic and religious composition. Ashville has experienced a steady decline in population since the Depression; its bank has long since closed, many businesses have failed and, recently, it has been threatened with the loss of its high school, which is recognized by the people as the last remaining focus of community organization.

The town of Solberg, with a population of 350 people, is next in size. It is a predominantly Norwegian-Lutheran community, and it was initially selected for study as representative of the relatively prosperous communities in the area. Although many of its residents are faced with economic problems, the presence of a new sunflower seed processing plant is providing some new wage labor opportunities, as well as increased incomes for farmers.

Draketon is a community of approximately 800 people. The village has commercial, educational, recreational and political facilities serving a large surrounding area of farming and logging people. Although it has a large Lutheran population, the town is relatively mixed in ethnic and religious composition. The economic situations of Draketon's families range from poverty to affluence. In our sample the range is from a low of $700 dollars a year income, to a high of $15,000.

The largest of the four communities is a town of 1500 people. As is true of Draketon, a few of James Lake's residents are well off, but the majority of people have marginal or substandard incomes. Although the town is institutionally well developed, with a village government, bank, newspaper, and many social clubs, it is also faced with many economic and social problems. Like all of the communities in the area, James Lake has seen its population dwindle since the days of the "great boom" in the 1920s.

Sociocultural and psychological data were gathered from randomly selected samples of households in each of the four communities. The sociocultural information was obtained by means of a lengthy structured interview. The psychological data were gathered with the MMPI (Minnesota Multiphasic Personality Inventory).

The MMPI is fairly well known as a standard clinical instrument. The 550 questions in the MMPI represent a distillation from a number of years of empirical searching for items that discriminate particular, defined psychiatric populations as distinct from normal people. Although this instrument has been used in a number of cross-cultural contexts, including Japan, Mexico, and Puerto Rico, anthropologists have been hesitant to use it since it is clear that the response norms, in terms of which the instrument is calibrated, are relatively ethnocentrically loaded. However, we felt it to be appropriate in the case of our research in No. Minnesota since the test was validated in Minnesota with a broad cross-section of respondents. We can also offer some direct contextual support for the validity of the instrument in No. Minnesota. In a control group of persons who contacted the mental health center in the area, for psychiatric help, MMPI responses are abnormal. The difference between these people and the ordinary, nonpatient local population is clearly significant, and in the manner in which the constructors of the MMPI instrument say it should be.

In our analysis we used the standard MMPI scales which measure the relative strengths of such characteristics as "depression," "paranoid tendencies," and "hysteria." We must emphasize that while the terminology is psychiatric, we do not intend that these terms be interpreted as referring to mental illness. Rather, the characteristics described should be regarded as psychological tendencies within the range of normal populations.

The staff of the mental health center had formed the opinion that depression was a major psychological problem in the population. The results of the MMPI strongly support this impression. With minor exceptions, both men and women, in all four of the communities, have depression scores that deviate markedly from the Minnesota norms. By the standards established for the MMPI, we would expect that three or four people in the research sample to have depression scores above two standard deviations from the mean. We find, instead, that eleven people in the sample have scores in this range.

A second distinctive characteristic that appears in the No. Minnesota population is what clinicians refer to as "hysteria." In the psychiatric handbooks, this psychological trait is described as including characteristics of "using physical symptoms as a means of solving difficult conflicts." This resort to physical disorder may appear only under stress. In addition, there is a tendency to deny troubles of any kind; there may also be denials of personal inadequacies and base impulses.

In another portion of research in the same area Stephen Schensul has found that, despite their cataloging of the economic and other deficiencies of life in No. Minnesota, respondents rate their own self image as remarkably close to their conceptualizations of the "ideal life."

Perhaps the classic expression of this mode of psychic adaptation was heard the morning after the 1968 presidential election when the losing candidate said, with tears in his eyes, "I don't feel bad, really. . . ."

In these No. Minnesota respondents the hysteria scale shows a statistically significant elevation for both males and females. This response is particularly important among males (see Table 1).

A basic hypothesis of our research was that a history of economic problems would be associated with evidence of psychological problems, but we also felt that ethnic and religious affiliation as well as other factors would have important effects on individuals' psychological states. Following the ideas of other researchers concerning the importance, for mental health, of community "health," we felt that some of these northern communities would be more conducive to psychiatric problems than others.

As a first step in the data analysis, the interview materials—social, economic, and cultural variables—were factor-analyzed by means of a standard computerized procedure.

Table 1: MMPI Scale Means by Community and Sex *

	ASHVILLE		SOLBERG		DRAKETON		JAMES LAKE	
SCALE	Male	Female	Male	Female	Male	Female	Male	Female
1	55	52	51	52	56	52	57	55
2	59	53	56	58	51	58	56	60
3	58	56	53	54	57	55	59	55
4	52	54	49	55	53	55	57	55
6	50	57	46	53	51	56	50	55
7	49	49	42	51	50	54	49	56
8	46	48	45	52	55	52	49	53
9	49	47	45	44	51	47	55	48

* The mean for the Minnesota population used to validate the test is set at 50 for all scales.

The second, more important, step consisted of a stepwise multiple regression analysis, by means of which we would examine the relative predictive efficacy of our battery of predictor variables as they affected individuals' MMPI depression scores. (See Tables 2 and 3.)

The computer continued to calculate the equation, adding articulation (low); organizational participation (low); unemployed; and occupation (farmer), so that the final multiple R was .66. However, these additional variables each accounted for less than one percent of the total variance and are not at a statistically reliable level.

The computer continued to add several variables to the equation: income (low), occupation (farmer), religiosity (low), and M.S.L. (low), education (low), to bring the final multiple R to .82.

In the factor analysis, the first major factor reflects the dimension of "socio-

Table 2: Sociocultural Predictors of Depression in Women (N = 41)

Variable	Direction of Association	Cumulative Multiple Correlation (R)
Religiosity	Low	.38
Lutheran	Yes	.43
Number of siblings in the area	None/few	.49
M.S.L.	High	.52
Income	Low	.55
Family cycle	Late	.61
Education	Low	.62
Scandinavian	Yes	.63
Household size	Small	.64

Table 3: Sociocultural Predictors of Depression in Men (N = 31)

Variable	Direction of Association	Cumulative Multiple Correlation (R)
Articulation	Low	.33
Place of residence	In town center	.49
Employment history—self-rating	Much unemployment	.56
Birthplace	In the area	.61
Siblings in area	None/few	.66
Lutheran	Yes	.68
Household size	Small	.70
Age	Older	.72
Organizational participation	Low	.74
Present employment status	Unemployed	.76
Family cycle	Late	.77
Scandinavian	Yes	.78

economic success-failure," * including the variables of income, employment, material style of life, and apparently closely related variables of education and articulation to the wider society. The multiple regression analysis shows that, on the whole, there is a greater incidence of depressive responses from those people who are toward the low end of the range of variation of socioeconomic success. This association between poverty and psychological stress is congruent with the findings of a number of other studies, both urban and rural. Although people who are poor, unemployed, and without many material comforts tend to be more depressed than their better-off neighbors, there are many other factors operating to produce psychological stress and the magnitude of the statistical association between depression scores and the economic variables is not extremely high. The correlations are on the order of .30–.35.

In the multiple regression analysis a second set of variables that are important in the prediction of depression involves aspects of "social marginality." People who live alone, who do not participate in community organizations, who have few or no relatives living nearby, and who apparently take less interest either in the events in their own community or in the outside world, are more likely to be depressed than those who are active community participants, and have frequent social contacts, including contact with children and relatives. We should note that social marginality and socioeconomic success are not independent of each other. In fact, there is a fairly strong association

* In using the term "socioeconomic success-failure" we are following the usage of people in the area who conceptualize economic concerns in terms of "success" or "failure." The expression does not imply anything about the "success" of an individual in other aspects of life, e.g., his/her "success" as a friend, neighbor, parent, etc.

among many of these variables. In general, the people who have higher incomes, steady jobs, a higher material life-style and more education are also active in community affairs and lead an active social life.

A number of writers have commented on the depressive characteristics of Scandinavian-Lutheran culture, and we hypothesized that ethnic-religious background would be a factor in predicting differential depression scores, since the area contains many people who have maintained some identity with their Scandinavian origins. Depressive tendencies did, in fact, appear more strongly among the Scandinavians in the research population than in other groups. People of Scandinavian-Lutheran background had higher depression scores. Also, the homogeneous Norwegian-Lutheran community of Solberg appears consistently in the analyses as a "variable" associated with higher depression.

There are many interesting differences in the four communities which were the focus of our research; but with the exception of Solberg, community of residence does not appear to be particularly significant in explaining variation in depression. However, there are intercommunity differences in rates of some of the other psychological measures, particularly in aggressiveness and "positiveness of outlook." Thus we feel that the factor—"community of residence"—must be included in the theoretical model.

In all of the statistical analyses "religiosity" shows up persistently as an important item; the direction of association is consistent—people who are "less religious" are more depressed! As operationalized in this research, "religiosity" includes measures of social participation as well as belief, and the variable is also correlated with measures of socioeconomic success, but not with religious denomination. While part of the association can be accounted for in terms of these two major factors it would appear that "religiosity"—in and of itself—acts as a buffer against psychological tension and helps to ease the stressful effects of living in an economically depressed area.

From the statistical analyses we have built a tentative model of psychosocial adaptation in the area which involves four main components that, in interaction, appear to have strong effects on "individual psychological well-being." These components are (1) socioeconomic success-failure, (2) social marginality-centrality, (3) cultural ideology, and (4) community of residence. In this research we conceptualized psychological state as a dependent variable and examined the effects of a number of independent variables. While we feel that "causal arrows" can be drawn—as in Diagram A—it is also clear that there is an interactive effect. People who suffer from psychological problems are, no doubt, more likely to experience economic failure and to withdraw from social contact, for example.

The variables analyzed in our research account for only 35–45% of the total variance in depression. Clearly, a number of other kinds of variables need to be incorporated into the model in order to enhance its predictive value. Some of the missing variables are well known. They include experiences of childhood, cohesion of natal family, and situational mishaps. The addition of those variables would not, we feel, detract from the significance of the sociocultural elements that have been the focus of this research.

DOMAINS OF FACTORS AFFECTING PSYCHOLOGICAL WELL-BEING

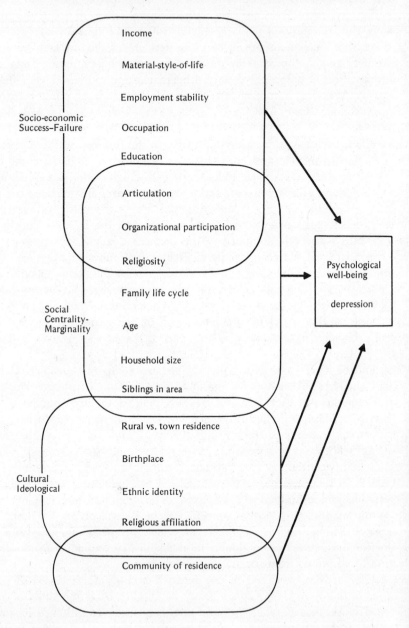

DIAGRAM A

In seeking to develop a model for predicting levels of psychosocial adaptation or "well-being" in marginal rural areas such as northern Minnesota we feel that many different kinds of economic, social and cultural factors need to be taken into consideration. There are many simple, one-variable models that concentrate on a single factor such as childhood experience, social integration of communities or class stratification. Each has "tapped" into a portion of the variation in psychological states; but each such single factor explanation, taken by itself, accounts for only a small proportion of the phenomena. To develop really effective predictive models, we must examine the interactions among an array of variables.

In this research, we placed a heavy emphasis on the materialistic variables of socioeconomic success, but we did not neglect to consider relatively nonmaterialistic sociocultural elements. The theoretical implications of our findings are that a psychosocial model must include both material and nonmaterial factors.

The relative weights of the significant predictive factors may vary from one behavioral setting or community to another, so that the shape of our multifactor model may take on quite different proportions under different circumstances, without changing its essential nature or its predictive power.

The model we are working with has implications for social science theory, and we hope to develop these through further research. But it should be clear that a major aim of research of this type is to provide analyses which are useful for community mental health centers and other agencies concerned with the social and psychological well-being of people.

8 Adaptations Through Contact with the Supernatural World

To many observers of the human scene, discussions of economics, politics, and health aspects of human adaptation come across as practical matters, in contrast to the "irrational, nonfunctional" behavior and thinking in the ritual and religious aspects of life. That is, many people make a sharp conceptual distinction between the "secular" and the "sacred." Anthropologists have observed, however, that the supposedly nonfunctional ritual and religious behaviors of people are widespread, found in all human societies at all levels of complexity. The worldwide nature of these behaviors leads one to suspect that they are indeed an essential part of the human adaptational story.

One of the first modern theories about religion and magic in human adaptation was offered by Bronislaw Malinowski, who argued that nonmodern peoples everywhere make clear distinctions between the practical, rational, and natural on the one hand, and on the other hand those areas of coping with nature in which their technical capacities are insufficient, and to which ritual and magic may be applied. In his day Malinowski was arguing against those people who claimed that practically all of the behavior of nonmodern peoples was shot through with magic and supernaturalism—a supposed "prelogical mentality." Malinowski's view held that non-Western peoples are just as rational and logical as industrialized Euro-Americans, and they apply "scientific methods" where possible in adapting to their environments.

The further assumption in this Malinowskian theoretical idea is that in every society there are areas of behavior that are dangerous, unpredictable, and threatening to individuals. The areas in which failures and disaster threaten are the domains in which our technologies are insufficient, and in which individual anxieties run high. Malinowski noted that people in dangerous occupations such as steeplejacks and airplane pilots are likely to carry good luck charms and other magical objects to help allay anxiety, and that in many phases of our modern living people still practice or believe in "little superstitions," especially in those situations of special attention. His argument can well be applied to the magical practices of many students during midterms and finals.

The perils of the sea have been an area of anxiety throughout human history, since fishermen and other sea travelers always face possibilities of unexpected storms and other trouble. No wonder, then, that fishing people have frequently had more than their share of magical and supernatural practices and beliefs. This extends down to modern times, as illustrated in the selection by Poggie and Gersuny. The final assumption in the theory of religion and magic offered by Malinowski is that the magical and religious practices are functional or practical for people because they allay anxieties, ease the mind, and make possible effective activity, just as the student who has avoided stepping on the sidewalk cracks on the way to class feels a shade more confident in tackling that final examination. The examples from Malinowski and from Rhode Island illustrate situations in which the environment is seen as the feature bringing about supernatural concerns.

In a somewhat similar vein Roy Rappaport has looked at the ritual regulation of environmental matters among a New Guinea people. However, the ritual activities concerned with pigs are not simply means of affecting individual anxieties or individual preoccupations, but, he argues, have direct impact on the relationships of the humans and their animals to the physical environment. This is a more complicated argument than the Malinowskian position. Ritual behaviors, after all, have many-sided and complex features including reflection of social relations, redistribution of food and supplies, expression of political power, and other facets. The American Thanksgiving festival can be looked at in the same way as having a number of different kinds of features, which have changed over time from a simple expression of thanks at harvest time to the social enactment of family togetherness and renewal of kinship ties.

Students can have a rich harvest of theoretical discussion and research if they go into examination of the multiple meanings and adaptive (and possibly maladaptive) functions of modern Christmas. An historical analysis of Christmas going back to old European times could add a very interesting time dimension to what has become the most important single ritual occasion in North American cultural life.

Contacts with the supernaturals are achieved in many different ways. Among many nonmodern groups the majority of persons in the community may have direct access to supernatural creatures for health and solace. North American Indians, for example, have emphasized individualized relationships to supernaturals through the institution of the "guardian spirit," and each individual sought out his or her own guardian spirit in vision quests and other psychological experiences. Such vision quests and other contact with guardian spirits usually required physiological stresses through fasting, endurance of cold in isolated places, as well as mortification of the flesh in a variety of ways. Thus the impact of relationships to the supernaturals has very clear ties to physiological processes. On the other hand, there are many societies in the world in which contacts with the supernaturals have been mediated by priest-specialists who alone have the special knowledge and means for dealing with supernatural beings. Such priestly special practices have often arisen in stratified societies in which elite peoples have superior access to the favors of supernaturals. Again, even in very complex societies with priests and other religious functionaries, individuals may have means of achieving contact with the nonnatural world through their own efforts.

In the paper by Weston LaBarre we note a modern North American phenomenon which excites the fascination of many, and brings at the same time strong negative reactions from police and other governmental officials, as congregations of people make contact with the supernatural through the handling of dangerous reptiles in their religious ceremonies. There are today many snake-handling cult groups in North America, but this is not a new thing. Throughout the ages there have been groups in Europe, Asia, and America who believed that serpents have special characteristics—some evil, some holy—which make them special objects of religious attention. This fascination with snakes may even have some biological basis, for it has been noted that many primate species other than *Homo sapiens* appear to have some instinctive fear or emotional reaction to snakes. The role of the snake in the Bible is another illustration of this special role of the serpent.

Widespread in human groups around the world has been the practice of using drugs and other mind-changing products to achieve relationships to supernatural things. As Richard Schultes noted, marijuana has been used for thousands of years as a mind-changing aid to supernatural and other experiences. In part of South America powerful drugs that are chemically similar to LSD have been used by shaman healers in their practice as well as by nearly everybody else. In seeking visionary experience, people in other parts of the world from Siberia to Central America have made use of mushrooms, including the dangerous fly agaric (*Amanita muscaria*) for contacting supernatural worlds and beings. Of course alcohol serves in many societies this same ritual function. Among many North American Indian groups the *peyote*, obtained from a desert plant in the Southwest, has had a central place in religious beliefs and practices.

It is fascinating to note that in many of the drug-using groups of modern times, however nonreligious the practice seems to outside observers, including police authorities, the "drug trip" is seen as a religious and sacred experience to many of the practitioners themselves, and the taking of the drug is usually imbedded in some kind of ritualistic context.

The last religious enactment of significance to the individual is that of death and burial. All human groups perform some kind of funeral rites for their departed dead. The funeral rites are of great variety, ranging from cremation to a variety of different ways to inter people in the ground, or drop them out in the ocean or other bodies of water. Some North American Indian groups have placed their departed dead on platforms high in trees or on cliffs, and in some societies the dead are rather unceremoniously dumped somewhere away from the community habitation sites.

Whatever the practice of burial may be, funeral ceremonials around the world usually provide the departed dead with help toward the other world to some sort of existence after death. Among many populations there is no happy hunting ground and no heaven or hell, only some kind of gray and shapeless limbo neither attractive nor awful. At the same time that funerals send off the dead, the bereaved may be highly concerned to enact ritual as protection against a newly created ghost, or they may be preparing for worship of a new ancestor. Funeral ceremonies obviously reflect important features of social structure, from the magnificent social stratification demonstrations of the burial tombs of the pharaohs of Egypt, the kings of Europe, and the magnificent tombs of many North American industrialists and politicians. In many societies the people about to die wish to be well remembered, and so they arrange for suitably splendid burials. At the same time it may be the wishes of their family, kin, and social stratum that their social position be indelibly inscribed on the landscape in the form of lavish tombs. Joan Ablon's description of funerals amongst Samoan people in urban America points to the ways in which funeral practices are modified in relation to socioeconomic realities.

While there are many different social and cultural messages involved in the rituals of death and dying, one panhuman characteristic is the mourning and sadness concerning the loss of members in social networks. "Death in Chamula" by Patrick Menget vividly portrays this aspect of funeral ritual. It may be argued that rituals of death and dying have little direct adaptative value for the deceased, and once again we can consider that adaptive features have many aspects for different participants in ceremonials. Clearly funeral ceremonials are among those enacted that have powerful psychological effects on the participants as well as diverse social and cultural meaning related to different forms of social organization and different environmental contexts.

Bronislaw Malinowski

Rational Mastery by Man of His Surroundings

The problem of primitive knowledge has been singularly neglected by anthropology. Studies on savage psychology were exclusively confined to early religion, magic and mythology. Only recently the work of several English, German, and French writers, notably the daring and brilliant speculations of Professor Lévy-Bruhl, gave an impetus to the student's interest in what the savage does in his more sober moods. The results were startling indeed: Professor Lévy-Bruhl tells us, to put it in a nutshell, that primitive man has no sober moods at all, that he is hopelessly and completely immersed in a mystical frame of mind. Incapable of dispassionate and consistent observation, devoid of the power of abstraction, hampered by "a decided aversion towards reasoning," he is unable to draw any benefit from experience, to construct or comprehend even the most elementary laws of nature. "For minds thus orientated there is no fact purely physical." Nor can there exist for them any clear idea of substance and attribute, cause and effect, identity and contradiction. Their outlook is that of confused superstition, "prelogical," made of mystic "participations" and "exclusions." I have here summarized a body of opinion, of which the brilliant French sociologist is the most decided and competent spokesman, but which numbers besides, many anthropologists and philosophers of renown.

But there are also dissenting voices. When a scholar and anthropologist of the measure of Professor J. L. Myres entitles an article in *Notes and Queries* "Natural Science," and when we read there that the savage's "knowledge based on observation is distinct and accurate," we must surely pause before accepting primitive man's irrationality as a dogma. Another highly competent writer, Dr. A. A. Goldenweiser, speaking about primitive "discoveries, inventions and improvements"—which could hardly be attributed to any pre-empirical or prelogical mind—affirms that "it would be unwise to ascribe to the primitive mechanic merely a passive part in the origination of inventions. Many a happy thought must have crossed his mind, nor was he wholly unfamiliar with the thrill that comes from an idea effective in action." Here we see the savage endowed with an attitude of mind wholly akin to that of a modern man of science!

To bridge over the wide gap between the two extreme opinions current on the subject of primitive man's reason, it will be best to resolve the problem into two questions.

Reprinted from Bronislaw Malinowski, Magic, Science and Religion *in* Science, Religion and Reality, *J. Needham (ed.), pp. 25–35, copyright © The Society for Promoting Christian Knowledge with permission of The Society for Promoting Christian Knowledge.*

First, has the savage any rational outlook, any rational mastery of his surroundings, or is he, as M. Lévy-Bruhl and his school maintain, entirely "mystical"? The answer will be that every primitive community is in possession of a considerable store of knowledge, based on experience and fashioned by reason.

The second question then opens: Can this primitive knowledge be regarded as a rudimentary form of science or is it, on the contrary, radically different, a crude empiry, a body of practical and technical abilities, rules of thumb and rules of art having no theoretical value? This second queston, epistemological rather than belonging to the study of man, will be barely touched upon at the end of this section and a tentative answer only will be given.

In dealing with the first question, we shall have to examine the "profane" side of life, the arts, crafts and economic pursuits, and we shall attempt to disentangle in it a type of behavior, clearly marked off from magic and religion, based on empirical knowledge and on the confidence in logic. We shall try to find whether the lines of such behavior are defined by traditional rules, known, perhaps even discussed sometimes, and tested. We shall have to inquire whether the sociological setting of the rational and empirical behavior differs from that of ritual and cult. Above all we shall ask, do the natives distinguish the two domains and keep them apart, or is the field of knowledge constantly swamped by superstition, ritualism, magic or religion?

Since in the matter under discussion there is an appalling lack of relevant and reliable observations, I shall have largely to draw upon my own material, mostly unpublished, collected during a few years' field work among the Melanesian and Papuo-Melanesian tribes of Eastern New Guinea and the surrounding archipelagoes. As the Melanesians are reputed, however, to be specially magic-ridden, they will furnish an acid test of the existence of empirical and rational knowledge among savages living in the age of polished stone.

These natives, and I am speaking mainly of the Melanesians who inhabit the coral atolls to the N.E. of the main island, the Trobriand Archipelago and the adjoining groups, are expert fishermen, industrious manufacturers and traders, but they rely mainly on gardening for their subsistence. With the most rudimentary implements, a pointed digging-stick and a small axe, they are able to raise crops sufficient to maintain a dense population and even yielding a surplus, which in olden days was allowed to rot unconsumed, and which at present is exported to feed plantation hands. The success in their agriculture depends—besides the excellent natural conditions with which they are favored—upon their extensive knowledge of the classes of the soil, of the various cultivated plants, of the mutual adaptation of these two factors, and, last not least, upon their knowledge of the importance of accurate and hard work. They have to select the soil and the seedlings, they have appropriately to fix the times for clearing and burning the scrub, for planting and weeding, for training the vines of the yam plants. In all this they are guided by a clear knowledge of weather and seasons, plants and pests, soil and tubers, and by a conviction that this knowledge is true and reliable, that it can be counted upon and must be scrupulously obeyed.

Yet mixed with all their activities there is to be found magic, a series of rites performed every year over the gardens in rigorous sequence and order. Since the leadership in garden work is in the hands of the magician, and since ritual and practical work are intimately associated, a superficial observer might be led to assume that the mystic and the rational behavior are mixed up, that their effects are not distinguished by the natives and not distinguishable in scientific analysis. Is this so really?

Magic is undoubtedly regarded by the natives as absolutely indispensable to the welfare of the gardens. What would happen without it no one can exactly tell, for no native garden has ever been made without its ritual, in spite of some thirty years of European rule and missionary influence and well over a century's contact with white traders. But certainly various kinds of disaster, blight, unseasonable droughts, rains, bush-pigs and locusts, would destroy the unhallowed garden made without magic.

Does this mean, however, that the natives attribute all the good results to magic? Certainly not. If you were to suggest to a native that he should make his garden mainly by magic and scamp his work, he would simply smile on your simplicity. He knows as well as you do that there are natural conditions and causes, and by his observations he knows also that he is able to control these natural forces by mental and physical effort. His knowledge is limited, no doubt, but as far as it goes it is sound and proof against mysticism. If the fences are broken down, if the seed is destroyed or has been dried or washed away, he will have recourse not to magic, but to work, guided by knowledge and reason. His experience has taught him also, on the other hand, that in spite of all his forethought and beyond all his efforts there are agencies and forces which one year bestow unwonted and unearned benefits of fertility, making everything run smooth and well, rain and sun appear at the right moment, noxious insects remain in abeyance, the harvest yields a superabundant crop; and another year again the same agencies bring ill luck and bad chance, pursue him from beginning till end and thwart all his most strenuous efforts and his best-founded knowledge. To control these influences and these only he employs magic.

Thus there is a clear-cut division: there is first the well-known set of conditions, the natural course of growth, as well as the ordinary pests and dangers to be warded off by fencing and weeding. On the other hand there is the domain of the unaccountable and adverse influences, as well as the great unearned increment of fortunate coincidence. The first conditions are coped with by knowledge and work, the second by magic.

This line of division can also be traced in the social setting of work and ritual respectively. Though the garden magician is, as a rule, also the leader in practical activities, these two functions are kept strictly apart. Every magical ceremony has its distinctive name, its appropriate time and its place in the scheme of work, and it stands out of the ordinary course of activities completely. Some of them are ceremonial and have to be attended by the whole community, all are public in that it is known when they are going to happen and anyone can attend them. They are performed on selected plots within the gardens and on a special corner of this plot. Work is always tabooed on such occasions, sometimes only while the ceremony lasts, sometimes for a day or two. In his lay character the leader and magician directs the work, fixes the dates for starting, harangues and exhorts slack or careless gardeners. But the two roles never overlap or interfere: they are always clear, and any native will inform you without hesitation whether the man acts as magician or as leader in garden work.

What has been said about gardens can be paralleled from any one of the many other activities in which work and magic run side by side without ever mixing. Thus in canoe building empirical knowledge of material, of technology, and of certain principles of stability and hydrodynamics, function in company and close association with magic, each yet uncontaminated by the other.

For example, they understand perfectly well that the wider the span of the outrigger the greater the stability yet the smaller the resistance against strain. They can clearly explain why they have to give this span a certain traditional width, measured in fractions of the length of the dugout. They can also explain, in rudimentary but clearly mechanical terms, how they have to behave in a sudden gale, why the outrigger must be always on the weather side, why the one type of canoe can and the other cannot beat. They have, in fact, a whole system of principles of sailing, embodied in a complex and rich terminology, traditionally handed on and obeyed as rationally and consistently as is modern science by modern sailors. How could they sail otherwise under eminently dangerous conditions in their frail primitive craft?

But even with all their systematic knowledge, methodically applied, they are still at the mercy of powerful and incalculable tides, sudden gales during the monsoon season and unknown reefs. And here comes in their magic, performed over the canoe during its construction, carried out at the beginning and in the course of expeditions and resorted to in moments of real danger. If the modern seaman, entrenched in science and reason, provided with all sorts of safety appliances, sailing on steel-built steamers, if even he has a singular tendency to superstition—which does not rob him of his knowledge or reason, nor make him altogether prelogical—can we wonder that his savage colleague, under much more precarious conditions, holds fast to the safety and comfort of magic?

An interesting and crucial test is provided by fishing in the Trobriand Islands and its magic. While in the villages on the inner lagoon fishing is done in an easy and absolutely reliable manner by the method of poisoning, yielding abundant results without danger and uncertainty, there are on the shores of the open sea dangerous modes of fishing and also certain types in which the yield greatly varies according to whether shoals of fish appear beforehand or not. It is most significant that in the lagoon fishing, where man can rely completely upon his knowledge and skill, magic does not exist, while in the open-sea fishing, full of danger and uncertainty, there is extensive magical ritual to secure safety and good results.

Again, in warfare the natives know that strength, courage, and agility play a decisive part. Yet here also they practice magic to master the elements of chance and luck.

Nowhere is the duality of natural and supernatural causes divided by a line so thin and intricate, yet, if carefully followed up, so well marked, decisive, and instructive, as in the two most fateful forces of human destiny: health and death. Health to the Melanesians is a natural state of affairs and, unless tampered with, the human body will remain in perfect order. But the natives know perfectly well that there are natural means which can affect health and even destroy the body. Poisons, wounds, burns, falls, are known to cause disablement or death in a natural way. And this is not a matter of private opinion of this or that individual, but it is laid down in traditional lore and even in belief, for there are considered to be different ways to the nether world for those who died by sorcery and those who met "natural" death. Again, it is recognized that cold, heat, overstrain, too much sun, overeating, can all cause minor ailments, which are treated by natural remedies such as massage, steaming, warming at a fire and certain potions. Old age is known to lead to bodily decay and the explanation is given by the natives that very old people grow weak, their oesophagus closes up, and therefore they must die.

But besides these natural causes there is the enormous domain of sorcery and by far the most cases of illness and death are ascribed to this. The line of distinction between sorcery and the other causes is clear in theory and in most cases of practice, but it must be realized that it is subject to what could be called the personal perspective. That is, the more closely a case has to do with the person who considers it, the less will it be "natural," the more "magical." Thus a very old man, whose pending death will be considered natural by the other members of the community, will be afraid only of sorcery and never think of his natural fate. A fairly sick person will diagnose sorcery in his own case, while all the others might speak of too much betel nut or overeating or some other indulgence.

But who of us really believes that his own bodily infirmities and the approaching death is a purely natural occurrence, just an insignificant event in the infinite chain of causes? To the most rational of civilized men health, disease, the threat of death, float in a hazy emotional mist, which seems to become denser and more impenetrable as the fateful forms approach. It is indeed astonishing that "savages" can achieve such a sober, dispassionate outlook in these matters as they actually do.

Thus in his relation to nature and destiny, whether he tries to exploit the first or to dodge the second, primitive man recognizes both the natural and the supernatural forces and agencies, and he tries to use them both for his benefit. Whenever he has been taught by experience that effort guided by knowledge is of some avail, he never spares the one or ignores the other.

He knows that a plant cannot grow by magic alone, or a canoe sail or float without being properly constructed and managed, or a fight be won without skill and daring. He never relies on magic alone, while, on the contrary, he sometimes dispenses with it completely, as in fire-making and in a number of crafts and pursuits. But he clings to it, whenever he has to recognize the impotence of his knowledge and of his rational technique.

I have given my reasons why in this argument I had to rely principally on the material collected in the classical land of magic, Melanesia. But the facts discussed are so fundamental, the conclusions drawn of such a general nature, that it will be easy to check them on any modern detailed ethnographic record. Comparing agricultural work and magic, the building of canoes, the art of healing by magic and by natural remedies, the ideas about the causes of death in other regions, the universal validity of what has been established here could easily be proved. Only, since no observations have methodically been made with reference to the problem of primitive knowledge, the data from other writers could be gleaned only piecemeal and their testimony though clear would be indirect.

I have chosen to face the question of primitive man's rational knowledge directly: watching him at his principal occupations, seeing him pass from work to magic and back again, entering into his mind, listening to his opinions. The whole problem might have been approached through the avenue of language, but this would have led us too far into questions of logic, semasiology, and theory of primitive languages. Words which serve to express general ideas such as *existence, substance,* and *attribute, cause* and *effect,* the *fundamental* and the *secondary*; words and expressions used in complicated pursuits like sailing, construction, measuring and checking; numerals and quantitative descriptions, correct and detailed classifications of natural phenomena, plants and animals—all this would lead us exactly to the same conclusion: that primitive man can observe and think, and that he possesses, embodied in his language, systems of methodical though rudimentary knowledge.

Similar conclusions could be drawn from an examination of those mental schemes and physical contrivances which could be described as diagrams or formulas. Methods of indicating the main points of the compass, arra ge-ments of stars into constellations, co-ordination of these with the seasons, naming of moons in the year, of quarters in the moon—all these accomplishments are known to the simplest savages. Also they are all able to draw diagrammatic maps in the sand or dust, indicate arrangements by placing small stones, shells, or sticks on the ground, plan expeditions or raids on such rudimentary charts. By co-ordinating space and time they are able to arrange big tribal gatherings and to combine vast tribal movements over extensive areas. The use of leaves, notched sticks, and similar aids to memory is well known and seems to be almost universal. All such "diagrams" are means of reducing a complex and unwieldy bit of reality to a simple and handy form. They give man a relatively easy mental control over it. As such are they not—

in a very rudimentary form no doubt—fundamentally akin to developed scientific formulas and "models," which are also simple and handy paraphrases of a complex or abstract reality, giving the civilized physicist mental control over it?

This brings us to the second question: Can we regard primitive knowledge, which, as we found, is both empirical and rational, as a rudimentary stage of science, or is it not at all related to it? If by science be understood a body of rules and conceptions, based on experience and derived from it by logical inference, embodied in material achievements and in a fixed form of tradition and carried on by some sort of social organization—then there is no doubt that even the lowest savage communities have the beginnings of science, however rudimentary.

Most epistemologists would not, however, be satisfied with such a "minimum definition" of science, for it might apply to the rules of an art or craft as well. They would maintain that the rules of science must be laid down explicitly, open to control by experiment and critique by reason. They must not only be rules of practical behavior, but theoretical laws of knowledge. Even accepting this stricture, however, there is hardly any doubt that many of the principles of savage knowledge are scientific in this sense. The native shipwright knows not only practically of buoyancy, leverage, equilibrium, he has to obey these laws not only on water, but while making the canoe he must have the principles in his mind. He instructs his helpers in them. He gives them the traditional rules, and in a crude and simple manner, using his hands, pieces of wood, and a limited technical vocabulary, he explains some general laws of hydrodynamics and equilibrium. Science is not detached from the craft, that is certainly true, it is only a means to an end, it is crude, rudimentary, and inchoate, but with all that it is the matrix from which the higher developments must have sprung.

If we applied another criterion yet, that of the really scientific attitude, the disinterested search for knowledge and for the understanding of causes and reasons, the answer would certainly not be in a direct negative. There is, of course, no widespread thirst for knowledge in a savage community, new things such as European topics bore them frankly and their whole interest is largely encompassed by the traditional world of their culture. But within this there is both the antiquarian mind passionately interested in myths, stories, details of customs, pedigrees, and ancient happenings, and there is also to be found the naturalist, patient and painstaking in his observations, capable of generalization and of connecting long chains of events in the life of animals, and in the marine world or in the jungle. It is enough to realize how much European naturalists have often learned from their savage colleagues to appreciate this interest found in the native for nature. There is finally among the primitives, as every fieldworker well knows, the sociologist, the ideal informant, capable with marvelous accuracy and insight to give the *raison d'être*, the function, and the organization of many a simpler institution in his tribe.

Science, of course, does not exist in any uncivilized community as a driving power, criticizing, renewing, constructing. Science is never consciously made. But on this criterion, neither is there law, nor religion, nor government among savages.

The question, however, whether we should call it *science* or only *empirical and rational knowledge* is not of primary importance in this context. We have tried to gain a clear idea as to whether the savage has only one domain of reality or two, and we found that he has his profane world of practical activities and rational outlook besides the sacred region of cult and belief. We have been able to map out the two domains and to give a more detailed description of the one.

John J. Poggie, Jr., and Carl Gersuny

Risk and Ritual in a New England Fishing Community [1]

Among certain groups and in certain behavioral settings in the United States, there is a greater use of ritual magic than is generally characteristic of the whole society. Coal miners and fiishermen as well as rodeo performers and gamblers are in occupations and situations that are replete with ritual magic. These groups and situations have in common a high degree of uncertainty associated with them. The "retention" of rituals in these cases, in an otherwise highly secularized society, functions to bridge the gaps of uncertainty. This interpretation is based on the classical theoretical formulation proposed by Bronislaw Malinowski.

Malinowski first related magic to different types of risks; the risks were associated with the interrelationship between technology and habitat in fishing activities among the Trobriand Islanders. Concerning fishing among the Trobrianders he states:

While in the villages on the inner lagoon fishing is done in an easy and absolutely reliable manner by the method of poisoning, yielding abundant results without

From John J. Poggie, Jr., and Carl Gersuny, "Risk and Ritual: An Interpretation of Fishermen's Folklore in a New England Community," Journal of American Folklore, 85:335 (January–March 1972), 68–72. Reprinted with permission of the American Folklore Society.

[1] This research, supported by the Marine Resources Committee and the Sea Grant Program at the University of Rhode Island, is part of a general socio-cultural study of a coastal New England community.

danger and uncertainty, there are on the shores of the open sea dangerous modes of fishing and also certain types in which the yield greatly varies according to whether shoals of fish appear beforehand or not. It is most significant that in the lagoon fishing, where man can rely completely upon his knowledge and skill, magic does not exist, while in the open-sea fishing, full of danger and uncertainty, there is extensive magical ritual to secure safety and good results.[2]

It is interesting to note that there are two elements of unpredictability in Malinowski's discussion of magic among Trobriand fishermen. On the one hand, there is the question of certainty or uncertainty of the catch, while on the other hand there is the uncertainty or danger to the fishermen themselves. This same distinction appears to apply to such activities in the United States as gambling and rodeo riding, where the risks are related most predominantly to "production" and "person" respectively. We feel that an important conceptual distinction must be made between these two types of uncertainty involved in "risk taking" activities. The distinction appears to be important in understanding why ritual is more prevalent in certain occupational groups and behavior settings than it is in others.

While it is true that man has continually increased his control over and predictability of the process of production, there has not been a comparable increase in technological control over the elements that endanger his life and limb. Man's cognitive image of his capacity to preserve his mortal self through rational technology can never reach the degree of confidence that he has in his ability to control his environment.

We thus wish to emphasize the distinction between ritual associated with production and ritual associated with protection of life and limb. We are hypothesizing that there is a differential rate of retention of ritual associated with these two types of risk. Production is much more secularized than the contemplation of mortality. This hypothesis applies to those domains of production where man has "allowed" technological innovation to occur. It does not apply to gambling, rodeo riding, or like activities, where the technology is purposely primitive.

Medical science is an example of an area in which great technological innovation has taken place, and the practice of medicine itself is largely devoid of ritual. On the other hand, when medical technology fails, as it always does in the end, it is a ritual practitioner and not the medical doctor who "takes care of us."

We have collected data on ritual from two occupational groups in a southern New England community. These two occupational groups are comparable in most respects, except that one is a high physical-risk occupation and the other a low physical-risk occupation. These are fishermen and textile mill workers respectively. Personal risk is higher among fishermen than among mill workers because of the differences in the environments in which the two types of work are carried out. Fishing is innately more dangerous

[2] Bronislaw Malinowski, *Magic, Science and Religion* (Garden City, N.Y., 1948), 30–31.

because it requires a technological coping with a marine environment by a terrestrial-arborial species even to start the work.

Precisely how dangerous fishing is as an occupation can be seen from a comparison of data on fatalities in commercial fisheries and coal mining, the most dangerous of land occupations. In 1965 the commercial fisheries of the United States recorded 21.4 deaths per million man-days, while in coal mining there were 1.04 deaths per million man-hours or 8.3 deaths per million man-days. In marked contrast is the rate of fatal accidents in textile mills in the United States which is 0.8 per million man-days.[3]

A comparison of the rituals of fishermen and textile workers will be the basis of testing the above hypothesis.

Danger and Rituals of Avoidance

Let us first briefly review the nature of rituals of avoidance as reported in the literature. Ritual, according to Leach, involves "non-instinctive predictable action . . . that cannot be justified by a 'rational' means-to-ends type of explanation."[4] In dangerous situations, especially where the perils besetting men are not susceptible to abatement by "rational" means, ritual is more likely to be developed than in safe and rationally controllable contexts. Avoidance rituals or tabus are thus an integral part of behavioral response to perceived danger.

Radcliffe-Brown referred to tabu as a "ritual prohibition" whose infraction results in undesirable change.[5] Tabu and danger are closely related, though in some cases the perception of danger arises from the tabu (as in the case of mother-in-law avoidance, perhaps, and certain food tabus), while in others it may be presumed that tabus arise in response to perils for which no technological remedy is known. Danger may thus be either the independent or the dependent variable in connection with tabu.

So far as ritual avoidances are concerned, the reasons for them may vary from a very vague idea that some sort of misfortune or ill-luck, not defined as to its kind, is likely to befall anyone who fails to observe the taboo, to a belief that non-observance will produce some quite specific and undesirable results.[6]

[3] Fatalities in fishing cited in Office of Merchant Marine Safety, A Cost-Benefit Analysis of Alternative Safety Programs for U.S. Commercial Fishing Vessels (Washington, D.C., 1971); fatality data in coal mining come from U.S. Bureau of the Census, Statistical Abstract of the United States, 91st ed. (Washington, D.C., 1970); data on fatalities in textile mills come from Bureau of Labor Statistics, Injury Rates by Industry—1969 (Washington, D.C., 1971).

[4] Edmund R. Leach, "Ritual," International Encyclopedia of the Social Sciences, vol. 13 (New York, 1968), 520–521.

[5] A. R. Radcliffe-Brown, Structure and Function in Primitive Society (New York, 1965), 134.

[6] Ibid., 142.

Steiner also elaborates on the theme of danger in his definition of tabu as follows:

Taboo is concerned (1) with all the social mechanisms of obedience which have ritual significance; (2) with specific and restrictive behaviour in dangerous situations. One might say that taboo deals with the sociology of danger itself, for it is concerned (3) with the protection of individuals who are in danger, and (4) with the protection of society from those endangered—and therefore dangerous—persons. . . . Taboo is an element of all those situations in which attitudes to values are expressed in terms of danger behaviour.[7]

The perils of the sea, compounded by the hazards of the labors peculiar to fishing, create a context conducive to the survival of tabus even in a society among whose dominant values rationality ranks very high.

Procedures and Findings

In order to obtain information on frequency and types of ritual associated with the two occupational groups, we administered an interview schedule asking the following question on superstition, the emic term used by the fishermen and mill workers themselves to describe ritual beliefs and behaviors:

Practically everyone has some superstitions such as walking under a ladder or knocking on wood. Are there any superstitions that are related to your type of work? If so, please describe as many as you can think of.

The interview schedule was administered to a sample of 27 fishermen and 29 factory workers. The sample of fishermen was a random one, while that of the factory workers was nearly a 100 percent sample of the work force in a small textile mill. Shoreville (pseudonym) is a predominantly "Yankee" coastal southern New England township of some 15,000 residents. The individuals involved in the fishermen and factory worker samples are for the most part local Shoreville people. The two groups are also similar in the sense that they are both blue-collar occupations. In educational attainment and age, the two groups are also quite similar. The mean age for both the fishermen and factory workers is 37, while their average number of years of education are 12 and 11 respectively.

There are three main types of fishing technology in Shoreville: pot lobster boats that work during the day, draggers that also return to port each day, and draggers that stay out for several days at a time. We surmised that these types of fishing might vary in risk, pot lobstering being the least dangerous, as it is mainly an inshore, daytime activity, and multiple day-trip fishing being the most hazardous, as it takes the men away from protected waters and involves being out of reach of rapid assistance. One-day dragging would be intermediate because it is carried out in offshore waters but only on a daytime basis. Thus we had the possibility not only of comparing factory workers with

[7] Franz Steiner, *Taboo* (New York, 1956), 20.

fishermen but also of comparing different types of fishermen within the general occupational group. There is no corresponding variation in personal risk among the mill workers.

The results of our interviews are tabulated in Table 1. It is of particular

Table 1: Fishermen's Tabus in Shoreville ($N = 28$; 6 pot lobstermen, 13 day fishermen, 9 trippers)

FREQUENCY OF TIMES MENTIONED BY ALL GROUPS	TABU
23	Don't turn hatch cover upside down—bad luck
	9–day; 8–tripper; 6–lobstermen
8	Don't whistle because it "whistles up a breeze"
	6–day; 2–tripper; 0–lobstermen
7	Don't mention "pig" on board
	4–day; 2–tripper; 1–lobstermen
4	Don't shave on a trip
	2–day; 1–tripper; 1–lobstermen
4	Don't turn against the sun, always into it
	0–day; 3–tripper; 1–lobstermen
4	Don't allow a man with a black bag aboard
	1–day; 1–tripper; 2–lobstermen
4	Don't serve beef stew aboard; it brings on a gale
	2–day; 2–tripper; 0–lobstermen
3	Don't bring women out on a trip
	1–day; 0–tripper; 2–lobstermen
3	Don't leave for trip on Friday
	2–day; 1–tripper; 0–lobstermen
3	Don't return a knife in any other way that the way it was given, open or closed
	1–day; 2–tripper; 0–lobstermen
3	Knock on wood for good luck
	1–day; 0–tripper; 2–lobstermen
2	Don't put hat in bunk
	2–day; 0–tripper; 0–lobstermen

Mentioned once by day fishermen:

Don't wash inside of wheelhouse windows
Don't wear a new hat—bad luck
No two-dollar bills—bad luck
No women on first trip of new boat
Don't wear yellow southwesters on board
Don't bring pork on board
Don't brag, it brings bad luck

Mentioned once by trippers:

Only coil a rope in the direction of the sun's path
Don't change name of boat
Don't leave dock twice in the same day

Table 1—Continued

Mentioned once by lobstermen:

Don't wear black sweater
Red sky in the morning—warning of bad weather
Calm before the storm, perfect day—be apprehensive
See rat leaving the boat—don't sail
Never use the number 13 in speech
Thirteen pot trawls—bad luck
Metal boats sink
Always refer to boat as "she"

significance to note that of the twenty-nine factory workers interviewed only one gave what he considered to be a superstition associated with his work. His response was, "I am afraid of getting my arms caught on something." This particular response appears to be more of an expression of a realistic fear than a ritual avoidance. On the other hand, the fishermen responded with numerous reports of superstitions associated with their work. The types of superstition and their frequency of mention are indicated in the following table. Only one out of twenty-seven fishermen reported that there were no superstitions associated with his work.

A striking pattern in these results is that the vast majority of the rituals are proscriptive in nature. That is to say, most of the ritual enjoins the avoidance of particular behavior patterns with the implication that misfortune will befall the actor if he does not avoid the proscribed behavior.

Discussion

The general hypothesis of this research is confirmed in that there is indeed considerably more ritual reported among the high-risk fishermen than among the low-risk textile workers. We argue that these differences are related to the differences in predictability and certainty of bodily integrity associated with these two occupational cultures. The textile workers are operating in a relatively safe environment, while the fishermen are operating in a much more hazardous one.

We have noted in our data that there is a preponderance of proscriptive norms or tabus reported by the fishermen. These beliefs deal with avoiding particular acts and are related to danger coming in the form of harm to the individual or his vessel. This situation is in contrast to prescriptive kinds of magic that prescribe necessary behaviors or acts, in this case in order to catch fish or to produce some other kind of output. Thus, if the general interpretation is correct, the prehistoric paintings of animals on the cave walls at Lascaux are prescriptive magic in that they were to ensure, among other things, the catching of animals. There is no logical connection between the clearly proscriptive types of ritual that were reported by our respondents and predictability in the catch. Rather, the types of ritual reported to us are strictly items that relate to preservation of body and its extensions. In the case of boxing and rodeo participation, even though physical danger is high, we are dealing with a select group of men whose physical self is defined as "all enduring" and where we think the major concern to the actor is more with the outcome (production). We find according to limited sources that magic rather than tabu predominates.[8]

It can be argued that the value system of the larger society in which this fishing subculture operates places great stress on technological rationality. The notion that technology can overcome the environment is pervasive in all sectors of American society. To a great extent this value system is consistent with the reality of technological competence that has been brought to bear on catching fish. The fishermen we have studied have at their disposal such efficient fish-tracking systems as sonar, aircraft for spotting schools of fish, as well as other devices that indicate the presence of particular species. Also at their disposal are the ecological data that deal with distribution of fish populations over the yearly cycle and that make locating fish a relatively predictable operation.

Thus we argue in Malinowski's terms that the uncertainty factor of the catch has been subjected by and large to technological remedies. Although it is possible for a fisherman from Shoreville to return to port after a day's work with few fish, it is unlikely for a fisherman to return with no fish. Furthermore, fishermen who do not come back with a large catch on one day have the prospect of a large catch another day to make up for a deficiency of the bad day. In the course of the year, fishermen do bring home large quantities of fish and realize a relatively high economic return for their efforts, at least in the Shoreville case.

Let us now consider the part of the environment with which the ritual reported to us is associated. Although it can be argued that man has brought ingenuity and technological competence to the task of overcoming the hazards of venturing out into the open ocean, we know that fishermen do lose their lives and do receive injury at a high rate because of their occupation. In contrast to a day with a poor catch, there is no second chance in losing one's life or in sustaining permanent injury. Thus, there is great risk involved in a man's going out onto the water to catch fish—more risk to his personal self than to his economic self. The risk we are talking about is characteristic of man's utilization of the marine environment. As a terrestrial species man is extending himself considerably by simply going out onto the water to carry out his work activities; in contrast, in a factory man does not need to build an artificial land environment under himself before he can even begin his

[8] S. Kirson Weinberg and Henry Arond, "The Occupational Culture of the Boxer," *American Journal of Sociology*, **57** (1952), 463–464; personal communication with ex-boxer–cowboy Tony McNevin.

activities. It is not only the artificial land environment (boat or platform) that man has made, but also the medium in which this artificial land environment operates that presents considerable hazard to the fisherman. Storms, rough seas, obstructions in the water, sudden changes in weather conditions, and other factors of the macro-environment along with the remote location of the work reduce predictability.

We had hypothesized that there would be a distinction between the rituals reported by pot lobstermen and those reported by day fishermen and multiple-day fishermen. The results, however, did not confirm this hypothesis. Each of the groups has about the same proportion of ritual beliefs except that there are certain specialized ones for particular types of fishing. Trippers, who are out for several days, have peculiar to their set of ritual beliefs items concerning food serving on board the boat and items related to the sleeping arrangements. The pot lobstermen, who do not usually prepare food or sleep on board, show zero responses to these items.

Although we do not have the data necessary to prove why this pattern occurred, we can suggest that the risk factors involved in each of those types of fishing have been equalized more or less. The pot lobstermen who generally do not venture out as far into the ocean, or stay out overnight in the darkness, are often operating in congested inshore waters devoid of ship-to-shore radio, radar, sonar, and other safety features that are a standard part of day and trip boats. Even though safety technology may tend to equalize risk between inshore and offshore fishing, it does not remove the basic danger, which is, according to our view, the basis of tabu associated with man's occupancy of the sea.

In our interviews with fishermen about their ritual beliefs, there was a degree of embarrassment expressed concerning these superstitions. Many times our respondents would disclaim believing in these superstitions but would often admit that they dared not "break the rule" of the superstitions aboard their own boats. The embarrassment, or ambivalence, as Goffman calls it,[9] associated with reporting about superstitions is, we feel, a manifestation of the divergence between the larger landbound culture that the interviewers represent and the occupational subculture of fishermen. Fishermen who are part of both cultures are sensitive to the values of general secularization that exist in the land setting. Nevertheless, while they are at sea they do observe the proscriptions of the tabus that embarrass them on shore.

It can be argued that the persistence of superstitions among fishermen is a relic of the past, "coming from a time" when fishing was much more hazardous than it is today. The wide distribution of the tabus reported seem to support this hypothesis.[10] However, this particular view of the "persistence of relics" says nothing about the functional nature of sociocultural traits. It

[9] Erving Goffman, *Interaction Ritual* (Garden City, N.Y., 1967), 179.

[10] Compare James G. Frazer, *The Golden Bough* (London, 1890); Richard M. Dorson, *Buying the Wind* (Chicago, 1964); Helen Creighton, *Folklore of Lunenburg County, Nova Scotia* (Ottawa, 1950).

can be argued that there is no such thing as a functionless trait and that "relics of the past" have contemporary functions. We have argued that, even though their form may be widespread, the contemporary functions of these rituals that are part of fishermen's folklore operate essentially as they did in the past —to help man cope with the uncertainties of operating in a personally hazardous environment.

Roy A. Rappaport

Ritual Regulation of Environmental Relations Among a New Guinea People [1]

Most functional studies of religious behavior in anthropology have as an analytic goal the elucidation of events, processes, or relationships occurring within a social unit of some sort. The social unit is not always well defined, but in some cases it appears to be a church, that is, a group of people who entertain similar beliefs about the universe, or a congregation, a group of people who participate together in the performance of religious rituals. There have been exceptions. Thus Vayda, Leeds, and Smith (1961) and O. K. Moore (1957) have clearly perceived that the functions of religious ritual are not necessarily confined within the boundaries of a congregation or even a church. By and large, however, I believe that the following statement by Homans (1941: 172) represents fairly the dominant line of anthropological thought concerning the functions of religious ritual:

Ritual actions do not produce a practical result on the external world—that is one of the reasons why we call them ritual. But to make this statement is not to say that ritual has no function. Its function is not related to the world external to the

Reprinted from Roy A. Rappaport, "Ritual Regulation of Environmental Relations Among a New Guinea People," Ethnology, **VI**:1 (January 1967), 17–29, with permission of Ethnology.

[1] The field work upon which this paper is based was supported by a grant from the National Science Foundation, under which Professor A. P. Vayda was principal investigator. Personal support was received by the author from the National Institutes of Health. Earlier versions of this paper were presented at the 1964 annual meeting of the American Anthropological Association in Detroit, and before a Columbia University seminar on Ecological Systems and Cultural Evolution. I have received valuable suggestions from Alexander Alland, Jacques Barrau, William Clarke, Paul Collins, C. Glen King, Marvin Harris, Margaret Mead, M. J. Meggitt, Ann Rappaport, John Street, Marjorie Whiting, Cherry Vayda, A. P. Vayda and many others, but I take full responsibility for the analysis presented herewith.

society but to the internal constitution of the society. It gives the members of the society confidence, it dispels their anxieties, it disciplines their social organization.

No argument will be raised here against the sociological and psychological functions imputed by Homans, and many others before him, to ritual. They seem to me to be plausible. Nevertheless, in some cases at least, ritual does produce, in Homans' terms, "a practical result on the world" external not only to the social unit composed of those who participate together in ritual performances but also to the larger unit composed of those who entertain similar beliefs concerning the universe. The material presented here will show that the ritual cycles of the Tsembaga, and of other local territorial groups of Maring speakers living in the New Guinea interior, play an important part in regulating the relationships of these groups with both the nonhuman components of their immediate environments and the human components of their less immediate environments, that is, with other similar territorial groups. To be more specific, this regulation helps to maintain the biotic communities existing within their territories, redistributes land among people and people over land, and limits the frequency of fighting. In the absence of authoritative political statuses or offices, the ritual cycle likewise provides a means for mobilizing allies when warfare may be undertaken. It also provides a mechanism for redistributing local pig surpluses in the form of pork throughout a large regional population while helping to assure the local population of a supply of pork when its members are most in need of high quality protein.

Religious ritual may be defined, for the purposes of this paper, as the prescribed performance of conventionalized acts manifestly directed toward the involvement of nonempirical or supernatural agencies in the affairs of the actors. While this definition relies upon the formal characteristics of the performances and upon the motives for undertaking them, attention will be focused upon the empirical effects of ritual performances and sequences of ritual performances. The religious rituals to be discussed are regarded as neither more nor less than part of the behavioral repertoire employed by an aggregate of organisms in adjusting to its environment.

The data upon which this paper is based were collected during fourteen months of field work among the Tsembaga, one of about twenty local groups of Maring speakers living in the Simbai and Jimi Valleys of the Bismarck Range in the Territory of New Guinea. The size of Maring local groups varies from a little over 100 to 900. The Tsembaga, who in 1963 numbered 204 persons, are located on the south wall of the Simbai Valley. The country in which they live differs from the true highlands in being lower, generally more rugged, and more heavily forested. Tsembaga territory rises, within a total surface area of 3.2 square miles, from an elevation of 2,200 feet at the Simbai river to 7,200 feet at the ridge crest. Gardens are cut in the secondary forests up to between 5,000 and 5,400 feet, above which the area remains in primary forest. Rainfall reaches 150 inches per year.

The Tsembaga have come into contact with the outside world only recently;

the first government patrol to penetrate their territory arrived in 1954. They were considered uncontrolled by the Australian government until 1962, and they remain unmissionized to this day.

The 204 Tsembaga are distributed among five putatively patrilineal clans, which are, in turn, organized into more inclusive groupings on two hierarchical levels below that of the total local group.[2] Internal political structure is highly egalitarian. There are no hereditary or elected chiefs, nor are there even "big men" who can regularly coerce or command the support of their clansmen or co-residents in economic or forceful enterprises.

It is convenient to regard the Tsembaga as a population in the ecological sense, that is, as one of the components of a system of trophic exchanges taking place within a bounded area. Tsembaga territory and the biotic community existing upon it may be conveniently viewed as an ecosystem. While it would be permissible arbitrarily to designate the Tsembaga as a population and their territory with its biota as an ecosystem, there are also nonarbitrary reasons for doing so. An ecosystem is a system of material exchanges, and the Tsembaga maintain against other human groups exclusive access to the resources within their territorial borders. Conversely, it is from this territory alone that the Tsembaga ordinarily derive all of their foodstuffs and most of the other materials they require for survival. Less anthropocentrically, it may be justified to regard Tsembaga territory with its biota as an ecosystem in view of the rather localized nature of cyclical material exchanges in tropical rainforests.

As they are involved with the nonhuman biotic community within their territory in a set of trophic exchanges, so do they participate in other material relationships with other human groups external to their territory. Genetic materials are exchanged with other groups, and certain crucial items, such as stone axes, were in past obtained from the outside. Furthermore, in the area occupied by the Maring speakers, more than one local group is usually involved in any process, either peaceful or warlike, through which people are redistributed over land and land redistributed among people.

The concept of the ecosystem, though it provides a convenient frame for the analysis of interspecific trophic exchanges taking place within limited geographical areas, does not comfortably accommodate intraspecific exchanges taking place over wider geographic areas. Some sort of geographic population model would be more useful for the analysis of the relationship of the local ecological population to the larger regional population of which it is a part, but we lack even a set of appropriate terms for such a model. Suffice it here to note that the relations of the Tsembaga to the total of other local human populations in their vicinity are similar to the relations of local aggregates of other animals to the totality of their species occupying broader and more or less continuous regions. This larger, more inclusive aggregate may resemble what geneticists mean by the term population, that is, an aggregate of inter-

---

[2] The social organization of the Tsembaga will be described in detail elsewhere.

breeding organisms persisting through an indefinite number of generations and either living or capable of living in isolation from similar aggregates of the same species. This is the unit which survives through long periods of time while its local ecological (*sensu stricto*) subunits, the units more or less independently involved in interspecific trophic exchanges such as the Tsembaga, are ephemeral.

Since it has been asserted that the ritual cycles of the Tsembaga regulate relationships within what may be regarded as a complex system, it is necessary, before proceeding to the ritual cycle itself, to describe briefly, and where possible in quantitative terms, some aspects of the place of the Tsembaga in this system.

The Tsembaga are bush-fallowing horticulturalists. Staples include a range of root crops, taro (*Colocasia*) and sweet potatoes being most important, yams and manioc less so. In addition, a great variety of greens are raised, some of which are rich in protein. Sugar cane and some tree crops, particularly *Pandanus conoideus*, are also important.

All gardens are mixed, many of them containing all of the major root crops and many greens. Two named garden types are, however, distinguished by the crops which predominate in them. "Taro-yam gardens" were found to produce, on the basis of daily harvest records kept on entire gardens for close to one year, about 5,300,000 calories [3] per acre during their harvesting lives of 18 to 24 months; 85 per cent of their yield is harvested between 24 and 76 weeks after planting. "Sugar-sweet potato gardens" produce about 4,600,000 calories per acre during their harvesting lives, 91 per cent being taken between 24 and 76 weeks after planting. I estimated that approximately 310,000 calories per acre is expended on cutting, fencing, planning, maintaining, harvesting, and walking to and from taro-yam gardens. Sugar-sweet potato gardens required an expenditure of approximately 290,000 calories per acre.[4] These energy ratios, approximately 17:1 on taro-yam gardens and 16:1 on sugar-sweet potato gardens, compare favorably with figures reported for swidden cultivation in other regions.[5]

Intake is high in comparison with the reported dietaries of other New Guinea populations. On the basis of daily consumption records kept for ten

[3] Because the length of time in the field precluded the possibility of maintaining harvest records on single gardens from planting through abandonment, figures were based, in the case of both "taro-yam" and "sugar-sweet potato" gardens, on three separate gardens planted in successive years. Conversions from the gross weight to the caloric value of yields were made by reference to the literature. The sources used are listed in Rappaport (1966: Appendix VIII)

[4] Rough time and motion studies of each of the tasks involved in making, maintaining, harvesting, and walking to and from gardens were undertaken. Conversion to energy expenditure values was accomplished by reference to energy expenditure tables prepared by Hipsley and Kirk (1965: 43) on the basis of gas exchange measurements made during the performance of garden tasks by the Chimbu people of the New Guinea highlands.

[5] Marvin Harris, in an unpublished paper, estimates the ratio of energy return to energy input ratio on Dyak (Borneo) rice swiddens at 10:1. His estimates of energy ratios on Tepotzlan (Meso-America) swiddens range from 13:1 on poor land to 29:1 on the best land.

months on four households numbering in total sixteen persons, I estimated the average daily intake of adult males to be approximately 2,600 calories, and that of adult females to be around 2,200 calories. It may be mentioned here that the Tsembaga are small and short statured. Adult males average 101 pounds in weight and approximately 58.5 inches in height; the corresponding averages for adult females are 85 pounds and 54.5 inches.[6]

Although 99 per cent by weight of the food consumed is vegetable, the protein intake is high by New Guinea standards. The daily protein consumption of adult males from vegetable sources was estimated to be between 43 and 55 grams, of adult females 36 to 48 grams. Even with an adjustment for vegetable sources, these values are slightly in excess of the recently published WHO/FAO daily requirements (Food and Agriculture Organization of the United Nations 1964). The same is true of the younger age categories, although soft and discolored hair, a symptom of protein deficiency, was noted in a few children. The WHO/FAO protein requirements do not include a large "margin for safety" or allowance for stress; and, although no clinical assessments were undertaken, it may be suggested that the Tsembaga achieve nitrogen balance at a low level. In other words, their protein intake is probably marginal.

Measurements of all gardens made during 1962 and of some gardens made during 1963 indicate that, to support the human population, between .15 and .19 acres are put into cultivation per capita per year. Fallows range from 8 to 45 years. The area in secondary forest comprises approximately 1,000 acres, only 30 to 50 of which are in cultivation at any time. Assuming calories to be the limiting factor, and assuming an unchanging population structure, the territory could support—with no reduction in lengths of fallow and without cutting into the virgin forest from which the Tsembaga extract many important items—between 290 and 397 people if the pig population remained minimal. The size of the pig herd, however, fluctuates widely. Taking Maring pig husbandry procedures into consideration, I have estimated the human carrying capacity of the Tsembaga territory at between 270 and 320 people.

Because the timing of the ritual cycle is bound up with the demography of the pig herd, the place of the pig in Tsembaga adaptation must be examined.

First, being omnivorous, pigs keep residential areas free of garbage and human feces. Second, limited numbers of pigs rooting in secondary growth may help to hasten the development of that growth. The Tsembaga usually permit pigs to enter their gardens one and a half to two years after planting, by which time second-growth trees are well established there. The Tsembaga practice selective weeding; from the time the garden is planted, herbaceous species are removed, but tree species are allowed to remain. By the time cropping is discontinued and the pigs are let in, some of the trees in the garden are already ten to fifteen feet tall. These well-established trees are

[6] Heights may be inaccurate. Many men wear their hair in large coiffures hardened with pandanus grease, and it was necessary in some instances to estimate the location of the top of the skull.

relatively impervious to damage by the pigs, which, in rooting for seeds and remaining tubers, eliminate many seeds and seedlings that, if allowed to develop, would provide some competition for the established trees. Moreover, in some Maring-speaking areas swiddens are planted twice, although this is not the case with the Tsembaga. After the first crop is almost exhausted, pigs are penned in the garden, where their rooting eliminates weeds and softens the ground, making the task of planting for a second time easier. The pigs, in other words, are used as cultivating machines.

Small numbers of pigs are easy to keep. They run free during the day and return home at night to receive their ration of garbage and substandard tubers, particularly sweet potatoes. Supplying the latter requires little extra work, for the substandard tubers are taken from the ground in the course of harvesting the daily ration for humans. Daily consumption records kept over a period of some months show that the ration of tubers received by the pigs approximates in weight that consumed by adult humans, i.e., a little less than three pounds per day per pig.

If the pig herd grows large, however, the substandard tubers incidentally obtained in the course of harvesting for human needs become insufficient, and it becomes necessary to harvest especially for pigs. In other words, people must work for the pigs and perhaps even supply them with food fit for human consumption. Thus, as Vayda, Leeds, and Smith (1961: 71) have pointed out, there can be too many pigs for a given community.

This also holds true of the sanitary and cultivating services rendered by pigs. A small number of pigs is sufficient to keep residential areas clean, to suppress superfluous seedlings in abandoned gardens, and to soften the soil in gardens scheduled for second plantings. A larger herd, on the other hand, may be troublesome; the larger the number of pigs, the greater the possibility of their invasion of producing gardens, with concomitant damage not only to crops and young secondary growth but also to the relations between the pig owners and garden owners.

All male pigs are castrated at approximately three months of age, for boars, people say, are dangerous and do not grow as large as barrows. Pregnancies, therefore, are always the result of unions of domestic sows with feral males. Fecundity is thus only a fraction of its potential. During one twelve-month period only fourteen litters resulted out of a potential 99 or more pregnancies. Farrowing generally takes place in the forest, and mortality of the young is high. Only 32 of the offspring of the above-mentioned fourteen pregnancies were alive six months after birth. This number is barely sufficient to replace the number of adult animals which would have died or been killed during most years without pig festivals.

The Tsembaga almost never kill domestic pigs outside of ritual contexts. In ordinary times, when there is no pig festival in progress, these rituals are almost always associated with misfortunes or emergencies, notably warfare, illness, injury, or death. Rules state not only the contexts in which pigs are to be ritually slaughtered, but also who may partake of the flesh of the sacrificial animals. During warfare it is only the men participating in the fighting who eat the pork. In cases of illness or injury, it is only the victim and certain near relatives, particularly his co-resident agnates and spouses, who do so.

It is reasonable to assume that misfortune and emergency are likely to induce in the organisms experiencing them a complex of physiological changes known collectively as "stress." Physiological stress reactions occur not only in organisms which are infected with disease or traumatized, but also in those experiencing rage or fear (Houssay *et al.* 1955: 1096), or even prolonged anxiety (National Research Council 1963: 53). One important aspect of stress is the increased catabolization of protein (Houssay *et al.* 1955: 451; National Research Council 1963: 49), with a net loss of nitrogen from the tissues (Houssay *et al.* 1955: 450). This is a serious matter for organisms with a marginal protein intake. Antibody production is low (Berg 1948: 311), healing is slow (Large and Johnston 1948: 352), and a variety of symptoms of a serious nature are likely to develop (Lund and Levenson 1948: 349; Zintel 1964: 1043). The status of a protein-depleted animal, however, may be significantly improved in a relatively short period of time by the intake of high quality protein, and high protein diets are therefore routinely prescribed for surgical patients and those suffering from infectious diseases (Burton 1959: 231; Lund and Levenson 1948: 350; Elman 1951: 85ff; Zintel 1964: 1043ff).

It is precisely when they are undergoing physiological stress that the Tsembaga kill and consume their pigs, and it should be noted that they limit the consumption to those likely to be experiencing stress most profoundly. The Tsembaga, of course, know nothing of physiological stress. Native theories of the etiology and treatment of disease and injury implicate various categories of spirits to whom sacrifices must be made. Nevertheless, the behavior which is appropriate in terms of native understandings is also appropriate to the actual situation confronting the actors.

We may now outline in the barest of terms the Tsembaga ritual cycle. Space does not permit a description of its ideological correlates. It must suffice to note that Tsembaga do not necessarily perceive all of the empirical effects which the anthropologist sees to flow from their ritual behavior. Such empirical consequences as they may perceive, moreover, are not central to their rationalizations of the performances. The Tsembaga say that they perform the rituals in order to rearrange their relationships with the supernatural world. We may only reiterate here that behavior undertaken in reference to their "cognized environment"—an environment which includes as very important elements the spirits of ancestors—seems appropriate in their "operational environment," the material environment specified by the anthropologist through operations of observation, including measurement.

Since the rituals are arranged in a cycle, description may commence at any point. The operation of the cycle becomes clearest if we begin with the rituals performed during warfare. Opponents in all cases occupy adjacent territories, in almost all cases on the same valley wall. After hostilities have broken out, each side performs certain rituals which place the opposing side in the formal category of "enemy." A number of taboos prevail while hostilities continue. These include prohibitions on sexual intercourse and on the ingestion of certain things—food prepared by women, food grown on the lower portion of the territory, marsupials, eels, and, while actually on the fighting ground, any liquid whatsoever.

One ritual practice associated with fighting which may have some physiological consequences deserves mention. Immediately before proceeding to the fighting ground, the warriors eat heavily salted pig fat. The ingestion of salt, coupled with the taboo on drinking, has the effect of shortening the fighting day, particularly since the Maring prefer to fight only on bright sunny days. When everyone gets unbearably thirsty, according to informants, fighting is broken off.

There may formerly have been other effects if the native salt contained sodium (the production of salt was discontinued some years previous to the field work, and no samples were obtained). The Maring diet seems to be deficient in sodium. The ingestion of large amounts of sodium just prior to fighting would have permitted the warriors to sweat normally without a lowering of blood volume and consequent weakness during the course of the fighting. The pork belly ingested with the salt would have provided them with a new burst of energy two hours or so after the commencement of the engagement. After fighting was finished for the day, lean pork was consumed, offsetting, at least to some extent, the nitrogen loss associated with the stressful fighting (personal communications from F. Dunn, W. MacFarlane, and J. Sabine, 1965).

Fighting could continue sporadically for weeks. Occasionally it terminated in the rout of one of the antagonistic groups, whose survivors would take refuge with kinsmen elsewhere. In such instances, the victors would lay waste their opponents' groves and gardens, slaughter their pigs, and burn their houses. They would not, however, immediately annex the territory of the vanquished. The Maring say that they never take over the territory of an enemy for, even if it has been abandoned, the spirits of their ancestors remain to guard it against interlopers. Most fights, however, terminated in truces between the antagonists.

With the termination of hostilities a group which has not been driven off its territory performs a ritual called "planting the *rumbim.*" Every man puts his hand on the ritual plant, *rumbim* (*Cordyline fruticosa* (L.), A. Chev; *C. terminalis, Kunth*), as it is planted in the ground. The ancestors are addressed, in effect, as follows:

We thank you for helping us in the fight and permitting us to remain on our territory.We place our souls in this *rumbim* as we plant it on our ground. We ask you to care for this *rumbim*. We will kill pigs for you now, but they are few. In the future, when we have many pigs, we shall again give you pork and uproot the *rumbim* and stage a *kaiko* (pig festival). But until there are sufficient pigs to repay you the *rumbim* will remain in the ground.

This ritual is accompanied by the wholesale slaughter of pigs. Only juveniles remain alive. All adult and adolescent animals are killed, cooked, and dedicated to the ancestors. Some are consumed by the local group, but most are distributed to allies who assisted in the fight.

Some of the taboos which the group suffered during the time of fighting are abrogated by this ritual. Sexual intercourse is now permitted, liquids may be taken at any time, and food from any part of the territory may be eaten. But the group is still in debt to its allies and ancestors. People say it is still the time of the *bamp ku*, or "fighting stones," which are actual objects used in the rituals associated with warfare. Although the fighting ceases when *rumbim* is planted, the concomitant obligations, debts to allies and ancestors, remain outstanding; and the fighting stones may not be put away until these obligations are fulfilled. The time of the fighting stones is a time of debt and danger which lasts until the *rumbim* is uprooted and a pig festival (*kaiko*) is staged.

Certain taboos persist during the time of the fighting stones. Marsupials, regarded as the pigs of the ancestors of the high ground, may not be trapped until the debt to their masters has been repaid. Eels, the "pigs of the ancestors of the low ground," may neither be caught nor consumed. Prohibitions on all intercourse with the enemy come into force. One may not touch, talk to, or even look at a member of the enemy group, nor set foot on enemy ground. Even more important, a group may not attack another group while its ritual plant remains in the ground, for it has not yet fully rewarded its ancestors and allies for their assistance in the last fight. Until the debts to them have been paid, further assistance from them will not be forthcoming. A kind of "truce of god" thus prevails until the *rumbim* is uprooted and a *kaiko* completed.

To uproot the *rumbim* requires sufficient pigs. How many pigs are sufficient, and how long does it take to acquire them? The Tsembaga say that, if a place is "good," this can take as little as five years; but if a place is "bad," it may require ten years or longer. A bad place is one in which misfortunes are frequent and where, therefore, ritual demands for the killing of pigs arise frequently. A good place is one where such demands are infrequent. In a good place, the increase of the pig herd exceeds the ongoing ritual demands, and the herd grows rapidly. Sooner or later the substandard tubers incidentally obtained while harvesting become insufficient to feed the herd, and additional acreage must be put into production specifically for the pigs.

The work involved in caring for a large pig herd can be extremely burdensome. The Tsembaga herd just prior to the pig festival of 1962–63, when it numbered 169 animals, was receiving 54 per cent of all of the sweet potatoes and 82 per cent of all of the manioc harvested. These comprised 35.9 per cent by weight of all root crops harvested. This figure is consistent with the difference between the amount of land under cultivation just previous to the pig festival, when the herd was at maximum size, and that immediately afterwards, when the pig herd was at minimum size. The former was 36.1 per cent in excess of the latter.

I have estimated, on the basis of acreage yield and energy expenditure figures, that about 45,000 calories per year are expended in caring for one pig 120–150 pounds in size. It is upon women that most of the burden of pig keeping falls. If, from a woman's daily intake of about 2,200 calories, 950 calories are allowed for basal metabolism, a woman has only 1,250 calories a day available for all her activities, which include gardening for her family, child care, and cooking, as well as tending pigs. It is clear that no woman can feed many pigs; only a few had as many as four in their care at the commencement of the festival; and it is not surprising that agitation to uproot the *rumbim* and stage the *kaiko* starts with the wives of the owners of large numbers of pigs.

A large herd is not only burdensome as far as energy expenditure is concerned; it becomes increasingly a nuisance as it expands. The more numerous pigs become, the more frequently are gardens invaded by them. Such events result in serious disturbances of local tranquillity. The garden owner often shoots, or attempts to shoot, the offending pig; and the pig owner commonly retorts by shooting, or attempting to shoot, either the garden owner, his wife, or one of his pigs. As more and more such events occur, the settlement, nucleated when the herd was small, disperses as people try to put as much distance as possible between their pigs and other people's gardens and between their gardens and other people's pigs. Occasionally this reaches its logical conclusion, and people begin to leave the territory, taking up residence with kinsmen in other local populations.

The number of pigs sufficient to become intolerable to the Tsembaga was below the capacity of the territory to carry pigs. I have estimated that, if the size and structure of the human population remained constant at the 1962–1963 level, a pig population of 140 to 240 animals averaging 100 to 150 pounds in size could be maintained perpetually by the Tsembaga without necessarily inducing environmental degradation. Since the size of the herd fluctuates, even higher cyclical maxima could be achieved. The level of toleration, however, is likely always to be below the carrying capacity, since the destructive capacity of the pigs is dependent upon the population density of both people and pigs, rather than upon population size. The denser the human population, the fewer pigs will be required to disrupt social life. If the carrying capacity is exceeded, it is likely to be exceeded by people and not by pigs.

The *kaiko* or pig festival, which commences with the planting of stakes at the boundary and the uprooting of the *rumbim*, is thus triggered by either the additional work attendant upon feeding pigs or the destructive capacity of the pigs themselves. It may be said, then, that there are sufficient pigs to stage the *kaiko* when the relationship of pigs to people changes from one of mutualism to one of parasitism or competition.

A short time prior to the uprooting of the *rumbim*, stakes are planted at the boundary. If the enemy has continued to occupy its territory, the stakes are planted at the boundary which existed before the fight. If, on the other hand, the enemy has abandoned its territory, the victors may plant their stakes at a new boundary which encompasses areas previously occupied by the enemy.

The Maring say, to be sure, that they never take land belonging to an enemy, but this land is regarded as vacant, since no *rumbim* was planted on it after the last fight. We may state here a rule of land redistribution in terms of the ritual cycle: *If one of a pair of antagonistic groups is able to uproot its rumbim before its opponents can plant their rumbim, it may occupy the latter's territory.*

Not only have the vanquished abandoned their territory; it is assumed that it has also been abandoned by their ancestors as well. The surviving members of the erstwhile enemy group have by this time resided with other groups for a number of years, and most if not all of them have already had occasion to sacrifice pigs to their ancestors at their new residences. In so doing they have invited these spirits to settle at the new locations of the living, where they will in the future receive sacrifices. Ancestors of vanquished groups thus relinquish their guardianship over the territory, making it available to victorious groups. Meanwhile, the *de facto* membership of the living in the groups with which they have taken refuge is converted eventually into *de jure* membership. Sooner or later the groups with which they have taken up residence will have occasion to plant *rumbim*, and the refugees, as co-residents, will participate, thus ritually validating their connection to the new territory and the new group. A rule of population redistribution may thus be stated in terms of ritual cycles: *A man becomes a member of a territorial group by participating with it in the planting of rumbim.*

The uprooting of the *rumbim* follows shortly after the planting of stakes at the boundary. On this particular occasion the Tsembaga killed 32 pigs out of their herd of 169. Much of the pork was distributed to allies and affines outside of the local group.

The taboo on trapping marsupials was also terminated at this time. Information is lacking concerning the population dynamics of the local marsupials, but it may well be that the taboo which had prevailed since the last fight— that against taking them in traps—had conserved a fauna which might otherwise have become extinct.

The *kaiko* continues for about a year, during which period friendly groups are entertained from time to time. The guests receive presents of vegetable foods, and the hosts and male guests dance together throughout the night.

These events may be regarded as analogous to aspects of the social behavior of many nonhuman animals. First of all, they include massed epigamic, or courtship, displays (Wynne-Edwards 1962: 17). Young women are presented with samples of the eligible males of local groups with which they may not otherwise have had the opportunity to become familiar. The context, moreover, permits the young women to discriminate amongst this sample in terms of both endurance (signaled by how vigorously and how long a man dances) and wealth (signaled by the richness of a man's shell and feather finery).

More importantly, the massed dancing at these events may be regarded as epideictic display, communicating to the participants information concerning the size or density of the group (Wynne-Edwards 1962: 16). In many species such displays take place as a prelude to actions which adjust group size or density, and such is the case among the Maring. The massed dancing of the visitors at a *kaiko* entertainment communicates to the hosts, while the *rumbim* truce is still in force, information concerning the amount of support they may expect from the visitors in the bellicose enterprises that they are likely to embark upon soon after the termination of the pig festival.

Among the Maring there are no chiefs or other political authorities capable of commanding the support of a body of followers, and the decision to assist another group in warfare rests with each individual male. Allies are not recruited by appealing for help to other local groups as such. Rather, each member of the groups primarily involved in the hostilities appeals to his cognatic and affinal kinsmen in other local groups. These men, in turn, urge other of their co-residents and kinsmen to "help them fight." The channels through which invitations to dance are extended are precisely those through which appeals for military support are issued. The invitations go not from group to group, but from kinsman to kinsman, the recipients of invitations urging their co-residents to "help them dance."

Invitations to dance do more than exercise the channels through which allies are recruited; they provide a means for judging their effectiveness. Dancing and fighting are regarded as in some sense equivalent. This equivalence is expressed in the similarity of some pre-fight and pre-dance rituals, and the Maring say that those who come to dance come to fight. The size of a visiting dancing contingent is consequently taken as a measure of the size of the contingent of warriors whose assistance may be expected in the next round of warfare.

In the morning the dancing ground turns into a trading ground. The items most frequently exchanged include axes, bird plumes, shell ornaments, an occasional baby pig, and, in former times, native salt. The *kaiko* thus facilitates trade by providing a market-like setting in which large numbers of traders can assemble. It likewise facilitates the movement of two critical items, salt and axes, by creating a demand for the bird plumes which may be exchanged for them.

The *kaiko* concludes with major pig sacrifices. On this particular occasion the Tsembaga butchered 105 adult and adolescent pigs, leaving only 60 juveniles and neonates alive. The survival of an additional fifteen adolescents and adults was only temporary, for they were scheduled as imminent victims. The pork yielded by the Tsembaga slaughter was estimated to weigh between 7,000 and 8,500 pounds, of which between 4,500 and 6,000 pounds were distributed to members of other local groups in 163 separate presentations. An estimated 2,000 to 3,000 people in seventeen local groups were the beneficiaries of the redistribution. The presentations, it should be mentioned, were not confined to pork. Sixteen Tsembaga men presented bridewealth or childwealth, consisting largely of axes and shells, to their affines at this time.

The *kaiko* terminates on the day of the pig slaughter with the public presentation of salted pig belly to allies of the last fight. Presentations are made through the window in a high ceremonial fence built specially for the occasion at one end of the dance ground. The name of each honored man is announced to the assembled multitude as he charges to the window to receive his hero's portion. The fence is then ritually torn down, and the fighting stones are put away. The pig festival and the ritual cycle have been completed, demonstrating, it may be suggested, the ecological and economic competence of the local population. The local population would now be free, if it were not for the presence of the government, to attack its enemy again, secure in the knowledge that the assistance of allies and ancestors would be forthcoming because they have received pork and the obligations to them have been fulfilled.

Usually fighting did break out again very soon after the completion of the ritual cycle. If peace still prevailed when the ceremonial fence had rotted completely—a process said to take about three years, a little longer than the length of time required to raise a pig to maximum size—*rumbim* was planted as if there had been a fight, and all adult and adolescent pigs were killed. When the pig herd was large enough so that the *rumbim* could be uprooted, peace could be made with former enemies if they were also able to dig out their *rumbim*. To put this in formal terms: *If a pair of antagonistic groups proceeds through two ritual cycles without resumption of hostilities their enmity may be terminated.*

The relations of the Tsembaga with their environment have been analyzed as a complex system composed of two subsystems. What may be called the "local subsystem" has been derived from the relations of the Tsembaga with the nonhuman components of their immediate or territorial environment. It corresponds to the ecosystem in which the Tsembaga participate. A second subsystem, one which corresponds to the larger regional population of which the Tsembaga are one of the constituent units and which may be designated as the "regional subsystem," has been derived from the relations of the Tsembaga with neighboring local populations similar to themselves.

It has been argued that rituals, arranged in repetitive sequences, regulate relations both within each of the subsystems and within the larger complex system as a whole. The timing of the ritual cycle is largely dependent upon changes in the states of the components of the local subsystem. But the *kaiko*, which is the culmination of the ritual cycle, does more than reverse changes which have taken place within the local subsystem. Its occurrence also affects relations among the components of the regional subsystem. During its performance, obligations to other local populations are fulfilled, support for future military enterprises is rallied, and land from which enemies have earlier been driven is occupied. Its completion, furthermore, permits the local population to initiate warfare again. Conversely, warfare is terminated by rituals which preclude the reinitiation of warfare until the state of the local subsystem is again such that a *kaiko* may be staged and completed. Ritual among the Tsembaga and other Maring, in short, operates as both transducer, "translating" changes in the state of one subsystem into information which can effect changes in a second subsystem, and homeostat, maintaining a number of variables which in sum comprise the total system within ranges of viability. To repeat an earlier assertion, the operation of ritual among the Tsembaga and other Maring helps to maintain an undegraded environment, limits fighting to frequencies which do not endanger the existence of the regional population, adjusts man-land ratios, facilitates trade, distributes local surpluses of pig throughout the regional population in the form of pork, and assures people of high quality protein when they are most in need of it.

Religious rituals and the supernatural orders toward which they are directed cannot be assumed *a priori* to be mere epiphenomena. Ritual may, and doubtless frequently does, do nothing more than validate and intensify the relationships which integrate the social unit, or symbolize the relationships which bind the social unit to its environment. But the interpretation of such presumably *sapiens*-specific phenomena as religious ritual within a framework which will also accommodate the behavior of other species shows, I think, that religious ritual may do much more than symbolize, validate, and intensify relationships. Indeed, it would not be improper to refer to the Tsembaga and the other entities with which they share their territory as a "ritually regulated ecosystem," and to the Tsembaga and their human neighbors as a "ritually regulated population."

Bibliography

BERG, C. 1948. Protein Deficiency and Its Relation to Nutritional Anemia, Hypoproteinemia, Nutritional Edema, and Resistance to Infection. Protein and Amino Acids in Nutrition, ed. M. Sahyun, pp. 290–317. New York.

BURTON, B. T., ed. 1959. The Heinz Handbook of Nutrition. New York.

ELMAN, R. 1951. Surgical Care. New York.

Food and Agriculture Organization of the United Nations. 1964. Protein: At the Heart of the World Food Problem. World Food Problems 5. Rome.

HIPSLEY, E., and N. KIRK. 1965. Studies of the Dietary Intake and Energy Expenditure of New Guineans. South Pacific Commission, Technical Paper 147. Noumea.

HOMANS, G. C. 1941. Anxiety and Ritual: The Theories of Malinowski and Radcliffe-Brown. American Anthropologist 43:164–172.

HOUSSAY, B. A., et al. 1955. Human Physiology. 2nd edit. New York.

LARGE, A., and C. G. JOHNSTON. 1948. Proteins as Related to Burns. Proteins and Amino Acids in Nutrition, ed. M. Sahyun, pp. 386–396. New York.

LUND, C. G., and S. M. LEVENSON. 1948. Protein Nutrition in Surgical Patients. Proteins and Amino Acids in Nutrition, ed. H. Sahyun, pp. 349–363. New York.

MOORE, O. K. 1957. Divination—A New Perspective. American Anthropologist 59: 69–74.

National Research Council. 1963. Evaluation of Protein Quality. National Academy of Sciences—National Research Council Publication 1100. Washington.

RAPPAPORT, R. A. 1966. Ritual in the Ecology of a New Guinea People. Unpublished doctoral dissertation, Columbia University.

VAYDA, A. P., A. LEEDS, and D. B. SMITH. 1961. The Place of Pigs in Melanesian Subsistence. Proceedings of the 1961 Annual Spring Meeting of the American Ethnological Society, ed. V. E. Garfield, pp. 69–77. Seattle.

Wayne-Edwards, V. C. 1962. Animal Dispersion in Relation to Social Behaviour. Edinburgh and London.

Zintel, Harold A. 1964. Nutrition in the Care of the Surgical Patient. Modern Nutrition in Health and Disease, ed. M. G. Wohl and R. S. Goodhart, pp. 1043–1064. Third edit. Philadelphia.

Weston LaBarre

Taking up Serpents

It is a hot night toward the end of July in a southern textile-mill town. In the middleclass part of town people sit on their porches drinking cokes or iced lemonade, quietly sweating and fanning themselves in a desultory fashion in the breathless air. From time to time someone remarks again, unhopefully, about the one topic—the relentless heat and the length of time the tobacco land has been without rain. A block away a jalopy full of highschool children careens around a corner, going nowhere much too fast in the hot night. Except for such occasional louder noises there are only the low murmur of voices from the darkened porches up and down the street, the slow rasp somewhere of a porch swing, the unreasonably cheerful steady orchestra of crickets, and the intermittent angrier protests of a cicada. Westward—must be several counties out toward the mountains—there is soundless heat lightning, but that is sure enough too far away to do this dry Piedmont section any good.

But down by the tracks of the Southern Railroad there are other signs of human life. On the corner diagonally across from the back end of the Sears Roebuck store, across the street from the Discount House, and down a bit from the Alcoholics Anonymous place, is the Zion Tabernacle. This is a plain one-room frame building, from which comes the warm-up singing of a church service just starting. The Tabernacle is a block behind Main Street, on the last street south before the railroad tracks, beyond which stretches "Haiti" (pronounced *Haý-tye*), the local Negro section. Eastward are warehouses, lumberyards, and nondescript businesses, and beyond that the white laboring-class section of town.

Many of the church members are already clapping, humming, and singing to guitar music. Most of them are whites who work in the cotton mill, in the tobacco plant, or for the Wright Machinery Company. The majority of the men wear their shirt sleeves folded loosely once upward above the wrist, but some wear shortsleeved sports shirts with their cheap cotton pants. The women have on standard ready-to-wear store dresses, of vivid cotton print or a quieter single color. Not counting the babies, the people present range from about seven to eighty years of age; children too old to be carried and those under seven have been left elsewhere, lest they be too great a bother to adults intent on their own emotional interests.

The minister begins his talk by stating that his first allegiance is to God. Holding up a white handkerchief striped with red and blue, he tells the following story: "I was on my way to visit a sick boy in Greensboro, and I was in such a hurry that I forgot my handkerchief. Because I felt that I would need one, I stopped along the way to buy it. When I reached my destination, Hettie, the Negro who usually prays with us—I like Hettie, don't you?—well, Hettie, she handed me a handkerchief. Now wasn't that phenomenal that Hettie should have thought that I needed a handkerchief? The other day when I took this handkerchief from my drawer, do you know what it reminded me of? Of this country; it's not what it used to be. More and more it's clamping down on religious freedom."

The minister continues: he thinks all people should have the right to worship as they wish. He plans to get as many names as possible in order to petition the state government to pass a religious freedom law. He would even go to the local Methodist divinity school and ask the students to sign this petition. One of these days, the fact that he had been denied religious freedom would be written up in the library at the state capitol. In years to come, people will be able to look back and see where religious rights were first being denied. He is glad that he lives in this country—it's still a nice place to live—but he owes his allegiance to no one nation, only to God.

The guitar-playing begins again, with the minister loudly leading the others into song. The verses are about the nature of heaven, "of a heaven where white, black, yellow, and brown can live and be happy together." At the end of the song, the minister adds that God loves all his children, no matter what color they are. The topic changes to his current problems with the police and a threatened jail sentence. He tells of the troubles his people are having in Tennessee and in Virginia, across the border in Georgia, and in North Carolina where they arrested a minister the previous winter. He speaks of two "brethern" up there who are already in jail for their religious beliefs. Some churches send their missionaries to foreign countries, but he is proud that his brethren would carry their mission to the prisoners. People may think that these incidents will divide the group, but instead it is bringing them closer and closer together.

The minister asks one of the men sitting on the platform to read from the Bible a passage ending, "And the man of righteousness will come with healing on his wings." The minister expands on the topic. Then two testimonies are announced, to be given by visitors from Chattahoochee. One, a pleasant-looking man of about thirty-five, says that he had had nervousness and trouble with his sleeping. But ever since last Sunday when the Reverend had prayed for him, all his troubles have disappeared. After him, his brother, in a high-pitched woman's voice, reports that he had had a cancer in his stomach and had hardly been eating anything. Since last Sunday, when the preacher blessed him and prayed for him, he has been able to eat everything and has had no pain. If no one believes that, he says, they can ask Dr. Lassiter in Tallahassee or they can call Stone General Hospital.

The preacher takes over again, saying that several people who had heard about him through the widespread publicity he had been receiving in the local papers have been writing him about his healing powers. He continues, speaking rapidly. "Every man carries his death wish with him, but if we have faith in God, we can prolong that Death. I have one sister in a sanitorium, two sisters under the grave, a father who died of a goiter on his neck, and when I was young I had TB. But look at me now! Glory be to God! Praise God! I don't believe the day will come when all men can be healed, because all men don't have faith. But I do believe that one of these days my hands will be able to heal. Maybe I won't be able to heal everyone. I can't heal people if they don't have faith. Even Jesus could not heal everyone. Faith is necessary! Glory be to God."

The next song is again about the life in heaven. About a fourth of those present join in with the words; others clap their hands and hum. The children especially seem to enjoy themselves, clapping and singing along very happily. The preacher says, "I once heard that I had to wait until I got to heaven until I had a happy life, but I can't wait that long! Heaven can be right now on this earth. I can live a happy life right now! Praise be to God." His manner of speaking is odd:* there are exaggerated intonations in the narrative, with unexpected rises and falls; but when he comes to phrases like "Praise the Lord," which one might expect would be uttered with some emphasis or emotion, he says these flatly, like punctuation, or like a hasty tic as he draws breath between sentences. The congregation puts far more feeling into these same phrases when they utter them.

More singing. The guitar music and singing gradually become louder. One man standing beside the woman guitarist shouts and sings even more loudly than the others present. Between fifteen and twenty women begin to have shaking reactions; it is hard to tell how many there are because the violence

---

* Olmsted has characterized with elegance and discretion the "old timey" style of preaching. "Without often being violent in his manner, the speaker nearly all the time cried aloud at the utmost stretch of his voice, as if calling to some one a long distance off . . . The speaker, presently, was crying aloud, with a mournful, distressed, beseeching shriek, as if he was himself suffering torture . . . Those who refused to kneel, were addressed as standing on the brink of the infernal pit, into which the diabolical divinity was momentarily on the point of satisfying the necessities of his character by hurling them off . . . I can only judge from the fact that those I saw the next morning were so hoarse that they could scarcely speak, that the religious exercises they most enjoy are rather hard upon the lungs, whatever their effect may be upon the soul" (Frederick L. Olmsted, "A Journey in the Seaboard Slave States in the Years 1853–54" [2 vols., New York: Putnam] in H. Becker [ed.], *Societies Around the World*, New York: Holt, 1956, 555–567, pp. 561–562).

of the shaking differs in degree. At least ten women are jerking their heads and bodies around wildly. Of these, several stand up from the benches where most of the women sit. Several of them perform a vivacious dance which looks something like jitterbugging in the fast movements, but with more rapid and extreme jerkings of the body. Others stand with their heads and bodies shaking, their heads forward and their necks jerking. Two men also begin dancing around, one of them a very small and meek-looking man who drives a laundry truck on a route on the west side of town.

Suddenly the minister begins to speak in unknown tongues. Others answer him in the same style. This language is quite unlike the tobacco auctioneers' chant, which has a singing change of pitch especially at the beginning and end of the monotone rapid nonsense syllables. Speaking in tongues is better described as a loud chattering at breakneck speed. The dancing continues, now both on the platform and below it. In many the shaking reaction and other bodily movements seem beyond the control of the trance-eyed individuals experiencing them; most of the women in this state have their eyes closed and their mouths open, even when not vocalizing. One woman who appears especially dazed, though no longer jerking, is hardly able to find her way back to her seat.

The music having quieted down, a woman who had been shaking and dancing rises and says, "Praise the Lord! All these people here don't know what it is like to love the Lord, but there is nothing like it! If you love the Lord, you love everybody: blacks, whites, yellows, and even your enemies. I wish I could show you how to love the Lord, but it is something you'll have to find out for yourselves." As the service grows somewhat quieter, the preacher assures everyone of the importance of praying to God in a way meaningful to the individual.

He continues, saying that he had planned to bring a snake tonight, but had decided not to because the snake looked sick. He could bring only one at a time now so that the police would not get all their snakes. Next week he planned to go to the mountains for some new ones. He then asks if there is anyone who wants to handle snakes tonight. Only one woman lifts a hand. "See!" he continues, "We can have a good time without snakes. Someone once asked me if we worshiped the snake. No! We surely do not! The snake represents evil, the Devil. We just show that God, good, has power over the Devil. You know, I don't advise anyone to handle snakes! In fact, no one should unless he has the feeling and faith that makes him want to do so."

The preacher requests the guitarist to sing the "Sampson song." It is in lively ballad form and tells the story of Samson and Delilah. At the end of the song, the preacher tells a story about a young boy who revealed to his mother that because Samson had laid his head in Delilah's lap, he had lost all his power. "The mother thought that her son had told her an evil story, but it wasn't! The head is the part of the body that has made man a higher animal. We shouldn't trust our head in anyone's lap but God's! Glory be to God!" He then talks about marriage laws. He had once written the state attorney general asking him if, as a preacher, he could perform his own marriage. "The attorney general didn't think so, but I sure did. No, I didn't get married then —won't tell you why! But I still think that a man has the right to conduct his own marriage service!"

More music and song. An attractive woman leaves her seat to go to the center of the tabernacle where she kneels and prays. After a few minutes the minister says, "You should pray to God any way that you like. If you still don't feel free, pray any way that you can, until you do. It doesn't matter where we kneel. The trouble with most of us is that we don't pray enough when we're alone, but if anyone has the desire to kneel and pray now, go right ahead!"

Several other women follow the first one to the front of the church where they all pray together. The preacher leaves the platform to come among his listeners. "I want to shake everyone's hand! Everyone stand! I want to be friends with you all. If you feel that you have the need to pass on to the front and pray, you go right ahead! But if you just want me to pray for you, come and shake my hand!" Many people come forth, stretching to the center aisle to shake his hand. About twenty women have now joined the first kneeling woman, many of them sobbing and crying out, a few shaking. The song and music end. Gradually the women straggle back to their seats. One boy about fifteen, who had also knelt to pray and had apparently been crying, gets up and stands close to the preacher. Slowly everyone leaves, with much enthusiastic conversation, and the service is ended.

This is not like it was last month, before snake-handling was forbidden by the town authorities. Surely troubled times have fallen upon the people, for now they cannot practice the religion they believe the Bible enjoins upon them. At that earlier time, when the observer entered the tabernacle there was already a mood of general excitement. Several people were fondling rattle-snakes and copperheads with apparent confidence. One deacon of the church twisted a snake around his head and arm and held the snake's head close to or just brushing his mouth. About twenty or thirty people were shaking violently. Many were dancing around, either alone or with others, some with persons of the same sex and others with persons of the opposite sex. Some were sobbing, shouting, and singing. A visiting minister did most of the preaching. He spoke dramatically, stressing the more spectacular aspects of the religion, such as faith cures and snake-handling. He loudly proclaimed that he believed every word in the Bible to be true. His sermon led into a healing ceremony which he, the local minister, and one of the latter's followers conducted in a somewhat unorganized manner.

As many men and women—but mostly women—came forward, the preachers and the other man grasped the heads of these communicants between the palms of their hands, repeated jumbled and at times incoherent words to them, and supported those who fell stiffly into their arms. With several women the local minister spent considerable time on the healing process. One young woman asked him to bless her foot, which had been giving her much trouble and pain. He asked her to remove her shoe. Then, while he held her foot in his hands and looked straight into her eyes, he encouraged her to have faith that her foot would be cured. He repeated his plea many times, emphasizing the importance of faith in the powers of God and in the many miracles that God could perform. After this, another woman, with a child in her arms, asked the preacher to bless and cure the child. Before he began, he asked the father to come forward, but only the mother was present. He then told her the importance of caring for the child and of showing the child the ways of the Lord. He pleaded with the mother to have faith in God and to do everything in her power to help her child get well. "With faith will come help," he said to her in a gentle and quiet but impressive voice.

Throughout the service the level of excitement was extremely high. The deacon's mother-in-law shouted, "This is the kind of thing we need more of!" A young woman in a dark suit-dress lay slightly twisted on her back upon the floor, the thumb of her half-opened right hand at her mouth, the left hand clasped at her turned-aside neck. The local preacher placed his left hand on her forehead, his right hand on her pubic region. Another woman lay flat on her back while he knelt on one knee and apparently massaged her throat. Still another, lying on her left side, he stroked on the shoulder with his left hand while he grasped the outside of her right thigh with his right hand. A plump girl in a black dress with a rhinestoned white collar, her eyes closed and mouth open in an expression half painful and half ecstatic, he held by both hands for a while; then she slid to the floor, her pelvis twisted downward, while the preacher held her right hand up in his left one and pressed her armpit with his right hand.

At one time there was a cluster of four middleaged men, two clasped in each other's arms, each weeping on the other's shoulder, while two other men stood, one behind and the other half behind, their left hands one atop the other on the shoulder of one of the embracing men. During part of the healing ceremony a young woman collapsed into the preacher's arms, where she remained stiff for several minutes. As she was coming out of her trance, the preacher began to speak of the wonders of a religion in which such phenomena could take place without their being the least intention of carnal desires. At least four men and four women handled snakes in this meeting. This time a young man accordionist supplied the musical accompaniment.

The service ended with shouting after the healing ceremony ceased.

Richard E. Schultes

Man and Marijuana

Strange things often happen to plants after a long and intimate association with man: they travel around the world; they grow in unusual and sometimes inhospitable soils and environments; and they often hybridize. They may escape cultivation and become weeds, or they may be altered by selection for characteristics associated with specific uses. These interacting forces frequently result in an organism greatly changed from its wild progenitor. To unravel and understand such changes, the biology and economic history of these plants must be considered together. Consequently, the investigation of the biological evolution of a cultivated plant and the evolution of its uses cannot be divorced from a study of the natural forces that may have shaped its new and perhaps unnatural role.

A prime example of this interplay between man and his useful plants is the relationship between man and *Cannabis*, known in the United States, according to its use, as hemp or marijuana. Marijuana has been around for thousands of years and has earned deep respect in many different societies. Botanists have usually considered *Cannabis* a single species, *C. sativa*, but recent research indicates that there may well be several species. The present biological variability of the genus may be traced in part to the complicated history of its various uses.

Cannabis has long been cultivated for five principal purposes: for hempen fibers; for its oil; for its achenes, or "seeds," which man has consumed as a food; for its narcotic properties; and as a therapeutic agent in folk medicine and modern pharmacopoeias.

Despite its long history as one of the major crop plants and its utilization by millions of people in many parts of the world, *Cannabis* is still characterized more by what is not known about its biology than by what is known. This lack of knowledge creates serious obstacles to an understanding of the moral, social, and legal aspects of its contemporary use or abuse and is the basis of many contradictions in the botanical, chemical, medical, and pharmaceutical literature.

There is no way of knowing which use of *Cannabis* represents the earliest. Plant uses normally proceed from the simpler to the more complex. Early man could hardly have missed seeing fibers exposed in naturally retted stems, and the production of hemp goes far back in the archeological record. *Cannabis* is

Reprinted from Richard E. Schultes, "Man and Marijuana," Natural History (August–September 1973), 58–63, with permission of Natural History Magazine. Copyright © The American Museum of Natural History, 1973.

probably man's oldest cultivated source of fiber and the first to have spread so widely. Remains of hempen fibers have been found in several of the earliest centers of civilization.

Curious stone beaters and crude tools for pounding hemp, as well as pottery in which impressions of cords were baked, have been discovered at an ancient riverside fishing site in Taiwan. There is evidence from several localities in China and Chinese Turkestan that nearly 5,000 years ago Neolithic man made thread and rope from hemp. In fact, the oldest known name of *Cannabis* is the Chinese *ta-ma*, which originally meant hemp. The character for the word represents plants growing near a house and would seem to indicate that the earliest and most important use of hemp in China was as a source of fiber. The Chinese believe that the legendary emperor Shen Nung, patron of medicine and inventor of agriculture, first taught cultivation of hemp in the twenty-eighth century B.C. Hempen fabrics have been excavated from sites in Turkey dated to the late eighth century B.C., older than the Taiwan finds, and an Egyptian tomb of between 3,000 and 4,000 years of age has yielded specimens of fabric thought to be hemp.

Ancient sites in the Altai Mountains of central Asia have provided remains of clothing made of hempen fibers. In 500 B.C. the Greek historian Herodotus stated that the Scythians, who originated in this mountainous area, grew hemp for its fiber and that the Thracians made garments of hemp that closely resembled linen.

Cannabis arrived as a fiber plant in Europe from the north, not from the south. The Greeks and Romans of classical times did not cultivate it, although it had arrived in Europe from Asiatic regions to the east before the Christian era. Fiber for ropes and sails was apparently imported into Sicily from Gaul as early as the third century B.C., and the Roman writer Lucilius mentioned the plant in 120 B.C. There is little evidence that *Cannabis* was cultivated as a major crop in western Europe before the Christian era. In the first century A.D., the Roman historian Pliny the Elder detailed the preparation and grades of hempen fibers, and hempen rope has been recovered in England from the site of a Roman fort dated A.D. 140–180, suggesting its introduction by the Romans from Gaul. Pollen studies have shown that there was a continuously increasing cultivation of hemp in England from the early Anglo-Saxon period into late Saxon and Norman times, from about 400 to 1100. Whether Viking sailors used hemp is not certain, but hempen fabrics and fishing lines have been retrieved from Viking graves in Norway, and the plant was grown in Iceland in the early Middle Ages.

In medieval England Henry VIII required English farmers to plant hemp, and in Elizabethan times England's maritime supremacy created such demand for the fiber that it was always in short supply, thus encouraging the cultivation of *Cannibis* in the New World. It was first introduced to North America apparently at Port Royal, Canada, in 1606. In Virginia the first crop of hemp was planted in 1611, and the Pilgrims brought it to Plymouth in 1632. Hemp was exported to England by the colonies, and in pre-Revolutionary America the fiber was used in making clothing.

There were undoubtedly a number of independent introductions of hemp into the Spanish and Portuguese colonies of the New World. *Cannibis* was known in Chili as early as 1545, and seeds were sent from Spain to Peru in 1554, but it never became a major crop.

The fiber became increasingly important in the United States. Extensive hemp plantations, centered around Kentucky, enjoyed prosperity until the middle of the last century, when disruption during the Civil War and rising labor costs killed the industry. By the 1870s, little hemp was being commercially produced in this country, but *Cannabis* seeds had spread from the abandoned plantations. The plant is now found as a weed mainly in the north-central area and the Middle Atlantic and New England states. Today hempen fiber is produced mainly in Russia and Poland, although the finest quality comes from Spain and Italy.

While the production of hemp represents one of the earliest uses of *Cannabis*, it is possible that consumption of the roasted achenes for food occurred even earlier. The ripened achenes are extremely nutritious and have undoubtedly been ingested as a fat-rich food by many peoples, especially in times of famine.

Archeologists have found hemp achenes in a receptacle excavated near Berlin, Germany, dated, with some reservation, at about 500 B.C. Since the mature achenes are devoid of the intoxicating principles, this find would seem to suggest their use as a food or their burial as a source of nourishment for the dead.

Sometimes eaten in eastern Europe, hemp is today cultivated for its seeds, especially in the Ukraine and Manchuria. In the United States hemp seeds are valued as a feed ingredient for birds and poultry.

It is as a substitute for linseed oil in the paint and varnish industry, in soap making, and as a lubricant that hemp seed oil has been chiefly used. The achenes contain from 19 to 35 percent of a drying oil, a greenish yellow fluid, which is also used for emulsions in pharmacy. In many areas of Russia peasants burn hemp oil in lamps to light their homes, but there is little evidence that oil production represents an early or widespread folk use of the plant.

Today it is seldom realized that, from the earliest periods of primitive cultures to modern times, hemp has been one of the world's major medicinal plants. Furthermore, many contemporary investigators believe that in the future wholly new therapeutic agents will come from *Cannabis* or from some of its chemical constituents.

The medicinal value of hemp—often, of course, closely related to its psychoactive properties—is perhaps its most significant, and was possibly even its earliest, role in cultural history. The oldest known record of *Cannabis* as a medicine goes back 5,000 years to Shen Nung, who prescribed hemp for malaria, beriberi, constipation, rheumatic pains, absentmindedness, and female disorders; an ancient Chinese physician, Hoa-Gho, recommended a mixture of hemp resin and wine to deaden pain during surgery.

In Indian mythology, hemp was a gift of the gods; its medicinal virtues lowered fevers, fostered sleep, relieved dysentery, and cured sundry other ills; it also stimulated the appetite, prolonged life, quickened the mind, and improved the judgment. In ancient India especially, the true medicinal use of *Cannabis* was closely associated with its magico-religious functions. As in many cultures, narcotics or hallucinogens represented the medicines par excellence, assuming, because of their psychoactive power, a far more important role than the merely physical active medicines. The several systems of Indian medicine valued hemp. The medical work *Sushruta*, for example, recommended hemp as an antiphlegmatic, as a treatment for catarrh accompanied by diarrhea, and even as a cure for leprosy. The *Bhavaprakasha*, written about A.D. 1600, termed the drug antiphlegmatic, digestive, bile affecting, pungent, and astringent and recommended it to arouse the appetite, improve the digestion, and heighten the power of the voice. At one time or other, Indian medicine ascribed curative properties for almost all ills to hemp; it was reputed to control dandruff and relieve headaches, mania, insomnia, gonorrhea, whooping cough, earaches, and consumption. *Cannabis* is still widely used in Indian medicine.

As hemp spread, its fame as a panacea spread with it. When it penetrated Africa, it became in some areas the preferred drug for treating malaria, dysentery, anthrax, and tropical fevers. Across Africa today, the most varied medicinal properties are ascribed to hemp. The Mfengu and Hottentots, for example, value the plant for snakebite; before childbirth Sotho women partially stupefy themselves by smoking the plant.

Even though *Cannabis* was used for a greater variety of medical purposes in India, it was in medieval Europe that it assumed most importance in both folk and "professional" medicine. Many of these European uses vary greatly from the Indian uses and can be traced directly to such early classical physician-writers as Dioscorides and Galen. Medieval herbals usually classified hemp as "hot and dry in the third degree." They distinguish the cultivated ("manured hempe") from the weedy ("bastard hempe") plant.

Little use was apparently made of bastard hempe, except as a remedy "against nodes and wennes and other hard tumours." Manured hempe, on the other hand, had a host of therapeutic applications. Boiled in milk, the achene was thought to alleviate a hot, dry cough. Crushed in white wine, it was held to relieve symptoms of jaundice. Fed to hens, the achenes were credited with increasing egg laying.

The medieval herbalists cautioned, however, that excessive use of hemp might bring on sterility. Parkinson, for example, stated in 1640 that "the seed . . . consumeth wind, and by much use thereof, doth disperse it so much that it dryeth up the naturall seed of procreation," while in 1619, Dodoens asserted that "it drieth up . . . the saede of generation" in men "and the milke of women's breasts."

Although not precisely a therapeutic use, it is worth noting the sixteenth-century report that a decoction of hemp "poured into the holes of earthworms will draw them forth, and that fishermen and anglers have used this feate to get wormes to baite their hooks." This curious use acquires added interest in view of the suggestion that in some Asiatic localities early man may have valued hemp as a fish-stupefying plant, a use that may have led to its domestication.

In spite of the plant's long role in medieval medicine, modern European and American medicine did not become seriously interested in the medicinal potentialities of *Cannabis* until the nineteenth century. During the last half of the century, more than a hundred articles on hemp appeared in medical journals. The principal effects of *Cannabis*, except for minor local irritant activity, concern the higher nerve centers. Consequently, in modern medicine the drug has been employed mainly as an analgesic, as a relief for insomnia, and to calm nervous restlessness. It usually takes the form of a tincture. It has also had limited use in inducing a euphoric condition helpful in reducing the pain of migraine headaches. Recently, hemp preparations have been shown to have antibacterial activity.

Cannabis is a difficult drug to use, since individual doses can be determined only by continued administration in increasing amounts until a desired effect is experienced. The most serious handicap in using hemp is difficulty in standardizing it, that is, the lack of certainty about the potency of the preparations.

At the present time, preparations of *Cannabis* are not available. It was included in the United States Pharmacopoeia and the National Formulary until 1937, but has been dropped from these American, as well as from most European, lists of official drugs.

Hemp's value in folk medicine was obviously associated closely with discovery of its euphoric and hallucinogenic properties, and knowledge of the narcotic effects of *Cannabis* may date almost as far back as its discovery as a fiber. Beset by hunger, early man experimented with all plant materials that he could chew. He could not have avoided discovering the intoxicating properties of *Cannabis*, for in his quest for the nutritious seeds and oil, he certainly ate the sticky tops of the plant, the most narcotic part. The euphoric, ecstatic, and hallucinatory aspects of the intoxication may have introduced him to an otherworldly plane from which emerged religious beliefs, perhaps even the concept of deity. The plant became accepted as a special gift of the gods, a sacred medium for communion with the spiritual world. And such it has remained in some cultures to the present.

While today *Cannabis* represents one of the most widely disseminated hallucinogens, its use as a narcotic, except in localized parts of Asia, seems to be relatively recent. As early as 5,000 years ago, Shen Nung, recommending hemp as a medicine, recognized its narcotic properties. One of its Chinese names meant "liberator of sin," indicating early condemnation of its use as an intoxicant. Eventually, however, its euphoric effects were accepted in China, as evidenced by a later name meaning "delight giver." A fourth-century report asserts that eating hemp causes the user to see spirits, and several hundred years later the Chinese were taking *Cannabis* for "the enjoyment of life."

The barbarian hordes of central Asia who lived west of China knew of the intoxicating properties of hemp. It was undoubtedly these nomadic tribes that spread the narcotic use of the plant. Among these people were the Scythians, who wandered widely in central Asia and southeast Europe, from the Altai Mountains to the Black Sea. There is evidence that they had a profound cultural influence on early Greece and eastern Europe.

Five hundred years before Christ, Herodotus described the Scythian use of *Cannabis*: "They make a booth by fixing in the ground three sticks inclined towards one another, and stretching around them woollen felts which they arrange so as to fit as close as possible: inside the booth a dish is placed upon the ground into which they put a number of red hot stones and then add some hemp seed . . . immediately it smokes, and gives out such a vapour as no Grecian vapour-bath can exceed; the Scyths, delighted, shout for joy. . . ."

Recent archeological finds in the Altai Mountains have validated this curious report. Frozen Scythian tombs dated 500 to 300 B.C. have yielded a miniature, tripodlike tent over a copper censer—a contrivance for the inhalation of *Cannabis* vapors. Hempen clothing and the remains of *Cannabis* achenes were also found at the site.

All classes of Hindus now consume *Cannabis* in such preparations as bhang, a decoction made from powdered hemp fermented in milk or water, and ganja, the form in which it is usually smoked. But the plant may not have been widely used as a narcotic until a relatively late date in India. Indian society, as can be adduced from oral folklore, often condemned the secular use of hemp. There are references stating that one's learning is diminished with the use of *Cannabis* and that he who smokes ganja forgets even his own father's name.

Hemp was one of the most sacred plants in India. Knowledge of its psycho-active effects seem to go far back in history, as suggested by the deep mytho-logical and spiritual beliefs about the plant. In ancient India, bhang was so sacred that it was reputed to deter evil, bring luck, and cleanse the user of sin. Harm and disaster visited those who trod upon the holy leaves of the hemp plant, and the most sacred oaths were taken on the hemp leaf.

The favorite drink of Indra, god of the firmament, was prepared from *Cannabis*. The Hindu god Siva taught that the word *bhangi* must be chanted prayerfully over and over at the time of sowing, weeding, watering, and harvesting the holy plant.

Thirty-five hundred years ago, the *Rig Veda* extolled the spiritual use of the narcotic god-plant soma, the identity of which has remained a deep mystery until recently. There was some suspicion that soma could be *Cannabis*, but recent studies by R. Gordon Wasson have identified it as the hallucinogenic mushroom *Amanita muscaria*.

Folklore holds that during the reign of Khusru (A.D. 531–79) the narcotic use of hemp was introduced to Persia by a pilgrim from India. The Assyrians, however, did employ hemp as an incense in the first millennium B.C., an indication that they may have used the drug for intoxication.

Knowledge and use of the inebriating properties eventually spread across Asia Minor. One of the enigmas of historical botany in this part of the world lies in the apparent absence of any direct mention of *Cannabis* or its products in the Bible. There are, however, several obscure passages in the Old Testament that have been interpreted as possible references to the intoxicating effects of hashish, the pressed, pure resin from the flowering tops of female plants.

Although at first prohibited among Islamic peoples, hashish spread widely. In 1378, the Emir Soudaun Sheikhouni tried to extirpate the plant from Arabian territory and imposed harsh punishments for the eating of hemp, but his efforts were in vain. As early as 1271, the use of hashish was so well known that Marco Polo described its consumption among the secret order of Hashashins, who used the narcotic to experience the rewards in store for them in the afterlife. Under the leadership of Hasan-Ibn-Sabbah, a Persian nobleman, this group of fanatics was dedicated—even to the point of committing murder—to the spread of an agnostic religious philosophy. Some philologists believe that the word *assassin* came into European languages from the Arabic *hashashin*, "eaters of hashish."

Although *Cannabis* was recommended as a medicine in classical Greece and Rome, its purposeful use as an intoxicant was apparently rare. By the first century A.D., however, the Romans customarily ate cakes containing hemp, which, according to Galen, were taken to promote hilarity but which, in excess, produced torpor.

Cannabis extended widely into Africa, partly under the pressures of Islamic influence. But the use of hemp far transcends Mohammedan areas and is found in primitive native cultures in such ingrained social and religious contexts that its arrival clearly predated that of Islam. In the Zambezi Valley, for example, there was an ancient tribal ceremony in which the participants inhaled the vapors from a pile of smoldering hemp; later, reed tubes and a variety of pipes were used, and the plant material was burned on an altar. The Kasai tribes of the Congo have revived the Riamba cult, a sect in which hemp, replacing ancient fetishes and symbols, became a god, a protector against physical and spiritual harm. Treaties and business transactions are sealed with puffs of smoke from a yard-long calabash pipe. In many parts of East Africa, especially near Lake Victoria, hemp-smoking and hashish-snuffing cults exist, and the plant is cultivated on a grand scale for its narcotic use. In southern Africa, the Hottentots, Bushmen, and Kaffirs customarily inhale the smoke of *Cannabis*, either burned free on the ground or in special pipes of horn and calabash.

Hemp has spread to many areas of the New World inhabited by large aboriginal groups, but the plant seems not to have penetrated significantly into native American religious life and beliefs. This may be because of the great number of native hallucinogens already firmly established in their magico-religious practices.

Modern use of *Cannabis* in the United States began in Texas about sixty years ago, when Mexican laborers introduced the smoking of marijuana. It spread across the south, and by the 1920s it was firmly established in New Orleans. In those early years, its use was confined mainly to the poor, especially to minority groups. The spread of the custom has resulted in a still unresolved controversy, despite the enactment, in 1937, of the Marijuana Tax Act, which made it illegal to grow or possess *C. sativa*.

What lies ahead for the man—hemp association? Certainly, the relationship will continue. There can be no doubt that a plant that has been in partnership with man since the beginnings of agricultural efforts, that has served man in so many ways, and that, under the searchlight of modern chemical study, has yielded many new and interesting compounds will continue to be a part of man's economy. It would be a luxury that we could ill afford if we allowed prejudices, resulting from the abuse of *Cannabis*, to deter scientists from learning as much as possible about this ancient and mysterious plant.

Joan Ablon

The Samoan Funeral in Urban America [1]

Culturally prescribed rituals relating to death function in significant ways to serve the living. Mandelbaum (1959:215) has noted that "Rituals for death can have many uses for life. And the study of these rites can illuminate much about a culture and a society . . . the melancholy subject of funerals may provide one good entryway to the analysis of cultures and to the understanding of peoples." The way a Samoan community in a new urban environment deals with death points to the significance both of continuing tradition and of adaptive modifications that have developed in the urbanization of a village people.

The Samoan funeral in West Coast cities of the continental United States dispatches the dead with elaborate Christian propriety and at the same time serves the living by reinforcing the social and economic security of relatives, friends, and the entire Samoan community. This paper will describe the ceremonies and ritual behavior that occur at the time of a death, and will examine the social and economic implications of these for family and community.

During the past two decades an ever-increasing stream of immigrants has come to West Coast cities from American Samoa. Some 15,000 to 20,000 Samoans now reside in Los Angeles, San Diego, Oceanside, and the San Francisco Bay area.[2] Samoans have adjusted with relative ease and poise to an environment that could hardly be more different from that of their native islands. Most have little difficulty in getting and keeping jobs. A large proportion of the men work in shipyards or in heavy industry, and the women are often nurse's aides in hospitals and nursing homes. Many families are buying their own homes and they live comfortably, although not extravagantly. They lead full and active lives centered about their families, their jobs, and their churches.

Reprinted from Joan Ablon, "The Samoan Funeral in Urban America," Ethnology, **IX** *(1970), 209–227, with permission of* Ethnology.

[1] The field research for this paper was supported in part by the National Institute of Mental Health, U.S.P.H.S. Grant No. MH-08375 to the Community Mental Health Training Program, Langley Porter Neuropsychiatric Institute; General Research Support Grant No. FR-67-23 (awarded to Langley Porter Neuropsychiatric Institute), from the General Research Support Branch, Division of Research Facilities and Resources, National Institutes of Health; and Ford Foundation Grant No. 690-0231 (administered through the Urban Research and Public Service Program, University of California).

I would like to thank Faatui Laolagi for assisting in the collection of the data on which this paper is based, and for his criticisms of the manuscript.

[2] There are no accurate census figures for the California Samoan population. The figures given here are estimates by Samoan ministers who travel widely between these cities.

This new mainland ethnic group has retained many features of Samoan life and custom. One of the most significant aspects of *fa'a Samoa*, Samoan tradition, that is carried on with ever-increasing vigor is a modified traditional pattern of funeral observances. Not only do these observances reify community solidarity, but the ritualized patterns of donations of money from relatives and friends provide an outstanding example of people helping one another, of mutual aid in an urban area where the cost of living and dying is very high.

The following discussion is based on field research in one of the above-mentioned cities of California, where there is a Samoan population of some 4,000 to 5,000 persons. Virtually all families are attached to one or another of the many all-Samoan Christian churches representing Congregationalist, Methodist, Pentecostal, Mormon, and Seventh-Day Adventist congregations. Catholics attend various parish churches in the city but unite in their own choir and Benevolent Association. Samoan funeral rites are carried on within the rituals and belief system of the Christian church. The accompanying social and economic activities are quasi-independent of these religious ceremonies and are prescribed by a developing modified Samoan cultural tradition.

Chronology of Family Activities Following a Death

Immediately following a death, the local minister of the church to which the family belongs is contacted, and he begins making plans for the various services to be held, as well as counseling the family of the deceased.

Telegrams are sent and telephone calls made to extended family members in Samoa, Honolulu, and any mainland cities where relatives reside. A number of these relatives prepare for the trip to attend the services. If there is no *matai*[3] (family chief) living in the urban area, a *matai* may come for the occasion to represent the extended family in Samoa.

During the days following the death, members of the nuclear family, close bilateral kin, and local *matai* or older and respected relatives meet to make the practical decisions for burial arrangements and for religious services and to decide the amount of money needed for necessary items. A spokesman for the family of the deceased is selected to speak on all occasions. If there is no *matai* (in this case, a talking chief, the recognized family orator) in the area, or one who can come from Samoa, an older relative or one who is respected and eloquent in speech is designated.

Soon after the death is announced to relatives and friends, a complex network of money-collecting activities goes into motion. The *aiga*,[4] the

---

[3] The *matai* is the family title holder who bears the responsibilities and privileges of leadership of the extended family. *Matai* are classified as chiefs and as talking chiefs or official orators.

[4] Mead (1930: 40) thus defined the term *aiga*: "*Aiga* means relative by blood, marriage and adoption, and although no native actually confuses the three ways by which the *aiga* status is arrived at, nevertheless a blanket attitude is implied in the use of the word. An *aiga* is

extended family—the parents, grandparents, children, siblings, aunts, uncles, and cousins of the deceased, the adopted kin within these categories, and the affines of all of these—are expected to contribute money from their respective households to the household of the deceased. The closer relatives contribute from $100 to $200 in cash. There is organized planning for these donations. For example, a group of siblings holds a meeting and decides how much they as a group should contribute. Arguments sometimes occur because one person might not feel that his household is able to contribute his proportionate share of the total at that time, but a consensus is finally reached. Probably $1,000 to $2,000 will be collected from the immediate bilateral kin. More distant relatives, such as cousins, take responsibility for gathering money from their relatives and affinal kin. Donations from each of these households range from $10 to $50, and are presented to the household of the deceased by the persons who organized the collection. Churchmates, friends, and other Samoans also contribute in smaller sums, from $5 to $20, as they are able and are inclined, depending on their relationship to the deceased. An intimate friend may in some cases donate more money than a close relative. Collections also come from other Samoan church congregations and usually are presented by the choirs of these churches during the funeral rites.

Complementing money donations from relatives and ritually even more significant is the custom of donating old fine mats, long a traditional item of economic and ritual exchange at weddings and funerals in the islands.[5] The fine mats, which are about 4 by 5 feet in size and made of the finest grade of pandanus, are no longer woven. The number in existence is limited, and the Governor of American Samoa in 1969 issued a declaration stating that they may no longer be taken out of American Samoa. Thus they are circulated in a closed and traditional manner in the United States. The closer relatives are expected to give two to five fine mats with the presentation of money. If a person has no fine mats to present, he tries to procure them from relatives or he may be able to buy them locally from others who might have a few extra. The set price of a fine mat (passing from Samoan to Samoan—

---

always one's ally against other groups, bound to give one food, shelter and assistance. . . . No marriage is permitted with any one termed *aiga* and all contemporary *aigas* are considered as brothers and sisters. Under the shadow of these far-flung recognized relationships children wander in safety, criminals find a haven, fleeing lovers take shelter, the traveler is housed, fed and his failing resources reinforced, property is collected for a house building or a marriage; and a whole island is converted into a series of cities of refuge from poverty, embarrassment, or local retribution." This functional definition is especially relevant for the understanding of the practical value of the retention of extended family bonds in the urban setting.

[5] Mead (1930: 73) offered a detailed discussion of the making and economic value of the fine mat, and noted: "Fine mats (i.e. *toga*) have often been called the Samoan currency. Their economic value is ceremonially enhanced by their age, by high lineage of the ladies who plaited them, and by the exchanges in which they have played a part. Some mats come to have the same sort of almost fictitious value which is attached to stamps or coins with us. Such mats have names, their history is well known, and is conventionalized into a formal account how and where the name was given."

they are rarely sold to non-Samoans) is $10 on the mainland and in American Samoa.

From the day of the death until the funeral and burial are completed, the immediate family and close relatives and *matai* who have come from other areas remain at the home of the deceased and receive callers who bring money and fine mats. Callers may also bring items of food such as chickens or turkeys. These gifts are presented with a formal speech to explain their purpose or the route or direction through which they come and why; that is, the relationship between the giver and the deceased or between the giver and various members of the family through whom the donations are directed. At that time, individual relatives representing both their own affinal kin and donors who are more distant kin make presentations for these kin groups as a unit. For instance, one representative may journey from San Francisco to San Diego at the time of death of his mother's cousin and take with him money and fine mats donated by his extended family and their affinal kin who reside in San Francisco. Those who come from Samoa bring a donation from their relatives there. Formal acceptance speeches are made by family spokesmen to the donors, and food is served to them. In the past, in this California city, money and fine mats were brought to the funeral services, but the formal presentations required a great deal of time; therefore, the ministers decided the giving of money and mats must take place in the household rather than at the public ceremonies.

A family may expect to receive from $2,000 to $10,000 or more in total financial gifts, depending on the social position of the deceased and his family and their standing in their church and the Samoan community, as well as the actual number of their relatives. Fine mats collected may number from 50 to 150 or more, usually in proportion to the money received. Gifts of money and mats are carefully recorded by certain family members who serve as secretaries. Mats are tagged with the giver's name, and following the funeral each fine mat is returned to the home of the person who presented it. This differs from the pattern in Samoa, where mats received by the family *matai* are redistributed to various other *matai* and family members. In the United States, because it is difficult to obtain these mats, the system of return of mats has developed. Some mats are especially prestigious and have been handed down in families; therefore, people may want the exact mats that they donated. The family of the deceased spends much time in the days and weeks following the funeral returning these beautiful mats to their donors.

Finances are carefully managed to pay the expenses of funeral and burial services. The cost of the casket (very handsome and ornate caskets often are chosen by the family) and mortuary services may amount to as much as $1,500. One mortuary official stated that most Samoan funerals handled by his establishment average about $1,200 in cost, somewhat higher than the average for his total client population. However, another stated that his experience has shown a broad range in the prices of caskets and services selected. The burial plot usually costs an additional several hundred dollars.

Several mortuaries customarily are used by the members of the various church groups. Funeral directors in these mortuaries are knowledgeable about Samoan preferences for arrangements, such as additional ceremonies held in the mortuary or church, and the holding of the body for a relatively long period of time before burial. The body is usually held in the mortuary for at least four days, and in some instances up to ten days, especially if the death is sudden and unexpected, to allow relatives to make the trip from Samoa. Samoans prefer to hold services on the weekend, because many persons do not work on these days.

A significant expenditure of money is made to provide food for relatives who have come from Samoa and other areas. Provisions for these relatives, who stay either in the home of the deceased or with other family members, may amount to $500 or more. Money is presented to ministers who participate in the memorial and funeral services. A donation of money and fine mats may be given by the family to the sponsoring church, as well as a special gift of money and a fine mat to the presiding minister. Another significant amount of money is expended on the elaborate feast that traditionally follows the funeral.

The money that remains after all the expenses are taken care of is then distributed between the immediate family and the bilateral kin. If, for instance, a man dies leaving a wife and small children, there is an obvious financial need for their support and they merit a larger share of the total. Cash may be distributed to more distant relatives from the core bilateral kin groups. One informant reported that her household and those of her five siblings each gave $100 for the collection at the death of her adopted mother. Some $6,000 was collected, and after the expenses were defrayed, there was enough left so that in the redistribution each of the six siblings received $300. Each made $200 above the return of his original donation. It is doubtful that such profits are frequent, because expenses and transportation costs are high. For example, many airplane fares may have to be paid for. The bank in Pago Pago has ready arrangements to finance travel in such emergency situations, suggesting that there is little problem about the loans being quickly repaid.

Ceremonies

The pattern of formal and informal services varies according to the church with which the family is affiliated. The following description portrays a generalized ideal pattern common to most of the church groups.

The body lies for viewing in the mortuary awaiting the formal services that may not begin for several days following death. Extended family, church members, and friends come in small numbers to sit with the casket, which usually is open, and hold informal services with prayers and hymn singing.

The first formal ceremony is held in the mortuary chapel, frequently on a

Saturday evening two nights preceding the funeral and interment. This service is regarded as the family service. The details of all services are worked out with the family by the minister of the church to which the family belongs (henceforth in this description called the host minister and the host church). The chapel usually is adorned with many large and elaborate flower sprays, and frequently fine mats are draped over the bier on which the casket rests. Larger weave, though handsome, utility mats may be used to carpet the aisles and platform area of the chapel. The family service generally is attended only by the extended family, the church members, and the church choir, in all some 50 to 100 persons. However, friends and acquaintances also may attend. The minister conducts the services, and prayers are said. All the services are conducted in the Samoan language. Speeches by siblings, parents, or children of the deceased concerning his life or Christian works, and by the *matai* or representatives of the family, are presented. Hymns are sung by the church choir. Those present file by to view the dead.

The largest of all of the funeral observances is usually the public service held the night before the funeral. This service is sometimes called the "opening service." It frequently is held on Sunday afternoon or evening in the mortuary or possibly in the church, and may be attended by as many as 400 persons, who represent most of the Samoan churches in the city and surrounding areas.

The minister of the host church arranges this service and may invite other ministers who represent all congregations. If the deceased held an important position in church affairs, ministers of that denomination come from the more distant California cities to represent their congregations. These ministers may hold a brief meeting immediately before the service and the host minister decides what parts each will take. Certain of them sit on the platform area and are honored with duties of presenting various parts of the service, such as the invocation, scripture reading, prayers, and sermon. These components are interspersed with hymns sung by the choir of the host church. Various speeches of gratitude for the participation of those attending are offered by the host minister and family spokesman. The formal public service lasts about an hour. The minister closes this service by turning over the second part of the evening, the choir singing, to his choir director.

The choir director of the host church then gives instructions concerning the order of singing to visiting choirs, who represent most of the Samoan churches of the area. There may be as many as twelve choirs in attendance, and rarely fewer than seven. The choirs then begin singing in rotation, in the order prescribed by the host choir director.

Representatives of the various churches all sing and constitute *ad hoc* choirs even though some may not be members of the official choirs of these churches. Each choir may sing one hymn only, or may be given the opportunity to sing a second, in rotation. After each finishes its choral contribution, its choir director offers a short speech and presents an envelope containing money for the family, as the financial donation of that church. The amounts vary; larger churches whose choirs number 30 to 50 persons contribute as much as $25 to $50, while the smallest choir made up of 10 to 20 persons ordinarily gives $15 for the death of an adult and $10 for the death of a child. A monthly collection may be held for these funeral funds.

After the seated choirs have completed their alloted turns, they frequently leave the building, with the exception of the host choir, which sings a closing hymn at the end of the service. The choirs which have been standing in the corridors enter and take the vacated seats. If there are more than seven or eight choirs the process may take two rotations until all have had their opportunity to sing. The rotations are necessary because there is always a problem of seating room at the choir service. Chairs are barely available for the family, church members, the host choir, and two or three other choirs at a time. One mortuary uses two connecting chapels when possible (a rarity for their non-Samoan services), but the crowd generally is such that there is still insufficient seating. Usually the family and church members of the host church are the only non-choir persons present.

The Congregational churches, which characteristically have more members in the area, always have the largest choir participation.[6] Some of the smaller denominations such as the Pentecostals and Seventh Day Adventists are sporadically represented. All churches take pride in their choirs, and generally hold choir practice at least one evening a week. The music is strong, with a uniquely moving quality and tone. With the exception of the Pentecostals, who frequently sing common American hymns in English as well as Samoan, the choirs all sing old Christian hymns translated into Samoan appropriate for this occasion.

After the last choir has had its turn, the host choir may sing once more, and then a closing speech of gratitude is presented by the *matai* or family representative and a closing prayer is given by one of the ministers. As the crowd disperses, members of the family of the deceased frequently pass out foodstuffs, such as tins of coffee or crackers, to the departing guests as they leave the building.

The following morning, frequently a Monday, the funeral service is held. This service usually is not as long nor as well attended as that of the evening before. Family, friends, church members, and the host church choir are present. Again, various ministers representing the churches of the area sit on the stage and take part in the service, which consists of prayers, exhortations, and hymns. A member of the family speaks about the personal life of the deceased. The minister or members of the various church associations or of the choir of the church attest to the dedication of the deceased individual to the church and to Christian life. Customarily those attending file by the casket to view the dead, and then warmly embrace or kiss the immediate

6 The London Missionary Society, which Christianized the Samoan Islands in 1830, constituted the first of the many Christian missionaries to Samoa. The majority of Samoans still attend LMS churches both in Samoa and in the mainland cities, where these churches frequently have affiliated with their American counterpart, the Congregational Churches.

family sitting near the casket. The funeral service is brief, no more than one hour in length. When it closes, people quickly go to their cars and follow the hearse for the last ride to the cemetery.

Of the many cemeteries in the area, several are chosen most frequently by Samoans for the burial of their dead. Large plot areas often are held by one religious denomination in common for all of their members regardless of individual church (Mormons or Catholics, for example), and Samoans of these religions are buried in the general plots. However, some Samoan churches have chosen sites bordering one another in one large cemetery.

The graveside service is a brief one. The family members are seated by the waiting open grave. The presiding minister conducts the service, the other ministers standing behind him. He presents several prayers and farewell statements to the dead, as hymns are sung by the crowd assembled around the burial site. The minister and relatives throw flowers on the casket symbolizing the proverbial "from dust to dust. . . ." Flowers, and the gloves worn by the pall bearers, are lowered with the casket. Sometimes relatives and friends bring cameras and take pictures of the casket with relatives encircling it. A family spokesman then offers the goodbye to the deceased and expresses his gratitude to the ministers and crowd for their participation. He invites them to a reception immediately following burial.

The cars then head for the announced site of a traditional reception or dinner. This may be held in the church fellowship hall, in which case the food is prepared and served by family and church members. The meal features traditional Samoan foods such as chicken, pork, taro, bananas, salt-corned beef, a specialized dish called "chop suey," and potato salad. Enormous amounts of food are served and guests are expected to take home what they cannot eat. Additional wrapped packages of salt-beef, pork, or chicken may be distributed to each guest to take home. Often, however, the dinner is catered and held in the banquet room of a large restaurant. In this case the food is of American style, but it is also served in great abundance. Guests are seated at long tables, with a special table for ministers or honored guests (aside from *matai*) at the head of the room. One of these ministers gives the blessing for the food.

When the diners are some 30 minutes into their meal, an exchange of oratory begins. The chief family spokesman, often a *matai* from Samoa, asks permission from the families and other high-ranking chiefs to speak for the family of the deceased. He gives thanks to God, then thanks the ministers who have taken part, relatives who have come from long distances, and local relatives and friends for their attendance. He prays for the safe journey of those who must return to Samoa or elsewhere. Then, local talking chiefs who have the right to represent the public thank the families of the deceased for the dinner and their courtesies. At times there is competition by title for this honor, and various talking chiefs may dispute the prerogative of one who rises to speak. The family may prefer that no such speech be given, and the spokesman indicates this to those who rise to speak.

During the course of the dinner the family presents envelopes with money to each of the ministers as a token of appreciation, and to thank them for their participation in the various services. The amounts of money range from $10 to $50 for the participating ministers and from $50 to $100 for the host minister who arranged and conducted the service.

The feast lightens the occasion somewhat, and the immediate family as well as friends may be seen talking and laughing during and after the meal, whereas lighter conversation is not so much in evidence during the preceding days. The crowd disperses and guests leave carrying bags, cartons, or boxes of food.

The old custom of observing a year of mourning is rarely followed now either in Samoa or the mainland cities, although the custom was recently observed in the case of the death of a prominent minister's wife. A graveside service and sumptuous dinner were held to close the mourning period.

Contrast with Contemporary Funeral Activities in American Samoa

Today in Samoa, immediately following a death, the family assembles and decides how long it will take relatives living outside of Samoa to arrive and how soon other necessary preparations can be made. If persons coming from the mainland or Hawaii will be delayed, there are facilities for the body to be kept at the hospital in Pago Pago. Otherwise, the whole funeral procedure is carried out within 24 hours. Embalming is not practiced, and burial is accomplished as soon as possible. All services as well as family exchange activities are centered in the home rather than in the mortuary.

Relatives and friends throughout the islands are alerted, and relatives gather to decide what each will contribute for the occasion. Contributions consist of fine mats and food. The need for cash is minimal, and only the closest of kin contribute money, which is used to pay for the food needed to serve the relatives who come. These relatives begin arriving soon after the death, or after the body is returned to the house from the hospital if there is a delay before the rites begin. Careful consideration is given to the number and kinds of mats given, depending on the status of the deceased and his relationship to the giver. Food donations vary also according to these criteria. Food is given in the form of large items such as kegs of salt-beef, pigs, and cases of sardines or biscuits. The mats collected by the family are then distributed to chiefs who may or may not be related to the deceased. Food collected is distributed to the bilateral kin in much the same fashion as cash is in the mainland cities.

Whereas in the United States the church is central in almost all the activities, there is a sharper dichotomy in Samoa between religious functions and family activities dictated by traditional cultural patterns at the time of death. The minister presides only in a set number of relatively short formal Christian services. He may say last rites before death and counsel with the bereaved following death. If death occurs at the hospital, the minister performs a short service there before the deceased is brought to the house. Only the family and church choir are present at the hospital. The body is then taken to the home, and another service is held, with a few church people and possibly ministers from several other villages. If the person who died was a minister, deacon, or lay preacher, all of the ministers of his district may participate in all of the services. Less often, ministers of other denominations may attend. The ministers and choir then leave, and the exchange of goods occupies the remainder of the day.

When evening comes, the minister and choir perform another service. Choirs come from other villages and sing the same kinds of traditional songs for the occasion as are sung at the public choir service here. When these choirs depart, they are given food by the family to eat after their return to their home villages. Following the singing of church choirs, the titled and untitled women's associations of the village of the deceased arrive. Throughout the night, these groups sing songs that have as their purpose the removal of the sadness of death and the return of the household to joy, while the family cooks and prepares for the next day's activities.

The following morning, the largest crowd at any of the services is present for the funeral. The body, which has been on public view on mats or in an open coffin, is then carried by family members to its resting place on family ground near the house or on the plantation. The plot is prepared by the young men of the family or of the village. A short service similar to the one described above for the mainland city is held at the grave, and the crowd returns for the dinner that follows burial.

Matai and their wives in attendance who are related to the family dine in the house of the deceased. Other *matai* not related to the family are assigned another house for their meal. Untitled relatives and guests are served outside. Formal speeches are made at this time in the houses where the *matai* are dining.

Historical Background of Contemporary Customs

Contemporary ritual elements, such as the presentation and redistribution of food and mats, the choir rotations, and even bookkeeping to identify goods presented can be traced from earlier accounts of Samoan funeral observances. The account by Turner (1884) of death and burial generally describes customs which have since disappeared. He does state that all who came to the burial brought presents which were all distributed again so that each person received something in return for what he had brought (Turner 1884:146).

Mead reported that at the time of her 1925–26 research the old Samoan death chants had been displaced by Christian hymns, and that Christian choirs had taken the responsibility from the untitled men's and women's groups for the customary singing in shifts at the time of an important death. Mead also documented the giving of food, fine mats, and tapa offerings. The food was consumed at the funeral feast, while goods either were returned to their donors or redistributed (Mead 1930:99–100).

A vivid and poignant description of a funeral is presented by Copp (1950), who also describes the choir singing, ritual exchange, and keeping of accounts of donations.

The History and Modification of Funeral Activities in the United States

Interchurch and community-wide interest in funeral activities is said to have developed in the West Coast cities in the early 1960s. The migration of Samoans to the mainland that began in the 1950s was rapidly increasing, and many older people who were knowledgeable about Samoan custom and who wished to perpetuate it in their homes had arrived. Before that time, when only a few of the many Samoan churches that now flourish in the area existed, the death of a Samoan aroused little interest or activity outside of his extended family.

Informants have suggested the key years of development of the present funeral customs were 1963 and 1964. Mats first were used as a covering for the casket, and later the traditional ritual exchange of mats began. In 1964 many Samoans died in a catastrophic fire that occurred at a Samoan community-wide dance. Concern over relatives and friends led the Samoan population and all churches to reach out in a co-operative endeavor to aid those families touched by the fire with services, money, and personal consolation. One Catholic informant reported that her husband, who was critically burned in the fire, requested that he be given a traditional funeral with many choirs present. She took this plea to church officials and Samoan Catholic laymen. Over some opposition she did arrange such a funeral, and this appears to have set the precedent for the coming together of all denominations for a Catholic funeral. Such an ecumenical movement was unknown before that time. Informants state that funeral customs in mainland cities are becoming more elaborate each year.

Some Samoans have observed that the customs now prevalent in the United States make use of familiar traditional elements, but that they have been confounded through purposeful modification or through ignorance of tradition. In contrasting funeral activities carried out in the California city with contemporary practices in Samoa, modifications in four areas will be pointed out: (1) changes in protocol concerning prerogatives of chiefs; (2) emphasis on collection and redistribution of money rather than goods; (3) centrality of the church; and (4) extension of the network of involved persons.

Changes in Protocol Concerning Prerogatives of Chiefs

In Samoa, traditionally, the funneling of donations of mats has been through talking chiefs who represent their family groups in presenting mats to the family of the deceased or in receiving mats in the redistribution. In the United States all categories of relatives individually present mats.

In the United States, the family spokesman, or the persons representing other families who choose to speak at events may not be talking chiefs, and in fact may hold no *matai* title at all. A chief may speak here, although traditionally the chief could only speak on certain specified occasions. Formal oration was the prerogative of the talking chiefs, as is still the custom in Samoa. Breaks such as these from traditional protocol can occur only in a geographic area far from the homeland, where there is an absence of the controls imposed by the total structural hierarchy, and where there is a genuine shortage of legitimate *matai*, a factor that must be a realistic consideration. Thus, "pretenders" may appear, through necessity or opportunism.

Emphasis on Collection and Redistribution of Money Rather than Goods

The emphasis on the donation of money in the United States recognizes the great expense of funeral and burial procedures in the mainland cities in contrast to Samoa, where an inexpensive coffin is used and there is no need to purchase a burial plot. A mutual aid function has developed in the United States to meet a practical need for immediate cash. However, it may be observed that in almost every instance the money accumulated far exceeds that needed for actual expenses. This overgiving might be explained in several ways. There appears to be a ritual need for a redistribution of surplus of a commodity that has the most practical value in this country, that is cash instead of corned beef. Also the "overgive" serves to reemphasize the cultural value placed on generosity of the greatest extent that a family can manage in this country, where living costs are high. In other words, in the United States, a conspicuous display of money is more impressive than a conspicuous display of food, although importance is still placed on great quantities of food being served and taken home.

Centrality of the Church

The church has become the focal point not only of religious but also of social life for Samoans in the United States. The church is the institution that supports and encourages and is itself supported and encouraged by the maintenance of traditional Samoan customs. In the absence of the traditional village, district, and island hierarchies of family chiefs, the church and its officials fill a structural vacuum. It should be noted that many persons migrated to the United States specifically to escape the strictures that the traditional *matai* system placed on their personal, social, and economic aspirations. In Samoa the *matai* still to a great extent dictate the daily activities of family members and may divide and distribute family resources. Frequently, *matai* are presented with family members' paychecks, which they then apportion as they see fit. A very small amount may be returned to the actual recipient of the check. Although there was a desire to escape these more personal controlling aspects of traditional social structure, there also was a need for certain familiar supports of the culture. Church structures quickly developed to meet the needs of the individual for religion and the fellowship of other Samoans, while allowing him and his family the same basic freedom to strive for social and economic mobility that has lured immigrants to the United States from all over the world.

Extension of Network of Involved Persons

In Samoa at all times, but especially at the time of death, the individual has not only large family groups to count on for practical and emotional support, but also the potential aid of a total village. There is a strong interpersonal network in a small circumscribed geographic area. In the large and alien metropolis, where one's neighbors are not known and can hardly be expected to give substantial aid in time of crisis, a sense of cultural and social unity has enlarged the network of persons that one can rely on and, conversely, that one feels responsibilities toward, to include all Samoans. The church choirs have served as actual and symbolic vehicles of this strengthening community feeling among Samoans. Although weddings also evoke community attention, it is significant that the coming together of churches of all denominations developed only at the time of death, the ultimate life crisis.

The Social Uses of Samoan Funeral Activities

Anthropologists have demonstrated that funeral rites are a particularly good area in which to examine the social functions of ritual (Mandelbaum 1959; Firth 1961; Vallee 1955; Nadel 1951). Firth noted that "a funeral rite is a social rite *par excellence*. Its ostensible object is the dead person, but it benefits not the dead, but the living. . . ." Firth suggested that funeral rites as he witnessed them in Tikopia served a variety of social functions. They provided a social symbol of finality, wherein the death was publicly acknowledged by family and community. Furthermore, he observed, as had Radcliffe-Brown before him, that such ritual reinforces the system of social sentiments of the group. This reinforcement is in part exhibited in the economic activities that take place at the time of death, e.g., the passage of goods between specified persons serves as a concrete expression and reinforcement of social forms and expectations (Firth 1961: 63–64).

The social uses of Samoan funeral activities fall in interlocking ways within the functions Firth defined. The social and economic elements are almost inextricable. But, in addition to these functions which Firth observed in the stable cultural tradition of Tikopia, Samoan customs, when viewed within the dynamic contextual situation of a migrant group in the process of developing a new life style, take on a greater significance. They perform a critical function of aiding in the social and economic survival of a village people in the most complex of metropolitan settings.

These social uses of the Samoan funeral can be summarized under four headings: (1) reinforcement of family and community solidarity; (2) reiteration of basic Samoan cultural themes; (3) reaffirmation of the significance of the Samoan Christian church; and (4) mutual aid for survival in the city.

Reinforcement of Family and Community Solidarity

The immediate rallying of kin and friends around the household of the deceased is both spontaneous and expected. The gathering of the closest bilateral kin who reside in the area and the arrival of relatives from Samoa and mainland cities contributes with studied efficiency to take the burden of decision and arrangment-making off the lone shoulders of spouse, parents, or children. There are many minds and hands to help with the numerous practical matters that must be attended to, to console the grieving, and to take care of children who suddenly may be left without a parent. Likewise the planning and conferencing necessary for the intricate money collection activities reinforce the cohesion of the family. Nadel (1951: 167) has noted that individuals participating in common activities may in the course of these activities share emotional experiences which develop a bond between them, a predisposition to work together more effectively in other contexts. The more emotionally charged the experience, the greater may be the strength of such bonds that develop.

Indeed, the coming together of the Samoan community at the time of death fosters an *esprit de corps* which serves them well in a new urban situation. One funeral director commented that he feels a chief reason that Samoans manage their grief so well is that they have "extraordinary financial and moral backing." He pointed out that many of his clients have only one other person to rely on for practical matters, and to comfort them, but Samoans have a whole "colony."

The Samoan identity establishes imperatives of responsibility to one's fellows. Death clearly evokes support not only of relatives but of other Samoans who may have been friends of the deceased, who migrated from the same village, or who had only a bare acquaintance with him. Because the Samoan population of the area is so large, people may know only relatives, friends, and persons attending their church. However, because of early village ties, schools attended in the islands, and wide affinal involvement, they know of other people. The feeling exists that one should contribute money and should attend the funeral services because the person who died was Samoan. It is said that the family of the deceased would be ashamed if only a handful of people or a few choirs came, or if their closing meal had few guests. However, given the number of relatives and affinal kin that any Samoan is bound to have in the area, and the fact that others come to show respect for the relatives and affines of the deceased, as well as for the deceased, a sizable crowd is always assured. If a relative cannot attend the services, he will at least stop by the house of the deceased to make his presentation and offer consolation. One comes to show respect; and if a person does not meet the needs of others, they may not meet his in similar circumstances. Indeed, this practical consideration may be more effective than the threat of having one's face blackened with soot, the punishment Mead (1930: 100) recorded for those who failed to appear to sing for the dead.

Having to work is often the only legitimate excuse one might have for not participating in the choir singing. As one informant put it:

Well, if I had to work, that's all right. You could be excused to work, but if somebody saw you going to a show instead of going to sing, then you or they would feel badly about it.

Samoans are ingenious in their ability to find ways of being excused from their jobs to attend funeral functions. Many women work in nursing homes where there are other Samoans on the staff, and they are able to trade shifts or days off. Also, many persons work swing or night shifts, and are thus free for morning activities. (Churches often arrange to have their main Sunday service in the morning or afternoon depending on the work shifts of the majority of members.)

The number of funerals each year in this area varies from five to fifteen. Most funerals are for older persons who die from natural causes. Younger persons usually represent traffic fatalities. The potential for depressive feelings at attending so many funerals was probed in interviews. It became apparent that even this suggestion reflected imposed cultural bias on the part of the investigator. The effect of melancholy is subordinated to the social obligations of attendance. Unless the person who died was a close relative or friend, an attitude of uninvolvement with the situation or the obvious grief of relatives seems to prevail. A woman who attends almost every funeral service held in the area was asked:

Q: How do you feel about being present at so many sad occasions? Does it make you feel sad?
A: I don't know too many people here except my relatives. I left the island in 1948. Unless it is someone you know, in this case you do feel sad, then you just sort of sit there.
Q: What do you think about?
A: Well, you sit there and you are curious. You wonder what is going to happen next on the program, or you just look around and see the people that are there. That is the way you spend your time.

Samoans view death as one of the natural events in the experience of the living. In contrast, death in the United States is a subject that is hidden away, or at least ignored as much as possible. As a commentary on this, there is little ritual at the time of death, and most persons attend only the funerals of those with whom they have had close interaction. Indeed, by age fifty, a person may only have attended a half dozen funerals. For Samoans, death has little of this mystique.

Mead (1961: 105–106) has discussed the way in which birth and death are presented matter-of-factly to the Samoan child. She vividly described the mode of primitive autopsy at the grave to determine the cause of death, and the postmortem Caesarean operation customary for women who died in pregnancy. Children routinely viewed these events. Mead stated that these "horrible but perfectly natural, non-unique occurrences" were presented as a legitimate part of the Samoan child's experiences. In contrast, the American child whose circle of intimates is much smaller, may only experience the death of one close relative in his years of growing up. All of the negative affect surrounding one highly charged emotional experience may be carried over to all other deaths that he encounters in his later life (Mead 1961: 158). The fact that Samoans, in contrast to mainland Americans, tend to view death as an aspect of the daily reality of life, allows the funeral rites and accompanying activities to provide a positive area for social interaction.

Reiteration of Basic Samoan Cultural Themes

Central themes of Samoan life are generosity, hospitality, reciprocity, and helping one another. This applies to the stranger in the path, as well as the relative in one's home; hence the importance of the ritualized presentations of money, fine mats, and food, and the expected attendance at ceremonies. Through his generosity, the donor honors himself and his extended family in the United States and in Samoa, as well as the recipient.

The giving of fine mats is a ritual documented by early chroniclers of Samoan life. In the United States, at the time of a funeral, mats must appropriately accompany the money presentations of relatives. Several informants expressed the opinion that the exchange of mats is an antiquated custom that still might "make sense" in Samoa, but one that they consider as useless (as contrasted to the very functional donation of money) in the United States. Yet these same persons feel their responsibility to contribute mats as long as the custom continues, and they unfailingly follow the elaborate protocol attending the presentation of the mats.

Generosity and hospitality are strongly evidenced by the supplying of food to visitors and the preparing and sponsoring of the elaborate dinner that is a requisite ending to the funeral ceremonies. The large crowd, the great quantity of food consumed and taken home—all honor and maintain the prestige of the family of the deceased, as well as serving to express gratitude to those who participated in the last rites. In discussing the social and symbolic significance of food for Samoan ceremony, Keesing (1956: 80) noted that a successful feast insured that the occasion and its business purpose would be publicly validated and would hold a place in the memories of the

guests, a most significant consideration in an oral culture. Samoan mainland custom has indeed maintained the tradition of elaborate feasting at
funerals and weddings, as well as at other less formal ceremonial occasions
held in the household or church.

Reaffirmation of the Significance of the Samoan Christian Churches

Reaffirmation of the daily importance of Christianity—whatever the particular denomination—in the life and death of parishioners is effectively accomplished in the course of the funeral observances. All of the formal rites
are couched within Christian form and dogma. Since the advent of the London Missionary Society and other Christian churches in Samoa, there has
been an effective integration of the Christian religion with the traditional
social structure. The church today remains a center of Samoan village life,
and church attendance and household family prayer are routine. In the
United States, the churches developed upon the mushrooming of Samoan
settlement and quickly became the centers of social activity for individuals
and families. It is fitting, therefore, that the churches take on the responsibility for the last rites of their members and elaborately dispatch the dead,
while drawing the living even closer to the bosom of church security in an
alien environment.

The development and elaboration of Samoan churches assume a special
significance when examined within the context of the migration process of
a non-Western village people entering an impersonal metropolitan area. The
integration of a religious dimension with as many life activities as possible
may serve to recapture some of the sacred nature of Samoan life, as opposed
to the secularism of daily life in urban America. Other ethnic migrants have
likewise turned to intensive organized religion in their attempts to re-establish
the sacred quality of life that their small communities had provided for
them.

At the time of death, religion appears to be the chief consolation for the
mourners. In the very act of withstanding the sacrifice of their loved one,
they are able to show their dedication to God and Jesus, much as Abraham
was privileged for the opportunity to sacrifice Isaac (this parallel was drawn
by a minister in speaking to a congregation about the recent loss of a much-
loved member). The continual reaffirmation of their faith allows some survivors to speak of this time of death as their happiest hour, of sacrifice
accompanied by understanding and blessing.

Frequently the speakers at the services are the choir director and representatives from the men's or women's associations of the deceased individual's church. They talk about the contributions of the deceased as a member
of these groups. The dead one may be pointed to as an example of Christian conduct or as the exemplary Christian mother or Christian father.
The significance of the person's relationship to the church is stressed. If

a person was especially active in the church or was a member of the minister's family, the services are more likely to be held in the church rather than the mortuary, and there may be additional special prayer services in the church to honor the family.

A Force for Survival in the City

The prospering of a new ethnic group in a metropolitan area is influenced by many complex factors, one of the most significant being the cultural heritage its members bring with them to their new environment. Their valued attitudes and forms of behavior greatly affect their economic and social adaptation in numerous and complex ways. A key cultural characteristic that has contributed to Samoan success in the city is that of family and community cohesion and loyalty. The responsibilities of loyalty extend in varying degrees to all Samoans. The time of death offers the opportunity for this loyalty and adhering mutual aid obligations to prove their most functional when kin and community are mobilized to aid and console a family in the throes of the ultimate life (death) crisis.

For many Samoans, the sympathy and desire to help are naïvely spontaneous responses, and they little question the obligation to give money, despite the continual drain on finances of large households. Some, in fact, comment on the security that the reciprocal nature of the cash exchange offers them for their own times of crisis.

When my son died, my relatives paid for the whole funeral—you know, I didn't have anything, any money. Look, if your husband should die, for instance, you would just have to sweat it out yourself—you wouldn't have any money. I was given $2,000 right away by the relatives that paid for all the expenses. It is very important that you have someone to help you at a time like that—to help with money. People come and give. Everybody helps. The thing is that you are giving and giving, but you know that you get it all back. There will come a day that it will all come back to you. If you don't give to anybody else, then when you have a death, when you have a wedding, when you have that time of trouble when you need money, you won't have anything. And it's like everybody is related. You know somebody and you just have to help them.

Nonetheless, ambivalence about giving is created by a conflict of cultural dictates and practical considerations of household finances in homes where there are many mouths to feed. Informants often refer to this conflict:

That's one thing with the Samoan people—when anything happens, other Samoans help you. Not just relatives, but other people care about you. Not like Americans here. Where no one cares and the people don't help you. You know—I might want to refuse.

Q: What do you mean?
A: Well, when we get our pay checks—my husband works hard to pay for us and our children and our house, but every month we always must help someone when there is a wedding or funeral, or someone goes back to Samoa. There is always this thing—we always have to pay money—$50, $100, $200, and so on.

Q: What do you do? Do you ever refuse?
A: No, I never refuse. We can never refuse. We always help. And it just means that we don't pay some of our bills then. But we can never refuse this.

And another comment:

Some people would like to cancel out that custom to give. They just don't want to have to give all that money. I have a lot of bills here just to pay for my house and to pay for my family, and then I am slapped with a bill to pay for somebody who needs it. But there are too many people around, and there is nothing you can do about it. You can't get away from it.

One informant, when asked if there are people who do not give, replied:

Nobody has to play that political game and particularly over here, and people don't give at one time because it just hits them at a bad time when they don't have money or something ahead, and they can't give. But another time of trouble will come and they will give. You don't just have one trouble in your life, you have many troubles. And when the next time of trouble comes, then they will give. So it will be all right. People know. Maybe if you can't help someone this time people know you would help them next time.

Other Samoans are more cynical about the necessity to give. One very active church member expressed his reservations as follows:

Nobody has to play that political game and particularly over here, and people don't realize it. What can they do to you? Like, people are always complaining to me. You have to give money, have to give this, have to chip in, have to help. I say to them, 'You're crazy, you don't have to do anything. What are they going to do to you?' Well, everyone's so afraid people are talking about them. I say, so let them talk. That's not going to harm you because you know they're not giving you your job or you're not dependent on them anymore. I don't give anything unless I want to.

However, this same informant was himself ambivalent; he makes it a point to attend every funeral, and commented on how badly a family would feel if "nobody showed up."

Every Samoan family contacted in the course of this research was asked what they most disliked about life in the United States, compared to Samoa. In response, most commented on the fact that people just do not care or feel responsible for others and their welfare. The Samoan, by contrast, has to care, has to help, has to be there. Persons in temporary need are aided by family or church. Informants generally disclaim knowledge of any family in chronic financial distress, but several stated that if it were known that a man could not support his family and his alternative was to receive public welfare, his relatives would collect money to send the family back to Samoa. The receiving of welfare benefits is considered shameful for a family; thus the fact is usually concealed from other Samoans. The number of families receiving public welfare appears to be very small proportionate to the size of the community.

Conclusion

Samoan funeral rites in urban America display a remarkable blending of Samoan tradition, elaborate Christian ceremony, and practical consideration and planning for the realities of a new environment. Differences from contemporary island practices reflect efforts to meet these realities as well as shifts that occur as a result of opportunities for deliberate changes in those aspects of the culture that Samoans wished to escape by their migration.

Funeral customs in this California community represent a rich area for the analysis of social process and cultural change. The ritual patterns described here have developed during less than a decade and have become more elaborate each year as the process of cultural reorganization takes place. Indeed, the occasion of death is an event that reflects the continuing reinforcement of the cultural and social identity of the individual, and the regirding of Samoan cultural and Christian tradition to meet the demands of urban life.

Bibliography

Copp, J. D. (1950) The Samoan Dance of Life. Boston.

Firth, R. (1961) Elements of Social Organization. Third edit. Boston.

Keesing, F. M., and M. M. Keesing (1956) Elite Communication in Samoa: A Study of Leadership. Stanford.

Mandelbaum, D. G. (1959) Social Uses of Funeral Rites. The Meaning of Death, ed. H. Feifel, pp. 189–217. New York.

Mead, M. (1930) Social Organization of Manu'a. Bulletins of the Bernice P. Bishop Museum 76:1–218.

———. (1961) Coming of Age in Samoa. Third edit. New York.

Nadel, S. F. (1951) The Foundations of Social Anthropology. London.

Turner, G. (1884) Samoa. London.

Vallee, F. G. (1955) Burial and Mourning Customs in a Hebridian Community. Journal of the Royal Anthropological Institute 85:119–130.

Patrick Menget

Death in Chamula

The voice of the old man droned on in the damp evening. He staggered away from the fresh moist clay of the open grave and turned to the small group of relatives and neighbors—all male—who had listened intently to his chant. A younger man stepped forward and pulled a bottle of white rum and a stained shot glass out of his ragged poncho. Slowly bowing to the reciter, he muttered a few indistinct words and then extended a full glass of liquor to the elder, who addressed a ritual toast, in turn, to each of the men standing by, from the oldest to the youngest. "I take it" said the old man. "Drink it" answered the younger ones. After the last exchange the elder gulped down the liquor, spat on the ground, and made a wry face—as one should to show that the liquor is nice and strong—then passed the glass to the next man in line. While the men were ceremoniously and gloomily emptying the bottle, the women stood silently a short distance away from the row of graves. A black cluster of weary and sad faces, huddling their children in the folds of their black shawls, they stared blankly at their husbands and relatives.

It had been a long, painful walk uphill, behind the men who stumbled on the muddy path under the weight of the casket. The rain made the children restive and unhappy, but the men had drunk too much to care. Now the men had finished the last bottle of liquor. A couple of boys quickly filled up the grave with earth and trampled it under their feet. They washed their hands with water from a bucket they had carried uphill to the graveyard, as did all the men. It would be dark before everyone was back home. The green valley had already turned gray and misty.

This burial took place one summer not long ago in the hills of central Chiapas, Mexico. The rugged mountains of the state of Chiapas were the last part of southern Mexico to open up to modern civilization, for not until the 1940's did the Pan-American highway connect the region of the Isthmus of Tehuantepec to San Cristobal and even farther to the Guatemalan border. As you drive along the highway you can see groups of brightly clad Indians and clusters of thatch-roofed huts among the cornfields. The region is inhabited by more than 150,000 Maya Indians. They speak either Tzotzil or Tzeltal, languages closely related to the ancient Maya of southern Mexico and Guatemala. But unlike the ancient Maya, who built the palaces and temples and erected the enigmatic and majestic stelae scattered in the jungle, the Indians of Chiapas do not have a writing system of their own. They use Spanish for their records and for all communications with the Mexican central government. They live in self-administered communities, each with its own dialect and customs. Chamula, the largest of those communities, with upward of 40,000 people, is to a great extent the most resistant to Mexican acculturation.

The Chamula are corn farmers, like all the Indians in the state of Chiapas, but their land is not overly fertile and they must supplement their income by working as wage earners on the coffee plantations in the lowlands. This work is seasonal—the coffee growers need extra manpower only for weeding and cleaning the fields and for harvesting. So the Chamula always manage to be back home for the major religious fiestas—Carnival, Holy Week, Saint John's Day (their patron saint), and *Todos Santos* (All Saints' Day).

It is only about seven miles from San Cristobal to Chamula. Both towns have churches, and the people in each place claim to be Catholic. Yet the differences between Catholicism in San Cristobal and what is called Catholicism in Chamula cannot be measured. In Chamula, the Catholic faith has given little more than a few concepts, a place of worship, and idols. Suffice it to say that in Chamula theology Christ is "our Father the sun"; the Virgin is "our Mother the moon." The Chamula will gladly accept baptism from the Catholic priest who visits irregularly, but all the other sacraments are unknown. The people have their own hierarchy of religious officers, replaced every year, that takes care of the arrangements for the fiestas.

The Chamula, it appears, were Christianized in the sixteenth century, fought this influence, and have largely succeeded in retaining their own system of beliefs, while adopting some Spanish terms and generously borrowing images, idols, and other religious paraphernalia. The Dominicans had to abandon evangelizing in the highlands in the early eighteenth century after a particularly bloody insurrection. More recently, the Mexican Revolution and the subsequent agrarian reform of President Cárdenas (1934) have given the Indians more control over their own affairs, and their religious organization has no room for a Catholic priest. In any case, their views of death and the hereafter reveal that their beliefs are heavily aboriginal.

The funeral I described took place in one of the outlying hamlets, Yalichin, about nine miles from Chamula. Neither the ceremony nor the beliefs inherent in it would be very different in any other part of the *municipio* (a self-administered territorial entity roughly equivalent to a county). Even though funeral ceremonies are private rituals and involve no more than a close circle of relatives and a few neighbors, the rules of behavior concerning death and the handling of it are rigid and strictly adhered to. This matter is important not only to insure a safe journey for the soul of the deceased but also for the well-being of the survivors. When someone dies from any cause other than murder or suicide, the body, if not already there, is brought back home. By the time it has been washed and dressed anew, most of the family are already aware of the death and on their way to the house. Since extended families tend to live in clusters of houses, each couple generally in a separate house, the gathering of kin does not take very long. Even a man's daughters, who often reside patrilocally with their husbands' families, will not live beyond the neighboring hamlets. All of the kin will come and stay in the house of the dead until the funeral is over. This may last from one to three full days, according to the resources of the deceased.

The Chamula believe that a man has two souls: one is an animal companion; the other an immortal principle. The animal companion is born and dies in a one-to-one correspondence with its owner and reflects the events of his life. It is, however, most active at night, in the mountains, where it fights for a living, wards off potent animals, and is exposed to many risks. A man will feel the repercussions of this second life, and in his dreams may even be aware of its happenings. But this animal dies when the man dies or vice versa, one death automatically provoking the other. After death the second soul, which has no special shape or appearance but is sometimes thought to be a manlike creature, will go to the underworld, where all souls live for a time equal to the earthly lives of their owners. Then it will be reincarnated in a person of the opposite sex and in a different situation. A myth describes life in the underworld as the inverse of earthly life. When the sun shines over the earth, it is moonlight down below, and at night the sun shines in the underworld. This is why a man has to be buried at sunset; he will accompany the sun on its westward path to the underworld.

A long wake is necessary for the soul to gather the pieces of the self lost during its lifetime, whether around Chamula or in the hot country (lowlands) where most of the Chamula have worked at one time or another. It is not until those bits (hair, nails, and in some cases, lost limbs) have been collected that the soul can undertake the long voyage to the "land of the dead." Additionally, the wake gives the family an opportunity to face together the dangers brought by death, help the deceased in his preparation for the voyage, and reunite the kin after a painful loss.

At the same time that the family is called, the professional musicians are summoned. There are some in every hamlet, and they will play without interruption, during the whole wake, the same monotonous funeral dirge day and night. A guitar, a harp, a two-stringed violin, and sometimes an accordion, will alternate and mix their chords, swaying in repetitious rhythm with the wailing and sobbing of the mourners. Music is a part of most Chamula ceremonies, whether public or private. As essential to a ritual as the smoke of incense and the flames of candles, it pleases the gods and keeps at bay the evil *pukuh* ("bad spirits") who hang around the corpse. Everyone in the village will know from hearing the melody that the house is mourning, and nobody will disturb the bereaved. For the wake the family of the dead buys many bottles of *posh*, the local rum produced by clandestine stills, for there can be no celebration without lots of *posh*. The Chamula seem to have an endless thirst for this cheap liquor, not so much for its taste, but because it is considered an offering to the gods. *Posh* is consumed in large quantities according to a strict etiquette, first by the oldest man, who has to address a toast to each of the men there in descending order of rank and seniority, then by the other men in the same order, finally by the women according to their husbands' positions. Although the order of drinking reaffirms the hierarchical principle, each drinker gets exactly the same amount of *posh*, reflecting a fundamental egalitarianism among the Chamula. Similarly, the property of the deceased will be equally divided among all heirs, male and female. So the drinking etiquette is a metaphor for social hierarchy, and at the same time, for equality among all members of society. The *posh* is always mentioned in prayers to the gods and often referred to as *nichim* ("flower"), a ritual euphemism. The men also pass around a bowl of ground wild tobacco, of which they take a pinch to eat. This powder, *moy*, which is extremely strong and bitter, gives strength and clairvoyance by enabling one to see through the night and to defend oneself against the evil spirits. The same substance, according to the myths, allows powerful shamans to transform themselves into strong animals, such as jaguars.

In the state of dangerous uncertainty brought about by the presence of someone who has ceased to live and is not yet in the land of the dead, men need to be as strong and united as they can, so they drink often "to warm their hearts," swallow lots of tobacco (very intoxicating) "to see better," and take great pains not to quarrel during the wake.

In one corner of the deceased's hut, dimly lit by a candle, the corpse lies, head toward the west. It is surrounded by female relatives, one of them wailing until she becomes tired and is replaced by another. In the smoke-filled hut—the hearth is right in the center on the dirt floor and the smoke escapes from the apex of the thatched roof—men keep milling around, drinking, talking, loudly lamenting. When I was introduced to the brother-in-law of the deceased, he burst out in tears, moaning the loss of his relative. As he poured me a drink, he spilled some of the liquor and suddenly switched from tears to a nervous laughter, in which the other men soon joined. Many men eventually become irritable under the influence of liquor, then crumble on the dirt, and pass out for a few hours. There is no contempt for such drunkenness, and the intoxicated ones will be shaken back to their feet if anyone needs them. As the wake goes on, the corpse is fed regularly with a few drops of *posol* ("corn gruel") placed between his teeth.

Women also prepare the goods that the dead will need on his journey: a set of new clothes, a blanket, little bags of food, a rosary stripped of its metallic parts, a few coins "for refreshment on the way," and a tiny drinking gourd. The food consists of the three staple elements of Chamula diet: tortilla, beans, and *posol*. But the dead are different from the living and the tortilla is completely burned, then ground to a fine black powder. Before putting it in small linen bags, each relative takes a pinch of it to his mouth with his left hand. This represents a communion with the dead, who, contrary to the living, cannot use the right hand for eating. If the deceased is a woman, she takes along three turkey feathers representing needles and a spindle; if a man, he is provided with three miniature sticks in order to fight back the animals on his way. From time to time an older relative will come near the corpse and recite a prayer for the dead that will assist him in gaining admittance to the land of the dead.

In a myth that bears an eerie resemblance to the Greek story of Orpheus, the Chamula tell that upon arriving in hell one has to be ferried across a large river by a black dog. On the other side of the river, a fire burns for which mules—symbolizing punished women—unload firewood. The last element, in spite of its probable Christian inspiration, brings to mind the daily activities of Chamula women who, indeed, collect all the firewood and tend the hearths as strenuously as mules.

The day of the burial proper, the close family of the dead kill all his chickens, which are eaten in equal shares by all present relatives. This reminds one of the ritual use of chicken, the most commonly sacrificed animal, particularly in curing ceremonies. Chickens are symbolically offered to the divinity so that he will admit the dead to the underworld. Upon leaving the house, red pepper is burned in the fire, producing an acrid and unpleasant smoke, the floor is carefully swept, and the door tightly locked. The soul of the dead should not linger around the house, and the smoke of pepper forces it to leave. Even though many relatives sincerely cry at this moment, people agree that they should behave more stoically, for fear that the soul might heed the lamentation and choose to remain in its home.

After this final separation, the procession starts toward the graveyard, located most often on a hilltop "so that the dead may look over the living." The procession stops often, not only to relieve the casket bearers but also to allow women to feed the dead a few drops of *posol*. They will stop more often if the person being buried was old, because then he tires more easily. The walk uphill is a symbol of the journey to the underworld. Once the interment is over and a cross has been erected on top of the fresh grave, the relatives will walk back to the house for a final gathering in order to share the property left by the dead. However, the separation is not completely ultimate. All people who die from natural causes, that is all those who are neither suicides nor the victims of murders, will come back to this world on *Todos Santos*, a time when they are treated with a feast. In each house, the ancestors in the male line will come back and eat the food that has been prepared for them. They will come back to the place where they used to live while the souls of a woman's ancestors will come back to her parents' house, since the Chamula are patrilineal. Those who did not leave anything to their descendants are not expected to return, as if this meeting between the dead and the living were a contractual bond. The Chamula only welcome those of their ancestors who have been beneficial to them. Most of the Chamula who go and work in the lowlands will come back to their parents' houses to join in the celebration of their forefathers. In the house an altar is set, with candles on each side, a sheet of pine needles on the table, a clay incense burner, and bowls of food. The vessels for food are old earthenware used only on this occasion and kept in the family chest the rest of the time. There is meat on the table, cabbage, tamales, *posol*, and salt, all rich and expensive foods. The house cross behind the altar has been decorated with a bow of greenery—pine boughs, branches of laurel, and flowers. Calling the souls of the ancestors, the oldest man in the family starts to sing, accompanying himself on a guitar.

The whole family stands around the altar in clean festive garments. They will wait till the end of the day, then eat what the dead have left. So that the ancestors can recognize the way, the family will have cleaned the grave and decorated it anew with pine boughs and flowers and will have marked the beginning of the path, at the grave, and the end of it, at the house, with pine needles and flower petals. Furthermore, a little stone in front of the house will indicate the entrance.

Meanwhile, at the center of Chamula, the whole body of religious authorities, most dressed in black *chamarras* (ponchos worn only on festive occasions), preceded by the musicians, followed by the civil officials and the ordinary people, will march to the graveyard, next to the old church of San Sebastian. The bells toll, calling for the dead, the music plays the sad melody of *bolomchon* (the "jaguar"). When the procession reaches the graveyard where the tall wooden crosses recently covered with fresh arches of greenery look as vigorous as a spring bush, everyone scatters around the gravesites to tend his dead. On each grave, women set candles, yellow flowers, such as the *flor de difuntos* ("marigold"), or wild orchids, and food offerings—perhaps an orange—presented on a little board. Those of the women who have recently lost their husbands kneel at the foot of the graves and moan and cry and complain of their miserable life. One of them, with her baby slung over her shoulder in a black shawl, might squat by the grave and pour a glass of liquor, muttering: "Ay, my lord, here I have come, I am lonely, here is some *posh*, drink one glass as you used to do, my companion" (the man probably died from excessive drinking!).

In the meantime, the *mash*, young boys wearing comic hats of monkey skin, will dance around the graveyard to the music of *bolomchon*. *Todos Santos* is a day when people are both content and sad. Their dead are among them, partake of the food and drink, listen to the music. But everybody knows that they will be gone tomorrow.

Yet, on this day, in front of the old church of San Sebastian, only one half of the graveyard is freshly cleaned and flowered. On the west side, beyond a little separation, the burial mounds do not even have crosses, only marking stones, and these are totally disregarded by the Chamula. No relatives around them, no music for these. Here lie the people who were murdered or who committed suicide. They will never be back, for they do not live in the underworld with the other dead and have quite a special status.

Murder is not infrequent among the Chamula. Among the mestizos of San Cristobal and also among other Indians, they are reputed to be violent, especially under the influence of alcohol. It seems that such a reputation is deserved, for the Chamula have a fairly high rate of murder (36 for 100,000 people per year). Yet compared to the incidence of murder in most large Western cities, Chamula is not a dangerous place. Murders usually occur when members of a family quarrel while drunk. There are some cases of women being murdered by their husbands or of presumed witches being killed. Rarely is someone killed by strangers. When a quarrel arises within a family and turns into violence, the murderer will often simply bury his victim in the backyard. But the news always leaks out, or some relative gets worried and warns the authorities. Besides, the Chamula do not try to escape justice when they have committed murder. Most cases of homicide are quickly solved, as if the murderers were too conscious of their religious plight to flee. They rarely resist arrest and appear resigned to their judicial fate.

When news of a murder is received at the municipal center, the president sends out a commission of *mayoles* (officials acting as policemen), headed by a judge. They march to the place of the killing, looking important with their black staffs of office and muzzle-loading guns. They force the alleged murderer to disinter the body. The expedition then walks back to the center, with the accused carrying the corpse, either wrapped in a mat slung over his back with a frontal tumpline, or on his back strapped on a kind of wooden sled. The *mayoles* follow (sometimes covering their noses with white handkerchiefs) along with possible witnesses. While authorities interrogate the suspects (later they will be sent to jail in San Cristobal), a doctor is called to perform the autopsy. The presumed murderer then is expected to dig a grave and bury the dead, all by himself, with no help. This always takes place in the western division of the graveyard of San Sebastian. West, where the sun sets, is the evil direction. Even if the family of the victim is present, there is no ceremony whatsoever, no prayer, no grave goods, and no set time for the interment. The complete absence of ritual contrasts sharply with the elaborate funerals for those who died normally. The only common element is that all are buried with heads to the west.

The Chamula justify their differential treatment of the dead by saying that in a case of homicide, the murderer assumes all the sins of his victim, and the latter goes straight to heaven. This is why in such cases the time of burial is of no importance since the soul does not have to follow the sun. As for suicide, the case is mostly hypothetical: the Chamula say that those people would also go straight up to heaven, but no one I talked to could recall a single instance of suicide. The Chamula are not afraid of the souls of such dead, since once they are in heaven, they are there forever. The murderers have a harsh afterlife in hell, even though they are buried with a regular funeral and on the good side of the graveyard (unless, of course, they were murdered in turn). Murderers never return to earth, neither on *Todos Santos* nor reincarnated.

Thus the cosmos for the Chamula is a sphere, with the sky in the upper portion, and heaven on top of it, the earth as a band in the middle, and the underworld (in Tzotzil, "the sky below") in the lower half, endowed by some with an outgrowth for the murderers. The sun travels visibly across the upper sky during the day, completing its cycle at night when it shines over the underworld. The over-all picture of the cosmos immediately brings to mind the concepts of the ancient Maya. For them, those who had died at war, or women who had died in childbirth, went to heaven and the others went to hell in the underworld. Yet, we do not understand why people meeting a violent end are not cared for in any way by the Chamula.

In European folklore we can still witness remains of a distinction between the kinds of death. The Church refused to bury murderers, witches, and people who took their own lives. In Russia people who were witches or those who were murdered were buried under public paths, as a sign of contempt. The theme of the castle haunted by one of its former owners who was murdered by his family is a very popular one in Britain. All those people who had not died normally linger on as nuisances and tricksters. At Halloween we are afraid, not of people who died naturally, but of those who died ambiguously. Whereas the "normal" dead are in a definite, well-known (at least in our belief) place forever, the abnormal ones have been denied, for some reason, a permanent haven. They have to be propitiated by men in order to avoid their tricks and malice. The Chamula have an exactly opposite conception: Whereas their "abnormal" dead are in a definite place forever, the normal dead come back periodically and will even come back to earth, eventually. They have to be respected, propitiated, venerated, lest they become harmful.

While the mist spreads around the trees, the old man's wife silently sobs, thinking of the ritual candle she has fixed in his right hand, all wrapped in red ribbons so that they can one day recognize each other and reunite in the underworld. Standing close by, the old reciter mumbles the end of the prayer:

"Where are we going to put him, what place do we have for him?
He lies there crying, he lies there moaning,
Under the cross, under the crucifix,
His face turned to the other side, he looks toward the other side.
Our Holy Father, Our sacred Ancestor,
Take him, receive him."

Rethinking Modernization: The Present and the Future

Modernization is many different things to different people. In some areas "modernization" comes in the form of missionaries and government officials bringing the "white men's law and order" to previously non-Europeanized people. In other places modernization is especially evident in the flow of commercial goods in places where barter and localized exchange systems had predominated. Again, conquest by foreign armies may be the shape of modernization to some people. Greater and greater complexities of national administrative systems, political bureaucracies, and economic corporations are all part of the flow of recent cultural and social evolution.

In our use, the words "modernization" and "evolution" do not imply that these processes are unmitigated progress or betterment for people. Quite the contrary. Sometimes they have real detrimental effects. In many cases modernization brings some positive features or apparently attractive changes in medical care, improvements of transportation, and new consumer goods that people regard as desirable. At least some parts of the affected populations may see these changes as beneficial to themselves, whereas other portions of the communities may experience the changes as negative or downright disastrous to their way of life. In addition, there are short-term attractive features that turn out, in the long run, to have serious side effects. In many areas of the world cash crops have been introduced which seemed at first to offer wealth and an easier way of life for peoples. In Central American areas many people have turned their attention to growing sugar cane, at first experiencing success, then finding themselves trapped in a fluctuating and uncertain world market, and unable to turn back to their adaptively more viable agricultural practices. Involvement in cash crops, and other complex commercialized ventures, usually involve people in purchases of equipment, long-term loans from banks, or governmental credit organizations which burden them with debts and obligations that cannot be easily erased once they are accepted. In the face of these kinds of changes in most areas there are "conservatives" who seem to resist or speak out against the introductions of new things and new policies, while there are other people who are looked on as "progressive" because they quickly accept the new economic ventures, political changes, and other signs of modernization.

Daniel Gross has studied in detail the effects of "the great sisal scheme" in northeastern Brazil. There we find a pattern of change that is becoming a familiar feature in many parts of the world. An interesting and hitherto little noted aspect of modernization and spread of commerce in many areas has been the deterioration of peoples' diets as they become more reliant on store-bought foods. In the case of the sisal in northeastern Brazil, there is the additional feature of the great expenditures of energy by man involved in sisal, cutting into the food available for their women and children.

Modernization in some areas takes the form of massive changes of the environment in roads, bridges and hydroelectric dams. The dams are usually constructed to provide sources of electrical energy, at the same time providing some control over unruly rivers. A first and obvious result of damming waterways is the production of large lakes, inundating previously rich agricultural lands. Often large-scale resettlement of population is necessary as in the case of the Kariba Dam in Zambia. Planners involved in the building of these massive works develop complex schemes for new crops, new land-use patterns, and new ways of adaptation for the affected populations. They do not always work out neatly, however. As Scudder notes, ". . . research stations have tended to develop new techniques without taking into consideration the total context. . . ."

Sometimes small-scale technological changes in the form of gasoline-driven machines have had profound effects. In some areas the coming of outboard motors has affected river and lake-dwelling populations, and of course the automobile has had massive impacts in most parts of the world. Air transport also has its major technological effects on peoples' lifeways. In the far north the decade of the 1960s saw sudden and very widespread changes of all sorts from the introduction of snowmobiles. Among reindeer-herding peoples of northern Europe, for example, the ways of herding and features of social organization were quickly transformed. Similar sweeping changes, especially in social relationships, have occurred in the Arctic north among Inuit and Indian populations.

The transformations related to modernization not only affect whole regions and social structures, but they also impinge on the lives of individuals. Uneven rates of economic development produce imbalances which lead people to seek their fortunes, or escape from poverty, through migration to more prosperous or more modernized areas and abandon their "less fortunate" areas of the world. In fact one of the most widespread aspects of the process of modernization is the movement of peoples from interior hinterlands to urban sectors, or from one nation to another, even involving travel from one continent to another. To this very day we see the influx of peoples from Europe, Latin America, and other parts of the world into the United States in search of the "American dream." Many of these people experience considerable difficulty and hardship in their adjustment to the new social and environmental setting. John Poggie has collected the story of an individual whose life was complicated by the migration of his family from Mexico to the southwestern United States. This individual is referred to by the Mexicans as *El Pocho*, which indicates that he is not culturally a pure Mexican but a mixture of Mexican and American culture. This term *pocho* may be thought of as the Mexican emic term for a marginal man. On the other side of the border this individual would be called a "hyphenated American," a Mexican-American who is straddling two quite different cultural worlds. Modernization creates the conditions whereby peoples become marginalized in a variety of ways. They may be marginalized in the sense of being of mixed cultural orientation or marginalized by being left outside the mainstream of their nation.

The many different complex processes involved in modernization have certain general features that all tend to contribute to "delocalization." Delocalization includes the loss of local political and economic autonomy; it involves the migration of peoples from their original locales to distant places, and various other uprootings of populations. Perhaps above all it involves the growing dependency of peoples on external energy resources. For example, delocalization in the Arctic is especially apparent in the dependence on gasoline and other power sources imported from the south. On the other hand, delocalization in connection with hydroelectric dams usually features the shifting of populations into new territories and the loss of autonomy in political, economic, and environmental terms. Another powerful aspect of delocalization is in the realm of information as people become more and more tied to external markets, international political developments, and other socioeconomic events far from the local scene. No wonder that the purchase of radios is one of the first steps of delocalization, followed by greater attunement to the economic attractions of the cities.

In the processes of delocalization, social stresses and tensions affect groups of people who may seek changes and "strike back at the system" in a variety of ways. The decade of the 1960s was particularly marked by the advent of "black power" and other movements. Luther Gerlach and Virginia Hine have analyzed some of the features of modern social movements and note that their organization has certain predictable and important aspects that contribute to their spread and success.

North American Indian groups were not far behind in organizing their own movements of "Red Power," in part modeled after the successes of the Black Power movement. One of the important means for mobilizing these organizations requires dramatic moments of confrontation with "the system" or with government or police groups. Such dramatic performances provide vivid symbolizing that can reach out and tighten the emotional commitments of members far from the actual scene of action. Such a dramatic symbolizing of the Indian movement was the take-over of Alcatraz Island in 1969.

Of course, different ethnic and racial groups have different degrees of success, and different foci in their movements of social change. Each time period has its own special features, and there is no limit to the number of minority groups or depressed or deprived populations likely to generate organizations of social transformation. The most recent phenomenon of this sort is perhaps the women's movement, which has a long history but which has only in the 1970s become widespread and effective in seeking changes of status for its membership.

In practically all aspects of culture and social organization, change and transformations have accelerated to a degree that produces alarm and anxiety in more and more people. The rates of change are increasing geometrically, and are at a level far removed from the gradual evolution of human cultural forms of just a few hundred years ago. A whole new crop of "futurologists" has arisen whose main concern is the predicting of things to come from present trends. The present trends involve everything from growth of environmental pollution and the coming depletion of the world's nonrenewable resources such as metals, fossil fuels, and chemical deposits. Some of the futurologists—in fact quite many of them—predict gloomy views of the world's ecological future. Pointing to the geometric expansion of world population and the extremely rapid growth of environmental degradation, groups such as the Club of Rome have forecast a coming collapse (some put the disaster at around the year A.D. 2020) which could only be averted if the nations of the world took massive steps to change the present trends of resource depletion and industrial output. Wound in with all of these problems, of course, is the state of the world's food supply, which has become more and more precarious during the mid-1970s, with the sudden discovery that the North American granaries are no longer brimming with surpluses of wheat, corn, and other commodities.

Many different groups, in and out of government, are pondering ways to effect more favorable outcomes in the future of human culture and society. Some people have turned their attention to developing new energy sources; others seek to bring changes in world population growth; still others focus on political changes to bring more balance in control of resources and access to consumption goods. Some people concerned about the environment have tried to develop simpler life-styles that might bring about a more efficient and satisfactory relationship to local resources. Among some communal groups there is an attempt to bring about "relocalization," especially by reduction of dependence on outside energy resources. Some people are giving up oil heating and going back to use of locally available wood and coal for their furnaces, and in some communal groups there is an attempt to develop local autonomy in food supplies as well. The article by Michael Corr and Dan MacCleod presents an analysis of some effects of communal life-style on energy utilization and related features. No one argues at this time that such small-scale communes are the answer for the whole world's population, but they represent nontechnological searches for solutions to our world predicament.

The delocalization of life-styles and cultural forms especially during the twentieth century has shifted human adaptive strategies away from concern with local environments and a greater concentration on relationships to complex social and political systems. This was an inevitable result of the growth in social complexity, but it led for a time to the wholesale and shortsighted neglect of the human cultural impact on the environment. Now the effects of that neglect have become evident, and have once again become of concern to adapting individuals worried about their health, their food sources, and where the next kilowatts of electricity are coming from. The forecasters of doom may be overstating the case somewhat about the nearness of cultural disaster, but it is clear that the next phases of human evolution will see very sharp revisions in life-styles and new cultural forms emerging in a changed world.

Daniel R. Gross

The Great Sisal Scheme

In northeastern Brazil, the lush green coastal vegetation almost hides the endemic human misery of the region. Unless you look closely, the busy streets of Salvador and Recife and the waving palm trees mask the desperation of city slums, the poverty of plantation workers. When you leave the well-traveled coastal highways and go—usually on a dusty, rutted road—toward the interior, the signs of suffering become more and more apparent.

The transition is quick and brutal. Within 50 miles the vegetation changes from palm, tropical fruit, and dark-green broad-leafed trees to scrawny brush only slightly greener than the dusty earth. Nearly every plant is armed with spines or thorns. The hills are jagged, with hard faces of rock exposed. This is the *sertão*, the interior of northeastern Brazil.

If the *sertão* were honest desert, it would probably contain only a few inhabitants and a fair share of human misery. But the *sertão* is deceitful and fickle. It will smile for several years in a row, with sufficient rains arriving for the growing seasons. Gardens and crops will flourish. Cattle fatten. Then, without warning, another growing season comes, but the rains don't. The drought may go on, year after dusty year. Crops fail. Cattle grow thin and die. Humans begin to do the same. In bad droughts, the people of the *sertão* migrate to other regions by the thousands.

The bandits, the mystics, the droughts and migrants, the dreams and schemes of the *sertão* hold a special place in Brazilian folklore, literature, and song. Even at its worst, the *sertão* has been a fertile ground for the human imagination.

For two years, I studied the impact of sisal crops—a recent dream and scheme—on the people of the *sertão*. Taking an ecological approach, I found that sisal, which some poetic dreamers call "green gold," has greatly changed northeastern Brazil. But the changes have not been what the economic planners anticipated. And misery has not left the *sertão*.

I lived in Vila Nova, a small village with a population less than 500 about an hour's drive from the town of Victoria in Bahia State. Vila Nova is striking only for its drabness. Weeds grow in the middle of unpaved streets. Facing the plaza is an incomplete series of nondescript row houses. Some have faded pastel façades, others are mud brown because their owners never managed to plaster over the rough adobe walls. The village looks decadent, yet the oldest building is less than 20 years old and most were built after 1963.

Cattle raisers settled the *sertão* 400 years ago when the expanding sugar plantations of the coast demanded large supplies of beef and traction animals. A "civilization of leather" developed, with generations of colorful and intrepid cowboys (*vaqueiros*) clad entirely in rawhide to protect themselves against the thorny scrub vegetation. As the population of the *sertão* grew, many *sertanejos* settled down to subsistence farming. Gradually the entire region became a cul-de-sac, with many small and medium-sized estates occupied by descendants of the *vaqueiros* and others who had drifted into the region.

Life was never easy in this thorny land, for the work was hard and the environment cruel. Yet cooperation and mutual assistance provided assurance of survival even to the poorest. The chief crops were manioc, beans, and corn, and most of what was grown was consumed by the cultivator's family. Most families received some share of meat and milk, and consumed highly nutritious foods like beans and squash, in addition to starchy foods like manioc flour.

When droughts menaced the region all but the wealthiest ranchers migrated temporarily to the coast to work on the sugar plantations. When the rains came again to the *sertão*, they nearly always returned, for the work in the cane fields was brutal and labor relations had not changed greatly from the time when slaves worked the plantations.

Originally from Mexico, sisal was introduced to Brazil early in this century and reached the *sertão* in the 1930's. Farmers found sisal useful for hedgerows because its tough, pointed leaves effectively kept out cattle. The cellulose core of the long sisal leaf contains hard fibers, which can be twisted together into twine and rope. When World War II cut off the supply of Manila hemp to the United States, buyers turned to Brazil for fiber. At first only hedgerow sisal was exploited, but the state of Bahia offered incentives for planting sisal as a cash crop. Since sisal plants require about four years to mature, Brazil did not begin to export the fiber in significant quantities until 1945. The demand persisted, and by 1951, Brazil was selling actively in the world market as prices rose.

In Vila Nova, a young entrepreneur who owned a mule team, David Castro, heard about the prices being paid for sisal fiber and planted the first acres of sisal in 1951. By 1968, in the county of Victoria where Vila Nova is located, so many people had caught "sisal fever" that half of the total land area was planted in the crop. Sisal is easily transplanted and cultivated, requires little care, and is highly resistant to drought. It has some drawbacks as a cultivated plant, however. At least one annual weeding is necessary or else the field may become choked with thorn bushes, weeds, and suckers (Unwanted small sisal plants growing from the base of parent plants). A field abandoned for two years becomes unusable, practically unreclaimable. Despite these difficulties, many landowners planted sisal, especially in 1951 and 1962, years of high prices on the world market.

From the outset, sisal produced differential rewards for those who planted

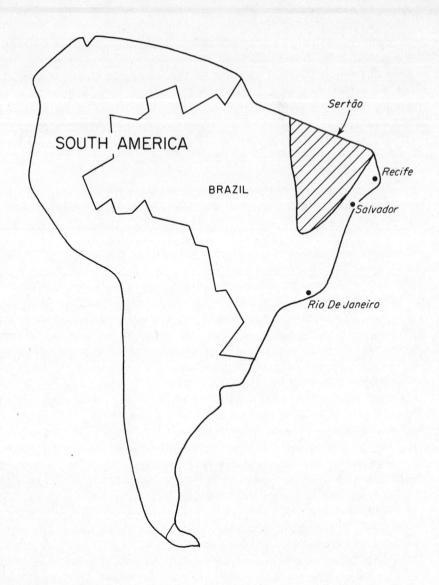

SOUTH AMERICA

BRAZIL

Sertão

Recife

Salvador

Rio De Janeiro

it. Owners of small plots (ten acres or less) planted proportionately more
of their land in sisal than did large landowners. Many who owned just a few
acres simply planted all their land in sisal in expectation of large profits.
This deprived them of whatever subsistence they had managed to scratch
out of the ground in the past. But work was easy to find because the need
for labor in the sisal fields grew rapidly. When, after four years, the crops
were ready to harvest, many small landholders discovered to their dismay
that prices had dropped sharply, and that harvest teams did not want to work
small crops. They had planted sisal with dreams of new clothes, new homes,
even motor vehicles purchased with sisal profits, but found their fields choked

with unusable sisal and became permanent field laborers harvesting sisal on large landholdings. In this way, sisal created its own labor force.

The separation of sisal fiber from the leaf is known as decortication. In Brazil, this process requires enormous amounts of manual labor. The decorticating machine is basically a spinning rasp powered by a gasoline or diesal motor. Sisal leaves are fed into it by hand, and the spinning rasp beats out the pulp or residue leaving only the fibers, which the worker pulls out of the whirling blades. Mounted on a trailer, the machine is well adapted to the scattered small-scale plantations of northeastern Brazil.

The decortication process requires constant labor for harvesting the year round. Sisal leaves, once cut, must be defibered quickly before the hot sun renders them useless. Each decorticating machine requires a crew of about seven working in close coordination. The first step is harvesting. Two cutters move from plant to plant, first lopping off the needle-sharp thorns from the leaves, then stooping to sever each leaf at the base. A transporter, working with each cutter, gathers the leaves and loads them on a burro. The leaves are taken to the machine and placed on a low stage for the defiberer to strip, one by one. A residue man removes the pulpy mass stripped from the leaves from under the motor, supplies the defiberer with leaves, and bundles and ties the freshly stripped fiber. Each bundle is weighed and counted in the day's production. Finally, the dryer spreads the wet, greenish fiber in the sun, where it dries and acquires its characteristic blond color.

For the planters and sisal buyers, this method of decortication operates profitably, but for the workers it exacts a terrible cost. The decorticating machine requires a man to stand in front of the whirling rasp for four to five hours at a shift, introducing first the foot and then the point of each leaf. The worker pulls against the powerful motor, which draws the leaf into the mouth of the machine. After half of each leaf is defibered, the defiberer grasps the raw fiber to insert the remaining half of the leaf. There is a constant danger that the fiber will entangle his hand and pull it into the machine. Several defiberers have lost arms this way. The strain and danger would seem to encourage slow and deliberate work; but in fact, defiberers decorticate about 25 leaves per minute. This is because the crew is paid according to the day's production of fiber. Although the defiberer is the highest-paid crew member, many of them must work both morning and afternoon shifts to make ends meet.

A residue man's work is also strenuous. According to measurements I made, this job requires that a man lift and carry about 2,700 pounds of material per hour. The residue man, moreover, does not work in shifts. He works as long as the machinery is running. The remaining jobs on the crew are less demanding and may be held by women or adolescents, but even these jobs are hard, requiring frequent lifting and stooping in the broiling semidesert sun.

With their own fields in sisal, to earn money the villagers had to work at harvesting sisal for large landowners. And because wages were low, more and more people had to work for families to survive. In 1968 two-thirds of all men and women employed in Vila Nova worked full time in the sisal decorticating process. Many of these were youths. Of 33 village boys between the ages of 10 and 14, 24 worked on sisal crews. Most people had completely abandoned subsistence agriculture.

Sisal brought other significant changes in the life of Vila Nova. Because most villagers no longer grew their food, it now had to be imported. Numerous shops, stocking beans, salt pork, and manioc flour, grew up in the village. A few villagers with capital or good contacts among wholesalers in the town of Victoria built small businesses based on this need. Other villagers secured credit from sisal buyers in Victoria to purchase sisal decorticating machinery.

The shopkeepers and sisal machine owners in the village formed a new economic class on whom the other villagers were economically dependent. The wealthier group enjoyed many advantages. Rather than going to work on the sisal machines, most of the children of these entrepreneurs went to school. All of the upper group married in a socially prescribed way: usually a church wedding with civil ceremonies as well. But among the workers, common-law marriages were frequent, reflecting their lack of resources for celebrating this important event.

The only villagers who became truly affluent were David Castro and his cousin. These men each owned extensive sisal plantations and several decorticating units. Most importantly, each became middlemen, collecting sisal in warehouses in the village and trucking the fiber into Victoria. David, moreover, owned the largest store in the village. Since the village was located on David's land, he sold house plots along the streets. He also acted as the representative of the dominant political party in Victoria, serving as a ward boss during elections and as an unofficial but effective police power. There was a difference between David and the large ranch owners of the past. While wealthy men were formerly on close terms with their dependents, helping them out during tough times, David's relations with the villagers were cold, businesslike, and exploitative. Most of the villagers disliked him, both for his alleged stinginess and because he never had time to talk to anyone.

During my stay in Vila Nova I gradually became aware of these changes in the social and economic structure. But I hoped to establish that the introduction of sisal had also resulted in a quantitative, ecological change in the village. At the suggestion of Dr. Barbara A. Underwood of the Institute of Human Nutrition at Columbia University, I undertook an intensive study to determine what influence sisal had on diet and other factors of a few representative households. When I looked at household budgets, I quickly discovered that those households that depended entirely on wages from sisal work spent nearly all their money on food. Families with few or no children or with several able-bodied workers seemed to be holding their own. But families with few workers or several dependents were less fortunate. To understand the condition of these families, I collected information not only on cash budgets but also on household *energy budgets*. Each household expends not only money, but also energy in the form of calories in performing work. "Income" in the latter case is the caloric value of the foods consumed by these households. By carefully measuring the amount and kind of food consumed, I was able to determine the total inflow and outflow of energy in individual households.

For example, Miguel Costa is a residue man who works steadily on a sisal unit belonging to a nearby planter. He lives in Vila Nova in a two-room adobe hut with his wife and four small children, ranging in age from three to eight. During the seven-day test period, Miguel worked at the sisal motor four and a half days, while his wife stayed home with the children. I was able to estimate Miguel's caloric expenditures during the test period. During the same period, I visited his home after every meal where his wife graciously permitted me to weigh the family's meager food supplies to determine food consumption. Each day the supply of beans diminished by less than one-half pound and the weight of the coarse manioc flour eaten with beans dropped by two or three pounds. Manioc flour is almost pure starch, high in calories but low in essential nutrients. At the beginning of the week about half a pound of fatty beef and pork were consumed each day, but this was exhausted by mid-week. The remainder of the family's calories were consumed in the form of sugar, bread, and boiled sweet manioc, all high in calories but low in other nutrients.

Estimating the caloric requirements of the two adults from their activities and the children's by Food and Agriculture Organization minimum requirements, the household had a minimum need of 88,142 calories for the week. The household received only 65,744 calories, or 75 percent of need. Since the two adults did not lose weight while maintaining their regular levels of activity, they were apparently meeting their total calorie requirements. Miguel, for example, had been working steadily at his jcb for weeks before the test and continued to do so for weeks afterward. Had he not been maintaining himself calorically, he could not have sustained his performance at

Calorie Budget of a Sisal Worker's Household

	AVERAGE DAILY CALORIC INTAKE	MINIMUM DAILY CALORIC REQUIREMENTS	PERCENT OF NEED MET	PERCENT OF STANDARD WEIGHT OF CHILDREN
Household	9,392	12,592	75%	
Worker	3,642	3,642	100	
Wife	2,150	2,150	100	
Son (age 8)	1,112	2,100	53	62%
Daughter (6)	900	1,700	53	70
Son (5)	900	1,700	53	85
Son (3)	688	1,300	53	90

his demanding job. Despite his small stature (5 feet, 4 inches) Miguel required some 3,642 calories per day to keep going at the job. And Miguel's wife evidently also maintained herself calorically—pregnant at the time of my visit, she later gave birth to a normal child.

The caloric deficit in Miguel's household, then, was almost certainly being made up by systematically depriving the dependent children of sufficient calories. This was not intentional, nor were the parents aware of it. Nor could Miguel have done anything about it even if he had understood this process. If he were to work harder or longer to earn more money, he would incur greater caloric costs and would have to consume more. If he were to reduce his food intake to leave more food for his children, he would be obliged by his own physiology to work less, thereby earning less. If he were to provide his household with foods higher in caloric content (for example, more manioc), he would almost certainly push his children over the brink into a severe nutritional crisis that they might not survive for lack of protein and essential vitamins. Thus, Miguel, a victim of ecological circumstances, is maintaining his family against terrible odds.

Miguel's children respond to this deprivation in a predictable manner. Nature has provided a mechanism to compensate for caloric deficiencies during critical growth periods: the rate of growth simply slows down. As a result, Miguel's children, and many other children of sisal workers, are much smaller than properly nourished children of the same age. The longer the deprivation goes on the more pronounced the tendency: thus Miguel's youngest boy, who is three, is 90 percent of standard weight for his age. The five-year-old boy is 85 percent; the six-year-old girl, 70 percent; and the oldest boy, at eight, is only 62 percent of standard weight. Caloric deprivation takes its toll in other ways than stunting. Caloric and other nutritional deficiencies are prime causes of such problems as reduced mental capacity and lower resistance to infection. In Vila Nova one-third of all children die by the age of 10.

When I surveyed the nutritional status of the people of Vila Nova, I found a distinct difference between the average body weights of the two economic groups formed since the introduction of sisal (shopkeepers and motor-owners on the one hand, and workers on the other). Since the introduction of sisal the upper economic group exhibited a marked improvement in nutritional status (as measured by body weight) while the lower group showed a decline in nutritional status. The statistics showed that while one group was better off than before, a majority of the population was actually worse off nutritionally.

This conclusion was unexpected in view of the widespread claim that sisal had brought lasting benefits to the people of the sertão, that sisal had narrowed the gap between the rich and the poor. Clearly, changes had come about. Towns like Victoria had grown far beyond their presisal size.

But outside the towns, in the villages and rural farmsteads, the picture is different. Having abandoned subsistence agriculture, many workers moved to villages to find work on sisal units. In settlements such as Vila Nova wages and profits depend on the world price for sisal. When I arrived in 1967, the price was at the bottom of a trough that had paralyzed all growth and construction. Wages were so low that outmigration was showing signs of resuming as in the drought years. In spite of local symbols of wealth and "development," my observations revealed a continuation of endemic poverty throughout most of the countryside and even an intensification of the social and economic divisions that have always characterized the *sertão*.

Sisal is not the only example of an economic change that has brought unforeseen, deleterious consequences. The under-developed world is replete with examples of development schemes that brought progress only to a privileged few. The example of sisal in northeastern Brazil shows that an ecological approach is needed in all economic planning. Even more important, we must recognize that not all economic growth brings social and economic development in its true sense. As the sisal example shows, a system may be formed (often as part of a worldwide system) that only increases the store of human misery.

Thayer Scudder

Koriba Dam:
The Ecological Hazards of Making a Lake

The impact of the Kariba Dam on alluvial cultivation below the damsite is an example of how man's engineering capacities can drastically reduce the productivity of an existing ecosystem. A glance at figures 1 and 2 is sufficient to show the extreme irregularity that has been introduced into the annual regime of the Zambezi River between Kariba gorge and the Kafue River as a result of the dam. Although commercial agriculture is of virtually no importance at present in the stretch of river involved, this is of little comfort to those thousands of Africans who desire to cultivate the fertile alluviums on a twice annual basis for their own subsistence. Here we have a pattern of increased risks for the farmer in an already high-risk environment. It is too early to predict how the farmer will respond, although it is already obvious

Reprinted from Thayer Scudder, "Kariba Dam: The Ecological Hazards of Making a Lake," Natural History (February 1969), 68–72, with permission of Natural History Magazine. Copyright © The American Museum of Natural History, 1969.

that he has suffered far more loss from man's manipulation of the Zambezi than he ever did during any equivalent time period in the past.

For the first three years (October, 1958–September, 1961), there was no Zambezi flood between the dam and the Kafue confluence; indeed, no water was released in the first seven months that the dam was sealed, except for a small trickle in March/April, 1959. During the rainy season, the agricultural implications of having the Zambezi restricted to its primary channel throughout this period were inconsequential for alluvium previously cultivated. On the other hand, the area that could be cultivated during the dry season was greatly reduced because of the absence of annual flooding. During the 1961–62 season, the dam-controlled regime approximated the original flow pattern for the first time since impoundment began. While this must have been a relief to those farmers who had suffered during the previous three dry seasons, it proved disastrous for those who had begun to cultivate rainy season gardens on the lower-level alluviums. This land had never been cultivated during the rains in the past because of flooding during the annual rise of the Zambezi. When this pattern was approximated in April, 1962, through nearly a sixfold increase in river flow over the previous month, these new

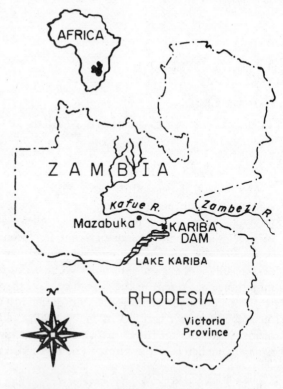

FIGURE 1

gardens were inundated by over ten feet of water within a single day. (According to the District Assistant for Lusitu, this loss of crops subsequently led to a food shortage in the Lusitu village of Kadabuka, which was most dependent on the gardens concerned.) The next year the man-made flood of the Zambezi came in February, again destroying crops in these lower-terrace alluvial gardens, but fortunately not rising sufficiently high so as to destroy the extensive maize gardens planted in the Lusitu Delta.

The case was altogether different, however, during 1963–64. Then three sluice gates were alternately opened and shut throughout most of the rains, so that virtually none of the Zambezi and tributary delta alluviums could even be planted during the most important agricultural season. Furthermore, since the river dropped rapidly in March, and no rain fell during April, dry-season crops planted at that time on the higher alluviums would have been subsequently heat struck. The next three years continued a similar pattern of extreme irregularity, with 1965–66 being a particularly disastrous year for the alluvial cultivator. Then early planted, rainy season crops would have been flooded out by the December rise, whereas most late-planted crops would have been destroyed by the April peak. Furthermore, planting during the middle of the season would, of course, have been impossible, because the water level remained up during most of December and January. As if this were not enough, those crops planted during the first part of the dry season would have also been flooded out, this time by the opening of two sluice

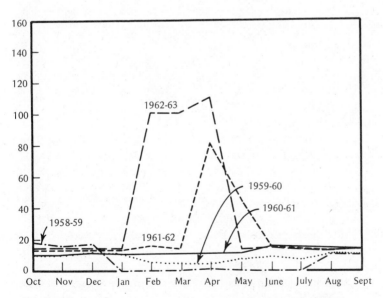

FIGURE 2. Zambezi River flows below Kariba Dam, October 1958 to September 1963. Average monthly flows in thousands of cubic feet per second. Data provided by the Central African Power Corporation.

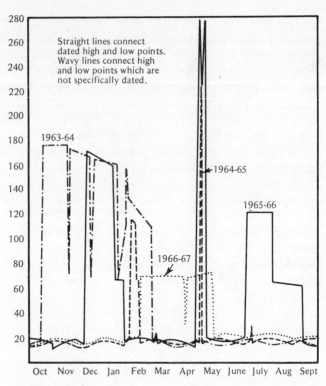

FIGURE 3. Zambezi River flows below Kariba Dam, October 1963 to September 1967. Flow indicated in thousands of feet per second. Data provided by the Central African Power Corporation.

gates in June. Under the circumstances, it is hard to imagine how those regulating the flow of water through the dam could have acted in a way more detrimental to downriver agriculture.

At this point it is important to emphasize, in all fairness, that Zambian population densities in the downriver area are low except in the Lusitu area where relocation was responsible for creating one of the highest rural densities in the country. Furthermore, practically all of the food grown on riverine alluviums is for local consumption. On the other hand, I am not aware that those planning for Kariba even considered the implications of alternate outflows for the future development of the downriver area. Nor am I aware that they considered the costs of possible food shortages arising from the present regime for the local people and for the government. I am protesting not so much against what happened as against the narrow viewpoint of those responsible for planning installations like Kariba. This project was essentially a unipurpose scheme. The population to be relocated was seen, not as a resource, but as an expensive nuisance, whose very existence was unfortunate. As for the future lake, it was strictly a by-product of the dam, whereas the needs of downriver inhabitants were considered only where backed up by political power, and then were seen as constraints by those who viewed the Kariba Project almost entirely as a means for generating power.

My study of a single Tonga village in 1956–57 showed that the large majority of farms in the Middle Zambezi Valley cultivated roughly one acre per capita, the expected harvest being sufficient to support the population during most years (Scudder, 1962). Unfortunately, just prior to relocation, the valley did not provide this minimum, in large part because of population increase and land degradation. (As used in this paper, land degradation includes both sheet and gully erosion and reduced fertility arising from overcultivation and overgrazing with or without accompanying erosion.) Though the annually inundated alluvial soils could support permanent cultivation for an indefinite period, over 20 per cent of the farmers in our five river villages did not have any access to such lands. Furthermore, of those who did, only a small proportion controlled large enough acreages to meet their consumption needs. In other words, most of the population also relied on the cultivation of less fertile, upper-level alluviums and on colluvial and karroo soils, which had to be periodically fallowed. Though the Tonga were quite familiar with the amount of fallowing that their various garden types required to restore fertility, lack of additional land was responsible for the overcultivation and hence exhaustion of certain alluvial gardens by the 1930's. This process continued during the 1940's, when certain farmers began to pioneer less fertile karroo soils well back in the bush. By 1957, most of the better karroo soils within walking distance were under cultivation, while extensive areas of upper-terrace alluvium were so degraded as to be under indefinite fallow. Although the situation would have continued to deteriorate, since the exhaustion of the karroo soils was only a matter of years away, relocation intervened. The overtaxed lands were flooded, and the people were moved toward the valley's outer margin or into the Lusitu area below the damsite.

Resettlement, however, did not solve the land problem. In fact, for many villages in the southern portion of the valley, it only made it worse; since those soils least susceptible to degradation through cultivation had been permanently flooded along the banks of the Zambezi and the lower reaches of the major tributaries. Table I shows the amount of land available for relocation within the valley. Under the local system of agriculture, less than 40 per cent of this land could support semipermanent cultivation (category 1),[1] which involves five to ten years of continuous cropping, followed by a fallow period of approximately equal length. The rest (category 2), ranging in quality from fair to poor, could support, at best, cultivation for about six years, followed by a twenty-year fallow. With almost all of the arable land

---

[1] This land consists mainly of deep woodland soils which had been only partially cultivated prior to relocation. Though their origin is still in doubt, apparently Bainbridge and Edwards (1963) believe that they were derived from non-karroo parent material, being transported into the valley from the adjacent escarpment and plateau. Mostly sandy clays, they are quite susceptible to erosion.

Table I: Cultivable Land and Population in Gwembe District Relocation Areas (1958)[1]

CHIEFTAINCY	POPULATION TO BE RELOCATED	LAND AVAILABLE FOR RELOCATION	TYPE [2]
Mwemba	9,000	20,000	Mostly category 2
Sinazongwe	9,000	30,000	At least 14,000 acres, category 1
Chipepo	9,300	8,000 (8,281)	Mostly category 2
Sinadambwe	none	4,550	Mostly category 2
Simamba	2,200	7,800	Mostly category 2
Lusitu	none	25,000	Mostly category 1
Mpendele-Mutulanganga	none	7,500	Categories 1 and 2
	29,500	102,850	Approx. 40,000 acres Category 1

[1] Information provided by the District Commissioner, Gwembe.
[2] Category 1: Supports "semipermanent agriculture" (5–10 years cultivation followed by 5–10 years fallowing).
Category 2: Supports "bush-fallow agriculture" (2–10 years cultivation followed by 20 years fallowing).

in the valley surveyed, this meant that semi-permanent cultivators needed an absolute minimum of two acres per capita, whereas bush fallow cultivators needed five or more. The situation was by far the worst in Mwemba, where 9,000 people had access to approximately 20,000 acres of category 2 soil, much of which fell in the less fertile and more easily erosible grades. To meet their needs, at least 40,000 more acres were needed.

The problem of land shortage presented by relocation was obvious from the start to all government officials concerned. After resettlement had been completed, it was known that approximately one-third of the population would find themselves in serious straits within ten years. The rest were more fortunate, although there was little room for population increase in some areas, and all areas could easily become degraded in the years ahead through erosion, overcultivation, and overgrazing.

The Department of Agriculture's response to this situation was to emphasize erosion control and agricultural intensification, although there was general agreement that the situation in the south of Mwemba was hopeless without further relocation. Two types of erosion control were stressed. The first would involve a prohibition of cultivation within 25 yards of the banks of major tributaries. The need for such an ordinance was obvious to all ecologically oriented personnel familiar with the tributary system on the plateau, in the escarpment, and in the valley. Referring to Mazabuka District on the plateau, Bainbridge and Edwards reported that "The amount of runoff, coupled with sheet and gully erosion that takes place during the heavy rains, is quite frightening." With much of their grass cropped right down to the roots, dambos along the upper reaches of rivers like the Lusitu are increasingly subject to abnormal flash floods. In the escarpment country leading down into the valley, the same authors refer to air photographs that "show clearly the denudation of the protective strips of woodland along the stream banks and the spreading of the cultivation away from the streams up the steep slopes." Without a protective cover, flash floods each year remove more of the soil, with the authors estimating that within ten to fifteen years "there will no longer be sufficient soil left in the escarpment to carry the present population." In the valley, flash floods periodically sweep the now unprotected banks of the major tributaries. When the Lusitu rose to record heights in a matter of hours in March, 1963, the extensive riverbank areas under cultivation since relocation were severely eroded. Clearly, this would not have occurred if the riverine fringe vegetation had not been systematically removed through the upper, lower, and perhaps middle reaches of the Lusitu. The second type of erosion control would stress the construction of contour ridges to keep relocation-area soils *in situ*.

The core of the program of intensification was a two- or four-crop rotation supplemented by the use of cattle manure, applied on departmental demonstration gardens and on the holdings of Peasant Farmers and Native Authority Improved Farmers. The first ten Peasant Farmers were selected by the District Commissioner in 1959. After receiving credit from a revolving fund under the DC's jurisdiction for their equipment and cattle needs, they became the responsibility of the Department of Agriculture. At first, each Peasant Farmer was restricted to a 20-acre holding. While building this up, he was supposed to follow a four-crop rotation, involving equal acreages of maize, sorghum, cotton, and a green-manure crop. Supplemental manure (at three tons per acre) was to be applied annually to half the acreage planted in grain, with each farmer told to build up a herd of twenty cattle to meet his ox traction and manure needs. The NA Improved Farmers had much smaller holdings on which they could receive a one pound sterling bonus per acre, provided they followed a simple, grain-legume rotation and manured half the grain plot each year.

If actually practiced, the recommended measures most likely would have been effective in maintaining soil fertility and preventing erosion. However, the degree of acceptance by the farmers has been minimal. No ordinance prohibiting cultivation within 25 yards of tributary beds was enacted. Even if it had been, it is unlikely that enforcement would have been possible. Throughout their known history, the Tonga have always cleared tributary banks, except for occasional shade and fruit trees, in order to cultivate the fertile alluvial soils. After relocation and the loss of Zambezi and delta alluviums, these soils became even more desirable, with tributary-bank clearing extended throughout much of the valley. While those Tonga involved were well aware of the resulting dangers of erosion, they saw no option but to continue as in the past, since no acceptable substitute for riverbank cultivation was presented to them.

While contour ridging was not actively opposed, the Native Authority was unwilling to back it publicly through its own regulations. Well aware that the valley residents did not really understand the basis for contouring, the Native Authority did not wish to associate itself with a potentially unpopular measure, since their support had always been low, especially after this relocation, which the NA councilors and chiefs had been pressured into supporting by the central government. Though some 1,230 miles of ridges, protecting 14,247 acres, were dug under the jurisdiction of agricultural staff members by October, 1964, they never received popular understanding, let alone sufficient support to provide for their maintenance. A year later, construction of the ridges apparently stopped in the Lusitu area, and thereafter I recall seeing only occasional references to them in agricultural reports. Though I do not know how these ridges are faring today, some Lusitu farmers broke them down in connection with the cultivation and extension of their gardens.

Intensification in the valley has fared no better as a degradation control device. Out of a total district farming population of well over 10,000 men, to the best of my knowledge there have never been more than 25 Peasant Farmers and 75 Improved Farmers. Moreover, the degree of intensification among these has decreased, if anything, through the years. According to the Agricultural Assistant at Lusitu, in 1965, those wishing to become Rural Council Improved Farmers wanted to grow unrotated cotton. In 1967, most Peasant Farmers had sown cotton or maize in plots that they were supposed to plant in green-manure crops. In the Kayuni block of the Lusitu, the most enterprising of the five Peasant Farmers was monocropping cotton during a four-year period, after which he planned to carry on a cotton-maize rotation. He had also stopped applying manure, although here the reason, as with other progressive farmers, was the breakdown of his Scotch cart, for which it was literally impossible to get parts owing to the Rhodesian crisis. Moreover, he had substantially increased his acreage with twenty acres now planted in cotton and nine in maize, versus only three in sun hemp and one in groundnuts during the 1966–67 season. As for the application of manure at the village level, no one in the village that I have been observing over the past ten years had applied it during the previous season or any other season. The same applied to any form of rotation. Indeed, I doubt that it is an exaggeration to state that no more than 1 per cent of the valley farmers have ever regularly practiced either animal manuring or crop rotation.

The present relocation areas just cannot support the existing population under these agricultural practices. In South Mwemba, the population has exceeded the carrying capacity of the land, and is once again subject to periodic food shortages that are bound to get worse with time. To prevent this, the government has decided to again relocate at least 6,000 people, and it is only a matter of time before this resettlement occurs. Elsewhere, the situation is still within the control of the local population, since exhausted fields can still be replaced by uncultivated land around the margins of the relocation areas or in the few areas that have yet to be settled. On the other hand, I expect all available land to be utilized within the next ten years unless there is a major reduction of population or a change in agricultural techniques. In the highly favored Lusitu area, the surplus population is already crossing into the previously unsettled Mpendele-Mutulanganga area. Although no one in my own Lusitu study village had joined this movement by 1967, some of the men had begun to clear distant gardens on the far side of the Lusitu. In all cases, no intensification was occurring; rather pioneer farmers were simply re-establishing the same extensive system of bush fallow cultivation.

Although the problem outlined in the last few paragraphs is a severe one, it is not my purpose in this paper to propose possible solutions. Rather I wish to emphasize, in closing, that what we are dealing with here are two incompatible systems of agriculture. One, proposed by the Department of Agriculture, is satisfactory from an ecological point of view, except that it is not acceptable to the farming population. The other, while satisfying to the farmer, has serious, indeed catastrophic, ecological implications under present population conditions. The problem is to design a compromise system acceptable to all involved.

Throughout Africa, research stations have tended to develop new techniques without taking into consideration the total context within which the farmer, for whom these techniques are designed, lives. Ecologists, I think, tend to make a similar mistake when they propose alternative land-use systems without asking the questions, "Can these support the existing human population, which, after all, is the ecological dominant in the area?" Or, "If not, is there an alternative way of life available for the people, which they are likely to accept?" If, for example, cattle pastoralists are to be driven out of an area to be used for game cropping or conservation purposes, the same concern must go into planning an acceptable future for them as relates to other communities within the habitat. Failure to do this is not only morally indefensible, but is also apt to be politically unacceptable. In other words, a technical or ecological solution to problems of environmental degradation is not of much use unless it is understood and implemented by the relevant people at the local and national levels.

References

BAINBRIDGE, W. R., AND A. C. R. EDMONDS. *Northern Rhodesia Forest Department Book for Gwembe, South Choma and Mazabuka Districts*, 1963.

SCUDDER, T. *The Ecology of the Gwembe Tonga.* (*Kariba Studies*, Vol. II); Manchester University for Rhodes-Livingstone Institute, 1962.

———. "The Economic Basis of Egyptian Nubian Labor Migration." A *Symposium on Contemporary Nubia*, ed. R. FERNEA. HRAF Press, New Haven, 1967.

Pertti J. Pelto

The Social Impact of the Snowmobile: Differentiation and Stratification

The results of the snowmobile revolution—the mechanization of herding, the increased costs of participation, the decimation of the herds, and the great increase in the speed of winter transportation—have all had very far-reaching effects on the lifeways of Sevettijärvi people. I will turn now to an examination of some of the changes in social organization and related characteristics of the Skolt Lapps that can be linked to this technological change. The data suggest the following:

1. The cash cost of effective participation in herding is beyond the resources of some families, so that they have had to drop out of serious participation in herding activities.
2. The use of snowmobiles drastically changed the role requirements of reindeer herding. These changes, in general, favor youth over age, so that older herders (who would be the persons most likely to wish to continue in that economic activity) are being forced out in favor of younger men.
3. The almost total loss of individual and family control of the reindeer has made it extremely difficult and unrewarding for small owners to stay in reindeer herding.
4. Aside from the individual differences of involvement in herding, the coming of the snowmobile has pushed the entire Skolt Lapp population sharply in the direction of cash dependency and debt.
5. The increased dependence on cash has forced many individuals to seek new types of employment, with the result that there is now greater diversity of occupations than had been the case ten years ago, as well as greatly increased out-migration. (Of course, the availabilty of nonreindeer-connected jobs in the area is not a direct result of the snowmobile.)
6. In the shift to cash income and regular employment, as well as in the readjustment to the changed reindeer industry, some persons have achieved considerable success, while others have tended to fall out of the contest. *A general increase in socioeconomic inequalities has resulted.*
7. The increased speed with which people can get from one place to another has increased the rate of social interaction, drastically reduced the amount of time required for some important activities (for example,

freight hauling), and has brought about changes in the scheduling and patterning of many group activities (for example, men return home from a roundup each night rather than camping out for many days at a time).

Changes in Role Requirements

By "role requirements" I mean the skills and characteristics (including motivation) that individuals must have in order to participate successfully in particular tasks, occupations, or other defined positions in the social system. For example, we usually assume that the role requirements for football players include a certain minimum of physical strength and hardiness; elementary schoolteachers should have skills in establishing positive relationships with children (among other important attributes); and political leaders should have decision-making capabilities. Most individuals occupying particular occupational roles are deficient in one or more of the needed skills or capabilities but manage nonetheless to perform their jobs sufficiently well because they have *most* of the requisite talents. Generally, the persons with the greatest skills (and resources) in the significant role requirements are the most successful in reaping the rewards (the profits, benefits, public acclaim) of particular social roles.

The following is a list of some of the principal requirements or skills in reindeer herding which *have been eliminated or drastically modified* by the snowmobile. Many of these activities were foci of conversation among reindeer men in 1958–59, as they compared experiences and indirectly assessed one another's performances and prestige.

1. Training, managing, and driving with draught reindeer.
2. Constructing harnesses and other equipment for draught reindeer use.
3. Lassoing reindeer in open country.
4. Recognizing individual reindeer (owner's marks, etc.) in open country.
5. All-day skiing in pursuit of straying reindeer.
6. Camping and "housekeeping" in forest and tundra.
7. Managing cows and calves during spring calving.
8. Controlled transporting of small herds of reindeer (for example, from roundup sites to home grazing grounds).
9. Training and managing herd dogs.

In place of these skills, the mechanized herdsman of the 1960s and 1970s must have:

1. Skills in maneuvering snow vehicles on rough terrain.
2. Ability to coordinate herding movements with other snowmobile drivers through visual cues (since voice communications do not carry over sound of motor).

3. Skills and resources (including money) for maintaining effective operation of motor vehicles.
4. Shrewd judgment concerning selling animals as they appear almost randomly in the various roundups.
5. Endurance and mobility required for attendance and participation *on relatively short notice* in different roundups at various locations throughout the year.

Comparing these two lists, one of the features we should note is that expertise in many of the skills that were important in the past was acquired through long years of experience, so that older herders were, in several respects, more competent than younger ones. Although physical endurance was important, many of the role enactments of reindeer herding were based on accumulated information, patience, and good judgment. In 1958–59 only one man in the community was definitely too old to participate actively in reindeer herding because of declining physical strength. He was seventy-one years old. Most of the other men of advanced years, including several in the sixty to sixty-five bracket, participated in many aspects of the work.

As the use of snowmobiles spread, the younger men were usually the more enthusiastic proponents of the machines, and they were the first to develop the skills for operating the machines in the backlands. Some of the more active young snowmobile herdsmen had never acquired the skills necessary for managing draught animals and other aspects of the pre-snowmobile herder's role; some of them were semidropouts until the machines made it possible for them to compete successfully in herding operations. Apparently the younger men were more willing to take physical and financial risks, and they were less concerned with the maintenance of the older herding regimen; also, many of them had had more experience with machinery as well as more exposure to new technical concepts as a result of both schooling and occasional wage-work activities. Their exposure to technical machinery during military training may have played a part in their readiness to work with the snowmobiles. In any case, they were quite successful in developing the new machine skills. We should also remind ourselves that the younger men had, for the most part, never experienced the intensive, "personalized" herding techniques that had characterized Skolt Lapp husbandry in prewar days. They therefore had less reason to put strong emphasis on intensive contacts between animals and men in the herding situation.

The slowness of the older men to develop proficiency with snowmobiles was almost certainly due to their attitudes toward reindeer herding rather than to a lack of mechanical capabilities as such. The prospect of eliminating many of the old herding practices was distasteful to many of the men who had been most active and successful in pre-snowmobile days. Whatever the causes, there has been a distinct shift toward a younger age group in reindeer operations, and this shift would not have come about if there had been no change to mechanized herding.

Dropping Out of Reindeer Herding

In 1960 a large percentage of the Skolt household heads were actively engaged in herding. Even those household heads who took no part in the official association work carried out a variety of tasks with their own family herds, especially during the latter part of the winter. In addition to the heads of families, some young men in their teens and early twenties also were involved with reindeer work. There were, in fact, very few other activities or occupations available to them.

Table 1 gives a breakdown by age categories of active reindeer herders of the Sevettijärvi area for 1960 and 1971.

The column labeled "Projected 1971" shows my estimate of the herding participation that would have been maintained if large-scale changes had not occurred in the system. It is based on the general assumption that active reindeer herdsmen maintain their participation in the system as long as health permits. Even serious losses of reindeer would not ordinarily cause a man to quit herding—provided such losses came about within the normal course of variations of "herding luck." Of the herdsmen active in 1960, only two or three have dropped out because of possibly attractive alternative sources of income. Some of the older men would have dropped out because of poor health and a few younger men not active in 1960 would have joined the ranks of association herdsmen. (Three herdsmen died during this decade.) The total number of herdsmen should have increased slightly.

The actual age profile of reindeer herders is quite different from this projection, however. We note in Table 1 that many of the men who were in the thirty-one to fifty age bracket in 1960 (and would be in their forties and fifties in 1971) have dropped out of active participation. Their place has been taken by the younger men. The trend is also clear if we compare the

Table 1: Age of Active Reindeer Herders, 1960 and 1971

AGE OF ACTIVE REINDEER HERDERS [a]	1960	PROJECTED 1971	ACTUAL 1971 [b]
15–20	4	4	7
21–30	13	8	10
31–40	7	12	13
41–50	12	6	2
51–60	4	10	2
61 +	1	3	3
Totals	41	43	37

[a] "Active" herders are those who participate in association work *in addition to* tending their own animals.
[b] Includes "part-time" herders.

number of *household heads* active in 1960 and in 1971. In spite of a small increase in the total number of households because of marriages contracted during the period (from forty-eight in 1960 to fifty-six in 1971), the number of household heads active in reindeer herding declined from twenty-five to nineteen. About a dozen men who were heads of households engaged in reindeer herding in 1960 have simply dropped out of the action because of the advent of snowmobiles.

These figures do not actually reflect the full extent of the decline in numbers of herders. As described earlier, before the snowmobile much of the reindeer-herding cycle was concerned with the care and maintenance of home herds. Some herders took relatively little part in association action, yet spent a great deal of time with their own animals, especially in the latter part of the winter. These men are not included in the list of "active reindeer herders" for 1960; yet their principal economic pursuits were basically aimed at reindeer husbandry. These "home herdsmen" now have *no* herds. Some of them have lost *all* their animals, but even those who still have a few head take no part in herding activities except for attending roundups occasionally.

Some of the older men who have "retired" from reindeer herding were pushed out because of physical or social complications in their herding effectiveness. Here are some samples.

Feodor Osipoff [1] was forty-six years old in 1960, and at that time had one of the largest herds in the Näätämö area. He was regarded as an effective herder in most respects, particularly in active operations in the backlands. However, at reindeer roundups he was thought to drink too heavily on occasion, and therefore he did not always maintain good control over the sales of animals and other transactions in the important festive atmosphere of the roundup enclosures.

In the early 1960s his herds began to decline. He did not buy a snowmobile during the first crucial years of the technological transition. Indeed, he did not have the cash for a snowmobile, probably in part because of occasional heavy expenditures on beer and other alcoholic drinks. By 1965–66 he no longer took part in herding operations, as most of the active herdsmen operated with snowmobiles. By 1971 his herd had dwindled from a pre-snowmobile high of nearly 200 to a mere seventeen reindeer.

Because of his growing needs for cash (including the expenses of the second-hand snowmobile purchased in 1969), Feodor signed up in the unemployment register of the Finnish employment service and has been working at various locations in Inari commune on road crews during recent winters. His sons have not continued in reindeer herding.

Maxim, who is Feodor's brother, was also an active herdsman in 1960, with a herd that numbered about seventy head in 1958. With a large and growing family, he apparently could not easily afford to buy a snowmobile during the mid-1960s, and in any case he was against the conversion to mechanized herding. He tried to maintain his string of draught reindeer until 1968 but finally had to give up. Even the draught reindeer could not be maintained effectively under the altered herding structure.

In addition to his opposition to snowmobiles, he was increasingly bothered by

[1] This and the following names are pseudonyms.

some health problems that hampered his effectiveness. Maxim's herd is down to thirteen reindeer, according to the official figures of 1971.

Boris Kotala is a member of the Vätsäri association and was an active herder in 1960, although he was already nearly sixty years old. Since the mechanization of herding in the Vätsäri district was slow in developing, one cannot say that he was forced out of herding by the advent of the machines. However, his son Eero had become an active herder by 1967 and had already purchased a snowmobile in the fall of 1966. Since then, Eero has been quite successful in building up the family herd and is reputed to be one of the most effective young men in the local association. Thus, Boris has been able to retire gracefully from reindeer herding because the family's interests are ably represented both at roundups and in herd-gathering operations.

A few of the dropouts from reindeer herding are younger men who were already effective herdsmen in the old system and were apparently doing very well in adjusting to mechanized herding when they made the decision to change their economic pursuits. For example:

Nikolai Asimoff was one of the very young but active herders of 1960. Since his father was fairly old and semiretired from reindeer herding, Nikolai was the primary representative of the family in herding activities. He bought his first snowmobile in 1966–67, when the first Moto-Skis appeared in the local area. He became one of the most active herdsmen in the new, mechanized system; and in 1968–69 he was the second most active herder in the Näätämö district, in terms of work days for the association.

Nonetheless, the following year he got word from one of his wife's relatives, who spoke of employment possibilities at a large Swedish factory. He has now been working in Sweden for three years and visits his kinsmen at Sevettijärvi during his summer vacations. The family still has a few head of reindeer, but except for obtaining an occasional animal for meat, the economic importance of their reindeer herding is minimal.

Mechanized herding attracted the interest of some younger men who were indifferent herders in pre-snowmobile days. The following is an example of a young man who was apparently becoming a successful mechanized herder when he made the decision to quit herding activity.

Evvan Andreev was a young man just back from military service in 1958–59 and seemed to be rather unskilled in reindeer herding, although his father showed great patience and care in grooming him for that occupation. The fact that the family had fairly sizeable herds (by local standards) certainly should have been an advantage in motivating him to improve his herding skills.

In the early 1960s he worked in logging camps somewhat more than he did in reindeer herding. With the advent of the snowmobile, the family was among the first Skolt Lapp households to acquire a machine. In fact, by 1966 their household owned two snowmobiles, while most families at that time still had none.

Evvan became active in reindeer herding. The old herdsman's skills that he had failed to acquire were now no obstacle, whereas his work with machinery in the logging camps aided in his adaptation to the new age of mechanization. For a few years he seemed to be successful at reindeer herding. Like some of the other more affluent herders, he and his brother (with their father's help) bought reindeer from the association in an attempt to build up their herds. Even though the family has had the advantages of early snowmobile ownership and sufficient economic resources to purchase more animals, they have reluctantly come to the conclusion that it is not economically advantageous to invest heavily in herding at the present time. Evvan has taken a full-time job in the government forest service, while his brother works full time for the government telephone-telegraph service. The aggregate family herd is still one of the three largest in the Näätämö association, but in spite of great personal efforts and monetary investment, even their herds have declined slightly.

Aside from the factor of age, the dropouts from reindeer herding can be divided into two main categories: "losers" and "adapters." Many of the men who have quit reindeer herding have done so because they effectively had no choice. They lost most of their reindeer, and they do not have the economic means to keep up snowmobile equipment and other aspects of involvement in reindeer-herding competition. On the other hand, Nikolai and Evvan, for example, seem to have had a clear choice, and they chose to leave reindeer herding because they perceived other alternatives to be more acceptable. Nikolai decided to take a chance on wage work in Sweden because of the promise of a steady income much greater than that possible from reindeer herding in the Näätämö region. Evvan also saw wage work opportunities as providing a better income for himself and family, although his employment is within the local area, thus involving fewer risks and sacrifices.

Men Who Stayed In

The men who have stayed in reindeer herding, at least on a part-time basis, are as varied in their adaptive responses as those who dropped out.

The Osipoff brothers, Sergei and Iutsa, are examples of men who have remained active in reindeer work all through the snowmobile transition, but with mixed success. In the old Suenjel days when their father was alive, the Osipoffs had more reindeer than any other family in the community. In fact, the ancestors of the Osipoffs may have been the originators of expanded reindeer herding in Suenjel in response to the sharp decline in wild reindeer during the early part of the nineteenth century.

During the period of rebuilding—in the 1950s—Sergei had managed to increase his herd to forty or fifty head, but he lagged well behind his brothers, especially Iutsa, who had about 130 animals in 1958–59. Both men had married after the war, and both had households totalling eight persons, of which there were as yet no sons old enough to participate in reindeer activities.

Sergei often talked of the successful reindeer herding methods of prewar days, and he was strongly insistent on the necessity for a separate Skolt Lapp association so that they could recover their former intensive control over the herds. Since Sergei was not as outgoing as his brothers, he did not participate directly in association herding as much as they did, preferring to spend a lot of time in his own home-herd activities. This arrangement may have reflected a division of responsibilities among the Osipoff brothers, for they cooperated quite closely in maintaining their joint winter herd.

From Sergei's point of view the herding situation had taken a turn for the worse in the early 1960s, and the advent of the snowmobile simply pushed them over the brink. He suffered rapid losses in both adult reindeer and calves, and he was insistent that the snowmobiles were ruining the reindeer herds completely. He did not want to participate in the mechanized herding, although he continued to operate as a ski-man during the periods when the conflicts and invidious comparisons between the ski-men and the snowmobile men were becoming increasingly painful.

In 1966–67, Sergei's oldest son acquired a used Evinrude machine and began to take part in some herding activities. The choice of the Evinrude as the family machine indicates that both Sergei and his son saw their primary transportation needs to be in household freight trips, wood hauling, and general travel. (By 1966–67, it was well known that the heavier machines were not suitable for intensive reindeer-herding action.)

In 1970–71, Sergei's total herd was tallied at just seven adult reindeer. He was, for all practical purposes, finished, and the family had to buy reindeer meat for household consumption. His son had signed up for unemployment and had been admitted to a carpentry course in Rovaniemi, from which he hoped to develop steady employment, although it might require that he live in the population centers of south Lapland.

Sergei's adaptation to the near-elimination of his stake in herding is probably a reflection of his deep identification with the reindeer industry. Although he has virtually no reindeer of his own, he continues to work for the association as a ski-man and, with the help of two of his sons, he has built coffee houses at two of the Näätämö roundup sites. Thus, he has tried to turn his continuing attendance at the roundups into a small source of income. Also, his boys haul meat for meat buyers and engage in other odd jobs, using the new Swedish Sno-trik that Sergei bought. In addition to the economic contributions of his three sons, Sergei's household economy also receives some help from daughter Anni's work. She has had occasional employment as a domestic servant in Kaamanen and was working on a farm in Norway during the summer of 1971.

Sergei has evidently been extremely careful with his very slender economic resources, for the household ranks well in the top half of households in terms of their material style of life. They have a telephone, snowmobile, and chain saw, in addition to which they have taken out government loans to expand their log cabin into a four-room frame structure. In addition to a long-term loan and a grant from the government, this expansion will cost Sergei about 4000 Finnmarks from his own pocket.

A hundred yards farther down the lakeshore, brother Iutsa's house was undergoing a similar expansion during the summer of 1971. From outward appearances, at least, he should be able to afford this expenditure somewhat more easily than Sergei, since he still has sufficient reindeer to provide a significant addition to his household economy. During the early part of the 1960s he was among the most active Skolt Lapp herdsmen in the Muddusjärvi association, and he was relatively quick to try his hand at mechanized herding.

Iutsa bought a Swedish Ockelbo in the winter of 1965–66 but found that the machine had serious design deficiencies for reindeer herding. The fact that he had more reindeer than most of his neighbors probably accounts for Iutsa's ability to invest in the machines at a fairly early date, since he was able to sell more reindeer for cash. His household economy is also given an important boost through his mother's old age pension, which amounted to something close to $80.00 a month in 1970.

Iutsa was one of several Skolts who bought the new Swedish Moto-Ski in 1966–67. He found this machine to be quite effective in herding, and he got a lot of service from it before he traded it in on a Sno-trik in 1969. In 1970 he again traded in his machine, thus maintaining his policy of frequent trade-ins as a way of minimizing out-of-pocket maintenance costs.

By 1970–71 Iutsa, like his brother, had a daughter working on a farm in Norway and two sons who were old enough for reindeer work and could make other contributions to the family economy. The official reindeer tally of 1970–71 listed Iutsa with forty adult animals and fifteen calves. Thus, Iutsa is still very much in competition to stay in the reindeer business, and the fact that his herd included fifteen calves in 1971 looks very good indeed. This represents a calf production of nearly forty percent—a rate that could result in a rapid rebuilding of his herd if it can be maintained.

One of the other Osipoff brothers died in the early 1960s; the fourth member of this once-powerful group is quite ill and has lost all his reindeer. Their cousins, who also had respectable herds in 1958–59, have suffered serious declines; although Demian Osipoff, with thirty-six head and nineteen calves, also seems to be making a comeback.

The younger men who have come into reindeer herding within the past few years represent two different types of households. On the one hand, several of them are sons of the most active older generation of herders. For example, there are five younger Osipoffs among the newer herdsmen. The other type of situation that has also produced a number of the younger herdsmen is a set of households that lacked able-bodied male protagonists for a long time. Thus, several of the new young herders are the sons of widows, or of crippled, nonherding fathers.

Aleksi Prokoff, for example, was just a young boy when his father died in 1958. His mother had always been active in all aspects of herding, however; and she continued to look after the family herds, working closely with her brother, whose house is only seventy-five meters away—practically in the same yard. The young Aleksi grew up in a household in which reindeer herding was particularly highly valued, and both mother and uncle provide role models and practical instruction.

The Prokoffs are in the Vätsäri district—in which the Skolts have fared somewhat better than their kinsmen in the Näätämö district; the young boys growing up in that area have not been faced with the degree of deterioration in morale that is so pervasive among their Näätämö neighbors.

There is only one Skolt Lapp family in the Näätämö association that can be regarded as really successful in the new herding situation. The Sergeev family's reindeer now constitute about thirty percent of the total association holdings. The two brothers, Peatt and Kiurel, are both very active herders; in fact, Kiurel was the single most active herdsman in the 1968–69 season (in terms of man-days of work) and Peatt was the herding foreman for the north end of the Muddusjärvi district. (At that time, the split between Muddusjärvi and Näätämö was not yet final, but the Skolt herders had been given partial autonomy in the organization of work.)

Kiurel was already a full-time herder in the late 1950s. Peatt was employed in wage labor until 1959–60, when he decided to become a herdsman. Since both brothers have had considerable experience in wage work, they have acquired economic means and skills with machines. Also, the fact that Kiurel is a bachelor and Peatt did not marry until the end of the 1960s placed them in advantageous positions with regard to personal mobility and financial flexibility.

It is interesting to note that Peatt's and Kiurel's father, who is still physically active, has never been much interested in reindeer herding. His special adaptation to local ecological posibilities has been to concentrate on lake fishing, leaving the care of family herds to his sons. On the other hand, his brothers were dedicated herdsmen; apparently they served as important role models for Peatt and Kiurel.

Although the Sergeev brothers did not invest in snowmobiles until the winter of 1966–67, they have expanded their "fleet" to the point where the family now owns four machines, one of which is driven by the father. Peatt owns two machines, one of which is regularly used by his nephew Andrei, who is regarded as his "right-hand man" in reindeer-herding activities.

Peatt and Kiurel have greatly increased their holdings by purchasing unidentified reindeer at the Muddusjärvi and Näätämö roundups. One or the other—often both men—have been present at practically all significant reindeer action around the district during the past several years, and they are frequently the directors of herding operations. In association meetings they are more vocal and outspoken than most of the rest of the membership and see themselves as formulators of policy.

The Sergeev brothers are probably the strongest local partisans of snowmobilized reindeer herding. From their point of view, the use of ski-men has entirely failed to produce results, and the improvement of herding in the district must depend on improved techniques of snowmobile use. This point of view is in opposition to the views expressed by many other persons in the association, who insist that snowmobile herding will not succeed in the rougher, forested part of the district. Many of the criticisms that have been made of the snowmobiles, Peatt notes, are criticisms of improper or careless handling and tactics. He argues that effective snowmobile herding is an art that many of the local people have not yet learned. But their mistakes of the past should not be used to deny the utility of the machines.

Figure 1 summarizes the shift in patterns of herding participation from 1960 to 1971. Of the forty-one Skolt herdsmen who were active in 1960, eight have died or retired for reasons of health; nineteen have dropped out of reindeer activities to take up wage-labor positions or other occupations; and only fourteen continue as active herdsmen. Most of the herding is now carried out by younger men, many of whom were too young to be reindeer herders in 1960. Twenty-three persons are now active, at least on a part-time basis, who were not involved in association herding in 1960.

If the snowmobile had been the only important new factor affecting the lives of the Skolt Lapps, my review of "drop-outs" versus "stay-ins" in reindeer herding would provide us with a set of cases from which we could assess the chief causes of socioeconomic "successes" and "failures." However, modernization processes in northern Finnish Lapland have introduced a number of alternative economic opportunities for the Skolt Lapps and their neighbors; so it is not possible to equate dropping out of reindeer herding with economic failure. Some of the cases described above (for example, Nikolai Asimoff and Evvan Andreev) illustrate the fact that a few of the men who have quit reindeer herding are among the more economically successful in-

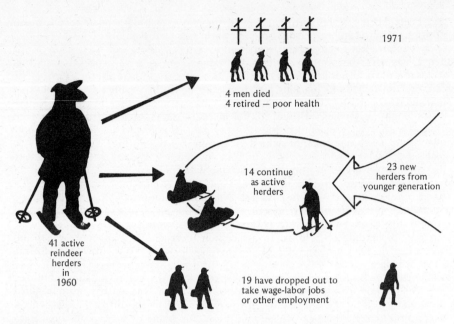

FIGURE 1. Only one third of the active Skolt herders were still participating in reindeer operations in 1971. Nearly half dropped out to pursue other economic activities.

dividuals. Assessment of "successful adaptation" must therefore include much more than reindeer herding.

New Patterns of Out-Migration

One of the new alternatives that some of the men have adopted is that of temporary or even permanent migration to other employment areas. The direct connection between events in reindeer herding and these recent increases in out-migration is evident when we contrast the Skolt males with their female counterparts. The Skolt girls have been eager to leave the Sevettijärvi area, either through marriage or through finding domestic work or other unskilled employment in the population centers. This pattern of female out-migration was already well established in the early 1950s.

Among the men, on the other hand, there was practically no out-migration until the middle and late 1960s. Their new search for wage employment outside the local area was brought about by several converging factors.

1. The snowmobile (and other newly available commercial goods) created very greatly increased needs for cash.
2. The advent of mechanized herding had created a situation of "tech-

nological unemployment" for the men who were forced out of full-time herding activities.

3. New policies of the Finnish employment service also had a strong influence on out-migration. The government has begun to pay unemployment compensation and has made increased efforts to find work for unemployed persons, particularly in road crews that are building and maintaining Finland's rapidly expanding network of paved roads.

4. The newest development in the Finnish employment service is the provision for schooling in various employable skills. Unemployed persons are given room and board, plus a small daily cash allowance, while they attend these courses. Skolt Lapps have attended training programs in automobile undercoating, manufacturing tourist souvenirs, windshield repair and replacement, carpentry and construction, assembly-line machine work, and others. This new program of the Finnish employment service will have a major impact on Lappish labor migration; however, it is important to note that the Skolts would probably have been much slower to participate in this program if the effects of the snowmobile had not pushed them out of their established winter activities.

5. The completion of the road to Sevettijärvi (1967), together with a very large increase in tourism all over Lapland, has led to contacts between the Skolts and persons in the south who are in positions to influence and aid in job placement. For example, several young Skolts are now in the industrial city of Tampere because of the efforts of one Finnish entrepreneur who befriended some of the local people during his vacation trips into the area.

In spite of the recent increases in male out-migration, a large imbalance between males and females still persists. Table 2 presents these out-migration data. Robert Paine has documented similar sex imbalances for a coastal Lapp community in Norway (Paine, 1965).

Table 2: Out-Migration of Severttijärvi Skolts

	PERMANENTLY EMIGRATED	STAYED IN COMMUNITY	TOTAL
Sons	28	58	86
Daughters	45	33	79

Note: These figures include sons and daughters of the original fifty households that settled in Sevettijärvi in 1949. They are approximately correct, although some of the daughters who emigrated in the early 1950s may have been "forgotten" in this tabulation. Exact figures fluctuate somewhat as unmarried persons, especially sons, return home for indefinite periods.

Incipient Social Stratification

When the snowmobile was first introduced into northeastern Lapland in 1961–63, the first Skolt Lapps to acquire them were individuals who were more socioeconomically successful than their fellows in the ways I have just suggested. In terms of ownership of material goods and participation in a number of different cash-earning activities, the first snowmobile owners were mainly from the upper quartile of the Skolt Lapp community (Pelto, *et al.*, 1968). This is, of course, to be expected, given the high cost of snowmobiles. The important fact, however, is that the acquisition of snowmobiles conferred additional adaptive advantages on those families who were already becoming socioeconomic leaders.

The snowmobile has had the effect of introducing a large element of "starting capital" into the economy such that some persons who may have the skills necessary for effective reindeer herding and other activities are unable to compete in these pursuits because they do not have the economic means to get started. Now, the difference that has come about is clearly a matter of degree, but the effect seems to be rather evident. Differentiation of the more successful families from those that are at the bottom of the economic hierarchy is, to a rapidly increasing degree, associated with the possession of costly technological devices and *cash reserves*. Economic competition in the region is structured more and more in terms of competing technological inventories rather than basic physical skills and wisdom. As the differentiation among the families increases, the competitive chances of the children in the poorer families are reduced, at least as far as participation in the reindeer-herding industry is concerned.

Table 3 shows the developing stratification of economic means among the fifty-one Skolt Lapp households. (I am including the Skolts from the Vätsäri association in these figures.) The same *general* economic forces are operating on them, even though they have not had to experience quite the degree of reindeer-herding disaster. Several points stand out in these illustrations. The "Material Style of Life" index shows that there is a rapidly growing differentiation in the household furnishings and technical goods available to the different households.

The index contains two different kinds of items: washing machines, gas lights, and oil heaters are "conveniences" which presumably add to the comfort and feeling of well-being in these families, but they are not "capital goods" in the sense of items that markedly improve the adaptive capacity of the household. The snowmobiles, chain saws, telephones, and automobiles, on the other hand, are technological features that are essential, or at least highly important, for improving an individual's physical mobility and speed of communication. Thus, people who are relatively high on the "Material Style of Life" scale are those families who have both "modern comforts" and technological aids for active socioeconomic competition.

Table 3: Scale of "Material Style of Life" among Skolt Lapps and Their Neighbors

	SCALE TYPE [a]	SKOLTS	OTHER LAPPS	FINNS	TOTAL
I	Household has all listed material items	1	0	1	2
II	All items except TV	2	1	1	4
III	All except TV and refrig.	3	0	0	3
IV	All except TV, refrig., and automobile	2	0	0	2
V	All except TV, refrigerator, auto, gas or electricity for both cooling and lighting.	2	1	0	3
VI	Chain saw, snowmobile, telephone, washing machine, gas or electricity for cooling or lighting.	9	1	0	10
VII	Chain saw, snowmobile, telephone, and washing machine.	3	0	0	3
VIII	Chain saw, snowmobile, and telephone.	8	1	2	11
IX	Chain saw and snowmobile.	15	3	5	23
X	Just a chain saw.	4	1	1	6
XI	Not even snowmobile or chain saw.	2	1	0	3
	Total households	—	—	—	—
					70

Note: Households with more than one nuclear family are considered single households in this list.

When we look at the relationship between significant participation in reindeer herding and position on our index, we find that households that have maintained a degree of involvement in the traditional economy are mainly in the upper half of the techno-economic scale. To a large extent this reflects the fact that active involvement in reindeer herding is now predicated, or at least enhanced, by ownership of several of the items in the Material Style of Life index.

It is interesting to note that the people in the upper half of our scale of techno-economic success control the major share of both the reindeer herding *and* the wage labor opportunities within the local area. Of the total of approximately twenty to twenty-four regular cash-earning jobs in the area that are held by Skolt Lapps, all except two or three of them are controlled by people in the *upper half* of the Material Style of Life index. This is not surprising, of course, in the case of the older employment cases, since the incumbents of these would have been expected to purchase the items in the Material Style of Life index from money earned on the job. However, almost all of the *new* occupations that have opened up in the past two years have also been captured by those people who needed them least—the people who were already economic leaders in earlier years (cf., Pelto, *et al.*, 1968). Thus, everything new that takes place in the increasingly differentiated economic pattern appears to work to the advantage of the families that *already have* the predominance of economic power as expressed in control of local inventories of scarce resources.

Until about 1960 the principal economic activity available to Skolt Lapp males was in reindeer herding. There was a moderate amount of differentiation in herding success, and there was also some differentiation among families in fishing activities, summer wage work, and other secondary economic pursuits. The advent of the road during the middle 1960s was accompanied by increasing economic complexity, expanded household needs, and greatly escalated contacts between the Skolts and the "outside world." Even if the snowmobile had never come to Lapland, these factors certainly would have contributed to further economic differentiation among the Skolt families. Trends of this sort were apparent in 1962—in differences in food supplies, upkeep of homes, dress styles of teenagers, and other aspects of life-style.

The remarkable transformation in the reindeer-herding situation during the 1960s greatly increased the tempo of differentiation and intensified the contrasts between the families with means and those who were increasingly handicapped in economic competition. Fortunately, many of the families in the lower end of the Material Style of Life index receive some income from the increasingly bountiful Finnish system of social security. They receive veteran's benefits, old age pensions, invalid's payments, and other transfer funds. Therefore, the material deprivation in food and other necessities among these Lappish families is not as serious as that found among the poor in many parts of the United States. Their socioeconomic situation is not nearly as desperate as that of most American Indian families, for example.

The social effects of the differentiation process are not particularly evident at this time. Although the differences in equipment, household goods, and other possessions provide signals of differential economic status, people who have been living in relatively egalitarian terms do not immediately begin practicing social exclusiveness to match their economic differences. There are some indications that differences in educational aspirations may be developing, but other clear signs of social stratification behavior are not evident—yet.

The process of developing inequality brought about by the snowmobile is most apparent as a growing "techno-economic differentiation," rather than an overall socio-cultural stratification of life-styles and social intercourse.

Who Made It to "The Top"?

One of my main concerns in this study has been to trace the internal processes through which economic and social differentiation occurs. In pursuing this interest, one important question which needs to be raised is: What are the characteristics of the individuals who "succeed" as compared with those who are less "successful"? Since the achievements of the families high on the index of Material Style of Life are not due to clearly inherited differences in starting capital, nor to more generalized class advantage, how can we account for their present situation? An assessment of the causes of individual success or failure during the postwar period would require a full-scale study. . . . Some suggestions can be set out, however, which are no more than rough hypotheses for future research.

A Comment on "Economic Success and Failure"

I should make clear that I am using the terms "success" and "failure" in a very limited range of meaning. From my research among the Lapps and their neighbors I found rather strong evidence that the majority of them desire material items such as those listed in [Table 3], and they want to have sufficient money to buy these and other goods, in order to attain a certain standard of living. They also appear to value successful performance of occupational roles (reindeer herding and other work) which produce goods and money. In addition to the evidence concerning the attitudes and motivations of the Lapps, it appears that acquisition of various technical items is a fairly effective indicator of economic flexibility among these people.

Therefore, I am using the term "economic success" to refer specifically to the acquisition of material items and financial means as reflected in the Material Style of Life index. This is not meant to imply that persons who are high on this scale are of greater excellence in other aspects of life. They are not necessarily more psychologically stable, better sexually adjusted, or higher in "moral" standards. "Successful adaptation" in my discussion simply refers to capability in "making a living" in terms that conform to current views among the Lapps.

Some of the relatively unsuccessful cases are perhaps easiest to analyze first. Poor health seems very clearly involved in several instances of men who have remained economically marginal. Since physical ability has been so closely related to success in reindeer herding and other economic activities, several individuals with uncertain health are among the emerging category of "techno-economic marginality."

Excessive alcohol use also seems to be implicated, for at least five of the more notable "dropouts" from reindeer herding were characterized by at least occasional heavy drinking in situations that required sober and effective action. Nearly everyone in the Sevettijärvi region uses alcohol at times, but there is a fine line between controlled drinking and the overuse of alcohol that reduces economic efficiency. (There are only one or two persons in the community who may be "alcoholic" in the usual medical sense.) A contributing factor in this picture is the loss of economic flexibility that comes from the high cost of alcoholic drink. A few of the men may have experienced an interaction effect between nascent economic failure and increased alcohol consumption.

The problem of financial flexibility was particularly central in the early years of the snowmobile transition. Several of the unsuccessful cases were men with insufficient cash and reindeer reserves to purchase machines in the period of 1965–68. It appears that herders who managed to get machines during that period were able to stay in the economic competition; those who did not were effectively squeezed out of reindeer activities, as well as some other economic niches.

Geographic marginality may have contributed to differential techno-economic success, for a few of the least successful members of the community are located in places that are far from the main lines of information flow. It may be suggested, however, that some of these individuals may have chosen their locations in order to stay out of the centers of social interaction. Also, a few of them appear to have been somewhat indifferent to prospects of economic success or failure. Thus, it is possible that a small number of these socially marginal individuals are not in any full sense "techno-economic failures," since they are uninterested in striving for the newly available material opportunities.

Some isolated instances of relative techno-economic failure appear to involve the following factors: lack of able-bodied men in the family (for example, in the homes of some widows); apparent lack of mental and physical capability, either from genetic inheritance or early experience; and misfortunes, accidents, or other chance events.

The characteristic that stands out most clearly in the case of the techno-economically most successful persons are those of physical mobility, high activity levels, nonspecialization, and centrality in information flow.

The men who appeared to be most well adapted and successful in 1958–59 were persons who were able to travel widely in order to take part in a great variety of activities. They were the men who went to all the roundups in the region, were active in all phases of herding, and who were in attendance at various social events as well. From my field notes I find that these more active persons tended to be frequent visitors and also were hosts more often than other people. They tended to have more physical equipment (such as boat motors) that aided their mobility.

Mobility and activity go hand in hand. These more successful individuals appeared, on the whole, to build more boats and fishing camps; they planted more potatoes; and they engaged in other economic and social activities. It is not possible to identify the focus of their activities as either "traditional" or "progressive." It seems to me that these men have been more active in *all* sectors of the social and economic system. Arto Sverloff, for example, has been reindeer herder, herding foreman, taxi driver, freight and passenger hauler, postman, and (incidentally) anthropological research assistant. Another "successful adaptor" has been a full-time reindeer herder under both old and new systems, and has been herding foreman. On the other hand, he has been active in snowmobile racing and was the first Skolt householder in the region to complete the building of a new four-room frame house to replace the old government-built log cabin. The activities of another successful family have included active reindeer herding (including herd foreman duties), salmon fishing, guiding for tourists and travelers, operating the telephone exchange, full-time employment in logging for the forest service, and other participation in wage work.

Several of the most techno-economically active families of the area are located near the hub of communications—at the village center which includes stores, school, health center, and church. The village center is the mail distribution point, the telephone exchange is located there, and the rather extensive influence of the local school is felt most strongly in this cluster of households.

To a certain extent the locations of the various families in the Sevettijärvi area were chosen by the families themselves, although it is clear that not all families had a clear choice in selecting house sites. Whatever may have been the benefits of information flow that have accrued to more centrally located families, they could not have been predicted from the situation in the planning stages of the move to the new area. And, to a certain extent, "centrality" in the communications network has been created and modified by the social interactions of the families.

Some external environmental factors, therefore, have been influential in affecting differential techno-economic expansion. We must also keep in mind that the vagaries of accident, sickness, and just plain bad luck are to a considerable extent (although not wholly) outside the realm of individuals' adaptive acting and deciding. Some well-founded folklore of reindeer herding also emphasizes the role of "luck" in promoting growth of herds and general success with reindeer.

But a very considerable part of the adaptive successes, however modest, of some of the Skolt Lapps compared with others appears to derive from the personal characteristics of particular individuals. Without attempting the difficult task of finding the "causes" for these personal differences, my argument can be summarized with the following observations.

On the whole, the more successful Skolts during this difficult time of rapid modernization are characterized by a very considerable flexibility of personal behavior, a self-confidence in individual task performance, and a high level of personal initiative in the accomplishment of economic work. These people are what David McClelland (1961) has referred to as "moderate risk takers." On the whole, the personal behavioral style that is particularly evident in the more successful Skolts is that of "individualism," which I have described at length in an earlier work (Pelto, 1962), following initial field research of 1958–59.

The characteristic individualism of the Skolts does not include any strong element of aggressive competition with other persons, although such competition is always present to some extent in fairly complex socioeconomic systems. Rather, individual Skolts have, at least in the past, focused on the struggle and "competition" between self and nonhuman environment instead of the complexities of social interaction and manipulation. In the past a man's adaptive success depended to a very great degree on his effective management of directly perceived information from and interaction with the reindeer, the physical terrain, and his personal equipment (sleds, harness, fishing gear, etc.).

Now the adaptive focus is shifting rapidly to much more socially involved sectors of behavior, especially to relationships with wage labor employers as well as commercial operators and tourists. But *some* of the socially *un*involved personal characteristics of these people have continued to be of adaptive significance (for example, in maintenance and repair of machinery, especially when operating in the backlands with snowmobiles). The more successful Skolt adaptors appear to exhibit a flexible mixture of individualistic *and* more socially involved personal style (cf., Pelto, 1971).

Increased Social Interaction

Snowmobiles have contributed in many indirect ways to increased social interdependence because of both technical and economic aspects of the machines. Also, the greatly increased speed of travel has added directly to the intensity of social interaction. Each individual traveling about by snowmobile can get around to more places in a shorter time. There are now about three times as many reindeer roundups as in pre-snowmobile days; and while there may be a slight dropoff in attendance at some of the more marginal roundups, the overall effect is a clear increase in the number of times that people come together at the roundup sites. (Many people continue to attend roundups quite regularly even though they do not participate in association herding and have very few reindeer of their own.)

Another contribution to social interaction comes from the fact that reindeer herders nowadays seldom stay out for long periods of time. Usually they return to their homes for the night, even if it requires driving several kilometers. With the men home every night, there is a net increase in the time spent in social interaction with people in the household, as well as with neighbors who may drop in for a visit. All trips to neighbors and to more distant families can be made much more quickly now than they were formerly, and the Skolts appear to have used this technological factor to increase wintertime interpersonal contacts. During the winter of 1966–67, movies were held biweekly at one of the local homes—an innovation that would scarcely have been possible in earlier times, since it was not possible to accumulate enough people for such a commercial venture except under fairly unusual circumstances, such as the Easter holidays.

At this time it is difficult to predict what the further effects of the increased intensity of social interaction will be, but the entire economic system now appears to depend on a much faster flow of information than was formerly the case. The speed-up of social contacts (as well as the rapid spread of telephone service to all the neighborhoods) is therefore a necessary concomitant of the new technology. Secondary effects of increases in social interaction are sometimes quite subtle and diffuse. Therefore, specialized research, perhaps over a long period of time, may be essential in order to trace these further ramifications of the snowmobile.

References Cited

McClelland, David (1961) *The Achieving Society*, Princeton: Van Nostrand and Co.

Paine, Robert (1965) *Coast Lapp Society II*. Tromsö: Museums Skriften IV, 2.

Pelto, Pertti J. (1962) *Individualism in Skolt Lapp Society*, Helsinki: [Finnish Antiquities Society] Kansatieteellinen Arkisto a6.

——— et al. (1968) "The Snowmobile Revolution in Lapland," Journal of the Finno-Ugric Society 69:3–42.

——— (1971) "Social Uninvolvement and Psychological Adaptation in the Arctic," paper presented at the Second International Symposium on Circumpolar Health, Oulu, Finland.

John J. Poggie, Jr.

El Pocho

They call me *El Pocho* * in my town because I live all my life in the States, and because at first when I came here to Mexico I didn't know how to speak very good Spanish. All the words that I used to speak I used to make. . . . Like for *push*, I used to say *"púshale,"* you know. That's not a Spanish word. In Spanish you say *"empújale."* But that's the way the pochos talk. They couldn't understand me here, so that's why they call me that.

Well, Pocho is my name. They nicknamed me El Pocho here in Mexico.

Reprinted by permission from Between Two Cultures: The Study of an American-Mexican, *John J. Poggie, Jr., Tucson: University of Arizona Press, copyright 1973.*

* The word *pocho* is used in Mexico as a pejorative term denoting one who is culturally prejudiced toward the United States, or one who has returned from the United States with little memory of Mexican language and culture.

I didn't have no trouble learning Spanish. Every time I heard somebody talk, I used to listen how they talk, you know, and right away I think, well, that word doesn't go that way. This friend of mine, Eduardo Lopal, he's a policeman in Mexico City. I used to help him in English, and he used to help me in Spanish. And he still says, "No, the word goes this way." He also used to work in the shop where I work, the Tienda Azteca. It took me about six months to learn how they speak Spanish here.

In the States we used to speak half English and half Spanish, you know. In Spanish if you want to say, "Let's go uptown" you say, "Vamos al centro." In pocho talk you say, "Vamos al tango." That's the way the pochos talk in California. Like another example, like they say *pantalones* for pants here in Mexico. In California a lot of the young guys, they don't call them *pantalones*. They call them *trabuchos*. And like *realist* is shirt. Here in Mexico it's *camisa*. Different words. Just like in the United States . . . like they have a different way of talking in New York; even English in New York they talk a different way. You don't understand them when you hear them talk. Pocho talk is slang, *calo*, that's what they call it. Like they say *mi gina*, my girlfriend. *Mi huisa* is a girl who likes to fool around and have relations with a lot of guys. She's a girl that's no good.

Well, I came here near Teotihuacán, near these pyramids, a year ago, you know. One day I went traveling with a guy, and we went to a place next to San Juan, a little town named La Laguna. They had a little store there where they sell beer. And we were drinking there, me, him, and his cousin. Then three guys from the pyramids came there. One guy, they call him *El Burro*, and another guy, I forget the other guy's name. But a short guy, you know, we called him *Chaparro*. In English we would call him Shorty.

So he came there and then he said, "So you're El Pocho." And I says, "Yeah, I'm El Pocho." And he says, "Do you think you're too good?" I says, "Why do you say that?" He says, "Because there are a lot of people that say you speak English." "That doesn't mean that I'm too good," I told him. "Well, to me it seems you think you're better than me. I speak English too." I told him, "I might speak better English than you, but that doesn't mean that I'm better than you. It's just that I know how to speak English better." So he said, "Come outside here!" And I told him, "I don't want to hit you because I know you people here don't know how to fight," and all that. So I hit him, you know. I hit him about two times and I knocked him out.

Now I go by the pyramids and he sees me and he don't talk to me. But I never let him get too close. I stay away from him, you know. He just knew a few words of English. Those guys sell souvenirs at the pyramids. They just speak a little English to sell to the tourists. So he got mad, because once I went to sell statues at the pyramids. That's why he was mad. Because I could talk better to the tourists so I sold more than he did. That's why I don't like to go around the pyramids or sell like that, because right away there's envy, you know. Because I speak better English than they do.

What I miss most about the States . . . over there you have a nice job, you know . . . maybe it's not yours when you rent a house, but you have everything that is necessary in your house, like you have your television, stove, and everything. Because in the States a house is all full of furniture, you know. Over there you can have a nice job, and you work good. That's what I miss. Like here I can't have nice furniture like you do in the States. It's not easy, because here the pay is too low. And you can't furnish a house in one year or two years, like that, because it takes a lot of money. It takes a long time before you can furnish a house. A nice comfortable house, a nice place to live in—that's what I miss most.

Because in the States you live a different life than here. When I was in the States, over there, I always was dressed good. Over there you can buy yourself three, four pairs of shoes, like that, and here it is not easy to buy them. Because the pay is maybe fifteen pesos a day, a little more than a dollar, and a suit costs you five hundred pesos. Twelve and a half pesos make a dollar, so that's forty dollars for a suit—not everybody makes forty dollars.

When I was in the States, I never did miss anything from Mexico. When I was in the States, I never did like to come to Mexico, you know. Because I was raised in the States. I lived all my life in the States. I never got to think of coming to visit Mexico or anything like that.

When they put me over the border, right away I would come back because I would never get used to Mexico. So as soon as the Immigration put me on this side, I wait only for one hour or two hours, like that. And then pretty soon I start looking up places where I could cross the border. And then I would cross and wait for a bus to pass, you know. I never thought the Immigration would pick me up. I just thought I'd go back, jump over the border. I jumped the border all total about nine times. And so many times they put me across, you know.

Finally I said, "I think I'll try to see if I can stay in Mexico." So I tried one time, you know, coming over here. I tried to stay here, for three months I stayed here. Finally I decided, "Ah, I'll go back to the United States." Because I was not used to the kind of life that the people lead here in Mexico.

Because, you know, it's hot in California, but after work you come home and take a shower, and then you dress up and go out. Maybe to a movie, or maybe to a drive-in, or maybe you go to a recreation hall, like the YMCA. You practice lifting weights or boxing or tennis, or play cards. Or you can play checkers or dominoes or chess. I used to go to the YMCA for recreation, play there, pass the time. They don't have that around here.

I haven't gone fishing since I left California. I'm done with fishing. In the States I used to do a lot of fishing. I would like to go, but it takes money to buy the fishing rod and all that. And then, here you have to go by car, and I have no car to go fishing. It's a long distance. You have to go maybe to Acapulco and go up in the mountains someplace where they have fishing. Like Mazatlán is a good point to go fishing. Mazatlán. It's a long ways from here to Mazatlán. In the States you work five days and a half, and then you have to go and get ready for Sunday. You make your plans where you are going to go. And here, the only place you go here is to the movies. Only to the movies.

We have time, but, I mean, here it is not as easy to go to those places like in the States. Over there, say you have a friend, you can ask him, "What are you going to do tomorrow?" He says, "Well, I have nothing in mind." You tell him, "Well, let's go fishing." You know, plan to do something. So he says, "How about going hunting, deer hunting?" Up in Watsonville we used to go deer hunting.

It's not because I have a wife. I still could go. In North America there would be places nearby where I could go and pass a Sunday or weekends, stuff like that. Maybe it's because I know so many people in the States, and here I don't know as many people. Here they don't do nothing. They don't go away like that. The only place they go is to Mexico City. That's the only place they invite me to go. Like I see somebody and they say, "Well, let's go to Mexico City to the movies." That's the only place they invite me.

The boys that I used to work with in the Tienda Azteca, they used to tell me, "Well, let's go to see this movie. It's a good one." And we would go to the movies. And that's the only thing we'd go to. The only place we go to here is to Chapultepec Park, in Mexico City. Lots of tourists there. They have boats, you get in and row, you know. That's the only place that I've been to. With my wife and her parents we went. Me, her, and my half sister, we all got in the boat. And then we never know how to row, and I got them all wet! They'd get all angry because I'd get them wet!

That's how come I used to come back and forth, because I didn't feel at home in Mexico, even though I was born here. To me, I felt that the States was my home because I lived there most of the time. And I know so many people in the States. Like here in Mexico I don't know very many people. Most of the people that I know are in the States. I know almost every town in California. I know the people, you know. There are families that I know. I stop in any town and they see me and know me. And here I go to any town and they don't know me. They don't know me because I never lived here.

Even now I feel like I would be more at home in the States. Even now that I have been away for, say, five years. When I go back, you know, right away a lady that knows me says, "Where have you been?" Or she says, "Oh, you've been in jail." These ladies were very well acquainted with my father; they were really friendly. I used to go back when they hadn't seen me for four or five years, and they would ask me, "Where have you been? Have you been in jail?" And I would tell them, "No, I have been in Mexico." And they would say, "Oh, we thought you were in jail or something." I still send Christmas cards to certain people in the States

The foods I like here in Mexico are like fried beans, fried potatoes, fried eggs, like that. Bread with butter. In the States, in the mornings I used to like toast with jelly, or hot cakes with coffee, waffles, or cornflakes. Then for dinner I used to eat like pork chops or fried chicken, with a soup, like chicken noodle soup. I used to like that very much. I like lamb chops, pork chops, tuna fish. Fried fish. Then hot dogs, hamburgers, cheeseburgers. I love those.

Here in Mexico they don't make them like they do in the States. Every time I go to Mexico City I see hamburgers, they call them *hamburguesas*. But, you know, they don't even taste like the hamburgers they make in the States. That's why I don't buy them. That's why I buy a *torta*. A torta is like a sandwich; they put ham, they put tomato, they put onions.

Over there I used to eat nothing but hamburgers, hot dogs, cheeseburgers, jumbo. A jumbo is a hamburger with a double layer. With hot dogs we used to buy french fries, and then coffee or a chocolate milkshake. I used to love it, to go to a restaurant like that. Sometimes we used to go, two, three boys, and invite two, maybe three girls, and then we used to go to this drive-in place. And you park and then a girl comes and asks you what you want, and then you order. I would order a cheeseburger, maybe a couple of cheeseburgers or hamburgers with french fries and coffee. I like ketchup with the hamburgers.

I used to like hamburger steak, you know. In the United States I used to go to a restaurant, and every time I went to this restaurant the lady knew right away what I was going to ask for. She used to say, "Oh, don't tell me—hamburger steak!" I used to say, "Oh you!" Because I used to laugh. Hamburger steak, you know, with a lot of ketchup. I used to love to go there. I used to go eat in that restaurant all the time. That place they give you good pork chops too. I used to drink only coffee and chocolate milkshakes.

I used to eat tortillas in the States. But tortillas in the States are different than the ones from here. The tortillas in the States are made out of flour, and here in Mexico they are made out of corn. So it's a different kind of tortillas. But see, in the Mexican restaurants over there, you can go and they have enchiladas, they have tacos, fried eggs, refried beans, just like here. They make a soup out of beef—you just put the beef in the pan, and then you put cabbage, carrots, rice, like that.

I like American food better than Mexican food. Even here, when I get a chance I eat American food. I told my wife to make like spaghetti, spaghetti with cheese, and steaks. Not just regular steaks—you get a steak and you press a lot of bread until it's just a powder, and then you fry it like that, and they come kind of brown on top. Yeah, breaded steak.

I haven't planned it yet, to go back. I would like to go back, just for a visit. I would like to go visit, to visit my relatives and friends, for maybe thirty days, and then I could return. And then if I decided that I could stay over there, then I would try to stay. But, I mean, jumping the border, I don't like to jump the border no more.

See, jumping the border, somebody picks you up and you probably go before a judge, and he has to sentence you for a certain time, say six months, one year, or eighteen months in the "facilities," they call it, where they have nothing but wetbacks. The last time I had to go before a judge, he gave me eighteen months of suspended sentence. Eighteen months suspended sentence with five years probation. That means that right now I could go back, but then, you see, the probation is over. But anyway, I would go before the judge. If I got caught I would go before a judge, and he would probably sentence me to hard labor, two years or eighteen months. That's why I don't like to go back.

A lot of time I stayed quite awhile waiting to be deported. One time I waited six months before I was deported. I never tried to get papers. It's just that a lot of people used to jump. At that time, thousands used to jump. The Immigration at that time didn't amount to much because the war was on. They needed people to work, so they didn't never watch the borders too close. Until the war was over, that's when they started getting tough. Then they really started getting tough.

I'm getting to be forty-five years now, not too old, but I don't like to cross the border no more. I got tired of it. It is better to work here and live. I used to do it, maybe because I didn't have a wife. Now I have a wife and decided to settle down. Sometimes I think about going back, or maybe going just to the border and get a permit to cross the border. I never tried to get papers. It just happened that it was so easy to cross that you didn't think of it, the papers. But maybe one of these days I will try to get some papers legally and cross the border.

That way you won't be afraid like when I was in the States illegally. When you would be in a city, right away when you see a cop, you think he is going to come and ask a question or so. Or when I was driving a car, in the mirror I used to look behind me and when I used to see a cop in back of me, right away I felt he was going to stop me or something. When I saw any Immigration that I would pass on the way, oh, I would go fast in the car, get them lost, you know.

I've been a few years here in Mexico now, working, and you don't have to be afraid of a cop in back of you. Because you don't have to be afraid of anything. You live here and you work. You don't make as much money as in the States, but you can live more happy here. In them days when I used to cross the border I used to make a lot of money, but still you didn't live a good life. You know, you don't even sleep good. You don't dare sleep good because right away you have to be awake in case you hear a noise of the Immigration coming in. Because they used to come at night. They used to come at night when everybody would be asleep. Pick you up. So sometimes I didn't even stay in a house. I used to stay out in the fields, take a blanket and sleep out in the fields. Here you don't feel like that. You can rest good, you work, you finish, you don't have to be afraid of somebody running after you. In the States you dress good, you buy your clothes, you have good meals and everything, but you are not free. Here you are free! I used to run back and forth before I had a wife. Then I said, "I am going to get married. Maybe if I get married I won't cross the border."

And sometimes I tell my wife, "I am going back to the States." She says, "You stay here. Oh no, you are not going." She says she wants me to stay here and be with her. But I talk. I tell her when I go to the border I will take her with me, just to the border. Maybe there I can get a better job than here. Even if I went to Mexicali or Tijuana I would stay in the tourist business. Because Tijuana is known as a tourist town; thousands of tourists cross every day and there are thousands of little shops for tourists that sell things. I would probably like to live in Tijuana, because in Tijuana it's very close to Mexicali, and then Tijuana's not hot. Just a climate like say here, by the pyramids. This is a good climate here. This kind of climate you would have in Tijuana. The ocean is very close. And then there's this town named Ensenada, where you can go fishing or something on weekends.

. . .

I heard the story of how my father wanted to move to the States years ago. See, my father borrowed some money to go to the States, from a friend. Not a friend, a relative—this man was married to my father's sister, and he loaned my father some money to go to the States. But he was telling my father not to go because my father had a beautiful wife, and he would lose his wife in the States. But my father wanted to go anyway, and so he borrowed the money, and he took my mother and me through El Paso. And from El Paso we went clear to California. You didn't need to have any papers or anything, you just pay. At the border there was a bridge there and they just paid five centavos.

I was about six months old. They went clear to Mendota, California. They just happened to go there because a friend, he was there before, and he came and told them about California, and then my father went back with him, see. They went to Mendota because that is in the San Joaquin Valley, and that is known for cotton-picking. Mendota is a big cotton place.

I heard that at first when we got there it was pretty hard because, you know, the wages in the States. . . . Maybe you've heard that they didn't pay enough money, they paid ten cents an hour in them days when I was small. They used to give just a little wage, so we had kind of a hard time. And then my mother used to have like a boardinghouse, so they could get money. They got a house like out in a lot of fields. The ranchers have a lot of houses for all the workers, you know, so in there she got a big place like a boardinghouse, but only for meals, not to sleep. My mother used to cook the meals for these men, Mexican workers. They worked out in the fields picking cotton. That's how they used to get by, you know. In Mendota they lived about six years.

The house where I lived was a small house just like a little room, a little kitchen, you know, and it had water inside. It was a wood house—all the houses in California are wood. We used to live out on a ranch, not in the city of Mendota. From Mendota to this little ranch was about two miles. The population of Mendota was then maybe eight thousand. I didn't go to school there.

We moved from Mendota to San Bernardino when I was about six years old. All my relatives lived in San Bernardino, that's how come we moved. Like a cousin of mine named Susanna, my mother's niece. She was born in Mexico but moved there, and they are still living there. And I have some other relatives on my father's side, like Vincente López. He has a lot of sons and daughters who still live there in San Bernardino, see. My relatives wrote to my father and told him to move to San Bernardino because there he could make more money picking oranges than he could on the cotton. So that's how come we moved there.

We moved over there and he picked oranges, and then I used to help him too, you know, on the bottom there picking oranges. I was small but I could pick a little bit and help him. He used to get, I think it was three cents a box. I used to help him on the weekends, and then summers when there was no school, vacation from school, I used to help him every day.

The first day of school my cousin took me, she must have been about twenty-one. I was about six or seven years old. That was in the first grade— I didn't go to kindergarten. The name of that San Bernardino school was Ramona School. I remember that first day when I went to school, she took me to the principal there, Mr. Harris I think it was, and they took me to a teacher named Mrs. Thorn. I still can remember her name because she was very nice to me, because I think that I was the only one that was from Mexico. There were Mexican kids but they were all from the city, born in the States. I was the only one that was born in Mexico.

The teacher was very nice, and she introduced me to all the students. Pretty soon they all started talking to me in Spanish. I didn't know any English at all; I went there to learn English. And they were very helpful, you know, try to teach me. Because when we used to go out to play I used to go out and sit by myself, see, because I wasn't very acquainted with all the boys. Pretty soon one boy told me, "Come on, let's go play." He's the one that every time I go back to the States I go visit him—his name was Jesús Valdez, but his nickname was Quityeo. So this Quityeo, he introduced me to all the other boys. Pretty soon we used to go out and play baseball, at school. It took about two months before I got to know them real good, to be playing with them. I was scared because I figured, you know, you're by yourself and they, you know, bunch on you.

Like one time when I was small, one boy told the other guy to pick a fight on me. You know how they put a little stick on your shoulder and knock it off? So they put that on me and told the boy to knock it off. Before he could knock it off I hit him. I hit the boy and they took me down to the principal, and the principal told me not to be fighting and all that. That was in 1928, I think, the first year that I went to school.

One time a bunch of guys beat up on me and then, well, I didn't say nothing that they beat me up, but I said one of these days I'll get even with them. My cousin asked me, "Why did you let them do that to you?" I says, "Oh, I let them do it but one of these days I'll get even. Let it go. One of these days I'll get even." But I never got even, because, how you say, I didn't hold no grudge against them. After that I got very friendly with them and then they told me they were very sorry that they beat me up.

They had an alley there and after school we used to go out there and fight over a new girl, or . . . you know how kids are. Everybody fought. Sometimes it was, "Why don't you go and fight with this boy in an alley?" I don't like to fight, but, if you don't fight you are a chicken. So I said OK. So we went out there and then when I was fighting with this boy, the brother of this boy wanted to fight with me. So then I said, "No, I don't want to fight you." They were two, you know, and I was only one. Then the father came over and told us that was enough.

We fought with fists, because in the town there was a prizefighter named José Gonzales, and he used to teach the boys with boxing gloves. He trained little boys. You know how little boys would go with boxing gloves, and fight with other schools. That's how he used to train us. And we knew how to fight.

In grammar school the boys used to form little gangs, and we used to fight. A gang of Mexican boys used to fight with other gangs of Mexican boys. Then a long time ago they used to fight with bicycle chains. You know, the chain on a bicycle? Well, they used to take it off and use it as a weapon, one gang against another one. I never done it because always the captain of the gang is the one that fights with it, with the captain of the other gang. I never was captain. When you get into bicycle chains, a lot of the guys get hurt and some get killed. And then they send you to prison. There are a few guys that I know who got in those fights and are in San Quentin right now, because they killed somebody.

. . . .

Mexico, Marriage, and Future Plans

You know, after I told my Aunt Guadalupe I wouldn't jump the border no more, I stayed there in Mexico City with her because I didn't have no job. So I took pictures, you know, photographs. I had them developed for maybe two pesos in Mexico City, and I used to resell them for maybe six pesos, whatever I could get. Like I take a photograph of you and develop it, and I take it to you and I sell it to you for a price. I worked at that for about six months, but I didn't like that, because we used to get tired, walking all the time. Like a postman, walking door to door.

Then I got a job in a moving van, one of those vans that move furniture from one place to another. We used to move furniture from Mexico City to Guadalajara, Monterrey, places like that. That job was pretty good, but I didn't like it. You had to sleep out on the highway in the truck. I had to help drive, too. And then afterwards when you are free all the boys would say, "Let's go to a cantina and get drunk." And I didn't like that. But we would all go to a cantina and drink. Drink beer, you know, and then we used to go to places where they had girls to entertain. This was in Monterrey.

In one of those places the girls weren't girls though. They were men dressed in women's clothes. But, like if you would go there, you would think they were girls by looking at them. One boy told me, "Why don't you dance with this girl?" And I said OK. I wanted to dance with her because she was really beautiful, just like a girl. And I asked her, "Would you like to dance?" And I started dancing with her, and everybody was laughing that I was dancing with her. "Why are they laughing?" I said.

And then we came and had a drink, and I invited her upstairs, you know. She wanted a drink. And then pretty soon she told me, "I am going to tell you something because you don't know. I am not a girl like you think. I am a man. But my feelings are just like a girl. I dress like a girl. Everything is just like a girl, but I am a man." I said, "Really?" He said "Yes." I said, "I don't believe you." He said, "You can ask your friends over there."

And that was sure a surprise for me. I thought she was a girl. She was really beautiful, and I thought maybe we could be friends, and I could take her out to different places. And then afterwards she told me she was not a girl but a man. So then my whole plan fell down about me trying to get acquainted with her, for she was not a girl after all, she was a man!

So I got real mad with my buddies, and I told them how cruel they were in letting me talk to and dance with this man, a man that was dressed in a woman's clothes. But they just laughed and told me that they were playing a joke on me. Before it got too far they would tell me that she was not a woman but a man. So my buddy told me, "Well, let's go to another place where we can see some girls."

So we went to another place, and there were a lot of girls. I didn't want to talk to the girls because I thought they were playing another joke on me. One girl came over and asked me to dance, and I didn't want to because I thought she was a man too, like in the other place we went to. Then this buddy of mine told the girl what happened at the other place. "I can prove it to you that I am not a man," she said. "Come on, let's dance." So I danced with her. We had a nice time there. We stayed there for a few hours, and then I left.

We came to Guadalajara, and there we picked up some furniture, and then we fooled around in a couple of places. Then from Guadalajara we went to Mexico City. And in Mexico City we went to a place where we had to leave the furniture. We unloaded this truck and got the furniture off, and then we went and rested for one day.

The next day we went back to the truck and loaded it with more furniture, and then we went to Saltillo to deliver this furniture. We went to a lot of places in Saltillo. And there in Saltillo I met a nice girl, a nice girl that belonged to a nice family. And I asked her if she would like to be my girl there, and she said yes. And then every time that we went to Monterrey I stopped in Saltillo and picked her up. And I got too serious about her and even considered marrying her. But I decided this girl was much too nice for me, because she came from a rich family, and I had no money. That's why I decided to cut her off.

I know how she felt, because she said, "I don't care if you have no money, because I have money and we can live very happy." But I don't like for a woman to support me. She was rich, and her father owned a couple of stores in Saltillo. I told her, "No, you are going to try and boss me around because you are the one with the money." "Well," she says, "if you don't want to, at least we can still be friends. When you come to Saltillo you can come and visit me, and if you decide we can talk it over again." "No," I said, "once I leave Saltillo I will never come back. I am even going to change jobs so I don't pass through Saltillo no more."

. . .

Since the last time I was deported, I think I have been here in Mexico maybe four years. Before I never stayed that long. Back and forth, only two, three months here in Mexico and then going back to the States. But now I have stayed quite awhile. I would never go back again, unless I get, you know, permission or something. Before I never used to have a wife, maybe that's why I used to run back and forth. But now I have a wife. I never had a wife in the States, just girlfriends, that I used to go live with. You know, be there maybe six months, maybe a year, two years, like that. But I never had one wife that I would be married to her. I never felt like it. I didn't want to be tied down, I guess.

When my wife has a baby, I think my life would change. Because of the baby, you know. That would change my whole life, because I think I would try to set up a home, you know, a decent home like I never had myself. That's what I would like to do. That's why I am buying little by little furniture, because I would like to have a good house where people would go in and say you had a nice house. Maybe I couldn't buy it all at once, but I figure having a baby like that, it would change me. And I don't think I would go no place else. I think I would stay here.

And I am going to try to progress in any way that I can. If I think I can make more money at farming, I'll do that. If I think that's not going to work, maybe I'll try and put up a tourist store someplace. I know it takes money, but maybe I'll get money somewhere. I have been thinking about trying to get help from somebody from the States—just get the store and then pay him back. I don't know, I don't know. I would have to write. It would take at least five thousand dollars, about sixty thousand pesos. For a good business, you know. And I would have a place, maybe in Mexico City. I don't know where, but I will give it a try.

Mexico City is really a good place where you can set up one of those stores, because in Mexico City they attract an awful lot of tourist business. But I think I am better off in the country. You see, Mexico City is too much . . . the life is just too fast. If you stay in Mexico City, you want to go out all the time. You spend more money in the city than you do out here in the country. Life is easier here, more slow. Mexico City is too fast, just like being in New York. Everything going one way, everybody running. Same thing in Mexico City. Everybody is running around.

I would like to have a business. I know how to sell everything to the tourists, because by working in these places I have enough experience in selling and in how to buy even the merchandise. Because when I was at the Tienda Azteca even that lady used to ask me, "Is this the right price to pay for this?" And I used to tell her, "Well, I think it is this price." And she used to ask me, because I worked in a lot of places, you know.

If I would move to the border it would be nice too. But if I get a place in Mexico City I don't think I would move to the border, because the climate is better in Mexico City than in Mexicali. In Mexicali it is too hot. Sometimes it gets to 120, 130 degrees. Just like fire. Very hot. In Mexicali I have a lot of relatives. My grandfather owns a ranch. I would like to go there, maybe go work for him. No, not work for him! No, because when you work for your relatives, you never have a moment free. That's why I say I would like to have a place of my own. Since I have been here in Mexico the last few years, I have thought about that. That way you can be thinking about the future. Maybe later on you can get a bigger place. Maybe start with a small one, then a bigger one.

It's kind of hard to save enough money to start a business. Because you don't make enough money here. You only make fifty, sixty pesos a day, or maybe seventy-five at the most. Seventy-five pesos is about the most that a man makes around here in Mexico. That's a salesman selling to the tourists. Any other man only makes about ten pesos, twelve, fifteen. Twenty-five is about the highest a man makes in a day. Look how long it would take you to save on twenty-five pesos a day! Yeah, I make more than that, but I mean, you know how high the food is in Mexico City. Look how much you spend. If you make twenty-five pesos, you spend it all on food and clothes. You never earn enough money to get a place. Here you can't get a loan like you can in the States. Here the only way you can get a loan is by having property. In the United States you can get a loan on your job. Here you don't have that kind of loan.

I'd like to own everything that I used to own in the States. Like a car, you know, and have a house. All good furniture inside. And then you can give the children education. That's why I would like to set up business or at least have a little money. And that way you can give your children education, so your children won't be running around like I did, you know.

And I want me and my wife to be together all the time. And then it won't happen like it happened to me. Like if I would ever leave my wife, then my children would be running around too. That's what I don't like, you know.

I want to stay with my wife. I've already told her that I would never leave her. And sometimes I even joke with her. I tell her I'm going away, I'm going to leave her, and she starts crying, and right away I get her and tell her, "No, I just tell you that for fun."

Luther P. Gerlach and Virginia H. Hine

The Black Power Movement

Black Power means many things to many people, both black and white. For some it means black separatism—the creation somewhere, somehow, of a separate black state. For some it simply means riots. For others it is the battle cry of violent mega-militants and connotes planned insurgency or guerrilla warfare. But the central concept of Black Power as defined by a growing number of black spokesmen, and as perceived by more and more members of the American public, implies the development by black Americans for black Americans of real economic and political power. It also implies the psychological transformation of blacks into a people proud of being black.

All of the ideological themes and the various approaches to methods of achieving Black Power goals can be traced back through the three hundred years of interracial history in America. Separatism is now advocated largely by the Black Muslims and the most radical of Black Power leaders. This approach, however, has been argued by various blacks since before the Civil War. Racial pride and solidarity have been unrealized but conscious goals of the black community since the days of slavery. Identification with an African heritage as a source of pride is more recent, and has been concurrent with the process of decolonization and independence in Africa.

Self-help is another theme running through Negro history; early in this century, it was clearly formulated in the United States by Booker T. Washington. His concept of blacks earning their place in white society is associated with the idea that blacks must take responsibility for their own inadequacy. Many whites and some conservative Negroes still hold this view. They criticize rioters for losing the respect and good will that "good Negroes" have so painstakingly earned for their race.

From People, Power, Change: Movements of Social Transformation, by Luther P. Gerlach and Virginia H. Hine, copyright © 1970, by The Bobbs-Merrill Company, Inc., reprinted by permission of the publisher.

However, a divergent ideological theme was introduced by one of the founders of the National Association for the Advancement of Colored People, W. E. B. DuBois. His argument that white racism, not black inadequacy, is responsible for existing inequalities made the NAACP a radical organization in its day. This same theme is now a basic tenet in Black Power ideology, and the *Kerner Commission Report on Civil Disorders* has inclined an increasing number of whites to accept it.

Integration, a traditional goal in Negro as well as in liberal white thought, has faded before the more radical proposals involving self-determination, racial pride, and black community. Integration implied that equality must be earned and could be charitably granted by white society to blacks who met white standards of behavior and proficiency. Black Power advocates reject the idea that self-fulfillment is possible only as blacks enter the mainstream of an unchanged white society, thereby abandoning their unique black history and heritage. There is increasing rejection of the idea that white society is automatically desirable. Even moderate blacks have come to realize that racism is not just a personal attitude but a product of social institutions as well. They are beginning to believe that the eradication of racism will require radical changes in American social, economic, and political structures.

There are three basic means by which Black Power participants seek to gain their ends. Conservative groups such as the NAACP and the Urban League believe in gradualism and legislative means. Moderates stand for non-violent direct action such as boycotts, sit-ins, and marches. More militant leaders advocate violence. All three methods have been used at various times by different Negro protest and action groups since the first slave ship arrived on American shores.

A new dimension has emerged with the focus of these themes and these means in the Black Power Movement. In the Civil Rights Movement the right to vote, the right to employment, the right to a good education, and all other benefits of desegregation were seen as goals in and of themselves. With the emergence of Black Power, civil rights have become simply the means to the further goals of economic and political power. Racial unity, also once seen as an end in itself, is now viewed as a means to communal bargaining power with the white power structure. This concept is now expressed in terms of black leadership of black groups and the relegation of white supporters to the status of followers. Previously, Negroes as individuals or in small groups obtained influence and position by cultivating white friends and patrons. Even in organizations established to benefit the black community, the leadership was originally largely white. The shift from whites to blacks in positions of power in these organizations has been accelerated by the advent of Black Power. Those groups which have come into being since that time reject white leadership, except in the case of certain individuals who are considered white radicals. Some even reject white support of any kind.

With the emergence of this emphasis on Black Power, the idea of black pride was transformed into the actual experience of pride for an increasing number of blacks. Such pride is often demonstrated by African dress, natural hair styles, and changes in terminology. Black militants reject the word "Negro" as a term of opprobrium assigned to black people by white masters. Many new terms have developed, of which "Afro-American" and "black" are among the most common.

Black Power was first advocated in a speech given by Stokely Carmichael during the march of James Meredith from Memphis to Jackson, Mississippi, in 1966. The decisive break with traditional methods of protest came six years earlier with the college student sit-ins.

When Black Power was first proclaimed and affirmed across the land, it expressed a mood and a stance rather than a program. It was still a loose collection of enthusiasms and protest tactics. The movement took shape using themes from the past in its emerging ideology; black debate over that ideology is still in progress. As one black put it, "I have the feeling that the movement is going out of its righteous mind trying to find unity and a program." In spite of—or . . . because of—this lack of ideological codification, black action groups of varied size, composition, and approach are springing up across the country. These groups of blacks, or of blacks and whites, have as their objective the implementation of one or another of the various themes that constitute Black Power ideology in its present form. The changing composition of each group, the backgrounds of its members, the situation it faces, and its competition with other groups for recognition, recruits, and support determine which of the major themes a particular group will emphasize. Each group reinterprets, modifies, and adds to the set of goals and means with which it was initially identified. Through this process, each group develops its own particular "style" and each "does its own thing" in its own way.

It must be stressed that these groups of which we are speaking exist at the local level. While many Americans have personally experienced manifestations of the Black Power revolt at the city, ward, or local community level, they characteristically perceive leadership, ideological direction, and method as something which emanates from some sort of central command or national mastermind. The large-scale national organizations such as the Urban League, the NAACP, the Southern Christian Leadership Conference, the Congress of Racial Equality, and the Student Non-Violent Coordinating Committee are often assumed to be monolithic entities which dictate policy from a national office to local branches. Even the *Kerner Commission Report* sometimes gives this impression. This is not correct in the Black Power world. . . .

Local NAACP, SCLC, CORE, and SNCC groups may have considerable independence of action and may vary in attitude and stance according to local conditions and personnel. The local NAACP youth league in one of the cities we visited was extremely militant even though the national organization is commonly considered an "Uncle Tom" outfit by other militants. Another example of such local autonomy is the Black Panthers. Even the brief history of the name illustrates the rapid organizational shifts characteristic of the movement. Originally, "Black Panthers" was the name of an independent black political party in Mississippi which was assisted by black and white SNCC members and which worked for voter registration. Later, a number of groups in different parts of the country—with widely divergent goals—called themselves Black Panthers. One was a youth group, another a black patrol, a third a West Coast militant action group. There was no organizational connection between these organizations at that time. Now, however, the name refers to the original West Coast militant organization which has developed a national structure and claims affiliated chapters in forty-five cities. However, even this attempt at unified national structure is frustrated by an intense rivalry among factions which has resulted in actual organizational splits. These countercurrents of unification and schism are characteristic of the whole Black Power Movement as well as of other movements.

Just as Pentecostalism is often assumed to be synonymous with the established Pentecostal sects, so the large-scale black organizations are sometimes assumed to encompass all of the groups identified with the Black Power Movement. We have seen that certain Pentecostal churches affiliated with one or another of the national or regional bodies can be far from representative of the Pentecostal Movement as a whole. The same is true of Black Power. Each urban center has a range of localized, locally organized and led, and locally named Black Power groups which owe no allegiance whatsoever to a higher body. Furthermore, it is often these groups which set the pace of change and manner of confrontation with the local white power structure. Branches of organizations with national reputations are often in the position of having to adjust to the pace and style set by the independent local groups. The term Black Power Movement as we use it here refers to the whole range of organizations and groups, at all levels of the Negro social structure, which are committed to the purpose of implementing Negro-enhancing social change in America.

These groups can conveniently be ranged along a continuum similar to that which we employed in discussing Pentecostal groups. In considering Black Power, the basis of our continuum is not degree of organizational routinization, as it was with Pentecostalism, but differences in goals-means orientation. The three points along the continuum may be referred to as the conservative, the moderate, and the militant stance. The more conservative civil rights organizations, such as the national NAACP or Urban League committees, may be placed at one end. The radical militant groups, such as those training for or engaging in urban guerrilla and terrorist tactics, are at the other extreme. Any other Black Power group may be placed somewhere in between. Each perceives the problems differently. For instance, to black conservatives, riots are riots. To moderates, they are rebellions. Militants see them as one aspect of The Revolution.

In one metropolitan area we studied, Negroes constitute about three percent of a total population of 480,000; most reside in two of four distinct core city areas. It is fair to say that before 1965 most of the white citizens of this urban area believed their city to be, in comparison with Chicago, New York, or the cities in the South, relatively free from racial prejudice, from slums, and from Negro unemployment. In fact, most white people in this area had little or no contact with blacks and no perception of what black citizens really thought or felt. On the other hand, blacks who moved to this urban area from elsewhere had heard from others that it was a good place for Negroes, but they found a great deal of subtle discrimination and latent hostility. Black Power developed here, as elsewhere, in the form of various groups committed to overt manifestation of anger, release of frustrations, and demands for change.

The first indications of racial "trouble" were incidents in which black youth clashed with white youth at public gatherings—especially at a monthly teen-age dance held by a large city firm for promotional and advertising purposes. There were the usual minor collisions with the police over what appeared to the public to be no more than unconnected criminal incidents.

A few militant blacks, including some at the local university, had participated in sit-ins, freedom rides, and demonstrations in the South and border states. Some liberal whites, again mostly college students, joined them in this, and a few moderate adult whites participated in the Selma demonstrations. More moderate blacks, along with various liberal white supporters, were active in the conventional programs of the NAACP and the Urban League, in several human rights commissions, and conventional social work programs.

Some blacks confronted various business establishments, landlords, real estate firms, agencies of city government, and the university with charges of racial discrimination. The means employed in these confrontations were essentially conventional legal actions in which the rules of the established order prevailed. Blacks often won such engagements, but their victories had little effect on the general public. Certainly they did not contribute much to the introduction of fundamental changes either in institutional practices or in the personal attitudes of white people.

Militant black activity picked up in this metropolitan area during 1966, especially after the long hot summer, when it began to appear that urban racial strife was becoming a new part of the American scene. Some far-seeing whites began to feel that "it *can* happen here," and some blacks not only agreed but also intimated that it would surely come to pass if remedial action were not taken at once.

Various measures were taken or contemplated in response to this threat. By the spring of 1967 a coalition of militant blacks, militant white university students, and influential white liberals developed a new type of community center in the heart of one black core area. A stated objective of this center was to "reach the unreachable"—the angry, depressed, and alienated youth of the area, both black and white. This objective reflected the prevalent and then-current white view that urban riots were caused by just such "down-and-outers" and could be prevented if only this group were "reached." Other activities and other community programs were contemplated, also reflecting a "deprivation causes riots" theory.

Then, in the late summer of 1967, this city had a civil disturbance of sufficient proportions to require the presence of National Guard units, although the disturbance involved less violence than that which gripped other northern cities that summer. Black Power activities and the formation of Black Power groups increased rapidly from this point on. White response was varied.

Some whites rushed in with offers of more jobs, more money for technical training and education for blacks, and more aid for community centers similar to the one mentioned above. Some developed programs to promote communication and understanding between white and black. Some focused attention upon the police and National Guard, pleading for more wisdom and less repressive force in dealing with the Black Power Movement. On the other hand there were some whites and a few Negroes who considered the disturbances as the rioting of delinquents and riffraff. Some saw the evil hand of Communist plotters at work. This faction demanded that the city counter rioting by punishing rather than rewarding the demonstrators. Whites taking this hard line urged the police to greater vigilance and to the use of more force in restoring "law and order." Acting out of a complex of motives, not the least of which was the desire for "fun and games," some young whites drove through the Negro areas on several occasions after the riots, shooting randomly at blacks. There have been a few other instances when whites openly sought conflict with blacks.

Since the single "breakthrough" riot of 1967, there have been additional minor clashes and confrontations, often with the police as a major target. Following the death of Martin Luther King, many whites in the city feared an outbreak of violence; tempers were running high. One response of the white power structure was to permit and to help blacks to establish their own force for what might be called parapolice activities. These are groups of blacks who patrol the black core neighborhoods to prevent the incursion of white troublemakers, to control the most militant black elements, and to reduce casual violence. Part of this force operated out of the community center already described. Another force was organized and operated from a technical school with black leadership and a predominantly black student body. Later, a third wing developed in another black community within the city.

While in theory having the same mission, the patrols compete with each other for recognition by whites as law enforcement bodies. They also compete for funds and equipment, patrol cars and radios, all donated by white individuals. A further basis for competition is the desire for recognition from conservative, moderate, and militant blacks. The three patrol groups differ in philosophy with regard to use of weapons, the degree of cooperation with whites and with police, and attitudes of hostility toward "the system." A fourth law enforcement group, composed of both blacks and whites, organized itself separately. It is a foot patrol which seeks to form a buffer between residents in the black community and white racists who have raided the area.

The development of these four independent patrol groups represents only one aspect of the proliferation of Black Power groups in this city. A brief description of some of the major organizations in this one metropolitan area will illustrate a variety of groups as characteristic of Black Power as it is of Pentecostalism.

The community center has grown since its inception, but retains its autonomy. It owes allegiance to no organization, although offers of alliance have been extended by representatives of several national organizations, both moderate and militant. The center itself has now divided, however, into a number of almost autonomous components—for example, the mobile black patrol and the integrated foot patrol mentioned above. In spite of rivalry, both groups use the center as headquarters. Among the other semi-independent sub-groups of the center is a group which teaches Afro-American history and culture, a group of very militant youths engaged in agitation and protest activities, and a group which works on drama and art. Many individuals share in the leadership of this center and focus on different aspects of the diversified activities.

There are many complex, bureaucratically organized institutions in our society which have equally diversified programs. For instance, YWCA programs and those of large churches often have leaders of various activities who know little or nothing of what other "departments" are doing. But in the YWCA or the large church, responsibility is vested in a single executive or board. There is someone who can speak for the organization. This is not true of this particular Black Power community center. Although the various sub-groups interact and are aware of each other's activities, there is no single leader who can speak for the whole group or whose decisions would be binding on all of the others.

Some of the original founders of this community center have since opened a similar center in another part of the city where blacks live. Although a kind of daughter of the first, this second center is now essentially autonomous. Its plans, programs, and leadership are independent. A third center, resembling these two in design and purpose, developed independently in a third black neighborhood in the same metropolitan area. These autonomous groups are linked only through the friendship and occasional cooperation of their leaders.

These community centers may be placed about halfway between the moderate center and the militant end of our Black Power continuum. There are forces at work within them and upon them which pull them now toward the middle, now toward the extreme of Black Power orientations. These forces include the activities and financial support of liberal whites and the activities of the angry black youths who participate in these centers. These youths constantly challenge the center leaders not to appear to be turning into "Toms."

There are still newer groups which are more militant than the centers. One of these units is composed of some core members of the local city planning and organizing committee for the Poor People's March. Blacks lead this group, but some whites participate. One of its objectives has been to unite poor people, both black and white, in common purpose. It has also proposed the formation of black representation in Washington which could appeal to various African countries for assistance in condemning racism in America.

There are several militant groups of high school and university students who meet for discussion and who are continually prepared to engage in protest activities. They are capable of rapid situational response to any statement, policy decision, or action of the establishment, and are adept at exploiting racial undertones. One group spearheaded opposition to a police handcuffing rule. This involved a demonstration which resulted in their being handcuffed. They threatened continued demonstrations to force arrest. Other Black Power groups protested in other ways. Eventually the rule was revoked. Sit-ins in the mayor's office, before police stations, and in front of police cars were other tactics used by these student groups to force police to abandon use of a controversial weapon. Changes in university and high school curricula, black studies programs, and administration policies remain favorite targets for these groups.

A common pattern in the Black Power Movement in all parts of the country is the initiation of protest action by black youth, followed by the consolidation of gains and continued activity by adult groups organized for this purpose. Black youth also function as gadflies to keep older, more established black organizations moving toward ever more radical goals.

The most militant group of all in the metropolitan area under study advocates violence for its own sake. They follow the manifesto of Frantz Fanon, a black Algerian psychiatrist, who describes violence as a cleansing force, one which frees the black from his inferiority complex, restores his self-respect, and invests his character with positive and creative qualities. Some of the members of this local group have armed themselves and talk about practicing urban guerrilla warfare.

These more militant groups are in considerable developmental flux. There is informal exchange of membership among them, leadership tends to shift, and they change rapidly in mission and composition. By the time this book appears in print, many groups such as those we observed will have disappeared and others come into existence.

Standing just to the left of the moderate middle of our continuum are a number of very small groups and certain independent individuals who consider the promotion of various forms of sensitivity training and interracial communication to be their major mission. These groups have formed in response to the statements of bewilderment on the part of whites who realize that they do not understand the problems or the orientations of black Americans. Some groups teach white groups about Afro-American history and culture. Others train whites to treat blacks in business and industry with more understanding. One group has developed around the production of a television series about blacks, their demands, and their ideas. These groups are cooperating with the white establishment, but they have a kind of vested interest in communicating the sentiments of black militants—hence, they must maintain a militant stance.

A more moderate position in this spectrum of Black Power groups is taken by a large technical training center. Its primary mission is the education and technical training of needy blacks and whites, so that they can obtain employment. Black staff members operate the center and teach in it, although some whites play important roles. Much of the money comes from influential white businessmen. Some of the students, faculty, and administrative personnel of this center are nonparticipants in the Black Power Movement. Others are interested but conservative. Still others speak out quite boldly in favor of revolutionary change. One of the key staff members is recognized as a leading militant spokesman. Some of his black militant rivals have labeled him a "Tom" for his willingness to work with conservatives, but the conservative members of the staff regard him as a local "Stokely." With its various stances, this group is a micro-continuum of Black Power. It also has loose links with similar training centers in other cities.

Another organization situated in the moderate middle of the continuum is a rumor control center staffed largely by blacks. One of the black patrol units shares its headquarters with this group. It represents an effort on the part of certain blacks and influential whites to provide a channel for community information about all pertinent activities in the metropolitan area. The rumor control center also represents an attempt at centralization of both Black Power groups and white positive response groups or "task forces." This function puts it in direct competition with the local Urban Coalition, which is attempting to do the same thing. For this reason, plus the autonomous nature of Black Power groups, the hope of centralization of efforts seems dim. At this writing (1968), three different national Black Power organizations are each trying to set up as the central information center for groups of all types across the country. Each holds national and regional meetings intended to unify the Black Power Movement. The very nature of the organizational autonomy observed in both the Pentecostal Movement and the Black Power Movement, however, would seem to militate against this hope for structural unity.

Toward the conservative end of the continuum observed in this particular city are the Civil Rights groups, the NAACP, and the Urban League. Certain individuals in local branches of these organizations are becoming quite forceful, but the general stance remains more conservative than militant. Also on the conservative end is a center designed to teach whites and blacks about Africa. One of its founders is a black professional man. The other is an African student attending the local university.

Perhaps the most conservative group in the city is one which endorses the advancement of the black cause but which also actively opposes militant extremism. In a sense it was founded in order to counter what its members considered to be the excesses of the community center previously described. Especially disturbing was the teaching, at the community center, of black youths to hate whites and to challenge the authority of their conservative black parents. Members of this conservative group are chiefly people of middle age who are in or moving into the middle class. Many are parents of the young people active at the community center. Some are white, most are black, and blacks are its chief spokesmen. Although it is regarded by many moderate and militant blacks as an "Uncle Tom" organization, it is in fact contributing to the Black Power Movement in various ways. It has organized previously isolated "integrated" blacks as a pressure group for the black cause. This pressure group, in turn, attracts moderate whites and exposes them to Black Power ideology. In spite of their more conservative stance, these blacks accept the long-range goals of Black Power. By interpreting such goals to other conservative blacks, however, members of this group tend to draw previously unorganized individuals closer to participation in the movement. Such groups appeal to blacks who have been integrated as individuals or as families into the white community.

It should be noted that the placement of these particular groups we have described along our conservative-militant continuum may not be the same by the time this book is published. The stance of any particular group is subject to change depending on local incidents or national events and upon shifts in leadership or membership within the group. The overall picture of such a continuum, however, and the variety of groups that may be ranged along it at any point in time will remain a fair description of the movement as a whole.

In addition to the relatively permanent Black Power groups, there are a great number of *ad hoc* groups of short duration and limited mission. These *ad hoc* groups are usually small, although on one occasion nearly all of the blacks in the entire metropolitan area were mobilized into one such group. In this way *ad hoc* groups sometimes constitute a structural cross-group linkage of temporary duration. These temporary groups come into being in response to specific incidents involving racial tension. They are not simply "spontaneous eruptions," for individuals step forward to take control and provide a minimum of organizational structure. On occasion an *ad hoc* group will become a permanently organized group under the initial or subsequent leader.

The pattern of the Black Power Movement in this metropolitan area includes, then, the following elements:

— a great variety of organizationally autonomous groups which work to implement various themes, use different means to achieve their goals, and often display rivalry and a spirit of competition;
— a conservative-moderate-militant continuum;
— certain ideological tenets that are common to all, even the most disparate groups; and
— shifting *ad hoc* alliances resulting in both fission and fusion.

This same pattern was evident in the two additional metropolitan areas we surveyed—one in the Midwest, one in the Southeast. Black Power groups in these and other cities are linked through the activities of traveling spokesmen-evangelists and organizers. Martin Luther King was such an evangelist and organizer for SCLC groups. Members of many local Black Power groups in a particular city came together to hear his speeches in the same way that Pentecostals from various types of churches and groups will come together for a revival meeting. An equally well-known traveling spokesman was Stokely Carmichael of SNCC. He also functioned as a traveling organizer among voter registration workers in southern states. Such groups supported efforts of southern blacks to register and to exercise their voting rights. They also organized mutual aid groups to protect black voters against the traditional means of white retaliation.

It would be misleading to describe the Black Power Movement even sketchily without mentioning the parallel development of what we will call white positive response groups. White response is as varied as the approaches to Black Power, ranging from enthusiastic acceptance of the concept of Black Power to total rejection. Some whites campaign militantly for Black Power groups while other whites prepare to repel the black advance. A characteristic middle-of-the-road response is based on the "I agree with your goals but cannot accept your means" orientation.

In the metropolitan area where we studied both Black Power and white response groups in some detail, the general community direction is toward significant social change. Both established white institutions and newer institutions such as the Urban Coalition argue the need for changes, but the shape of the changes or the means by which they will be made is far from clear.

It has become increasingly apparent that the conventional responses of white institutions are not effective and do not bring about the kinds of change that are necessary. The initiative for change is thus shifting to a host of small grass roots groups which are springing up in response to specific local situations and problems. These groups are as varied in goals and means as those within the Black Power Movement. In some cases they even overlap so that one is tempted to classify them as Black Power groups or as "white auxiliaries." While Black Power has achieved full status as a movement, the white response groups may be considered an incipient or proto-movement.

A very brief list of examples drawn from several metropolitan areas will serve to indicate the nature of the white response groups:

— two black and two white housewives met and started to recruit others in an attempt to start cross-racial communication;
— discussion groups of whites formed to discuss racial issues and explore their own reactions;
— a group of wealthy businessmen took trucks into the ghetto area and collected garbage because city schedules tended to neglect this area;

— one group was organized to collect clothing, food, and supplies for participants in the Poor People's March from their area;
— one couple volunteered their home as a collection center for whites who believed all guns should be turned in as a demonstration of commitment to white non-violence;
— concerned clergymen organized to recruit participants for various demonstrations;
— several groups organized to provide shelter and collect food, clothing, household equipment, and medical supplies for blacks who were hurt or homeless after the riots;
— groups of white university students organized to support blacks in their demands for black studies programs;
— several lawyers organized to provide voluntary legal aid for blacks;
— one group had "stamp out racism" buttons made and sold them. They also put "white racism must go" signs up in their yards and recruited others who were willing to do likewise;
— one individual started a very successful "buy black" campaign;
— one young couple who had formerly owned an import business helped a black couple set up channels for importing African items, and turned over to them all their address lists and similar business information.

There is some question as to whether the Black Power Movement, the white positive response groups, and even the student campus rebellions are all part of the same social movement. We take the position here that although they may all be part of a single social revolution, at least for purposes of analysis Black Power may be identified as a separate movement. For the purposes of this study, a Black Power group will be defined as *any group (a) which accepts and attempts to implement the goals of black economic and political power, black unity, black self-determination, and racial pride for blacks, and (b) in which the locus of decision-making power, control of funds, and ownership of property is in, or is shifting to, the hands of blacks.*

Alvin M. Josephy, Jr.

"We Must Hold On to the Old Ways"

Indians of All Tribes
Alcatraz Island, December 16, 1969

The striving for self-determination, nurtured by a new pride in Indian identity and background and symbolized by the slogan "Red Power," enlisted no more dedicated partisans than those Indians who lived away from reservations—at universities and in urban centers of the United States. By the end of the 1960's several hundred thousand—perhaps more than half a million—Indians lived in Chicago, Minneapolis, Denver, Los Angeles, and other major cities. Many of them had been lured there by World War II defense jobs, others by Bureau of Indian Affairs postwar relocation programs, and still others had gotten there on their own.

Adjusting to the alien "mainstream" of white culture was difficult for large numbers of them, and their lives were filled with social and economic problems every bit as serious as those of the reservations. Far from home, also, the urban Indians were cut off from the federal services to which they were entitled on the reservation. In their loneliness they tended to find each other, even though they came from different tribes and different parts of the country, and grouping together in urban Indian centers, they found strength and sustenance in their Indianness.

Among the young city and university Indians particularly, loyalty to their individual tribes and to the Indian people in general began to blaze high during the 1960's. From that point, militant advocacy of Indian self-determination and bitter hostility toward the Bureau of Indian Affairs and all other white oppressors of the Indians were a short step. Indian protest songs, sung by Johnny Cash, a descendant of Cherokee, Floyd Westerman, a Sioux, and Buffy Sainte-Marie, a Cree, inspired them, as did the writings of the young Standing Rock Sioux, Vine Deloria, Jr. (*Custer Died for Your Sins*), and the Red Power and Indian nationalist speeches of Clyde Warrior, Wallace "Mad Bear" Anderson, Hank Adams, Lehman Brightman, Tillie Walker, and other Indians.

At many colleges Indian students formed their own clubs, conducted seminars and conferences on Indian problems, pressured for the introduction of Indian studies, and talked of off-campus activism in behalf of all the Indian peoples. In the cities so-called urban Indians formed activist organizations of their own, such as the American Indian Movement (AIM), under the direction of Clyde Bellecourt and Dennis Banks in Minneapolis, and the United Native Americans, Inc., led by Lehman Brightman in San Francisco. Some of the groups, together with previously existing Indian centers in various cities, joined in a nationwide federation called American Indians United, whose first head was Jess Six Killer, an Indian member of the Chicago Police Department.

Within the national context of non-Indian activist activities, marked especially by youth and minority group demonstrations, it was inevitable that Indian acts of protest would soon occur also. Old and new grievances were focused upon: the indifference of the government to long-standing injustices being suffered by tribes; the continued deafness by official Washington to the demand for self-determination; "stacked cards" against the Pyramid Lake Paiutes' right to water, the Taos Pueblos' right to their sacred Blue Lake, the Puget Sound Indians' right to fish, the Alaskan natives' right to their lands; exploitation of Indians by white promoters and advertisers; discrimination against Indians by federal, state, and local agencies of government; and the initial "realignment" of the Bureau of Indian Affairs, which failed to get at the heart of problems. These and other grievances stirred anger among the steadily growing groups of activists.

Then on November 20, 1969, a landing party of seventy-eight Indians calling themselves Indians of All Tribes suddenly occupied Alcatraz Island, in San Francisco Bay, electrifying Indians all over the United States and Canada and giving new inspiration to the cause of Indian freedom. Alcatraz, taken originally from Indians, had been employed in recent times by the federal government as a prison site. But the prison had been closed, and save for the operation of a lighthouse, the government no longer had use for the island. The Indians, most of whom lived or attended colleges in the San Francisco Bay area, moved onto the island under an old law that permitted certain tribes to reclaim land taken from them by the federal government when the government no longer needed it. They proclaimed Alcatraz to be Indian Land, and, though suffering hardships because of lack of water, food, and electricity, set about making their stay permanent.

Most of the non-Indians of the nation gave them their sympathy and support, and the government, not wishing to provoke a confrontation, let them stay—though wondering how, eventually, to oust them. San Franciscans sent food, medical supplies, and other assistance; tourists ferried to the island to give words of encouragement; and enthusiastic Indians from reservations and other urban areas came to live there temporarily or permanently.

Typical of the reactions of non-Indian well-wishers were the following sentiments by the Chairman of the American Bar Association's Committee on the American Indian, Monroe E. Price, a professor of law at UCLA and Deputy Director of California Indian Legal Services: "The taking of Alcatraz may begin a new era of Pan-Indian awareness and activity. That hard and lonely settlement has been greeted not with tear gas but with a sense of hope and promise. The band of Indians on the prison island have formed a policy for themselves and by themselves. They are staking a claim for the restoration of a culture and a strength of community that should not be lost. The wager they are asking the country to make is a safe one: that they cannot be more wrong than the great white fathers of the past."

Alcatraz was self-determination brought about by the Indians themselves. A community of, by, and for Indians was created. But the occupation of the island and the establishment of a settlement were not ends in themselves. On December 16, 1969, the group on Alcatraz addressed a letter to all the Indians of North America, inviting them to send delegates to a meeting on the island the following week. The letter set forth their ultimate goal, the establishment of an Indian cultural and educational center on Alcatraz. Many Indians from across the United States and Canada responded, and some stayed on the island, adding to its population, which soon represented fifty tribes.

The letter sent by the Alcatraz Indians on December 16, announcing the reason for the occupation of the island and the goal of the occupiers, follows.

Dear Brothers and Sisters:

This is a call for a delegation from each Indian nation, tribe or band from throughout the United States, Canada, and Mexico to meet together on Alcatraz Island in San Francisco Bay, on December 23, 1969, for a meeting to be tentatively called the Confederation of American Indian Nations (CAIN).

On November 20, 1969, 78 Indian people, under the name "Indians of all Tribes," moved onto Alcatraz Island, a former Federal Prison. We began cleaning up the Island and are still in the process of organizing, setting up classes and trying to instill the old Indian ways into our young.

We moved onto Alcatraz Island because we feel that Indian people need a Cultural Center of their own. For several decades, Indian people have not had enough control of training their young people. And without a cultural center of their own, we are afraid that the old Indian ways may be lost. We believe that the only way to keep them alive is for Indian people to do it themselves.

While it was a small group which moved onto the island, we want all Indian people to join with us. More Indian people from throughout the country are coming to the island every day. We are issuing this call in an attempt to unify all our Indian Brothers behind a common cause.

We realize that there are more problems in Indian communities besides having our culture taken away. We have water problems, land problems, "social" problems, job opportunity problems, and many others.

And as Vice President Agnew said at the annual convention of the National Congress of American Indians in October of this year, now is the time for Indian leadership.

We realize too that we are not getting anywhere fast by working alone as individual tribes. If we can gather together as brothers and come to a common agreement, we feel that we can be much more effective, doing things for ourselves, instead of having someone else doing it, telling us what is good for us.

So we must start somewhere. We feel that if we are going to succeed, we must hold on to the old ways. *This is the first and most important reason we went to Alcatraz Island.*

We feel that the only reason Indian people have been able to hold on and survive through decades of persecution and cultural deprivation is that the Indian way of life is and has been strong enough to hold the people together.

We hope to reinforce the traditional Indian way of life by building a Cultural Center on Alcatraz Island. We hope to build a college, a religious and spiritual center, a museum, a center of ecology, and a training school.

We hope to have the Cultural Center controlled by Indians, with the delegates from each Indian nation and urban center present for the first meeting on December 23, and at future meetings of the governing body.

We are inviting all our brothers to join with us on December 23, if not in person, then in spirit.

We are still raising funds for Alcatraz. The "Alcatraz Relief Fund" is established with the Bank of California, Mission Branch, 3060 16th Street, San Francisco, California 94103, and we are asking that donations of money go to the bank directly.

Many Indian Centers and tribal groups from throughout the country have supported the people of Alcatraz by conducting benefits, funded drives, and so forth. We are deeply appreciative of all the help we have received, and hope that all Indian people and people of good will, will join us in this effort.

We are also asking for formal resolutions of support from each organized Indian tribe and urban center. We can have great power at the bargaining table if we can get the support and help of all Indian people.

We have made no attempts at starting a hard and fast formal organization. We have elected spokesmen because someone has had to be a spokesman. We feel that all Indian people should be present or represented at the outset of a formal national Indian organization.

We have also elected a Central Council to help organize the day-to-day operation of the Island. This organization is not a governing body, but an operational one.

We hope to see you on December 23rd.

Indians of All Tribes
Alcatraz Island

Time Magazine

The Worst Is Yet to Be?

The furnaces of Pittsburgh are cold; the assembly lines of Detroit are still. In Los Angeles, a few gaunt survivors of a plague desperately till freeway center strips, backyards and outlying fields, hoping to raise a subsistence crop. London's offices are dark, its docks deserted. In the farm lands of the Ukraine, abandoned tractors litter the fields: there is no fuel for them. The waters of the Rhine, Nile and Yellow rivers reek with pollutants.

Fantastic? No, only grim inevitability if society continues its present dedication to growth and "progress." At least that is the vision conjured by an elaborate study entitled *The Limits to Growth*. Its sponsors are no latter-day Jeremiahs, but the 70 eminently respectable members of the prestigious Club of Rome. These include Aurelio Peccei, the Italian economist (and former Olivetti chief) who now heads the management firm of Italconsult in Rome; Kogoro Uemura, president of the Japan Federation of Economic Organizations; and Britain's Alexander King, director general for scientific affairs of the Office for Economic Cooperation and Development. It is as if David Rockefeller, Henry Ford and Buckminster Fuller suddenly came out against commerce and technology.

The club was founded by Peccei back in 1968 with the avowed purpose of exploring the large issues confronting society. "We needed something to make mankind's predicament more visible, more easy to grasp," says Peccei. To that end, the Volkswagen Foundation granted the club $250,000 in 1970. Peccei turned to an international team of scientists led by M.I.T. Computer Expert Dennis Meadows and told them to study the most basic issue of all—survival.

Meadows, 29, had studied the new field of "systems dynamics." His mentor was M.I.T. Professor Jay Forrester, the brilliant developer of a computer model that could simulate the major ecological forces at work in the world today. Forrester's model begins with the recognition that all these factors are interlocked. Human population cannot grow without food for sustenance. Since just about all the globe's best land is already under cultivation, farm production can rise only through use of tractors, fertilizers, pesticides—all products of industry. But more industrial output not only demands a heavier drain on natural resources that are scarce even now; it also creates more pollution. And pollution ultimately interferes with the growth of both population and food.

Using this model, Meadows and his team fed M.I.T.'s megacomputer with an array of data ranging from expert opinion to hard, empirical facts—the world's known resources, population growth rates, the incidence of pollution connected with nuclear power plants, etc.

The question Meadows had to answer was: How long can population and industrialization continue to grow on this finite planet? Unlike the doomsday ecologists who predict that man will drown in pollution or starve because of overpopulation, Meadows' system concludes that the depletion of nonrenewable resources will probably cause the end of the civilization enjoyed by today's contented consumer.

END IN COLLAPSE. The sequence goes this way: As industrialization grows, it voraciously consumes enormous amounts of resources. Resources become scarcer, forcing more and more capital to be spent on procuring raw materials, which leaves less and less money for investment in new plants and facilities. At this stage, which might be about 2020, the computer's curves begin to converge and cross (*see chart*). Population outstrips food and industrial supplies. Investment in new equipment falls behind the rate of obsolescence, and the industrial base begins to collapse, carrying along with it the service and agricultural activities that have become dependent on industrial products (like medical equipment and fertilizers). Because of the lack of health services and food, the world's population dwindles rapidly.

In an attempt to find a way out of this basic dilemma, Meadows postulated other scenarios. He assumed that there are still huge, undiscovered reserves of natural resources, say, under the oceans. Testing that possibility, Meadows' computer shows that industrialization will accelerate—and the resulting runaway pollution will overwhelm the biosphere. Might not new technological devices control pollution? Sure, says the computer, but then population would soar and outstrip the ability of land to produce food. Every advance in technology consumes scarce natural resources, throws off more pollutants and often has unwanted social side effects, like creating huge and unmanageable unemployment. What if pollution was abated, the birthrate halved and food production doubled? The readouts are no less glum. There would still be some pollution from every farm and factory, and cumulatively it would still trigger catastrophe. After running thousands of such hypotheses through the computer, Meadows sums up his conclusion tersely: "All growth projections end in collapse."

The Meadows team offers a possible cure for man's dilemma—an all-out effort to end exponential growth, starting by 1975. Population should be stabilized by equalizing the birth and death rates. To halt industrial growth,

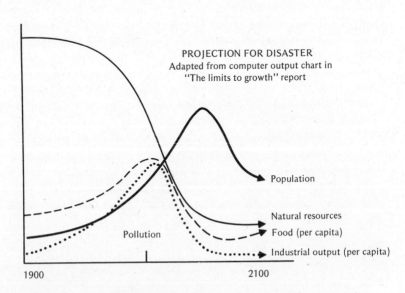

FIGURE 1. Projection for disaster. Adapted from computer-output chart in "The Limits to Growth" report.

investment in new, nonpolluting plants must not exceed the retirement of old facilities. A series of fundamental shifts in behavioral patterns must take place. Instead of yearning for material goods, people must learn to prefer services, like education or recreation. All possible resources must be recycled, including the composting of organic garbage. Products like automobiles and TV sets must be designed to last long and to be repaired easily.

As the report presents it, the result is a sort of utopia—not the stagnation of civilization. "A society released from struggling with the many problems imposed by growth," the report says, "may have more energy and ingenuity available for solving other problems." Research, the arts, athletics might well flourish in a no-growth world. Nor would developing nations necessarily be frozen into everlasting poverty. Without the burden of an increasing population, they might provide fewer citizens more amenities.

"The report makes one thing abundantly clear: there is a limit to everything," says Japan's Yoicha Kaya, a club member and systems analyst now working for the Battelle Institute in Geneva. "There is no use in wringing hands. We can and must try to do what is humanly possible, and we must act soon." Even the club members were startled by the computer's findings but were unable to raise any important objections to them. The study is now being polished and refined by Potomac Associates, a public policy "think tank" in Washington that will publish *The Limits to Growth* in March. After translating it into a dozen languages, the Club of Rome will use its influence to place *Limits* in the right hands, where its message may influence policy and stir public debate.

One glaring weakness nonetheless remains in the report. It lacks a description of how a society dedicated to upward and onward growth can change its ways. Dennis Meadows, thoroughly aware of the problem, is trying to raise funds for a computer study of the possibilities. To date, he has had little success. Why? Mainly because Americans still tend to believe that continual growth is the solution to all problems.

The Club of Rome is not alone in its concern. Last week Britain's *Ecologist* magazine devoted 22 pages to a "Blueprint for Survival" that also projects disaster and argues for quick action to end exponential growth. The article gains its authority not from computer studies but from the endorsement of 33 of the U.K.'s most distinguished scientists, including Biologist Sir Julian Huxley, Geneticist C. H. Waddington and Naturalist Peter Scott. Unrestricted industrial and population expansion, they warn, must lead to "the breakdown of society and of the life support systems on this planet—possibly by the end of this century and certainly within the lifetime of our children."

Why has this dangerous trend not received wider attention? "Governments," reported the article, "are either refusing to face the relevant facts or are briefing their scientists in such a way that the seriousness is played down." As a result, "we may muddle our way to extinction."

Rather than wait, the scientists suggest urgent efforts to encourage a steady or declining population and heavy new taxes on raw materials. The taxes would penalize industries that consume great amounts of non-renewable natural resources and favor those that are labor intensive, thus keeping employment levels high. Another new tax would be based on the life of industrial products. A consumer buying a machine-made product that lasts one year would pay a 100% tax on it, while a product built to last 100 years would be taxfree. Stiff as such measures may seem now, the *Ecologist* says, they will avoid imposing infinitely greater hardships on future generations of British citizens.

Michael Corr and Dan MacLeod

Getting It Together

We build power plants, tolerating air, water, and thermal pollution as well as massive alterations of the landscape, in order to create certain products and comforts for ourselves. Exactly which products and comforts our power resources are used to produce are determined by our life-style, defined here as the manner in which resources are used to fulfill human needs. Life-style, in turn, can be looked at as being dependent on family structure, values, and so on, and as these factors vary, so does life-style. Viewed in this manner, life-style can yield some interesting insights into home energy consumption.

The historical trend and recent policy preferences have been to small families, and as the number of large household operations has decreased, many of the advantages of large families have been lost. For instance, in 1900, with an average of 4.8 people in the household, chores like dishwashing, laundry, gardening, and canning could be shared among several people; now, with an average household of 3.2 people, the dishwasher, the automatic laundry, and the freezer seem like necessities to the housewife.

Nuclear families, consisting of mother, father, and children and extended families, which include grandparents or other relatives as well, are not, however, the only kinds of large households (with size-related advantages) possible. During the past few decades considerable interest in various patterns of communal living has been exhibited by young people. Students, artists, young working people, political activists, and religious people have formed numerous large households with varying degrees of success.[1] A true commune is defined as a household with a common pool of income and property, allocated by means of a single budget; a common home, in which all goods and facilities (for example, kitchen and bathroom) are fully accessible to all members, with consensually determined provisions for privacy; and a common provision for the care and education of children. A life-style that leads to communal use of facilities would appear to make a pronounced difference in personal energy consumption.

Unfortunately, only meager data to support an analysis of life-style as a function of family structure are available through the Bureau of Census of the Department of Commerce. The bureau data only indicate that major appliance ownership, and therefore presumably domestic energy consumption, increases with family income.[2] In addition, thorough analysis of communal use of resources relative to use by other types of households is complicated by the wide variety of life-style innovations among urban and rural communes.

In an attempt to gain insight into commune resource use, a group of twelve communes, with a total of 116 members, in the Minneapolis area were visited, and a questionnaire was administered to determine patterns of natural gas, electric power, and motor fuel consumption, as well as appliance and automobile ownership.

The limitations of this study are many. The houses were selected rather arbitrarily through personal acquaintances and may not be a representative sample of the entire communal counter-culture. Minneapolis has a relatively severe winter requiring more energy use for heating. Most groups did not keep accurate records. Utility bills were sometimes paid with the rent. Odometers in some communes' automobiles were broken. Thus, some figures must be considered rough estimates. Nevertheless, the study does give some interesting indications of the degrees of reduction in energy consumption which could result if large numbers of people began sharing consumer goods and otherwise simplifying their life-styles. For example, computed on a per household member basis, natural gas, on the average, was consumed by the commune members at a rate 40 percent below that for an average Minneapolis house of 900 square feet occupied by 2.6 people, electric power at a rate 82 percent below the Minneapolis average, and gasoline at a rate 36 percent below the national average.

Natural gas consumption by all of these groups was similar, whereas power use varied widely from group to group, and the consumption of gasoline varied even more widely (in some cases being even higher than the national average). This results perhaps from the fact that the consumption of power and gasoline is dependent on personal habits as well as the size of the household (see Table 1).

This low rate of energy consumption was voluntary and was not considered by the people involved as a lowering of their standard of living. Most of the people in these groups are young political activists who decided to live collectively for social and financial reasons. The reduction in energy consumption

Table 1: Summary of Direct Commune Energy Use

	NATURAL GAS (MINNEAPOLIS)	ELECTRICITY (MINNEAPOLIS)	GASOLINE (NATIONWIDE)
Average per household	120.6 thousand cu. ft./yr.*	6,651 kwh/yr.**	905 gallons/yr.***
Average per person	3,860 cu. ft./mo.	213 kwh/mo.	285 gallons/yr.
Commune use per person			
low	1,700 cu. ft./mo.	17 kwh/mo.	60 gallons/yr.
average	2,300 cu. ft./mo.	39 kwh/mo.	181 gallons/yr.
high	3,000 cu. ft./mo.	66 kwh/mo.	444 gallons/yr.
Percentage reduced per person			
low	56%	92%	79%
average	40%	82%	36%

* Based on estimated average housing unit size of 900 sq. ft. A. L. Pooler, Minneapolis Gas Co., and Allan Anderson, Minnesota State Planning Agency.

** Personal communication, Margaret Brian, Northern States Power, Minneapolis; and U.S. Dept. of Commerce, Bureau of Census, *1970 Census of Housing, Minneapolis-St. Paul Urbanized Area, Block Statistics*, Aug. 1971; figure for average household of 2.6 members.

*** *U.S. Statistical Abstracts*, 1971, p. 36, 3.17 people per household. U.S. Bureau of Consumer Buying Expectations, unpublished data, 1.291 vehicles per household. *U.S. Statistical Abstracts*, 1971, 700 gallons of motor fuel consumption in 1969 per automobile year.

was a result of this desire to live collectively and to de-emphasize the materialistic aspects of life. Some of the people were making conscious attempts to reduce their consumption of energy; others were not. Some were apologetic about their high bills and the number of appliances they owned; others had not given energy conservation much thought.

Appliances

In an attempt to quantify the difference in appliance use between communes and other households, appliance ownership was computed on an average per capita basis for the commune sample and compared with the averages for all households in the U.S. Some striking differences were observed.

Whereas about 25 percent of Minneapolis homes had air conditioning,[3] the communes had none. The communes had no dishwashers or food freezers and only two clothes dryers for the 116 members, 0.02 dryers per person, or only one-eighth the national average. Some commune members may be hanging their clothes on clotheslines to dry, but most are probably using dryers at the Laundromat where they wash their clothes.

Washing clothes at a Laundromat may not save any "laundering energy," but as a communal facility, Laundromat machines will typically do the work of several home laundry devices, thereby saving considerable secondary energy, that is, manufacturing and materials extraction. Obviously, it takes more energy to produce washers for several individual families than it does to produce one Laundromat machine, which can serve the same number of families.

It is difficult to estimate the possible impact of communal living on energy required for manufacturing. It seems likely that appliances in large households are used more intensively than those in average-sized households. There is more food to cool, cook, or blend; more work for toasters, irons, and record players. Commune appliances would therefore seem more likely to wear out, rather than be retired due to obsolescence. (This does not necessarily hold true for such appliances as refrigerators, which run all day regardless of how many people use them.) When consumers use articles until they wear out, instead of discarding them for other reasons such as obsolescence, they help relieve the energy burden of manufacturing.

In an attempt to evaluate the demands of "the new life-style" on the manufacturing sector, saturations were computed from the commune data for nineteen appliances or conveniences. Household saturation for a convenience is the percentage of all households which own or are furnished with that convenience. Because the average commune had ten members, more than three times the national average for households, appliance saturations were computed on a per capita, as well as a household, basis. These data are listed in Table 2.

The national average household saturation for the nineteen conveniences considered was 74 percent, and the commune average household saturation was 62 percent, somewhat lower, certainly, but not strikingly so. What was striking was the difference among per capita saturations. The national average was 24 percent, the commune average only 6 percent.

Note that every one of the conveniences considered, from cars to blenders, can serve a communal function. It can be argued that as long as a household has a convenience, all the members enjoy its services. From this general observation, one can see that the commune members are being served much better by their investment in appliances than are average occupants. Their per capita *access* to conveniences is almost equal to that of the average U.S. household member even though their per capita *consumption* is only 25 percent of the national average, measured in terms of saturation. Thus, such a life-style clearly consumes much less secondary energy through the nation's manufacturing sector than does the average household, on a per capita basis.

Table 2: Selected Convenience Saturation for New Life-style Communal Groups Compared to the National Average

Convenience *	NATIONAL AVERAGE				SAMPLE COMMUNES		
	Approx. Price (if new) **	No. per House-hold ***	No. per Indivi-dual	Weighted Price per Individual	No. per Commune	No. per Commune Member	Weighted New Price per Commune Member
Cars and Trucks	$2,910 retail	1.291†	0.41††	$1,192	1.84	0.19	$533
	$2,195 wholesale			900			418
Air conditioner	250	0.25†††	0.09	23.20	—	—	—
Dishwasher	200	0.21†	0.07	14.00	—	—	—
Freezer	225	0.33‡	0.10	22.50	—	—	—
Television	175	1.22†	0.38	66.50	0.68	0.07	12.23
Refrigerator	300	0.998‡	0.32	96.00	1.36	0.14	42.00
Radio	50	0.998‡	0.32	16.00	1.65	0.17	8.50
Electric iron	15	0.997‡	0.32	4.80	0.75	0.08	1.20
Toaster	12	0.93‡	0.29	3.48	0.87	0.09	1.08
Water heater	100	0.92‡‡	0.29	29.00	1.07	0.11	11.00
Vacuum cleaner	75	0.92‡	0.29	21.75	0.68	0.07	5.25
Coffee maker	14	0.89‡	0.28	3.92	0.19	0.02	0.28
Mixer	25	0.82‡	0.26	6.50	0.29	0.03	0.75
Washing machine	175	0.74‡	0.23	40.25	0.17	0.02	3.50
Range	275	0.59‡‡	0.19	52.30	0.97	0.10	27.50
Frypan	20	0.56†	0.18	3.60	0.2	0.03	0.60
Electric blanket	16	0.50‡	0.16	2.56	0.39	0.04	0.64
Clothes dryer	150	0.47†	0.15	22.50	0.17	0.02	3.00
Blender	25	0.37‡	0.12	3.00	0.39	0.04	1.00
Average saturations		0.74	0.24		0.62	0.06	

	NATIONAL	COMMUNE
Weighted new retail value per person		
Without autos and trucks	$ 431.86	$ 118.53
With autos and trucks	1,623.86	671.53
Weighted new retail value per household		
Without autos and trucks	$1,356.40	$1,185.30
With autos and trucks	5,116.40	6,715.30

* Since national household saturation data were available for only 19 of the 32 conveniences, such items as hairdryers, waffle irons, electric tools, and one mimeograph machine were omitted from the calculations.

** Approximate prices for all appliances are from *Sears and Roebuck's Fall and Winter 1971 Catalogue*, except for the air conditioning price, which was taken from their 1972 Spring and Summer catalogue.

*** Except for ranges and water heaters, all saturations are for 1971.

† U.S. Bureau of Census, Survey of Consumer Buying Expectations, July 1971, unpublished data.

†† Assumes 3.17 people per household, the national average for 1970; U.S. Dept. of Commerce, 1971, op. cit.

††† Saturation of air conditioners for Minneapolis only; personal communication from an undisclosed source at Northern States Power.

‡ U.S. Dept. of Commerce, *Statistical Abstracts*, 1971, Table 1117.

‡‡ U.S. Office of Science and Technology, *Patterns of Energy Consumption in the United States*, household saturations for 1968.

When the convenience saturations were weighted by the approximate new retail value of the conveniences involved, the pattern apparent in the saturation averages was reinforced, in spite of the wide range of prices between toasters and cars. The average commune had $6,715.30 worth of the conveniences considered, 31 percent more than the $5,116 computed from national household saturations for the conveniences considered. The average new value per commune individual was $671.53, which was 59 percent below our estimated national average per household individual. In terms of energy required for producing, promoting and retailing such conveniences, input-output table calculations indicate that the average U.S. household member has indirectly used 123.9 million British Thermal Units (BTU) of energy through the nineteen conveniences considered. The average commune member has used only 49.97 million BTU, or 59.6 percent less.[4] These energy savings can be amortized over an estimated ten-year appliance lifetime, yielding a saving of about 7 million BTU per person each year for commune individuals. It can be estimated that U.S. energy consumption per capita was about 351 million BTU per capita in 1971. Therefore by saving 7 million BTU (after amortization) the commune member is achieving a 2 percent saving in per capita energy use.

The energy economies in actual use of the conveniences turn out to be comparable in magnitude. As noted earlier, the average commune member used 40 percent less natural gas and 82 percent less electricity than the average household individual. This yielded a 71 percent energy saving over average per capita residential consumption.[5] Residences account for 19.2 percent of end use of energy;[6] thus the commune members achieved an additional saving of 13.6 percent of national average per capita energy consumption through their economies in direct natural gas and electricity use (assuming 1968 proportions of energy use for 1971). Moreover, the commune members used 36 percent less motor fuel than the per capita average of 285 gallons per household member, a saving of 104 gallons. This is a saving of 13.09 million BTU per person, or a saving of 3.7 percent of national per capita energy consumption. Altogether the *savings* of energy by commune individuals amount to 19.3 percent of total U.S. national per capita energy consumption. (See Table 3.)

Since consumption of household goods (new value) for commune members was 60 percent below the national average, it can be surmised that the cash needs of commune members were considerably less than the national average for adults. Many communes have special businesses, such as running a bakery, a repair shop, a printing shop, a radio station, a newspaper, a free school, a Yoga school, or a documentary film operation. Communes also save energy in such cases where home and work are the same place for the members. For instance, one bakery and restaurant commune manages to get by with only two small buses for seventeen adult members and two children.

Table 3: Average Per Capita Energy Savings Tabulated for
New Life-Style Participants

SAVINGS CATEGORY	USAGE REDUCTION (IN MILLIONS OF BRITISH THERMAL UNITS)	SAVINGS AS PERCENT OF NATIONAL PER CAPITA ENERGY CONSUMPTION *
Motor fuel	13.1	3.7
Gas, oil, and electricity	47.7	13.6
Amortized energy for manufacture and distribution of household conveniences (over ten-year period)	7.0	2.0
Totals	67.8	19.3

* Base national per capita energy consumption: 351 million British Thermal Units in 1971.

Transportation

In the commune sample there were 32 vehicles, and the average fuel consumed per vehicle was 655 gallons per year, 6 percent below the national average. Motor fuel consumption per individual was 36 percent below the national average, and the automobile mileage per individual was 68 percent below the national average. However, the average commune automobile was driven about the same mileage as the average domestically owned U.S. automobile. By ride sharing, economies were possible in going to school, work, and for shopping and other errand running. Mass transit use by commune members was minimal; only four individuals of the 116 members commuted by bus, a method of passenger travel with about one-fourth the impact on energy resources per passenger mile as auto travel.[7] The twelve communes also had 45 bicycles, more than one for every three people. Bicycles use about 4 percent as much energy as automobiles per passenger mile.[8]

In 1968 the total energy used to produce and distribute new cars in the U.S. was 2,040 trillion BTU.[8] This amounted to 3.8 percent of all energy available for end use in the economy. The automobile's large share of the national energy budget as well as its relative importance in the family and commune budget, suggest that it is worth considering whether communal auto use patterns offer any advantages beyond the lower per person mileages observed in the communes.

Another approach to insuring that social capital invested in the auto is used in a manner which minimizes impact on the environment would be to look for ways in which the individual auto could be used more intensively. If Americans drove the same number of passenger miles by auto but did it in fewer autos (that is, more passengers per auto on the average) then the individual auto would be producing more social good per unit of auto production.

That higher total mileages are possible can be seen from the experience of the taxicab industry. Taxi companies often get 150,000 miles of service before the engine needs a major overhaul.[9] The taxi is usually given an engine overhaul a couple of times, and total mileage in the neighborhood of 300,000 miles is not uncommon. By contrast, the average family drives 10,000 miles per auto each year.[10] In order to put the taxicab's 300,000 miles on their auto a family would have to drive it, on the average, 30 years, but in 1970 the average age of the auto on the road was only 5.6 years.[11] Thus, when the energy required for production is considered, it appears that present patterns of family auto usage are resource wasteful, since most autos are taken out of service due to accidents or psychological obsolescence, rather than, as in the case of the 300,000-mile taxi, due to being worn out.[12] The fact that the autos of the commune sample were receiving slightly less than average mileage, even though the average commune had three times as many members as the average U.S. household, suggests that optimal use of the auto as commune social capital might be affected through sharing autos between communes, so that they receive intensive use, and are at least not retired due to psychological obsolescence. In Washington, the May Valley Coop (about six households) and the Ploughshare Collective (three households) have experimented with inter-household, shared vehicle ownership. In the latter case two vehicles serve seventeen adults, two children, and the bakery and restaurant which support the collective. The Ploughshare vehicle mileage per individual is about 40 percent below the national average, while the vehicles are receiving about 60 percent more use than the average family auto.[13]

Commune ownership of autos (for functions which cannot be met by bicycle or bus) also offers the possibility of organized community maintenance of vehicles. Another option which would extend the useful life (total mileage) of autos would be the selection of mechanically simple vehicles for community use. This would encourage community members to perform a larger proportion of the maintenance and repair of community vehicles, a policy already followed by the Ploughshare Collective.

Clearly these notes on communal use of vehicles are not intended as the basis for curing the complex environmental problems of U.S. transportation. From previous articles on transportation appearing in *Environment*, it is clear that mass transport offers great reductions in personal energy consumption where population densities are sufficient to support it.[7] Such work also indicates that there may be great gaps in the services which can be provided by mass transit in the U.S., and that therefore additional energy savings might by necessity be required to come from changes in the cultural pattern of use of the automobile.

Examination of the transportation problem suggests that it is deeply related to cultural *and* technical factors. Evaluations of energy consumption through the materials used in autos and comparison of auto durability relative to that of trucks and buses, suggests a change in the design of automobiles could yield an auto which could provide more miles of use with less investment in energy during the vehicle production process.[14] However, as indicated in the case of taxis, social factors dictate against giving full use to a vehicle because of the psychological obsolescence factor, and the fact that the individual family has no chance to drive an auto as intensively as would be optimal. The idea is to use fewer machines more intensively, to minimize production while still meeting transportation needs. Large communes with few vehicles offer this advantage of intensive vehicle use.

A small example of cultural adroitness of implementing life-style alterations in transportation was highlighted in a recent news release from Poland. For the past ten years, at a small fee, Polish authorities have provided hitch-hikers with travel coupons which are lottery tickets for the drivers who pick them up. The hitchhikers' fees support an insurance system protecting both parties in a hitchhiking-related accident, and the coupon book which is used to flag motorists assures them that everything is on the up-and-up.[15] While in Poland hitchhiking was first encouraged because of an auto shortage, in the U.S. it may someday be encouraged to alleviate the problem of traffic jams due to excessive reliance on personal transportation.

When many of the young talk about the implications of life-style, their interest goes far beyond what happens in the commune kitchen to encompass questions of prevalent culture and economic structure. Paul Goodman's book, Communitas, begins to deal with these cultural questions on the national scale, considering life-style as a variable.

Home Heating and Life-Style

As a life-style problem, the transportation question immediately invites one's inquiry to the quality of urban planning and production in the automobile industry, the largest industry in the nation. By contrast, questions regarding home heating are tightly coupled to personal values and are subject to individual decisions.

Home water and space heating and cooking accounted for about 90 percent of domestic energy consumption in 1968 (exclusive of transportation).[6] Of the twelve communes surveyed, only two possessed electric space heaters. In both cases the heaters received little or no use, and heating was done primarily by gas. Minneapolis housing units have an average of 2.6 occupants,[16] and in our comparison of gas consumption, the commune units were compared to 900-square-foot homes assumed to be occupied by 2.6 people, using approximate data supplied by the Minneapolis Gas Company. Thus the homes used in our comparison averaged 346 square feet per inhabitant, while the large dwellings used by the communes averaged 2,340 square feet, or 242 square feet per inhabitant. The commune members had adequate, though slightly less, space per individual than Minneapolis families living in average-sized dwelling units, while using considerably less gas and electricity for all purposes including space heating (40 percent less gas and 82 percent less electricity).

In this comparison it appears the saving for space heat is due both to more intensive use of space, and to space heating economies of scale offered by large dwellings, with their favorable surface to volume ratio. It should be noted that multiple dwellings also offer the heating advantage, provided space utilization is achieved to as full a degree as in the case of the communes. In space heating, as in the cases of automobile use and appliance use, the communes seem to be enjoying per capita advantages of scale which are not available to the nuclear household living in their own single family structure.

Since interest in Oriental and American Indian philosophies is often high among new life-style groups, it is appropriate to examine the question of space heat through the eyes of those cultures to see if there are adaptations which might help a new life-style group reduce their energy consumption.

The cultures of Tibet and the American Indian offer an extreme in the attitude towards cold. Some Tibetan Yoguns believe that they can endure extremes of cold and heat through chanting religious verses, a practice involving breath control, and hence, perhaps, control over metabolism.[17] The Tlinget Indians of the Northwest American coast report in their myths having used cold salt water baths regularly to increase their endurance.[18] The Zen meditation halls of lowland Japan are usually unheated, reflecting Buddhist attitudes of indifference towards "pain." Cultural factors, no doubt, temper the attitudes of the people of India towards heat. They are reported to tolerate ten more degrees of heat at comparable humidity than Americans, before considering themselves uncomfortable.[19]

In correspondence with the shared Tibetan and American Indian practice, or discipline, of functioning in the extremes of the elements, one author points out that work under conditions of heat or cold can be moderately adapted to through repeated short exposures and the use of appropriate clothing, but the conditions may severely limit output. For instance, a man can do five times as much work at 90 degrees F. and 60 percent humidity as at 120 degrees F. and 60 percent humidity, and work in heat or cold can easily result in debilitating heat prostration or in the case of cold, frostbite sometimes resulting in gangrene and loss of limbs.[20]

The widely accepted technical approach to thermal comfort involves the determination of what spatially uniform combination of temperature, humidity, and air movement are necessary for a man to work comfortably with a given degree of clothing. For instance, one author calculates that in a room with relative air velocity zero and relative humidity 50 percent, a lightly clothed man doing light work would require an ambient air temperature of 75 degrees F., whereas the same man doing light work in heavy clothing would require an air temperature of 60 degrees F.[21] Such criteria for optimum comfort have increased steadily by about 10 degrees F. since 1900, a *cultural change* attributed to the year-round use of lighter weight clothing, changing diet, and new comfort expectations.[22] Similarly, a decision to use twice as much energy to achieve air conditioning for weather above 70 degrees F. rather than above 75 degrees F. in New York City reflects a cultural judgment as well as the characteristics of human physiology.

Following the preference for uniform space heating noted earlier, central space heating is the prevalent approach in the U.S. at this time. One can see intuitively that this approach must require much more energy than localized heating methods, but few data are available comparing the respective energy costs. Obviously climate places severe limitations on the application of localized heating in homes.

Aside from intuitive advantages of the English system of local heating by small fireplaces rather than space heating, a 1920s heating engineer reported that the English also accustom themselves to a room temperature of 60 degrees F.[23] Such a practice could yield considerable energy savings in the U.S. in regions with a climate similar to that of England, that is, the East and West Coasts.

Much of the American South and West coast is subtropic, as is Japan, a culture in which the art of localized heating has been perfected to a surprising degree. The nucleus of the traditional Japanese home energy system, which was common until well after World War II, consisted of a wood-fired bath, a charcoal-fired cooking fire, charcoal hibachis and low tables with charcoal heaters under them. The hibachi may be built into a low wooden chest, or it may be a crockery cylinder from 5 to 25 gallons in volume. It is usually lined with ashes, and the charcoal fire is built underneath a brazier which holds an iron kettle for hot water. During the coldest portion of the year, the hibachi may be supplemented with a kotatsu, or low table with a quilt bib to hold in the heat produced by a well protected tray of hot coals beneath the table.

Four Japanese-American women, who matured in early post-war Tokyo, estimate that their households used from two to four tewara-bags of charcoal per month in the winter, plus a kindling ration for the bath. Rough calculations indicate that their subsequent energy bill for heating and cooking was from one-tenth to one-fifth that of an American apartment in a city with comparable, subtropic winter.[24]

The Japanese informants claimed that throughout World War II they had no difficulty at all in obtaining ample supplies of charcoal, the surplus of which was perhaps contributed to by the saturation bombings of Japanese cities. Since World War II small gas heaters, gas heated baths, instant water heaters, and electric hibachis, etc. have come into common use, preserving only to a certain extent the traditional pattern of localized heating. Thus our comparison of Japan and the United States must be considered historical with Japanese reliance on fossil fuels for home energy consumption growing rapidly.[25]

Typical of Japanese culture, the sophistication of their adaptation to winter goes far beyond conveniently designed "spot heaters." For instance, in contrast to Western costume, several kimonos can be worn on top of each other, providing great warmth. When this method is applied in moderation, there is no undue loss of comfort, since the sleeves, collars and waists, aside from being elegant, fit together conveniently.

Hot Water, Culture, and the Bath

In addition to the energy consumed in space heating, the heating of water accounted for another 15 percent of U.S. domestic energy consumption in 1968, an increase of 2 percent from the 1960 level. Analysts usually focus on the method of heating water when discussing the increased energy bill for hot water, since an electric water heater uses about twice as much energy per gallon of water heated as a gas heater.

One expert estimates the bath might account for about 30 percent of domestic hot water use,[26] or 5 percent of total domestic energy consumption. Table 4 demonstrates the important roles of both cultural and technical factors in this aspect of domestic energy consumption. As would be expected, a big, electrically-heated tub bath uses twice as much energy as the same bath heated by gas. A more energy-economical, conventional bath is a gas-heated, small tub bath using about 22 percent as much energy as the big, electrically-heated bath.

The large Japanese style iron tub bath heated directly by a wood fire provides the luxury of the large American tub bath at 22 percent of the energy cost per person. In the Japanese case, however, there is a heavy cultural cost attached: the loss of privacy. The Japanese achieve their economical bath by an ingenious system of sharing the bath water. The members of an extended family all bathe in the same tub of water, some scrubbing with soap outside the tub while each person takes a turn soaking (with no scrubbing) in the tub. Since no scrubbing is done inside the tub, the water is clean enough after five or more people have bathed to still wash a tub of dark clothes in the water. Using the conventional electric hot water heater and automatic washer, a bathing and laundry function which costs the Japanese 86,300 BTU of energy would cost an American household 470,000 BTU, or about 5 times as much. Using gas technology, it would cost the American household 207,700 BTU, or 2.4 times as much. The strength of the Japanese adaptation to bathing rests on the cultural factor of willingness to tolerate family nudity, and the technical factor of a directly heated bath enclosed in a small room which is also heated by the fire directly under the tub. Undoubtedly the fact that hot water was obtained for laundry as a by-product of the bath contributes to the low energy consumption by the traditional Japanese system.

A large Finnish-style wood-fired sauna studied in the Sierra Mountains of California achieved a level of efficiency similar to that of the Japanese system when shared by about ten people. The common bath or sauna would be ac-

Table 4: Energy Use and Bath Technology

BATH STYLE	HOT WATER (GALLONS)	RESOURCE (BTU)	PERSONS SERVED	BTU PER PERSON	COMMENT
Big tub bath (electric water heater)	30	81,000	1	81,000	Electric power generation and transmission efficiency of 27.3%
Big tub bath (gas water heater)	30	35,000	1	35,000	Assumes tank temp. increase of 87°F. and 62% efficient gas water heater
Small tub bath	15	17,500	1	17,500	Gas water heater
Five-minute light shower	5	5,850	1	5,850	Gas water heater
Wood-fired Japanese bath and one tub laundry	46	86,300	5	17,300	Doing tub wash after bath saves 27,700 BTU
American machine load laundry	24	27,700	1	27,700	Gas water heater
Electric sauna and cold showers		82,000 (space heat)	5	16,400	
Electric sauna and one hot shower per person	25	29,300 (water) 82,000 (space) ——— 111,300	5	22,200	300 cu. ft. room with 7.5 kilowatt heater operating 0.88 hours out of 1.25 hours (MacLevy Products Corp., Elmhurst, N.Y.)
Gas-fired sauna and cold showers	—	22,000	5	4,400	350 cu. ft.; 25,000 BTU/hr. unit operating 0.88 hours out of 1.25 hours (Viking Sauna, San Jose, Ca.)
Gas sauna and one hot shower per person	25	29,300 (water) 22,000 (space) ——— 61,300	5	12,300	
Solar heated bath	30	—	1	—	Capital investment of from $500 to $800 for solar collector and elevated insulated storage tank.

ceptable in many communes since many members have a more relaxed attitude toward nudity. Under such special cultural circumstances where nudity is a value or at least not a cost, American technology can actually provide a gas-fired sauna bath at an energy cost below that of the Japanese or Finnish system. Including a short, hot shower in addition to the gas-fired sauna, the energy cost per person becomes one-sixth that of the big electrically-heated bath, and about one-third that of a big gas-heated tub bath. The flexible cultural attitudes common in communes, combined with good technology, offer the commune considerable energy savings beyond those observed in the presence of conventional technology.

Conclusion

We have seen that attitudes toward energy use in the home can be tightly coupled to cultural attitudes about the nature of comfort and leisure as well as cultural perceptions of the desirability of hand labor. For example, it is a common insight that when dishwashing is shared by both sexes, the labor is lighter because there are more hands doing it, and because it is not a symbol of oppression. Thus in many homes a cultural change in attitudes toward sex roles may end up having the environmental effect of making hand-dishwashing feasible, reducing energy used for hot water for dishwashing by a factor of four [26] and eliminating the use of strong machine dishwashing detergents.

Many of today's young are interested in eastern religions, and such teachings may have a profound influence on how individuals view labor. For instance, Zen teaches that the insights possible through disciplined meditation are also possible when the disciplined alertness of meditation is carried to manual labor, and ultimately to every corner of one's life, with the preferred states of mind being possible through manual labor. Thus a chore like dishwashing loses the onus which some sectors of our culture attach to manual as opposed to mental or spiritual endeavors. Of course this insight is also available through such native sources as Henry David Thoreau and some American Indian patriarchs.

From this viewpoint the claim that household labor saving devices "liberate man" may be viewed with skepticism by followers of the new life-styles. The dishwasher and the vacuum cleaner (with its wall to wall carpet) may ultimately be discarded by some as encumbrances. This concept may be more applicable to a commune with six adults and two children than to a nuclear household with two adults and six children.

In considering personal energy consumption and life style, it is convenient to examine the interplay between social structure, cultural expectations, and technology. The material goods enjoyed by the Minneapolis commune sample were similar to those enjoyed by most middle-class households, with the exception that dishwashers and air conditioners were entirely absent from the twelve communes visited. The low personal energy budgets appeared to be basically economies of scale. However, the same cultural flexibility that brought the 131 commune members into voluntary associations might be an indication that individual adherents of the new life style would consider other adaptations, if they were available.

About 90 percent of the average American domestic energy budget is devoted to cooking, space heating, and water heating. Considerable savings in energy in those areas are possible through the use of localized heating combined with cooking, and baths designed for community use, and more clothing. In addition, adaptations to greater variations in home temperatures seem promising, though poorly researched at this time.

Thus in an era when Americans are staggering before the environmental and economic problems associated with a rapidly expanding industrial economy, this paper is intended to suggest that the assumptions commonly made about domestic energy needs are not based on absolutes. They are a function of decisions of taste and culture, as well as of the absolutes of physiology and technology.

Notes

1. Snyder, Gary "Why Tribe" and "Buddhism and the Coming Revolution," *Earth Household*, New Directions, New York, 1969.
2. Commoner, Barry, and Michael Corr, *Power Consumption and Human Welfare in Industry, Commerce and the Home*, paper for the Energy Crisis Symposium, AAAS Annual Convention, Philadelphia, Dec. 1971. *Survey of Consumer Buying Expectations*, U.S. Bureau of Census, unpublished data, July 1971.
3. Brian, Margaret, Northern States Power, personal communication, 1972.
4. "Input Output Table of the United States Economy," *Scientific American*, publisher, New York, 1970. Hirst, Eric, *Energy Consumption for Transportation in the U.S.*, ORNL, Oak Ridge, Tenn., 1972.
5. In 1968 the residential sector satisfied 34.8 percent of its requirements by petroleum, 50.1 percent by gas, and 15.1 percent by electricity according to the Office of Science and Technology (see next note). However, if energy losses of 72% during generation of electricity are included, these figures for direct home energy dependence become 25% for heating oil, 36% for gas, and 39% for electricity. Multiplied by the commune saving in each case, this yields a total home energy saving of 71% $(1.0 \times 0.25 + 0.40 \times 0.36 \times 0.82 \times 0.39 = 0.25 + 0.14 + 0.32 = 0.71)$.
6. *Patterns of Energy Consumption in the United States*, White House Office of Science and Technology, unpublished, 1971.
7. Luszczynski, K. H., "Lost Power," *Environment*, April 1972.
8. Hirst, loc. cit.
9. Knaus, William, Colonial Taxicab Co., Pittsburgh, personal communication.
10. Lansing, John B. and Gary Hendricks, *Automobile Ownership and Residential Density*, Institute for Social Research, University of Michigan, Ann Arbor, 1967 p. 24.
11. *1971 Auto Facts and Figures*, Automobile Manufacturers Association, New York, 1971, p. 22.

12. Hearings on Disposal of Junked and Abandoned Vehicles, Senate Public Works Committee, Y4, p. 96/10: J96, 1970
13. Shakow, Don Ph.D. economics, personal communication, 1972.
14. Commoner and Corr, loc. cit.
15. Walker, Connecticut, "Hitchhiking in Poland—Licensed, Safe, Profitable," *Parade Magazine, St. Louis Post-Dispatch*, July 30, 1972.
16. *1970 Census of Housing, Minneapolis-St. Paul Urbanized Area*, Block Statistics, Bureau of the Census, Dept. of Commerce, Aug. 1971, Table 1.
17. Evans-Wentz, W. Y., *Tibetan Yoga and Secret Doctrines*, Oxford University Press, N.Y., 1970, p. 160.
18. Garfield, Viola E., et al., *The Wolf and the Raven*, University of Washington Press, Seattle, 1961, p. 77.
19. Banerji, S. K., "Comfort Zone," *Climate, Environment and Health*, National Institute of Sciences of India, New Dehli, 1959, p. 28.
20. Basu, N. M., "Life in Cold and Hot Climates," *Climate, Environment and Health*, Ibid., pp. 32–35.
21. Fanger, P. O., *Thermal Comfort*, Danish Technical Press, Copenhagen, 1970, p. 49.
22. *Handbook of Fundamentals*, American Society of Heating, Refrigeration and Air Conditioning Engineers, New York, 1972, p. 136.
23. Trane, R. N., "Heating Practices in England," *Domestic Science*, Feb. 1923, p. 364.
24. Corr, Michael, and Dan MacLeod, "Home Energy Consumption as a Function of Life Style," *Electric Power Consumption and Human Welfare*, AAAS/CEA Power Study Group, Aug. 11, 1972, review edition.
25. *Japan Statistical Yearbook*, 1968, Bureau of Statistics, Office of the Prime Minister of Japan, 1968.
26. New, R. E., "The Electric Utility Looks at the Domestic Appliance and Electric Heat Load," paper presented at the IEEE Industry and General Applications Group Annual Meeting, Chicago, Oct. 3–6, 1966.

Epilogue:

The Present and Future of Anthropology

Anthropology, like every other cultural institution, is undergoing considerable change in this terminal phase of the twentieth century. The "environmental crisis" that became evident in the 1960s in North America brought immediate response in an upsurge of ecological research by anthropologists, frequently teamed up with environmentalists and other disciplines. Some of the focus of attention in anthropology has shifted from supposedly static or slow-changing marginal populations to a study of urbanization, revitalization movements, Black Power, Red Power, and other political movements. There is at this time a rapid development of anthropological work concerning human population dynamics. As these changes of topical orientation have progressed, the work of anthropologists has brought them into contact with a new array of other academic disciplines sharing overlapping research objectives.

The applied branch of anthropology has continued to grow as more researchers direct their concerns to practical problems—seeking ways to modify the effects of rampant delocalization, trying to increase the awareness of the hidden and not-so-hidden side effects of modern technologies; and trying to counteract the tendencies for social planners and developers to think only in terms of Euro-American cultural and social forms. Until now, developers and governmental planners have operated on a principal of "unlimited growth" and "unlimited good." Anthropologists seek to help in the application of a more environmentally sensitive and socioculturally compatible view of change.

Students who take courses in which this book is used will become part of a world in which delocalization of all sorts will increase; there is a call for new modes of thinking and new modes of coping with the business of living. We have seen recently the effects of curtailment in the free flow of oil on the economic and social system of the United States. This dramatic example of the interdependence of diverse parts of the world is not a unique example, but is an indication of a trend of increasing delocalization and interdependence. As more parts of the world become linked together in thicker social, economic and political networks, the need for cross-culturally sensitive ways of dealings and exchanges will increase dramatically. Although anthropology is not the only discipline that deals with cross-cultural communication and meaning, it is the one that has dealt with this most extensively. The goal of anthropology has not been to create more and more anthropologists (however, we are not trying to discourage interested individuals from entering the discipline), but the prime mission of anthropology is to develop in people the cognitive maps necessary to appreciate and be sensitive to the importance of a cross-cultural perspective in all aspects of life. Students who become fishery biologists, petroleum geologists, agricultural economists, teachers, public health workers, and business people can all benefit from the application of cross-cultural understanding.

By cross-cultural understanding we do not simply mean a positivistic, goodwill orientation toward other human beings—as valuable as that may be—for we are advocating the adaptive and pragmatic consequences of being able to understand the complexity of the many different adaptational modes found around the world. It should be clear to every one using this book that there are different ways of accomplishing the same basic human adaptive goals of survival and the creation of a meaningful life.

In coming decades various segments of the world community will need to have great innovative flexibility, coupled with understanding of the complex interrelations of humans with their social and physical environments in order to develop new modes of adaptation and new ways of maintaining satisfactory lifeways under conditions of continued rapid sociocultural evolution. Such an understanding and flexibility can be generated from an informed consideration of the human biocultural past, plus knowledge of the different human adaptations in these most recent centuries. Adaptive flexibility comes from the realization that many different cultural forms are possible and that, however successful a system may be at a given point, its very best features may become maladaptive in other contexts and environments.

The knowledge of human adaptive systems is not simply a social and cultural concern but also requires a realization of the biological characteristics, as well as psychological patterns among human individuals. The complex network of interaction among the different aspects of human behavior is beyond the reach of any one single academic discipline, and anthropologists cannot pretend to be expert in all of the ramified biological, social, economic, and other aspects of life in the way the specialists may be within their disciplines. The attempt of anthropology is to develop a systematic multifactoral model of human behavior such that particular questions and crises can be approached with understanding and flexible modes of planning and adjustment.